JO⋯N S
VIR⋯A RAID

John Brown's Virginia Raid

Philip F. Rose

Trafford rev. 01/17/2013

 www.trafford.com

North America & international
toll-free: 1 888 232 4444 (USA & Canada)
phone: 250 383 6864 ♦ fax: 812 355 4082

TABLE OF CONTENTS

Compiled From Contemporary
Source Material

By

Philip F. Rose

John Brown
From a Painting by Nathum B. Onthank

Introduction

ONE OF THE first publications on John Brown's raid at Harper's Ferry was "The Life, Trial and Conviction of Capt. John Brown: Being a Full Account of the Insurrection at Harper's Ferry, Va." It appeared in print in New York City at the end of 1859. This pamphlet was one hundred pages long, had eight wood cut engravings, and was priced at 25¢.

It was a compilation of material from official reports and current newspaper accounts assembled by New York publisher Robert M. DeWitt. DeWitt gave no account of life at the Kennedy Farm before the raid, but plunged into the first night of the assault on October 16, 1859. The capture of Brown and his trial followed newspaper accounts closely and the pamphlet ended with John Brown being found guilty.

The next major publication to appear about John Brown was the "Report of the Select Committee of the Senate Appointed to Inquire into the Late Invasion and Seizure of the Public Property at Harper's Ferry." This report was ordered to be printed on June 15, 1860. Senator Mason presented the Majority Report and the Minority Report was presented by Senators Collamer and Doolittle.

This report is invaluable for the live examination of the witnesses relative to the raid. Thirty-two contemporary witnesses were interrogated and their testimony recorded. Colonel Robert E. Lee made a comprehensive report as to the actions of the Marines making the final assault on the Engine House.

Senator Mason reported that upon the whole testimony there could be no doubt that Brown's plan was to commence a servile war on the borders of Virginia, which he expected to extend, and which he believed his means and resources were sufficient to extend through that State and throughout the entire South. Senator Mason further reported that the point chosen for the attack seems to have been selected from the two-fold inducement of the security afforded the invaders by a mountainous country, and the large deposit of arms in the arsenal of the United States there situated. It resulted in the murder of three of the most respected citizens of the State of Virginia without cause, and in the like murder of an unoffending free Negro. Of the military force brought against them, one Marine was killed and one wounded; while eight of the militia and other forces of the neighborhood were wounded, with more or less severity, in the several assaults made by them.

The first major book about John Brown was written by James Redpath who knew John Brown intimately. "The Public Life of Capt. John Brown was published by Thayer and Eldridge of Boston in late 1860. This book was dedicated to Wendell Phillips, Ralph Waldo Emerson and Henry D. Thoreau.

In December of 1859 Mary Brown wrote Messrs. Thayer and Eldridge that she was satisfied that Mr. Redpath was the man to write the life of her beloved husband, as he was personally acquainted with him, and that he would do him justice! James Redpath said, "When the news of the arrest of John Brown reached Boston, I could neither work nor sleep; for I loved and revered the noble old man, and had perfect confidence in his plan of emancipation.

Osborne P. Anderson, one of the black members of the Virginia raid wrote "A Voice From Harper's Ferry. A Narrative of Events at Harper's Ferry; With Incidents Prior and Subsequent to its Capture by Captain Brown and His Men." It was published in Boston for the author in 1861. In Anderson's preface he said, "My identity as a member of Captain Brown's Company cannot be questioned, successfully, by any who are bent upon suppressing the truth; neither will it be by any in Canada or the United

States familiar with John Brown and his plans, or those who knew his men personally, or by reputation, or who enjoyed his confidence sufficiently to know thoroughly his plans."

With the advent of the Civil War no new documentation appeared relative to John Brown and his men. During the period of time after the war both Frank Sanborn and Richard Hinton, as well as C. B. Galbreath gathered documentation and background information from the John Brown family directly. Since some of the insurrectionists were still alive they were followed closely by these men.

Frank Sanborn published his "Life and Letters of John Brown" in 1885. He dedicated the volume to John Brown Jr., Owen Brown and Ruth Thompson. In compiling the text he remarked, "I could not have completed this task of nearly thirty years but for the constant and friendly aid of the family of John Brown, who have placed without reserve their papers in my hands."

Richard J. Hinton wrote "John Brown and his Men" published in 1894. Hinton said that the work was written because he was compelled and desired to do it. Hinton was one of the men involved in the aborted rescue attempt of Aaron Stevens and Albert Hazlett from jail back in 1860.

At the turn of the century an article appeared by Joseph Barry of Harper's Ferry, and a biography of the Coppoc Brothers appeared in the Journal of the Ohio Historical Society by C. B. Galbreath somewhat later.

The next milestone appeared in 1910. It was a well crafted book entitled "John Brown, 1800-1859: A Biography Fifty Years After," by Oswald Garrison Villard. Villard was the son of Henry Villard the former owner of the New York Evening Post, and—on his mother's side—the grandson of William Lloyd Garrison, the famous abolitionist.

"John Brown 1800-1859" is an impressive achievement of narrating the facts of John Brown's life. Villard did not pursue Brown's racial agenda in depth, however. As Mr. Villard said, "Fifty years after the Harper's Ferry tragedy, the time was ripe for a study of John Brown, free from bias, from the errors in taste and fact of the mere panegyrist, and from the blind prejudice of those who can see in John Brown nothing but a criminal." Villard's book was updated in 1943 with a new forward, textual corrections, a critical addenda and a revised bibliography.

In 1973 Richard O. Boyer's book, "The Legend of John Brown" appeared. Boyer's book did not focus on John Brown's raid, but on the long cold war between the North and the South which shaped Brown into a symbol and a prime actor. The book focused on the important Abolitionists who were alive when John brown was executed. As author Richard Boyer said, "This book concerns the time and its temper, the long cold war over slavery between South and North, the large and violent land steeped in almost permanent crisis that formed John Brown and his contemporaries." Boyer remarked, "There are two different ways of viewing John Brown. They are the way he was regarded by many during his lifetime and the way he has been seen by most since."

The most recent study (2005) of John Brown was by David S. Reynolds called "John Brown, Abolitionist." Reynold's book argues for Brown's achievements in bringing about Civil Rights by planting the seeds for the movement by making a pioneering demand for social and political equality for America's ethnic minorities. Reynold's book attempts to explain how and why he did it. It is not a study of the details of the Virginia raid.

The present volume, "John Brown's Virginia Raid" does not focus on abolition but on the lives and actions of the men who joined John Brown in his raid upon Harper's Ferry. This book attempts to present the unvarnished facts of exactly what happened after Brown was taken prisoner, tried and executed. Much dependence was placed upon contemporary newspaper accounts, and material gathered from various historical societies.

Chapter 1

JOHN BROWN

THE FOLLOWING ARE excerpts from John Brown's own account of his childhood and youth, written for Harry Stearns, a boy of thirteen:

Red Rock, Ia., 15th, July, 1859

Mr. Henry L. Stearns.

MY DEAR YOUNG FRIEND: I have concluded to send you a short story of a certain boy of my acquaintance, and for convenience and shortness of name, I will call him John.

John was born on May 9, 1800 at Torrington, Connecticut of poor but respectable parents. When he was five years old his father moved to Ohio, then a wilderness filled with wild beasts and Indians. They traveled by ox team, and after getting to Ohio in 1805 John hung around with the Indians and learned a bit of their talk.

At age six he wandered about the wild country finding birds and squirrels and sometimes even a wild turkey's nest. A poor Indian boy gave him a yellow marble, the first he had ever seen. A while later he lost the marble and it took years to heal the wound and he cried about it many times.

John was never quarrelsome, and was excessively fond of the roughest kind of play. For a short time he was sent to school but the opportunity it afforded him to wrestle and throw snow balls, and run and jump offered him the only compensation for the confinement and restraint of school. He would always choose to stay at home and work rather than be sent to school.

When John was eight years old his mother died and soon afterwards his father remarried. John never felt close to her and pined over his own mother for years.

When war broke out with England his father supplied the troops with beef cattle. Military affairs disgusted John and he played the Quaker until his age cleared him of military duty. During the war with England he ran into the facts of slavery. He was temporarily staying with a landlord who held a slave boy near his own age who was an intelligent and active young man. The Negro boy was badly bloated, poorly fed, and beaten with iron shovels and any other thing that came in his master's hands. This brought John to reflect on the wretched hopeless condition of slave children. John would often raise the question *is God their Father?*

At the age of ten he started to acquire a taste for reading which framed the principal part of his early education. He never attempted to dance in his life, nor did he ever learn to play any kind of card game. By the time he was twelve he was sent off more than a hundred miles on a cattle drive.

John had been taught from earliest childhood to "fear God—and keep his commandments." He became very familiar with the Bible and possessed a most unusual memory of its entire contents. He joined the Congregational Church at Hudson, New York in 1816.

From age fifteen to twenty he spent most of his time working at the tanner and courier's trade. He began to make himself tolerably well acquainted with common arithmetic and surveying.

Soon after age twenty he married a neat and industrious lady by the name of Dianthe Lusk on June 21, 1820. He discovered that he had a great liking for cattle, horses, sheep and pigs. He now began to be the practical shepherd.

You will discover that in using up my *half sheets to save paper*, I have written two pages, so that one does not follow the other as it should. I have no time to write it over; and but for unavoidable hindrances in traveling I can hardly say when I should have written what I have. With an honest desire for your best good, I subscribe myself,

Your Friend,

J. BROWN

Of John Brown's life after marriage there is a reliable record. In May 1825, despite the successes of his tannery and his having built himself a substantial house the year before, John Brown moved his family from Ohio to New Richmond, Pennsylvania near Meadville, where he cleared twenty five acres of timberlands, built a fine tannery, sunk vats, and had leather tanning in them all by the first of October. He surveyed new roads, was instrumental in erecting school houses and procured teachers. Being instrumental in obtaining the first post office in that region he received the appointment of postmaster from President John Quincy Adams.

In August 1832 Dianthe Brown died. Nearly a year later Brown married Mary Anne Day. The family lived at New Richmond, Pennsylvania for nearly ten years, but then for business reasons Brown felt compelled to return to Ohio. He then moved to Franklin Mills, to go into the tanning business with Zenos Kent, a well-to-do businessman of that town.

The partnership of Kent and Brown was not destined to be of long duration. Brown secured a contract for the construction of part of the Ohio and Pennsylvania Canal, from Franklin Mills to Akron, Ohio. About that time Brown, with twenty-one other prominent men, formed the Franklin Land Company and purchased the water-power, mills, lands, etc., in both the upper and lower Franklin villages from Zenos Kent and others.

Brown's enterprises failed during the bad times of 1837, and he lost most of his properties. In 1837 Brown left Franklin Mills and lived briefly with his family in Hudson, Ohio. In December 1838 he drove some cattle from Ohio to Connecticut. On this trip he purchased ten Saxony sheep for $130—this being the beginning of his long career as John Brown the shepherd.

In June 1839 when his family was again at Franklin Mills he made another trip to the East on cattle business. In the interval of sheep and cattle trading, he and his father conceived of the idea of buying some land belonging to Oberlin College in Virginia. Through Brown's own fault, however, negotiations dragged on for so long that the whole plan fell through.

As a result of this disappointment Brown went back to sheep-herding, taking charge of the flocks of Captain Oviatt at Richfield, Ohio in the spring of 1841. He speedily became known as a suave and professional shepherd, able to tell at a glance the presence of a strange animal within the flock. Brown moved his family to Richfield in 1842. In 1843 he had the misfortune of losing four of his children who died of various diseases.

The transformation of the peaceful tanner and shepherd into an avowed abolitionist seems to have taken place in the latter part of his fourth decade. Brown decided to establish a headquarters in Springfield, Massachusetts along with Samuel Perkins Jr. of Akron, Ohio to classify wool for the wool-growers in order that they might obtain a better value for their product. The practical shepherd felt his blood racing when he moved to Springfield in 1846. There he had the opportunity to come into contact with the militant Boston abolitionists. Brown's residence in Springfield gave him the opportunity not only to attend anti-slavery meetings, but also to meet many people of color.

The Springfield business continued through 1848 but it was evident that John Brown, who lacked a merchant's training, was not fitted for this work. It was his all-compelling desire to help the colored people that led him to move his family to the Adirondacks. Gerrit Smith of Peterboro, Madison County, New York, offered to give 120,000 acres of land in that area to worthy colored people. By April of 1848 Brown had decided that he would settle among the Negro colonists there. Gerrit Smith was greatly pleased at the prospect of so experienced a farmer settling on his land, and thus began a warm friendship between the two.

Brown moved his family to North Elba in the spring of 1849. North Elba was a dreary and an inaccessible place, especially in the winter. Brown was at North Elba shortly after the passage of the Fugitive Slave law in January 1851. The reasons for John Brown's abandonment of North Elba in 1851, after only two years there were the burdens of lawsuits against Perkins and Brown, which kept him involved with traveling from one place to another. In March, 1851 he moved his family back to Akron, Ohio. The record breaking drought of 1854 ruined many farmers in Ohio, but Brown fared tolerably well.

John Brown's two sons Jason and Owen were living on a large farm belonging to Mr. Perkins, but they decided that they would seek new homes in Kansas in order to help stem the slave movement. Brown decided to go back to North Elba in March, 1855. He had to sell off some of his cattle so it wasn't until June 1855 that he was able to make the move. When he and his family finally arrived at North Elba they moved into a plain four room house built for him by his son-in-law, Henry Thompson, who had married his daughter Ruth.

Brown felt a strong urge to join his sons in Kansas. So did all his other sons except Watson, then in his 20th year. Brown turned to his family and said, "If it is so painful for us to part with the hope of meeting again, how of poor slaves?" Owen, Frederick and Salmon Brown pulled up stakes and left Ohio for Kansas, arriving in that state on April 20, 1855. When they reached Osawatomie, Kansas they joined Jason and John Brown Jr. who had left Ohio with their families at the opening of river navigation.

Meanwhile John Brown was trying to dispose of his cattle and wind up the odds and ends of his businesses in Illinois, Ohio and New England. On June 28, 1855 he went to Syracuse to attend a convention of anti-slavery men who called themselves Radical Political Abolitionists. Frederick Douglass, Gerrit Smith, Lewis Tappan and Samuel J. May were among the speakers, as well as John Brown himself. There was a proposal to raise money for Brown, that he might collect arms for his sons. He received about sixty dollars and was able to ship a box of firearms to Cleveland, which he subsequently picked up on his way West.

On August 15 Brown took leave of his family at North Elba and headed West with his son-in-law Henry Thompson. They stopped at Cleveland for the firearms and continued on to Detroit where they met Oliver Brown and prepared at once for their overland journey. They paid $120 for a nice young horse. The poor creature had all he could do to drag the load when Brown and his son-in-law left Chicago for the West.

It was on October 6, 1855 that the caravan reached the family settlement at Osawatomie, Kansas. They arrived with but sixty cents between them. Brown, himself, being very tired, did not cover the last mile or two until the next day. There was no shelter there save tents. For pure misery the pioneer tales of Kansas from 1855 to 1858 were not surpassed by any others in the history of the winning of the West!

John Brown came to Kansas with no thought of settling. Surveying was to give him a livelihood while he remained, but he came to fight. He liked the Kansas country. He told his sons that if he were a younger man he would certainly stay with them, but that so long as he had a good farm at North Elba he felt he could maintain his wife and daughters there while his sons settled where they wished.

Three days after Brown's arrival he and his sons went to the election for a free state delegate. Brown said they went "most heavily armed, but no enemy appeared nor have I heard of any disturbance in any part of the territory." Free state killing began in earnest on October 25, at Doniphan, Kansas when Samuel Collins, owner of a saw mill was shot by a pro-slavery man named Patrick Laughlin. John Brown organized his sons and others into a group called the "Liberty Guards." He himself received the title of captain for the first time. As a matter of fact the Liberty Guards were in existence for only two days during which time peace negotiations were under way. Brown and his sons remained at Lawrence, Kansas until December 12th, when the company disbursed and the men left for their homes.

On December 14th, 1855 Brown, his four sons and their half-starved horse were back at Osawatomie. On January 5th Brown was appointed chairman of a convention called for the purpose of nominating state officers. His son John Brown Jr. was nominated for the legislature and was elected. Only fifteen of the Topeka legislators signed the measure to Congress asking for the admission of Kansas as a free state. John Brown Jr. was, of course, one of the fifteen.

During the morning of Saturday, May 24, 1856 when John Brown's party of avengers lay in the timber between two deep ravines above Dutch Henry's Crossing, Brown insisted that it was now necessary "to strike terror in the hearts of the pro-slavery people." At 10:00 PM the party, armed with swords, revolvers and rifles proceeded North crossing Mosquito Creek. Soon after crossing the creek one of the sons knocked at the door of a cabin. There was no reply, but from within came the sound of a gun rammed through the chinks of the cabin wall. The Brown party did not disturb that man. It was then but a short distance to the Doyle residence, where two savage bull dogs were on guard.

Mrs. Mahala Doyle said, "It was about 11:00 PM when my family heard a knock. My husband Mr. Doyle, a pro-slavery man, opened the door, and several pushed their way in. They told my husband that he and the boys must surrender. These men were armed with pistols and large knives. They took my husband and my two sons William and Drury outside. My youngest son John was spared because I asked them in tears to spare him. A short time afterwards I heard the report of pistols. I went out next morning in search of them, and found my husband and William, my oldest son, lying near each other dead on the road about two hundred yards from the house. I did not see my other son Drury until the day he was buried." Young John Doyle who was spared later testified that he saw his brother Drury near a ravine. His fingers were cut off, his arms were cut off, his head was cut open, and a hole was punched in his jaw. "My father," he said, "was shot in the forehead and stabbed in the breast."

The next man to meet his fate at the hands of John Brown's party was Allen Wilkinson. The same procedure was adopted. The last man to die was William Sherman. He was marched into the Pottawatomie Creek where he was stabbed by Brown's two youngest sons and left dying in the creek. The rising Sabbath sun shone on five mutilated bodies. Their bloody night's work was over. What did John Brown assign to the reason for the murders? Assuming the powers of a judge he stated that the Doyles, Sherman and Wilkinson deserved of death because they had murder in their hearts.

John Brown and those who had participated with him in the Pottawatomie murders arrived at Jason Brown's claim and went into hiding on May 26, 1856. On May 27th the news of the Pottawatomie crimes was posted all over Leavenworth. Captain Henry Clay Pate, the fighting correspondent of the *Missouri Republican* went at once with his company of men to assist the United States Marshal in arresting the

Pottawatomie Creek murderers. On June 2nd the so called Henry Clay Pate skirmish took place at Black Jack.[1] Captain Pate always attested that he had been taken prisoner by John Brown by trickery and thievery when under a flag of truce. Governor Shannon, on hearing of the Black Jack episode, reported it to President Franklin Pierce as a sign of the unrest of the territory. President Pierce telegraphed the governor to "maintain the laws firmly and impartially, and take care that no good citizen has just ground to complain of the want of protection." On June 5th Major Abbot with his company of free state men assailed Franklin, some four and a half miles from Lawrence.

Brown remained in hiding at Ottawa Creek near Palmyra throughout June awaiting the recovery of his sick and wounded sons, and gradually he recruited new men for his group. In their hot, primitive quarters, in which the flies were an extreme torment, Owen Brown and Henry Thompson were in misery and Salmon Brown was crippled. Henry Thompson, Oliver, Owen and Salmon declared that they had enough of Kansas. They did not want to fight any more.

The opening of the Presidential campaign between Frémont and Buchanan kept Kansas in the news. On June 17th the Republican National Convention resolved that Kansas would be admitted to the Union with her present free constitution. John Brown left Kansas and went to Nebraska City. He didn't stay there long and joined a party of thirty men headed by Captain Samuel Walker and General Lane. Captain Walker declared his belief that Brown was insane. On August 7th John Brown met Aaron Dwight Stevens who at that time went by the name of Captain Charles Whipple. Stevens had just escaped from the military prison at Fort Leavenworth while serving a three year sentence for taking part in a soldier's mutiny in New Mexico.

On August 28th Brown returned to Osawatomie, traveling slowly because of the 150 herd of cattle he drove before him. A plan to raid Osawatomie and finally destroy it had carefully matured in the minds of

---

[1]   A spot on the Santa Fé trail named for a group of "black jack" oaks.

the pro-slavery leaders. On the 29th of August General Reid with 250 mounted men and one six-pound cannon was detached to proceed to the abolition settlement. On his way Reid's men were joined by the Reverend Martin White who had a malignant hatred of all Free Soil men. They reached Osawatomie early the next morning. It was here that Frederick Brown 2nd was killed by the Reverend White. John Brown himself was preparing breakfast when the news of his son's death reached him. He seized his arms and cried, "Men, come on!" But it was too late. Reid's ruffians had reduced Osawatomie to ashes.

After the battle of Osawatomie a report of the death of Frederick Brown persisted for a few days. Brown made no attempt to rally his forces after they were driven across the Marias des Cygnes River. The news of Brown's defeat, the burning of Osawatomie, the restoration of peace, the release from jail of his son John Brown Jr., and the approach of winter were the reasons why Brown decided to leave Kansas for the East in search of rest and additional funds to carry on his war.

On departing from the territory, Brown left his Osawatomie volunteers under the command of James H. Holmes, with instructions to "carry the war into Africa." By October 10th Brown and his sons were safely at Tabor, Iowa. There Brown, weak and ill, met with a hearty reception. It was the most congenial soil upon which John Brown had set foot on since his departure from Ohio. Brown stayed a week in Tabor and then set out for Chicago by way of Iowa City arriving there on the 23rd of October. Brown pushed on to Rochester and Peterboro. Just after the New Year he arrived in Boston, there to begin a series of new friendships. Here he met Frank B. Sanborn who was acting as a secretary for the Massachusetts State Kansas Committee. At once Mr. Sanborn took him to visit Dr. Samuel G. Howe and Theodore Parker. George L. Stearns, Wendell Phillips, and William Lloyd Garrison were some of the other friends Brown made.

Mr. Parker soon became one of the five men who grouped themselves as an informal committee to aid Brown in whatever attack he might make on slavery. John Brown's first practical encouragement came on January 7th when the Kansas Committee voted to give him 200 Sharp's rifles together with 4000 cartridges, and 31,000 percussion caps. On Sunday January 11, 1857 Brown was invited to George L. Stearn's mansion, and he entertained the family at the dinner table with an account of the Black Jack affair.

Brown again went to Peterboro, by way of Vergennes, Vermont to visit Gerrit Smith who was always ready to help him out. From Peterboro Brown, accompanied by his son John Brown Jr. made a trip to his family at North Elba whom he had not seen for a year and a half. But he was back in Boston again on February 16, 1857.

At about the beginning of March 1857 Brown met Charles W. Blair at Collinsville, Connecticut. Blair was a blacksmith who had attended one of Brown's lectures and heard his plea for funds. Brown showed him a spear blade about eight inches long and he remarked that, "If I had a lot of these spears attached to poles about six feet long they would be a capital weapon of defense for the settlers of Kansas." He asked Blair what it would cost to make a thousand of them and Blair replied about a dollar apiece. Brown then made a written contract with him.

John Brown was now busy trying to raise money to pay for the pikes and other weapons. On March 18th at New Haven he received a promise of $1000. While in New Haven Brown turned to Amos A. Lawrence for aid. In Hartford, Connecticut $600 was raised for him. From the 21st to the 26th Brown was a guest of Eli Thayer. Thayer gave him $500 worth of weapons—a cannon and a rifle.

Brown's financial progress to the end of March was characteristically bad. The winter was slipping away rapidly; spring was at hand and he knew he would have to return to Kansas. His benefactors expected him to be there in the spring to meet any fresh aggression by the Border Ruffians.

Brown was not able to make the first payment of $500 for his pikes from Blair within ten days as required by the contract. Instead he sent only $350 and did not make his next payment of $200 until April 25th.

After Blair made some 550 pikes he waited for more payments which did not arrive.

Late in March 1857 on one of Brown's trips to New York he met Hugh Forbes who had fought in Italy under Garibaldi in the unsuccessful revolution of 1848-49. Brown was impressed with Forbes and believed he would be the perfect lieutenant for his upcoming raids. The result was that Forbes was hired as an instructor at $100 per month for Brown's volunteer company to operate first in Kansas and possibly later in Virginia.

Forbes soon became a burden on Brown. He used up most of Brown's money, and showed very little inclination to follow Brown westward. Forbes's excuse was the burden of writing his two volume manual of warfare. By late April Brown's hope of further frontier funds had evaporated, so he visited for a few weeks in North Elba before leaving for Iowa by way of Vergennes, Vermont. On May 13th he wrote to George L. Stearns, "I leave here for the West today." Stearns estimated that Brown had supplies worth in the neighborhood of $13,000.

Brown visited Milwaukee on June 16, 1857, and then went on to Chicago to meet Gerrit Smith. On June 24th he returned to Ohio to attend the Tallmadge semi-centennial of the founding of that town. On June 29th Brown wrote Colonel Forbes that he would leave Cleveland for Tabor, Iowa. Brown reached Iowa City on July 6th, and at last on August 7th he reached his old quarters at Tabor. By this time it was apparent that there was to be no bloodshed in Kansas that summer. Free State elections were held in Kansas just two days after Brown's arrival at Tabor. Hugh Forbes arrived at Tabor two days later, but there was no need to train Brown's "volunteer-regulars."

Hugh Forbes didn't stay long. He had found no one at Tabor to drill except his employer, Jason Brown, and a few others. They discussed tactics and a possible raid into Virginia. Although anxious to return to Kansas, Brown didn't leave Tabor for the territory until the day he saw Forbes off for the East on November 2nd, 1857 at Nebraska City.

Brown went straight to the vicinity of Lawrence, Kansas stopping at the home of E. B. Whitemen on November 5th. He stayed two days with Mr. Whiteman obtaining tents and bedding, besides some money which came from the Massachusetts Kansas Committee. Within a week Brown was back in Kansas.

The most important result of Brown's arrival back in Kansas was the recruitment of his first men for the future Virginia incursion. No sooner had he reached Mr. Whitemen's than he sent for John E. Cook, whom he had met after the battle of Black Jack. When Cook arrived Brown told him simply that he was organizing a company of men for the purpose of putting a stop to the aggression of pro-slavery forces. Cook agreed to join him. Brown and Cook went to Topeka where they were joined by Aaron D. Stevens, Charles W. Moffet and John H. Kagi. On November 17th they left Topeka heading for Iowa.

At this point of time Brown was wrapped up in his plan to go to Harper's Ferry in Virginia. Kansas was crossed off his mind. It was during the long wintery journey to Springdale, that the details of the Virginia venture were gradually worked out. On Christmas Day they passed Marengo, a town about thirty miles from Iowa City. They reached Springdale, fifteen miles beyond Iowa City three days later. On December 29th the ten members of Brown's party boarded with John H. Painter, a friendly Quaker, with whom they remained until January 11, 1858. They then they moved to the farm of William Maxson some distance from the village. The room and board was $1.50 a week, "not including washing nor extra lights."

On January 15th Brown and his men left for the East from Springdale. John Brown was at Frederick Douglass's home in Rochester on January 28th. There he had numerous talks informing Douglass that the time was ripe for his long cherished undertaking in Virginia. Brown stayed three weeks with Frederick Douglass, and then had a meeting with his wisest and most generous supplier, Gerrit Smith in Peterboro from February 18th till the 24th. On February 24th Brown left for the home of Dr. and Mrs. John Gloucester, a well-to-do colored couple of Brooklyn, New

York. Brown revealed his Virginia plan to them and received both counsel and funds. Then Brown went to Philadelphia, meeting a group of colored men on March 15th. To these men he also stated his project and appealed for men and money.

From Philadelphia John Brown and his son John Jr. went to New York City and then up to North Elba for a farewell visit, arriving on March 23rd. A particular disappointment was Brown's inability to reenlist his son-in-law Henry Thompson, whose services and bravery in Kansas had been so invaluable. By April 2nd they were at Gerrit Smith's place at Peterboro and left for Rochester where John Brown went on alone to St. Catherine's in Canada West. There he visited Harriet Tubman known as the "Moses of Her People." There was a large enclave of escaped slaves living in Canada West and Brown hoped that Harriet Tubman would be a chief guide to the North of the slaves he wished to set free in the neighborhood of Harper's Ferry. He stayed three weeks in Canada and then departed for Detroit, Michigan, arriving there on the morning of Thursday, April 29th.

John Brown was in his organizational stage and had put together a large meeting scheduled to take place in Chatham, Canada. Chatham was the chief town of Kent County and a favorite place for the colored men who had found the personal liberty denied to them under the Stars and Stripes under the British flag. Here were some well-to-do colored farmers and mechanics. Brown made up his mind that this would be the best place for the convention of his followers. Brown and his men were present for the meeting on May 8th. None of the Eastern backers were present, not Gerrit Smith, Wendell Phillips nor Frank B. Sanborn. Brown's party now consisted of himself, Leeman, Stevens, Tidd, George B. Gill, Taylor, Luke F. Parsons, Kagi, Charles W. Moffet, Cook, Richard Realf and Owen Brown—twelve in all. The colored men were thirty-four in number, among them Richard Richardson, Osborne P. Anderson, James H. Harris and Dr. Delany. The presiding officer of the meeting was William C. Munroe, pastor of a Detroit Colored Church and the secretary was John H. Kagi. Brown delivered a long talk and then presented his plan of organization entitled, "Provisional Constitution and Ordinances for the People of the United States." The convention appointed John Brown Commander-in-Chief and John H. Kagi Secretary of War. On May 10th Richard Realf was made Secretary of State, George B. Gill Secretary of the Treasury, Owen Brown Treasurer and Osborne Anderson and Alfred M. Ellsworth members of Congress. A definite and immediate result of the Chatham convention was the complete exhaustion of Brown's treasury. Most of Brown's men left Chatham by May 11th and went to Cleveland in search of work.

Just what the plans for the new raid were could be gleaned from excerpts of the following long letter written by Hugh Forbes on May 14, 1858 to Dr. Samuel G. Howe[2], detailing his differences of opinion with Brown and demanding that he and his men be stopped.

Washington, D.C., May 14, 1858

SIR: Yours of the 10th came to hand yesterday. You mention one of my letters as being anonymous. I am at a loss to account for this, unless I may have sent that one which I intended to have reserved as a copy; or perhaps the copy of the letter to John Brown Jr., inclosed in mine, was not signed . . .

Since you warn me that if you do not like the "spirit" of my reply you will throw it in the fire without perusing it to the end. It is possible that it may not have survived your wrath even thus far; therefore, I shall forward

---

[2] Dr. Howe as a youth fought six years for the independence of Greece and was thrown into a Berlin prison for aiding Polish patriots. As one of Boston's foremost citizens he was a noted editor as well as a physician. Dr. Howe was the founder of one of the nation's first school for the blind, the Perkins Institute. His wealthy wife was the gifted Julia Ward Howe. Dr. Howe had proposed movements of actual force against slavery in the South as early as 1844. Howe acted as an unofficial manager for his good friend, Charles Sumner, elected in 1851 by an anti-slavery coalition as U. S. Senator from Massachusetts.

sundry copies to your associates, and to abolitionists, that it may at least reach them. The caprice of refusing to read anything distasteful is so like a pouting, spoilt kid, that I should not be surprised at your being easily hood-winked by anyone who were to approach you with flattery and a pleasing story. I shall, however, humor no such nonsensical notions, and I would recommend that you read this attentively all through.

As this must of necessity (for you may throw it in the fire unread) be sent to many abolitionists, some of whom may be ignorant of the details of the case, I will here recapitulate a few essential points. When John Brown applied to me last Spring in the name of the committees and leading humanitarians, I answered, as you are well aware, that being an anti-slavery man, I would not stir *merely* to get *"Kansas for free white people,"* and on his answering me that he himself and the leading minds among his associates had views similar to my own, I considered that the application being put upon that basis, I ought to go. Brown could not then discuss those details. We examined the respective merits of our plans at Tabor.

Mine was as follows: With carefully selected colored and white persons to organize along the Northern slave frontier (Virginia and Maryland especially) a series of stampedes of slaves, each one of which operations would carry off in one night, and from the same place, some twenty to fifty slaves; this to be effected once or twice a month, and eventually once or twice a week along non-contiguous parts of the line; if possible without conflict, only resorting to force if attacked. slave women, accustomed to field labor, would be nearly as useful as men. Everything being in readiness to pass on the fugitives, they could be sent with such speed to Canada that pursuit would be hopeless. In Canada preparations were to be made for their instruction and employment. Any disaster which might befall a stampede would at the utmost compromise those only who might be engaged in that single one; therefore we were not bound in good faith to the abolitionists (as we did not jeopardize that interest) to consult more than those engaged in this very project. Against the chance of loss by occasional accidents should be weighed the advantages of a series of successful "runs." *Slave property would thus become untenable near the frontier; that the frontier would be pushed more and more southward, and it might reasonably be expected that the excitement and irritation would impel the pro-slavery people to commit some stupid blunders.* The Missouri frontier being so far from the habitable part of Canada, and the political parties—anti- and pro-slavery—being in that state (Missouri) so nearly balanced, suggested a peculiar action in that quarter, which would depend in a great measure on affairs in Kansas.

Brown had a different scheme. He proposed, with some twenty-five to fifty, (colored and white mixed) well armed, and bringing a quantity of spare arms, *to beat up a slave quarter in Virginia.* To this I objected that, no preparatory notice having been given to the slaves, (no notice could, with prudence be given them) the invitation to rise might, unless they were already in a state of agitation, meet with no response, or a feeble one. To this he replied that he was sure of a response. He calculated that he could get on the first night from 200 to 500. Half, or thereabouts, of this first lot he proposed to keep with him, mounting 100 or 80 of them, *and make a dash at the Harper's Ferry manufactory, destroying what he could not carry off.* The other men not of this party were to be subdivided into three, four or five distinct parties, each under two or three of the original band, and would beat up other slave quarters, whence more men would be sent to join them.

He argued that were he pressed by the United States troops, which after a few days might concentrate, he could easily maintain himself in the Alleghenies, and that *his New England partisans would in the meantime call a Northern convention to restore tranquility and overthrow the pro-slavery administration.* This, I contended, could at most be a mere local explosion. A slave insurrection, being from the very nature of things deficient in men of education and experience, would under such a system as Brown proposed, be either a flash in the pan, or would leap beyond his control or any control—when it would become a scene of mere anarchy, and would assuredly be suppressed.

On the other hand Brown considered foreign intervention as not impossible. As to the dread of a Northern convention, I consider it as a total fallacy. Brown's New England friends would not have the courage to show themselves, so long as the issue was doubtful.

After days of discussion, Brown (whom you reiterate underlined in your letter of the 10th, enjoys your entire confidence) acquiesced or feigned to acquiesce in a mixed project styled "the well matured plan." I consented to make that concession to secure mutual cooperation, and in consideration of the prospective committee of management which was at the proper time to be established. I preferred, however, my original plan of stampedes, unalloyed by anything else. Your assertion that I want to take the management is wholly unfounded; my insisting upon a committee of management is conclusive on that head. John Brown, had he been truthful, might have been useful in some capacity; almost every one might, if zealous, be useful in some place, whereas the same man might be mischievous in another place. This mixed plan in which I am compromised more than you (lying, as you do, out of sight), having been definitely settled upon, I deny the right of Brown, or you, or any one, from caprice or speculation, to set it aside for the Brown project, pure and simple, or for any other. *It is a breach of confidence which I will not tolerate,* especially when your first act is to assail my own family. You must be worse than insane—you must be depraved—to expect it of me. Now, however, after what has passed, *I would not undertake the intended mixed plan, or even my own project of stampedes in connection with any of you,* because I can place no more faith in New England humanitarians.

My first thought after discovering Brown's complicity in the New England breach of faith was—let him try. Though justly irritated at the horrible treatment of my family, 1 did not, till towards the end of April, utter a syllable, even to Mr. Sanborn, which might tend to check the supplies. I spoke to but one abolitionist after my arrival here, and he thought much as I did. On reconsidering the matter, with other abolitionists, they advanced such sound reasons that I conceived my first impression to have been erroneous, and they say that Brown must be stopped.

The more I reflect the more I become confirmed in the opinion of the last named abolitionist. First, because a man who deviates from truth, betrays his associate, and ill-treats a friendly family, should not be trusted with any humanitarian enterprise. Second, because Brown, with his bigoted mind and limited vision, has not the capacity necessary to direct such an enterprise. Third, because the crude project which he and his confederates have in their heads is not likely to succeed, but is merely suited for a grand speculation in the sudden rise of cotton on the exchanges. Fourth, because some of the hands engaged by him are highly objectionable; for example, when Brown was in the first Kansas troubles he was, by his own men, robbed of horses, etc. Now, a young man whom he asserted had helped to rob him has been re-engaged, for the reason that he did an audacious act, going with three others to Missouri, to the house of another John Brown, whence they took money and horses, after the troubles in Kansas were over, and Brown had left; thence they went to another house and did in the like manner, and though pursued, they got away with the booty. Reprisals and foraging for the common stock are justifiable in war, when ordered by the directing power, but such things, if permitted to be done by individuals, for private gain, constitute brigandage; the robbery of comrades is, however, the worst of all pillage. I remonstrated against the engagement of that person, but Brown told me he had already done it; his admiration for the desperate feat effaced every other feeling.

For these and many other reasons, *I call on you and your associates to stop Brown, and to take from him your arms, etc.* I have a right to exact this, and I do exact it. To your assertion that to stop Brown I would denounce and betray, I echo what the abolitionists here say, that if you do not, by taking from him your arms, etc, stop him, you betray them; for this concerns the abolitionists, and they have a right to be heard . . .

You have as strange a notion of what is gentlemanly as you have of what is just. Last autumn, when I was asked to write strong tracts . . . United States troops, pointed against the United States government and the border ruffians, I complied with the request and the productions were pronounced to be admirably adopted to the purpose. I was urged to continue them, and because they suited you and yours, nothing was hinted as to their being ungentlemanly or that "that which cometh out of the mouth defileth the man and him only."

Very Truly,

H. FORBES

John Brown left Chatham, Canada and headed for Boston where he held many a conference with his friends there. The outcome of the Boston meetings was the temporary abandonment of the Virginia plan and his departure again for Kansas. The Kansas Committee had put some $500 in gold in his hands and politely told him to leave as soon as possible. Brown swallowed his disappointments and went straight to North Elba where he was on June 9th. He was in Cleveland on June 20th and tried to call his scattered followers together and notify them of the decision of his Boston friends.

A general breakup of Brown's followers ensued. Realf went to New York to watch Forbes; Owen went to his brother Jason's house at Akron, Ohio, while Kagi and Tidd left with John Brown for Kansas by way of Chicago. Moffet worked his way home to Iowa after staying for some time in Cleveland, while George Gill and Stevens went back to Springdale on their way to Kansas, where they later joined John Brown. Cook went to Harper's Ferry to live there in order to reconnoiter the vicinity. He arrived there on June 5, 1858. Luke Parsons spent the summer on Forbes's farm and then returned to his home at Byron, Illinois. He had lost all his enthusiasm for the venture. Leeman and Taylor drifted about in Ohio and Illinois.

On Friday, June 25th Brown was back at Lawrence, Kansas, and on Monday he was off to Southern Kansas in disguise. He even had a new name—Shubel Morgan! One of the most atrocious of crimes had occurred just recently there. Charles A. Hamilton, a graduate of the University of Georgia, and a few friends had captured eleven reputable free state citizens, tied them up in a little ravine, and then proceeded to shoot them. To make sure of their work the brutal and brazen murderers then kicked the prostrate men to see who still lived. Those that twitched were shot in the head. It will forever be remembered as the Marias des Cygnes Massacre, and inspired a commemorative poem by John Greenleaf Whittier. After the massacre a week of extreme lawlessness ensued, although Federal troops had been ordered out into the area.

On July 9th, at the site of the Hamilton massacre, John Brown drew up his "Articles of Agreement for Shubel Morgan's Company." In early August Brown tried to get the revolvers sent to him in 1856 by the National Kansas Committee, but was unsuccessful. In the same month Brown started to suffer from his recurrent ague or malarial fever. He was taken by William Partridge to the Reverend Mr. Adair's cabin at Osawatomie where he lay for a month nursed by the devoted Kagi and the Adair family.

On September 13, Brown wrote his wife that he was still very weak. On the 30th of October an attempt was made to assassinate free state leader James Montgomery, his wife and his children, by pro-slavery men, who attacked his cabin at night and fired a volley into it. This event led Brown's men to strongly fortify Montgomery's cabin. George Gill, Tidd and Stevens did most of the work since Brown was not fully recovered.

On Thursday, December 16th James Montgomery attacked Fort Scott in order to release Benjamin Rice, a free state settler. Two days earlier Montgomery had organized a force of a hundred men and invited John Brown to join in. Montgomery was obviously a border chieftain after his own heart. This Brown did together with Kagi and Stevens. During the melée Kagi was hit by buckshot, but his heavy overcoat saved him from severe injury. Brown was subsequently wrongfully charged by Governor Robinson with the leadership and instigation of the Fort Scott attack, both of which questionable honors clearly belonged to Montgomery.

On December 19th a slave by the name of Jim Daniels told George Gill the story of his impending fate—to be sold at an administrator's sale in the immediate future. Shubel Morgan decided to lead a party of ten men to the home of Harvey G. Hicklan, Daniels's temporary master, while Stevens, Tidd, Hazlett and five others were to visit other plantations and rescue slaves who desired their liberty. On the night of December 20th the two bands made their way into Missouri.

At midnight Harvey Hicklan's door was pried open and he was informed of the mission of the raiders. The slaves were liberated and Brown's men plundered the home. From Hicklan's it was three-quarters of a mile to the residence of John Larue where five more slaves were freed. Brown and his men then returned to Kansas.

The President of the United States offered a reward of $250 apiece for the arrest of Brown and Montgomery, and the governor of Missouri upped the ante and offered $3000 for the capture of Brown. As for Brown he was now ready to leave the territory for the last time. Brown said goodbye to his people at Osawatomie and on January 20, 1859 set out with the liberated slaves for the long journey East. On February 4th Brown stood on Iowa soil having eluded a posse of fifty men who were hot on his trail. One day more and he was in the familiar town of Tabor. The slaves were put up in a little school-house and the teams unloaded on the public commons. Brown rested and recuperated for the long overland trip across Iowa towards Springdale.

On February 25th the caravan was enthusiastically welcomed at Grinnell, Iowa, the home of Josiah B. Grinnell, the most prominent abolitionist in the state. The party reached Springdale and remained there until March 10th. Gill parted from the group here because of a bad case of inflammatory rheumatism. The rest departed for Chicago by train. At Chicago Brown, with Kagi, Stevens and others awakened Alan Pinkerton, of detective fame, at 4:30 AM on March 11th for help. Pinkerton got them under cover, sending John Brown to his friend John Jones, a Negro, and taking the others into his own home. Pinkerton made some breakfast for them and then hurried over to Jones's to see Brown, who explained that he was on his way with the slaves to Canada. At 4:45 PM the same day the party left for Detroit, Michigan under Kagi's charge, and arrived at 10:00 AM on March 12th. Brown went to Detroit on an earlier train to see Frederick Douglass, who was visiting in that town. Brown was on hand to have the happiness of seeing his black charges on the ferry-boat for Windsor, where they were soon rejoicing in their freedom under the Union Jack.

Kagi and Brown went on to Cleveland and spent a week with Mrs. Charles M. Sturtevant who was a sister of Charles W. Moffet. While there Brown sought to raise money by giving a lecture or two and selling some horses. As he walked the streets of Cleveland, Brown saw numerous posters announcing the President's offer of $250 for his arrest. On March 25th Brown sent $150 from the proceeds of his horse-sale to his family at North Elba. Brown went to Jefferson on the next day at the invitation of Joshua R. Giddings to deliver a lecture for which he was paid $3.00.[3] Brown finally reached North Elba on April 19th. On May 9th he spent his birthday at Concord, Massachusetts, with Mr. Sanborn. From Boston Brown went to Collinsville, Connecticut to ask about his pikes. Appearing at Mr. Charles Blair's door on June 3rd, he said, "I have been unable, sir, to fulfill my contract with you up to this time; I have met with various disappointments; but now I am able to do so." Brown came back the next day and gave Blair a check for $100.00 and fifty dollars in cash. Three days later, writing from Troy, New York, Brown sent a draft for three hundred dollars more to Mr. Blair. Blair agreed to finish off the pikes for the $450 he had received, and deliver them to Brown at Chambersburg, Pennsylvania early in September.

At Brown's final visit to North Elba he did everything possible for the comfort of his family. He remained less than a week. It was probably on Thursday, June 16th that he started out on his final adventure to Virginia. There was no record of their parting, a last earthly one for several. Nor was it probable that there was much feeling displayed; the Browns were

---

[3] This figure was swelled to $300 by reporters from Harper's Ferry after the raid.

neither emotional nor demonstrative. On the 23rd of June he mailed a letter home from Akron, Ohio, his first report since leaving them. He did not hesitate to mention that he had arms and men, and was contemplating an attack upon Virginia.

John Brown Family Statistics

John Brown was born in West Torrington, Connecticut on May 9, 1800. John married Dianthe Lusk on June 21, 1820 in Hudson, Ohio. She died on August 10, 1832 in New Richmond, Pennsylvania. John and Dianthe had seven children as follows:

Name	Born	Location	Married	Date	Died	Location	Notes
John Brown Jr.	July 25, 1821	Hudson, Ohio	Wealthy C. Hotchkiss	July 20, 1847	May 2, 1895	Put-in-Bay, Ohio	He did not participate at Harper's Ferry.
Jason Brown	January 19, 1823	Hudson, Ohio	Ellen Sherbondy	July 15, 1847	December 24, 1912	Akron, Ohio	-
Owen Brown	November 4, 1824	Hudson, Ohio	-	-	Jan. 8, 1889	Pasadena, California	-
Frederick Brown	January 9, 1827	New Richmond, Pa.	-	-	March 31, 1831	New Richmond, Pa.	-
Ruth Brown	February 18, 1829	New Richmond, Pa.	Henry Thompson	Sept. 26, 1850	January 18, 1904	Pasadena, California	Married at North Elba.
Frederick Brown 2nd.	December 21, 1830	New Richmond, Pa.	-	-	August 30, 1856	Osawattomie, Kansas	Murdered by the Reverend Martin White.
Unnamed	August 7, 1832	New Richmond, Pa.	-	-	August 7 1832	New Richmond, Pa.	Buried in the same grave with his mother.

John Brown married Mary Anne Day, daughter of Charles Day of Whitehall, New York, on July 11, 1833 at Meadville, Pennsylvania. Mary Brown wanted to go West with her young daughters. In 1864, when her son Salmon planned to take his family out West, Mary decided to go along.

They joined a train of 40 wagons and settled in Red Bluff, California until 1870. They later moved to Humboldt County and Mary bought a house in Rohnerville. Salmon and his family moved next door. Mary's daughter Annie, Sarah and Ellen also settled in Rohnerville. Salmon went on to become a pioneer sheep rancher. Mary Anne Brown left Rohnerville in the winter of 1881 and took up residence in the Santa Clara community of Saratoga. She contracted cancer within a few years and died in San Francisco on February 29, 1884. She was buried in the Madronia Cemetery at Saratoga, California. She had thirteen children as follows:

Name	Born	Location	Married	Date	Died	Location	Notes
Sarah Brown	May 11, 1834	New Richmond Pa.	-	-	Sept. 23, 1843	Richfield, Ohio	-
Watson Brown	October 7, 1835	Franklin Mills, Ohio, now Kent, Ohio	Isabella M. Thompson	Sept. 1856	October 19, 1859	Harper's Ferry, Virginia	Slain in Va. insurrection.
Salmon Brown	October 2, 1836	Hudson, Ohio	Abbie C. Hinckley	Oct. 15, 1857	May 10, 1919	Portland, Oregon	Married at North Elba. Despondent over illness he committed suicide.
Charles Brown	November 3, 1837	Hudson, Ohio	-	-	September 11, 1843	Richfield, Ohio	Got ill on Sept 4, 1843.
Oliver Brown	March 9, 1839	Franklin Mills, Ohio	Martha Evelyn Brewster	April 7, 1858	October 17, 1859	Harper's Ferry, Virginia	Died in Va. insurrection. Martha died in childbirth early 1860.
Peter Brown	December 7, 1840	Hudson, Ohio	-	-	September 22, 1843	Richfield, Ohio	-
Austin Brown	September 14, 1842	Richfield, Ohio	-	-	September 21, 1843	Richfield, Ohio	-
Anne or "Annie" Brown	December 23, 1843	Richfield, Ohio	Samuel Adams	Nov. 1869	October 3, 1926	Shively, California	Married at Red Bluff, California.
Amelia Brown	June 22, 1845	Akron, Ohio	-	-	October 30, 1846	Akron, Ohio	-
Sarah Brown 2nd	September 11, 1846	Akron, Ohio	-	-	June 30, 1916	Campbell, California	-

Ellen Brown	May 20, 1848	Springfield Mass.	-	-	April 30, 1849	Springfield Mass.	-
Unnamed	April 26, 1852	Akron, Ohio	-	-	May 17, 1852	Akron, Ohio	Died of Pneumonia
Ellen Brown 2nd	September 25, 1854	Akron, Ohio	James Fablinger I	1876	July 15, 1916	Saratoga, California	Married at Rohnerville, California.

Chapter 2

HARPER'S FERRY

ON JUNE 26, 1859 John Brown and his son Oliver arrived at Bedford Springs, Pennsylvania, having come from North Elba, in upstate New York. Bedford Springs was the site of the summer White House for President Buchanan and there were many influential men there to talk to. From Bedford Springs they went to Chambersburg where they were joined by Jeremiah Goldsmith Anderson and Brown's son Owen. Jeremiah Anderson was an Iowan who had fought in Kansas for over a year for the free state cause. They identified themselves as "I. Smith & Sons." On the 30th they left for Harper's Ferry, Virginia and John Brown announced his departure to his second in command as follows:

Chambersburg, Pa., 30th of June, 1859

JOHN HENRIE ESQR

DEAR SIR: We leave here today for Harper's Ferry via Hagerstown. When you get there you had best look on the hotel register for I. Smith & Sons without making much inquiry. We shall be looking for cheap lands near the railroad in all probability. You can write I. Smith & Sons at Harper's Ferry should you *need* to do so.

Yours in truth,

I. SMITH

At Hagerstown the four men spent the night at the Hagerstown tavern. From there they went on, partly on foot, and partly by train, arriving at the town of Harper's Ferry on July 3rd, 1859. When they got off the train Brown inquired where they could get the cheapest room and board in town. They were informed that they could get it cheaper at Sandy Hook, about a mile below the Ferry, and consequently they went there.

At 8:30 AM on July 4th a genial Southerner named John C. Unseld, a slaveholder and resident, bumped into John Brown and the three young men while walking to Harper's Ferry. Unseld said, "Good morning, Gentlemen, How do you do?" John Brown said that his name was "Smith" and he introduced his two sons and Jeremiah Anderson.

Unseld, noticing that Brown was carrying a heavy-looking carpetbag, said "I suppose you are out hunting for rare ore?" Brown's reply was, "No we are not, we are out looking for land. We want to buy some property, but we only have a little money and we want to make it go as far as possible." Brown then asked the price of land in the area and Unseld told him that it ranged from $15 to $30 an acre. Brown exclaimed, "That's high; I thought I could buy land for a dollar or two per acre." Unseld asked them where they came from and Brown's answer was, "I am from the northern part of New York State." Brown said "I was a farmer there but the frost had been so heavy it killed all my crops and so I decided to sell out and come South."

Unseld then left Brown and went on to Harper's Ferry. On returning he met his new acquaintances in the same vicinity. Brown asked, "Do you know of any farm that is in the neighborhood for sale?" Unseld answered, "I just think I might; there is a farm about four miles from here, owned by the heirs of a Doctor Robert F. Kennedy. Doctor Kennedy purchased the 194 acres of land and cottage from the Antietam Iron Works in 1852. Soon after he had a one story-high stone foundation built and raised a one-room cottage on it. He then added a larger two-story wing to the northeast. Dr. Kennedy recently died. His farm is empty, and it's up for sale."[1] Brown remarked that he wanted to lease for awhile till he got better acquainted with the area, and he asked Unseld if he knew of any property to rent.

Unseld said that perhaps the Kennedy farm could be rented, but he wasn't sure. Brown immediately told his sons, "Boys, you had better go back and tell the landlord at Sandy Hook that we will not be there for dinner." Unseld then gave Brown instructions on how to find the farm. He remarked that it was difficult to make a living on a farm these days, and Brown replied that he planned to buy up fat cattle and sell them up North.

About three days later Brown met Unseld on the road and exclaimed, "Well, I think that place will suit me just fine. Where can I find the widow and the administrator?" Brown and Unseld met again in a few days and Brown told him that he would send one of his sons to pay the rent. The following week they met again. He said, "Well, we have the property, and we paid the rent of $35 for the two houses, pasture and firewood, from now until March 1st. In fact here is my receipt." A week later Brown was seen taking notes about compass directions for the five mile route from the farm to the arsenal. Unseld said that he bumped into Brown, and Brown told him that the compass would tell him whether there were any ore deposits in the area. Unseld was impressed and made it a point to stop by quite often, which became an annoyance to the Brown party.

Brown emptied out the Kennedy cabin in the swamp across the road from the main farm house so as to conceal his weapons, ammunition and his team of men. The two buildings were separated by about six hundred yards and the small cabin was hidden among the shrubbery. In the meantime Brown put on an act that he was an ordinary farmer and a

---

[1]   The Kennedy farm was eventually purchased by a black Hagerstown Minister, the Reverend Leonard Curlin in 1949, and sold to a white private developer, South T. Lynn, who restored it to its 1859 appearance with the help of a historic architect from the National Park Service. It is a now a Maryland historic landmark.

family man. He sent his son Oliver back to North Elba with the following letter to his wife:

DEAR WIFE: I would be most glad to have you and Anne come on with Oliver and make me a visit of a few weeks while I am preparing to build. I find it will be indispensable to have some women of our own family with us for a short time. I don't see how we can get along without you, and on that account I have sent Oliver at great expense to come back with you. If you cannot come, I would be glad to have Martha and Anne come on . . .

You need not bring anything but your *plain* clothes and a few sheets and pillow cases. What you could pack in a single trunk and an extra bag would be quite sufficient. A few towels and something for milk strainers would be useful. Have your bag or bags marked I. Smith . . . Do not consult with your neighbors about the trip. Oliver can explain to you the reasons why we want you now.

Your Affectionate Husband,

I. SMITH

Mrs. "Smith" was not ready to leave her home and children, but she wished her husband health and success in his endeavors. Martha, Oliver's wife, and Anne promptly responded to the call. Both were very young, seventeen and sixteen years old, respectively. Oliver Brown accompanied them. On Saturday, July 16th, the two young girls arrived near the Kennedy farm, and boarded with a farmer named Nicholls for a few days until they moved in and began housekeeping on the 19th of July.

Brown's second in command was John Henry Kagi, twenty-four years old, and a Kansas correspondent of the New York *Tribune* in Cleveland. He had grown up in Maryland and Virginia and was now stationed at

Chambersburg, Pennsylvania. Chambersburg was the nearest railhead to the farm and was about fifty miles distant. He had the job of getting the arms in from Ohio and Connecticut, and assembling the team. Brown bought a wagon, a horse and a mule to bring the supplies on. His son Owen was to handle the details of the trip.

Watson Brown, William Thompson and Dauphin Thompson (brothers of Henry Thompson) arrived at the Kennedy farm on August 6th followed by Charles Plummer Tidd and Aaron Dwight Stevens on the 8th, and shortly thereafter by Albert Hazlett, Stewart Taylor and the Coppoc brothers.

Brown's daughter Anne took charge of the arrivals in the swamp. These men were called the "Invisibles." The men had to spend most of their time in the attic, but they all knew that they were going to make history. This kept them in good spirits. They assembled the pikes that had been secretly shipped in. They also cleaned the Sharp's rifles. A little fat woman named Jane Hoffmeister (with a passel of children) had rented a patch from the Kennedy in-laws and was raising vegetables down the road. Her curiosity was insatiable, and sometimes she would show up at dinner time and Anne would have to decoy her out into the garden while Martha hid the food and the "Invisibles" scurried up into the attic. In the meantime Martha kept the farmhouse and put on an appearance of domestic tranquility. Brown spent his time brooding over the question of man's emancipation and how he would achieve it.

As the hiding place filled with men and guns, tensions began to build. Charles Tidd, who had been with Brown in Kansas was especially annoying and quarrelsome. He would argue with his crony, Aaron Stevens about everything. He also wrote letters back to Iowa telling his friends about the operations. Little did Brown know that some of these letters would be leaked to United States Secretary of War John B. Floyd.

One day Brown received a letter from his son John Brown Jr., who was his Northern recruiting agent. He told his father that Frederick Douglass wanted to visit him at Chambersburg. Brown was elated because he knew that with Douglass at his side the plan could not fail. Before starting out for this meeting Brown had a final briefing with John E. Cook at the farm. When Cook first arrived at Harper's Ferry he got a job on the locks of the canal which fed water power to the gun shops. He also took a job as a school teacher on the Maryland side of the river and learned about the families living on the farms outside the Ferry. He would have valuable intelligence. Brown also knew that Cook talked too much. With a little encouragement Cook would display his gun collection and hint that he was soon to take part in a daring raid to free slaves. But he was loyal and Brown depended on him. Cook insisted that the local residents were not unsympathetic to anti-slavery ideas and might be recruited for the cause. He argued that a team should be sent to the plantation of Lewis Washington. It was situated further from town than Brown wanted to go, but Cook pointed out that Washington would be an excellent hostage as a colonel in the Virginia State Militia, and how important it would be to liberate his slaves.

Brown then went to Chambersburg and stayed in an abandoned quarry west of town waiting for Douglass to show up. He finally arrived accompanied by a young black recruit named Shields Green. Douglass said that he was instantly recognized in town and was pressed to make a speech which he complied with. Douglass and Brown talked for the better part of two days and Brown told him that he was also at Chambersburg to pick up two hundred carbines, two hundred revolvers and a load of pikes to empower those who would dare to be free. Brown patted Douglass affectionately on the back and said, "Now it is yourself, Frederick, that we need more than anything."

Douglass argued that Brown's plan would be fatal to the purpose of running off slaves from nearby plantations. He said his field of labor for the abolition of slavery did not include an attack upon a United States arsenal—"**Nothing as rash and wild as that!**"

"Rash and wild," Brown repeated sadly. "Have you lost confidence in me Frederick?" "By no means," protested Douglass, but "Virginia will blow you and your hostages sky high before they will allow you to hold Harper's Ferry for an hour! Why don't you forget about this Ferry attack and resume the policy we have agreed on of gradually drawing off the slaves to the mountains."

"Because," Brown said, "gradually but ultimately the slave holders will surround us and slaughter us, and the world will know nothing about it until we are dead." There was no reply to this and a long silence fell between the two men. Finally Douglass said that he had no match for this argument, but seeing that it was getting dark he would return to the village and visit Brown again the next day. Douglass and Shields Green left and Brown settled down in the quarry while Kagi stood guard all night.

The next day was a Sunday. Douglass and Green appeared as the church bells began to ring. Owen Brown joined his father, having brought up the mule wagon to carry back a load of rifles to the Kennedy farm. Douglass wanted to discuss Hugh Forbes who was in on the plan. When Forbes left Iowa and made the rounds of his supporters, he denounced Brown as a religious bigot, and said that his revolutionary movement was a complete failure. Douglass thought that Forbes' betrayal would make Brown give up his plan. Douglass said that Forbes told anybody who would listen, from editor Horace Greeley to various government officials, what Brown was up to. Douglass said, "You must have known that he was a Judas to you, and yet you plan to go on?" Brown shrugged his shoulders and lectured Douglass, "I'm not afraid of him. After hearing that he informed Senator William H. Seward of my intentions, the Senator made a most remarkable address predicting an *"Irrepressible Conflict"* between the free and slave states."

Douglass made one more attempt to discourage Brown by disclosing the news that some black militants in New York and Philadelphia on whom Brown was counting were not going to show up. Brown said, "Then *you* must come with me Douglass. I will defend you with my life. *When I strike the bees will swarm, and I shall want you there to hive them."*

The encounter was over. When about to leave Douglass asked Shields Green what he had decided to do. He was surprised by Green's exclaiming, "I believe I'll go wid the Old Man." Douglass made his way out the rutted road back to the village and Kagi remarked to Brown, "We'll get him yet, Captain. I know just how to do it."

Brown remained at Chambersburg but his son Owen and Shields Green, traveling at night, returned to Harper's Ferry. It was dangerous for a white man and a black man to be seen together. When they got back to the farm Owen was openly skeptical of his father's plans. He was Brown's only son who dared meet his father head-on in an argument. Owen told the men about Frederick Douglass' refusal to come with them, and he found that most of the men agreed with his objections. Feeling responsible to tell his father about these doubts he made his way back to Chambersburg on foot.

Brown received the news calmly. He conceded that he was also discouraged about the lack of recruits. Owen now began to defend the plan, saying they shouldn't give up after going this far. Kagi, who was present at the time agreed and spoke with enthusiasm about the project. Brown asked Kagi to come back with him and talk it over with the men. They arrived back at the farm on the dawn of the next day, August 18, 1859. Brown called all his men together and told them he was aware of their dissatisfaction with his plans. He even told them they could choose another leader; that he, John Brown, would faithfully serve under him.

Aaron Stevens asked Brown what his thoughts were after the disagreement with Fred Douglass. Brown declined to comment. Both these men were associated with Brown in Kansas and were not afraid to speak their mind. Charles Tidd was mad and asked Brown what he would do if all decided against it. Brown said he would find others and do it all by himself. He then told the men he would leave the room and await their decision.

In about an hour Owen came out and handed his father a note:

DEAR SIR: We have all agreed to sustain your decisions, until you have *proved incompetent*, and many of us will adhere to your decisions as long as you will.

Your Friend,

OWEN SMITH

It said that the men upheld the decision to strike with Brown. Brown asked Owen how Tidd had taken the verdict. Owen said, "He was a little bit mad, but he's going to stay with the group, and in fact he said he would stay with Cook at the Ferry for a few days."

Dangerfield Newby was the most restless of the "Invisibles." He always told Brown that he wanted to go out blazing and get it over with. Getting his freedom had broken up Newby's family. He had lived with his wife and family at Fauquier County, Virginia. When his white father died he was given his freedom in the will, but he was forced to leave the state. No freed slaves were allowed to live in Fauquier County. Dangerfield Newby now hoped to buy his family's freedom.

Brown allowed his men to vent their pent-up energies in argument and he made a point of reading a chapter of the Bible to them every day. At the end of the reading he would offer a prayer and ask God for the liberation of the oppressed all over the world. He got no argument with this ploy. One of Brown's younger followers from Chatham who had arrived was a Canadian by the name of Stewart Taylor. Taylor was twenty-two and beardless. He was a pessimistic young fellow and always said he would be the first to fall in battle. He even described the exact manner in which he would meet his maker. The men knew that Taylor had tried harder than anyone else to join the group.

Then there were the two Iowa farm boys, Edwin and Barclay Coppoc who joined the group a little earlier. They knew all about farm animals, but never had a gun in their hands. Barclay was the younger brother at twenty-one and Edwin was twenty-four. The brothers had been raised by a mother who taught her boys that slavery was the greatest human sin. In fact all of Brown's men hated slavery and all were intelligent.

It was the middle of September when the final shipment of pikes arrived. The next Saturday night Brown went to his usual church meeting up the road with his daughter Anne. He preached there several times a week and concentrated on making anti-slavery comments to the congregation. When he returned home he found that Mrs. Hoffmeister had dropped in unannounced, and saw three black men cleaning off the table. She immediately accused the two white men present of using the farm to keep "runaway niggers." Brown told Anne to try and bribe her into silence with a few gifts and reassurances.

The women would now have to be sent back to North Elba. Brown had to borrow $40 from Barclay Coppoc to give to his son Oliver so that he could accompany Anne and his wife Martha as far as Troy, New York. Martha was pregnant and was aware of the risks her husband would make in a few days. Brown could not begrudge the couple this good-bye journey together. Brown made an unsuccessful recruiting trip to Philadelphia at the time Oliver left. On the way back he met Oliver and the two ladies at Harrisburg. It was a sad parting. When Brown got back to the farm he learned from Kagi that there would be a search of the two buildings at the Kennedy farm to satisfy the suspicions of cautious neighbors.

Brown hoped that any new men coming after the middle of the month would stay at Chambersburg or Harrisburg until the attack on Harper's Ferry was well in motion. Brown tentatively told his men that the attack would take place at some time after the 6th of October. John E. Cook then joined the group. He had sent his wife away from Harper's Ferry and into the care of Kagi at Chambersburg. On September 25th Osborne P. Anderson arrived at the farm from Canada and carried the promise of several more recruits who were on the way. Osborne Anderson had been a printer and reporter working for a black press in Canada. Brown now had a new problem. The carbines which he considered his most important weapons had arrived without percussion caps. Brown needed 40,000 of them which would cost about a hundred dollars. He didn't have the money.

An event in Boston provided the solution. John Brown had sent one of his last-minute recruiting letters to Lewis Hayden, a leader of Boston's black community. Hayden was devoted to Brown's mission and was trying to raise money to pay the train fare for six black recruits. One day Hayden bumped into Francis Jackson Merriam, a young abolitionist who had just turned twenty-one and inherited some money. Hayden came right to the point and asked for $500 for Brown's cause. Merriam said, "If you tell me where John Brown is, you can have my money and me along with it."

Merriam outfitted Hayden's black recruits and set out for Chambersburg where he eventually located Kagi. Kagi told him about the pressing need for caps, and he and Merriam went to Philadelphia and Baltimore to acquire these items. Brown met Merriam in Philadelphia and made a final try at some understanding with Frederick Douglass. When Brown returned to the farm two new recruits had arrived from Cleveland, Lewis Sheridan Leary and John Anthony Copeland, Jr. Leary was an excellent leather worker and saddler. Copeland had been a student at Oberlin College. Both these men were black.

Harper's Ferry is situated in Jefferson County, Virginia,[2] at the confluence of the Potomac and Shenandoah rivers, on a point just opposite the gap through which both waterways pass the Blue Ridge on their way to the ocean. The Ridge here is about twelve hundred feet in height, showing bare, precipitous cliffs on either side on the river, and exhibiting some of the most beautiful and imposing natural scenery to be found in the country. The town was originally built on two streets stretching along a narrow shelf between the base of the bluff and the rivers, meeting at the point at nearly a right angle, and named respectively Potomac and Shenandoah Streets. To accommodate its increasing population the town extended up the steep bluff, and, in detached villages and scattered

---

[2]   Now West Virginia.

residences, occupied the level ground about four hundred feet above the streams.

In 1859 Harper's Ferry had altogether a population of five thousand residents. It was distant from Richmond by 173 miles; from Washington City 57 miles by turnpike road; and from Baltimore 80 miles by railroad. Here the Baltimore and Ohio Railroad crossed the Potomac over a magnificent covered bridge 900 feet long, and passed along Potomac Street westward, its tracks lying forty feet above the river. The Winchester and Harper's Ferry Railroad, lying along Shenandoah Street, connected with the Baltimore and Ohio Railroad at the bridge. Potomac Street was entirely occupied by the workshops and offices of the national armory, and its entrance was inclosed by a handsome gate and iron railing. Nearly at the angle of the junction the old arsenal buildings were located, where usually from 100,000 to 200,000 stand of arms were stored. The other buildings on the point, and nearer the bridge, included railroad offices, hotels, eateries, stores, shops, etc. Shenandoah Street contained a few stores and dwelling houses for half a mile or more, followed by Hall's Rifle Works, which was situated on a small island in the Shenandoah River.

John Brown had arrived at Harper's Ferry with what he considered a well engineered plan. With his sons Owen and Oliver and his bodyguard Jeremiah G. Anderson he had made himself familiar over a period of time with the city, the arsenal and both entry bridges. John Cook had been working there and informed Brown that the arsenal personnel were mostly indifferent and were not fanatical defenders of slavery. Nor were they well armed. Brown planned on occupying the enclosure within which stood the government buildings. Just outside this enclosure stood a large three-story armory which, it was rumored, stored some forty-five thousand rifles. To the west, along the banks of the Shenandoah River Hall's Rifle works could be seen. It was one-half mile from the point and would have to be occupied.

On Sunday morning, October 16, 1859 Brown read his Bible passage and after the service Jeremiah Anderson was made the chairman of the revolutionary council. The new recruits were sworn in under Brown's constitution, which was the document declaring the independence for the enslaved men of the country. The men were told that they would move out that night, and it was important that the new recruits read over the provisional constitution that morning. Brown read article 32 to them which stated that they should not treat anyone with cruelty, insult or needless severity.[3] In the afternoon Brown called the men together again and issued a series of written orders covering in detail their actions. They were to move into battle that night. The men were told to get some rest, but many wrote letters of farewell and hope.

At 8:00 PM John Brown exclaimed, "Men, arm yourself; we will then proceed to the Ferry." The last thing Brown said was, **"Do not take the life of anyone needlessly, if you can possibly avoid it; but if it is necessary to take life in order to save your own, then make sure work of it."**

It took but a minute to bring the horse and wagon to the door. They then started out on a damp starless October night—nineteen men ready to take on the slavery and tyranny of the state of Virginia. Three men were left behind to guard the arms and direct any unknown recruits. These were Brown's son Owen who had a withered arm, Francis Merriam who had a missing eye and the youngster Barclay Coppoc. Brown rode the wagon wearing his colorful "Kansas Cap." He had 20 pikes, a crowbar, a sledge hammer and some incendiary material aboard. It was five miles to the Maryland end of the Potomac bridge. Most of the man marched behind the wagon down the rutted road. Cook and Charles Tidd went first; they were to cut the telegraph wires to Washington and Baltimore on the poles just outside the bridge.

As they arrived at the bridge Brown ordered the men to lock and load their carbines. John Kagi and Aaron Stevens moved out at 10:30 PM towards the Virginia end of the bridge in the dark. The rest of the men waited at the Maryland entrance. A track watchman came toward them with his lantern in hand, alarmed at the activity which was unusual for this normally quiet hour of night. A few of Brown's men grabbed him and

---

[3]   An abridged copy of the Constitution appears in the appendix.

he was told that he was their prisoner, but that no harm was intended him. Stevens took the watchman's lantern, entered the bridge, and peered down the rails. He then turned around and waved the lantern in a wide arc to tell Brown and his men that it was safe to enter.

The watchman who was quite submissive stood quietly by. When Cook and Brown's son Watson came along, cradling their Sharp's rifles in their arms and revolvers in their belts, the watchman actually snickered because the men looked so stupid. Brown drove his wagon into the covered bridge and was soon out on the Virginia side. There were no shots, no screams, and all was quiet. The bridge head emptied out into the Harper's Ferry public square. To the right was a railroad depot joined to a hotel called the Wager House and on the left was a saloon called the Galt House.

To the right just beyond the Wager House, was Brown's target—the government armory, less than 150 feet away. Also in the armory complex was a brick building called the engine house, so called, because two bays of the building held fire-fighting equipment. The third bay, called the watch house, was a make-shift office and assembly room for the watchmen. It had a door and two windows cut into its front. Brown planned to use the watch house as his headquarters.

The armory gate was locked shut so Tidd and Aaron Stevens tried to force it open. Daniel Whelen, a 39 year old building watchman, who was relaxing in the watch house, heard the commotion and came out shouting, "Hold on—you can't open that gate!" Two of Brown's men grabbed him by the coat. Whelan shoved them aside, so five more of Brown's men ran up and placed their guns against his breast. They said, "Give up your keys, or else!" Whelan said he couldn't let them have his keys, so they knocked him down on the ground and went to the wagon for a crowbar and a large hammer. They broke open the chain on the fence and poured into the enclosure. Then the wagon was driven in. Brown left one man at each side of the gate as a guard and then walked over to Whelan with Bill Williamson, the bridge watchman who had just been captured. He told these men that he came from Kansas and wanted to free all the Negroes in Virginia. He said that he now had possession of the United States armory, and that if the citizens interfered with him he would torch the town and blood would surely flow.

As it now stood two of Brown's men were on the bridge. Three men (including Brown) occupied the arsenal, and another group under the command of Kagi went off to take possession of Hall's Rifle Works, about a half-mile up the river off of Shenandoah Street. Brown knew that this move was chancy because it tied up Kagi who was Number Two in command. After Kagi, Copeland and the others were sent off, Brown remained outside the engine house and questioned Whelen about the personnel of the government works. Brown learned that they would all be reporting to work at daybreak and he planned to take them into custody at that time.

At precisely midnight another bridge watchman, Patrick Higgins, came to his post to work his twelve hour shift. He noticed that the lights supposed to be burning at each end of the bridge were out, and that his fellow watchman was missing. He started down the length of the dark bridge and called out "Bill, where are you Bill?" About half-way in he bumped into Oliver Brown and William Thompson. Oliver seized Higgins and told him to come along quietly. Oliver intended to put him into the watch house at the arsenal with the other watchman. Higgins walked along quietly for a while but when Oliver got distracted by some sounds he was able to wrench his arm from Oliver's grasp. Oliver swung around, only to be smacked by Higgins' hot lantern. Thompson fired his rifle at the escaping Higgins, putting a bullet through his hat and grazing his scalp.

This shot, however, awoke some town residents including Dr. John D. Starry and the night clerk who was dozing on a couch in the lobby of the Wager House. Starry had no idea why a shot was fired, but Throgmorton, the night clerk recalled seeing a wagon coming over the bridge two hours earlier. Throgmorton went out on the hotel porch where he saw Oliver and Thompson guarding the bridge and taking a few night-owl citizens into custody. Throgmorton had heard rumors that the men at the arsenal were striking for higher wages and thought that this might be the explanation for the late night activity.

The first side thrust was put into motion at just past midnight. Aaron Stevens was put in command of three blacks and two whites to go up High Street and then go west for about five miles to the plantation of Lewis Washington. The blacks were Osborne Anderson, Shields Green and Lewis Leary. The whites were John Cook and Charles Tidd, both very good friends of Aaron Stevens. They arrived at the plantation and broke into the rear gate at 1:30 AM. Then they called Washington's name out in a very low voice. He was in bed and asleep. Washington supposed it to be some friend who had arrived late, and being familiar with the house, had been admitted in the rear by the servants. Washington opened the door in his night shirt and slippers. As he opened the door he saw four armed men with guns pointed at him. Three had rifles and one a large revolver. The man with the revolver held a glowing torch in his left hand. Stevens, the man who was in charge, asked him what his name was. On being told that he was Lewis Washington, Stevens said, "You are our prisoner!" "Oh God," said Washington, "What's going on?"

Washington was a colonel on the staff of Governor Wise of Virginia and a prominent citizen. He recognized Cook instantly as the man he had invited to his home some time back and exhibited his historic treasures to. Cook knew that Washington had two rare pistols given George Washington by Lafayette. Cook had also seen the sword presented by Frederick the Great to General Washington which was used by the latter as his dress sword. Stevens demanded that the sword be handed over to Osborne Anderson. Stevens told Colonel Washington that they wanted his slaves and were going to take him into town as well. He said they had come to abolish slavery and they would not be hurt if they did not resist. Cook ransacked the house taking a shotgun, a small rifle, the two pistols and another sword supposedly used by General Washington.

After a short while the male slaves were brought around a large four-horse wagon belonging to Washington which had been hitched up by Shields Green. The slaves called him "Emperor." The slaves seemed willing to go along with the intrigue. Washington's private carriage was also loaded for the ride into Harper's Ferry. Down the road the carriage stopped at the home of Mrs. Henderson, widow of Richard Henderson. Washington remarked, "There is no one here but ladies, and it would be a shame to wake them up at this hour of the night." Tidd jumped out, went back to the wagon, made some remarks, and they went on.

They then arrived at the residence of John Allstadt and broke in his front door with a fence rail. Stevens, Tidd and Cook climbed over the broken door and dragged Allstadt out of bed and told him to dress immediately as he was being taken into town as a hostage. His eighteen year old son[4] came downstairs and was also taken as a hostage. His daughters were ignored even when they yelled for help out the front windows. As Allstadt was being ushered out the door he saw that six of his slaves had been rounded up and loaded on the wagon. On the road back they met some colored men who agreed to join them. Stevens asked some of them to go around to the colored people and circulate the news that they were liberating slaves.

At 1:25 AM the train from Wheeling, Virginia, bound for Baltimore came in. It was a mail train, but carried some passengers. Patrick Higgins, who had escaped Brown's men earlier, ran into the train shed and shouted to the engineer to stop. Higgins yelled out that the bridge was in possession of some crazy people who had extinguished the lights, were taking prisoners, and were heavily armed. The engineer put the train in reverse and moved it back to the loading platform, and two or three nosy passengers hopped off the train to see what was going on. The engineer climbed nervously down from his cab and had a conference with Higgins and Mr. Throgmorton who had arrived breathlessly from the hotel.

Higgins told his story of being captured and showed his fresh wound. He predicted dire consequences if the train proceeded. Phelps,

---

[4] Newspapers had reported his age as sixteen, but Mr. Allstadt said his son "was either eighteen or nineteen years old" when interrogated later by the U. S. Senate Select Committee.

the conductor, said he doubted if anyone would stop the U.S. mail, but that they ought to check it out. They were joined by the porter from the depot, a black man by the name of Shephard Hayward, who was in the employment of the Baltimore & Ohio Railroad Company. Hayward was a big smiling man, well liked by the station personnel, and he served them with great courtesy. As the group of men moved down the dimly lit shed where there was a "Y" joint in the rails, they faintly saw four men ahead with rifles pointed at them. Oliver, thinking it was Higgins back with reinforcements yelled out, "Halt!" Thompson fired a shot over their heads, but Hayward kept coming in their direction. Thompson yelled, "Damn you, halt!" and fired his rifle. It ricocheted off the walls of the tunnel. He fired a second round which passed through Hayward's back and entered his chest. Hayward staggered back and flung his arm around Higgins, who dragged him to cover in the depot office.

Harper's Ferry also had its Paul Revere. He was John D. Starry, a physician of the town, who lived just a stone's throw from the Wager House. The shot which mortally wounded Hayward aroused him, as did the injured man's cry of distress. He went at once to Hayward's side, only to find he was near death. He heard the firing on the street which made the conductor beat a retreat, but Dr. Starry was not to be scared. He stood at the corner of the station and watched three of the raiders approaching. He notified the alarmed passengers who had crowded into the train depot that he would follow the strangers into the armory and find out what it was all about. He did so, but got no answers and returned to the station.

John Brown did not know that Hayward had been shot but he was not pleased to hear the sounds of the train across the armory yard. Someone put out the train's lights. A panic seized some of the train passengers, and the women were brought into the Wager House and given smelling salts. The men clutched their money belts expecting the worst. Brown didn't want to contend with the train passengers, but when, after a few hours, he still saw the train standing there, he made an attempt to get it moved out. At 3:00 AM he sent an elderly man named Grist, who had been picked up on the Shenandoah Bridge, to tell Conductor Phelps he should go on. Grist first went to the hotel, but it was locked up and dark. He then went to the depot where he found Phelps, the conductor, who had left his car. Phelps inquired angrily, "What the hell is this all about?" Mr. Grist answered patiently, "The parties who arrested me have instructed me to tell you that you should cross the bridge with your train as fast as possible." Phelps replied that he wouldn't take the train through until it was daylight and he could see that it was perfectly safe.

Grist could do no more but to report back to Brown that the train would not move. Brown told Grist that he was free to go home, but Grist went back to the hotel where he remained for the rest of the night. In his desire to keep the action bloodless Brown reasoned that men not in arms were not against him. That, of course, was a mistake.

John Brown was elated to see Stevens when he arrived back at the armory yard at 3:45 AM on Monday morning. The captured armory personnel stared in wonderment as the Washington and Allstadt entourage trooped in. Brown welcomed Colonel Washington and told him he would be treated with respect as a valued hostage. Washington was shivering as it was damp and drizzling that Monday morning, and Brown told him to warm himself up at a stove which was inside. The freed blacks were also brought in to be warmed. They were then pressed into duty to stand guard by the gate. Osborne Anderson handed each one a pike to be used if anyone tried to rush them.

Thomas Boerley, a small grocery store keeper who lived down the street, saw what was going on. He grabbed up his gun and ran to the nearest corner of the armory gate and fired into the ranks of the black men with the pikes. Shields Green, standing near by, fired back, killing him instantly. Then deadly silence reigned again. Brown was told of the shooting and shrugged his shoulders knowing that things like that would occur. He was busy holding about forty-five men hostage between the armory gate and the engine house.

At 5:05 AM on Monday morning the big four-horse wagon was sent back into Maryland. Riding it were John E. Cook, Tidd, William Leeman and four of the liberated slaves. The hostages believed that the wagon was loaded with government rifles which were taken to Brown's men waiting in the Maryland woods to be armed and brought into the attack. The last thing the hostages saw was a nondescript young black man carrying Lewis Washington's fine shotgun who jumped on the wagon as it pulled out. At this time the hostages guessed that the liberated slaves just might fight with John Brown.

Brown's orders to Cook were to go as far as the plantation of forty-two year old Terrence Byrne, a Maryland slave owner. They were to take Byrne a hostage and then liberate his slaves. Some of the men were to continue on to their farm one and a half miles further north and bring the guns to the school house. Cook, riding up front on the big wagon, saw Byrne as he was riding towards Harper's Ferry on his horse. At 5:30 AM, just as Byrne passed the tail gate of the wagon he heard a voice call out, "Mr. Byrne, stop right now." Byrne reigned up his horse and looked back. He recognized John E. Cook whom he had known in the neighborhood. Cook got off the wagon and approached Byrne on the right side of his horse, and remarked, "I am very sorry to inform you that you are my prisoner." Byrne looked at him and smiled, and said, "You are certainly joking!" Cook said, "I certainly am not." Byrne saw the barrel of a rifle protruding under Cook's coat, and he kept jerking it around. Tidd poked his rifle menacingly at Byrne's chest and said, "No parley here, or I will put a ball through you. You must go with us to your place. We want your Negroes." Byrne then replied, "Well I would rather go back with you than get shot."

So they went back to Terence Byrne's house where Byrne met his brother at the porch. He whispered the words, "It's war!" to him and walked in. It was now 5:50 AM. Cook, Leeman and Tidd seated themselves uninvited. Byrne nervously paced up and down the room while Cook lectured Byrne's brother on slavery. Byrne's paid very little attention to what Cook said. Byrnes's cousin, a lady of considerable nerve, came downstairs and the first thing she said was, "Cowhide these scoundrels out of the house; why do you suffer them to talk to you?" Byrne said, "Cook told my brother that he wanted our slaves. His reply was, Captain Cook you must do what I do when I want them—hunt for them." The servants had left on Saturday evening and had not returned as yet. Only the women and children were left at home.

Cook and Leeman remained with Byrne while Tidd took Colonel Washington's wagon and five or six slaves back up the road to the Kennedy farm where Owen Brown had been left in charge. At the farm they started loading the big wagon with powder and other implements next to the boxes containing the Sharp's rifles. Owen fed them a late breakfast and then they continued their task of loading the wagon. It was a slow process and it was almost 9:15 AM before they started off again. When the wagon got back to Terrence Byrne's house, he was told that he must be taken along as a hostage. Cook explained to him that Brown's men had possession of the armory, the railroad bridge, and the telegraph, and that Colonel Washington was a prisoner. So they left with Byrne as their hostage.

They first went to the school house where the arms were deposited. They had to pass by it on the road. When the wagon halted Tidd went in and asked Mr. Currie, the school teacher to suspend school for a while. He said they wanted to deposit some boxes there. Mr. Currie asked the children to stay. At one point he came out and Byrne whispered across the fence to him that he was a prisoner and remarked to him, "You have nothing to fear, you are not a slave holder," but Currie whispered back, "Oh yes I am!" Tidd, Cook and the slaves unloaded the arms, while Leeman and the hostage Byrne set out for Harper's Ferry on foot.

William Thompson appeared on the road with a blanket over his shoulders and armed. He extended his hand and said, "How are you Mr. Byrne?" Byrne replied, "Good morning Mr. Thompson; I am quite well, and how are you?" Byrne asked him about the news at Harper's Ferry, and Thompson said that the Ferry was completely under the control of the liberators. Thompson then left to tell Cook at the school house to hurry up the loaded wagon as the weapons were sorely needed by Brown.

It then commenced raining very hard and Leeman suggested they get under a tree until the shower passed. They took refuge and Byrne pulled out his umbrella. He asked Leeman to share it with him while they were waiting for the rain to let up. While sitting under the tree Leeman remarked to Byrne, "Did you know that our captain is not Isaac Smith but the famous John Brown of Kansas notoriety." When the rain let up they proceeded on to Harper's Ferry. When Leeman and Byrne crossed the bridge they were greeted by Oliver Brown, who shook hands with Byrne. Put among the other hostages Byrne greeted them with feigned cheerfulness, "Good morning gentlemen, I hope I am in good company."

Brown and Stevens returned from the bridge after the train had left. Brown sent some of the hostages home to eat breakfast and the bar keeper was sent over to the hotel with a note to prepare "a good breakfast for forty-seven men." A friendly, middle-aged man, Mr. Throgmorton, wandered over to the enclosure from the hotel to see what was going on. He had noticed that armed blacks were going in and out of the watch house to get warm at the stove. While shivering at the armory grounds he was invited by Brown to come in and get warm himself. Then Brown asked him if he would go to the hotel to pick up the breakfasts he had ordered. Throgmorton left and returned a little later with a young black pushing a handcart loaded down with a large assortment of hot food. Both Colonel Washington and Mr. Allstadt refused to eat saying the food might be poisoned. Brown was also too preoccupied to eat. Soon after breakfast Brown sent Osborne Anderson and Shields Green to back up the men in the arsenal and he sent Lewis Leary and three freed slaves down to Hall's Rifle Works to reinforce Kagi. Lastly he sent William Thompson over the bridge to find Cook and tell him to get the rifles to the armory.

After everyone had breakfast a strange hold-off persisted at the engine house. Some of the hostages went into the watch house and napped on the floor. John Brown walked around checking the bridge, the arsenal, and the men around the engine house. Brown realized that things were much too quiet. This submission of the towns people was puzzling. Brown wanted to openly negotiate with them for more slaves and then move into the mountains. This wasn't happening. Brown sent Jeremiah Anderson to see how Kagi was doing at the Rifle Works, and Anderson brought back the urgent message that Kagi thought they should move out immediately. Brown sent a reply for Kagi to hang on a little longer as he did not want to leave the men and the Sharp's rifles abandoned on the Maryland side of the river.

Edwin Coppoc was on guard at the gate at 6:40 AM, when the train conductor asked him what he wanted to do with his train. Coppoc looked at him in surprise. "We don't want to injure you or detain your train. You should have left when you were requested to at 3:00 AM, so you better go talk to the captain." After locating Brown he inquired what security he would have to get his train safely through the tunnel and on its way East. Brown said he would walk over the bridge ahead of the train with Phelps. Brown then asked Stevens to join him and the three of them started out to cross the bridge. The train slowly followed them and at the other end Brown shook hands with Conductor Phelps and asked him not to reveal what was going on at Harper's Ferry. Phelps agreed and jumped on the train as it departed.

The train flew down the track towards Baltimore, stopping at about 7:05 AM at Monocacy Station where Conductor Phelps sent a telegram on to W. P. Smith, the master of transportation at Baltimore, saying that an insurrection had broke out at Harper's Ferry where an armed band of hoodlums had full possession of the government arsenal and the town. He said the bridge was guarded by insurgents, all armed. Phelps said the insurrectionists planned to free all the slaves and intended to do so at all hazards. He suggested that the Secretary of War be notified at once. Phelps said the local telephone wires were cut and that Monocacy was the first station where he could send off his dispatch. The President of the railroad, John W. Garrett saw the conductor's dispatch and lost no time in acting upon it. By 10:30 AM he had telegraphed to the President of the United States, to Governor Wise, of Virginia, and to Major General George H. Stewart, commanding the First Light Division, Maryland Volunteers, in Baltimore, that an insurrection was in progress in Harper's Ferry, in which free Negroes and whites were engaged. Moreover, from Monocacy word had reached Frederick, a short distance away, and by

10:00 AM the military company of that place was under arms. President Buchanan called in Colonel Robert E. Lee and told him he was going to send a company of ninety marines to the Ferry, by special train, under the command of Lieutenant Israel Green.

Back at Harper's Ferry John Brown held a number of conversations with the hostages. He asked Armistead Ball, the master machinist, if he would deliver into his possession all the war munitions belonging to the government in exchange for his freedom. Ball answered, "They are already in your possession, as we are." Brown could not understand why some city official was not there bargaining for the hostages release. An unhealthy stalemate existed.

Fontaine Beckham, the mayor of Harper's Ferry and railroad agent was at the Wager House and knew it was his responsibility to do something about the unfolding insurrection. He was aware that time, however, was on the side of the townspeople because surely military help would soon be coming from the outside. At a little past noon on Monday Brown heard the echo of a body of men moving down the road to the bridge on the Maryland side. Perhaps Cook had a small band of men to escort the Maryland arms across the bridge. Aaron Stevens and Brown went out to the gate to offer a welcome. Then they heard heavy firing and saw Oliver, Stewart Taylor and Dangerfield Newby come running out from the bridge; firing at some fleeting shadows behind them. It was foe and not friend that they heard.

Hearing the gunfire, Osborne Anderson, Albert Hazlett and Shields Green ran out of the arsenal while Watson Brown came over from the Shenandoah Bridge. Captain Brown shouted, "Let go on them!" Brown's men fired at the approaching troops and several of them fell. The troops scattered, some of them trying to carry off their wounded buddies. They didn't seem to realize that Brown's men would fire at them. The consequence was that after leaving several wounded on the field they beat a confused retreat back over the bridge and stayed there waiting under cover for reinforcements.

ATTACK AT THE BRIDGE

Brown had driven back this first attack but some of the soldiers found their way into deserted houses in the vicinity of the town square. Dangerfield Newby stepped out and looked down a deserted street in the direction of his home in the Virginia mountains. Suddenly a shot rang out and Newby became the first Brown casualty. The missile tore into his neck and blood gushed out from his severed jugular vein. He fell to the ground and expired immediately. Shields Green, standing beside him saw a man on horseback pointing a gun. Green instinctively shot and killed the stranger. Osborne Anderson took Green by the arm, telling him that he had to take cover or suffer the same fate as Newby. Anderson urged Green to come back with him to the arsenal building, but Shields seeing that Brown was under fire at the armory yard, shook him off and said, "I'm going to go with Captain Brown."

Shortly after Dangerfield Newby's death a number of hogs came rooting about him. They tugged away at him and Joseph Barry, a village shop keeper, saw that one black and white porker had run his snout into a wound and dragged out a sinew of some kind. It appeared to be very long and elastic. One end was in the hog's mouth and the other in Newby's body. "This circumstance," remarked Barry, "could not fail to improve the flavor and value of pork at Harper's Ferry next winter."

Another eye-witness of the day's events was John G. Rosengarten, who was a Northerner on his way back East from Chicago on the Baltimore train. It had stopped at a small station some miles west of the Ferry, held there by the rumor that there was trouble at Harper's Ferry caused by a strike of the workmen at the arsenal.

Rosengarten got off the train and took the long walk on to Harper's Ferry. He finally reached High Street which leads down Bolivar Heights to the arsenal yards. He was joined by a man on horseback carrying an army musket. The man was a retired officer, a West Point graduate, and he told Rosengarten that his name was George W. Turner, and that he was from Wheatland, about five miles from Charlestown. He said that a band of abolitionists were gathered down there to set all the slaves free. Rosengarten noticed that he and Turner were the only two men standing in the middle of a seemingly deserted street. Looking down the hill not a soul was visible and only a few persons could be seen moving about in the arsenal inclosure. George Turner, hearing the shot that felled Dangerfield Newby, raised his musket to his shoulder. A sudden gun shot rang out killing George Turner instantly. Coming from nowhere a few towns people came out the side street holding a white flag and carried off the body of Turner without a question or a word of explanation.

Rosengarten was completely bewildered by what he had just witnessed, and beat a hasty retreat down High Street toward the arsenal, "with some vague notion of being a peacemaker." On the way he was accosted by a small group of men who took him to the Galt House to be turned over as a suspicious person. Rosengarten protested that he was only an ordinary traveler from a stalled train and showed his ticket stub as proof of his innocence. It only convinced the authorities of his guilty intent. Rosengarten pleaded that he was not an abolitionist and that Governor Wise would vouch for him.

When John Brown got back to the engine house he found that all the hostages had run into the watch house. The forty-odd frightened men in the watch house crowded around Brown as if they needed his protection. Brown announced that he was picking out ten hostages to take into the engine house with him. He first picked Colonel Washington. One man, not picked, said bitterly, "I suppose you are going to leave the rest of us here to be shot down at random." "No, sir," said Brown, "I am going to defend you as well as all the others. I give you my pledge that you will come out of this unharmed and sent home to your families, and I will keep my word."

As Brown walked the chosen men into the engine house a group of militia stationed on the railroad trestlework, which ran on the north boundary of the armory enclosure, opened fire. "They will kill us," moaned one of the hostages. A stranger came out from one of the houses on Shenandoah Street and ran over to the inert body of Dangerfield Newby. He took out a sharp knife from his shirt and quickly sliced off the ears of the cadaver as a souvenir. The ferociousness due to a slave rebellion was out of hand. Brown looked back and saw that several men on the trestlework were firing at the engine house. "Their guns are no good," said Brown, "they're falling short." Stevens went out and began firing his Sharp's rifle at them. The snipers inched their way to the water tower beside the trestlework. Mr. Kitzmiller, the armory superintendent intervened. "This is getting to be hot and dirty work. If you will allow me a suggestion, I think I can accommodate matters. Mr. Brua has been won over to your cause. We are not your enemies."

A gentleman by the name of Reason Cross joined in on the conversation. He suggested that a paper be drawn up signed by all the hostages that would ask for a cease fire in exchange for their release and Brown's retention of the arsenal and the slaves, the question of which to be settled at a later time by the government. This was agreed to. William Thompson was selected to escort Mr. Cross over the yard to the hotel. Reason assured everyone that Mayor Beckham was a fair man and would listen to "reason."

As they started out sniper fire issued forth from the water tower. Brown shouted, "tell the mayor to get those sharpshooters away from the water tower. They will kill their neighbors." Thompson had a white handkerchief tied on his gun and when he got out of range of the engine house, some man ran out and seized him. He was tied securely and dropped on the ground. Reason Cross protested loudly, but the man threatened to tie him up as well. Thompson was taken to the hotel and locked up in a room there.

Things were not going well at the engine house either. There was increased militia fire. Colonel Baylor, the militia commander had complained that they did not have enough rifles. But this deficiency was corrected, as new guns were now in the hands of the Virginia militia, and were being used against the engine house. Mr. Brua asked for permission for a short parole. With no sign of William Thompson coming back with Reason Cross, Captain Brown gave his permission. Mr. Brua walked out confidently and returned some fifteen minutes later. According to Colonel Washington he had "brought back a promise that the militia would not act while negotiations were pending."

Mr. Kitzmiller now made his plea that he be allowed to carry out the negotiations for the release of the hostages. Here John Brown made another mistake. Brown figured that his rear guard was holding the bridge and he agreed to let Kitzmiller go out and negotiate. "Take Stevens and Watson along," he said. "There is a company of my riflemen on the bridge." Kitzmiller put his white handkerchief on his walking stick and the three started out. When they got to the bridge Kitzmiller recognized some local people and went out in front to talk to them. Stevens called him back.

At that moment George Chambers, owner of the Galt House and town clerk, drew a bead on Aaron Stevens and shot him in the thigh. Stevens screamed in pain, but remained standing. He started firing into the bridge opening, clearing out the militia men. But then another good shot from Chambers, who was firing from the second floor of his saloon brought Stevens down. A stray shot from the bridge hit Watson Brown in the chest. He crawled back to the engine house dragging his rifle with him. John Brown lost his temper. "What kind of dogs are they, shooting down my men, butchering them under a flag of truce?" Mr. Brua told Brown that he would go out and see if he could do something for Stevens. He also said he would try for some halt in the slaying. Brown said, "You go at your own risk, I will not send out any more men!"

As Mr. Brua was leaving Willie Leeman decided to go along behind Kitzmiller, using him for cover, and then break for the river. Brown asked him to try and rescue Steven's rifle so that it would not be used against them, to which Leeman agreed. Leeman successfully walked out under Brua's cover and then ran over to Steven's side, snatched his gun, and ran into the hotel. He accidentally dropped the gun going through the front door, but kept on running through the hotel and out the back door. He made his way through a culvert which was nearby and followed it to the river where he got into the shallow water. Holding his own gun over his head he made his way in breast-high water to a rock in the river. He pulled himself onto it and collapsed with exhaustion. The militia men spotted him and began firing at him from the railroad trestle. Leeman raised his arms in surrender. A Virginia militiaman waded out and blew Leeman's head off with his pistol. Waving to his buddies on the trestle, he cut off Leeman's shirt for a trophy. He then propped the body up on the rocks, where the militiamen used it for target practice the rest of the afternoon.

When Mr. Brua got to Steven's side he knew the young man was close to death. He was covered with blood and dazed with shock. Brua tried to lift him up but could not do it alone. Throgmorton came gallantly to his assistance and the two of them dragged Stevens into the hotel and got him into a spare room. Stevens groaned. "What can I do for you Stevens? Brua asked. "Take my body from this place," came the whispered answer and he then slipped into unconsciousness. Brua folded Steven's arms across his chest and ran back to John Brown at the engine house.

SNIPER FIRE FROM THE WATER TOWER

Mayor Beckham could see the men firing from the water tower. He decided to investigate and made his way down to the trestlework near the tower. He looked around to see where the firing was coming from. Edwin Coppoc, watching Beckham from the engine room door, was upset and said. "If he keeps on peeking I'm going to shoot him." One of the prisoners shouted, "Don't shoot for God's sake." They'll shoot in here and kill us all. But it was too late. Coppoc shot and Mayor Beckham fell to the ground dead.

These actions increased the bloodlust of the militia. Without hesitation George Chambers of Williamsport and Henry Hunter[5] ran to the rooms where Stevens and William Thompson were located. Hunter leveled his gun at Thompson whose hands were tied behind his back. A young lady by the name of Christine Fouke begged him not to kill Thompson before her

---

[5]   Henry Hunter was the son of the State's Special Attorney, Andrew Hunter.

eyes. Chambers and Hunter took Thompson by the throat and dragged him outside and dropped him off the edge of the bridge. Standing three or four feet away they fired into his body again and again as they flung him off the bridge. They continued to fire at him with their revolvers until he landed into the water forty feet below. Thompson's will to live was so strong that he was able to climb on to an abutment for a minute or two. He was finally terminated by another fuselage of bullets Chambers and Hunter, having heard about the members of Brown's team at Hall's Rifle Works started off there hoping to add new trophies. At the works Kagi was disheartened by the long hours of separation from the rest of Brown's men. He was getting ready to abandon the post with his comrades and some of the slaves. Looking out of the window at the Rifle Factory he saw that he was hemmed in by hundreds of men. Kagi and his men decided to escape by the back way and waded out into the shallow waters of the Shenandoah River. Leary, Kagi and John Copeland made for a flat rock in the river out of gunshot range. About 50 militia men were firing at them. Kagi was hit and died before they got to the rock. Leary was then badly wounded while climbing up, but Copeland hid behind some stones and floated down river. A militia man came out into the river and spied Copeland as he was floating past. He was going to kill Copeland like Leeman had been killed. He lifted his rifle, aimed and pulled the trigger, but nothing happened. His ammunition was wet. Dr. Starry, still on his horse, saw what was going on. While a gang of men were knotting their handkerchiefs together to hang Copeland, Starry rode into their group and succeeded in staving off the execution. John Copeland was then taken to the armory office under guard.

Brown, knowing nothing about any of these killings, still hoped that his rear guard was coming. At about four in the afternoon a company of railroad workers, under the command of Captain Alburtis decided that they could do what the Virginia militia could not—take Brown in the engine house. Brown only had seven of his men in the engine house, including his son Watson who was fatally wounded. Osborne Anderson and Albert Hazlett, still occupying the armory, were as yet undetected. Captain Alburtis's company marched through the armory yard from the West just as some of Brown's men came out of the engine house, looking for a possible escape route. The assailants were no match for the Sharp's rifles and eight of Alburtis's men were shot. The company succeeded in getting to the watch house section of Brown's headquarters and found some thirty or forty prisoners who had been held by the outlaws. The windows were broken in by Alburtis's men and three men escaped. All of Brown's men were now driven into the engine house.

WILLIAM THOMPSON SHOT & THROWN OFF THE BRIDGE

Watson Brown, bleeding internally, fired repeatedly and fainted after the battle. It was obvious that he would die soon. The demoralized Virginia militiamen, who lurked under cover behind the water tower, fired intermittently into the engine house. They were also drinking freely and the hostages warned Brown that they were drunk enough to come head-on and fire blindly into the door of the engine house. Oliver or Edwin Coppoc went to the door and fired a few shots, thus keeping the yard clear from an enemy advance.

During one of the shooting flurries Oliver stepped to the door where a militiaman spotted him and fired. Oliver fell to the floor, fatally wounded. It was now too late for Captain Brown to shoot his way out, so he grimly held on to his hostages hoping that the standoff could be resolved somehow. Shortly after Oliver was hit an elderly citizen approached the engine house and told Brown through the door that he was Samuel Strider and that Brown should surrender. Brown scribbled out a note saying that he would take all his prisoners and cross the Potomac bridge, at which point he would set them at liberty; and after which he would negotiate about the government property as might be best. Mr. Strider ran back to the militia with the note and returned shortly with a reply:

> Sir, I cannot accept the terms proposed. Under no consideration will I consent to a removal of our citizens across the river.
>
>
>
> Robert W. Baylor
> Colonel, Commandant
> 3rd Regiment, Cavalry
>
>

When old man Strider left, Brown asked him if he would send a doctor to look at his wounded.

Cook and the rear guard who were alone at the school house had heard firing in the distance but did not know what was happening. Tidd and the liberated slaves had gone back to the farm for another load of rifles. When Cook first arrived at the school he wanted the students to carry on as if nothing happened. Mr. Currie, the school master said this was impossible and the boys were so frightened that they were unable to do their school work. Cook sent them all home. One boy was hysterical and Currie asked Cook to let him accompany the child home. Cook said he would allow this if Currie would swear to return. In the meantime the slaves unloading the wagon told Cook that Currie was a slave owner and lived only a mile up the road from Colonel Washington. Cook felt obligated to stay at the school house and guard the arms.

When Tidd, who had been gone for over three hours on his second trip, finally arrived Cook snatched up a rifle and started for the Ferry. Behind him followed one of the free slaves with a shotgun. Cook called him Joe. At the canal lock-keeper's house, just above the bridge a woman told Cook that Brown's men were hemmed in at the arsenal and several of them had been shot. Cook wanted to go on but Joe demanded that they go back for reinforcements. Cook ordered Joe to explain the situation to Tidd and allow him to prepare accordingly. Cook continued his scramble down the Maryland Heights cliff. At one point he could see the men on High Street pouring fire into the armory inclosure. He even tried to fire a few shots at them himself but was unsuccessful.

After this he climbed down and came out by a small store near the canal. Seeing several people he pointed his gun at them and motioned for someone to come forward. A man approached Cook who knew him and said that John Brown was dead and that all his company were killed or taken prisoner.

"John Brown was shot at 4:00 PM," the man repeated. Cook was distraught and the man took him into the store and made him a cup of coffee. Cook then decided to go back to the school house. When Joe got to Tidd and the small group at the school house, he told them that Brown's men were hemmed in across the bridge and action was necessary to help them get away. Tidd cried out, "It's hopeless, hopeless!" While Tidd was sulking Joe rode back to the Kennedy farm and told Owen and the others they must leave at once to join in the fight at the Ferry.

When given the word to abandon the farm, Barclay Coppoc, Merriam and Owen loaded up all the guns they could carry and started down the road. They realized that they were Brown's last hope. The rain and coming dusk obscured their passage. Owen saw someone in the distance who raised his rifle. Then a face emerged and Owen called out, "Tidd!"

Tidd ran up and said he thought the best thing they could do was to get away from where they were as fast as possible. "We can't leave my father and the men," Owen said, "We better go to the school house, get all the slaves that were left there, and return to the location where Cook had been. Tidd just kept repeating, "It's hopeless! It's hopeless!" Just before they got to the school house they ran into Cook. Cook broke into tears while telling Owen the news that his father was killed at four o'clock, that the rest were killed or captured, and that they should escape immediately at the risk of being captured themselves. Owen heard shots coming from the direction of the armory but Cook insisted they were drunk and were firing without reason.

Owen and Tidd went back to the school house. Tidd followed Owen into the school, revolver in hand. It was empty, but battered school books were scattered all around. Owen and Tidd came out and stood there emotionless, crying out for the liberated slaves from time to time. They went back to the farm, packed up some blankets, and some other small supplies. Owen told the boys that if they stuck by him he felt pretty sure he could get them safely through to the North and Canada. The plan was to travel northwest at night, making no fires, and being silent until they got past Chambersburg. Thus the rear guard left the struggle without firing a shot.

Back at the armory the men were fearful that the militia would try to take them by storm, and night would make it impossible to distinguish between friend and foe. Brown was calm and at one point asked "Big" Phil, who was a stout black fellow, if he could knock a hole through the wall next to the door and handed him a hammer and chisel. Phil and the slaveholder Allstadt soon knocked out a loophole from which to fire into the guard.

Now that it was fairly dark squads of militiamen stood on the trestlework and fired at the engine house without being picked off by Brown's men. Colonel Washington was upset with Shields Green who was constantly watching everybody like a hawk. There was no doubt that the hostages would not attempt to rush Brown, seize the weapons and escape as long as Shields Green stalked among them and the freed slaves stood by them with pikes in hand.

It was now quite dark but John Brown saw a man coming through the armory gate with a white handkerchief showing. Brown pushed the heavy door open a bit and motioned the stranger to come in. He said he was Captain Sinn, commander of a volunteer company from Frederick, Maryland. Sinn was introduced to the hostages and then he asked Brown if he was ready to capitulate. Brown told Sinn he had a proposition, "If I am allowed to take my wagon and my party across the bridge to the edge of the mountain, then you may take me if you can."

Captain Sinn said it was no longer just a question of slavery, that Brown and his men had ruthlessly killed citizens of the town. Brown countered that he did not shoot at any unarmed man. But this was a case of innocent men being caught up in the heat of battle. Brown said that he only fought those who chose to fight him. His hostages were protected, but his two sons were dying,—one shot under a flag of truce.

Looking at the dying boys, Sinn said to Brown, I consider you a brave man. It's a shame that some honorable end can't be arranged." Sinn told Brown how William Leeman died and how his body was being used for target practice. He said he saw Stevens dying in a hotel room. Then he told Brown, "But I have no sympathy for your acts and I am here to bring you to justice." Up until this time Brown had been wearing George Washington's sword. Now he took it off and picked up a gun and said to Sinn, "Please send a doctor to look at my boys, if you can." He pushed open the door and ushered Captain Sinn out. Sinn obliged Brown and a few minutes later a military surgeon attached to Sinn's Company arrived and tendered aid to the wounded. He said he would return at daybreak.

The hostages and freed slaves tried to make themselves comfortable on the brick floor that night. After an hour or so young Oliver died. He had been in agony and his father had told him, "I cry for you, but if you must die, die like a man!" There were now only four of them left besides John Brown; Edwin Coppoc, Jeremiah Anderson, Dauphin Thompson and Shields Green. They waited for the attack Tuesday morning which they knew would come.

Osborne Anderson and Hazlett slipped out of the arsenal building under the cover of darkness before the marines arrived. They walked along the railroad tracks along the Shenandoah River and crossed over to the Virginia side. They found an old boat tied to a tree. They crossed the Potomac in the boat and then went to a farm house which they found ransacked and deserted. They then went on to the school house where they saw no trace of their comrades. They decided that they should make their escape North.

Back at the yard, the marines were taking their position for the final assault under cover of darkness. Robert E. Lee lined up his forces for the attack. He had offered the honor to the Virginia militia, but Colonel Baylor declined, somewhat indignantly. He said he had only come to protect the people of Harper's Ferry, not to attack some insurgents in the engine house. He could not expose citizens to such a risk when there were mercenaries present to do the job.

When the first glimmer of light appeared Shields Green, standing on guard, saw a soldier intently studying the engine house doors. Green took a bead on him with his Sharp's rifle. Brown saw that the man was unarmed and told Green not to shoot. Brown saw well armed marines at every corner and angle of the adjoining buildings. He made some feeble preparations for resisting them by pushing the fire apparatus against the doors and securing them.

Lieutenant J. E. B. Stuart arrived at the door of the engine house with a flag of truce. Brown cracked open the door a bit and they talked. Brown offered the same things as he proposed before. He said the only way he would surrender was that he and his party be allowed to escape across the river. Stuart said, "That is out of the question. All you can do is surrender on the spot." All Brown could do was to trust to the clemency of the United States government. Brown said, "I am prepared to die right where I am." Stuart stepped back from the door and took off his hat and waved it towards Colonel Lee. That was the signal for the attack began.

Twelve marines led by Lieutenant Israel Green ran up to the door with huge sledge hammers and started pounding. The door didn't budge, and the men inside held their fire. Lewis Washington remarked how cool and firm John Brown was at that very moment. With one son dead at his feet and another mortally wounded, he leaned over and felt the pulse of his other dying son with one hand and held his rifle with the other. The hostages were told to take whatever cover they could.

Seeing that the door was not budging Lee sent some men in with a ladder which had been standing against one of the armory buildings. At the second stroke of the ladder the lower left corner of the door broke off. Lieutenant Israel Green, a small wiry man, crawled through the hole and jumped on the fire engine standing near by. Both sides started to fire at each other.

Leaping from the fire engine Lieutenant Green tried to stab Brown to death, but his sword blade was deflected by Brown's cartridge belt. Green started to strike Brown over the head and Brown fell down across Watson's body. As the marines followed their leader through the hole in the door Shields Green fired the last shot, killing Private Luke Quin instantly. The marines stabbed Dauphin Thompson and one of them drove his bayonet into Jeremiah Anderson's body with such force that the blade stuck into the wall leaving Anderson impaled there. Another marine made a few vicious jabs at Brown as he lay apparently unconscious over the body of his son. Soon everything became quiet and the bloodshed at Harper's Ferry was finally at an end.

Chapter 3

AFTERMATH

Aᴌᴌ ᴛʜᴇ ʀᴇsɪᴅᴇɴᴛs of Harper's Ferry showed up early on Tuesday morning the 18th of October to see John Brown, dead or alive! He was spread out on the floor of the engine house in a fetal position and apparently in great pain. At that moment, the hostages poured out of the building and the first of a number of cheers went up. As he came out, John Daingerfield told the crowd to leave Brown to heaven, *"He is dying. He won't last another hour. Let him die peacefully."*

The first man to reach Brown's side was John Rosengarten, the friend of Governor Wise. Brown asked him, "Where is my son?—is he still alive?" Rosengarten told him that his son Watson was still living and was being cared for. Reporters rushed in and began their questioning, and Brown seemed to gain strength from the interrogations.

The dead and wounded were carried out of the engine house and laid on the grass of the armory yard by the marines. The prisoners were greeted with loud execrations, and only humane considerations saved them from immediate execution. The crowd, nearly every man of whom carried a gun, swayed with tumultuous excitement, and cries of "Shoot the bastards!" "Shoot them!" rang from every side. The appearance of the liberated hostages, however, all of whom escaped injury through the steadiness of the marines changed the current of feeling, and prolonged cheers again took the place of the howls and loud swearing. In the assault, Private Ruppert of the marines had received a ball in the stomach, and was badly wounded. Another marine had received a slight flesh wound. They were also gently placed on the lawn.

To all of the onlookers, the lawn presented a dreadful sight. Laying upon it were the bodies of two men killed on the previous day and found inside the building, three wounded men—one of them just at the last gasp of life—and two others groaning in pain. One of the dead was Brown's son Oliver. The wounded Brown and his son Watson, were laying on the grass; the father presenting a gory spectacle. He had a severe bayonet wound in his side and his face and hair were clotted with blood.

A short time after Captain Brown was brought out, he revived somewhat and talked calmly to those about him, defending his course of action and avowing that he had only done what was right. He replied to questions submitted to him as follows:

Question: Are you Captain Brown, of Kansas?
Answer: I am sometimes called so.

Question: Are you Osawatomie Brown?
Answer: I tried to do my duty there.

Question: What is your present object?
Answer: To free the slaves from bondage.

Question: Were any other persons except those with you now connected with the movement?
Answer: No.

Question: Did you expect aid from the North?
Answer: No, there were none connected with the movement but those who came with me.

Question: Did you expect to kill people in order to carry your point?
Answer: I did not wish to do so, but you forced us to it.

Various questions of this kind were put to Captain Brown, which he answered clearly and freely, with seeming anxiety to vindicate himself. He stated that the town had been at his mercy—he could have burned it down and murdered the inhabitants, but did not; he had treated the prisoners with courtesy. He complained that he was hunted down like a beast. He spoke of the killing of his son Watson, which he alleged was done while he was bearing a white flag of truce. He also seemed very anxious about the safety of Oliver, his other wounded son. His conversation expressed his conviction that whatever he had done to free slaves was right, and that, in the warfare in which he was engaged, he was entitled to be treated with all the respect of a prisoner of war. He seemed fully convinced that he was being badly treated and had a right to complain. Although at first he was considered to be dying, an examination of his wounds proved that they were not necessarily fatal. He expressed the desire to live and to be tried by his country.

In his pockets over $300 in gold were found. Several important papers found in his possession were taken charge of by Colonel Lee, on behalf of the government. One such note was as follows[1]:

TO CAPTAIN JOHN BROWN:

Dear Sir: I have been disappointed in not seeing you here ere this to take charge of your freight. The boxes have been here now two weeks, and as I had to superintend the storage of them, it has imposed upon me no small task; besides, if not soon shipped out, some of them will go back to Missouri. I wish to know definitely what you propose on doing. They cannot be kept here much longer without risk, and if any of them are sent back to that state, it will be a bad termination of your enterprise.

---

[1] The note was written in pencil on a page of fine straw-tinted notepaper. It was obviously written by a person of education. It was undated. The freight referred to was undoubtedly that which was usually carried on the underground railroad.

Besides Captain Brown, the prisoners taken were his son Watson, who was seriously injured in the abdomen and was not likely to live, Edwin Coppoc of Iowa, and a Negro named Shields Green, who came from Pittsburgh to join Brown. The stories given by all were precisely the same. They agreed as to the objects proposed to be established, and the number of persons in the movement. Young Brown, in answer to a question, said there were parties in the North connected with the movement, thus differing with his father on this point. Coppoc, twenty-four years old, seemed less shrewd than the others. He said he had not wished to join the expedition, and when asked, gave a reply which revealed the influence which Brown had over him: "Oh, you gentlemen don't know Captain Brown; when he calls for us we <u>never</u> think of refusing to come."

Edwin Coppoc, the brave Iowa boy reported:

I was with Watson Brown at 10:00 AM on Monday morning when he was shot. Even though mortally wounded he fought bravely against the men who charged us at three o'clock in the afternoon. When the enemy was repulsed and the excitement of the charge was over, he began to sink rapidly.

After we were taken prisoner, he was placed in the guard house with me. He was suffering greatly. He complained of the hardness of the bench on which he was lying. I begged hard for a bed for him, or even a blanket, but could obtain none for him. I took off my coat and placed it under him, and held his head in my lap. It was in this position he died this morning at 3:00 AM without a groan or a struggle.

Several slaves were found in the room with the insurrectionists, but it is believed that they were there unwillingly. Indeed, Brown's expectation as to slaves rushing there was entirely disappointed. None seem to have come to him willingly, and in most cases they were forced to desert their masters. Only one instance in which slaves made a public appearance with arms in their hands was related. A slave who had been abused by one of the townspeople took up a pike, and used his brief authority conferred by his possession of that weapon, to arrest a citizen and have him taken to the armory. The citizens imprisoned by the insurrectionists all testified to their lenient treatment. They were neither tied nor insulted, and—beyond the outrage of restricting their liberty—were not ill-treated. Captain Brown was courteous to all of them, and at all times assured them that they would not be injured. He explained his purpose to the workmen, and while he had them in confinement he made no abolition speeches to them. Colonel Lewis Washington spoke of him as a man of extraordinary nerve. Brown never blanched during the assault, though he admitted in the night that escape was impossible, and that he would probably have to die.

Alexander Boteler, the Congressman from Shepherdstown in the Harper's Ferry district, arrived at the engine house shortly after the marines stormed it. He described the end of the fighting as follows:

> I heard a shot, some inarticulate exclamations, and finally the rescued men emerged from the smoke filled building, followed by marines bringing out prisoners. The pent-up feelings of the spectators found appropriate expression in a number of shouts.

> As Colonel Lewis Washington came out of the building I hastened over to him with my congratulations and a query, "Lewis, old fellow, how do you feel?" He replied, "Feel! Why I feel as hungry as a hound and as dry as a powder-horn; for, only think of it, I've not had anything to eat for forty odd hours, and nothing better to drink than water out of a horse-bucket!"

> Colonel Washington told me that when Lieutenant Israel Green leaped into the engine house he greeted him with the exclamation, "God bless you Green! There's Brown!" at the same time pointing out to him "the brave but unscrupulous old fanatic," who, having discharged his

rifle, had seized a spear, and was yet in the half-kneeling position which he had assumed when he fired his last shot. Washington said also, that the cut which Green made at Brown would undoubtedly have cleft his skull if the point of his sword had not caught on a rope and weakened the force of the blow; but it was sufficient to cause Brown to fall to the floor and relax his hold upon the spear. I took possession of that spear as a relic of the raid.

Inside the engine house one of Brown's party was found lying dead on the floor, and another, Watson Brown, was stretched out on a bench at the right-hand side of the door, and seemed to be in a dying condition. John Brown himself had been brought out and was then lying on the grass; but so great was the curiosity to see him that the soldiers found some difficulty in keeping back the crowd, and Colonel Lee consequently had him removed to the superintendent's room in an adjoining building, strictly guarded by sentinels, where, shortly afterward, I had an interview with him, the particulars of which I think you will find most interesting. On entering the room where he was I found him alone, lying on the floor on his left side, and with his back turned towards me. The right side of his face was smeared with blood from the sword-cut on his head, causing his grim and grizzly countenance to look like that of some aboriginal savage with his war-paint on. Approaching him, I began the conversation with an inquiry, "Captain Brown, are you hurt anywhere except on your head?"

"Yes, in my side—here," he said, indicating the place with his hand.

I then told him that a surgeon would be in presently to attend to his wounds, and expressed the hope that they were not very serious. Thereupon he asked me who I was, and on my giving him my name Brown muttered as if speaking to himself, "Yes, yes,—I know now,—member of Congress—this district."

I then asked the question, "Captain, what brought you here?"

"To free your slaves," was the reply.

"How did you expect to accomplish this with the small force you brought with you?"

"I expected help," he said.

"Where, whence, and from whom, captain, did you expect it?"

"Here and from elsewhere," he answered.

"Did you expect to get assistance from whites here as well as from the blacks?" was my next question. "I did," he replied.

"Then," I said, "you have been disappointed in not getting it from either?"

"Yes,' he muttered, "I have—been—disappointed."

I then asked him who planned his movement on Harper's Ferry, to which he replied, "I planned it all myself" and upon my remarking that it was a sad affair for him and the country, and that he trusted no one would follow his example by undertaking a similar raid, he made no response. I next inquired if he had any family besides the sons who had accompanied him on his incursion, to which he replied by telling me he had a wife and children in the state of New York at North Elba, and on my then asking if he would like to write to them and let them know how he was, he quickly responded, "Yes, I would like to send them a letter."

"Very well," I said, "you will doubtless be permitted to do so. But, captain," I added, "you probably understand that, being in the hands of the civil authorities of the state, your letters will have to be seen by them before they can be sent."

"Certainly," he said.

"Then, with that understanding," I continued, "there will, I'm sure, be no objections to your writing home; and although I myself have no authority in the premises, I promise to do what I can to have your wishes in that respect complied with."

"Thank you—thank you, sir," he said, repeating his acknowledgment for the proffered favor and, for the first time, he turned his face towards me. In my desire to hear him distinctly he had placed himself by my side, with one knee resting on the floor; so that, when he turned, it brought his face quite close to mine, and I remembered well the earnest gaze of the gray eye that looked straight into mine. I then remarked, "Captain, we too have wives and children. This attempt of yours to interfere with our slaves has created great excitement, and naturally causes anxiety on account of our families." Now let me ask you, "Is this failure of yours likely to be followed by similar attempts to create disaffection among our servants and bring upon our homes the horrors of a servile war?"

"Time will show," was his significant reply. Just then a Catholic priest appeared at the door of the room. He had been administering the last consolations of religion to Quinn the marine, who was dying in the adjoining office; and the moment Brown saw him he became violently *angry,* and plainly showed, by the expression of his countenance, how capable he was of feeling "hatred, malice, and all uncharitableness."

"Go out of here—I don't want you about me—damn it, leave me!" was the salutation he gave the priest, who, bowing gravely, immediately left. Whereupon I arose from the floor, and bidding Brown good-morning, likewise left him.

In the entry leading to the room where Brown was placed, I met Major Russell, of the U.S. Marine Corps, who was going in to see him, and I detailed to him the conversation I had just had. Meeting the major subsequently he told me that when he entered the superintendent's room Brown was standing up—with his clothes unfastened—examining the wound in his side, and that as soon as the major saw him he forthwith resumed his former position on the floor; which incident tended to confirm the impression I had already formed, that there was a good deal of vitality left in the old man, notwithstanding his wounds. I left soon after these observations.

When Colonel Lee's marines broke through the engine house barricade earlier that morning, Jeremiah G. Anderson was pierced with three bayonets as his smoking rifle fell from his grasp. Mortally wounded, he was dragged out and thrown down on the stone flagging, and left to the mercy of the crowd. He was then suffering from an intestinal hemorrhage and was actively vomiting bodily fluids. While he was in this state a young gang of boisterous Virginians mustered enough courage to approach this disarmed and dying man, and kicked his face with their heavy boots. They forced open his eyes and spat tobacco juice into them. After an hour

Samuel Troy, a local farmer, came by and viewed him in silence, but with a scornful look. He went away and then returned almost two hours later. Troy noted that Anderson was still breathing, and said to him, "Well it sure takes you a hell of a long time to die!" Shortly afterwards Anderson's weary eyes closed forever.

Some physicians from the medical school at Winchester picked Anderson out as a good subject for dissection and they immediately took possession of his body. In order to take him back to the school they procured a barrel and proceeded to pack him into it. They rammed him in head first, but they could not bend his legs so as to get them into the barrel with the rest of his body. In their attempt they cracked a number of bones but the job was eventually carried out. The praiseworthy exertion of these sons of Galen in the cause of science and humanity elicited approval from the townspeople who looked on. Anderson was finally loaded on to a cart and dragged off to Winchester.

John C. Unseld volunteered his involvement at Harper's Ferry to the authorities. His testimony was as follows:

> I arrived early on Tuesday morning at Harper's Ferry. When I got there the engine house had just been stormed. I saw an old acquaintance, Captain Butler, of the Hamtramck Guards, which was a volunteer company in Jefferson County, Virginia, and I asked him to take his company over to the school house, on the other side of the river. Butler remarked, "My company is dismissed," and left in a huff. I was sure that Cook, Tidd, and the Negroes they had taken were in the school-house, and had arms with them, guns, pistols, etc. I had learned from others the day before that Cook and his friends were at the school-house where my child, a young school-boy, attended. After leaving Captain Butler, I came across Captain Rowan, another captain of a volunteer company of Jefferson County, and said to him, "Captain Rowan, please take your company and go over to the school-house;

they are over there; the danger is there." Rowan remarked, "I will, if John will go," pointing to Mr. Avis, who stood a few feet away. I asked him "What do you say, John?" "Well," John said, "I will see about it directly," and he walked across the street as though he were going to attend to some unfinished business.

I went on around the hotel, and came across Captain Rhinehart, who was a captain of another Jefferson County company. Again I asked him to take his company and go to the school house and capture anyone who was there. Rhinehart replied, "My company is dismissed." I turned around—I was now at the back of the railroad station, and at the back porch of the tavern. Coming back, I met Mr. Faulkner at the front door, and I asked him if he knew Colonel Lee. Faulkner replied that he did. "Well," I said, "I wish you would get him to send a company over to the school house; because the insurgents are over there now. My friend Pitcher, who says he just came from there, said they opened the door and pointed a gun at him." "Well," said Faulkner, "come along and I'll get him." We were then in the superintendent's office, or under that roof in one of the offices.

Faulkner went in and saw Colonel Lee. While he was in the house Colonel Baylor, of the Virginia militia, came to the door, and I said to him, "Colonel, send a company over to Maryland to the school house." Baylor told me, "I have no right to send a company to Maryland." By this time I was quite mad and said, "The devil you haven't; I would send them anywhere at such a time as this." "I won't do it," he said, and he turned away and left. I was outside and Faulkner was inside. Mr. Faulkner came out and said, "Colonel Lee says they have gone an hour ago." I asked, "What company has gone."

"The Baltimore Greys," Faulkner replied. There was a man standing in the street who had a uniform on, and I hailed him and asked what company he belonged to, and he told me the Baltimore Greys. "Where is your captain?" The soldier said, "He has gone up on Camp Hill to get his breakfast." "Well," I said, "come with me and point hum out."

We started up on foot and overtook the captain before he got to the top of the hill. I told him my business, and the officer said that after he got something to eat he would go with me. I went back to the ferry, and passing the armory gate I met Captain Sinn, of the company belonging to Frederick, Maryland, who was just entering. I asked him "Are you the captain of that company?" "Yes," he said. "Well," I said, "come take them, and go to the school-house and capture those fellows." The captain said, "I can't do it now." I then began to get a little out of humor. I came to the square and met Mr. Boteler, member of the House of Representatives. I said to him, "Aleck, do you know Colonel Lee?" He said he did. "Now," I said, "I wish you would go and see him and get him to send a company over to our school house. Nobody it seems will go there, and those strangers to the area are over there." Mr. Boteler went and talked to Colonel Lee and then came back and told me, "Colonel Lee says they went some two hours ago." Exasperated I said, "they haven't gone at all; I know they haven't; where is Colonel Lee anyway?" Boteler pointed him out, and I went over and introduced myself.

Lee said to me, "My dear friend, my men have been gone for over two hours." "No," I said, "Colonel, they haven't gone at all; I just came from there." Lee asked, "Are you certain of it? Would you lead men there?" "Yes, of course" I said. "Then," said Lee, "come and I will get you a company." He went down towards the gate and met the lieutenant of the Baltimore company and asked him why he didn't go to the school house in Maryland, as he had been ordered. "They told me the order was countermanded," the lieutenant said. While Lee was talking to him, the captain came up and Colonel Lee said to him, "Why didn't you go to the school house when I ordered you?" "Why," he said, "my men were hungry, and I thought a short time would not make any difference, so we went to Camp Hill to get breakfast, and when we came back they told me the order was countermanded."

Colonel Lee said, "I didn't countermand it, and nobody else had any authority to do so. I want you to get your company and go with this man who says he will lead you there." The Baltimore Grays proceeded at "double-quick" time, along a constantly ascending and rocky road, to execute the order. About a mile from the Ferry, we arrived within sight of the school-house, a cabin situated in a gloomy hollow, and, apparently, closely barricaded. Halting for a few moments, the Grays formed into platoons, under the respective commands of Lieutenant's Simpson and Kerchner, and, at a given signal, dashed down the declivity of the road, and with the butt-ends of their muskets, battered in the doors and windows, through which they entered. *The cabin was entirely void of any occupants.* Against the front door were piled sixteen long and heavy boxes, one of which, upon being burst open, was found to contain ten newly-manufactured Sharps's breech-loading rifles, evidently fresh from the hands of their maker. There was also discovered one large square wooden box, exceedingly heavy, which we didn't open; a large and heavy black trunk, a box filled with bayonets and sabers, and several boxes of rifle cartridges and ammunition. There were in all twenty-one boxes, several of which were filled with Maynard's large-sized patent revolvers, with powder flasks accompanying. The room was littered with Sharps's rifles, revolvers, and pikes, evidently distributed with a view to their immediate use, either for the purpose of defense or an aggressive action. I think there were also a few grubbing hoes and picks and shovels—not many in any event. They were new and never had been used. I was present when the pikes were taken.

We opened some of the boxes and distributed a number of rifles to the Baltimore company, and to some young men who came along. Every man who was there got a gun and a pistol or two. After that the captain said, "Let's take the rest of these back to the Ferry, and when we get there we will open the balance and distribute them." I made some remarks to the captain who had came to the door and asked me if they couldn't get a wagon. There was a man who lived close by, and I went over to see him. I said to him, "Mr. Beck, would you hitch up your horse and bring some items to the Ferry." He started off, but after he left I checked out a ravine south from the school-house, and saw a wagon sitting among the bushes. I remarked to someone, "There's a wagon down there now, just come along with me and we will go down and see what's going on." We went down and found a very large wagon and three horses—one horse hitched to the wagon and the other two loose. We caught the two, hooked them up to the wagon, and drove it to the school-house. There we put a large number of items into that wagon, and some of the boxes into the other wagon belonging to Mr. Beck. After we loaded them in, nobody appeared to be willing to drive the horses, so I said to some one, "Here, get on my horse, and I'll drive them." One of the soldiers got on my horse and I got on the wagon containing the guns and drove the team down to the Ferry.

The arms were delivered to Mr. Kitzmiller, who was then acting as superintendent of the armory, for safe keeping in the arsenal of the United States, though the Grays asserted an exclusive right to their possession, as the lawful prize of the captors. The stores found included 10 kegs of gunpowder, 13,000 Sharp's rifle cartridges, 23,000 percussion rifle caps, 100,000 percussion pistol caps, 14 pounds of lead balls, 55 old bayonets, 483 pikes, shovels, clothes, tents, envelopes, pencils, paper, twine, medicine, one large trunk and a horse wagon besides.

Now that the fighting was over, the weary Virginians started to flock back to Harper's Ferry on Tuesday afternoon. Given an hour's notice, the First Virginia Regiment, accompanied by Governor Wise, set out for Harper's Ferry and were joined at Washington by another force from Alexandria. Owing to delays in Washington and at the Relay House, Wise did not arrive with the volunteers until after 1:00 PM. The governor was disappointed to find that the fight was all over, and when he was informed of the mere handful of men who had created all this ruckus, he boiled over. In his wrath he did say a few useful things. Indeed it was universally seen and felt that Governor Wise was just the man for such an occasion. After ridiculing the people, Wise decided to visit the prisoners. The interview was personal and none but the bitterest enemies of the liberators were present during this confrontation of the representatives of the North and South.

Accompanied by Andrew Hunter, Esq., a distinguished lawyer of Jefferson County, the governor went to the paymaster's office in the armory room where the two wounded prisoners lay, and there had a protracted conversation with John Brown. It had more the character of a conversation than a legal examination, for the governor treated the wounded man with a stately courtesy that evidently surprised and affected him. Brown was lying upon the floor with his feet next to the fire and his head propped upon pillows on the back of a chair. His hair was a mass of clotted gore, so that one could not distinguish its original color, and his beard, originally sandy, was white and blood-stained. His speech was frequently interrupted by deep groans, not awakening sympathy like those of the young soldier dying in the adjacent office, but reminding one of the agonized growl of a ferocious beast.

A few feet from the leader lay Stevens, not in pain apparently, conversing in a voice as full and natural as if he were unhurt. His hands lay folded upon his breast in a child-like, helpless way—a position which the governor observed was assumed by all those who had died or were dying of their wounds. Only those who were fatally shot lay as they fell.

Brown was frank and communicative, answering all questions without reserve, except such as might implicate his immediate associates not yet killed or taken. During the conversation with Mr. Hunter some notes were extracted by a correspondent as follows:

> Brown said that the small pamphlet, many copies of which were found on the persons of the slain, and entitled "Provisional Constitution and Ordinances for the People of the United States," was prepared principally by himself, and adopted at a convention of abolitionists held about two years ago at Chatham, Canada West, where it was printed. That under its provisions he was appointed "Commander-in-Chief." His sons and Stevens were captains, and Coppoc was a lieutenant. They each had their commissions, issued by himself.

> He said that the whole number operating under his organization was but twenty-two, each of whom had taken the oath required by Article XLVIII; but he confidently expected large reenforcements from Virginia, Kentucky, Maryland, North and South Carolina, and several other slave states, besides the free states—taking it for granted that it was only necessary to seize the public arms and place them to the hands of the Negroes and non-slave holders to recruit his forces indefinitely. In this calculation he reluctantly and indirectly admitted that he had been entirely disappointed.

Concluding that the prisoner must be seriously weakened by his vigils and his wounds, the governor ordered some refreshment to be given him and, appointing a meeting for the following day, took his leave. As some officials lingered behind, the old man referred again to his sons, of whom he had spoken several times, asking if they were both dead. He was assured that it was so.

"How many bodies did you take from the engine house?" John Brown asked.

He was told three.

"Then," he said, quickly, "they are not both dead; there were three dead bodies there last night. Gentlemen, my son is doubtless living and in your power. I will ask for him what I would not ask for myself; let him have kind treatment, for he is as pure and noble-hearted a youth as ever breathed the breath of life."

There was some show of human feeling in the old felon at last, but his prayer was vain. Both his boys lay stark and bloody by the armory wall.

I observed Stevens holding a small packet in his folded bands, and feeling some curiosity in regard to it, it was handed to me. It contained miniatures of his sisters; one, a sweet girlish face of about fourteen, the other more mature, but pretty. What strange reflections these incidents awakened in my mind! This old man craved a boon for his noble boys which neither pain nor death could bring him to ask for himself. The other clasped to his dying breast a remembrance of his gentle sisters and his father's elm-shaded cottage far away in peaceful Connecticut. Is this pity that thus dims my eyes?"

The bodies of Leary and William Thompson were taken out of the river early in the afternoon and were buried in shallow holes along the river bank. Oliver Brown's body was thrown on its back into the shallow trench grave and in his arms was placed the body of Dangerfield Newby. Later in the afternoon the local town dogs dug them up and started to chew at the remains. They were discovered and the dogs chased away, but the remains were left laying on the river bank.

John C. Unseld continued his story:

> I had a group of men at the Ferry ready to go with me to Brown's residence. The superintendent said we should have guns. When we got the company formed, Dr. Murphy said we shouldn't have any guns. The guns were in Murphy's charge, and he couldn't give any more out. He said he had given out a large number the day before. I then went to Colonel Lee again, and I said, "Colonel, the company that was with me at the school-house have left me, and I want another company to go to Brown's house." "Well," Lee said, "if you will lead them there, I'll give you another company." So he hunted up Lieutenant Israel Green, of the marines, and told him to take his men with me up to Brown's residence. "How far is it?" Green asked. I said, "it is about four and a half miles." We took along the wagon and horses we found at the school-house, which I had learned was Lewis Washington's wagon. Mr. Washington told me so himself at the arsenal, and we took it by his permission to the Kennedy farm.
>
> Following the same path which the Grays had pursued in making their discoveries, and which is known as the "County Road," leading into the heart of Washington County, Maryland, we continued our course until we reached the houses occupied by Brown, under the name of Isaac Smith. We discovered that there had been some citizens from the neighborhood of Sharpsburg at one

of the houses before we got there. The dwelling, a log house, containing two unfinished basement rooms, used apparently for storage, and in which were several empty gun boxes; two rooms and a pantry upon the second floor; and one large attic room in which were six husk mattresses—was discovered to be unoccupied, save by a huge savage-looking mastiff, tied with a rope to the railing of a small piazza outside the house; but there was abundant evidence of its recent hurried vacation. The floors of all the rooms were littered with hooks, papers, documents, and wearing apparel of several persons, hastily snatched from eight or ten trunks and an equal number of valises and coarse carpet bags strewn around, the fastenings of all of which had been forcibly broken, as if their violators were too much pressed for time to adopt the tardier method of entrance by looking up keys. In the pantry, which appeared to have been used for kitchen purposes, besides an almost new cooking stove, and an abundance of tin utensils, were two barrels of flour, a large quantity of sausage meat and cured hams, together with several pounds of butter, lard, etc. The fire was yet smouldering in the stove, and the water in the boilers was quite hot at the time of our entrance.

The most valuable discovery was a carpet bag belonging to Captain Brown, containing a great number of highly important papers, documents, plans, and letters from private individuals throughout the Union—all revealing the existence of an extensive and thoroughly organized conspiracy. The bag contained documents throwing much light on the affair, printed constitutions and by-laws of an organization showing or indicating ramifications in various states of the Union. In this bag were also found various unimportant notes, from prominent persons in different states; letters to "J. Henrie," meaning Kagi; and "Friend Isaac," meaning Captain Brown referring chiefly to the old man's Kansas work; brief entries, in journals, of subscriptions received, and journeys made, and hardships endured in Iowa, the Eastern states, and Canada; copies of his constitution, and books of military tactics, with numerous receipts and bills for stock and provisions purchased for the war of liberation.

We found a number of trunks there, and a quantity of bundled printed papers. The words "Patriotic Volunteer" appeared on the outside. It was a drill-book for soldiers, gotten up by Hugh Forbes, I believe. There was a number of them in a large box, but no furniture there at all save one table and a cook stove. We found a pamphlet "The Laws of Kansas; a Speech of Schuyler Colfax, of Indiana, in the House of Representatives, June 21, 1856," and a map of the Kansas territory. My little boy tore up the map. We found no arms at all at the house where he lived. We put the trunks and papers in the wagons. Some of them were destroyed and carried off by citizens, but there were a good many taken to the Ferry—and some trunks; I do not think any boxes were. Lieutenant Israel Green and myself went in the cabin. He placed one of the soldiers at the door. In the lower part of the house we found a quantity of bed-clothing, such as comforters and canvass for tents, and some axes. There were two cast-iron hominy mills, as I was informed they were, and a good deal of clothing boxed up—new clothing; but the boxes had been opened when we got there. There was clothing for men, and some boots. The clothing was all given away and carried off by the citizens of the neighborhood.

There was a pile of counterpanes that looked to be new and very good, that was piled up, I suppose, between two and three feet high, doubled up and piled nicely, laid outside the boxes. There were some knives and forks and spoons, also new, which had never been used. I had

a number of them in my hands. I picked them up and
threw them down. In the upper part of the house, in the
loft, we found a large number of pikes. They were put
in the wagon which we took up there. A number of the
pikes were distributed there, and Green gave the men a
great many. He told me to break the window open and
throw them out. I helped him to throw out a good many
until I got tired, and then I told him I would not throw
any more out. He said "send up a couple of soldiers and I
will tell them to throw them out." He told the neighbors
who were present that they could have as many as they
wanted. He said to them, at first, "you can each have
five." Afterwards he told them ten a piece, and finally, he
said, "you may each have up to fifty." They took as many
as they wanted and the rest were put in the wagon. The
pikes had handles on them. There were two straw ticks
on the floor, and on turning them up I found two pikes
under them, one under each, without handles. We found
picks at the school house, not pikes, and they were for
grubbing. We also found some picks and shovels in the
cabin. We found only a very few. Apparently they were
taken there to be used. There were perhaps half a dozen
shovels, short and long handles together, at his house, but
they were carried off by the citizens. We carried all that
were not distributed back to the Ferry. The pikes were
lying loose, piled up in a corner, as though you would
put something up here to hold them from rolling down.
They were piled up in one corner right close to where
the window had been, but it was nailed up. Handles had
been put on the pikes by Brown's men, as I was told by
Cook afterwards. They were delivered to Mr. Kitzmiller,
the acting superintendent, and taken to the store-room in
the armory, just as the guns were.

In the late afternoon the body of Kagi was taken from the Shenandoah
river, and the other corpses were rounded up. Burial of the other bodies in

one of the village cemeteries was, in view of the popular excitement, out of the question. The body of Watson Brown had been crammed into a box and carried off for preservation at the Winchester Medical College as an anatomical specimen. Oliver's remains, with those of seven other raiders who died at Harper's Ferry, were buried in two large sturdy boxes by James Mansfield, to whom the county gave $5.00 for his services. He procured two large "store boxes" and into these receptacles thrust the remains of the eight men, and buried them about half a mile from the Ferry upon the banks of the Shenandoah River almost at the water's edge. He wrapped them in the blanket shawls they had worn over their shoulders as they went to their deaths. Besides Oliver Brown and John Henry Kagi the grave contained Lewis Leary, Dangerfield Newby, Dauphin Thompson, William Thompson, Stewart Taylor, and William H. Leeman.

Tuesday night soon came, bringing with it the drunken clamor and turmoil of the crowd in the village. Matters were made worse by the impressment of all the horses in town. The men of Harper's Ferry had to trudge home rather out of humor with their patriotic sacrifice; while the tipsy and pot-valiant militia fought and squabbled with each other between rounds of drinks. They only ceased that sport to pursue and hunt down some poor fugitive Negroes, and one or two half maddened drunken fellows who in their frenzy proclaimed themselves John Brown's men.

Tired out from the day's activities, Governor Wise took refuge in the Wager House. For some time he stood on the porch haranguing an impatient crowd as "Sons of Virginia!" Inside the Wager House the scene was stranger still. Huddled together in the inn's worst room the governor's staff sat around a large table lit by tallow candles. The Richmond Grays were lying around the floor in a novel pursuit of "soft planks," and a motley audience was gathered to hear about the papers captured at the Kennedy farm on Maryland Heights a few hours before. John Rosengarten said of the scene, "the most innocent notes and letters, commonplace newspaper paragraphs and headlines were distributed and twisted by the reading and by the talking into clear instructions—and positive plots."

Rosengarten added, "However my main impression was of the picturesqueness of the soldiers resting on their knapsacks, and their arms stacked in the dark corners,—of the governor and his cronies, some of whom were decked out in full military array, seated around the lighted table,—and of the grotesque eloquence with which either the governor or some of his prominent friends would now and then burst out into oratorical tirade, all wasted on his sleepy audience, and lost to the world for want of some clear shorthand writer."

At 7:30 AM on Wednesday morning John Rosengarten was elated to hear that his belated train had spent the last two days at Martinsburg, and was now arriving. He did not at all regret the two days which had been so full of adventure and incident. Waiting for the train, he walked slowly through Harper's Ferry again. As he was strolling near the armory, one of the watchmen who had been captured by John Brown and spent the night with him in the engine house came over and spoke with him for a few minutes. Then Rosengarten looked up Governor Wise, thanked him, and said his good-byes. He was duly thanked for his valiant service to Virginia, and rewarded by being offered the honorary and desirable title of A. D. C. to the Commander-in-Chief of Virginia, both for past services and for the future tasks to be met of beating off an invading host from the North. He politely declined this handsome offer and got on the train which departed almost immediately.

Chapter 4

INTERROGATION

THE NEW YORK *Times* of Wednesday October 19, 1859 in an article titled "The Virginia Insurrection" reported:

The insurrection at Harper's Ferry, though sufficiently alarming at the outset, proved to have been but a short-lived affair. It was very speedily crushed by the formidable military forces brought against it from Washington, Baltimore and Virginia,—but, unhappily, not without a serious loss of life. The parties actively engaged in it seem never to have numbered over fifty or sixty, though ten times that number were induced or coerced into an apparent support of the movement before the close of the affair. So far as appears, it was not the result of any combination among the slaves themselves, but it was merely the explosion of a clumsy plot concocted by a single man, John Brown, of Kansas notoriety, with the aid of his two sons and one or two other accomplices.

Brown, it will be remembered, suffered severely in the loss of his property and in the death of one of his sons, during the reign of ruffianism in Kansas. He was a fearless, fanatical, energetic old man to begin with, and the death of his son made him nearly frantic. Having sworn vengeance against the authors of his calamities, he made himself very conspicuous, and universally dreaded by the ruffians, during the subsequent troubles in Kansas.

He was the leader of the fight at Osawatomie, where he was said to have killed several of the invading borderers with his own hand. After the troubles in Kansas had been quieted, Brown's uneasy spirit extended its resentment to the Missourians, and especially to the slave holders whom he regarded as the authors of his wrongs. He entered into plots for promoting the escape of their slaves, and succeeded in getting twenty or thirty of them away, and in so alarming the slave holders throughout that section of the state, that they forthwith commenced sending their slaves to the Southern states. He himself escaped unharmed, and came, it now appears, over a year ago to the neighborhood of Harper's Ferry, and commenced preparations to renew his operations in Virginia. It was the very general belief of those who knew him in Kansas that Brown, after the death of his son, became insane upon this subject; and his proceedings in this affair certainly give countenance to that belief. A wilder and more hopeless project than that in which he embarked cannot well be imagined.

There seems to be no reason for believing that the plot had any extensive ramifications, or that any further danger is to be apprehended. Yet the affair can scarcely fail to startle the public mind in Virginia, and it may have the same effect as Brown's movements had in Missouri, and increase, largely and rapidly, the transfer of slaves from Virginia to the more Southern states. Every such outbreak, from whatever causes it may spring, quickens the public sense of the insecurity of slave property on the borders of the slaveholding states, and so tends to the removal southward of that frontier.

As a matter of course, the violent partisans will seek to make the most of the affair. But we see no reason for supposing that it had any connection whatever with any political movement, or that any party can with justice be held responsible for it. It seems to have been the work of a single man,—smarting under a sense of personal wrong, and insanely seeking to avenge them upon a whole community. He will probably pay the penalty of his rash insanity with his life, and leave, we trust, no inheritors of his passion or his fate.

By noon on Wednesday October 19, 1859 the armory office was crowded with local Harper's Ferry residents and military officers. Soon thereafter an agent of the associated press from Baltimore connected with the Baltimore *American* of that city showed up. General Strouther, an artist working for *Harper's Weekly*, was also among the earlier arrivals. Senator James M. Mason arrived, having come from his home at Winchester, 30 miles distant. Colonel James Faulkner, member of Congress, lived but a few miles distant and arrived next. A number of other distinguished gentlemen also arrived, including Andrew Hunter; local resident Colonel Lewis Washington; Congressman Alexander R. Boteler from the Harper's Ferry district; and of course Virginia Governor Henry A. Wise. The special reporter for the New York *Herald* did not arrive until shortly after 2:00 PM.

Word was soon announced that Brown was awake. Standing about Brown, black coated and hatted, the dignitaries waited for Governor Wise to start his interrogation. The courteous Colonel Lee began the interview by saying that he would exclude all visitors from the room if the wounded men were annoyed or pained thereby. To this John Brown answered that he was "glad to make himself and his motives clearly understood."

Senator Mason stepped up and started questioning Brown, ignoring Governor Wise who had walked over to the side of the room. Mason, a noted speaker in the Senate and the author of the Fugitive Slave Bill, began in a calm but commanding voice:

Senator Mason: Can you tell us, at least, who furnished you all the money for your expedition?

John Brown: I furnished most of it myself. I cannot implicate others. It is by my own folly that I have been taken. I could easily have saved myself from it had exercised my own better judgment, rather than yielded to my feelings.

JOHN BROWN & AARON STEVENS ARE INTERROGATED ON OCTOBER 19, 1859 BY THE NEW YORK *HERALD* CORRESPONDENT, SENATOR MASON, GOVERNOR WISE, CLEMENT VALLANDIGHAM AND OTHERS.

Senator Mason: You mean if you had escaped immediately?

John Brown: No; I had the means to make myself secure without any escape, but I allowed myself to be surrounded by a force by being too tardy.

Senator Mason: Tardy in getting away?

John Brown: I should have gone away, but I had thirty odd prisoners, whose wives and daughters were in tears for their safety, and I felt for them. Besides, I wanted to allay the fears of those who believed we came here to burn and kill. For this reason I allowed the train to pass the bridge, and gave them full liberty to pass on. I did it only to spare the feelings of those passengers and their families, and to allay the apprehension that you had got here in your vicinity a band of men who had no regard for life and property, nor any feeling of humanity.

Senator Mason: But you killed some people who were passing along the streets quietly.

John Brown: Well, sir, if there was any thing of that kind done, it was without my knowledge. Your own citizens, who were my prisoners, will tell you that every possible means were taken to prevent it. I did not allow my men to fire, nor even to return a fire, when there was danger of killing those we regarded as innocent persons, if I could help it. They will tell you that we allowed ourselves to be fired at repeatedly, and did not return it.

Bystander: That is not so. You killed an unarmed man at the corner of the house, over there, (at the water tower) and another besides.

John Brown: See here, my friend; it is useless to dispute or contradict the report of your own neighbors, who were my prisoners.

Senator Mason: If you would tell us who sent you here,—who provided the means,—that would be information of some value.

John Brown: I will answer freely and faithfully about what concerns myself—I will answer any thing I can with honor, but not about others.

At this point there was a commotion in the room as Clement L. Vallandigham, the Democratic Congressman from Ohio, entered. Vallandigham announced his belief that the plot was the work of Ohio abolitionists. He then turned to question Brown.

Mr. Vallandigham: Mr. Brown, who sent you here?

John Brown: No man sent me here; it was my own prompting and that of my Maker, or that of the Devil which ever you please to ascribe it to. I acknowledge no master in human form.

Mr. Vallandigham: Did you get up the expedition yourself?

John Brown: I did.

Mr. Vallandigham: Did you get up this document that is called a constitution?

John Brown: I did. They are a constitution and ordinances of my own contriving and getting up.

Mr. Vallandigham: How long have you been engaged in this business?

John Brown: From the breaking out of the difficulties in Kansas. Four of my sons had gone there to settle, and they induced me to go. I did not go there to settle, but because of the difficulties.

Senator Mason: How many are engaged with you in this movement? I ask these questions for your own safety.

John Brown: Any questions that I can honorably answer, I will, not otherwise. So far as I am myself concerned, I have told every thing truthfully. I value my word, sir.

Senator Mason: What was your object in coming?

John Brown: We came to free the slaves, and only that.

Senator Mason: How many men in all did you have?

John Brown: I came to Virginia with eighteen men besides myself.

A young man wearing the military uniform of a volunteer company next spoke up. There is no record as to his exact identity.

Volunteer: What in the world did you suppose you could do here in Virginia with that amount of men?

John Brown: Young man, I don't wish to discuss that question here.

Volunteer: You couldn't do anything.

John Brown: Well, perhaps your ideas and mine, on military subjects, would differ materially.

Senator Mason: How do you justify your acts?

John Brown: I think, my friend, you are guilty of a great wrong against God and humanity.—I say it without wishing to be offensive—and it would be perfectly right for any one to interfere with you so far as to free those you wilfully and wickedly hold in bondage. I do not say this insultingly.

Senator Mason: I understand that.

John Brown: I think I did right, and that others will do right who interfere with you, at any time, and all times. I hold that the golden rule—"Do unto others as you would that others should do unto you,"—applies to all who would help others to gain their liberty.

Lieutenant Stuart: But you don't believe in the Bible.

John Brown: Certainly I do.

Mr. Vallandigham: Where did your men come from? Did some of them come from Ohio?

John Brown: Some of them.

Mr. Vallandigham: From the Western Reserve? None came from Southern Ohio.

John Brown: Yes, I believe one came from Steubenville, down not far from Wheeling.

Mr. Vallandigham: Have you been in Ohio this summer?

John Brown: Yes, sir.

Mr. Vallandigham: How lately?

John Brown: I passed through to Pittsburgh on my way, in June.

Mr. Vallandigham: Were you at any county or state fair there?

John Brown: I was not there since June.

Senator Mason: Did you consider this a military organization in this paper? (Showing a copy of John Brown's constitution and ordinance.) I have not yet read it.

John Brown: I did in some measure. I wish you would give that paper your close attention.

Senator Mason: You considered yourself the Commander-in-Chief of these "provisional" military forces.

John Brown: I was chosen, agreeably to the ordinance of a certain document, Commander-in-Chief of that force.

Senator Mason: What wages did you offer?

John Brown: None.

Lieutenant Stuart: The wages of sin is death!

John Brown: I would not have made such a remark to you, if you had been a prisoner and wounded, in my hands!

Another bystander, the identity of whom was unknown, next spoke.

Bystander: Didn't you promise a Negro in Gettysburg twenty dollars a month?

John Brown: I did not.

Bystander: He says you did.

Mr. Vallandigham: Were you ever in Dayton, Ohio?

John Brown: Yes, I must have been.

Mr. Vallandigham: This summer?

John Brown: No; a year or two ago.

Senator Mason: Does this talking annoy you?

John Brown: Not the least.

Mr. Vallandigham: Have you lived long in Ohio?

John Brown: I went there in 1805. I lived in Summit County, which was then Trumbull County. My native place is in Connecticut; my father lived there until we moved in 1805.

Mr. Vallandigham: Do you recollect a man in Ohio named Brown, a noted counterfeiter?

John Brown: I do. I knew him from a boy; his father was Henry Brown; they were of Irish or Scotch descent, and he had a brother also engaged in that business; when boys they could not read or write; they were of a very low family.

Mr. Vallandigham: Have you been in Portage County lately?

John Brown: I was there in June last.

Mr. Vallandigham: When in Cleveland, did you attend the Fugitive Slave Law convention there?

John Brown: No. I was there about the time of the sitting of the court to try the Oberlin rescuers. I spoke there, publicly, on that subject. I spoke on the fugitive slave law, and my own rescue. Of course, so far as I had any influence at all, I was disposed to justify the Oberlin people for rescuing the slave, because I have myself forcibly taken slaves from bondage. I was concerned in taking eleven slaves from Missouri to Canada, last winter. I think that I spoke in Cleveland before the convention. I do not know that I had any conversation with any of the Oberlin rescuers. I was sick part of the time I was in Ohio. I had the ague. I was part of the time in Ashtabula County.

Mr. Vallandigham: Did you see anything of Joshua R. Giddings there?

John Brown: I met him.

Mr. Vallandigham: Did you converse with him?

John Brown: I did. I would not tell you, of course, any thing that could implicate Mr. Giddings; but I certainly met with him, and had a conversation with him.

Mt. Vallandigham: About that rescue case?

John Brown: Yes, I did. I heard him express his opinion upon it very freely and frankly.

Mr. Vallandigham: Justifying it?

John Brown: Yes, sir. I do not compromise him, certainly, in saying that.

Bystander: Did you go out to Kansas under the auspices of the Emigrant Aid Society?

John Brown: No, sir; I went out under the auspices of John Brown, and nobody else.

Mr. Vallandigham: Will you answer this: Did you talk with Giddings about your expedition here?

John Brown: No, sir! I won't answer that, because a denial of it I would not make; and to make an affidavit of it, I should be a great dunce.

Mr. Vallandigham: Have you had any correspondence with parties at the North on the subject of this movement?

John Brown: I have had no correspondence.

Bystander: Do you consider this a religious movement?

John Brown: It is, in my opinion, the greatest service a man can render to his God.

Bystander: Do you consider yourself an instrument in the hands of providence?

John Brown: I do.

Bystander: Upon what principle do you justify your acts?

John Brown: Upon the golden rule. I pity the poor in bondage that have none to help them. That is why I am here; it is not to gratify any personal animosity, or feeling of revenge, or vindictive spirit. It is my sympathy with the oppressed and the wronged, that are as good as you, and as precious in the sight of God.

Bystander: Certainly. But why take the slaves against their will?

John Brown: I never did.

Bystander: You did in one instance, at least.

Stevens: (to the bystander, interrupting Brown) You are right, sir; in one case. (a groan from the wounded man) In one case, I know the Negro wanted to go back.

Stevens: (to Brown) Captain, the gentleman is correct in his statement.

Bystander: (to Stevens) Where did you come from?

Stevens: I lived in Ashtabula County, Ohio.

Mr. Vallandigham: How recently did you leave Ashtabula County?

Stevens: Some months ago. I never resided there any length of time. I have often been through there.

Mr. Vallandigham: How far did you live from Jefferson?

John Brown: (to Stevens) Be very cautious, Stevens, about an answer to that; it might commit some friend. I would not answer it at all.

Stevens, who had been groaning considerably, as if the exertion necessary to conversation seriously affected him, now seemed content to abide by his captain's advice. He turned partially over, with another groan of pain, and then became silent.

Mr. Vallandigham: (to Captain Brown) Who are your advisers in this movement?

John Brown: I cannot answer that. I have numerous sympathizers throughout the entire North.

Mr. Vallandigham: In Northern Ohio?

John Brown: No more there than any where else—in all the free states.

Mr. Vallandigham: But are you not personally known in Southern Ohio?

John Brown: Not very much.

Mr. Vallandigham: (to Stevens) Were you at the convention last June?

Stevens: I was.
Mr. Vallandigham: (to John Brown) You made a speech there?

John Brown: I did, sir.

Bystander: Did you ever live in Washington City?

John Brown: I did not. I want you to understand, gentlemen,—(and to the reporter of the *Herald*) You may report that—I want you to understand that I respect the rights of the poorest and weakest of the colored people, oppressed by the slave system, just as much as I do those of the most wealthy and powerful. That is the idea that has moved me, and that alone. We expected no reward except the satisfaction of endeavoring to do for those in distress—the greatly oppressed—as we would be done by. The cry of distress, of the oppressed, is my reason, and the only thing that prompted me to come here.

Bystander: Why did you do it secretly?

John Brown: Because I thought that necessary to success, and for no other reason.

Bystander: And you think that honorable, do you? Have you read Gerrit Smith's last letter?

John Brown: What letter do you mean?

Bystander: The New York *Herald* of yesterday, in speaking of this affair, mentions a letter in this way:

Apropos of this exciting news, we recollect a very significant passage in one of Gerrit Smith's letters, published a month or two ago, in which he speaks of the folly of attempting to strike the shackles off the slaves by the force of moral suasion or legal agitation, and predicts that the next movement made in the direction of Negro emancipation would be an insurrection in the South.

John Brown: I have not seen a New York *Herald* for some days past; but I presume, from your remarks about the gist of the letter, that I should concur with it. I agree with Mr. Smith, that moral suasion is hopeless. I don't think the people of the slave states will ever consider the subject of slavery in its true light until some other argument is resorted to than moral suasion.

Mr. Vallandigham: Did you expect a general rising of the slaves in case of your success?

John Brown: No, sir; nor did I wish it. I expected to gather them up from time to time and set them free.

Mr. Vallandigham: Did you expect to hold possession here till then?

John Brown: Well, probably I had quite a different idea. I do not know that I ought to reveal my plans. I am here a prisoner, and wounded, because I foolishly allowed myself to be so. You overrate your strength when you suppose I could have been taken if I had not allowed it. I was too tardy, after commencing the open attack, in delaying my movements through Monday night, and up to the time I was attacked by the government troops. It was all occasioned by my desire to spare the feelings of my prisoners and their families, and the community at large.

Mr. Vallandigham: Didn't you shoot a Negro on the bridge, or did not some of your party?

John Brown: I knew nothing of the shooting of a Negro.

Mr. Vallandigham: What time did you commence your organization in Canada?

John Brown: That occurred about two years ago. If I remember right, it was, I think, in 1858.

Mr. Vallandigham: Who was the secretary?

John Brown: That I would not tell if I recalled it; but I do not remember. I think the officers were elected in May, 1858. I may answer incorrectly, but not intentionally. My head is a little confused by my wounds, and my memory of dates and such like is also somewhat confused.

At this point Dr. Biggs, the physician who had examined George Turner spoke up.

Dr. Biggs: Were you in the party at Dr. Kennedy's house?

John Brown: I was the head of that party. I occupied the house to mature my plans. I would state here that I have not been in Baltimore to purchase percussion caps.

Dr. Biggs: What was the number of men at Kennedy's?

John Brown: I decline to answer that.

Dr. Biggs: Who lanced that woman's neck on the hill?

John Brown: I did. I have sometimes practiced in surgery, when I thought it a matter of humanity or of necessity—when there was no one else to do it; but I have not studied surgery.

Dr. Biggs: It was done quite well and scientifically. These men have been very clever to the neighbors, I have been told, and we had no reason to suspect them, except that we could not understand their movements. They were represented as eight or nine persons; on Friday there were thirteen.

John Brown: There were more than that.

Questions were now put in by almost every one in the room.

Question: Where did you get the arms to obtain possession of the armory?

John Brown: I bought them.

Question: In what state?

John Brown: That I would not state.

Question: How many guns?

John Brown: Two hundred Sharp's rifles, and two hundred revolvers—what are called the Massachusetts Arms Company's revolvers, a little under Navy size.

Question: Why didn't you take that swivel you left in the house?

John Brown: I had no occasion for it. It was given to me a year or two ago.

Question: In Kansas?

John Brown: No, I had nothing given to me in Kansas.

The special reporter for the New York *Herald* next asked a question:

Reporter: I do not wish to annoy you; but if you have anything else you would like to say, I will report it.

John Brown: I do not wish to converse any more; I have nothing to say. I will only remark to these reporting gentlemen, that I claim to be here in carrying out a measure I believe to be perfectly justifiable, and not to act the part of an incendiary or ruffian; but, on the contrary, to aid those suffering under a great wrong. *I wish to say, furthermore, that you had better—all you people of the South—prepare yourselves for a settlement of this question. It must come up for settlement sooner than you are prepared for it,* and the sooner you commence that preparation the better for you. You may dispose of me very easily; I am nearly disposed of now, but this question is still to be settled—this Negro question, I mean. The end of that is not yet. These wounds were inflicted upon me, both the saber cut on my head, and the bayonet stabs in the different parts of my body,—some minutes after I had ceased fighting, and had consented to surrender for the benefit of others, and not for my own benefit.

This statement was vehemently denied by many of the interrogators. Without seeming to notice the interruption, Brown continued:

John Brown: I believe the major here (pointing to Lieutenant Stuart) would not have been alive but for me. I might have killed him just as easily as I could kill a mosquito, when he came in; but I supposed that he came in only to receive our surrender. There had been long and loud calls of surrender from us, as loud as men could yell, but in the confusion and excitement I suppose we were not heard. I do not believe the major, or any one else, wanted to butcher us after we had surrendered.

An officer who was present then stated that special orders had been given to the marines not to shoot anybody. But, when they were fired upon by Brown's men, and one of them had been killed and another wounded, they were obliged to return the compliment.

Captain Brown insisted, with some vehemence, that the marines fired first.

Officer: Why didn't you surrender before the attack?

John Brown: I did not think it was my duty, or in my interest, to do so. We assured our prisoners that we did not wish to harm them, and that they should be set at liberty. I exercised my best judgment, not believing the people would wantonly sacrifice their own fellow-citizens. When we offered to let them go upon condition of being allowed to change our position about a quarter of a mile, the prisoners agreed by a vote among themselves to pass across the bridge with us. We wanted them only as a sort of guarantee for our own safety—that we should not be fired into. We took them, in the first place, as hostages, and to keep them from doing any harm. We did kill some men when defending ourselves; but I saw no one fire except directly in self-defense. Our orders were strict not to harm any one not in arms against us.

Charlestown resident: Well, Brown, suppose you had every nigger in the United States, what would you do with them?

John Brown: (in a loud tone, and with emphasis) Set them free, sir!

Charlestown resident: Your intention was to carry them off and free them?

John Brown: Not at all.

Bystander: To set them free would sacrifice the life of every man in this community.

John Brown: I do not think so.

Bystander: I know it. I think you are a fanatic.

John Brown: And likewise I think you are fanatical. "Whom the gods would destroy, they first make mad;" and you are mad.

Charlestown resident: Was your only object to free the Negroes?

John Brown: Absolutely our only object.

Bystander: But you demanded and took Colonel Washington's silver and watch.

John Brown: Yes; *we intended freely to appropriate the property of slave holders to carry out our object.* It was for that, and only that; and with no design to enrich ourselves with any plunder whatever.

Charlestown resident: Did you know Sherrod in Kansas? I understand you killed him.

John Brown: I killed no man except in a fair fight. I fought at Black Jack, and at Osawatomie; and if I killed anybody, it was at one of those places.

John Brown was now coughing rather regularly and was clasping his wounded side. Governor Wise made his way forward and waved the people out, signifying that the interview was over. Mr. Hunter strongly advised Governor Wise to move Brown and the other prisoners immediately to the jail at Charlestown since it was obvious that Brown was not conveniently going to die from his wounds.

After a public exhibition of more than thirty-four hours, as they lay unattended and bloody on the floor of the guard house, interrogated by unmanly politicians and insulted by the brutal mob, the surviving liberators were ordered to be conveyed Wednesday evening to the jail at Charlestown, under an escort of marines.

After the political inquisitors had finished with the whites, a United States marshal from Ohio endeavored to extort confessions from Copeland and Green, so that abolitionists in Ohio might be implicated. He did not succeed in procuring a confession, but only a few brief answers to his leading questions, which served to show at once his political purpose and the depravity of his heart.

The prisoners were given some plain soup and some stale bread and were told that they were being moved to the jail. A local journalist described their journey to Charlestown. He reported:

> On Wednesday evening, October 19th, at around 6:00 PM the prisoners were conveyed to the jail at Charlestown. This town was the government seat of Jefferson County, Virginia. A flourishing town of 1650 citizens, Charlestown was the center of a region called the Garden of Virginia. George Washington's brother Charles, who like many other Washingtons settled in this area.
>
> The removal to the train occurred under circumstances that called for marine guards rather than a local military company. The prisoners were in the joint charge of the sheriff of Jefferson County and the United States Marshall of the Western District of Virginia. They were escorted by a marine company commanded by Lieutenant Israel Green Stevens and Brown had to be taken in the wagon, but the Negroes Shields Green, John Copeland and Edwin Coppoc, being unhurt, walked between the file of soldiers, followed by hundreds of excited men, exclaiming, "Lynch them! Lynch them!" Governor Wise, who was standing on the platform at the station, yelled to them as they arrived, "Listen to me, it would certainly

be a cowardly act to do so now," and the crowd fell back, and the prisoners were safely placed on the train. Most of the militia then returned to their homes leaving one company on duty after the departure of the prisoners.

Aaron Stevens was placed on the floor of the car, being unable to sit up. Brown was propped up on a seat with pillows, and Edwin Coppoc and Shields Green were seated in the middle of them; the former was evidently much frightened, but looked calm, while the latter was the very impersonation of fear. His nerves were twitching, his eyes were wild and almost bursting from their sockets, and his whole manner indicated the dreadful apprehensions that filled his mind. This fellow was a member of congress, under his provisional government, and had been very daring while guarding the arsenal, and very impudent while in the engine house, but when the marines entered it, he jumped back among the imprisoned, and cried out, "I'm just another prisoner!" Mr. Washington thrust him forward, and informed the besiegers that he was one of the guerillas, upon which a stab was made at him, but missed him, and he still lives to expiate his guilt on the gallows. John Copeland sat in the corner of the car and said absolutely nothing.

Governor Wise and Mr. Hunter accompanied the prisoners all the way to Charlestown, where they were taken to the jail, and placed under the charge of the jail officials. They entered through the main entrance at the center of the southern facade. The jailor's quarters occupied the southwestern front of the jail on the main street, and the yard inclosing the brick jail was surrounded on the other three sides by a sturdy wall fourteen feet in height.[1]

---

[1]   The Charlestown prison was greatly expanded after the Civil War. All available photographs show the enlarged view of the building. The prison

**PRISON HOUSE AT CHARLESTOWN
SHOWING REAR WALL**

The jail building was guarded by a heavy force, including two cannons which were planted to cover the buildings. The number of inside guards in the main jail complex was greatly increased when John Brown arrived. Inside the east wall of the jail there was a reception room for visitors. A prison cell adjoined the reception room and was used for transients.[2] The cell next to the outside wall was selected to house Brown and Stevens. Two special cots were installed when Brown arrived. The recovery of Stevens remained doubtful, and he was carefully examined by the prison doctor. Shields Green and John Copeland

---

was demolished in 1919.

[2]   This cell was occupied by Albert Hazlett when he was jailed. He was moved in with Stevens when John Brown was executed.

were assigned a cell next to Brown and Edwin Coppoc was put in a third cell.

On the same evening there was another panic back at Harper's Ferry. It was Cook, this time, who was murdering all the people at Sandy Hook! The marines hastened out to protect the citizens, but found neither Cook nor a broil there. When they returned to Harper's Ferry, the Virginia militia, who had been afraid to follow, now valiantly offered to go out to defend their fellow citizens.

The prisoners were formally committed to the jail on Thursday morning, October 20th, by a Justice of the Peace of Charlestown, on the oaths of Henry A Wise and two others, "for feloniously conspiring with each other, and other persons unknown, to make an abolition insurrection and open war against the commonwealth of Virginia," and for the additional crimes of murder and "conspiring with slaves to rebel and to make insurrection." On the same day a warrant was issued to the sheriff, commanding him to summon eight Justices of the Peace to hold a preliminary court of examination on the 25th of October.

A letter for counsel was posted by Brown:[3]

CHARLESTOWN, JEFFERSON Co., Oct. 21, 1859.

TO THE HON. THOMAS RUSSELL:

DEAR SIR: I am here a prisoner, with several saber cuts in my head, and bayonet stabs in my body. My object in writing is to obtain able and faithful counsel for myself and fellow-prisoners, five in all, as we have the faith of Virginia pledged through her governor, and numerous prominent citizens, to give us a fair trial. Without we can obtain such counsel from without the slave states, neither

---

[3] A copy of this letter was sent to Judge Daniel R. Tilden, of Ohio, and another to Reuben A. Chapman, of Springfield Mass.

the facts in our case can come before the world, nor can we have the benefit of such facts as might be considered mitigating, in the view of others, upon our trial. I have money on hand here to the amount of two hundred and fifty dollars, and personal property sufficient to pay a most liberal fee to yourself, or any able man who will undertake our defense, if I can be allowed the benefit of said property. Can you, or some other good man, come on immediately, for the sake of the young men prisoners at least? My wounds are doing well. Do not send an ultra abolitionist.

Very respectfully yours,

JOHN BROWN

Indorsed, "The trial is set for Tuesday next, the 25th instant.— J. W. CAMPBELL, *Sheriff Jefferson Co.*"

One of Mr. John Allstadt's Negroes died on Saturday, October 22nd. Mr. Allstadt reported that he came out of the engine house not feeling well. On Friday Allstadt went into Charlesown and saw his Negro at the jail crying profusely. He was very sick with pneumonia, complicated by all the outward fears of that which had befell him, so much so that Allstadt could not move him home. He was about twenty years old.

The honorable Clement Vallandigham had this to say today about his interview with John Brown:

The Cincinnati *Gazette* of Friday, October 21st contained what purported to be a conversation between John Brown, the Harper's Ferry insurgent, and myself. The editorial criticism in that paper, while unjust, was, nevertheless, moderate and decent in temper and language. Not so the vulgar, but inoffensive comments of the *Commercial* and the *Ohio State Journal* of today.

Self-respect forbids to a gentleman any notice of such assaults. But the report and editorial of the *Gazette* convey an erroneous impression, which I desire briefly to correct.

Passing of necessity through Harper's Ferry on Wednesday last, on my way home from Washington City, I laid over at that place between morning and evening trains for the West. Through the politeness of Colonel Lee, the commanding officer, I was allowed to enter the armory inclosure. Inspecting the several objects of interest there, and among them the office building, I came to the room where Brown and Stevens lay, and went in, not aware that Senator Mason or any reporter was present till I entered, and without any purpose of asking a single question of the prisoners, and had there been no prisoners there I should have visited and inspected the place, just as I did, in all these particulars.

No "interview" was asked for by me or any one else of John Brown, and none granted, whether "voluntarily and out of pure good will," or otherwise, Brown had no voice in the matter, the room being open equally to all who were present within the armory inclosure. All went and came alike, without consulting Brown, nor did he know myself or the other gentlemen with whom he conversed. Entering the room, I found Senator Mason, of Virginia, there, casually together with eight or ten others, and Brown conversing freely with all who chose to address him. Indeed, he seemed eager to talk to every one; and new visitors were coming and going every moment. There was no arrangement to have any reporter; nor did I observe for some minutes after I entered that any were present. Some one from New York was taking sketches of Brown and Stevens during the conversation, and the reporter for the *Herald* made himself known to me a short time afterward; but I saw nothing of the *Gazette* reporter till several hours later, and then at the hotel in the village.

Finding Brown anxious to talk and ready to answer any one who chose to ask a question, and having heard that the insurrection had been planned at the Ohio State Fair held at Zanesville in September, I very naturally made the inquiry of him, among other things, as to the truth of the statement. Learning from his answers that he had lived in Ohio for fifty years, and had visited the state in May or June last, I prosecuted my inquiries to ascertain what connection his conspiracy might have had with the "Oberlin Rescue" trials then pending, and the insurrectionary movement at that time made in the Western Reserve to organize forcible resistance to the execution of the fugitive slave law; and I have now only to regret that I did not pursue the matter further, asking more questions, and making them more specific. It is possible that some others who are so tenderly sensitive in regard to what was developed, might have been equally implicated. Indeed, it is incredible that a mere casual conversation, such as the one held by me with John Brown, should excite such paroxysms of rage and call forth so much vulgar but impotent vituperation, unless there be much more yet undisclosed. Certain it is that three of the Negroes, and they from Oberlin, and at least six of the white men, nine in all out of the nineteen, including John Brown, the leader of the insurrection, were, or had been, from Ohio, where they had received sympathy and counsel, if not material aid in their conspiracy.

But the visit and interrogations were both casual, and did not continue over twenty minutes at the longest. Brown so far from being exhausted volunteered several speeches to the reporter, and more than once insisted that the conversations did not disturb or annoy him in the least. The report in the New York *Herald*, of October 21st, is generally very accurate, though several of the questions attributed to me, and particularly the first four, ought to have been put into the mouth of "Bystander," who, by the way, represented at least half a score of different persons.

"As to the charge preferred of breach of good taste and propriety," and all that, I propose to judge of it myself, having been present on the occasion. There was neither "interviewing, catechizing, inquisition, pumping," nor any effort of the kind, but a short and casual conversation with the leader of a bold and murderous insurrection, a man of singular intelligence, in full possession of all his faculties, and anxious to explain his plans and motives so far as was possible without implicating his confederates otherwise than by declining to answer. The developments are important; *let the galled jades wince.*

And now allow me to add that it is vain to underrate either the man or his conspiracy. Captain John Brown is as brave and resolute a man as ever headed an insurrection, and in a good cause, and with a sufficient force, would have been a consummate partisan commander. He has coolness, daring, persistency, the stoic faith and patience, and a firmness of will and purpose unconquerable. He is tall, wiry, muscular, but with little flesh—with a cold, gray eye, gray hair beard and mustache, compressed lips and sharp aquiline nose; of cast-iron face and frame, and with powers of endurance equal to anything needed to be done or suffered in any cause. Though engaged in a wicked, mad and fanatical enterprise, he is the farthest possible remove from the ordinary ruffian, maniac or madman; but his powers are rather executory than inventive, and he never had the depth or breadth of mind to originate and contrive himself the plan of insurrection which he undertook to carry out. The conspiracy was, unquestionably, far more extended than yet appears, numbering among the conspirators many more than the handful of followers who assailed Harper's Ferry, and having in the North and West, if not also in the South, as its counselors and abettors, men of intelligence, position, and wealth. Certainly, it was among the best planned and executed conspiracies that ever failed.

For two years he had been plotting and preparing it with aiders and comforters a thousand miles apart, in the slave states and the free; for six months he lived without so much as suspicion in a slave state, and near the scene of the insurrection, winning even the esteem and confidence of his neighbors, yet collecting day by day large quantities of arms, and making ready for the outbreak. He had as complete an equipment, even to intrenching tools, as any commander in a regular campaign, and intended, like Napoleon, to make war support war. He had Sharp's rifles and Maynard's revolvers for marksmen, and pikes for the slaves. In the dead hour of night, crossing the Potomac, he seized the armory with many thousand stand of arms and other munitions of war; and making prisoners of more than thirty of the workmen, officers and citizens, overawed the town of Harper's Ferry with its thousand inhabitants. With less than half a score of men surviving, he held the armory for many hours, refusing, though cut off from all succor, and surrounded upon all sides, to surrender, and was taken with sword in hand, overpowered by superior numbers, yet fighting to the last. During this short insurrection eighteen men were killed and ten or more severely wounded—twice the number killed and wounded on the part of the American force at the Battle of New Orleans.

John Brown failed to excite a general and most wicked, bloody and desolating servile and civil war, only *because the slaves and non-slave holding white men of the vicinity, the former twenty thousand in number, would not rise.* He had prepared arms and ammunition for fifteen hundred men, and captured, at the first blow, enough to arm more than fifty thousand; and yet be had lees than thirty men—more, nevertheless, than have begun half the revolutions and conspiracies which history records. But he had not tampered with slaves, nor solicited the non-slaveholding whites around him, because he really believed that the moment the blow was struck they would gather to his standard; and expecting, furthermore, the promised reinforcements instantly from the North and West. This was the basis upon which the whole conspiracy was planned; and had his belief been well founded, he would unquestionably have succeeded in stirring up a most formidable insurrection, possibly involving the peace of the whole country, and requiring, certainly, great armies and vast treasure to suppress it.

Here was his folly and madness. He believed and acted upon the faith which for twenty years has been so persistently taught in every form throughout the free states, and which is but another mode of statement of the doctrine of the "*irrepressible conflict*"—that slavery and the three hundred and seventy thousand slave holders of the South are only tolerated, and that the millions of slaves and non-slaveholding white men are ready and eager to rise against the "oligarchy," needing only a leader and deliverer. The conspiracy was the natural and necessary consequence of the doctrines proclaimed every day, year in and year out, by tho apostles of abolition. But Brown was sincere, earnest, practical; he proposed no mild works in his faith, reckless of murder, treason, and every other crime. This was his madness and folly. He perishes justly and miserably, an insurgent and a felon; but guiltier than he, and with blood upon their heads, are the false and cowardly prophets and teachers of abolition.

An Associated Press article appeared on Monday, October 24th:

The trial of John Brown and his accomplices in the attempt to stir up a slave insurrection in Virginia is expected to commence tomorrow morning. Knowing the general interest felt in the subject, the associated press has made arrangements to receive full telegraphic reports of the proceedings from day to day. Whether these men will be charged with murder, or with the attempt to incite slaves to insurrection—which is probably, in Virginia, a still more serious crime—we are not yet advised. If the charge of the presiding judge may be taken as any indication of the temper with which the trial will be conducted, the prisoners will have no reason to complain of any unfairness or undue prejudice. It is hardly possible, however, that a jury should be found, taken from the people of the menaced neighborhood, entirely free from impulses of hostility towards the accused. There can be little question of their guilt, as they themselves do not seem inclined to deny any of the facts needed to establish it

These men will doubtless be hung for the crime they have committed. Conceding their guilt, it is not easy to complain of its penalty. Their crime was the most heinous which can be committed against a community, and the fact that they believed themselves to be doing right cannot be admitted as a bar to punishment, however it may modify our impressions of their personal culpability. We cannot think the ferocious tone generally held towards them by the Southern press likely to be of service to the Southern cause. It only tends to make these men martyrs, and to screen their enterprise from the just detestation and abhorrence which it everywhere inspires.

Probably strenuous efforts will be made in the trial to trace this plot to its origin and through all its ramifications. It is generally believed in the South to have had very extended and formidable support in the Northern states. We believe this to be an error; but if there is any such plot in the North, we shall be very glad to have it exposed by the developments of this trial. It is not at all likely that any such crime can be brought home to Northern men in this connection as will warrant Governor Wise in demanding their surrender; it is only "*fugitives* from justice" who can be thus demanded, and the use of this word implies that their crime must have been committed within the state from which the demand proceeds. But public sentiment will punish severely and permanently, any man who shall be proved to have aided in the nefarious crime for which Brown and his accomplices will suffer in person.

Chapter 5

THE TRIAL OF THE CENTURY

T HE CRIMINAL PROCEEDINGS involving John Brown and the other Harper's Ferry conspirators commenced in Charlestown on Tuesday, October 25, 1859 in the magistrate's court. Colonel Braxton Davenport was the presiding justice, and the following magistrates were associated with him on the bench: Dr. Charles Alexander, John J. Lock, John F. Smith, Thomas H. Willis, G. W. Eichelberger, C. H. Lewis and Moses W. Burk.

At 10:30 AM the sheriff was directed to bring in the five prisoners, who were conducted from the jail under a guard of eighty armed men. A guard was also stationed around the court. The courthouse was bristling with bayonets on all sides.

Charles B. Harding acted as attorney for the county, assisted by Andrew Hunter, counsel for the commonwealth. The prisoners were ordered to be brought forth. First to arrive were John Brown and Edwin Coppoc, who were manacled together. Brown seemed weak and haggard, his eyes swollen from the effects of the wounds on his head. Coppoc was uninjured. Aaron Dwight Stevens was then brought in. He looked haggard and depressed, and had several wounds on his head, but was far less injured than Brown. Next came John Anthony Copeland, Jr., a light mulatto about twenty five years old. Lastly, Shields Green a dark Negro, *alias* Emperor, marched in.

Sheriff Campbell read the indictment against the prisoners, who were charged with high treason and murder. Mr. Harding asked that the court might assign counsel for the prisoners, if they had none. The court then inquired if the prisoners had counsel, at which time Mr. Brown addressed the court as follows:

> VIRGINIANS: I did not ask for any quarter at the time I was taken. I did not ask to have my life spared. The governor of the state of Virginia tendered me his assurance that I should have a fair trial; but under *no circumstances whatever will I be able to have a fair trial.* If you seek my blood, you can have it at any moment, without this mockery of a trial. I have had no counsel. I have not been able to advise with any one. I know nothing about the feelings of my fellow prisoners, and am utterly unable to attend in any way to my own defense. My memory doesn't serve me. My health is insufficient, although improving. There are mitigating circumstances that I would urge in our favor, if a fair trial is to be allowed us. But if we are to be forced with a mere form—a trial for execution—you might spare yourselves that trouble. I am ready for my fate. I do not ask for a trial. I beg for no mockery of a trial—no insult—nothing but that which conscience gives, or cowardice would drive you to practice. I ask again to be excused from the mockery of a trial. I do not even know what the special design of this examination is. I do not know what is to be the benefit of it to the commonwealth. I have now little further to ask, other than that I may not be foolishly insulted, only as cowardly barbarians insult those who fall into their power.

At the conclusion of Brown's remarks, the court assigned Charles J. Faulkner and Lawson Botts as counsel for the prisoners. Faulkner, after a brief consultation with Brown and the others, addressed the court as follows:

> I was about to remark to the court that, although I feel at any time willing to discharge any duty which the court can legally claim, and by authority of law, devolve

upon me, I am not aware of any authority which this court has, sitting as an examining court, to assign counsel for the defense. Besides, it is manifest, from the remarks just made by one of the prisoners, that he regards the appearance of counsel under such circumstances, not as a *bona fide* act, but rather as a mockery. Under these circumstances, I do not feel disposed to assume the responsibility of that position. I have other reasons for declining the position, connected with my having been at the place of action and hearing all the admissions of the prisoners, which render it improper and inexpedient for me to act as counsel. If the court had authority to order it peremptorily I should acquiesce and obey that authority. I am not aware that there is any such power vested in this court, but as it is the prisoners' desire I will see that full justice is done them.

Lawson Botts said he did not feel it to be his duty to decline the appointment of the court. He was prepared to do his best to defend the prisoners, and he hoped the court would assign some experienced assistant in case Faulkner persisted in his declination.

Mr. Harding addressed Brown, and asked him if he was willing to accept Mr. Faulkner and Mr. Botts as his counsel. This question led to the following exchange:

Mr. Brown: I wish to say that I have requested counsel from elsewhere. I applied through the advice of some persons here, to some persons whose names I do not now recollect, to act as counsel for me, and I have sent for other counsel who have had no possible opportunity to see me. I wish for counsel if I am to have a trial, but if I am to have nothing but the mockery of a trial, as I said, I do not really care anything about counsel. It is unnecessary to trouble any gentleman with that duty.

Mr. Harding: You are to have a fair trial.

Mr. Brown: There were certain men—I think that Mr. Botts was one of them—who declined acting as my counsel, but I am not positive about it. I cannot remember whether he was one, because I have heard so many names. I am a stranger here; I do not know the disposition or character of the gentleman named. I have applied for counsel of my own, and doubtless could have them, if I am not, as I said before, to be hurried to execution before they can reach me. But if that is the disposition that is to be made for me, all this trouble and expense can be saved.

Mr. Harding: The question is, do you desire the aid of Messrs. Faulkner and Botts as your counsel? Please answer either yes or no.

Mr. Brown: I cannot regard this as an examination under any circumstances. I would prefer that they should exercise their own pleasure. I feel as if it is a matter of very little account to me. If they had designed to assist me as counsel I should have wanted an opportunity to consult with them at my leisure.

Mr. Harding: Stevens, are you willing that those gentlemen should act as your counsel?

Mr. Stevens: I am willing to have that gentleman (pointing to Mr. Botts).

Mr. Harding: Do you object to Mr. Faulkner?

Mr. Stevens: No. I am willing to take both.

Mr. Harding addressed each of the other prisoners separately, and each stated his willingness to be defended by the counsels named. The court issued a peremptory order that the press should not publish detailed testimony, as it would render the selection of a jury before the circuit court impossible.

Eight witnesses were then called for a pre-examination. All but one had been hostages at Harper's Ferry. In general they said Brown had treated them with courtesy and respect.

Colonel Lewis Washington, the Jefferson County planter and a great-grandnephew of George Washington, stated that at about one o'clock on Monday morning he was in bed asleep, and was awakened by a noise. He heard his name called, went down stairs, and was surrounded by six men. Stevens appeared to be in command; Cook, Coppoc and two Negro prisoners were along, and another white man, whom he afterwards recognized as John Henry Kagi, was with them. Mr. Washington then proceeded to detail all the particulars of his being taken as a prisoner with his Negroes to the armory, and the subsequent events up to the attack by the marines; and his delivery.

A. M. Kitzmiller gave the particulars of his being taken prisoner and locked up; saying:

> I subsequently had several interviews with Brown, who always treated me with a great deal of respect and courtesy. I endeavored to ascertain from Brown what object he had in mind, and Brown repeatedly told me that his only object was to free the slaves, and he was willing to fight the pro-slavery men to accomplish that object. On one occasion during the attack I said to Brown, "This is getting to be hot work, and, if you will allow me to interfere, I can possibly accommodate matters." I went out with Stevens under a flag of truce on Monday afternoon. I requested that Stevens remain while I went forward; at which point Stevens was fired on and fell. I recognized only Brown and Stevens. I counted twenty-two men early in the morning, armed with Sharp's rifles. When Stevens was lying wounded there he remarked to me, "I have been cruelly deceived," to which I dumbly replied that I wished I had remained at home.

Mr. Washington then stated that he recalled a conversation with Governor Wise, in which Brown was told he need not answer questions unless he chose to. Brown replied that he had nothing to conceal; he had no favors to ask. He said that he had enough arms for two thousand men, and could get enough for five thousand if they were needed.

Armistead Ball told the particulars of his being taken by the insurgents:

> I had an interview with Brown after my capture, who stated that he did not come for child's play, but was prepared to carry out his designs; that his object was not to make war against the people, and they would not be injured if they remained quiet; his object was to place the United States arms in the hands of the black men, and he proposed to free all the slaves in the vicinity. Brown repeatedly said his whole object was only to release the slaves. I asked him if some plan could not be arranged for the liberation of myself and the other prisoners. He said we could only be released by furnishing able-bodied slaves in the place of each. I only recognized Stevens, Green and Brown. Captain Brown told the prisoners when the charge of the marines was about to be made, that although he did not intend to injure them himself they should equally occupy the post of danger with himself; that if they were not dear enough to their fellow citizens to accept the terms he had proposed to secure their safety they must be barbarians. Coppoc, on the other hand, told me and friends to get behind the engines, because he did not wish to see any of us injured. I heard one of the insurgents, Mayor Beckham say, "I have dropped him." I did not see Captain Brown fire once from the engine house; I don't think he fired at any time, but Green fired several times. The prisoners were never unreasonably exposed.

At this point Stevens appeared to be fainting, and a mattress was procured for him, on which he laid down during the balance of the examination.

John Allstadt, one of the slave owners, who was brought into the armory with his slaves, described how the door to his home was battered down, and how he was seized by six armed men. He went on to say, "I think Brown fired several times, I know I saw him with a gun leveled at the crowd. I saw all the prisoners, except the yellow man, Copeland."

Alexander Kelly detailed the particulars of the collision with the insurgents, and the exchanging of several shots; but could not identify any of the prisoners.

William Johnson testified to the capture of the yellow man Copeland, who was attempting to escape across the river. He was armed with a spear and a rifle in the middle of the Shenandoah River. He said that he had been placed in charge of Hall's Rifle Factory by Captain Brown.

Andrew Kennedy was at the jail when Copeland was brought in. Kennedy questioned Copeland, who said that he had come from the Western Reserve of Ohio, and that Brown came there in August and employed him at $20 per month.

Mr. Faulkner objected to this testimony as implicating the white prisoners. The presiding judge said his testimony could only be received as implicating himself.

Mr. Kennedy resumed his story saying, "Copeland said that their object was to release the slaves of this country; that he knew of nineteen in the party, but there were several others he did not know."

Joseph A. Brua, who was one of the prisoners in the engine house, said, "I was permitted to go out several times with a flag of truce. During the exchange of firing, Coppoc fired twice, and at the second firing, Brown remarked "that man is down." I then asked permission to go out, and found that Mr. Beckham had just been shot, and I had no doubt that Coppoc had shot him."

Mr. Allstadt recalled, "I think that Captain Brown shot the marine who was killed; I saw him fire."

The preliminary examination being concluded, the court remanded the prisoners for trial before the circuit court. The preliminary examination had merely been to see whether the charges were of sufficient importance to go before the grand jury. On the following day the jury would undoubtedly report the bill, and the case would then be immediately called for trial. There was evidently no intention to hurry the trial through, and execute the prisoners as soon as possible, fearing attempts to rescue them. In the case of servile insurrection, thirty days were not required between conviction and execution, as in other capital convictions.

The circuit court of Jefferson County, Judge Richard Parker on the bench, assembled at 2:00 PM. The grand jury were called in and the magistrates' court reported the result of the earlier examination in the case of Captain Brown and the other prisoners. The grand jury retired with the witnesses for the state. At 5:00 PM they returned into court and stated that they had not finished the examination of witnesses, and were therefore discharged until 10:00 AM the next morning.

It was rumored that John Brown wanted to make a full statement of his motives and intentions through the press, but the court refused all further access to him by any reporters, fearing that he might put forth something calculated to influence the public mind and to "have a bad effect on slaves." The mother of Cook's wife was in the court house throughout the examination. The general belief was that Cook was still in the mountains, somewhere near Harper's Ferry. On Sunday night a woman who kept a canal lock said Cook came to her house and asked the privilege to warm himself by her fireside. She knew him well, as she was a relative of his.

Coppoc said that he had a brother in the party, and that Brown had three sons in it. He further said that there were two other persons engaged, named Taylor and Hazlett, so that, including Cook, five had escaped, twelve were killed, and five captured, making twenty-two men in all. Nobody doubted that the trial would commence on the following morning, although much difficulty was anticipated in selecting a jury.

Captain Brown's object in refusing the aid of counsel was that, if he had counsel, he would not be allowed to speak himself, and Southern counsel would not be allowed to express his views. The reason given for hurrying the trial was that the people of the whole county were in a state of high excitement, and a large armed force would be required to prevent attempts at any rescue. It was presumed that the prisoners would demand separate trials. After conviction, only a few days would be given to them before their execution. It was thought that all but Brown would make a full confession.

The prisoners, as brought into the court, presented a pitiable sight, Brown and Stevens being unable to stand without assistance. Brown had three sword wounds in his body, and one saber cut over the head. Stevens had three balls in his head, one in his breast, and one in his arm. He was also cut on the forehead with a rifle bullet, which had glanced off, leaving a bad wound.

The first day of the trial commenced on Wednesday, October 26, 1859 at the Charlestown court house. The circuit court, Judge Parker presiding, met at 10:00 AM. The grand jury were called in and they retired to resume their examination of the witnesses. The court took a recess awaiting the return of the grand jury. Mr. Johnson, U. S. Marshal of Cleveland, Ohio arrived that morning. He visited the prisoners, and identified Copeland as a fugitive from justice in Ohio. His object was supposed to be to ferret out testimony implicating the other parties.

The excitement of the people was unabated and crowds of persons from the surrounding county were in town. The event was regarded as proving the faithfulness of the slaves, and no fears were entertained of them, but a military guard was kept up, fearing an attempt to rescue the prisoners. Consternation among the slaves of Colonel Washington was caused by the fear of being seized, and they firmly believed the object of the prisoners was to carry them South and sell them. Not a single slave was implicated as sympathizing with the insurrectionists. Those carried off were all recaptured and returned to their masters.

Brown made no confession, but said he had full confidence in the goodness of God, and was confident that He will rescue him from the perils that surrounded him. He said he has had rifles leveled at him, knives at his throat, and that his life has often been in as great peril as it is now, but that God has always been at his side. He said that he knew that God was with him, and he feared nothing.

Alexander R. Boteler, member elect of Congress of the district, had collected from fifty to one hundred letters from the citizens of the neighborhood of Brown's house, who had searched it before the arrival of the marines. The letters were in the possession of Andrew Hunter, Esq., who had a large number of letters obtained from Brown's house by the marines and other parties. Among them was a roll of the conspirators, containing forty-seven signatures; also, a receipt from Horace Greeley for letters, etc., received from Brown, and an accurately traced map from Chambersburg to Brown's house; copies of letters from Brown, stating that as the arrival of too many men at once would excite suspicion, they should arrive singly; a letter from Merriam stating that of the twenty thousand dollars wanted, G. S. was good for one-fifth; also, a letter from J. E. Cook stating that the Maryland election was about to come off, the people would become excited, and that they would get some of the candidates to join their side.

Cannon were stationed in front of the court house and an armed guard patrolled around the jail.

Captain Brown consented to allow Messrs. Faulkner and Botts to act as his counsel; they assured him that they would defend him faithfully, and give him the advantage of every privilege that the law would allow.

Stevens declared that he did not desire to be defended by Northern counsel, preferring Southern, and that the court should name them. There was a decided sympathy for Stevens, not only on account of his sufferings, but because he had shown none of that vindictiveness and hardness that characterized Brown. His regret was regarded as caused by the consequences of his folly, and the examination yesterday indicated that the other prisoners lost their confidence in Brown, and are not disposed to follow him in his defiant course.

At twelve noon the court reassembled, and the grand jury reported a true bill against the prisoners. The grand jury members were then discharged. Charles B. Harding, assisted by Andrew Hunter, represented the commonwealth, and Charles J. Faulkner and Lawson Botts were counsels for the prisoners. A true bill was found against each prisoner included the following charges:

> *First*—For conspiring with Negroes to produce insurrection.
>
> *Second*—For treason to the commonwealth; and
>
> *Third*—For murder.

The prisoners, who were accompanied by a body of armed men, passed through the street and entered the court house without the slightest demonstration on the part of the people.

Brown looked somewhat better, and his eye was not overly swollen. Stevens had to be supported, and reclined on a mattress on the floor of the courtroom, evidently unable to sit; he was described as having the appearance of a dying man, breathing with great difficulty. Before the reading of the arraignment, Mr. Hunter called the attention of the court to the necessity of appointing additional counsel for the prisoners, stating that one of the counsel appointed by the county court, Faulkner, considered his duty in that capacity as having ended, and he had left. The prisoners, therefore, had no other counsel than Mr. Botts. If the court was about to assign them other counsel, Hunter said, it might be proper to do so now.

The court stated that it would assign them any members of the bar they might select. After consulting with Captain Brown, Mr. Botts said that the prisoner had retained him, and desired to have Mr. Green, his assistant, to assist him. If the court would accede to that arrangement it would be very agreeable to him personally. The court requested Mr. Green to act as counsel for the prisoners, and he consented to do so. Mr. Brown, on rising said:

> I do not intend to detain the court, but barely wish to say, as I have been promised a fair trial, that I am not now in a circumstance that enables me to attend to a trial, owing to the state of my health. I have a severe wound in my back, or rather in one kidney, which enfeebles me greatly. But I am doing well, and I only ask for a very short delay of my trial, and I think I may become able to listen to it; and I merely ask this, that as the saying is "the devil may have his dues," no more. I wish to say, further, that my hearing is impaired, and rendered indistinct in consequence of the wounds I have about my head. I cannot hear distinctly at all. I could not hear what the court said this morning. I would like to hear what is said in my trial, and I am now doing better than I could expect to be under the circumstances. A very short delay is all I would ask. I do not presume to ask more than a very short delay, so that I may in some degree recover, and be able at least to listen to my trial, and hear what questions are asked of the citizens and what their answers are. If that could be allowed me I would feel very much obliged.

Mr. Hunter replied, "Your request is rather premature. An arraignment must be made, and then this question can be considered."

The court ordered the indictment to be read, so that the prisoners could plead guilty or not guilty and it would then consider Mr. Brown's request.

The prisoners were compelled to stand with difficulty during the arraignment, and Stevens was held upright by two bailiffs. The artist Porte Crayon was present, and made sketches of the prisoners as thus arraigned. The reading of the indictment occupied about twenty minutes. Each of the prisoners responded to the question "not guilty," and desired to be tried separately. The prisoners were removed from the court room.

Mr. Hunter began by stating that the state elected to try John Brown first.

Mr. Botts responded by saying, "I am instructed by Mr. Brown to say that he is mentally and physically unable to proceed with his trial at this time. He has heard today that counsel of his own choice will be here soon, and he will, of course, prefer that. He only asks for a delay of two or three days. It seems to me a reasonable request, and I hope the court will grant it."

Mr. Hunter's reaction was as follows, "I do not think it the duty of the prosecutor for the commonwealth, or for anyone occupying that position, to oppose anything that justice requires, nor to object to anything that involves a simple consideration of humanity where it can be properly allowed. In regard to this proposition to delay the trial of John Brown two or three days, we deem it our duty that the court, before determining matters, should be judiciously put in possession of all the facts and circumstances that they were aware of in the line of our duties as prosecutors. My own opinion is that *it is not proper to delay the trial of this prisoner a single day,* and that there is no necessity for it."

Mr. Hunter then alluded to the conditions surrounding the case in general terms. He believed that they made it dangerous to delay the trial, and placed excessive pressure upon the physical resources of the testimony. He said, "Our law, in making special provisions for allowing at the discretion of the court, briefer time than usual in case of conviction for such offenders, between the condemnation and execution, evidently indicates indirectly the necessity for acting promptly and decisively, though always justly, in proceedings of this kind."

In reference to the physical condition of Brown, Mr. Hunter asked the judge not to receive the unimportant statements of the prisoners as sufficient grounds for delay, but that the jailor and physicians should be examined. As to expecting counsel from abroad, he said that no impediment had been thrown in the way of the prisoners procuring such counsel as they desired, but on the contrary every facility had been afforded. Able and intelligent counsel had been assigned them here, and he felt there was little reason to expect the attendance of those gentlemen from the North, who had been written to.

Mr. Harding concurred in the objections of Mr. Hunter, on the ground of danger in delay, and also because Brown was the leader of the insurrection, and his trial ought to be proceeded with on account of the advantage thereby accruing in the trial of the others.

Under the circumstances Mr. Green thought a short delay was desirable as he had not been given opportunity of consulting with the prisoner, or preparing a defense for him. The letters for Northern counsel had been sent off, but it was too early to have received any answers. Mr. Botts added that at present the excitement was so great as, perhaps, to deter Northern counsel from coming out, but now that it had been promised that the prisoners should have a fair and impartial trial, he presumed that they would come and take part in the case.

Judge Parker stated that if physical inability was shown, a reasonable delay must be granted. As to the expectation of other counsel, that did not constitute a sufficient cause for delay, as there was no certainty about their coming. Under the circumstances it was natural that the prisoners should seek delay. The brief period remaining before the close of the term of the court rendered it necessary to proceed as expeditiously as practicable, and to be cautious about granting delays. The judge would request that the physician who had attended Brown be present, to testify as to his condition.

Dr. Mason understandingly thought Brown was able to go on with the trial. He did not think his wounds were such as to affect his mind or recollection. Dr. Mason had heard him complain of debility but not of hardness of hearing. Mr. Cockerell, one of the guards at the jail, said that Brown had always been ready to converse freely.

Mr. John Avis, Brown's jailor, was sworn in. He testified, "I heard Brown frequently say to persons visiting him that his mind was confused and his hearing affected; and he would not like to give any opinion as to his ability to . . ."

At that point the telegraph from Charlestown ceased working, owing to a storm prevailing there. The record of the proceedings then continued somewhat later.

A jailor was ordered to bring Mr. Brown into court. He found him in bed, from which Brown declared himself unable to rise. He was accordingly brought back into court on a cot. The prisoner was laying down most of the time with his eyes closed, and the counterpane drawn up close to his chin. He was evidently not injured greatly, but he was determined to resist the rushing of his trial by all the means in his power.

The jury pool were then called in and sworn. They were questioned as to having formed or expressed any opinion that would prevent their deciding the case impartially on the merits of the testimony. The court excluded those who were present at Harper's Ferry during the insurrection, and had seen the prisoners perpetrating the acts for which they were to be tried. They were all from distant parts of the country, mostly farmers, some of them owning a few slaves, but others none. The examination was continued until twenty-four were decided upon by the court and counsel to be competent jurors. Out of these twenty-four the counsel for the prisoner had a right to strike off eight, and then twelve were drawn by ballot out of the remaining sixteen. The following were the questions put to the jurors:

—Were you at Harper's Ferry on Monday or Tuesday?

—How long did you remain there?

—Did you witness any of the proceedings for which this party is to be tried?

—Did you form or express any opinion from what you saw there with regard to the guilt or innocence of these people?

—Would that opinion disqualify you from giving these men a fair trial?

—Did you hear any of the evidence in this case before the examining court?

—What was your opinion based on?

—Was it a decided one, or was it one which would yield to evidence, if the evidence was different from what you supposed?

—Are your sure that you can try this case impartially, from the evidence alone, without reference to anything you have heard or seen of this transaction?

—Have you any conscientious scruples against convicting a party of an offense to which the law assigns the punishment of death, merely because that is the penalty assigned?

The following were finally fixed upon as the twelve jurors: Joseph Allyers, George W. Boyer, Isaac Dust, John C. McClure, William A. Martin, Jacob Miller, Thomas Osborne, William Rightodale, George W. Tapp, Richard Timberlake, Thomas Watson Jr., and John C. Wiltshire.

The jury were not sworn in at this time, but the judge charged them not to converse upon the case, nor to permit others to converse with them. They were dismissed at 5:00 PM, and the prisoner was then carried back over to the jail on his cot, and the court adjourned until the next morning.

It was learned that John Copeland, the mulatto prisoner from Oberlin, Ohio, had made a full confession to United States Marshal Martin, of Virginia; and also to Marshal Mark Johnson, of Cleveland, representing the Northern District of Ohio. John Copeland gave the names of the parties at Oberlin who induced him to go to Harper's Ferry, and who furnished the money for his expenses. He also stated that a movement of a similar character had been contemplated in Kentucky at about the same time. Many people in Northern Ohio, whose names had not been heretofore mentioned, were directly implicated. Governor Wise ordered that Copeland's confession be withheld from the public until the Brown trial was over.

Marshal Johnson displayed a large number of important letters implicating Gerrit Smith and a number of prominent men of Oberlin, Cleveland and other points in Ohio. Among those letters was the following:

Tribune Office, April 30 1850.

Mr. J. H. Kaji

SIR: Yours is received and we inclose our check for $41, for seven letters from Kansas and two from Ohio. Yours, etc.

HORACE GREELEY & CO.

Kagi, it will be remembered, was one of the men killed in the insurrection.

There was also a letter from Captain Brown to one of his sons, dated April 16, 1859, detailing a visit to Gerrit Smith at Peterboro. The letter said that Gerrit Smith gave him $180; that he also, at his house, received a note that he considered good for $200 more; and that Gerrit Smith had written to his friends in the East, saying that $2,000 must be raised for Brown, of which he himself would agree to furnish one-fifth. There was also notice of a draft from the cashier of the New York State Bank for $100, sent him by direction of Gerrit Smith. This was dated "Albany, New York, Aug. 29, 1859."

Marshal Johnson desired to furnish this mass of correspondence to the court, but Mr. Hunter, by direction of Governor Wise, objected to its immediate publication. The correspondence contained a list of officers of the provisional government and a list of contributors to the project. Marshal Johnson left for Cleveland that evening, taking copies with him.

The examination made by the United States marshals settled the fact that Brown's movement had long been maturing; that many prominent men in the Northern states had given money and influence in its behalf; and that, when the facts would be made public, an unparalleled sensation would be expected.

The second day of the trial commenced on Thursday, October 27, 1859 and met at the Charlestown court house in Virginia. Mr. Brown was brought into the court walking, but upon his arrival he laid down on his cot at full length within the bar. He looked considerably better than he had on the previous day, the swelling having left his eyes.

Senator Mason, taking an interest in the case, was present in the court room. Messrs. Harding and Hunter again appeared for the commonwealth, and Messrs. Botts and Green for the prisoner. Mr. Botts read the following dispatch which he had received that morning:

Akron Ohio, Wednesday, Oct. 26, 1859.

To C. J. Faulkner and Lawson Botts:

SIRS: John Brown, leader of the insurrection at Harper's Ferry, and several of his family, have resided in this county many years. Insanity is hereditary in that family. His mother's sister died with it, and a daughter of that sister has been two years in the lunatic asylum. A son and daughter of his mother's brother have also been confined in the lunatic asylum, and another son of that brother is now insane and under close restraint. These facts can be conclusively proven by witnesses residing here, who will doubtless attend the trial if desired.

A. H. LEWIS

William C. Allen, the telegraphic operator at the Akron office, added to the above dispatch that A. H. Lewis was a resident of that place, and that his statements were creditable.

Mr. Botts testified, "On receiving the above dispatch I went to the jail with my associate, Mr. Green, and read it to Brown, and the latter desired to say that in his father's family there had never been any insanity. On his mother's side there had been repeated instances of it. He added that his first wife showed symptoms of insanity, which were also evident in his first and second sons by that wife. Some portions of the statements in the dispatch he knew to be correct, and of some of the other portions he was ignorant. He did not know whether his mother's sister died in a lunatic asylum, but he believed that a daughter of that sister had been in the asylum for two years. He also believed that a son and daughter of his mother's brother had been confined in an asylum, but he was not apprized of the fact that another son of that brother was now insane and in close confinement."

Brown desired his counsel to say that he does not plea insanity, and if he had been at all insane he was totally unconscious of it. Yet he added that those who are most insane generally suppose they have more reason and sanity than those around them. For himself he disdained to put in that plea, and he seeks no immunity of that kind. This movement was made totally without his approbation or concurrence, and it was unknown to him till the receipt of the above dispatch. Brown raised himself up on his cot and said:

> I will add, if the court will allow me, that I look upon it as a miserable artifice and pretext of those who ought to take a different course in regard to me if they took any at all, and I view it with contempt more than otherwise. As I remarked to Mr. Green, insane prisoners, so far as my experience goes, have but little ability to judge of their own sanity, and if I am insane of course I should think I know more than all the rest of the world. But I do not think so. I am perfectly unaware of any insanity, and I reject, so far as I am capable, any attempts to interfere in my behalf on that score.

Mr. Botts further stated that he was instructed by Mr. Brown to say that, rejecting this plea entirely and seeking no delay for that reason, he does repeat to the court his request made on the previous day, that time be given for the foreign counsel to arrive that he has now reason to expect. A dispatch was received from Cleveland, Ohio, signed "Dan Tilden," dated October 26th asking Brown whether it would be of use for counsel to leave on the previous night. To this dispatch an answer was returned that the jury would be sworn in on the following morning, and that Brown desired the counsel to come at once.

The telegraphic operator then stated that this dispatch would be sent off at once, in advance of the dispatches sent by reporters, and he had learned that morning that it was sent before the previous night's storm-interrupted communication, and that counsel might reach the courthouse by twelve midnight or one o'clock the next morning.

The course taken by Brown made it evident that he sought no postponement for the mere purpose of delay, as he rejected the plea of insanity. Still, in his opinion, he could have a fairer trial if the defense were conducted by his own counsel than if he were defended by the present counsel.

Mr. Hunter observed that the prisoners' counsel, having renewed the motion of the previous day to delay for a specific period, based upon information received in the telegram, questioned whether there was sufficient grounds in this additional information to change the decision announced by the court on that motion. If the court did not at once deem this circumstance verbally insufficient, before the decision was made, the counsel for the commonwealth would deem it his duty to call attention to two or three other matters connected with the affair. Though desirous to avoid forestalling the trial of this case, in regard to the present prisoner at the bar, they were prepared to prove that he had made open, repeated, and constant acknowledgments of everything charged against him.

"What does John Brown mean by wanting a delay for the purpose of having a fair trial?" asked Mr. Hunter. In a proper sense, and in the only sense in which it can be regarded by the court, it was a fair trial according to the laws of Virginia, and the safeguards against wronging the prisoner which these laws throw around him. If the prisoner's idea of a fair trial was to have it so shaped, so as to produce a fairness in his conception outside of what the laws recognized, it became the duty of the commonwealth and, as Hunter apprehended, of the court, to resist any attempts of that kind. Considering the circumstances, there could be no justification to claim any delay, except so far as the prisoner could show, in a reliable form, that such delay was necessary to do justice in his particular case according to the laws and policies of the state of Virginia.

In regard to the telegram that was read, Hunter didn't know who Mr. A. H. Lewis was. He didn't know whether he was to come here as counsel for the prisoner, or whether he wanted to head a band of desperadoes. The jurors had a right to believe the latter as well as the former. There had been enough time since the letter for Northern counsel was mailed last Saturday for it to reach him, and for Lewis to arrive, if he had designed coming. It was fairly obvious that he did not intend to come. But might it not be an attempt to gain time, and learn the latest day when a rescue could be attempted? While commending the earnestness and zeal of the prisoner's counsel, Hunter asked the court to reject the motion, and proceed with the trial at once.

Mr. Harding was reluctant to withhold from a prisoner charged with a crime of the greatest enormity, as in the present case, anything calculated to afford him the amplest opportunity of justice; but Brown had able and intelligent counsel assigned to him, who would see that he was fairly and impartially tried, and Harding, therefore, fully concurred with the remarks of his colleague, in opposing the motion. He referred, also, to the fact that Brown had pretended that he was unable to walk, and was brought into court on a cot, yet he walked back to the jail after the close of the trial seemingly without difficulty. He thought these were pretenses for a delay which the court should overrule.

Mr. Green remarked that one days' delay would be sufficient to ascertain whether the expected counsel would come or not, and no prejudice could result to the commonwealth from a small delay of that character. In reference to the new matter brought to the consideration of the court, he did not believe the prisoner had made any acknowledgment upon which he could be convicted. All the acknowledgments, so far as he knew of their character, referred to the treason. Those confessions, according to Virginia law, were insufficient to convict a party who may have acknowledged the fact in the plainest manner to one hundred witnesses—for if that was all the evidence upon which the commonwealth relied, the prisoner could not be convicted, because our code provides that such a confession shall be made in open court, and the prisoner has denied in open court by putting in a plea of not guilty.

As to sufficient time having elapsed for counsel to reach here, it was a reasonable supposition that the persons to whom Brown wrote were absent, and did not immediately receive the letter. The commonwealth attorney did not know who Tilden was, but he was an ex-member of

Congress, and was said to be a man of respectability. As for what was called Brown's sham sickness, it should be remembered that it was not made the grounds of application for delay. Brown did not think this trial should be hurried through for the reason that a rescue might be apprehended, for such fears were idle.

The judge stated that, in this case, he must see, as he would have to in any other case, that a proper cause for a delay was made out before granting such an application. In the present case, he did not see that the telegram gave any assurance that the additional counsel intended to come. It was seen that the prisoner was now defended by counsel who would take care that no improper evidence was adduced against him, and that all proper evidence in his behalf would be presented. The judge did not see that a proper cause for delay was made out. The expected counsel might arrive before the case was closed, and they could then see all the testimony which had been taken, and thus the prisoner might have the benefit of their advice, even in mid-case. As for the matter of insanity, it was not presented formally. Instead of mere statements, the judge expected affidavits or something more firm. He thought that the jury should be sworn in and the trial proceed.

Once the jury swore to fairly and impartially try the prisoner, the judge directed that the prisoner might forego standing while arraigned, if he desired it. Mr. Botts put the inquiry to the prisoner, who continued to lie prostrate in his cot while the long indictment, filling seven pages with its three counts of Insurrection, Treason and Murder, was read.

Mr. Harding addressed the jury. He presented the facts of the case, detailing the scenes at the armory, the killing of the bridge-keeper, and the subsequent killing of the citizens named in the indictment. He further described the seizure of Lewis Washington and Mr. Allstadt with their slaves, the forming of a government within the limits of the commonwealth, the holding of the citizens as prisoners of war, and their subsequent capture. He read the law on treason, levying war against the state, giving comfort to its enemies, and establishing any other government within its limits, punishable by death; the law against advising a slave to produce insurrection, punishable by death; and the law on the murder of citizens, punishable by death. All these charges, he said, would be distinctly proved beyond any possibility of doubt in the minds of the jury. He said that he would show that the prisoners' whole object was to rob citizens of their slaves, and carry them off by violence, and he further said, against the wills of the slaves, all of whom escaped and rushed back to their masters at the first opportunity. He concluded by urging the jury to cast aside all prejudices, and give the prisoners a fair and impartial trial, and not to allow their hatred of abolitionists to influence them against those who had "raised the black flag on the soil of this commonwealth."

After giving the law applicable to the case Mr. Green, on behalf of the prisoner, said that the jury must bear in mind that they are judges of the law and the facts, and that if they had any doubt as to the law, or the fact of the guilt of this prisoner, they were to give the prisoner the benefit of that doubt. On the first charge of treason, a specific act of treason must be proved. It must be proved that he attempted to establish a separate and distinct government, and it must also be proved what was purported to be treasonable acts before you could convict him on those charges. If the intent was to rely on Brown's confessions to prove treason, the law distinctly said, "No conviction can be made on a confession unless it is made in open court." There must be sufficient evidence to prove the charge, independent of any confession out of court, and it requires two distinct witnesses to prove each and every act of treason.

In regard to the second charge, namely that of conspiring with slaves to rebel and make insurrection, the jury must be satisfied that such a conspiracy was done within the state of Virginia, and within the jurisdiction of the court. If it were done in Maryland the court could not punish the act as if it were done within the limits of the armory at Harper's Ferry. It was not done within the limits of that state; and so the government of the United States holds an exclusive jurisdiction within the said grounds. Attorney General Cushing had decided this point with regard to the armory grounds at Harper's Ferry. This opinion was read to the jury, showing that persons residing within the limits of the armory cannot even be taxed by Virginia, and that crimes committed within the said limits are punishable by the federal courts.

Mr. Green then reminded the jury that, although they might have had doubts about the laws on this subject, they must give the prisoners the benefit of that doubt upon the trial. As for the charge of murder, if it were committed within the limits of the armory the court would have absolutely no jurisdiction. In the case of Mayor Beckham, if he was killed on the railroad bridge, the crime was committed within the State of Maryland; and that state claimed jurisdiction up to the armory grounds. Green reminded the jury that, although he may be guilty of murder, it must be proved that it was deliberate and premeditated murder to make it a capital offense; otherwise, the killing was murder in the second degree, punishable with imprisonment. "If you have any doubt on the points," he said, "you must give that doubt to the prisoners." Mr. Green was satisfied that the jury would not allow any outside excitement to affect them, and that they would do their duty faithfully and impartially.

Mr. Botts next addressed the jury, "This case is an unusual one, and the crime charged is in many respects unknown. The jury trial calls for calm, unimpassioned deliberation, and not the seizure upon loose statements for a conviction. The jury must be above all prejudices and influences, and deliberate calmly, and free of all resentment, bearing in mind that the mission of the law is not to wreak vengeance, and that the majesty of the law is best maintained when judges, counsel and jury rise above these influences. The burden of proof is on the commonwealth, and if she fails to substantiate her charges, you are bound to do your duty impartially, and find your verdict on the law and testimony that the commonwealth may be able to present to you."

Mr. Botts then proceeded to go over the same grounds covered by Mr. Green on each of the three points of the indictment, treason, insurrection and murder. He said, "No matter how much a jury may be convinced in their own minds of the guilt of the prisoner, it is essential that they have tangible proof of positive guilt in a case like this, involving both life and liberty."

Mr. Botts, reviewing the law bearing upon the case, expressed a determination to avail himself of every advantage that the law allowed, and to do his duty to the prisoner earnestly and faithfully. It was beholden on the prisoner to state that he believed himself to be actuated by the "highest and noblest feelings that ever coursed through a human breast," and that his instructions were to destroy neither property, nor life. They would prove by those gentlemen who were prisoners that they were treated with respect, and that they were kept in positions of safety, and that no violence was offered to them. These facts must be taken into consideration and have their due weight with the jury.

Mr. Hunter followed. He stated that his purpose was to avoid anything by way of argument or explanation not immediately connected with the particular issue to be tried. He intended to march straight forward to the attainment of the ends of justice, by either convicting or acquitting the prisoner at the bar. With a single preliminary remark explaining his position as that of assistant, a position which had been assigned to him by the governor of the commonwealth, as well as His Honor the judge, he passed at once to a review of what the law was in reference to the case, and what he expected to be able to prove to the satisfaction of the jury. He remarked that this was probably the first case of high treason, or treason against the state, that had ever been tried there by the state courts, and he fervently hoped it would be the last that would ever occur. But this result, he said, would depend not only upon the court's decision but upon the prompt return of a verdict in the case by the jury.

Hunter thought his friends on the other side of the fence were totally mistaken in their view that the law as it then stood on the statute-books in reference to overt acts was, either in language or substantially, that contained in the constitution of the United States. On the contrary, the phraseology had been varied from that of the constitution, and, as he conceived, for a plain and palpable purpose. All the powers vested in the federal government were given with great jealousy. This was a perfectly familiar historical fact, and consequently, while treason against the United States consists only in levying war against them, or adhering to their enemies and giving them aid and comfort, there is no provision that no person shall be convicted of treason unless upon the testimony of two witnesses of some overt act or confession in open court.

State law was more explicit, and included within its definition of treason the establishing, without the authority of the legislature, of any government within its limits separate from the existing government, or the holding or executing of such government of any office; professing allegiance or fidelity to it, or resisting the execution of laws under the color of its authority; and it went on to declare that such treason, if proved by the testimony of two witnesses to the same overt act, or by confession in court, should be punished with death. Any one of these acts constituted treason against the commonwealth, and Hunter believed that the prisoner had been guilty of each and all of these acts, which would be proved in the clearest manner, not by two, but by a dozen witnesses, unless limited by the impact of time. Hunter said, "The prisoner had attempted to break down the existing government of the commonwealth, and establish on its ruins a new government; he had usurped the office of commander-in-chief of this new government, and, together with his whole band, professed allegiance and fidelity to it. He resisted not only the civil authorities of the state, but our own military; he is doubly, trebly and quadruply guilty of treason!"

Mr. Hunter then turned again to the question of jurisdiction over the armory grounds, and examined the authority cited on the other side by Attorney-General Cushing. The latter was an able man, but, said Hunter, "He came from a region of the country where opinions were very different from ours in relation to the power of the federal government as affecting states rights. Our courts are decidedly adverse to Mr. Cushing's views. In time past the jurisdiction of Jefferson County in criminal offenses committed at Harper's Ferry had been uninterrupted and unchanged, whether they were committed on government property or not. He cited an instance twenty-nine years ago where an atrocious murder was committed between the very shops in front of which these men fought their battles. The criminal was tried here, convicted and executed under our laws!"

Hunter pointed out that there was a broad difference between the cession of jurisdiction by Virginia to the federal government and mere assent of the states that the federal government should become a landholder within its limits. The law of Virginia, by virtue of which the grounds at Harper's Ferry were purchased by the federal government, ceded no jurisdiction. Brown was also guilty, on his own notorious confession, in advising and conspiring. In regard to the charge of murder, the proof will be that this man was not only actually engaged in murdering our citizens, but that he was the chief director of the whole movement. No matter whether he was present on the spot or a mile off, he was equally guilty.

In conclusion, Mr. Hunter said that he hoped the case would be considered with fairness and impartiality, and without fear, favor or affection; and he only asked that the penalty might be visited on the prisoner which the law denounces, which reason denounces, which our safety requires, and which the laws of God and man approved.

The afternoon session assembled at 3:30 PM. An examination of the witnesses commenced,

Dr. Starry: I heard a shot fired at the Ferry on Sunday night and heard a cry. I looked out and saw two men coming towards the armory gate. A tall man came from the armory gate and two men from the cars halloed "there he goes now." The man stopped and raised his rifle. They followed him to the armory gate and exchanged shots with him. Conductor Phelps was one of those men. Afterwards I found the black man Shephard Hayward dying in the railroad office; he said he was commanded to stop by the men on the bridge, and when he refused they fired upon him. I saw several men patrolling during the night and go into the bridge. I did not know what to make of it, and went to inquire of the armory watchman what it all meant. I then met a man who leveled his rifle at him; asked him where the watchman was, and was answered that he was not there, but that there were "a few of us here." Afterwards, in the morning, I saw a wagon pass with three armed men following it. I had gone to Mr. Kitzmiller and Mr. Ball and told them that an armed body of men had possession of the armory, and not to go near it; I also gave information to the other persons employed in the armory and saw three of them at Hall's Works. I did not see more than thirty all told, and recognized them by a peculiar hat they wore. I rode to Charlestown to give the alarm and get assistance and returned about eleven o'clock. I assisted in issuing orders and guiding the armed forces to the best place of attack. I did not see or recognize Brown there at all. As I rode past the armory armed men were at the gate; but they did not attempt to stop me. *I was determined not to be stopped.*

Conductor Phelps: On Monday morning, the 17th, my train arrived at 1:25 AM eastward bound. I didn't see any watchman at the bridge, and I thought that was strange, as his business was to be there. I talked to the engineer, and was in the act of starting ahead when the missing watchman came up to me in an agitated state and said that he had been attacked on the bridge by men carrying rifles. Mr. Harvey was also standing there with my light. Before starting the train; the baggage-master and a passenger accompanied him, and when they entered the bridge some one said, "Stand, and deliver." I had previously told the engineer to follow Harvey slowly, but I immediately saw the muzzles of four rifles resting on a railing and pointing at us. I told the engineer to back up, as something was wrong on the bridge, which he did.

As I got on the trestle I heard the report of a gun, and Hayward, the colored porter, came running up to me and said, "Captain, I am shot." The ball had entered his back and came out under his right nipple. I carried him to the railroad office, and started out for a doctor, when I saw a man come to the bridge and go towards the armory gate. I yelled, "There he goes now," and Throgmorton, clerk of the Wager House, fired at him. The shot was returned by two men at the armory gate. I was close behind Throgmorton, who exchanged several shots with them. About ten minutes after Hayward was shot I heard the men loading their rifles again. The reports were very loud, and I wondered why the people were not aroused. I walked back to the railroad office, and one of the party on the bridge came out and said, "You can come over the bridge with your train;" I replied, "I would rather not after all this," and I asked "What do you want?" He replied, "We want liberty, and we intend to have it." I then asked, "What do you mean?" He replied, "You will find out in a day or two."

I then felt alarmed for the safety of myself and the passengers, and decided to wait until daylight before proceeding. Men were passing back and forward from the bridge to the gate of the armory, and each appeared to be in blankets. The passengers were very excited. I went to the back of the train and saw from twenty to thirty men about the engine house. At about 4:00 AM I saw a wagon driven in the yard, and nearly a dozen men jumped out of it; also a carriage, but I didn't see any one get out of it. I saw men go back and forth who seemed to be putting something in the wagon. They were also going up and down the street leading from the armory, and all seemed busy at something. This continued until nearly daylight, when the wagon left the yard and passed over the bridge to the Maryland side. At about three o'clock, before the wagon left, an old gentleman came to me and said, "The parties who captured me allowed me to come out on condition that I would tell you that you could cross the bridge with your train." Afterwards I learned that this was Mr. Krouse, a citizen of the town. I replied that I would not cross the bridge until daylight, so that I might see whether it was safe or not."

Afterwards I saw a man coming down Shenandoah Street with a lantern, and an armed man arrested him. Then I saw a short, stout man walking with a staff with one of these men. I couldn't see what was in the wagon. Later a black boy brought a note to the clerk of the Wager House, ordering breakfast for forty-seven men. I determined to go out and ascertain what it meant, and met a man whom I now recognize as Coppoc, and asked what they were up to. He replied, "We don't want to injure you or detain your train. You know you could have gone at three o'clock. All we want is to free the Negroes." I then asked if my train could now go, and went to the guard at the gate who said, "There is Captain Smith, he can tell you what you want to know." I went to the engine house and the guard called Captain Smith, and said that somebody wanted to see him. The prisoner at the bar came out and I asked him if he was Captain of those brigands and he replied that he was. I asked him if I could cross the bridge, and he peremptorily responded, "No, sir." Then I asked him what he meant by stopping my train. He replied with a question, "Are you the conductor on that train?" I told him I was, and he said, "Why, I sent you word at three o'clock that you could pass."

I told him that after being stopped by armed men on the bridge, I would not pass with my train. He replied, "My head for it you will not be hurt," and he said he was very sorry, and it was not his intention that any blood should be spilled; that it was bad management on the part of the men in charge of the bridge. I then asked him what security I would have for my train to pass in safely, and asked him if he would walk over the bridge ahead of my train with me. He called a large stout man to accompany him, and one of my passengers, a Mr. McByrne, asked to accompany me, but Brown ordered him to get into the train, or he would take them all prisoners in five minutes. Brown and the other man accompanied me; both had rifles, and as we crossed the bridge the three armed men were still in their places. When we got across Brown said to me, "You doubtless wonder what a man of my age is doing here with a band of armed men, but if you knew my past history you would not wonder about it so much." My train was then through the bridge, and I bid him good morning. I jumped on a car and thank God, I was gone.

I returned to Harper's Ferry on Tuesday, and went in with Governor Wise and others to see Brown who was a prisoner. I heard his conversation with Wise and Hunter. Governor Wise said he "was sorry to see a man of his age in that position." Brown replied that he "asked no sympathy, and had no apologies to make," and that he knew exactly what he was about. The governor asked him if he didn't think he was doing wrong in running off with other people's property. Brown said, "No I don't," hesitated, and said that he never had but twenty-two men in his party, but expected large reinforcements from Maryland, Virginia, North and South Carolina, and, I think, some of the New England states and New York. He said that arms were sent to them from Massachusetts. I think he spoke of Sharp's rifles, revolvers and spears; he said he could arm from fifteen hundred to two thousand men. He said he had Harper's Ferry in his eye as the place for his operations, that he had rented a farm four miles off from Dr. Kennedy, that he had paid the rent up to March, and that all his arms were sent to him there from Chambersburg, Pennsylvania. He said those who brought the arms there did not know what they were, as he had taken the precaution to pack them in double boxes. They were all addressed to I. Smith & Sons. Brown told Governor Wise that he had books in his trunk that would explain to him his whole proceedings, and what the purpose of his business was. Colonel Lee said he had one, and handed it to Governor Wise.

John Brown asked Governor Wise to read two of its first preambles, and four of the last sections, which he did, and Brown said it was a correct copy. In reply to a question of Governor Wise, Brown said he was Commander-in-Chief of the forces under the provisional government, and that he then held that position. He said the constitution was adopted in a place called Chatham, in Canada. Brown said there was a Secretary of War, Secretary of State, Judge of the Supreme Court, and all the officers for a general government; he said there was a House of Representatives, and that there was an intelligent colored man elected as one of the members of the House. (This created a sensation!) Governor Wise asked Brown if he had taken the oath of allegiance provided for in the forty-eighth article, and he replied that he had. Brown said that there were appointed and commissioned officers—that Stevens, Tidd, and his sons were Captains, Edwin Coppoc and William Leeman were lieutenants, and that Cook held a captain's commission. Brown said something about a battle in Kansas, and having one of his sons shot. Governor Wise asked Brown if he thought he had been betrayed by the Secretary of War. He said he thought he had been betrayed, but had practiced the ruse to prevent suspicion. The governor asked him what the ruse was, but he refused to answer; said he knew exactly the position he had placed himself in, and if his life was forfeited he was prepared to suffer the consequences.

Mr. Green, counsel for the prisoner, interrupted the witness and said to the court that he had just received a dispatch from Cleveland, Ohio announcing that counsel was coming, and would almost certainly be here that night. As this was a very important witness, and as it was late in the evening, he would ask the court to adjourn until morning, in order that counsel might have an opportunity to cross examine the witness. He did not intend to conduct the case longer than the arrival of counsel selected by the prisoner. As only two scraps of a conversation of two hours with Governor Wise had been picked out and given to the jury, he desired that the witness should be questioned as to the other parts of the conversation.

Mr. Hunter replied that there were several other witnesses to be called of the same character, to whom such questions could be put by new counsel tomorrow. If the case were not pushed on the whole balance of the term would be sufficient to try these men. He thought there was no reason for delays, especially as it was uncertain whether counsel could get here before tomorrow.

The judge decided that the witness should proceed.

Conductor Phelps, cross-examined by Mr. Green: In conversation, Mr. Brown said it was not his intention to harm anybody or anything, and that he was sorry men had been killed. It was not by his orders or his approbation, and would not occur again provided the people were peaceable and quiet. When Brown spoke of taking them all prisoners if they did not get into the cars, he appeared to want the train to go on as soon as possible. It was advice more in the form of a threat. I did not recognize Brown until I talked with him in the armory yard; don't think Brown was with the party on the bridge in the wagon, for if he had been I think I would have recognized him from his peculiar beard.

Mr. Hunter: When Brown was parleying with us at the bridge the three armed men remained on the bridge. I saw what seemed to be a man dressed in woman's clothing pass, followed by a boy with a box or a bundle.

Colonel Lewis W. Washington was then sworn in. He reiterated the details of the incident with no change from his previous day's testimony. He was then cross-examined.

Colonel Washington, cross examined by Mr. Green: I cannot say whether the marines fired after they broke into the engine house because the noise was so great. Several shouted from the inside that some one had surrendered the prisoners; we were kept in the rear engine house, and allowed to seek a safe position, so that there was no effort to endanger us. Brown's conduct was not rude or insulting towards us.

Mr. Hunter: I was present at the conversation with Governor Wise on Tuesday. Governor Wise asked Brown if he had not selected Harper's Ferry as a border place between Maryland and Virginia for the establishment of his provisional government, and he answered, "Certainly!" He avowed that his object was to free the Southern slaves, and said that his party consisted of twenty-two men, nineteen of whom came over with him; he said he had 200 Sharp's rifles, 200 revolvers and he did not remember how many spears. Brown said that he had enough equipment to arm about 1,500 men.

The governor asked if he expected that number. He said there was no doubt of that number, and fire thousand more if he wanted them. He detailed the conversation respecting the provisional government substantially as the last witness.

Mr. Botts: At the time of the attack on the engine house the prisoners remained in the rear at the suggestion of Brown and his party. I heard Brown direct his party not to fire on any unarmed man; he gave that order more than once.

Mr. Hunter: Cook said Brown had been studying this subject twenty or thirty years, and had reconnoitered Harper's Ferry repeatedly.

Mr. Botts: The prisoners were allowed to go out and assure their families of their safety. Some were out several times. He told men not to return from their dwelling-house. There were numerous shots towards the water tower where Beckham was killed. Brown assured me that they should be treated well, and their property should not be destroyed.

Mr. Hunter: While I was a prisoner in the engine house I overheard a conversation between Stevens and another party not known to me, about slave-holding. Stevens asked the man if he were in favor of slavery. He said, "Yes," although he was not a slave holder. Stevens said, "You are the first man I would hang."

Mr. Harding: One of the three Negroes taken with me was kept in the armory room; another escaped and went home. I saw no connection, in particular, between myself and the Negroes who were taken there. All the Negroes were armed with pikes, while in the armory yard. They walked about the armory grounds, and one came over and warmed himself. No Negro from this neighborhood appeared to take up arms voluntarily. I saw no wounded men dragged into the engine house.

At seven o'clock the court adjourned until the next morning. Orders were given to the jailors to shoot all the prisoners if any attempt was made to rescue them.

The third day of the trial of John Brown commenced on Friday, October 28, 1859. News arrived that Captain Cook who had been captured on the 26th at Chambersburg had been taken under heavy guard to the Charlestown prison. He arrived at the jail in chains at 1:00 AM this morning. Before being assigned to his cell he said that if Brown had taken his advice in relation to the attack, a thousand men could not have taken them. There was great rejoicing at his arrest. Cook said that Fred Douglass acted the coward, having promised to be there in person.

George H. Hoyt, of Athol, Massachusetts, counsel for Brown, also arrived early on Friday. Although he was twenty-one years old, he appeared to be no older than eighteen or nineteen. The court met at 11:00 AM, and Brown was led over from the jail, walking very feebly. He laid down upon his cot. Senator Mason entered the Court with Mr. Hoyt, the Boston counsel for Mr. Brown. John Brown remarked that the testimony of Colonel Washington and Mr. Phelps yesterday was strictly truthful.

The jury were called and answered "present" to their names.

Mr. Botts announced the arrival of Mr. Hoyt, who had come to assist the counsel for the prisoner. Hoyt said that, at present, he really did not feel disposed to take part in the case, but he would do so. There had been an attempt to retain Benjamin Franklin Butler, the noted Massachusetts lawyer, but his caseload was overbearing. Mr. Hunter warned that Mr. Hoyt had better be qualified as a member of the bar and that he should produce proof. Mr. Hoyt had not brought his credentials of admission. The court said it was not required in order to be strictly legal; to that fact any citizen's evidence would answer. Mr. Green said his partner had read letters from fellow-students of Hoyt, alluding to him as a member of the bar. Mr. Hoyt then took the customary oath, and testimony was resumed. Conductor Phelps was recalled.

Mr. Botts: (The questions put to him were prepared by Mr. Brown.) The firing was commenced by those men on the bridge, who shot Hayward. The next firing was by Throgmorton. I do not know whether the firing at Hayward was intentional. There was no attack on Brown's men until after Hayward was shot. He was shot by armed men on the Winchester span of the bridge.

Colonel Lewis W. Washington was then recalled.

Colonel Washington: Negotiations were opened with Brown for the release of prisoners before the general firing commenced on Monday; I do not know whether all the prisoners signed the proposition for a suspension of firing. In the opening negotiations Brown frequently suggested that the prisoners should cross the bridge with him to the second canal, and the lock was not to be fired upon until they reached that point. None of the prisoners made any objection to the proposition. Brown said he was too old a soldier to yield the advantage he possessed in holding hostages. During the day Brown's son was wounded in the breast, the ball passing around to the side, but he took his weapon again and fired frequently before his sufferings compelled him to retire. I heard Captain Brown frequently complain of bad faith in his people with regard to a flag of truce, but I didn't hear him make any threat or even express any vindictiveness against the people. Mr. Joseph A. Brua went out and brought in a promise that the people would not fire while negotiations were pending. I really can't say that all the firing of Captain Brown or his men was in self-defense. I heard Brown give frequent orders not to fire on unarmed citizens and the first firing was against the engine house. Brown said the people appeared to pay but little regard to the lives of the citizens, and we must take the chances with them. After the first attack on the engine house by the marines, there were no general cries of "surrender." One cried surrender, but the others fought on; Brown had a rifle in his hand when he was struck down by the marines, and received a cut over his head from a sword thrust by Lieutenant Israel Green.

Mr. Hunter then laid before the jury the printed constitution and ordinance of the provisional government, reading the first two clauses of the preamble, the 7th, 45th and 48th articles, and briefly summing up other portions of the constitution. Sheriff Campbell knew the handwriting of the prisoner and would vouch for it. Campbell had copied a letter for him.

Brown said he would himself identify any of his handwriting, and save all that trouble. He was ready to face the music.

Mr. Hunter: I would prefer proving them through Mr. Campbell.

Mr. Brown: Either way as you please.

A large bundle of letters was produced. Each was identified by Campbell, and handed to Brown, who, at first glance replied to each in a loud voice, "Yes, that is mine." The papers and letters were about fifty in number.

On receiving a list of members of the convention, Mr. Hunter read it. It was headed, "William Charles Morris, President of the Convention, and H. Kagi, Secretary of the Convention." It was handed to Brown who exclaimed, with a groan, "Yes, there's my signature."

In reference to another paper Brown said, "I really have nothing to say about that."

Mr. Hunter next read a letter from Mr. J. R. Giddings, acknowledging the receipt of a letter from Brown, and saying that he would be pleased to see him at his house this summer. Mr. Hunter then read a letter from Gerrit Smith about the "Kansas work," which has already been published. It had "June 13, 1859," endorsed on the back, in Brown's writing. Here Mr. Botts insisted on the right of examining the letters before they were read.

Armistead Ball, Master machinist at the armory, was next sworn in.

Mr. Ball: Early in the morning I was aroused by Benjamin Hobbs, who announced that persons were at the armory carrying off government property. I reached the gate and was accosted by two armed men. They seized me as their prisoner and refused to make any explanation until we were within the armory yard. Stephens was a sentry at the gate. I was conducted to Captain Brown, who told me his object was to free slaves, and not the making of war on the people; that my person and private property would be safe; that his war was against the accursed system of slavery; that he had power to do it, and would carry it out. He said it was no child's play that he had undertaken. He then gave me permission to return to my family and assure them of my safety, and get my breakfast.

I started back home, and was accompanied by two armed men, who stopped at the door. As breakfast was not ready, I went back, and was allowed to return home again under escort at a later hour. On returning again Captain Brown said it was his determination to seize the arms and munitions of the government and to arm the blacks to defend themselves against their masters. Brown also made a proposition to himself and other officers of the armory to deliver into his possession the munitions of war belonging to the government. We replied that they were already in his possession, as we were. Brown frequently told us that our safety depended on the good conduct of our citizens. When the firing commenced we all felt we were in danger, and almost any proposition that was made to us was accepted to secure our safety. Brown said if the citizens were willing to risk their lives and those of the prisoners to capture him, they must abide by it. Brown made but one proposition and that was to go to the canal-lock, give up their prisoners, and fight it out with the military.

At daylight on Tuesday morning I appealed to Brown, on the ground of humanity to the prisoners, as well is to the men who appeared so bound to him, not to persist in spilling more blood. Brown replied he was well aware what he was about, and knew the consequences—that he was already proclaimed an outlaw, and $3,500 was on his head. With regard to the killing of Beckham, one of Brown's party fired in that direction several times. I remonstrated with him when he leveled his rifle at an old man named Grist, that he was not a combatant, and he desisted. Afterwards I heard him fire, and heard him say, "I dropped him." When we heard that Beckham was dead, the man who fired turned to us and asked who he was. We told him he was an old and respectable citizen, and mayor of the town, and the man who fired expressed himself very sorry. I am sorry to say that this man was killed later when the marines charged in. Captain Brown certainly made preparations for resisting the marines. He was always armed, but I do not think I saw him fire.

The rest of Mr. Ball's testimony was merely a corroboration of Colonel Lewis Washington's.

Ball, cross-examined by Mr. Green: We, as prisoners, agreed to such terms of capitulation as our citizens were willing to accept. The proposal was written by Mr. Daingerfield and dictated by Mr. Brown. I do not know whether Brown's son and Stevens were wounded while they accompanied the citizens with a flag of truce. In fact I didn't know that any of them were Brown's sons until I heard Captain Brown sadly say to Captain Sinn, "There lies one of my sons dead, and here is another dying." Brown frequently remarked that the citizens were acting with impunity in persisting in firing on their own citizens. He suggested a different position all the time. Brown repeatedly said he wouldn't injure anyone but in self-defense. One of Brown's men, Coppoc, frequently urged us to seek places of safety, but Brown never did. He appeared to desire us to take care of ourselves, and at the time of the charge of the marines he told us we must equally occupy the post of danger with themselves. There were three or four slaves in the engine house and they had spears, but they all seemed badly scared. One of them, Washington Phil, was ordered by Brown to cut a port-hole through the brick wall. He continued at this task until a brisk fire commenced outside, at which point he said, "this is getting too hot for old Phil," and he quit and squatted down. Brown then took up the tools and finished the hole.

John Allstadt: On Monday morning, at about 3:00 AM, I was awakened from sleep. I asked who was at the door and the reply was, "Get up quietly or we will burn you up." I asked what they intended to do and they said, "Free the country of slavery." They told me they were going to take me to Harper's Ferry. I dressed myself, and when I got to the door they had rounded up all my blacks, seven in number. We were all put into a wagon. The Negroes were then all armed with pikes. All the men who took us were armed as well. We went to the armory yard, where I was put in the charge of one of Brown's party. Afterwards we were ordered into the watch house where I saw Colonel Washington. Brown came over and spoke to us about getting two Negroes to take our places. If we did so he would then release us, but nothing further was said about it. I saw that Brown's rifle was cocked at all times. The Negroes were placed in the watch house with pikes in their hands, but the slaves showed no disposition to use them. I was afterwards transferred to the engine house. Several Negroes were there and I saw Phil making port-holes by Brown's order. The other Negroes were doing nothing, and had dropped their pikes. In fact most of them slept nearly all the time. (At this point there was considerable laughter in the courtroom.) When the marines made their assault, Brown's party took positions behind the engines, and aimed at the door. Brown was in front squatting, and he fired in the direction of a marine. In my opinion he killed the fellow.

Allstadt, cross-examined by Mr. Green: I did not see any others shoot, and I guess I really cannot state certainly which shot killed the marine. He might have been killed by shots fired before the door was broken open. There was so much confusion and excitement at the time. I heard some regrets expressed at Mayor Beckham being killed.

Alexander Kelly was then sworn. Mr. Kelly described the manner in which Thomas Boerley was killed on Monday.

Kelly: Brown's party fired at me and I returned the fire. Boerley was with me, and was armed with a gun. I saw him right after he was killed. The shot came from the direction of Shenandoah Street.

Kelly was not cross-examined.

Albert Grist, sworn in: On Sunday night I had been to a meeting with my son. Coming home across the Shenandoah bridge I was seized by two men with rifles. When we got to the end of the bridge we were stopped by a man with a spear. I asked what in Hell was the matter—was the town under martial law? He told me that I wouldn't be hurt, and asked me whether there were many slave holders around Harper's Ferry. I told him "Hell, no." Brown came up and observed, "Great, you have some prisoners." They took us to the armory where there were other citizens being held. Being tired, we laid down. Brown told us his object was to free the slaves; I said there were not many there. He replied, "The Good Book says we are all free and equal, and, if we were peaceable, we should not be hurt." There was some firing about that time. Afterwards, at about 3:00 AM, I was sent to tell the conductor that the train might pass unmolested. I saw Mr. Beckham, and delivered the message. Brown then dismissed me and said I could go, but I didn't go home, because I was afraid that some of Brown's men wouldn't know this and shoot me. I saw Hayward brought in wounded.

Mr. Kelly, recalled: I saw George W. Turner killed on High Street. He was shot while in the act of leveling his gun. The shot came from the corner of Shenendoah and High Streets, and the men who fired used rifles. One of those men had a shawl on.

The morning session here ended, and reassembled at the court house at 3:00 PM in the afternoon.

Henry Hunter, sworn in: I went to Harper's Ferry with the Charlestown Guard. I stayed for a while on the bridge, and then I left the company, going off fighting on my own hook. I saw Beckham fall when he was shot. I could actually hear the whistling of the ball. I undertook to go to his assistance, but was held back by a friend. Soon thereafter another person went out to remove his body, saying that he would "help the squire." I heard the whistle of another ball. I think that Beckham had a pistol in his coat pocket, judging from the weight and shape of his pocket. I didn't see it, and I don't think the people from the armory yard saw it. I am sure the shot that killed Beckham came from the engine house. Numerous shots were fired from there near the water tower.

The cross-examination of this witness elicited nothing new.

Colonel Gibson, sworn in: I went with the militia of Jefferson County to suppress the insurrection. The Jefferson Guard and other detachments were all in the action. They were called out by authority of the law. Three of the insurgents were killed at the rifle factory, and a man called Copeland was captured.

Colonel Gibson, cross-examined by Mr. Green: There was firing by outside citizens, and the three killed were not under my command. I don't think the insurgents fired a gun at the rifle factory, but endeavored to make their escape across the river.

Benjamin T. Bell, sworn in: I went to Harper's Ferry armed. I did not join the military; but was stationed in the Galt House, with Captain Botts' company. In the evening I walked out on the platform and saw Mayor Beckham shot. I went as near to him as was safe, and perceived he wasn't breathing. There was firing from the engine house towards the railroad. Private Young, a member of the Jefferson Guards, was wounded while making a charge against the insurgents. I saw others shot; there were probably 30 or more shots fired from the engine house towards the water tower, and in other directions.

Bell, cross-examined by Mr. Green: There was general firing in almost every direction. The fellow McCabe was about to fire when he was shot. There were 20 or 30 men firing at the engine house when Young and McCabe were wounded.

Lewis Starry was then examined. He testified in respect to the death of Turner.

The prosecution rested here.

The counsel for the defense called Joseph A. Brua who testified that he was one of the prisoners in the engine house with Washington and the others.

J. A. Brua: I heard Brown remark that the prisoners should share their danger. They were allowed to shelter themselves as best they could. Reason Cross went out with a flag of truce. Another went out and came back wounded. Stevens and Kitzmiller went out, and Stevens was shot. After that it commenced raining very hard. I supposed that Stevens was dead. We lay near the corner of the depot and heard groaning. I heard Stevens moving and asked Brown to send a man to relieve Stevens. Brown refused to send any one, because he said he would be shot. I was allowed to go and assist Stevens to the hotel. I returned to the engine house; according to my pledge. I was sent several times by Brown to request the citizens not to shoot, as the lives of the prisoners were endangered.

Negotiations were going on between Brown and the prisoners before the general firing commenced, and Brown proposed that he should retain possession of what he held, including the armory and Negroes. Colonel Washington and the others seemed to acquiesce in this arrangement. Reason Cross was sent out to confer with Beckham and others on the subject. A guard went with him, who was fired upon. After that Stevens wanted to shoot back, but Kitzmiller appealed to him, and they went out together to stop the firing. When they did not return, Brown seemed to show temper, and there was a change in the arrangements. After that Brown said he had it in his power to destroy the whole place in half an hour, but wouldn't do it unless he was resisted. I think a shot from the water tower struck Coppoc. Coppoc then returned the fire and some one said, "That man's down." My special object was in going out to see who was firing from the water tower. This was annoying to those in the guard house.

A. M. Kitzmiller, sworn in: I made repeated efforts to communicate my thoughts and other matters with Brown. He just said his object there was to free the slaves from bondage, and, if necessary, fight the pro-slavery men for that purpose. I was first surprised, then indignant, and finally disgusted with Brown. At one point he said to me, "There is a company of riflemen on the bridge, get them to go in company with Stevens." Mr. Hunter told them I was sorry they did not leave their guns. Stevens remarked that would not do. I had no white flag, and did not consider myself the bearer of a flag of truce. As to the rifle company on the bridge, I saw they were our own men. I waved my handkerchief and told Stevens and the other man to remain. I soon heard firing very close. Stevens fired back in rely to a bullet which struck him. It came from a house by the side of the Winchester Railroad depot. Stevens swore and the other man returned fire. I think it was Brown's son. I am sure Stevens was shot before he fired back. Thompson, one of Brown's men, was a prisoner on the bridge.

At this point Brown described the circumstances connected with the death of Thompson.

A. M. Kitzmiller: I was not there, and did not see the death of Thompson. The last I saw of Thompson he was a prisoner with the Ferry people on the bridge. Moore, Berkhardt, Anderson and twenty or thirty others were there. Mr. Beckham was killed at or about the time Thompson was taken; I did not return to the engine house. My object was to prevent unnecessary shedding of blood and I went out at the request of Brown to use my influence for that purpose.

James Beller, sworn in: I was at the Galt House with Chambers on Monday morning. Chambers fired, and I clearly saw the man lying there who Chambers shot. I didn't know the man. I suppose now it was Stevens. I did not see any one with him when he was shot. Stevens was definitely shot before Captain Botts and his company reached the Galt House.

Mr. Green stated to the court that he desired to bring out testimony relative to the shooting of' Thompson, and one of the insurgents on the bridge, but the state objected to it unless Brown had a knowledge of that shooting.

Mr. Hunter said that there was a great deal of testimony about Brown's forbearance in not shooting citizens who had "no more to do with the case than the dead languages." If he understood the offer, it was to show that one of these men, named Thompson, a prisoner, was dispatched after Beckham's death. The circumstances of the deed might be such as he himself might not at all approve. He did not know how that might be, but he desired to avoid any investigation that might be used. Not that it was so designed by the respectable counsel employed in the case, but because he thought the object of the prisoner in getting at it was for out-door effect and influence. He therefore said if the defense could show that this prisoner was aware of these circumstances and the manner in which that party was killed and still exerted forbearance, he would not object. But unless the knowledge of it could be brought home to the prisoner, and his after conduct, he could not see its relevancy.

Mr. Botts observed that they had already proved that, for hours after that, communications were held between the parties.

The court thought these facts were admissible as evidence.

Mr. Hunter, the witness, called to the stand: After Mr. Beckham, who was my grand-uncle, was shot, I was completely exasperated and started out with Mr. Chambers to the room where the second Thompson was confined. My purpose and the purpose of others was to shoot him. We found several persons in the room, and leveled our guns at him. At this point Mr. Fouke's sister threw herself before him, and begged us to leave him to the mercy of the law. We then caught hold of him, and dragged him out by the throat. I heard him saying, "Though you may take my life, eighty thousand millions will rise up to avenge me, and carry out my purpose of giving liberty to the slaves." We carried him out to the bridge, and two of us, leveling our guns at him in our moment of wild exasperation, fired. Before he fell a dozen or more balls were buried in him. We then threw his body off the trestle-work and returned to the bridge to bring out the prisoner Stevens and serve him in the same manner.

We found him suffering from his wounds and probably dying, so we concluded to spare his life, and start out after the others, and shoot all we could find. I had just seen the best friend I ever had and my beloved uncle shot down by those villainous abolitionists, and I felt justified in shooting any and all whom I could find. I felt it was my God given duty, and I have no regrets.

William M. Williams, the watchman on the bridge, was then sworn. He related the particulars of his arrest and his confinement in the watch house.

William Williams: Brown told the prisoners to hide themselves, or they would be shot by the people outside. Brown said the would not hurt any of them. He told Mr. Grist to tell the people to cease firing, or he would burn the town, but if they didn't molest him he wouldn't molest them. I heard two shots on the bridge about the time the express train arrived, but I did not see Hayward killed.

At this point Mr. Brown started to conduct some of the defense himself.

Brown: State what was said by myself, and not about his being shot!

William Williams: I think you said that if he had taken care of himself he would not have suffered.

Reason Cross, sworn in: I made a proposition that Brown should retain possession of the armory. I said he should release us, and that the firing should stop.

Brown: Were there two written propositions drawn up while you were present?

Reason Cross: Yes, there was another paper prepared by Kitzmiller and some others. I went out to stop the firing. A man went out with me and they took him prisoner and tied him. That was Thompson, who was afterwards taken out and shot. Brown's treatment of me was kind and respectful. I heard him talk roughly to some men who were going in to where the blacks were confined.

Several witnesses for the prisoners were then called but did not answer the subpoenas. They had not been returned to the court. Brown arose from his mattress, evidently excited, and, standing on his feet, addressed the court as follows:

> May it please the court, I discover that, notwithstanding all the assertions that I have received of a fair trial, nothing like a fair trial is to be given me, as it would seem. I gave the names, as soon as I could get at them, of the persons I wished to have called as witnesses, and was assured that they would be subpoenaed. I wrote down a memorandum to that effect, saying where those parties were, but it appears that they have not been subpoenaed, so far as I can learn, and now I ask, if I am to have anything at all deserving the name and shadow of a fair trial, that this proceeding be deferred until tomorrow morning. For I have no counsel, as I have before stated, in whom I feel that I can rely, but I am in hopes counsel may arrive who will attend to seeing that I get the witnesses who are necessary for my defense. I am myself unable to attend to it. I have given all the attention I possibly could to it, but am unable to see or know about

them, and can't even find out their names, and I have
nobody to do any errand, for my money was all taken
from me when I was sacked and stabbed, and I leave not
a dime. I had two hundred and fifty or sixty dollars in
gold and silver taken from my pocket, and now I have
no possible means of getting anybody to do my errands
for me, and I have not had all the witnesses subpoenaed.
They are not within reach, and are not here. I ask at
least until tomorrow morning to have something done,
if anything is designed. If not, I am ready for anything
that may come up.

Brown then lay down again, drew his blanket over him, and closed his
eyes, and appeared to sink into a tranquil slumber.

Mr. Hoyt, who had been sitting quietly all day at the side of Mr.
Botts, arose amid great sensation and addressed the court.

Mr. Hoyt: May it please the court, I would add my voice to the appeal
of Mr. Brown, although I have had no consultation with him, that the
further hearing of the case be postponed until morning. I would state
the reason of this request. It was that I was informed and had reason to
believe that Judge Tilden, of Ohio, was on his way to Charlestown, and
would undoubtedly arrive at Harper's Ferry at 7:00 PM tonight. I have
taken measures to insure that gentleman's arrival in this place tonight if he
reaches the Ferry. For myself, I have come from Boston, traveling night and
day, to volunteer my services in defense of Brown. I could not undertake
the responsibility of the defense as I am now situated. The gentlemen who
have defended Brown have acted in an honorable and dignified manner
in all respects, so far as I know, but I cannot assume the responsibility
of defending him myself for many reasons. It would be ridiculous for
me to do it, because I have not read the indictment through—have not,
except so far as I have listened to the case and heard counsel this morning,
got any idea of the line of defense proposed, and have no knowledge of
the criminal code of Virginia, and had no time to read it. I had no time
to examine the questions arising in this defense, some of which are of

considerable importance, especially that relative to the jurisdiction over armory grounds. For all these reasons, I ask the continuation of the case until tomorrow morning.

Mr. Botts: In justice to myself, I must state that on being first assigned as counsel to Mr. Brown, I conferred with him, and, at his instance, took down a list of the witnesses he desired subpoenaed in his behalf. Though it was late at night I called up the sheriff, and informed him that I wished subpoenas issued early in the morning. This was done, and Messrs. Phelps, Williams and Grist are here, and they have all been examined.

Sheriff Campbell stated that the subpoenas had been placed in the hands of an officer, with the request to serve them at once. "He must have served them," the sheriff said, "as you can see that some of the witnesses were here. The process has not been returned, and may have been sent by private hands, and failed to arrive."

Mr. Botts thought they had shown, and he was confident he spoke the sentiment of the whole community, when he said that they wished Mr. Brown to have a fair trial.

Mr. Hunter: I do not rise for the purpose of protracting the argument or interposing the slightest impediment in any way to a fair trial. This is fair. Whether it was promised to Brown or not, it is guaranteed by our law to every prisoner; and, so far as I am concerned, I have studiously avoided suggesting anything to the court which would in the slightest degree interfere with it. I beg leave to say in reference to this application, that I supposed the court, even under these circumstances, will have to be satisfied in some way, through counsel or otherwise, that this testimony is material testimony. So far as any witness has been examined, the evidence relates to the conduct of Captain Brown in treating his prisoners with leniency, respect and courtesy, and this additional matter that his flags of truce—if you choose to regard them so—were not respected by the citizens, and that some of his men were shot. If the defense chose to take that course, we are perfectly willing to admit these facts in any form they desire, unless the court shall be satisfied that the testimony (which I have no doubt is, every particle of it, here) which could be got, is really material to the defense. I submit that the application for delay on that score should not be granted. Some of these witnesses have been here and might have been asked to remain. A host of witnesses have been here and have gone away without being called on to testify. I simply suggest that it is due, in justice to the commonwealth, which has some right, as well as the prisoner, that information be given to the court showing that additional testimony is relevant to the issue. I do not think the simple statement of counsel is sufficient.

Mr. Green: Mr. Botts and myself will now both withdraw from the case. We can no longer act on behalf of the prisoner; he having got up now and declared here that he had no confidence in the counsel who were assigned him. I feel confident that I have done my whole duty so far as I have been able to. After this statement of his, I should feel myself as an intruder upon this case were I to act for him from this time forward. Actually I had no disposition to undertake the defense, but I accepted the duty imposed on me, and under the circumstances when I felt compelled to withdraw from the case, the court insisted that I should remain in that unwelcome position.

Mr. Harding: We have been delayed from time to time by similar applications, in the expectation of the arrival of counsel, until we have now reached the point of time when we are ready to submit the case to the jury upon the evidence and law, when another application arises for a continuance. The very witness that they now consider material, Mr. Daingerfield, came here, actually summoned by ourselves. But deeming that we had testimony enough, we did not examine him.

Judge Parker: The idea of waiting for counsel to thoroughly study our codes can not be admitted. As to the other ground, I do not know whether the process has been executed or not, as no return has been made.

Mr. Botts: I have endeavored to do my duty in this matter, but I cannot see how I can perform that duty, consistent with my personal feelings. I can no longer remain on this case, when the accused, whom

I have been laboring to defend, declares in open court that he has no confidence in his counsel. I make the suggestion that I now quietly retire from this case, especially since there is now here a gentleman from Boston who has come on to volunteer his services for the prisoner. I ask that the court allow him this night for preparation. My notes, my office, and my services shall be at his command. I will sit up with him all night to put him in possession of all the law and facts in relation to this case. I cannot do more; and in the meantime the sheriff can be directed to have the other witnesses here tomorrow morning.

Judge Parker would not compel the gentleman to remain on the case, and accordingly granted the desired postponement. The court adjourned at 6:00 PM that evening

Meanwhile the town was greatly excited by all these events. The guard was increased. The conduct of Brown was generally regarded as tricky. Governor Willard, of Indiana, brother-in-law of Cook, accompanied by J. E. McDonald, Attorney-General of the same State, and D. W. Voorhees and M. M. Randolph, arrived in the afternoon and had a long interview with Cook.

The fourth day of the trial of John Brown commenced on Saturday, October 29, 1859, at the Charlestown court house in Virginia. The court met at 10:00 AM.

The judge announced that he had received a note from the new counselors for the prisoner, requesting a delay for ten minutes or so, to enable them to have an interview with the prisoner. He would accordingly wait a short time. Fifteen minutes later Brown was brought in, and took his usual recumbent position on the cot.

Samuel Chilton, of Washington City, appeared as additional counsel for the prisoner, and was qualified. Henry Griswold, of Cleveland, Ohio was introduced to the court as counsel for the prisoner, and also qualified.

Mr. Chilton, thinking it necessary to make an explanatory statement before the trial, described how he was unexpectedly called upon to come and aid in the defense of the prisoner. Knowing from the newspapers that the trial was in progress, he took time to consider and consult his friends as to the propriety of accepting the proposition. He would have had no hesitation if he had been spoken to in time, but his friends advised him to come, and he did so with the expectation of merely assisting the gentlemen already conducting the defense. Upon reaching the court he found that they had withdrawn from the case, and he then hesitated in undertaking it; but upon consultation with the prisoner and his friends, they insisted he should do so, and he would do the best he could, not feeling at liberty under the circumstances to refuse. These circumstances, however, would render it impossible for him to discharge the full duty of counsel, since he had not had the time to read the indictment and examination already given. He made no motion for delay; this was a matter entirely within the discretion of the court, and if Judge Parker thought it proper to refuse to grant any postponement, he knew it would be done under a sense of duty. These extraordinary circumstances would also render it impossible for his associate, Mr. Griswold, to discharge his full duty as counsel. A short delay of a few hours, if the court thought proper to grant it, would enable them to make some preparation.

Judge Parker decided that the trial must go on. Counsel had been assigned to the prisoner here, of his own selection, who had labored zealously in his behalf and had withdrawn because the prisoner had yesterday evening declared in open court that he had no confidence in them.

No obstacle had at any time been thrown in the way of the prisoner's having an ample defense. If this was the only case of the kind before this court, he would at once grant the request, but several similar cases remained to be disposed of. The court term would very soon end, and it was his duty to endeavor to get through with as many cases as possible, in justice to the prisoners and in justice to the state. The trial must therefore proceed.

Mr. Hoyt remarked that, on the previous day, the attorney for the commonwealth had produced various papers in court which were identified—for what purpose he knew not, but presumed he should be informed—some as being in Captain Brown's handwriting, and some as bearing his endorsement. He had hastily examined those papers, and wished to object to some of them. The learned gentlemen associated with him in the trial had not examined them, but he supposed the court would not regard that material under the prevent ruling.

Mr. Hunter (interrupting): There is no need of argument about the matter. Designate those you wish to object to.

Mr. Hoyt: I desire to know the object of the counsel in introducing those papers.

Mr. Hunter: The papers will speak for themselves. If you will designate which of them you wish to object to, we will go on at once.

Mr. Hoyt: I object to the autobiography of Captain Brown, as having no bearing on this case.

Mr. Hunter: I withdraw it.

Mr. Hoyt: I object to the letter of Gerrit Smith.

Mr. Hunter: I withdraw that, also.

Mr. Hoyt: I handed a list of names to the clerk last night whom we wished summoned as witnesses: Samuel Strider, Henry Ault, Benjamin Mills, John E. P. Daingerfield and Captain Sinn. I received a dispatch just now, informing me that Captain Sinn had gone to Frederick, and would return by the first train this morning, and come on to Charlestown this afternoon. I should like to inquire whether the process summons has reached Captain Sinn at Harper's Ferry.

Sheriff Campbell replied that the officer stated that Captain Sinn had gone to Frederick.

Mr. Hunter: He was here yesterday. I hope we will proceed with some other witnesses.

John E. P. Daingerfield was called, and he testified that he was an officer of the armory; and had been a prisoner in the hands of Captain Brown at the engine house. Negotiations had been going on for the release of all the prisoners before the firing commenced. About a dozen black men were there, armed with pikes. They were lying about asleep, some of them having crowded under the engines. Mr. Daingerfield remarked, "I am free to say that from Captain Brown's treatment of me I had no fear of him or his men during my confinement. I saw one of the men shot in the engine house. He fell back exclaiming, 'Its all up with me,' and died in a few moments. This man, I learned, was one of Captain Brown's sons. I saw another young man who came in wounded and commenced to vomit blood. He was also a son of Captain Brown, and was wounded while he was out with Mr. Kitzmiller. Captain Brown frequently complained that his men were shot down while they were carrying a flag of truce."

Mr. Hunter complained that they were again going over the same facts that had already been elicited; and that all this was freely admitted by the defense.

Mr. Hoyt said that he regarded it as the only feasible line of defense to prove these facts. It was the duty of counsel to show, if possible, that Captain Brown was not guilty of treason, murder or insurrection, according to the terms of this indictment. Mr. Hoyt said, "We hope to prove the absence of malicious intention."

Mr. Hoyt reminded the court that the course being pursued was not only in accordance with their conviction of duty, but in accordance with the express commands of their client. The judge remarked that counsel was responsible to the court to conduct the case according to the rules of practice. Mr. Hoyt thought the language of the prosecution was calculated to impugn the honor of the counsel for the prisoner.

Mr. Hunter: Nothing of the kind was intended. It is presumed the gentlemen will conduct the case in accordance with their duty as counsel, and their responsibility to the court.

Mr. Daingerfield resumed: I heard Captain Brown say that he had it in his power to lay the town in ashes, and carry off all the women and children, but that he had refrained from doing so. I didn't hear him make any threats that he would do so. The only threat I heard from him was at the commencement of the storming of the engine house. He then said that we must all take equal shares with him; that we could no longer monopolize the places of safety. He, however, made no attempt to deprive us of the places we had taken. Brown promised safety to all descriptions of property except slave property. At the time of the assault by the marines, one of the men cried out for quarter. I heard the same man in conversation during the night ask Brown if he was committing treason against his country by resisting the marines, to which Brown replied that he was. The man then said, "I'll fight no longer;" that he thought he was merely fighting to liberate the slaves. After the attack was made on the engine house, two of Brown's men cried for quarter and laid down their arms, but after the marines burst open the door, they picked them up again and renewed the fight. After the first attack, Captain Brown cried out to surrender, but he was not heard. I never saw him fire afterwards. I did see Coppoc attempt to fire twice, but the caps misfired. I saw that Brown was wounded in the hip by a thrust from a saber, and he also several cuts on his head. When the latter wounds were inflicted Captain Brown appeared to be shielding himself, with his head down, but making no resistance. The parties outside appeared to fire as they pleased.

Mr. Mills, Master Armorer, sworn in: I was one of the hostages of Captain Brown and confined in the engine house. Before the general firing commenced negotiations were pending for the release of the prisoners. A paper was drawn up, embracing certain terms, and borne by Mr. Brua to the citizens outside. The terms were not agreed to. The last time Mr.

Brua was out there was severe firing, which, I suppose, prevented his return. Brown's son went out with a flag of truce, and was shot. He limped back wounded; and I attended him, and gave him water. I heard Brown frequently complain that the citizens had acted in a barbarous manner. He did not at that time appear to have any malicious feelings, and he undoubtedly seemed to expect reinforcements. He said it would soon be night, and he would have more assistance. His intentions were not to shoot anybody unless they were carrying or using arms. He said if they did, "Let them have it!" This was while the firing was going on.

At this point Captain Brown asked Mr. Mills whether he saw any firing on his part which was not purely defensive.

Mr. Mills: It might be considered in that light, perhaps. The balls came into the engine house pretty thick.

Question by Counsel: Didn't you frequently go to the door of the engine house?

Mr. Mills: No, indeed! (laughter)

A general colloquy ensued between John Brown, lying on his cot, and the witness as to the part taken by the prisoner in not unnecessarily exposing his hostages to danger. No objection was made to Brown's asking these questions in his own way, and interposing verbal explanations relative to his conduct. The witness generally corroborated his own version of the circumstances attending the attack on the engine house, but could not testify to all the incidents that he enumerated. Mr. Mills did not hear Brown say that he surrendered. The witness' wife and daughter were permitted to visit him unmolested, and free verbal communication was allowed with those outside. They were treated kindly, but were compelled to stay where they did not want to be. Brown appeared anxious to effect a compromise.

Samuel Strider was sworn in and proceeded to detail the whole circumstances of the two days that John Brown was in Harper's Ferry, with what he saw, what he thought, and what he heard. Nothing new was elicited. He confirmed the statement of the other witnesses, that Brown endeavored to protect his hostages, and constantly said that he wished to make terms, more for their safety than his own.

Mr. Hoyt, at 1:30 PM, complained of indisposition from the heat of the room, and asked that the usual recess for dinner be taken.

The court then adjourned for one hour. At 2:30 PM the court reassembled, and Mr. Griswold, taking his seat by the side of the prisoner, prepared to question the witnesses, and to receive from him such suggestions in the course of the examination as he had to make.

Captain Sinn, commander of the volunteer company from Frederick, Maryland, sworn in: The report came to Frederick that seven hundred and fifty blacks and abolitionists combined had seized Harper's Ferry. I started for the Ferry with the volunteers under the command of Colonel Shriver, and was glad to find their numbers were exaggerated after I reached there on Monday afternoon. I saw that the door of the engine house was partially open, and I was hailed from there. Two shots had been fired from there, and as I said, I was hailed, and went in. I met Mr. Daingerfield and others there. Captain Brown said to me that he had a proposition to make, to which I listened intently. He wanted to be allowed to go over the bridge unmolested, and we then might take him if we could. He said he had fought Uncle Sam before, and was willing to do it again. Brown complained that his men had been shot down like dogs while bearing a flag of truce. I told him that they must expect to be shot down like dogs if they took up arms in that way.

Brown said he knew what he had to undergo before he came there; he had weighed the responsibility and would not shrink from it. He said he had full possession of the town, and could have massacred all the inhabitants had he thought proper to do so, but as he had not, he considered himself entitled to some terms. Brown said he had not shot anyone who had not carried arms. I told him that Mayor Beckham had been killed, and that I knew he was altogether unarmed. He seemed sorry to hear of the mayor's death and said sadly, "I fight only those who fight me." I then told the prisoner that I did not think any compromise could be effected. Brown said he only kept the hostages for his own safety. They did not appear to fear any injury from him or his men, but only from the attacks from the outside. Every man had a gun, and four-fifths of them were not under any command. The military had ceased firing, but men who were intoxicated were firing their guns in the air, and others were firing at the engine house. Brown, or any of his men could not have ventured outside the door of the engine house that night without being shot. I saw Stevens in the hotel after he had been wounded, and shamed some young men who were endeavoring to shoot him as he lay in his bed apparently dying; told Stevens that if he could stand on his feet with his pistol in his hand, they would all jump out of the window.

Captain Sinn's testimony continued on at great length, but little new was elicited.

At the conclusion of his testimony, Captain Sinn stated that he had returned at the summons of the prisoner to testify in his behalf with as great alacrity as if he had come to testify against him. He had no sympathy for the acts of the prisoner, or for his movement; on the contrary, he would be one of the first to sentence him to punishment. But he regarded Captain Brown as a brave man, and being informed that he wanted him here as a witness, he had returned with pleasure, as a true Southern man would, to state the facts about the case, so that Northern men wouldn't have any opportunity of saying that Southern men were unwilling to appear as witnesses in behalf of one whose principles they abhorred.

Israel Russell was then sworn in and testified, "I was the bearer of a flag of truce from Brown's party to the citizens of the Ferry." His further testimony was merely in corroboration of the facts stated by the previous witness.

Terrence Byrne was next sworn in and testified, "I was taken prisoner by Captain Cook and two others, and was one of the ten hostages confined in the engine house. Brown had five or six of his men there. He did not give any reason to us why we were put there, except that it was for his safety. He said he did not think any attack would be made upon the engine house while us hostages were there."

Here the defense closed their testimony. None of the witnesses for the defense were cross-examined by the state.

Mr. Chilton, speaking for the prisoner, rose and submitted a motion that the prosecution be compelled to elect on the indictment, and abandon the others. The indictment consisted of four counts and was endorsed thus: "An indictment for treason, and advising and conspiring with slaves and others to rebel." The charge of treason was first, and the second count alleged a charge different from that which was indorsed on the back of the indictment, and which was upon the record. The second count was under the following statute, "If a free person advise or conspire with a slave to rebel or make an insurrection, he shall be punished with death, whether such rebellion or insurrection be made or not." But the second count of the indictment was that those parties who were charged by the indictment, "conspired together with other persons to induce certain slaves, namely the property of Messrs. Allstadt and Washington, to make rebellion and insurrection." A broad distinction was made between advising and conspiring with others to induce slaves to rebel, and conspiring with others to induce slaves to rebel. Whether Mr. Chilton was to avail himself of their irregularity by instruction from Judge Parker to the jury to disregard this second count entirely, or whether it would be proper to wait until the conclusion of the trial, and then move an arrest of judgment, he left the judge to decide.

Mr. Chilton then proceeded to argue the motion that the prosecution be compelled to elect one count and abandon the others, quoting Archibald's *Criminal Pleading* in support of his views. He further alluded to the hardship which rested upon the prisoner to meet the various and distinct charges in the same trial. From the authority he read, it would be seen that in a case of treason different descriptions of treasons could not be united in the same indictment. That is, high treason could not be associated with other treason. If an inferior grade of the same character could not be included in separate counts, still less could offenses of a higher grade be included. "Treason," Mr. Chilton expounded, "is high treason in this county. Treason against the state of Virginia is treason against her sovereignty. We have no other description of treason, because treason can only be committed against a sovereignty, whether that of the United States or of a sovereign state."

Mr. Harding could not see the force of Chilton's objection. In regard to separate offenses being charged, he saw them as but different parts of the same transaction. Harding said, "Treason against the government was properly made the subject of one of the counts. But we also have a count of murder. It can hardly be supposed that treason can exist without being followed or accompanied by murder. Murder arose out of this treason, and was the natural result of this bloody conspiracy; yet after all the evidence has been given on all these points, the objection was made that we must confine ourselves to a single one of them. I hope that no such motion will be granted."

Mr. Hunter followed and replied further to the arguments of Mr. Chilton. He said, "At the discretion of the court, compelling the prosecution to elect one count of the indictment, was only exercised when great embarrassment would otherwise have result for the prisoner. As applied to this particular case it involved the point, as had been disclosed by the evidence, that it was one transaction, a continued closely-connected series of acts, which, according to our apprehension of the law of the land, involved the three great offenses of treason, conspiring with, advising slaves to make insurrection, and the perpetration of murder." Hunter further expounded, "Whether in cases of this character, it is right and proper for the court to put the prosecution upon its election as to one of the three, and bar us from investigating the two others entirely, even though they related to facts involved in one grand fact. Notwithstanding the multiplicity of duties devolving upon the prosecutor and assistant prosecutors, we have found time to be guarded and careful in regard to the mode of framing the indictment. It is my duty, and I propose to defend it in a right and proper manner."

Hunter then proceeded to quote Chitty's *Criminal Law* and Robinson's *Practice* to prove that the discretion of the court, there spoken of, in reference to the furtherance of the great object in view—the attainment of justice—was applicable in the present case. He said further, "Where the prisoner is not embarrassed in making his defense, this discretion is not to be exercised by the court, and no case can be shown where it has been thus exercised, where the whole ground of the indictment referred to one and the same transaction. This very case in point would show the absurdity of the principle; if it were as broad as contended for by his learned friend. As to the other point of objection it was too refined and subtle for his poor intellect."

Mr. Chilton responded, "In order to ascertain what a party is tried for, we must go to the findings of the grand jury. If the grand jury returned an indictment charging the party with murder, finding a true bill for that, and he should be indicted for manslaughter, or any other offense, the court would not have jurisdiction to try him on that count in the indictment. The whole question turns on the construction of the section of the statute which has been read, viz: whether or not advising or conspiring with slaves to rebel is a separate and distinct offense from conspiring with other persons to induce it."

Judge Parker said that the differences might perhaps be taken advantage of to move an arrest of judgment, but the jury had been charged and had been sworn to try the prisoners on the indictment as drawn. The trial must go on, and counsel could afterwards move an arrest of judgment. As to the other objection, the judge made this answer, "The very fact that the offense can be charged in different counts, varying the language and circumstances, is based upon the idea that distinct offences may be charged to the same indictment. The prisoners are to be tried on the various counts as if they were various transactions. There is no legal objection against charging various crimes in the same indictment. The practice has been to put a party upon election where the prisoner would be embarrassed in his defense, but such is not the law. In this case these offenses charged are all part of the same transaction, and no case is made out for the court to interfere and put the parties upon an election."

Mr. Chilton said he would reserve the motion as a basis for a motion in arrest of judgment.

Mr. Henry Griswold remarked that the position of all the present counsel of the prisoner was one of very great embarrassment. They had no disposition to interfere with the course of practice, but it was the desire of the defendant that the case should be argued. He supposed that counsel could obtain sufficient knowledge of the evidence previously taken by reading notes of it. But it was now nearly dark. If it was to be argued at all, he supposed the argument for the commonwealth would probably occupy the attention of the court until the usual time for adjournment, unless it was the intention to continue with a late evening session. From what had heretofore transpired, he felt a delicacy in making any request of the court, but knowing that the case was now ended, except for mere argument, he did not know that it would be asking too much for the court to adjourn after the opening argument on behalf of the prosecution.

Mr. Hunter said that he would cheerfully bear testimony to the unexceptional manner in which the counsel who had just taken his seat had conducted the examination of witnesses today. It would afford him very great pleasure, he said, in all ordinary cases, to agree to the indulgence of such a request as the gentleman had just made, and which was entirely natural, but he was bound to remember and respectfully to remind the court that this state of things, which places counsel in a somewhat embarrassing position in conducting the defense, was entirely the act of the prisoner. His counsel would not be responsible for it; the court would not be responsible for it, but the unfortunate prisoner was responsible for his own act in dismissing his faithful, skillful, able and zealous counsel on yesterday afternoon. He would simply add that not only were the jurors kept away from their families by their delays, but there could not be a female in this county, who, whether with the good cause or not, was not trembling with anxiety and apprehension. While, then, courtesy to the counsel and humanity to the prisoner should have due weight, yet the commonwealth has its rights, the community has its rights, the jury have their rights, and it was for the judge to weigh these on opposite sides of the scale, and determine whether they should go on, or bring the case to a close tonight.

Mr. Chilton said that their client desired that they should continue to argue his case. It was impossible for him to do so now, and he could not allow himself to make an attempt at argument on a case about which he knew so little. If he were to get up at all, it would be for the unworthy purpose of wasting time. He had no such design, but having undertaken this man's cause, he very much desired to comply with his wishes. He would be the last man in the world to subject the jurors to inconvenience unnecessarily; but although the prisoner might have been to blame, may have acted foolishly, and may have had an improper purpose in so doing, still he could not see that he should therefore be forced to have his case submitted without argument. "In a trial for life and death," he said, "we should not be too precipitate."

Judge Parker here consulted with the jurors, who expressed themselves to be very anxious to get home, as it was getting late. His Honor said that he was desirous of trying this case precisely as he would try any other, without any reference at all to outside feeling.

Mr. Hoyt remarked that he was physically incapable of speaking that night, even though he was fully prepared. He had worked very hard the previous night to get the points of law, until he fell sick and unconscious from exhaustion and fatigue. For five days and nights he had only slept ten hours, and it seemed to him that justice to the prisoner demanded the allowance of a little extra time in a case so extraordinary in all its aspects as this.

The judge suggested that the jury might hear the opening argument for the prosecution at any rate.

Mr. Harding said that he would not like to open his arguments right away, unless the case was to be finished that night. He was willing, however, to submit the case to the jury without a single additional word, believing they would do the prisoner justice. The prosecution had been met not only on the threshold, but at every step with obstructions as to the progress of the case. If the case was not to be closed that night, he would like to ask the same indulgence given to the other side, that he might collate the notes of the evidence he had taken.

The judge inquired as to what length of time the defense would require for arguments on Monday morning. He could then decide whether to grant the request or not. After consultation, Mr. Chilton stated that there would be only two more speeches; one by himself and one by Mr. Griswold, and that they would not last more than two and a half hours.

Mr. Hunter again entered an earnest protest against delay.

The judge replied, "Then you can go on yourselves."

Mr. Harding commenced the opening argument for the commonwealth, and spoke for only about forty minutes. He reviewed the testimony as elicited during the examination, and dwelt for some time on the absurdity of the claim or expectation of the prisoner—that he should have been treated according to the rules of honorable warfare. He seemed to have lost sight of the fact that he was in command of a band of murderers and thieves, and had forfeited all title to protection of any kind.

The court then adjourned at 5:00 PM, to meet again at 10:00 AM on Monday morning, at which time Mr. Chilton would deliver his opening speech for the prisoner. On Sunday, October 30, 1859 a Day of Holy Rest was observed.

On Sunday evening at 4:00 PM the United Guards of Frederick City, under the command of Captain Sinn, reached the jail from Harper's Ferry. They requested to be allowed to see the prisoners, and were admitted by authority of Judge Parker—going in by squads. They first visited the cell of Brown and Stevens. Brown was in good spirits. He rose from his couch and took his visitors by the hand, and remarked, "I am glad to see you fellows."

In reply to their questions he said that he was still suffering some pain about the left kidney. He said he was treated with all humanity, and bore testimony to the efficiency of the volunteer soldiers. He thanked Captain Sinn for the manly and truthful manner in which he had testified, and said he would always remember him for his many noble traits of character. During the conversation Brown occasionally played with the little children of the jailors, who were present. He remarked that he had fought on the frontiers in 1812, and that during all his life he had endured hardships and knew how to bear them. Stevens was suffering a great deal, although he was getting better. He shook all the company by the hands. Coppoc said he was prepared to bear his fate like a man. He told Sinn he wanted him to testify at his trial, which Sinn promised to do. They all stated that they were well treated. Cook's cell was not entered. He had been busy all day writing, and was preparing a full confession at the advice of Governor Willard, in the hopes of a pardon. During the visit the jail was surrounded by a large crowd, but good order prevailed. Mr. Hoyt, the prisoner's counsel, continued to be very ill Saturday night, but was feeling much better on Sunday.

The fifth day of the trial took place on Monday, October 31, 1859 at the Charlestown court house in Virginia. The court met at 9:00 AM. The prisoner was brought in, and the trial proceeded without delay. Brown looked better than he had before, and his health was evidently improving. He was placed on a cot as usual. The court house and its approaches were densely crowded.

Mr. Griswold made the opening speech for the defense, taking up the several charges in the indictment and replying to the points made in the opening argument for the prosecution. He alluded to the peculiar circumstances surrounding the case, and hoped the jury would give it calm and dispassionate attention, divesting their minds as far as possible from all prejudice, and disregarding outside influences. The prisoner was entitled to an impartial trial under the laws of Virginia, and let him be acquitted or convicted according to those laws and the evidence given in the case. With regard to the charge of treason brought against the prisoner, Mr. Griswold argued that Brown could not be guilty of treason, as he was not a citizen of this commonwealth, and none but a citizen could commit treason. Never having sworn allegiance to Virginia he could not be a rebel against her authority. He was also charged with levying war against the state, but the evidence given did not support the charge. There was a great difference between levying war and resisting authority. Men congregated together to perpetrate crime have their rules and regulations. When assailed they defend their lives to the utmost, sacrificing and intending to sacrifice the lives of others—but that was *resistance* and not levying war. He would not shrink from the admission, and the prisoner openly confessed, that those men came for the purpose of running off slaves.

That was a crime under the laws of Virginia for which the prisoner was amenable to punishment to the extent of those laws. In carrying out that purpose he temporarily took possession of the arsenal at Harper's Ferry, and attempts were made to arrest him. Mr. Griswold had no complaint to make about that. But it was in resisting those attempts that the blood was shed and the lives were taken, and not in levying war against the commonwealth. It was resisting that which was claimed to be the legal authority of Virginia—seeking to arrest those men assembled in violation of law. Such things have often happened. Jails have been broken open and men taken thence and executed in defiance of the law, after being acquitted by a jury of their countrymen, and the power of the sheriff trampled under foot. Neither does it necessarily constitute levying war if murder ensues, because the commission of the offense of shedding blood may not have been contemplated.

Mr. Griswold said, "Now let us inquire whether the offenses charged in this indictment are a leveling of war, or simply resisting the constituted authorities of the land with a high hand." He alluded to an organized government and that charge was sought to be sustained by evidence, particularly by a pamphlet which had been prepared, and which was taken from the prisoner. Griswold said, "But gentlemen, it would not necessarily follow that overthrowing the commonwealth of Virginia was contemplated due to anything which appeared in that pamphlet." The most harmless organizations in the country have been created with all the outside forms and machinery of government. In debating societies governments have been established, a Congress created, and resolutions and laws discussed. One reading the bulletins of those associations, and knowing nothing about them, would suppose them miniature governments, organized within the limits of the existing government. No matter what names or what officers they may have, that is not sufficient. Bands of robbers and desperadoes have their rules and regulations, their officers, and prescribe death as the punishment for the violation of their laws, but that does not imply that they contemplated the overthrow of a legitimate government. Griswold argued that the jury could not find Brown guilty of treason, unless they found him guilty of associating with others to organize a government to subvert and overthrow the government of Virginia.

If the pamphlet proved anything, it showed that an attempt was made to organize a government in opposition to the government of the United States, and not of Virginia, for all the tools used, all the officers appointed, had reference to a government like that of the United States. It was in vague, unmeaning language, which really proved nothing at all. However, there was a chance in it which must be taken, for it was all in evidence, notwithstanding a distinct and positive statement that it contemplated no overthrow of the general or state government, but simply the repeal of obnoxious laws in the constitution. Mr. Harding, the learned authority who opened the case seemed to occupy that ground entirely, not even going over the evidence to show wherein the treason was proved; said the prisoner was guilty of giving aid and comfort to the enemies of the commonwealth, and that was the only specification he made charging the defendant with treason. He was surprised to hear that gentleman burst forth in such a sublime apostrophe of freedom in terms and language and with action of such surpassing eloquence that no one need be told he had been reared in the land that *urned* the ashes of Patrick Henry.

Mr. Griswold alluded to the distinguished associate of the prosecution, Mr. Hunter, who had brought into his remarks "the disheveled tresses of heightened beauty." He then proceeded to discuss the charge of conspiring with slaves, and said there was a manifest distinction between the effort to run off slaves, or steal slaves, and conspiring to induce them to rebel. Rebellion and insurrection was rising up, not running away—although freedom might be the ultimate object—but rising up against masters, against whites, or against the state. It contemplated riot, rapine, murder, arson, and all the crimes which follow insurrection. The question was as to the object and intention. Griswold maintained that none of the testimony showed that Brown, or anyone with him, said or did anything to incite any slave to rebel. Slaves were taken possession of for a temporary purpose and placed in the arsenal; but Colonel Washington, who knew more about it than any other witness, testified that no slaves took part in the matter except Phil, who at the suggestion of the prisoner attempted to drill a porthole—and that was not done for the purpose of insurrection and rebellion, but to protect themselves.

True, they were engaged in an unlawful act, but not the act charged. They were amenable to punishment, but not as they were indicted. Death ensues as is; they are punishable in some way, but not as charged. Griswold then proceeded to consider the count charging murder in the first degree. This was a crime involving premeditated murder, but he argued that no such malice had been exhibited. First, Hayward was killed; how it happened, nobody knew. It was done in the dark, and whether accidental or intentional, does not appear in the evidence, or by whom. Perhaps those men were guilty in some form, but it was not proved to be murder in the first degree due to deliberate premeditated malice. Griswold could only say, as Captain Brown said to him, "Why should we shoot a Negro? That was not our object." He did not justify these men in staying there and resisting the authority of the country, but he said they were there to protect themselves from arrest. Guns were fired in all directions, and they fired or intended to fire only on armed men.

Without excusing that conduct for one moment, he would remark that it refuted the idea of premeditated malice; they had not the time for thought and reflection which the law contemplates. Not that he would say these men should be allowed to sin within the Commonwealth of Virginia, perpetrate these crimes and go un-whipped of justice, but charge and convict them according to their own law. Virginia has laws and institutions sufficient for her protection, has thrown over the lives of her citizens every safeguard she deems necessary and essential, and has made laws necessary for the protection of property, and the punishment of those who deprive the owners of it. It is the boast of our citizens that no man can be punished beyond what the law requires, and if the law is not severe enough, the proper remedy lies within the legislature.

Captain Brown knew he was committing an offense on slave property. He had repeatedly confessed it, and was willing to abide by the consequences.

Mr. Griswold said:

> Indict him for that offense, and don't convict him of an offense he never dreamed of committing. Nothing in the circumstances of this case demands such a course of procedure. Public safety doesn't require him to be punished contrary to law, if he is a man of indomitable energy and perseverance. If Brown could be engaged five months in prosecuting such an enterprise, and only gather together twenty on white and black men throughout the United States, when there was nothing in the world to oppose him, how in Heaven's name can it be supposed, with him and all his companions struck down, the South awake, everybody alert to enterprises of this kind, that there is the remotest danger of another scheme similar to his?

> It is hardly necessary to make these remarks, it is the duty of the jury to be blind to all outside of this case. The physical courage of those who suppressed the insurrection has been highly commended, but it is moral courage superior to that which can resist prejudice and passion. Let simple justice be meted out to the prisoner. He asked no more, and called on the jury to preserve their oaths intact, their honor untarnished, and the reputation of the commonwealth for justice, magnanimity and chivalry sustained.

Mr. Griswold closed by saying, on behalf of his client, that he had no exception to take to a particle of the evidence given in the trial, but deemed it a wonder, under the circumstances, that the truth should have been as fully developed as it has been. He especially bore honorary testimony to Captain Sinn, who voluntarily came from another state with the simple purpose of doing justice.

Mr. Chilton spoke of the embarrassment under which he undertook the case. He intended to do his duty faithfully, and had come to deal with the prisoner not as Captain Brown, leader of the foray, but simply as a prisoner under the charge of violating the law. If that law did not warrant a conviction, he should endeavor to make that appear to the jury. Still, he would say he had no sympathy with the prisoner. His birth and residence, until within a few years ago, had been in Virginia, in connection with the institution of slavery. Although now a resident of the District of Columbia, he had returned to his native state, to spend the remainder of his days, and mingle his dust with her soil. No other motive operated on him than a distinguished one, to do his duty faithfully. He regretted the excitement respecting the case, but was glad to hear the judge say, on Saturday, that he desired to try this case precisely like all others. He desired, and the whole state desired, and the whole South desired that the trial should be fair; and it had been fair in his estimation.

Circumstances had interrupted their progress; counsel was here without proper preparation; but indulgence had been granted, and they made no complaint. They should do the best they could under the circumstances, and could not complain of the excitement. It was natural. Chilton hoped it would not interfere with the course of justice, or cast a stain on the honor of the state. The jury had sworn they were unbiased, and he presumed they would firmly discharge their oaths in bringing in a verdict. He could not understand from the opening of the prosecution on what ground these charges against the prisoner were attempted to be sustained. The commonwealth attorney indulged in a strain of abuse of the prisoner, and pronounced sentence on him without waiting for the verdict of the jury, thus usurping the place of the judge. There were these distinct charges. The first was of treason. This was an offense of common law. The word was derived from a French word signifying betrayal. Treason meant betrayal of trust or confidence, the violation of fidelity or allegiance to the commonwealth. He maintained that treason could not be committed against a commonwealth except by a citizen thereof. In the present case the whole proof shows that this prisoner was not a citizen of Virginia, and he, therefore, could not be found guilty of treason.

The indictment charged the prisoners with committing every act composing treason. They were charged with levying war against the state, and exciting slaves to insurrection, but there was no proof that they committed the acts charged, no proof that they resisted any process issued against them as violators of authority of the commonwealth. They were rather guilty of resisting Colonel Robert E. Lee, which was resistance to the federal government, and not to the commonwealth of Virginia.

He had carefully read John Brown's provisional constitution, and had regarded it as ridiculous nonsense, a wild chimerical production. It could only have been produced by a man of unsound mind. It defined no territory over which it was intended to operate and said that the signers of the document, not all citizens of the United States, do establish a provisional government. Mr. Chilton said, "What is it? Is it an association or a co-partnership? Citizens are to own property in common, and regulate its tenures. This constitution did not contemplate a government, but merely a voluntary association to abolish slavery. It did not even undertake to levy taxes, which is an essential to any government. It did not appear that this association was to be established in Virginia, or where it was to go into effect. Was it the adoption of a constitution or was it the establishment of a government? The answer—by no means! Those parties had a mere imaginary government to govern themselves and nobody else, just like governing a military company or a debating society. Even if they intended to set up a government over the other, they did not do it."

There was a principle that every piece of evidence was to be construed most favorably to the accused, who should have the benefit of every doubt. In considering the evidence the jury must consider the whole of it—they must take the declarations of the prisoner in his own favor as well as against himself. Now look at the forty-sixth article of this provisional constitution, which expressly declared that the foregoing articles should not be construed to encourage the overthrow of any state government or general government, and look to the dissolution of the Union, but simply as amendment and repeal. This was on evidence before the jury, being submitted by the prosecution.

Again, the prisoner was charged with conspiring with slaves to make an insurrection. No proof was shown that the slaves entered into a conspiracy, and unless that was the case there was no conspiracy. One party cannot conspire alone. Each charge is to be considered alone by the jury. If they believe the evidence, it does not warrant the conviction of treason, and they must consider the charge of conspiracy just as if no charge of treason had been made. One count in the indictment was not to be brought in to aid another. He considered the prisoner had a right to be tried on one charge at a time, entirely disconnected with any other. The court had, however, overruled that motion on Saturday, and hence the importance of making this point clear to the jury, so that they might not confuse the various offenses and the evidence relating to each.

Next, as to murder. Five prisoners were charged with the murder of four men. That they might have jointly done it, he could understand, but that they could have severally done it he declared it was almost impossible for the prisoner to make a defense against such a charge. It was too loose and too vague. By the laws of Virginia, there was but one specific murder charge punishable as a capital offense, and that was deliberate, premeditated murder. The prosecution charged the prisoner with murder with murder in the first degree, but he argued that the evidence in this case did not sustain the charge. The prisoner's conduct in the engine house showed no malice, according to the testimony of Colonel Washington and Mr. Allstadt. However ridiculous his project, which it would seem could never have entered the mind of a sane man, he might still have believed he could carry out that project without bloodshed. At any rate, no sane man could suppose he expected to accomplish his object by force with a mere handful of men, and it is but fair to take his declarations, especially when coupled with his acts, that he intended to shed no blood, except in self-defense, unless you should believe beyond the slightest doubt, that those declarations were untrue, and that the prisoner was actuated by malice in taking the lives of those who never did him harm, and against whom no cause for malice existed. As to Hayward, there was no proof as to how he met his death, or who killed him, or for what cause, and, as his colleague had remarked, the prisoner had no motive to kill Negroes.

The subsequent conflict resulted in loss of life, but the prisoner endeavored to avoid that conflict for the purpose of saving life, and therefore could not have been actuated by malice, which is necessary to constitute murder in the first degree. Even if the prisoner were guilty of murder in the second degree, or manslaughter, neither was a capital crime, and not the crime charged in the indictment. He did not know if Brown was justified in returning the fire, when fired upon under such circumstances. It was a sort of self-defense, and, very probably, had a little more time been allowed, those men could have been taken into custody without loss of life.

Chilton charged the jury to look on this case, as far as the law would allow, with an eye favorable to the prisoner, and when their verdict should be returned—no matter what it might be—he trusted that every man in the community would acquiesce in it. Unless the majority of the law were supported, dissolution of the Union must soon ensue, with all the evils which must necessarily follow in its train.

Mr. Hunter closed the argument for the prosecution. He said that he proposed to argue this case precisely like any other. He had hoped the counsel for the defense would have omitted any outside matters, and to a great extent he had been gratified. One remark he would allude to in the opening speech of the defense this morning, where he had been represented as having drawn the picture of the disheveled locks of an alarmed beauty. His friend had done him some injustice in attributing to him a design of exciting alarm, or disturbing the minds of the people unnecessarily. He had endeavored to march straight forward with the sole purpose of discharging his duty in procuring the attainment of justice in respect to the prisoners.

He would commend to Mr. Griswold the testimony he had borne in the opening of the court; that not only, have the forms of a fair trial been extended to the prisoner, but the substance also—that in the midst of all temptations, to the contrary, in the midst of all the solid reasons that have been urged why a different course—he did not mean an irregular course—a different legal and constitutional course by the governor of Virginia might have been pursued of declaring martial law, and administering drum-head justice.

Mr. Hunter said, "That the chief magistrate had taken high conservative grounds, we as Virginians are justly proud of, and that we did not force this thing beyond what prudence requires of us, and that in regard to the power and patriotism of the commonwealth of Virginia we are sufficient for it, come when it may, and in whatever form."

He proceeded to remove the objections founded on the plea that might have been made as to the power of the court to try a case where the offense was committed. It was hardly necessary to show that it was within the county of Jefferson and within the jurisdiction of this court. There was a law in Virginia making the Potomac River the boundary between Maryland and Virginia, giving either states power, by a solemn compact, to execute a criminal process to the further bank. It was unnecessary to prove through witnesses these matters, which were contained in the code of Virginia. The jury could read the code for themselves.

Another law defined the limits of Jefferson County, showing that it embraced the locality where these events occurred, and giving jurisdiction to this court. It was hinted in a preliminary stage of the proceedings, and an attempt was made to argue, that the United States held an exclusive jurisdiction over the armory grounds but no stress was now laid on that point, because not one murder out of the four lives taken was committed on the armory grounds. Mr. Hunter then took up the argument of treason, which he understood to be, that none but an *attaché* of the commonwealth can commit treason against it. Mr. Hunter said:

It is limited to no parties—it did not require that the offender should be a citizen according to our system of government, and the complicated machinery of federal and state governments, under which we live. In some respects, as citizens of Virginia, we are unfortunately bound to recognize those who have proven themselves, within our borders, as in this case, and, without them, as in others, our deadliest enemies. The constitution of the United States provides that citizens of each state shall be entitled to all the immunities of citizens of the several states. Brown came here with the immunities given by the constitution. He did not come divested of the responsibilities belonging to those immunities. Let the word treason mean breach of trust, and did he not betray that trust with which, as a citizen, he was invested, when within our borders? By the federal constitution he was a citizen when he was here, and did that bond of union—which may ultimately prove a bad bond to us in the South—allow him to come into the bosom of the commonwealth with the deadly purpose of applying the torch to our buildings, and shedding the blood of our citizens? Again, our code defines who are citizens of Virginia, as all those white persons born in any other state of this Union who may become residents here.

The evidence in this case shows, without a shadow of a doubt, that when this man came to Virginia, and planted his feet on Harper's Ferry, he came here to reside and hold the place permanently. It is true that he occupied a farm four or five miles off, in Maryland, a short time ago, but not for the legitimate purpose of establishing his domicile there. It was for the nefarious and hellish purpose of rallying forces into this commonwealth and establish himself at Harper's Ferry as a starting point for a new government. Whatever it was, whether tragical or farcical, and ridiculous as his counsel has presented it, his conduct showed, if his declarations were insufficient, that it was not alone for the purpose of, carrying off slaves that he came there. His provisional government was a real thing, and not a debating society, as his counsel would have us believe; and in holding, office under it, and exercising its functions, he was clearly guilty of treason. The forty-sixth section has been referred to as showing it was not treasonable, but he supposed that the new government was to be a union of separate states, like the present, with the difference that all were to be free states. The whole document must be taken together. The property of slave holders was to be confined to the South, and any man found in arms was to be shot down. Their conduct at Harper's Ferry looked like insanity, but there was too much method in Brown's madness. His purposes were too well matured, and he and his party declared there were thousands in the North ready to join them, while the jury are to take the whole declaration.

The law books expressly declare they may reject, if they see good cause to do so, that which would extenuate the guilt of the prisoner. They are bound to consider it—that's all. As to conspiring with slaves or rebels, the law says the prisoners are equally guilty, whether insurrection was accomplished or not. Advice may be given by actions as well as words. When you put pikes in the hands of the slaves, and hold their masters captive, that is advice to slaves to rebel, and it is punishable with death. The law does not require positive evidence, but only enough to remove every reasonable doubt as to the guilt of the party. Sometimes circumstantial evidence is the strongest kind, for witnesses may perjure themselves or be mistaken. The defense say we don't know who killed the Negro Hayward; that Brown did not do it, because he had no reason to, but that it was dark, and the supposition is that Hayward was killed by mistake. They say Brown did not shoot any unarmed men, but Beckham was killed when unarmed, and therefore he thought the whole case had been proved by the mass of the arguments.

With regard to malice, the law was that if the party perpetrating a felony, undesignedly takes life, it is a conclusive proof of malice. If Brown was only intending to steal Negroes, and in so doing he took a life, it was murder with premeditated malice. So the law expressly lays down, that killing committed in resisting officer's attempting to quell a riot, or in arresting the perpetrator of a criminal offense, was murder in the first degree. Then why do we need all this delay? The proof that Brown treated all his prisoners with leniency, and did not want to shed blood. Brown was not a madman, to shed blood when he knew the penalty for so doing was his own life. In the opening of the campaign he had sense enough to know better than that; but only wanted the citizens of Virginia calmly to hold arms, and let him usurp the government—manumit our slaves, confiscate the property of slave holders, and, without drawing a trigger or shedding blood, permit him to take possession of the commonwealth, and make it another Hayti.

Such an idea is too abhorrent to pursue; so, too, the idea that Brown shed blood only in self-defense, was too absurd to require argument. He gloried in coming here to violate our laws, and said he had counted the cost, knew what he was about, and was ready to abide the consequences. That proves malice. Thus admitting everything charged, he knew his life was forfeited if he failed. Then is not the case made out beyond all reasonable doubt—even beyond any unreasonable doubt indulged in by the wildest fanatic? We, therefore, ask his conviction to vindicate the majesty of the law.

While we have patiently borne delays, as well here as outside in the community, in preservation of the character of Virginia, that plumes itself on its moral character, as well as physical, and on its loyalty and its devotion to truth and right, we ask you to discard everything else, and render your verdict as you are sworn to do. As to the administrators of civil jurisdiction, we ask no more than it is your duty to do—no less. Justice is the center upon which the Deity sits. There is another column which represents its Mercy. You have nothing to do with that. It stands firmly on the column of justice. Administer it according to your law. Acquit the prisoner if you can, but if justice requires you by your verdict to take his life, stand by that column uprightly, but strongly, and let retributive justice, if he is guilty, send him before that Maker who will settle the question forever and ever.

Mr. Hunter concluded his lengthy arguments at 1:30 PM.

During most of the day's arguments, Brown lay on his back with his eyes closed.

Mr. Chilton asked the judge to instruct the jury that, if they believe the prisoner was not a citizen of Virginia, but of another state, they could not convict him on a count of treason. Judge Parker declined, saying the constitution did not give rights and immunities alone, but also imposed responsibilities. Mr. Chilton asked another instruction to the effect that the jury must be satisfied that the place where the offense was committed was within the boundaries of Jefferson County, which the court granted.

The jury was then sent out to deliberate the case and a recess was taken for about thirty-five minutes. Soon after the recess the jury returned with a verdict. There was intense excitement. Brown sat up on his cot while the verdict was being read. It didn't take long. The jury found him <u>guilty</u> of treason, advising and <u>conspiring</u> with slaves and others to rebel, and for <u>murder</u> in the first degree. Brown lay down quickly and said nothing more.

There was no demonstration of any kind.

Mr. Chilton moved an arrest of judgment, both on account of errors in the indictment and errors in the verdict. The objection in regard to the indictment had already been stated. The prisoner has been tried for an offense not appearing on the record of the grand jury,—the verdict was not on each count separately, but was a general verdict on the whole indictment. The prisoner had also been found guilty on both murder counts for the murder of the same persons. It was manifest that he could not be guilty of both. It was agreed that these arguments could be argued on the next day.

Brown was remanded back to jail.

Mr. Harding announced that he was ready to proceed with the trial of Coppoc, who was brought in. The ceremony of passing him between files of armed men was dispensed with. Coppoc took his seat between Messrs. Griswold and Hoyt, who appeared as his counsel. He seemed calm and composed. The remainder of the day was spent in endeavoring to select a jury for the Coppoc case, but the panel was not complete at 5:00 PM, so the court adjourned.

The sixth day of the trial commenced on Tuesday, November 1, 1859 at the Charlestown court house in Virginia. The court met at 10:00 AM. Coppoc was brought in. Previous to proceeding to his trial, Mr. Griswold stated the points on which an arrest of judgment was asked for in Brown's case. In addition to the reasons mentioned yesterday, he said it had not been proved beyond a doubt that Brown was even a citizen of the United States, and he argued that treason could not be committed against a state, but only against the general government, citing the authority of Judge Story; also stating that the jury had not found the prisoner guilty of the crimes as charged in the indictment. They had not responded to the offenses charged, but found him guilty of offenses not charged. They found him guilty of murder in the first degree, when the indictment did not charge him with the offenses constituting that crime.

Mr. Hunter replied, quoting the Virginia code to the effect that technicalities should not arrest the administration of justice. As to the jurisdiction over treason, it was sufficient to say that Virginia had passed a law assuming that jurisdiction, and defining what constitutes that crime.

The Court reserved its decision. Mr. Brown was present during the argument.

The jury was assembled and sworn in for Coppoc's case. The testimony was similar to that given earlier, but it was much more brief. The examination of witnesses for the prosecution was not concluded at the time of adjournment. Cook waived an examination before the magistrate's court.

On Wednesday, November 2, 1859 the seventh day of Brown's trial at Charlestown commenced. Messrs. Russell and Sennott, arrived here from Boston today. Cook was brought before the magistrate's court, and waived an examination. Coppoc's trial was resumed. No witnesses were called for the defense. Mr. Harding opened for the commonwealth; Messrs. Hoyt and Griswold followed for the defendant, and Mr. Hunter closed for the prosecution. The speeches were of marked ability. Mr. Griswold asked to give several instructions to the jury, which were all granted by the court, and the jury retired.

Brown was then brought in, and the court house was immediately thronged.

The court gave its decision on the motion for an arrest of judgment, overruling the objections made. On the objection that treason cannot be committed against a state, Judge Parker ruled that where allegiance is due, treason may be committed. Most of the states have passed laws against treason. The court regarded as insufficient the objections as the form of the verdict rendered.

The clerk then asked Mr. Brown whether he had anything to say as to why sentence should not be pronounced upon him.

Mr. Brown immediately rose, and in a clear, distinct voice addressed the court:

> I have, may it please the court, a few words to say. In the first place, I deny everything but what I have all along admitted—that is a design on my part to free slaves. I intended, certainly, to have made a clean thing of that matter, as I did last Winter when I went into Missouri and there took slaves without the snapping of a gun on either side, moving them through the country, and finally depositing them in Canada. I designed to have done the same thing again on a larger scale here. That was all I intended. I never intended murder or treason, or the destruction of property, or to excite or incite slaves to rebellion, or to make insurrection. I have another objection, and that is, it is unjust that I should suffer such a penalty. Had I interfered in the manner which I admit, and which I admit has been fairly proved—for I admire the truthfulness and candor of the greater portion of the witnesses who have testified in this case—had I so interfered in behalf of the rich, the powerful, the intelligent, the so-called great, or in behalf of any of their friends, either father, mother, brother, sister, wife or children, or any of that class, and suffered and sacrificed what I have in this interference, it would have been all right; every man in this court would have deemed it an act worthy of reward, rather than punishment.
>
> This court acknowledges, too, as I suppose, the validity of the law of God. I see a book kissed, which I suppose to be the Bible, or at least the New Testament, which teaches me that all things whatsoever I would that men should do to me, I should do even so to them. It teaches me further, to remember them that are in bonds, as bound with them. I endeavored to act up to that instruction. I say I am yet too young. to understand that God is any

respecter of persons. I believe that to have interfered as I have done, as I have always freely admitted I have done, in behalf of His despised poor, no wrong, but right. Now, if it is deemed necessary that I should forfeit my life for the furtherance of the ends of justice, and mingle my blood further with the blood of my children, and with the blood of millions in this slave country whose rights are disregarded by wicked, cruel and unjust enactments, I say let it be done.

Let me say one word further. I feel entirely satisfied with the treatment I have received on my trial. Considering all the circumstances, it has been more generous, than I expected. But I feel no consciousness of guilt. I have stated from the first what was my intention and what was not. I never had any design against the liberty of any person, nor any disposition to commit treason or to excite slaves to rebel, or make any general insurrection. I never encouraged any man to do so, but always discouraged any idea of that kind.

Let me say also, in regard to the statements made by some of those who were connected with me. I fear it has been stated by some of them that I have induced them to join me, but the contrary is true. I do not say this to injure them, but as regretting their weakness. Not one but joined me of his own accord, and the greater part at their own expense. A number of them I never saw, and never had a word of conversation with till the day they came to me, and that was for the purpose I have stated. Now, I have done.

While Mr. Brown was speaking perfect quiet prevailed, and when he had finished the judge proceeded to pronounce sentence. After a few prefatory remarks, he said that no reasonable doubt could exist of the guilt of the prisoner, and sentenced him to be hung in public on Friday, the

2nd of December next. Mr. Brown received his sentence with composure. The only demonstration made was by the clapping of the hands of one man in the crowd, who was not a resident of Jefferson County. He was promptly suppressed, and much regret was expressed by the citizens at its occurrence.

JOHN BROWN ON HIS WAY TO THE PRISON
AFTER HEARING OF THE SENTENCE OF
DEATH PRONOUNCED UPON HIM.

After being out for one hour the jury came in with the verdict that Coppoc was also guilty on all the counts in the indictment. His counsel gave notice of a motion for arrest of judgment, as in Mr. Brown's case. **The court then adjourned, and the Trial of the Century was over.**

Chapter 6

INTERLUDE

THE FIRST OF several friendly visitors to John Brown from the North after the trial were Judge Thomas Russell and his wife, the daughter of the famous seaman's preacher, "Father" Taylor. As Mrs. Russell stepped into Brown's cell on the evening of November 2nd, 1859 she was struck by how calm and relaxed he looked. Brown exclaimed, "Oh my dear, this is no place for you."

Mrs. Russell threw herself into Brown's arms and sobbed uncontrollably. Judge Russell told Brown he had not been prepared for the unusual haste in which the trial had been carried out. He had received Brown's letter and intended to defend him but he had not been able to clear his docket in time. He said he had brought a brilliant young Boston lawyer named George Sennott to defend the other men. The Russell's had been present in the court house when the sentence of death was given. Judge Russell congratulated Brown on his speech. Brown said that it did him a great deal of good to know that the Russell's had come to stand at his side when others were calling him a mad man.

Mrs. Russell wept on seeing the pillow on Brown's cot clotted with blood. She noticed that Brown's coat was torn and stained with blood as well. She made him take his coat off and lay it on the table. She had needle and thread in her bag and repaired his coat with her skillful hands, while her husband, as they conversed, was looking at the wide fire place in the room and conjecturing whether this might be a perfect escape route. Judge Russell said, "Two good Yankees could easily arrange your escape."

Mrs. Russell called a guard and when he appeared she gave him Brown's clothing for cleaning and repair. "At last," said Mrs. Russell, "we had to take our leave, and I kissed Mr. Brown's forehead, weeping. His mouth trembled, ever so little, but he only said, "Now go." The Russell's left rather subdued and walked back to their hotel. On the train platform near the jail they saw Lewis Washington. He questioned them suspiciously regarding their intimacy with the prisoner. "I am not quite sure I am doing the right thing," he said, "of letting them get away from here so easily."

The New York *Commercial Advertiser* begged the executive of Virginia not to make a martyr of Brown; that being a fanatic he was certainly insane to some degree, and they feared that direful consequences would spring from his execution. That as the blood of the martyrs was the seed of the Church, so from the grave of John Brown the *Advertiser* feared a crop of armed fanatics might spring up destructive both to Virginia and the South. It would, perhaps, have been more to the point to have shown that the pardon of Brown would have lessened the number of existing fanatics rather than by suggesting their increase from a due course of justice. The *Advertiser* staff apprehended that the executive of Virginia would not turn an attentive ear to suggestions coming from such a source as the New York *Commercial Advertiser*. The Republican Party, of which the *Advertiser* was an organ, was too deeply implicated in the actions of their chief leaders to offer suggestions with regard to the just punishment of one of their number.

The *Advertiser* made the following comments:

> The constitution of Virginia has placed the mercy seat in the enlightened conscience of her executive, and that the high prerogative of pardon has not been mercilessly exercised, and we point to a long list of executive clemencies that grace the administration of Governor Wise. But in all the pardons granted by him neither the crime nor the motives of Brown find any place. *To cool and calculating crime, to murder, pillage and plunder, to servile wars and its attendant horrors, the executive of Virginia will always turn*

a deaf ear, and soil not the robes of mercy with the crime of permitting such wickedness to go unpunished.

Violated laws and murdered citizens demanded a victim at the hands of justice; if Brown was a crazed *fanatic,* irresponsible either in morals or law, there are yet guilty parties. He is then the agent of wicked principals. If the Northern people believed Brown insane, what punishment is due to those who have poisoned his mind with the *"irrepressible conflict"* and spurred his fanaticism to deeds of blood and carnage? He may be insane, but there are other *criminals,* guilty wretches, who instigated the crimes perpetrated at Harper's Ferry. *Bring these men—bring William Seward, Horace Greeley, Giddings, Hale and Smith to the jurisdiction of Virginia, and Brown and his deluded victims in the Charlestown jail may hope for pardon.* In the opinion of Virginia, the five Republican leaders above mentioned are more guilty than even John Brown and his associates. An ignorant fanaticism may be pleaded in palliation of the crime of Brown, but the five Republican leaders would spurn such a stultifying plea! They would not compromise their intelligence even at the cost of their morality. Let the friends of Brown, let all who believe him to be insane, and all who intend to represent him as a crazy fanatic, for whose folly, no party is responsible, *deliver up Seward, Greeley, Giddings, Smith and Hale.* A fair trial, at their own time, with their own counsel, will be freely given them; and if Virginia does not prove them guilty, they too shall go unhurt.

A correspondent of the Boston *Traveller* who made a quick visit to Charlestown the previous week, and who was present when the sentence upon Brown was pronounced, wrote:

Captain Brown was then led in, and the motion in arrest of judgment in this case was refused. After reading his opinion on this question, Judge Parker asked the prisoner if he had any reason why sentence should not be pronounced and then Brown delivered his remarkable speech, speaking with perfect calmness of voice and mildness of manner, winning the respect of all for his courage and firmness. His self-possession was more wonderful, because his sentence, at this time, was unexpected, and his remarks were entirely extemporaneous.

Sentence was pronounced, and it was received in perfect silence, except for a slight demonstration of applause from one excited man, whom the judge instantly ordered into custody. It illustrates the character of the people, that several officials and members of the bar hastened to inform us that this man was not a citizen of the county. They take pride in thinking that Jefferson is a county of gentlemen.

During my interviews with Brown at the jail, he repeated what he said in court, that he was perfectly satisfied with the fairness of his trial, and the kindness of his treatment. He said that Captain Avis, his jailor, showed as much kindness in treating him, as he had shown courage in attacking him; "It is what I should expect from a brave man." Seeing that one of the deputy-jailers was present, he added: "I don't say this to flatter—it isn't my way. I say it because it is true." (For the same reason I here repeat it.) Judge Parker appears to have conducted the trial with remarkable candor, dignity and impartiality and when we consider what a servile insurrection is, the self-control of the people was wonderful.

Brown has not been in irons since the first night, and every possible indulgence was shown him, except the indulgence of delay. Even the speed of the trial was, in part, accounted for by the accident that the term of the court happened to be held just at this time.

Captain Brown appeared perfectly fearless in all respects and said that he had no feeling about death on a scaffold, and believed that every act, "even all the follies that led to this disaster, were decreed to happen ages before the world was made." The only anxiety he expressed was in regard to the circumstances of his family. He asked and obtained leave to add a postscript to a letter to his wife, telling her that he was to be hanged on the 2nd of December, and requested that it should be directed to Mrs. John Brown, "for there are some other widow Browns in North Elba." He spoke highly of his medical attendants, but rejected the offered counsel of all ministers who believed that slavery was right. He will die as fearlessly as he has lived.

Stevens was on a bed in the same large room, dangerously wounded. He probably will not be tried during this term, as the judge will not be so inhuman as to try a dying man. And it is the wish of many Virginians that he should die of his wounds rather than recover to be executed.

The bill of exceptions in Brown's case will be argued before the court of appeals, now sitting at Richmond. Some of the main points would certainly secure a new trial in this state; and they may be sufficient to do so, under the looser practice of Virginia. Mr. Chilton is one of the ablest advocates in the country, and will probably be aided by another gentleman of great ability. Some of the same points occur in the cases of Coppoc and of the colored prisoners, who are defended by Messrs. Griswold and Sennott. The treason count cannot be sustained against the colored men, as it will be held under the Dred

Scott decision that they owe no allegiance, and therefore could not commit that crime.

John Brown wrote the following letter from his jail cell:

CHARLESTOWN, JEFFERSON CO., Va,

Oct. 31, 1859

MY DEAR WIFE AND CHILDREN, EVERY ONE: I suppose you have learned before this by the newspapers that two weeks ago today, we were fighting for our lives at Harper's Ferry; that during the fight Watson was mortally wounded, Oliver killed, Wm. Thompson killed and Dauphin slightly wounded; that on the following day I was taken prisoner, immediately after which I received several saber cuts in my head, and bayonet stabs in my body. As near as I can learn, Watson died of his wound on Wednesday the second, or on Thursday the third day after I was taken.

Dauphin was killed when I was taken, and Anderson, I suppose, also. I have since been tried, and found guilty of treason, &c., and of murder in the first degree. I have not yet received my sentence. No others of the company with whom you were acquainted were, so far as *I can learn,* either killed or taken. Under all these terrible calamities, I feel quite cheerful in the assurance that God reigns, and will overrule all for his glory and the best possible good. I feel *no* consciousness of *guilt* in the matter, nor even mortification on account of my imprisonment and iron; and I feel perfectly assured that very soon no member of my family will feel any possible disposition to "blush on my account." Already dear friends at a distance, with kindest sympathy, are cheering me with the assurance that *posterity* at least will do me justice. I shall commend you all together, with my beloved, but bereaved, daughters-in-law, to their sympathies, which I have no doubt will soon reach you.

I also commend you all to Him "whose mercy endureth forever"—to the God of my fathers, "whose I am, and whom I serve." "He will never leave you or forsake you" unless you forsake him. Finally, my dearly beloved, be of good comfort. Be sure to remember and *to fellow my advice,* and my example too, so far as it has been consistent with the holy religion of Jesus Christ, in which I remain a most firm and humble believer. Never forget the poor, nor think any thing you bestow on them to be lost to you, even though they may be as *black* as Ebedmelech, the Ethiopian eunuch, who cared for Jeremiah in the pit of the dungeon, or as *black* as the one to whom Philip preached Christ. Be sure to entertain strangers, for thereby some have—"Remember them that are in bonds as bound with them." I am in charge of a jailer *like* the one who took charge of "Paul and Silas;" and you may rest assured that both *kind hearts* and *kind* faces are more or less about me, whilst thousands are thirsting for my blood. "These *light* afflictions, which are but *for a moment,* shall work out for us a far *more exceeding and* eternal weight of glory." I hope to be able to write you again. My wounds are doing well. Copy this, and send it to your sorrow-stricken brothers, Ruth, to comfort them. Write me a few words in regard to the welfare of all. God Almighty bless you all, and make you "joyful in the midst of all your tribulations." Write to John Brown, Charlestown, Jefferson Co., Va., care of Captain John Avis.

Your affectionate husband and father,

JOHN BROWN

Nov. 3, 1859.

P. S.—Yesterday, Nov. 2nd, I was sentenced to be hanged on Dec. 2nd next. Do not grieve on my account. I am still quite cheerful. God bless you.

Yours ever,

JOHN BROWN

The following resolutions relative to the insurrection in Virginia were passed by the Georgia Legislature on Thursday, November 3, 1859:

Whereas, The late attempt at Harper's Ferry, in the State of Virginia, to excite a portion of the slaves of the South to insurrection, has produced the highest degree of indignation in the minds of the Southern people against the perpetrators of that outrage, their aiders arid abettors, and affords just ground to apprehend a renewal of their efforts in other places and whereas, the action of Governor Wise and President Buchanan meets with our unqualified approbation, we deem it incumbent upon the members of the legislature of the state of Georgia to give the most authoritative expression of their sentiments; therefore

Resolved, That we regard the effort to excite the slaves of the South to a servile insurrection with the most intense indignation, and trust that the parties to this insane and treasonable plot may meet with the most prompt and signal punishment, believing, as we do, that while it will be meting out a just retribution for their crime, it will exert a wholesome influence in deterring others from countenancing similar movements.

Resolved, That the prompt and energetic action of Governor Wise, of Virginia, and of President Buchanan, in suppressing the outbreak at Harper's Ferry, and in their efforts to capture the insurgents, evince a degree of manliness and patriotism, honorable alike to them and worthy of our warm admiration.

Resolved, That we pledge the state of Georgia to uphold and support the state of Virginia and the President of the United States in the position they have assumed in connection with this unfortunate affair, and we earnestly counsel the utmost vigilance in guarding against the recurrence of a similar conspiracy in our own borders, or elsewhere at the South.

Resolved, That a copy of the foregoing preamble and resolutions be transmitted by the governor of the state of Georgia to the governor and legislature of Virginia, and to the President of the United States.

The same was then ordered to be transmitted to the Senate without delay. Frederick Douglass' announcement of Friday, November 4, 1859 was as follows:

DEAR READERS AND FRIENDS: As I am about to leave my post as editor for a long contemplated visit and lecturing tour in Great Britain, which may detain me for many months from my editorial duties, the peculiar circumstances of the occasion seem to justify me in saying to you a few parting words. In ordinary conditions, considering the rapidity, safety and certainty with which a journey is now made to Europe—almost converting the two continents into one—a simple voyage from America to Great Britain would not seem to warrant a very ceremonious and formal parting, or to require apology or explanation.

In any circumstances, however, I should be most freely pardoned by all right-feeling man and women, if while looking around upon the scores of kind and earnest friends who, during the last eighteen years have cheered and sustained me by their sympathy and cooperation, in my humble labors to promote the emancipation and elevation of my people, I should let fall a tearful word at the thought of parting, and breathe one heart-prayer that the cause of justice and benevolence, the bond of our friendship may continue to fill their hearts and command their best exertions for its ultimate triumph. Neither the long experience of partings and meetings, nor the calmness borrowed from philosophy, avail me anything, as I say to my friends and readers, farewell. Even the delightful prospect of renewing the *bonds-fraternal* formed in Great Britain and Ireland, during my visit to those countries fourteen years ago, fails to shield me from the keen edge of regret at leaving my friends here in the present state of the anti-slavery question. Dark and perilous as is the hour—maddened and vengeful as is the slave power—the infuriated demon of slavery never seemed to me more certain of extirpation than now. At the present moment, slavery seems to have gained an advantage. The audacity of the attack made upon it by that stern old hero, who looks death full in the face with a steady eye and undaunted heart, while pierced with bayonet wounds and covered with saber gashes, had created for the moment perhaps, a more active resistance to the cause of freedom and its advocates, but this is transient. The moment of passion and revenge will pass away and reason and righteousness will all the more, for this sudden shock, roll their thundering appeal to the ear and heart of this guilty nation.

The Christian blood of old John Brown will not cease to cry from the ground long after the clamors of alarm and consternation of the dealers in the bodies and souls of men will have ceased to arrest attention. Men will soon begin to look away from the plot to the purpose—from the effect to the cause. Then will come the reaction—and the names now covered with execration will be mentioned with honor, as noble martyrs to a righteous cause. Yes, sad and deplorable as was the battle of Harper's Ferry, it will not prove a total loss to the cause of liberty. The sharp crack of the rifles there, proclaiming liberty to the captive, cruelty left in bondage by our boasted religion and law, may rouse a dead church and a dumb ministry to the duty of putting away this dark and dangerous sin. The silent heights of the Alleghanies, leaning in grandeur against the pure blue sky, will hereafter look down and speak to the slave with a loving and wooing voice. The benumbed conscience of the nation will be revived and become susceptible of right impressions. The slave holders of Virginia and the South generally, are endeavoring to make the impression that the Negroes summoned to the standard of freedom by John Brown, viewed the effort to emancipate them with indifference. An eye witness, and a prominent actor in the transactions at Harper's Ferry, now at my side, tells me that this is grossly aside from the truth. But even if the contrary were shown, it would afford small comfort to the slave holders. The slaves were sensible enough not to shout before they gained the prize, and their conduct was creditable to their wisdom. The brief space allowed them in freedom was not sufficient to bring home to them in its fullness the real significance of the occasion. All the efforts to disparage the valor of the colored insurgents are grounded in the fears of the slave holders, not in the facts of the action. They report many dead insurgents, and few killed among those who opposed them. I have at last seen one man among the insurgents reported killed, who is still alive and bids fair to live yet many years. On many accounts were the thing possible, I should be glad to use the event at Harper's Ferry, and the state of feeling it has produced, before the American people. But there is work abroad as well as at home. Efforts will be made in England as well as in America to turn the Harper's Ferry insurrection to the account of slavery. I may, for a time, be useful there, in resisting and counteracting these efforts.

It will probably be charged, by those who delight in any pretext for aspersing me, that I go to England to escape the demands of justice for my alleged complicity with the Harper's Ferry insurrection. I am not ashamed of endeavoring to escape from such justice as might be rationally expected by a man of color at the hands of a slave holding court, sitting in the state of Virginia. I am not a favorite in that state, and even if acquitted by the court, with my knowledge of slaveholding magnanimity and civilization, I could scarcely hope to re-cross the slave holding border with my life. There is no more dishonor in trying to keep out of the way of such a court, than there would be in keeping out of the way of a company of hungry wolves. Nevertheless, it is only due to truth to state that, for more than a year past, I have been making arrangements *not* to go to Harpers's Ferry but to England. This has been known alike to both friends and foes. My going, too, has been delayed, rather than hastened, by the occurrence of that outbreak. The fact of my known intention to visit England in November, and my published lecturing engagements in different parts of the state of New York, plainly show that no man had any right to expect my personal cooperation elsewhere. I am, however, free to confess that I deem England a safer asylum for me than any afforded by the president of the United States.

I have once before found shelter and protection in a monarchy from the slave hunters of this Republic, and am indebted not to democratic humanity or justice for the liberty I have enjoyed during the last dozen years, and amid all the atrocities under the Fugitive Slave Bill in America—but to humane British men and women who bought my body and bones with British gold, and made me a present to myself—a free, and unsolicited gift. In other words, they gave me back the body originally given me by my Creator, but which had been stolen from me under the singularly just and generous laws of a Republican slave state! I thank God that there is at least one Christian country on this globe, where a colored man as well as a white man may rest secure from the fury and vengeance of alarmed and terrified slave holders, the meanest tyrants that ever cursed the earth by their cruelty, or insulted Heaven by their blasphemous arrogance.

Almost ever since the Harper's Ferry disturbance, I have been assured that United States marshals, in strong force, have been in search of me at many different points, but chiefly at Rochester. A government which refuses to acknowledge—nay, denies that I can be a citizen, or bring a suit into any courts of justice—in a word, brands me as an outlaw in virtue of my blood, now professes a wish to try me for being a traitor and an outlaw! To be a traitor two conditions are necessary: First—one must have a government; secondly—he must be found in armed rebellion against that government. I am guilty of neither element of treason. The American government refuses to shelter the Negro under its protecting wing, and makes him an outlaw. The government is therefore quite unreasonable and inconsistent. Allegiance and protection are said to go together, and depend upon each other. When one is withdrawn the other ceases. But I think Mr.

Buchanan is not only unreasonable and inconsistent in his design upon me but a little cowardly withal.

The plan seems to be to strike where his blows are likely to meet the least resistance. It cannot be that I am worthy of extra attention paid me by the government. The Rochester *Union* very properly raises the inquiry as to why I am especially singled out. Am I more involved than others whose names have been mentioned in connection with the name of dear Old Osawatomie Brown? The eagerness to get hold of me, while the other and more popular men happened to be equally compromised; are merely threatened. It shows that my color, as well as my alleged crime, enters into the calculations of the government, and that it professes to arrest first those who can be arrested easiest. In this it acts with its usual cowardice.

But really, dear readers, I am much to highly concerned by the importance given me in connection with the Harper's Ferry affair. My relation to it is perhaps less important than friends or enemies would seem to suppose. A letter sent for publication elsewhere, and which I hope will be inserted here, will give you a pretty clear idea of my true relation to that transaction.

In conclusion, I hope to be able to continue the regular publication of my paper during my absence, and to keep in correspondence with those who shall continue to stand by my little anti-slavery sheet. If this shall be done, (and I have very little doubt it will be) I shall take my old post again and do battle as of yore.

I am most happy to be able to announce that a competent and experienced friend of the cause will edit the paper in my absence, so that nothing will be lost to its readers on this score. The principles of Liberty, Justice and Humanity, which have found expression and advocacy in the paper, will continue to be upheld as firmly as ever. No abatement need be expected in heart or hope.

With every sentiment of regard and grateful friendship,
I am yours to the end of slavery,

FREDERICK DOUGLASS

Mr. George H. Hoyt, counsel for John Brown and Coppoc, arrived at the court house on Friday evening, November 5, 1859. Mr. Griswold will continue the defense of the remaining cases. Mr. Hoyt released the following letter to John Brown for newspaper publication:

NEWPORT, R. I., Tenth month, 27th, 1859.

Captain John Brown

DEAR FRIEND: Since thy arrest I have often thought of thee, and have wished that, like Elizabeth Fry toward her prison friends, so I might console thee in thy confinement. But that can *never* be, and so I can only write thee a few lines, which, if they contain any comfort, may come to thee like some little ray of light.

You can never know how very many dear Friends love thee with all their hearts, for thy brave efforts in behalf of the poor oppressed, and though we, who are non-resistants, and religiously believe it better to reform by moral and not by carnal weapons, could not approve of bloodshed; yet we know thee was animated by the most generous and philanthropic motives. Very many thousands openly approve thy intentions, though most Friends would not think it right to take up arms.

Thousands pray for thee every day; and, oh, I do pray that God will be with thy soul. Posterity will do thee justice. If Moses led out the thousands of Jewish slaves from their bondage, and God destroyed the Egyptians in the sea because they went after the Israelites to bring them back to slavery, then, surely, by the same reasoning, we may judge thee a deliverer, who wished to release millions from a more cruel oppression. If the American people honor Washington for resisting, with bloodshed, for seven years an unjust tax, how much more ought thou to be honored for seeking to free the poor slaves.

Oh, I wish I could plead for thee as some of the other sex can plead, how I would seek to defend thee! If I had now the eloquence of Portia how I would turn the scale in thy favor! But I can only pray "God bless thee!" God pardon thee, and through our Redeemer give thee safety and happiness now and always.

From thy friend,

ELIZA BARCLAY

John Brown replied:

Charlestown, Jefferson County, Va.,
Tuesday, 1st November, 1859.

MY DEAR FRIEND E. B. OF R. I.: Your most cheering letter of 27th October, is received, and may the Lord reward you a thousand fold for the kind feeling you express toward me; but more especially for your fidelity to the "poor that cry, and those that have no help." For this I am a prisoner in bonds. *It is solely my own fault, in a military point of view, that we met with our disaster*—I mean that I mingled with our prisoners and so far sympathized with them and their families, that I neglected my duty *in other* respects. But God's will, not mine, will be done.

You know that Christ once armed Peter. So also in my case, *I think he put a sword into my hand, and there continued it, so long as he saw best, and then kindly took it from me. I mean when I first went to Kansas.* I wish you could know with what cheerfulness I am now wielding the "Sword of the Spirit," on the right hand and on the left. I bless God that it proves "mighty to the pulling down of strongholds." I always loved my Quaker friends, and I commend to their kind regard my poor bereaved widowed wife, and my daughters and daughters-in-law, whose husbands fell at my side. One is a mother, and the other likely to become so soon. They, as well as my own sorrow-stricken daughter, are left very poor, and have much greater need of sympathy than I, who, through Infinite Grace and the kindness of strangers, am "joyful in all my tribulations."

Dear Sister, write them at North Elba, Essex County, N. Y., to comfort their sad hearts. Direct to Mary A. Brown, wife of John Brown. There is also another—a widow—wife of Thompson, who fell with my poor boys in the affair at Harper's Ferry, at the same place.

I do not feel conscious of guilt in taking up arms; and had it been in behalf of the rich and powerful, intelligent, the great—as men count greatness—if those who form enactments to suit themselves and corrupt others, or some of their friends that I interfered, suffered, sacrificed and fell, it would have been doing very well. But enough of this.

These light afflictions, which endure for a moment, shall work but for me *a far more exceeding and eternal weight of glory.* I would be very grateful for another letter from you. My wounds are healing. *Farewell.* God will surely attend to his own cause in the best possible way and time, and he will not forget the work of his own hands.

Your friend,

JOHN BROWN

William Harrison, *alias* Albert Hazlett, was surrendered from Carlisle, Pennsylvania to the authorities of Virginia, upon the requisition of Governor Wise, as implicated in the Harper's Ferry troubles. He left for Virginia at 3:00 PM Saturday afternoon, November 5, *via* Chambersburg.

If the information was reliable, Hazlett, one of the insurgents was well known in Pennsylvania. It was said by some there that they claimed to be cognizant of the fact that Hazlett was reared in Westmoreland County, and that some years ago was employed in the capacity of a boat man on the Pennsylvania Canals. While so engaged he was intrusted with the care of a section boat belonging to one John McGovern. During one trip, when he reached his destination on the other side of the mountain, he disposed of the boat and team and pocketed the proceeds. He was afterwards arrested, but the matter was doubtless adjusted by the disgorging of the money, as he never came to trial.

His next appearance was in connection with a band of horse thieves, one of whose depredations were committed near Wilmore, in this county, and as such was arrested, but upon turning state's evidence and giving testimony against his confederates, during their trial at Elmira, New York, he was discharged, and again appeared in this part of the country. While here he expressed his intention of leaving for parts unknown, as he feared the vengeance of those whom he had betrayed into the hands of justice. Shortly after this he departed, and was lost sight of until he turned up as one of the desperadoes led on by the infamous John Brown at Harper's Ferry, where he was reported as shot and killed, after cowardly taking to the water and imploring for life.

The article to which the subjoined letter replies appeared in the Philadelphia *Inquirer* of the 26th of October last, and contained the following extract:

> Mr. Charles J. Faulkner was one of the lawyers assigned as counsel for the prisoners. He denied the right of the court to assign counsel, and said that he could not enter upon the defense on such short notice, as it would, "indeed, *be a mockery of justice*." Mr. Faulkner having said this, there can be no misinterpretation of our motives when we declare that we *echo* the opinion.

The following letter from Mr. Charles Faulkner not only afforded a denial of the remarks therein attributed to him, but was a reply to the entire article:

> Boydsville, near Martinsburg, Saturday, Nov. 5, 1859.

> DEAR SIR: Your favor of yesterday has been received, inclosing to me a copy of the Philadelphia *Inquirer,* containing nearly a column of comments upon a remark which the editor ascribes to me as having been made when I declined to act as counsel for John Brown and others, charged with treason, murder, and an attempt to excite to insurrection our slaves. No such remark ever fell from my lips. And it is a striking illustration of editorial license, that he should attribute any such language to me, in the face of the telegraphic report of my remarks contained in the same paper, embraced in an authentic account of the proceedings of the cause, and which contradict every idea that he imputes to me.

> So far from having declined to act as counsel for the prisoners, because of the haste with which the examining court was held, or because I believed the trial under the circumstances to be a mere mockery of justice, I feel free

to say that I have never in the course of my life witnessed an examination which was entered upon and conducted with more deliberation and decorum, and with a more sacred regard to all the safeguards and requirements which the humane system of our criminal law throws around the life and liberty of the accused, than was extended to those wicked disturbers of our peace. And the reasons which the examining court gave why they determined to assign me as counsel for the prisoners, but which I do not regard it proper for me to detail, would, if disclosed, be additional evidence of the determination of that tribunal to exercise the high responsibilities which devolved upon it, with the most scrupulous regard to the reputation of the court, and to the honor and dignity of the state.

As the circumstances under which I was assigned by the court as counsel have nowhere been fully stated, nor my reasons for declining to act on the trial, and as they have been the subject of some misrepresentation in one of the Baltimore Opposition papers, and you request, as a friend, to know them, I will state them to you with circumstantial precision.

My residence, as you are aware, is by railroad 28 miles from Charlestown, the place of trial, and about 17 miles across the county. I made a visit to that place on Monday, the 24th of last month, to attend to some chancery business, not intending to remain more than two days, and having, after that time, urgent and imperative engagements elsewhere. Shortly after the prisoners were conducted to the court house on Tuesday morning, to undergo their examinations preliminary to a regular trial, and while I was standing in the street, Mr. Botts, an able and promising young lawyer of Charlestown, called upon me, and informed me that the examining court had decided to assign me, in conjunction with himself, to act as counsel for the prisoners. I promptly expressed to Mr. Botts my objections to the position. He told me the magistrates were all upon the bench, and that I had better go into the court house and see them. I did so, and in a private interview with the members of the court, stated my objections to the position they proposed to assign me. My objections were overruled by the court, and in a few moments afterwards I was, by the president of the court, assigned to act in conjunction with Mr. Botts in the defense of the prisoners. This preliminary examination was closed in a few hours, and the prisoners remanded to jail to await their regular trial before the circuit court, then in session at Charlestown.

In the evening of the same day Judge Parker informed me that if the counsel expected from abroad had not arrived in time to act on behalf of the prisoners, that he would assign Mr. Botts and myself to appear in their defense. This caused me to state to Judge Parker, more at length than I had done to the examining court, the reasons which rendered it inconvenient to me, and improper in itself for the court to assign, or for me to accept, the position of counsel for the prisoners at their regular trial.

I stated to him that I was then upon a brief visit, to that place, with urgent and imperative engagements elsewhere; that the prisoners would each ask, and be entitled to, separate trials, which would occupy some ten days or two weeks, and that I could not, without great inconvenience to myself, and disregard of existing engagements elsewhere, spend that time in the County of Jefferson; that I thought the duty should be devolved upon some of the resident members of the bar of Charlestown and its vicinity, among whom were to be found many able and experienced lawyers.

He referred to the fact that I had (under protest, however) appeared as counsel and cross-examined the witnesses in the examining court. I said that was true, but I had been assured that the examination would occupy but a few hours, and besides it was but a mere preliminary proceeding, involving none of the results and responsibilities of a regular trial—a proceeding very often waived by the prisoners themselves, and of no practical importance in view of their speedy trial; and that while I felt there was some objection to my appearing as counsel even in that preliminary examination, still the objections were not of so grave a character as they would be to my appearance in a trial involving the lives and liberties of the prisoners. I then stated to him the facts growing out of my antecedent relation to the transaction, which rendered it inexpedient and improper for the court to assign me as counsel at the regular trial.

These facts were: that I, as one of the citizens of Virginia, had on Monday, with arms in my hands, repaired to the scene of the disturbance to aid in repulsing the invasion, and the punishment of the perpetrator of this outrage upon our peace and security; that I had on Tuesday freely and publicly expressed my opinion of their guilt and of the summary punishment which should follow their crime; that on Wednesday I was engaged with Governor Wise in the examination of witnesses, papers and other evidences of guilt found upon the persons or in the recent possession of the prisoners, and in advising the preliminary steps for the prosecution of the offenders; that I had heard from the lips of Brown and Stevens a full confession of their criminal acts, and criminal motives of action; and that, upon the basis of their own admissions, as well as what I had seen, I had freely and publicly expressed my opinion of their guilt, and of the just punishment that awaited their crimes;

that my feelings and declarations would utterly disqualify me as a juror, and with my high estimate of the relation of counsel and client, they would equally disqualify me from acting as counsel for the prisoners.

Judge Parker conceded that my objections were perfectly satisfactory and conclusive, and, with his full approval of my course, I left Charlestown by train on Wednesday morning before the bills of indictment were brought in by the grand jury.

The reasons given by the examining court and by Judge Parker why they desired to assign me the position of counsel, I shall not state; but they were honorable to the court and judge, and honorable to me.

Very truly yours,

CHARLES J. FAULKNER

To M. W. Cluskey, Esq., Washington City.

Edwin Coppoc wrote his parents over the week-end from the Charlestown jail as follows:

CHARLESTOWN, Nov. 5th, 1859.

DEAR MOTHER AND FATHER: It is with much sorrow that I now address you, and under very different circumstances than I ever expected to be placed, but I have seen my folly too late and must now suffer the consequences, which I suppose will be death, but which I shall try and bear as every man should; though it would be a source of much comfort to me to have died at home. It has always been my desire, that, when I came to die, my last breath should be among my friends; that in my last moments they could be near me to console me. But alas! such is not my fate. I am condemned and must die a dishonorable death, among my enemies, and hundreds of miles from home.

I hope you will not reflect on me for what I have done, for I am not at fault, at least my conscience tells me so, and there are others that feel as I do. We were led into it by those that ought to have known better, but who did not anticipate any danger; but after stopping at Harper's Ferry we were surrounded and compelled to fight, to save our own lives, for we saw our friends falling on all sides. Our leader would not surrender and there seemed to be no other resort than to fight, though I am happy to say that no one fell by my hand, and am sorry to say that I was ever induced to raise a gun. I was not looking for such a thing. I am sorry, very sorry, that such has been the case. Never did I suppose that my hand would be guilty of raising a gun against my fellow men. After our capture, which was on the morning of the 18th, we were kept there until the evening of the 19th when we were removed to this place, where we have been ever since. We are well cared for. The jailer seems to do all he can to make us comfortable.

November 6th.—I have just finished a letter to Mr. Painter, which I expect to send out tomorrow with this. I sent one yesterday to Doctor Gill, stating to him that it was not worth while for any of you to come, but on thinking more about it, I concluded that I would like to see some one from there, so tomorrow I intend to telegraph for the doctor to come.

I have written J. Painter and told him what to do with my land, but whatever money is spent by anyone coming here, I wish to have it replaced out of the land.

The captain has had some apple pies and preserves sent him from Ohio, by some friends. I presume they do not go bad though I have not had a taste.

If the Doctor has not started when this gets there, and you have any sweet cakes or other nick-nacks, just send them along. They will go very good here between the iron bars. We get plenty to eat here, but *it is not from home.* It is not baked by the hands of those we love at home, or by those whom I never expect to see.

I don't feel like writing more. I hope and trust the doctor will come, and if anything is in the way so he cannot come, I hope some one else will come in his stead. I believe I have nothing more to say. This may be the last letter you may get from me. If it is, think of me as one who thought he was doing right.

Give my love to Brigss' and Maxsons' folks and to all inquiring friends for such I feel I have a large circle, and I trust that what I have done will not make them enemies. My love to all the family.

No more,

EDWIN COPPOC

The Reverend James Freeman Clark, of Boston, made the Harper's Ferry business the topic of his sermon on Sunday; November 6th, availing himself of the text, "And Herod feared John, knowing he was just a man." (Mark, VI., 20) In the course of his remarks, he related the following anecdote illustrative of Brown's strict and impartial sense of justice: "Some years ago, when living in Western Pennsylvania, or on the Ohio Reserve John Brown found a man whom he believed a horse-thief. He had him arrested and taken to jail. The man was convicted and sent to prison. But while he was in prison, Brown furnished that man's family with provisions and clothing. The man had committed a crime, and Brown's sense of justice required that he should be punished. His wife and children had not, and Brown's sense of justice would not allow them to be punished for another's fault. The man who told this story to my brother-in-law is now deputy-sheriff in Crawford County, and was at that time a boy in Brown's family, and was himself sent to town to buy flour, etc., and carry it to the house of the convict."

The Richmond *Enquirer* of Monday, November 7th presented the following statements:

The sympathy that has been enlisted for the Charlestown prisoners, has overstepped the bounds of wise discretion, and, in assailing the State of Virginia, her people and executive, has defeated its object.

The trial has been denounced as begun too soon, and conducted with "indecent haste." What is the great fundamental principle of "criminal prosecutions" as embodied in the Constitution of the United States, and the Bill of Rights of the several states of this Union? "A Speedy Trial by an Impartial Jury" is demanded by the Bill of Rights of twenty-five states in the American Union—and the amendment of the Federal Constitution also provides, in the words of George Mason's Bill of Rights, for a "SPEEDY TRIAL." The universal presumption of innocence on the part of the accused demands a "speedy trial"—and, until the mawkish sympathy recently manufactured in the North began its preaching of "indecent haste," a "speedy trial" was esteemed the guaranteed right of the accused, to have denied which would have been in violation of our own Bill of Rights.

Fanatical love for the criminal, now designates a "speedy trial" as conducted with "indecent haste," and endeavors to compromise the dignity and justice of Virginia with insinuations against her courts of justice. Such conduct is not calculated to allay the excited feelings of Virginia, or to temper justice with mercy; nor does such sentiments and conduct tend to reconcile an injured people with the Union. It serves no good end—either to the prisoners, the country, nor the Northern people—and the sooner returning reason asserts her sway the better for all, for the prisoner, the government and the people.

John Brown has had his just rights, "speedy trial by an impartial jury;" he has had the "nature and cause of his accusation" explained to him; he has been "confronted with his accusers and witnesses;" he has had all the "evidence in his favor" that he desired. By the "unanimous consent of an impartial jury" he has been "found guilty;" he was not "compelled to give evidence against himself;" nor was his voluntary confession used upon his trial; but he will be "deprived of his life by the law of the land and the judgment of his peers."

Thus every right secured "in criminal prosecutions" by our "Bill of Rights" has been freely and fully extended to the prisoner; and that prisoner has expressed his satisfaction with the trial and all its incidents.

Shall John Brown be pardoned? The law of Virginia, chapter 17, section 18, provides—

> The governor shall not grant a pardon in any case before conviction, nor to any person convicted of treason against the commonwealth, except with the consent of the general assembly, declared by joint resolution. Neither shall he grant a reprieve to any person convicted of treason for a longer period than until the end of the session of the general assembly, during which it may be granted, or, than until the end of the succeeding session, when it is granted during the recess.

> Here, then, is an end to all pardon by the executive. He has not the power to pardon John Brown, convicted of treason. He has not the power to reprieve longer than the end of the approaching session. If John Brown is sane he ought not to be pardoned—if insane he ought not to be punished.

The Virginia Code, chapter 208, sections 16, 17 and 18, sets forth the law as follows:

16. No person shall, while he is insane, be tried for a criminal offense.

17. If a Superior Court, to which an examining court remands a person for trial, sees reasonable ground to doubt his sanity at the time at which, but for such doubt, he would be tried, it shall suspend the trial, until the jury inquire into the fact as to such insanity. Such jury shall be impaneled at its bar. If the jury find the accused to be sane at the time of their verdict, they shall make no other inquiry, and the trial in chief shall proceed. If they find that he is insane, they shall inquire whether or not he was so at the time of the alleged offense. If they find that he was so at that time, the court may dismiss the prosecution; and either discharge him, or, to prevent his doing mischief, remand him to jail, and order him to he removed thence to one of the lunatic asylums of the state. If they find that he was not so, at that time, the court shall commit him to jail, or order him to be confined in one of said asylums, until he is so restored that he can be put upon his trial.

18. *If,* after conviction, and before sentence of any person, the court sees reasonable ground to doubt his insanity, it may impanel a jury to inquire into the fact of his sanity, and sentence him, or commit him to jail, or to a lunatic asylum, according as the jury may find him to be insane or sane.

Thus by the laws of Virginia *an insane man cannot be tried*; the plea of insanity arrests the trial for guilt, and the jury must first ascertain the fact of sanity. Should the insanity not be discovered until after "conviction and before sentenced," the 18th section provides the relief. But, should sentence have been passed, relief may still be had, by a postponement of the execution by the Executive, until the question of sanity is definitely ascertained.

If John Brown, in the opinion of any persons, be not sane, we hope they will not fail to institute proceedings for the trial of the fact of sanity. If those persons who now profess to believe him insane are sincere, they will not fail to institute the necessary proceedings. *All hopes of executive clemency should be abandoned, for, as we have shown, the executive, if he had the disposition, has not the power.*"

The Baltimore *American* of November 7th said: "Mrs. Mary A. Brown, wife of Captain John Brown, now under sentence of death at Charlestown, Va., arrived in this city yesterday morning, from Philadelphia, intending to start for Harper's Ferry on the train this morning. In the course of the afternoon, however, she received a dispatch from the North, requesting her to return immediately to Philadelphia, and she left again for home on the evening train. She is about thirty-five years of age, very tall and masculine, and was evidently in great distress of mind."

In Cynthiana, Kentucky, some person originated great excitement by writing an anonymous letter to the local newspaper, forewarning the inhabitants of the town of another servile insurrection. At once a stringent police was organized to check the slightest movement on the part of the supposed conspirators, and all the pistols in the stores of the town were confiscated. Nothing further was heard of the matter until another supply of firearms was procured.

There was a considerable stir in Charlestown on Saturday, November 5th, when it was announced that Mrs. Lydia Maria Child, an authoress and poet of some repute, had arrived on the afternoon train from Boston. On inquiry it was ascertained that the lady was a Mrs. Spring, and <u>not</u> Mrs. Child. Mrs. Spring was a fine-looking lady, about fifty years of age, and dressed with much taste.[1] She was accompanied by a young man,

---

[1]   In 1851 Rebecca Spring's husband, Marcus Spring, purchased an estate the couple named Eagleswood. It was to be their primary family home as well

who represented himself as her son. He was of a very genteel appearance. Immediately after their arrival in town they proceeded to the jail and made application for admittance, which was refused. After a short consultation and several inquiries, they made their way to the residence of Mr. David Howell, one of our most wealthy and respected citizens, and a member of the Society of Friends, where the lady made known her mission and desired Mr. Howells aid in getting an interview with Brown and his fellow prisoners. She was in a very polite but candid manner informed by Mr. Howell that he would do nothing toward furthering her wishes, as he was decidedly of the opinion that she was doing no honor to the respectable society with which she claimed to be connected, by running about the country and offering her services to "nurse" and "soothe" the perpetrators of the terrible crimes of which Brown and Co. have been convicted. Nothing daunted, she made application to Dr. Mason, the physician of the jail, who informed her that permission to enter would be granted her the following day, which was the Sabbath.

When Brown was informed of her arrival, he said he did not want to see her, and immediately had a dispatch forwarded to Mrs. Child and other Northern volunteers, telling them to stay at home, and stating that, if they had any money to spare, he would prefer that his wife should have it. But Mrs. Spring visited Mr. Brown on the Sabbath, according to her appointment, accompanied by her son, and was kindly received by Brown and Stevens. She remained with them for some time, and visited them again in the afternoon. No objection was made by the state's officers to her

---

as the site of a utopian community they had long been planning. Located in Perth Amboy, New Jersey, Eagleswood became the home of the Raritan Bay Utopia in 1854. This community emphasized social progress and reform grounded in education, and included a school run by Theodore Weld. The community dissolved in 1859, but the Welds continued to manage the school and the Springs continued to live at Eagleswood in their own private mansion.

The Springs participated in abolition by using their estate as a station on the Underground Railroad. Rebecca Spring and her son Edward did indeed travel to visit John Brown in prison prior to his execution. Marcus Spring died in 1874 and the Spring family left Eagleswood in 1890.

giving the prisoners any attention she may desire, although they were being treated with the utmost possible kindness by the officers in command of the jail. Considerable suspicion was aroused towards the young man who professed to be her son. It was thought that he might actually have been a brother of the prisoner, Stevens, and had availed himself of this *ruse* to obtain an interview.

The excitement in regard to the trial of the Harper's Ferry conspirators continued even as fair progress was made by the court in the disposal of cases. The case of Copeland, the free Negro, was brought to a close on Saturday afternoon, November 5th, the jury finding a verdict of not guilty of treason, as charged in the first count of the indictment, he not being recognized as a citizen; and guilty of conspiracy with slaves to rebel, and of murder, as charged in the second and third counts. The case was ably argued by Andrew Hunter, Esq., on behalf of the state. The prisoner was defended by George Sennott, of Boston, who labored with much zeal for his client. A bill of exceptions, and a motion for arrest of judgment were entered by the prisoner's counsel, and will be disposed of the next morning.

The court assembled at 10:00 AM on Monday, and was called to order by Judge Parker. The grand jury was then sworn and immediately proceeded to their room, to consider the case of Captain Cook. A number of witnesses were summoned, and the jury were absent about two hours. On the reassembling of the court, Mr. Harding, the prosecuting attorney, stated that as a number of the witnesses in the case of Cook, who would not be in the Stephens case, were present, he would, if agreeable to the counsel on the other side, move to take up the case of Cook first.

Thomas C. Green, Esq., one of the counsels for Cook, said that he had not yet had time to read the indictment, and had not yet decided what plea to enter to the charge. He was unable to proceed in the case, and would prefer that the commonwealth should proceed with the case of Stephens, which would allow them time to prepare for the case of Cook.

A. D. Stephens was accordingly brought into court and placed upon a mattress. He looked pale and haggard; his abstinence from food and the large quantity of medicine taken by him having had a decided effect. But it was observed that he seemed to bear his wounds with much fortitude and was seldom heard to murmur. His counsel, Mr Sennott (who had endeavored to have his trial moved to an adjoining county but was refused) appeared, and the impaneling of the jury proceeded. After a considerable number of jurymen had been obtained, Mr. Hunter arose and said that he had just received a dispatch which would probably interfere with the further proceedings in impaneling a jury. He then read the following telegraphic dispatch from Governor Wise:

RICHMOND, Nov. 7, 1859.

ANDREW HUNTER:

DEAR SIR: I think you had better try Cook and hand Stephens over to the federal authorities.

Respectfully,

HENRY A. WISE

Mr. Hunter stated that he has for several days been in correspondence with Governor Wise, and had in his possession a number of facts important to the development of this case, which were unknown to the public, and which would for the present remain so. He had, since his last letter to the governor, come into possession of other facts which pointed to Stephens as the most available party to be handed over to the federal authorities, as he *felt assured that enough would be ascertained to result in bringing before the federal bar, a number of the prominent abolition fanatics in the North.*

Mr. Harding objected to these proceedings, and insisted that the case should be proceeded with. He was not in league with Governor Wise or anyone else, and was not fed by any one. He would only receive as a compensation for his arduous labors the small pittance allowed by the circuit court.

Mr. Sennott remarked that he had not consulted with his client, and as the jury had partly been chosen he would not consent that the state should hand the prisoner over to the government. For what purpose it was to be done was known to Governor Wise, and had been foreshadowed by the remarks of Mr. Hunter. If time had been allowed him the trouble had in impaneling the jury would have been dispensed with. Mr. Hunter then would proceed immediately with the case of Stephens, and hand over the prisoner, Hazlett, who has not yet been indicted, to the federal court. It was immaterial to him whether Stephens would prefer a trial or not.

Mr. Sennott then asked a delay of a moment for consultation with Stephens, after which he announced that the prisoner accepted the offer of the state to hand him over to the federal authority, and would, therefore, prefer to be remanded to jail. Mr. Harding desired the clerk to enter his earnest protest against the whole proceedings. He considered the proceedings wrong, and wished it to be shown on the docket.

Judge Parker told the clerk, "Do no such thing. I wish no such protest entered on the docket of this court." The prisoner was then handed over to United States Marshal Martin, and lodged in jail, where he would remain until the term of the federal court at Staunton, which would not meet for some time.

The jury was then discharged, and a large number of freeholders of the court were summoned to appear the next morning at 9:00 AM, when the case of Cook would be taken up. Cook was defended by J. E. MacDonald, Attorney-General, and Mr. Voorhies, District-Attorney, of Indiana, and Messrs. Lawson Botts and Thomas C. Green, of our own Bar. The prosecution was conducted by Andrew Hunter, Esq. The prisoner seemed to be in fine spirits, and not without hope of a verdict in his favor. Governor Willard and Mr. Crowley, his brothers-in-law, would be present during the entire trial.

The governor of Virginia was determined that the *"irrepressible conflict,"* which he so much delighted to denounce, should not be suffered to die away because its sponsor, Mr. Seward, chose to turn his back upon American politics and disport himself for a while among the pyramids of Egypt and over the sands of the desert. Mr. Wise either possessed, or fancied that he possessed, the cipher of a mighty conspiracy against the peace and dignity of the Union, and he was bent upon pursuing the dread secret of which he had caught a glimpse through all the ramifications of the Republican labyrinth.

The New York *Times* of November 9, 1859 had this to say in an article titled "Too Much Zeal:"

> On Monday, November 7th the case of Andrew Stevens, one of John Browns lieutenants, was on the point of being tried, when Mr. Hunter, the prosecuting attorney, interrupted the proceedings by stating that he had received a telegram from Governor Wise, requesting him to reserve Stevens for trial by the federal authorities. This condescension to a government which Mr. Wise's organ, the Richmond *Enquirer*, had so vehemently assailed as effete, incapable and unworthy of receiving any consideration from the commonwealth of Virginia, was speedily explained by Mr. Hunter. On a mere question of convicting and hanging the culprits actually in her grasp, the Old Dominion needs no help from the Union. If necessary she could, no doubt, find a headsman to decapitate and executioners to draw and quarter these high-traitors in the old chivalric fashion. But there are other victims whom Governor Wise desires to sacrifice, and these can only he readied through the national executive. The federal courts are, therefore, to be charged with the duty of listening to the revelations of at least one of the Harper's Ferry insurgents, in order that the president may take steps for securing the arrest and punishment of certain distinguished Northern

accomplices of John Brown. Stevens was at first selected for the honor of swinging from a national gibbet; and when Mr. Hunter showed a disposition to relegate that opportunity to another of the prisoners, Stevens loudly urged his claims, and finally succeeded in procuring his deliverance from the short shrift of the sitting jury, before him. The proceedings against Cook at once began; and Stevens awaits the action of the national authorities.

This new feature in the pending state trials will attest, of course, very general attention. If it should prove eventually that the expectations with which Stevens has been reserved to act as a conductor between the national feeling and the electrifying revelations which Governor Wise so confidently awaits, are as baseless as the charges originally fished up from the recesses of Colonel Forbes's famous carpetbag, the indefatigable agitator of Virginia will find himself playing a very undesirable part before the country. It is no light thing to assume the responsibility of urging accusations against prominent Northern statesmen, which all rational men must be very slow to entertain seriously. And if (as we by no means wish even remotely to hint) this formal expansion of the "plot" and its implications has been attempted mainly to support a preconcerted course of political and partisan intrigues, the experiment will not be likely, by its results, to encourage the inventors to a repetition. The feeling of the Northern people, as we have repeatedly taken occasion of late to show, is just now particularly friendly to the South, and particularly hostile to all superfluous political disturbers of our common peace. But the Northern people cannot be expected to take any special pleasure in listening to vague and sweeping accusations of treason against Northern public men of standing and character; and unless these accusations are to be really sustained by something more presentable than the wild inferences by which alone up to this time they have been connected with the names of various prominent leaders of one great political party in the North, the irritating process of turning them over and over before the whole country in a federal court can do nothing but harm.

Governor Wise, and his sensationist friends in the North as well as in the South, appears to us to be in very great danger of disregarding the diplomatic maxim which forbids all excess even in the most political zeal.

They could hardly do their partisan antagonists a better service, than to interrupt the general and decided crystallization of the national sentiment in regard to the nature and tendency of the strictly sectional opposition to the slave-power, by attacking individual men with charges of complicity in purposes which the whole North indignantly repudiate. This is a case in which a single failure on the part of the government to maintain its allegations will outweigh in mischievous results all the good that can be looked for from a dozen victories.

It may be important to bring "prominent abolition fanatics before the Federal Bar." But we venture to think it decidedly more important to bring the principles and mainsprings of the political agitation which alone invests the said fanatics with a transient power, calmly and dispassionately before the bar of public opinion. And this is assuredly not to be done by clamorous exaggerations, pompous mystifications, or a perpetually rising tide of passionate invective.

Chapter 7

A TIMELY DISCOURSE ON THE VIRGINIA INSURRECTION

*T*HE *HONORABLE JOSHUA* R. *Giddings,*[1] *of Ohio, delivered a discourse Friday evening, October 28, 1859, at the National Guard Hall in Philadelphia on the subject of the "Harper's Ferry Insurrection, and John Brown, of Osawatomie," before a large audience. The applause was frequent and emotionally expressive.*

There is at this time an unusual excitement in the community. One week ago nineteen men invaded the Old Dominion, captured two thousand of her inhabitants, and sent consternation throughout her vast territory. Her governor has taken the field in person, called out her military forces, and placed arms and troops at all available points. Maryland, too, has supplied her quota of men and arms; while the President of the United States has ordered such portions of our army as were within convenient distance, to repair to the scene of conflict, and placed the militia in the District of Columbia in active service, to protect the public property. He has also placed arms and ammunition in the city hall, to be used in case of emergency.

---

[1]   Joshua Giddings, an anti-slavery congressman for twenty-one years from Ohio's Western Reserve testified that during the summer of 1859 John Brown had appeared at public meetings throughout the Reserve asking for public funds.

The invading force is nearly all slain—perhaps four of them still remain alive, but they are nearly dead of wounds. Others have fled, and probably all are by this time prisoners. Yet, even in this city, and in several states, there appears to be a degree of excitement and consternation. It is, in truth, the first instance in which any number of white men have combined for the purpose of giving freedom to the slaves of our nation.

Such visions have long been foretold. More than seventy years ago, Mr. Jefferson pointed his country to the time when this condition of things must take place, and solemnly warned them that in such a contest, God had no attribute that would enable Him to take sides with the slaveholder. Nearly twenty years later, Mr. Adams, said with prophetic assurance that the day of the deliverance of the slave *must* come. Whether it came in peace or in blood, he could not tell, but let *it come*.

The sympathy of the Christian world is with the slave. For their liberation our ministers and Christians pray, our statesmen labor, and their freedom is the subject of desire with all candid, intelligent men, and all feel unwilling to see their freedom stained with blood. Men of age and of experience look coolly upon these facts. They should not be moved, nor permit themselves to become excited. I deplore the loss of human life as deeply as any man. I never witness human woe, nor can I look upon human suffering without being moved; and yet I would not ask for the slave, nor for the master, for Brown nor for his fellow-citizens, anything more, nor anything less, than justice.

This interesting incident in our country's history stands connected with some well-defined cause. The subject which excited the invaders to action is unmistakably set forth in the accounts we have received. The institution of slavery was the moving cause. Whether Brown and his men are as guilty as they are represented, or not, their object seems to have been the liberation of the slaves of that region. Pennsylvania had slaves. She emancipated them, and now enjoys the quiet and prosperity consequent upon her justice. Virginia retains her slaves, and is consequently subjected to annoyance. Thus cause and effect are always connected.

I make these remarks to show the certainty with which every effect may be traced to its appropriate cause. Unthinking men seldom trace events to their remote origin. This event may be as clearly traced to the exciting cause as any other event of the present age. If we ascribe the cause, we cannot fail to see clearly the remedy. In order to properly trace out the more remote, as well as the proximate causes of this lamentable occurrence, it seems necessary to allude to some historic facts, and to some important, immutable principles.

Virginia held slaves while she was a colony. From the landing of the first Dutch ship in 1620, with her small cargo of human chattels, the Old Dominion has cherished this peculiar institution up to this very day. All the other colonies held slaves until after the close of the Revolution.

At the formation of the federal government a new doctrine was adopted. The Declaration of Independence became the bond of the Union, and by that it was agreed that the new government should be *free*, each state holding its slavery subject to the will of its own people, without reference to the federal organization. At the adoption of the constitution, the states each retained the entire and supreme power over the institution within its own territory, having the right to abolish it at pleasure, and to consecrate its soil and its institutions to freedom. I do not intend to argue this point. I merely lay them down as incontrovertible principles. I, therefore, assert that each state may at pleasure establish liberty within its limits, and that no other power has any right to interfere. Pennsylvania has the undoubted right to be free, while Virginia has the power and privilege to maintain her slavery.

Another proposition I lay down as incontrovertible is that every attempt of the federal government to involve the people of Pennsylvania or any other free state, in the expense, the crime or disgrace of slavery, constitutes an over-stepping of its legitimate, and its constitutional powers.

In saying this, I am certainly aware that Virginia, and all the slave states deny this proposition, and insist that although we had the right to abolish slavery in our own states, we are nevertheless bound to aid them to uphold it in Virginia. I am aware that this now constitutes the great issue between political parties. But I repeat, it is no part of my present purpose to argue these points. It is sufficient for my present purpose to say that nearly all of our people of the free states maintain and believe the doctrine as I have laid it down—that our obligation to defend the slave states against invasion or domestic violence, has no more reference to slavery than to her imprisoned offenders.

Perhaps, for the better illustration of my subject, I ought to say that, through the constitution, Pennsylvania and all the states covenanted with each other to surrender fugitive slaves, and to grant to the citizens of each state all the immunities and privileges of citizens of the several states. Both these covenants have proved inconvenient. The slave states say they cannot grant to the colored citizens of our own free states the same immunities and privileges which their own citizens enjoy without endangering the institution of slavery. That is doubtless true. Neither can the free states seize and return fugitive slaves without establishing slavery to that extent within their own territories. The covenants are mutual and dependent. If one be performed, both doubtless will be. If one be violated, the other ought not to be performed. I do not argue this point. I lay it down as a plain proposition, saying that the people of the free states generally believe it. This belief of the great body of our people is the predicate from which I draw deductions.

I certainly hazard nothing in saying that the people of all the free states desire to do their duty towards each other, and are willing that each state shall enjoy all its constitutional privileges, and that patriotism demands that they shall maintain their own rights and the rights of these states.

Pennsylvania and other states have abolished the institution, her people desiring to be free and entirely purified from the contagion of oppression. However individuals may labor to subject her people to the support of slavery from political or interested motives. I hesitate to say that nine-tenths of her citizens, of all parties, wish to be entirely separated and divorced from any and from all participation in the support of slavery, and this is the prevailing sentiment in all the free states.

It is certain that a strong feeling of dissatisfaction exists throughout all the free and most of the slave states. Indeed, the term *dissatisfaction* does not express the popular feeling. In some of our Northern states it has risen to that of *indignation* against those who have prostituted and are now prostituting the influence and power of our government to the support and extension of slavery instead of freedom—to invade the rights of the free states instead of maintaining the rights of all the states. This feeling has been produced by the constant encroachments upon the rights of the free states for many years. One outrage after another has been perpetrated, each exciting remark, denunciation and deeper feeling, until they culminated in the despotism exerted in Kansas, and the murders committed there. There they drove Brown and his associates to that desperation which will long mark an era in our political history. This is not the time to speak of Brown and his companions. Those who most bitterly assail his movements speak of him more highly than I could at this time. I must speak for the future. I must not unnecessarily excite feeling on the one hand, nor omit important truths on the other.

Most of Brown's companions are dead, at least the more fortunate among them have departed. The others will, probably, soon follow. Their sad fate will occupy a brief page in the history of our nation. Those who yet survive seem to have anticipated this result, and are now waiting its consummation. I recall an instance of somewhat similar character. When the Africans of Algiers seized and enslaved Americans, we sent an army and a navy to butcher them, declaring them unworthy of existence. While our fleet lay off the port of Algiers a large ship was in sight lying under the protection of the guns of that immense fortress. The American commander proposed to send a boat for the purpose of blowing up the ship. The plans were laid, arrangements were perfected, and at the silent hour of midnight about twenty men solemnly and silently shook hands with their companions, entered the boat and struck out boldly to capture an immense ship, in order to liberate their fellow-men from bondage. They *died; not one returned*. Their plan was ill-conceived, and it failed, but their motives were sublime, and we honor their memories.

Right and wrong are immutable. If slavery were wrong then it is now. If it were wrong for Africans to enslave Americans, it is no less wrong for Americans to enslave Africans. In all our words, and thoughts, and actions, we should ever keep in view those attributes of Deity—*Truth* and *Justice*. I never look upon human woe without emotion. I deplore the loss of life as deeply as any person can, and yet I would not ask for Brown nor his associates aught but justice; nor would I withhold justice from the slave nor from his master.

I proceed to call attention to some of the causes which have produced the present feeling in the free states. In 1801 Congress passed the law which sustained the slave-trade in the District of Columbia to this very day. The people of the free states appear to have been unconscious of the national dishonor until John Randolph, of Roanoke, himself a slaveholder, called attention to it, and, in his own nervous style of eloquence, denounced it, declaring it *inhuman* and *disgraceful* saying he would expose it at his own expense if Congress refused to assist him. He was the first man who appears to have been excited to indignation by a traffic which continues at our seat of government to this very day.

John Minor, of Pennsylvania, (I am honored by his memory.) next made an official report in regard to this traffic, which aroused the Quakers and other religious people, and that body next became excited, and adopted gag-rules suppressing the right of petition in regard to this slave-trade, and all other matters relating to slavery, prohibiting all debate on those subjects.

This outrage aroused a large portion of our people who were anxious to maintain the constitutional right of petition and the freedom of debate, as well as the rights of the free states, although they took but little interest in the subject of humanity.

Among the prominent men of our nation, John Quincy Adams stood forth as the leader among the advocates for the right of petition. He denounced the gag-rules; said they were a violation of the constitution, and called on the people to stand forth in defense of their rights. He did not, like some of the statesmen of the present day, say it was *a law,* although unconstitutional, and must be obeyed until repealed. He declared the gag-rules to be no law, deserving no respect. He trampled upon them—he abhorred them. Throughout all the free states the people sympathized with him, and when he was arraigned and tried for presenting a respectful petition of the people, the whole population of our free states were deeply moved.

It was the fortune of your humble speaker to mingle in those scenes. I was constrained to sit in that hall with my lips sealed upon the great truths on which our government was based. I then declared the doctrine which for two hundred years had been uttered by all Christian writers, that human governments are limited in their legitimate powers to the support of human rights, and that they neither have nor can have any just powers to rob the humblest individual who treads the earth of the life or the liberty which God has given him. Conscious of the correctness of this position, and believing that every act of any government which attempts to invade this natural law is despotic and void and that it should be so treated by officers and people, I did what I could in a humble way, to direct the public mind to the support of these self-evident truths.

(Owing to the delinquency of the messenger to whom the package was intrusted, the talk ended at this point. The telegraph, however, supplied briefly the close of this address.)

Alluding to the prisoner on trial at Charlestown, Virginia, Mr. Giddings stated that he had invited Brown to Jefferson County, Ohio, where he delivered a lecture one Sunday, after church, relating to his adventures in Kansas. After the lecture Mr. Giddings had prompted the audience to contribute relief to the lecturer. Afterwards, Brown took tea at his residence, where, as may readily be preconceived, the conversation turned to slavery. Though Brown did not say he intended to visit the slave states to free slaves, Mr. Giddings inferred he would do so, if opportunity offered, mainly from his having practiced that business in Missouri. These were the only times Mr. Giddings saw Brown; and he asserts that neither in his lecture nor in his conversation did Brown refer to any assistants or associates. No mention was made of a Harper's Ferry or Virginia organization, or of a provisional government. He acknowledged giving three dollars to Brown's son towards the necessities of his father, after the rescue of Doy from the kidnappers, a matter in which Mr. Giddings acknowledged taking strong interest. In bestowing this gratuity, he had little idea that it would be used in fitting out an expedition to capture Harper's Ferry, to effect the conquest of the Old Dominion, to strike terror to the executive, or to imperil the government. To use the emphatic language of the speaker, *"I never at any time heard of his being, or intending to be, in Virginia. I never heard from him, nor from any person, his aim or intentions connected with that state, or with Harper's Ferry, and when I read the account of his long residence there, I was as much astonished as any other man."*

Mr. Giddings concluded his remarks as follows: These despotic acts have aroused the spirit of the people, and there is, in serious truth, an *"irrepressible conflict"* now in progress. It is that irrepressible conflict between freedom and slavery, which has been in progress for centuries. It is one of those revolutions which never go backward. Our statesmen have misapprehended the philosophy of free governments. They have attempted to rule a free people by brute force, instead of a just administration of legitimate powers. They have preferred the crime of slavery to the God-given rights of liberty. They have trampled upon the rights of our free states to obtain political favor with the slave power.

They have stained the soil of our free states with innocent blood. Men are captured in our Northern villages, their limbs manacled, and they are carried to slavery as though our territory lay upon the African coast, subjected to the pollution of slave-dealing pirates, while the Stars and Stripes, those emblems of liberty, are prostituted to the protection of an execrable commerce in human flesh.

The indignation of our people is awakened. In some localities it is intense. Let no man mistake or belittle that feeling. It has long been foreseen. All reflecting men knew it must come. In fifteen years I have constantly pointed it out to Southern men. Recent events will increase and strengthen it. Let those in power understand it cannot be trifled with. Let timid men keep silent. Let demagogues no longer sneer nor threaten. The time for intimidation is gone by. All must see that if the cause of the excitement continues the excitement will not cease. But of the future I will no longer speak. It is written upon the tablet of Heaven. It is read in every circumstance around us. All must see that the men now in power are incompetent to the duties of their station. If they continue to guide the ship of state, all must be lost. Let them retire. Let the past policy of the government be abandoned. Let the despotic acts alluded to be repeated. Let the free states be placed upon an equality with the slave states. Let our territory be consecrated to freedom. Let us cease to maintain a piratical commerce in the bodies of men and women. Let our federal government be purified from the contagion of slavery. Let us leave that institution where the constitution left it, "with the states" in which it exists.

I repeat, the people of the free states will not support it. They will not be involved in its crimes or its disgrace. Our emancipation from the slave power must come, and in the words of my illustrious and lamented friend, John Quincy Adams, let me say, "**It will come**; whether in peace or in blood I knew not—but whether in peace or in blood, **let it come!**"

Chapter 8

HENRY WARD BEECHER'S SERMON

*M*R *HENRY WARD Beecher, in his sermon at the Plymouth Church in Brooklyn, New York, on Sunday evening, October 29, 1859 spoke as follows about the Harper's Ferry outbreak:*

I avail myself of the present state of our land to utter some sentiments on the subject of slavery, though I have not done so for a considerable time. The nation is now greatly excited, and deeply concerned about the recent sudden and unexpected attack at Harper's Ferry. Seventeen white men, without organization, without a military basis of operations; without the countenance or approval of any legal or deliberative body, most unexpectedly and openly attack an entire state to release and rescue an enslaved race. They were not called upon by the sufferers, nor expected even by them. They undertake all themselves. Yes, these seventeen white men summoned two thousand people to surrender to them, and they did as they were required and these seventeen men held them all in durance for two full days. They waited until the forces of two states were massed to release them. I do not wonder that the Virginians feel humiliated. Every one feels for them. No one doubts the bravery of the Virginians—not at all. (laughter) But people may be sometimes surprised and taken unawares. However this may be, it seems to us strange that this invasion of seventeen men should have caused so much alarm, so much confusion and noise.

It is no wonder the Virginians try to make the most of it. They feel ashamed of the facts, and every one is sympathizing with them. There was full enough of the matter, and I think we shan't have any more of it, or anything like it. There is something in the matter which cannot be got over, in the fact that seventeen men held two thousand people prisoners for two days. They cannot hide the significance of this single fact, do what they will. It cannot be concealed. These seventeen men invaded a state, seized upon the government armory, and held two thousand of the inhabitants of that state prisoners for two days, till two suns had risen and descended on their actions. The Virginians feel piqued, to be sure, but they only remind us of the story of the fox which got his tail cut off in a trap and then endeavored to get the other foxes to get theirs cut off in a like manner, but none of them would do it. There is something, there must be something, underlying all this, which caused two thousand Virginians to submit to the power of seventeen men till the forces of two whole states should be brought against them—till the United States forces should arrive at the scene with their artillery—till the whole South should be excited and alarmed, and till the North should wonder and sympathize. I will not say any more about this riot.

THE REVEREND HENRY WARD BEECHER

There was one who figured throughout it, however, to which some allusion should be made. An old, honest, industrious man peacefully went to settle with his family in the West. His lot was cast in Kansas. A great slave state adjoining the territory marches her armed men in among the peaceful settlers to dragoon them to uphold slavery by force of arms. They cross the boundary and subvert the laws, the order, and commence a civil war. They pollute the ballot-box, and carry destruction among the harvests and death among the quiet cultivators of the soil. There were no marines, no militia sent to oppose them—none. There were forces there, but they acted on their side; it was on the side of the wrong-doers, the invaders. It was here that Brown learned his first lesson on the slavery system; here that old man endured his first sufferings in the death of his first-born, who was dragged manacled across the country by the slavery men in the heat of a broiling sun, and afterwards beaten by inhuman officers of these men. Another son was shot down by the same men. Revolving the indignation in his mind against the system that would tolerate and countenance such cruelty and bloodshed, he is goaded by his own feelings to a mad but fixed determination to oppose it to the end of his life. And now, as he is in the depressing, the most trying circumstances, no one can fail to discover in this same old man a manly, straightforward, independent soul, which rises high above all those among whom he is at present, however insane he may be.

I shrink from the folly of the bloody fray in which he was engaged; I shrink further from the bloody fray which will follow it; but while I do, I feel that by-and-by, when people will read the record of the whole tragic scene, they will wonder at and admire the bearing of the old man who through all his misfortunes, woes and suffering, maintained a dignity and independence and a sentiment which only shines in full brilliancy when contrasted with the conduct of his accusers, who possess their reason. But one word more for those states which have powder for their cargoes. Suppose seventeen men seized the armory at Springfield, Massachusetts, do you think they would subject the inhabitants of that place; that all the militia of New York and Massachusetts and other neighboring states, and the federal troops, would have to be called out to release them and to overcome the seventeen? Do you suppose that the government would be alarmed, and that the president would have to deliberate with the Secretary of War on what was to be done? (laughter) Not at all. You cannot. You and every one else would rest satisfied that the people of Springfield would be fully able to manage the business themselves, and nobody would feel alarmed. But there is a dread hanging over the Southern states which paralyzes them on the very shadow of danger arising.

Chapter 9

THE TRIAL OF JOHN E. COOK

T HE TRIAL OF John E. Cook commenced on Tuesday, November 8th, 1859. The court room, as usual, was noisy and crowded. Governor Willard and Mr. Crowley, brothers-in-law of the prisoner, were seated beside him. He pleaded guilty to all the counts in the indictment except that of treason. The prisoner was well dressed, firm and dignified. The demurrer to the treason count was argued and overruled by the court. The jury were then sworn in, and the same questions put to them as in Brown's case. The opening speech was made by Mr. Harding. Mr. Green, for the prisoner, admitted the fact of a conspiracy with the slaves to rebel, which was punishable with death or imprisonment for life. Mr. Hunter then rose and read the confession of Cook, as written by Cook himself. There were 25 foolscap pages of it. Nothing new was revealed by it, except that he implicated Frederick Douglass and Dr. Howe, of Boston. The confession will be published in a pamphlet form for the benefit of Samuel C. Young, who was wounded at Harper's Ferry.

The following letter, received from Cook by his mother-in-law, residing in Williamsburg, New York, was released for publication:

Charlestown Jail, Virginia, Nov 6, 1859.

MY EVER DEAR WIFE AND SON: A dungeon bare confines me, a prisoner's cell is mine. Yet there are *no bars* to confine the immortal mind, and *no cell* that can shut up the gushing fountain of undying love. Distance cannot part the twining tendrils of affection, nor can Time sever the golden links of that eternal chain which binds my throbbing heart to *my life's partner* and my child.

The love I cherished for you in my hours of freedom, has grown deeper and stronger while gazing through my prison bars. Alone, within my cell, my heart is ever turning to the fond memories of its loved ones; recalling from memory's history of life; all the dear words, the loving acts, and kindly smiles of those whose deep affection here has strewn the buds of hope and promise all along the pathway of my life.

And bright upon my memory now are their loved faces beaming. But oh! amid them all, thine own is beaming brightest, with our dear child in your arms. Words have no power to tell the strength and depth of that love I bear for my boy and *thee.* Nor have they power to tell my deep regret for every harsh or ungentle word I ever gave to thee. And the memory of every unkind act, like Banquo's Ghost, is with me *now* to tell me of the wrong. But oh! for every unkind act and each ungentle word, I humbly ask forgiveness. And I feel and know thy deep devotion and thy love wilt pardon all. Forgive my errors—all my faults forgive, and love me still, although I wear a prisoner's chains.

You know that in the scheme which has resulted in the death of most of my companions, and which made me a prisoner, that I was actuated only by the tenderest feelings of sympathy and humanity. I had been led to believe, as had my comrades, that it was the daily prayer and the life-wish of the masses of the slaves for freedom. That they were groaning beneath the yoke of oppression, with no hand to aid them, or point them to the light of freedom. I knew how dear my own freedom was to me; and every sympathy of my heart was aroused for them. It had been represented to me and my comrades that when once the Banner of Freedom should be raised, they would flock to it by thousands; and that their echoing shout of Freedom would be borne by the breeze to our most Southern shore, to tell of freedom there. I gave heart and hand to a work which I deemed a noble and as holy cause. The result has proved that we were deceived; that the masses of the slaves did not wish for freedom. There was *no rallying beneath our banner.* We were left to meet the conflict all alone, to dare, and do, and die. Twelve of my comrades are sleeping now with the *damp mold over them, and five are inmates of these prison walls.* We have been deceived; but found out our error when too late. Those who are dead, died like brave men, though mistaken. Those who still live will not shame, I trust, their comrades who are gone. If they too, must die, I hope they will meet it in a way that will prove them worthy of a better fate. Let not the world judge them too harshly for whatever wrong they have done, for they but erred on the aide of sympathy and love. It was an error of their judgment, not of their hearts. *Braver men never lived: truer ones to their plighted word never were banded together.* Let the veil of charity be dropped over their errors. *Remember them only for their Spartan courage, and their fidelity to their leader.*

What my be my fate I know not, but whatever it may be, I trust that I may meet it as a brave man should—unflinchingly. There is but one thing that makes me waver, and that is the remembrance of the ties that bind me. The thoughts of *my wife and child,* of my father and mother, brothers and sisters. Did not these ties exist, I could meet my doom, whatever it might be, without a murmur. But, oh! when I think of *you and my child,* my poor heart is wrung with agony. I have no words to tell my feelings when I think of the terrible grief that this has brought on all who have loved me so fondly and so well.

Thoughts like these crush down the spirit that would sternly meet whatever doom might be in store for me, without a murmur or a word. It is a fearful struggle of despair and hope. Were I alone in the world, with none to whom this blow would be a thunder-stroke of agony, I could meet it calmly, and *my soul,* with no sin of *intention upon its robes,* could gaze unmoved upon the scaffold or the tomb.

The wrong I have done has not been one of intention. In this work, no man's blood rests upon my hands. I had no part in the death of those who were killed at the Ferry. My orders were to remove the arms from Captain Brown's house to the school house, and to guard them there. I obeyed orders to the very letter. I was anxious to know what was the cause of the firing at the Ferry, and as quick as I could go without violating the orders I received, I hurried on to learn. I found my brave comrades surrounded—saw them fired upon from every side. I contrived to draw the fire of a part of their opponents upon myself, and succeeded. I tried my best to discover some means to save them, but I could not. I left them with a heavy heart. It was the saddest day of my life. Those who fell there were more than comrades—they were brothers.

Whatever may be my fate, I trust that you will hear it with fortitude and submission. We all *must die,* and a brave man *dies* but once. Should such be my fate, then *you must be* for my child its guard and guide. *Teach him to love the memory of his father. Teach him to love and worship God.*

JOHN E. COOK

George Sennott, the lawyer sent from Boston to defend the balance of Brown's fellow prisoners, created quite a sensation on the second day of the trial. He pitched in at every point with such freedom and pertinacity as completely to shock the dignity and decorum of the Virginia court. In defending Shields Green, one of the Negroes, he picked all sorts of flaws in the indictment, and was so generally irreverent that the court and the spectators began to feel wolfish, and it was with difficulty that they kept their chivalrous hands off him.

Mr. Brockett, a Boston artist, also arrived at Charlestown on Wednesday, to procure a likeness of Brown and a measurement of his head, to aid in making a bust, for which he had received a commission, but he found it difficult to obtain access to Brown on account of the new excitement raised by Sennott, and it is doubtful whether he will be allowed to take Brown's daguerreotype. The idea of a statue to the man who has plotted treason against Virginia does not suit the court's idea of the fitness of things.

Brown's wounds, except the cut on the back of his head, were now all healed, and the scars were scarcely visible. He attributed his rapid recovery to his abstemious habits throughout his life. He occupied a room in jail with Stevens, whose recovery was still doubtful at that point. Brown said that he was preaching, even in jail, with great effect, upon the enormities of slavery, and with arguments that everybody failed to answer. His friends said, with regret, that in many of his recent conversations, he gave even stronger reason for a belief that he was insane than he did ever before.

George H. Hoyt, who acted as junior counsel for John Brown at Charlestown, returned from Boston to Virginia on Wednesday, November 9th from Boston to assist his client in the disposal of his personal effects. He proposed to remain at Charlestown until after Brown's execution. Mr. Hoyt's first visit had been in the capacity of a messenger, to obtain the services of Montgomery Blair, to whom he carried letters of recommendation. Mr. Blair was unable to assume the duties of counsel for Brown, but was instrumental in securing the services of Mr. Chilton who subsequently acted so effectively in his case. It was not until after Mr. Hoyt had ascertained that the services of Mr. Blair could not be obtained that he resolved to act as assistant counsel for Brown.

November 9th was spent mainly in taking testimony and opening the argument for the state. The public feeling against Cook was stronger than against any of the other prisoners. He was regarded as having been a spy for the insurrectionists. Strong efforts were made by his friend Governor Willard, of Indiana, to save his life. Governor Willard was sworn in the defense of Cook, not to rebut the case of the prosecution but to show the antecedents of the prisoner. Mr. Willard stated:

> I became acquainted with the prisoner in the year 1847, when I married Cook's sister. Cook was then a mere youth, and was regarded by his family and friends as kind-hearted and generous; after that I saw nothing of him for two years, until I met with him in Philadelphia, where he was engaged at Congress Hall. Cook returned to his family after an absence of three years, and was engaged in the store of his brother-in-law, Mr. Crowley. He remained there a short time, after which he went into the law office of Mr. Stearns, in 1854. I have not seen him since that time, until I saw him in prison here. Cook had been absent for some time, when a brother went to Kansas in search of him, but did not succeed. When I saw the name of Cook mentioned in connection with the Harper's Ferry invasion, I did not know whether it was his brother-in-law or not, but determined to make a visit here and ascertain that fact. When I arrived I met with Senator Mason, who was a friend of his, and who accompanied me to the jail. When I entered Cook commenced a conversation, detailing his connection with the affair. I then told him that he had better not make any statement in regard to the affair then, because I would be called on to testify before the court. I told John Cook that he had better make a confession, stating all he knew about the matter. I thought it would the best thing for himself, and it was due the family. Cook coincided with me, and hence the confession. I again repeated that the

prisoner was considered kind-hearted and honest by all who knew him.

Gerrit Smith was confined in the State Lunatic Asylum in Utica, New York. He was brought there by his relatives on Monday, November 7th. He was seriously deranged. It was stated in Richmond, on the very highest authority, that no requisition had been made by Governor Wise on Governor Morgan, of New York, for Smith.

The Cincinnati *Gazette* of November 10th published the following letter received from its correspondent at Charlestown, Virginia:

> Let me state the particular evidences of present fear. Every train that passes, although it be not searched by men passing through, is inquired of. The conductor is put through an examination—to what effect I could not learn—so that if any suspicious characters are abroad they may be detected. Every man who stays at the station is placed under surveillance, and egress from the hotel generally results in arrest. Last week has been prolific in arrests; they included a Presbyterian clergyman, who, on his way to the synod, stopped over to avoid traveling the whole night; also a gentleman from Kansas, whose name I could not learn, who incautiously stated that he knew Brown; a Mr. Bartlett, from Louisville, who *en route* for the East allowed his curiosity to induce him to look at the water tower in Charlestown, beside several other places.

> This is not all. The brave Mr. Washington, the nearest relative living of the "Father of his Country," does not sleep at home at night, lest his slaves should murder him or his family, and Mr. Allstadt and others follow his example. This is said to be explained by the fact, that suspicion has been aroused, that not all of the people of Harper's Ferry were innocent of knowledge of the proposition of Brown to free the slaves of the Old Dominion. Upon this point

considerable silence is attempted, but when the insurgent chiefs are disposed of, there will be a considerable stir among the citizens here. Certain it is that at least the Negro of Washington, who is claimed to have been drowned as he was returning to his enslaver, was doing nothing of the sort. He was well armed, had been at the rifle works, and like the unfortunate white man, whose cruel butchery I recounted in my last report, he was escaping when overcome by the waters.

The visit of Governor Willard, of Indiana, and his political allies, United States District-Attorney Voorhies, and Attorney-General McDonald, is much canvassed in connection with the fate of Cook. This man finds but few friends. He is regarded as a bad man, who, having set a machine in motion, had not the courage to wait the result of its working. Fears are generally expressed that he will escape, and yet there is a settled conviction that his is the primal guilt. From conversations with several who have watched the progress of the entire affair, I am inclined to think that Cook will be used as state's evidence.

The pardon of Brown was urged upon Governor Wise by two classes of persons—the abolitionists, who desired it from sympathy with the man and his crime, and the anti-abolitionists, who desire to deprive the abolitionists of the damaging stimulus of his martyrdom. It was scarcely to be expected that the interference of the first class would have any other result than to aggravate the panic and augment the general disorder of the Virginia mind. But it was hoped that the advice of the conservative portion of the Northern people, based, as it was, exclusively upon friendly feeling for the South, and an earnest wish to allay the anti-slavery agitation, already so perilously ripe throughout the country, might be met in a corresponding spirit by the parties most directly concerned.

If the leading organs of Southern opinion were to be regarded as authority, every consideration of expediency in connection with this affair was deliberately cast aside. The Southern public has been thrown into a state of irrational and senseless alarm by this paltry invasion at Harper's Ferry, which it was very difficult to understand or conceive in the Northern States. And Governor Wise and his partisans in Virginia seemed determined to play upon this panic for the promotion of their political ends, and for his own elevation to the presidency. It is to be used as the great engine for sweeping away all Southern toleration for moderate sentiments on the slavery question, for ending all thought of accepting Mr. Stephen A. Douglas as the Presidential candidate, and for rallying the excited political feeling of the South to the most ultra and extreme demands. It seems sad that there should be inability anywhere to see the disastrous tendency of such a course, and that personal ambition should so far overbear patriotism as to permit any public man openly to enter upon it. The Richmond *Enquirer* has distinctly proclaimed its purpose to feed the flame of Southern excitement with all the "fuel" which ultra-abolitionism may supply, and then leave the responsibility to the Northern states. This equals the wisdom of the man who, living near a powder magazine, makes a fire on the spot, out of the tinder which others may send him, and then throws upon them the responsibility of the explosion.

Since the South resented the suggestions of Brown's pardon, we trust they will be discontinued. That he has fairly forfeited his life, no one doubts. We certainly have never uttered a word against the essential justice of his sentence:—the only ground on which we have advocated commutation of his doom has been the great public good which seemed to us likely to result therefrom. If those whom it was likely to benefit reject the offer, we have not the slightest disposition to press it. Brown himself has no special desire to live, nor do we suppose his life would be of any special service to the world. His crime merits death, and he has personally no claim to mercy. But we can tell the South that Brown on the scaffold will do them more damage, and involve them in far more peril, than a hundred Browns at large in the Northern states.

There are various ways of assisting people in affliction, but the mode adopted by the Virginia authorities of soothing the sorrows of the citizens who were wounded at Harper's Ferry, certainly had the advantage over any other we have heard of in point of originality. Cook, Brown's Captain, made a full confession of his sins, twenty-five foolscap pages in length, implicating, it is said, Dr. Howe, of Boston, and Frederick Douglass, late of Rochester; and this document is about to be published in a pamphlet form for the benefit of Samuel C. Young, who, whether in advancing or retreating was not stated, received a wound at the battle of Harper's Ferry.

Nothing can be more just than that a criminal's avowal of his enormities should be made to minister to the necessities of those whom he has injured; but we regret to say that we fear in this instance Mr. Young will not be greatly benefitted by the sale of Mr. Cook's great work. In other words, it seems to us that its sale will be somewhat limited. If the author had it ready for publication the morning after the fight, and it had forthwith been committed to the care of an enterprising house, it might possibly have run through several editions in a few days. Or even if it had been furnished to the Fifth Avenue Vigilance Committee in time for use in their manifesto, those gentlemen would doubtless have paid a handsome sum for the copyright. In either case Mr. Young would have profited by it. But at this moment we are afraid the market for this species of literature is overstocked. Most readers are heartily sick of old Brown's enterprise, and certainly do not want to go back upon it, and begin at the beginning once more. The Virginia press has kept us so well supplied with intelligence about the plot and its ramifications, that we really have no stomach for another syllable. If Cook's confession tells us nothing more remarkable than that Dr. Howe and Fred Douglass were implicated in the conspiracy, we don't believe many people will pay anything to learn how their connection with the plot came about. In other words, nobody here cares whether they were or not. The fact, if it be a fact, possesses no sort of significance. So much the worse for them both; but we must say we never heard of a worse basis for commercial speculation than the knight-errantry of these two personages. Douglass has, moreover, seriously damaged the sale of the pamphlet by his departure for England. The only way we know of in which this individual could now be made to help its sale, would be by a demand from Governor Wise upon the British government for his extradition. The certainty of its meeting with a refusal would make it all the better as an advertisement.

An episode of some little interest in regard to the alleged revelations of the Harper's Ferry affair by Colonel Forbes occurred in New York City on Friday, November 11th. The colonel had been vehemently accused by the New York *Tribune* and other journals of having betrayed the plans and movements of Brown, and of having publicly thrown suspicion upon prominent abolitionists and Republicans in connection with the affair. This he has always denied. He alleged on Friday that he was not a party to the original publication of his letters upon which these charges were based,—but that they were procured in some secret and surreptitious manner.

It seems that Colonel Forbes returned from Kansas in December, 1857, and went to lodge at No. 767 Broadway, where his letters to Sanborn and Dr. Howe were dated. On his return from Washington, in the succeeding June, he lodged at the same place. About the middle of the month he departed, leaving behind a debt of $120, and a trunk full of books, papers and *private letters,* among them being a correspondence concerning the intended invasion of the slave states for the emancipation of their slaves.

Colonel Forbes went to Toronto, Canada. On the afternoon of November 10th, 1859 his agent called at No. 767 Broadway in New York City to reclaim the trunk and its contents. The person who had possession of it declined to give it up except on payment of his debt. He *had broken it open* and examined the papers;—whether it was through his agency that they were made public did not clearly appear. An arrangement was made for the satisfaction of the debt, and the colonel regained possession of his documents.

A gentleman who saw and conversed with Gerrit Smith, shortly after the affair at Harper's Ferry, told the Albany *Atlas & Argus* on Friday, November 11th that he was insane; not merely excited by fear and agitated by the emotions which his complicity in the affair might produce, but mentally deranged. His eyes were wild, and his appearance haggard, and his motions spasmodic and uncertain, but unceasingly restless.

He was in constant fear of being arrested and carried off to Virginia, and suspected his friends of an intention to betray him into the hands of justice. When the cruel electioneering hoax was circulated that Governor Wise had issued a requisition upon Governor Morgan for him as a fugitive from justice, he seems to have become so frantic that his friends saw no other hope than to send him to an asylum.

The following is from a private letter upon this subject, which gives some particulars of this sad end of a well-meant but misdirected career, fatal in its consequences alike to him and to all with whom he involved in his fanaticism:

Utica, N.Y., Tuesday, Nov. 8, 1859.

MY DEAR SIR: Gerrit Smith was brought to our asylum yesterday, and is quite deranged intellectually as well as morally; and he is also feeble physically. He refused to take an anodyne, alleging that they only wanted to put him to sleep for the purpose of shipping him off to Virginia. When informed that he must take it, voluntarily or by compulsion, he opened the door and screamed (into the hall) "I won't!" He then reluctantly took it. I deem his madness a sign of the times. He is a victim of the excitement which he helped to make general, and which, in various degrees, is now pervading all the free states. It is much akin to the excitement against witches that prevailed at Salem and other parts of New England, and the time will come when our descendants will look back at it as we look back on the doings in Salem. I am not sure but that the Harper's Ferry outbreak will intensify the excitement.

Very truly,

A. Carson, M. D.

The trial of John Cook, the Harper's Ferry insurgent, was closed at the Charlestown court house late in the afternoon of Wednesday, November 9th. Notwithstanding the utmost efforts of his counsel, the jury rendered the verdict, guilty of murder and of exciting insurrection, and the court overruled the prisoner's bill of exceptions. Hazlett would not be tried until the May term of the court.

The convicts, Cook, Coppoc, Copeland and Green were brought into court on Thursday, November 10th, at 12:00 noon, to receive the sentence of Judge Parker. The courtroom was crowded, and the anxiety to get another view of the prisoners was great. They were brought into court chambers by the deputies, and placed at the bar, in a row of chairs facing the judge. Near Cook was seated Governor Willard and Mr. Crowley, both of whom seemed bent beneath the weight of sorrow this affair had cast over them and their families.

The prisoners were then directed to stand up, and asked if they had anything to say as to why sentence should not be passed upon them. Cook and Coppoc then proceeded to deliver short addresses, the former being somewhat vehement in his manner of speaking, while the latter made a firm impression by his great and collective style of delivery. Both protested their ignorance of the attack on Harper's Ferry, until the Sabbath before the night of the attack, when they were called on to swear to obey the orders of their commander, Brown. Coppoc said, "The charges that have been made against me are not true. I never committed any treason against the State of Virginia. I never made war upon it. I never conspired with anybody to induce your slaves to rebel and I never even exchanged a word with any of your servants. What I came here for I always told you. It was to run off slaves to a free state and liberate them. This is an offense against your laws, I admit, but I never committed murder. When I escaped to the engine house and found the captain and his prisoners surrounded there, I saw no way of deliverance, but by fighting a little. If anyone was killed on that occasion it was in fair fight. I have, as I said, committed an offense against your laws, but the punishment for that offense would be very different from what you are going to inflict now. I have no more to say." The Negroes declined to say anything.

Judge Parker then proceeded to deliver the sentence on the prisoners, which was received by them with great firmness. Judge Parker then said with great emotion:

> Your trials, on which we have been so long employed, have at length ended, and all that remains to be done to complete these judicial proceedings, is to pronounce and record the judgments which by law must follow upon the crimes for which you have been tried, and of which you have been found guilty.
>
> These crimes have all grown out of a mad inroad upon this state, made with the predetermined purpose to raise in our midst the standard of a servile insurrection. In the execution of this purpose, in the darkness of a Sabbath night, you seized upon a portion of our territory, captured several of our best citizens—holding them as hostages of war until your party was itself overcome by force—armed such of our slaves as you could seize upon, with deadly weapons, which they were to use against their owners whom you denounced to them as their oppressors; and in your efforts to push your bold and unholy scheme through to a successful conclusion, you have taken human life in no fewer than five instances. The evidence most abundantly proved that all these things had been done, and by the force of that evidence, jury after jury has felt itself compelled to bring in its verdict of guilty, against each one of you.
>
> Happily for the peace of our whole land, you obtained no support from that quarter whence you so confidently expected it. Not a slave united himself to your party, but, so soon as he could get without the range of your rifles, or as night gave him opportunity, made his escape from men who had come to give him freedom, and hurried to

place himself once more beneath the care and protection of his owner.

When we reflect upon all the mischief and ruin, the dark and fearful crimes, which must have attended even your partial success—men everywhere should be thankful that you were so soon and so easily overpowered.

For these offenses the law demands the penalty of **death,** and imposes upon me the duty of pronouncing that sentence. It is the most painful duty I have ever been called on to perform.

In spite of your offenses against our laws, I cannot but feel deeply for you, and sincerely, most sincerely, do I sympathize with those friends and relations, whose lives are bound up in yours, and whose hearts will be so wrung with grief when they shall hear of the sad fate which has overtaken you, the objects of their warmest and holiest affections. For them we all do sorrow; whilst a due regard for our safety may not permit us to forgive the offenses of which you have been guilty, I hope that they will turn for consolation, and you for pardon, to that good Being, who in his wrath remembereth mercy. Make then your peace with him—for you must soon be ushered into his presence, there to be dealt with as His justice and His mercy may ordain.

To conclude this sad duty, I now announce that the sentence of the law is, that you, and each one of you, John E. Cook, Edwin Coppoc, Shields Green and John Copeland, be hanged by the neck until you be dead—and that the execution of this judgment be made and done by the sheriff of this county, on Friday, the 16th day of December next, upon you Shields Green and John Copeland, between the hours of eight in the forenoon and twelve, noon, of that day—and upon you John E. Cook and Edwin Coppoc between twelve (noon) and five in the afternoon of the same day. And the court being of opinion that the execution of this sentence should be in public; it is further ordered that this judgment be enforced and executed, not in the jail yard, but at such public place convenient thereto as the said sheriff may appoint—and may God have mercy upon the soul of each one of you.

During the delivery of the sentence the utmost silence was observed, and the solemnity was very marked. A large number of the spectators wept, as also did the judge. The prisoners were then remanded back to the jail, there to await the execution of this judgment.

Governor Willard, Attorney-General McDonald, Mr. Voorhees and Mr. G. Crowley had left the previous day for Washington City, and it was then supposed that he would also visit Richmond for the purpose of consulting with Governor Wise. The feeling in favor of Cook was then very great, and it was thought that a commutation of his punishment to imprisonment would give great satisfaction to a large majority of the thinking portion of the community.

The Charleston correspondent of the Baltimore *American* wrote:

> Cook states in his confession that he met Captain Brown in Kansas some two years ago, and was led by the representations of Brown to join his band, not knowing at the time what would be the field of their operations. After some time had elapsed, Brown informed him that the town of Harper's Ferry was the place he contemplated making his stand at, and that he wished him (Cook) to proceed there and try and ascertain whether or not the man Forbes had divulged the plan to any one at Harper's Ferry, as a rumor had reached him to that effect.

Cook strongly objected to any such move as contemplated, but was replied to by Brown that he had taken the oath to stand by him, and that he must not now desert him. Cook, therefore, started for the Ferry, and took up his residence. After having been there some time he was introduced into society, which resulted in his courting and marrying a Miss Kennedy, at South Bolivar. He then determined, by all possible means, to change the determination of Old Brown, but all his arguments and entreaties failed when brought to bear against the iron will of the Kansas outlaw.

The more important portions of his confession were those which told of the convention held in Canada, at which the well-known constitution was framed; of the military training under Stevens which Brown's party went through, altering their original intention, which was to be instructed by Colonel Forbes; and of his own exploration of Jefferson County, Virginia, under Brown's directions, to prepare the way for the insurrection.

John Brown sent the following reply to Mrs. Lydia Maria Child's letter of condolence on Friday, November 11th:

MY DEAR FRIEND: Such you prove to be, though a stranger—your most kind letter has reached me, with the kind offer to come here and take care of me. Allow me to express my gratitude for your great sympathy, and at the same time to propose to you a different course, together with my reasons for wishing it. I should certainly be greatly pleased to become personally acquainted with one so gifted and so kind, but I cannot avoid seeing some objections to it, under the present circumstances. First, I am in charge of a most humane gentleman who with his family, have rendered me every possible attention

I have desired, or that could be of the least advantage; and I am so far recovered of my wounds as no longer to require nursing. Then, again, it would subject you to great personal inconvenience and heavy expense, without doing me any good. Allow me to name to you another channel, through which you may reach me with your sympathies much more effectually. I have at home a wife and three young daughters, the youngest but a little over five years old, the oldest nearly eighteen. I have also two daughters-in-law, whose husbands have both fallen near me here. There is another widow, Mrs. Thompson, whose husband fell here. Whether she is a mother or not, I cannot say. All these, my wife included, live at North Elba, Essex County, New York. I have a middle-aged son, who has been, in some degree, a cripple from his childhood, who would have as much as he could well do to earn a living. He was a most dreadful sufferer in Kansas, and lost all he had laid up. He has not enough to clothe himself for the Winter comfortably. I have no living son, or son-in-law, who did not suffer terribly in Kansas.

Now, dear friend, would you not as soon contribute fifty cents now, and a like sum yearly for the relief of those very poor and deeply-afflicted persons? To enable them to supply themselves and their children with bread and very plain clothing, and to enable the children to receive a common English education? Will you also devote your own energies to induce others to join you in giving a like amount, or any other amount, to constitute a little fund for the purpose named?

I cannot see how your coming here can do me the least good; and I am quite certain you can do me immense good where you are. I am quite cheerful under all my afflicting circumstances and prospects; having, as I humbly trust, "the peace of God, which passeth all understanding," to rule in my heart. You may make such use of this as you see fit. God Almighty bless and reward you a thousand-fold.

Yours, in sincerity and truth,

JOHN BROWN

Francis Jackson Merriam, of Boston, who was reported to have been with Brown in the Harper's Ferry insurrection, and subsequently to have died of his wounds in Philadelphia, was actually alive in November 1859, and lived in Canada.

Some surprise, perhaps some complaint, had been expressed in some of the Northern newspapers, that John Brown, and others of the Harper's Ferry prisoners should have been brought to trial so soon after their capture. This was, however, in exact obedience to the Virginia statute on the subject which enacts that "when an indictment is found against a person for felony, he *shall*, unless good cause be shown for a continuance, be arraigned and tried at the same term." Thus the law was strictly pursued in these cases. No good cause was shown for a continuance; indeed a continuance was not as much as asked. Hazlett, who was afterwards arrested, was not tried, because he could not be indicted during the term.

Quick as these trials may seem to have followed the perpetration of the offense, the records of the Jefferson court have shown cases of felony where the trial was even more speedy. A correspondent remembered one which occurred but a few years ago, where during the session of the court, a horse was stolen, taken to Maryland, and there offered for sale; the prisoner was arrested, brought back to the county, and having waived his right to an examining court, was tried and on his way to the penitentiary within a week from the time he committed the larceny.

Had Brown deferred his attack for a few weeks, he could not have been brought to trial until the Spring. He chose his own time for the attack, and his sympathizers have no ground to blame a Virginia court for dealing with him precisely as their law required, and as it had again and again dealt with its own citizens.

Mr. Hoyt was told that it was stated by a correspondent of the New York *Times*, that Judge Parker, before whom these unfortunate men were tried, had ordered that they be shot in case of an attempt to rescue them. This is altogether a mistake, unintentional, of course. No such order was made, nor an order of any kind respecting their custody. The judge would not, and did not, interfere with duties pertaining to others. He merely tried the prisoners; the sheriff and jailor are responsible for their safe custody, and they could not be in kinder hands. This mistake should be corrected to prevent all misapprehension, and because more or less importance was attached to everything connected with these trials.

Mr. Hoyt also referred to a statement which appeared in various papers, that the judge had decided that the Sharp's rifles and other arms used by the insurgents belonged to Brown, and were ordered to be delivered to his heirs. No such question ever came before the judge—and the statement had no other foundation than some idle, vague rumor.

Matters are more quiet in Charlestown, *now* that the court has adjourned, but considerable excitement still exists. The mayor issued a proclamation, and appointed a committee to look over strangers, and bring them before a Justice of the Peace. Mr. Hoyt and Mr. Jewett, the latter Frank Leslie's artist, received notice from Colonel Taylor that they were not safe, and accordingly left, arriving in Baltimore on Friday, November 11th. Mr. Jewett was <u>accused</u> of being the correspondent of the New York *Tribune*, whose letters had caused considerable ill-feeling. Everybody wanted to learn who the snooping Charlestown correspondent of the New York *Tribune* was. The New York *Times* man was offered $20 for the release of his name, but he was as ignorant of it as the man making the offer. If found out, the *Tribune* man will certainly fare badly.

Thomas C. McDonough supposed to be one of Brown's party and now under arrest, was nothing but a miserable vagrant lately discharged from the workhouse in Louisville, Kentucky. He passed Harper's Ferry a week ago, was detained one night, and was then released. He had no connection whatever with the Harper's Ferry insurgents.

The Cleveland *Herald* was permitted to publish this letter from John Brown, addressed to a half-brother residing in Ohio:

Charleston, Jefferson County, Va.,
Nov. 12, 1859.

DEAR BROTHER JEREMIAH: Your kind letter of the 9th inst. is received, and also one from Mr. Tilden, for both of which I am greatly obliged. You inquire, "Can I do anything for you or your family?" I would answer that my sons, as well as my wife and my daughter, are all very poor, and that anything that may hereafter be due me from my father's estate, I wish paid to them, as I will endeavor *hereafter to describe*, without legal formalities to consume it all. One of my boys has been so entirely used up as very likely to be in want of comfortable clothing for the Winter. I have, through the kindness of friends, fifteen dollars to send him, which I will remit shortly. If you know where to reach *him*, please send him that amount at once, as I shall remit the same to you by a safe conveyance. If I had a plain statement from Mr. Thompson of the state of my accounts, with the estate of my father, I should then better know what to say about that matter. As it is I have not the least memorandum left me to refer to. If Mr. Thompson will make me a statement and charge my *dividend fully for his trouble*, I would be greatly obliged to him. In that case you can send me any remarks of your own. I am gaining in health slowly; and am *quite cheerful* in view of my approaching end, being fully persuaded that I am worth inconceivably more to *hang* than for any other purpose. God Almighty bless and save you all.

Your affection brother,

JOHN BROWN

P. S.—Nov. 13.—Say to my poor boys never to grieve for one moment on my account, and should many of you live to see the time when you will not blush to own your relation to Old John Brown, it will not be more strange than many things that have happened. I feel a thousand times more on account of my sorrowing friends than on my own account. So far as I am concerned, I "count it all joy." I have fought the good fight, and have, as I trust, "finished my course." Please show this to any of my family that you may see. My love to all, and may God, in infinite mercy, for Christ's sake, bless and save you all.

Your affectionate brother,

J. BROWN

The following letter from John Brown was received by an acquaintance in Boston:

Charlestown, Jefferson Co., Va., Nov. 13, 1859.

MY DEAR SIR: Your kind mention of *some* things in my conduct here which you approve, is very comforting indeed to my mind, yet I am conscious that you do me more than justice. I do certainly feel that through Divine grace *I have endeavored* to be "faithful in a very few things," mingling with even these much of imperfection. I am certainly "unworthy even to suffer affliction with the *people of God*," yet in Infinite grace he has thus honored me. May the *same* grace enable me to serve him in *"new obedience,"* through my little remainder of this life; and to rejoice in Him forever. I cannot feel that God will suffer even the poorest service we may any of us render him or his cause to be lost or in vain. I do feel, "dear brother," that I am wonderfully "strengthened from on high."

May I use that strength in *"showing his strength* unto this generation," and his power to every one that is to come. I am most grateful for your assurance that my poor, shattered, heart-broken family *"will not be forgotten."* I have long tried to recommend them to "the God of my Fathers." I have *many* opportunities for *faithful plain dealing* with the more powerful, influential and intelligent classes in this region, which I trust are not entirely mis-improved. I *humbly trust that I* firmly believe that "God reigns," and I think I can truly say, "Let the Earth rejoice." May God take care of his *own cause, and of his own great name,* as well as of those who love their neighbors. Farewell.

Yours in truth,

JOHN BROWN

The Cleveland *Leader* published the following letter from John E. Cook, addressed to Mr. and Mrs. Charles Sellers, of that city:

CHARLESTOWN JAIL, Va.,
November, 16, 1859.

DEAR BROTHER AND SISTER OF MY ADOPTION: After a long interval of silence I sit me down to write to you. Not as of yore, in freedom, but a doomed man in a prison cell, wearing a prisoner's chains;

as one who has heard his death sentence spoken, and whose hours of life are numbered.

Oh! you little thought when last we parted, nor no more did I, that *such* a doom was then in store for me. That he to whom your friendship and affection gave the endearing name of brother, should, ere two short years had passed, have been styled a traitor and *murderer*. Yet so it is.

One short month more and He whom your generous hospitality welcomed to your happy home will stand upon the scaffold to take his last look of earth. Surrounded by a gaping crowd who are eager for our blood, my comrades and myself, amid their scoffs and jeers, must die. The dread of death with me is small, for I have faced it oft before, unflinching and untrembling. I only dread the mode in which it now must come, and the disgrace attendant on it. The only ties that bind me are the ties of kindred and affection. These, it is true, bring with them death's deep agony, and almost crush the spirit with their weight of woe.

Brave men have fallen in this brief, fatal struggle. Comrades who to me were brothers, companions of many a scene of danger, and many a happy hour, sleep in their bloody *grave,* with the cold earth above them. They died as they had ever lived, brave men and true. Eleven of twenty-two fell in the contest. Five more were already doomed. Another but awaits his trial to meet the same sad fate.

Those who fell, died like brave men. Those who yet remain will not shame, I trust, their comrades who are gone. We, I trust, shall calmly meet our doom untrembling and unshaken, and our souls, with no guilt of intention upon their robes, will seek a mightier Judgment Throne, where mercy is not guilt. We will appeal to that *Higher Court,* which judges of the motives which actuate and govern us.

Our days of earthly life are numbered. But beyond the grave's dark confines we shall spring to a higher, holier life amid the undying radiance of eternity. There only can the inmost heart be read—there only can we truly know each other.

Oh! oft through the long interval of silence which has past, have my thoughts wandered back to the circle of your home. The memory of your disinterested and devoted affection has dwelt with me ever as a bright beacon of the past—joy's landmark in the log-book of my life. A footprint on the shore of time on which my heart has longing gazed with love and hope. Oft in the silence which has passed have I anticipated a happy meeting and a fond reunion round your joyous hearth. And fancy's pencil these bright hopes has tinged with love's own rainbow light. But now we meet no more on this side of the river of death. But I trust that we, beyond the shadowy stream may meet amid those bright Elysian bowers where friends no more may part, and farewells are unknown. But before I go hence, I will bid you in these hasty lines, farewell—farewell forever on the shore of earth. And with these parting words accept my love and deep affection for all your kindness to the wayward and erring brother of your adoption. Bid your father and mother, sister and brother farewell for me. Tell them, though absent, they are not forgotten; that their names are still fresh and green upon the tablet of my memory. That here, within these prison walls, I bear their image with me, and their kindness to the stranger is graven in undying letters upon his heart.

Remember me to your dear children. Kiss them for me; and with that kiss give them my love and best wishes for their earthly and eternal welfare.

And oh! when I am gone, think of me sometimes; and let your hearts cherish the name of him to whom in your love and friendship you gave the name of Brother.

And let me still, although an inmate of these prison walls, share as in days of yore in your love; and let me also through the tongue of the absent still hold conversations with you in your happy home. Write to me and let me know of your welfare and your happiness. Forgive my errors, all my faults forgive, and remember me still with the same love and affection that you were wont to feel for me in by-gone days. Accept my love and best wishes for your happiness and prosperity. Good-bye, and may God be with you and bless you, is the prayer of him who here subscribes himself the brother of your adoption.

JOHN E. COOK

P. S.—Direct to me in care of Sheriff Campbell, Charlestown, Jefferson County, Virginia, as all the letters are opened and read by him before I receive them.

I remain, as ever, your adopted brother,

JOHN E. COOK

The following letter was written by John E. Cook to his brother and sister:

Charlestown Jail, Monday, November 21, 1859

MY EVER DEAR SISTER AND BROTHER: Your kind and welcome letter postmarked Nov. 14th, I received the following day. I have no words to tell the deep, pure joy it gave me. So kind, so full of love and affection that while it gave new life, still made me feel that I was all unworthy of such a fond and devoted sister. You cannot know my feelings as I read o'er and o'er again the dear lines your hands had penned. Confined within my lonely cell, shut out from society your letter came like the "olive-branch" to those who for long, long days, had floated o'er a deluged world. It came to me as the "olive-branch" of love, borne from a dear sister's heart. Those lines came to me but to wake responsive echoes to your tones of love, which thrilled through all my soul like some wild burst of seraph music, over whose sounds we love to linger. Those dear lines are engraven on my heart's core and on my memory, stamped in bright, eternal characters. It made my lonely cell more cheerful, for, from every word and line beamed love's own sunshine o'er my heart. It awoke to newer life every chord of affection and every kindred tie. *I know that you do not believe that any stain of murder rests upon my soul. Though doomed to die for such a crime, I feel a conscious innocence from such deep stains of blood. Whatever may be my fate, I shall meet it calmly.* If we are thus early parted here, I hope that we again may meet where partings are unknown.

Governor Wise arrived here with about 400 troops last Sunday night. Two companies had come up from Alexandria the Friday previous; in all, between 500 and

600 men, with five pieces of artillery. They have all sorts of rumors here about an attempt to rescue us. *I have no idea that any one at the North has any such ideas. At least, I hope they have not.* Guards are stationed at every avenue, and I believe are relieved every hour. Within the last few days, they have stationed a guard in the hall in front of my prison door, soon after dark, which they change every hour. Governor Wise has not been in to see me yet, but I expect him this morning. Edwin Coppoc is in the same cell with me. Yesterday we had about 400 visitors, mostly soldiers, many of whom expressed a great deal of sympathy for us.

WEDNESDAY MORNING, Nov. 23.

When I left off writing yesterday morning, I did not think that this letter was destined to be delayed another day. But so it is. We had about 400 more visitors yesterday. Among them were three young ladies from Harper's Ferry, two of whom I was acquainted with. They gazed on me a moment with deep earnestness, and then burst into tears. They sympathized deeply with me in my sad position. I was glad to see them . . .

I have but a very poor chance to write here, as so many are constantly coming in to see us; some through sympathy, but more through curiosity. But there are many with whom I have become acquainted since I have been here, that I know do most truly sympathize with me. The jailor, Mr. Avis, is a kind hearted and a noble man. All the attendants about the prison are very kind to us all. Sheriff Campbell has also done us many favors. Edwin Coppoc, one of my comrades, is now in the same cell with me. We have been together about ten days. He is a noble-hearted fellow. But I must close. Accept my love and best wishes for the welfare of you and yours. Good bye.

As ever, your affectionate brother,

J. E. COOK

John Brown wrote the following letter to his younger children:

Charlestown, Jefferson County, Va., Nov. 22, 1859.

DEAR CHILDREN, ALL: I address this letter to you, supposing that your mother is not yet with you. She has not yet come here, as I have requested her not to do at present, if at all. She may think it best for her not to come at all. She has (or will), I presume, written you before this. Annie's letter to us both, of the 9th, has but just reached me. I am very glad to get it, and to learn that you are in any measure cheerful. This is the greatest comfort I can have, except that it would he to know that you are all Christians. God in mercy grant you all may be so! That is what you all will certainly need. When and in what form death may come is but of small moment. I feel just as content to die for God's eternal truth and for suffering humanity on the scaffold as in any other way; and I do not say this from any disposition to "brave it out." I would readily own my wrong were I in the least convinced of it. I have now been confined over a month, with a good opportunity to look the whole thing as "fair in the face" as I am capable of doing; and I now feel it most grateful that I am counted in the least possible degree worthy to suffer for the truth. I want you all to "be of good cheer." This life is intended as a season of training, chastisement, temptation, affliction, and trial; and the "righteous shall come out of" it all. Oh, my dear children, let me again entreat you all to "forsake the foolish, and live." What can you possibly lose by such a course? "Godliness with contentment is great gain, having the promise of the life that now is, and of that which is to come. Trust in the Lord and do good, so shalt thou dwell in the land; and verily thou shalt be fed." I have enjoyed life much; why should I complain on leaving it? I want some of you to write me a little more particularly about all that concerns your welfare. I intend to write you as often as I can. "To God and the word of his grace I commend you all."

Your affectionate father,

JOHN BROWN

To his older children he wrote:

Charlestown, Jefferson County, Va., Nov. 22, 1859.

DEAR CHILDREN: Your most welcome letters of the 16th inst. I have just received, and I bless God that he has enabled you to bear the heavy tidings of our disaster with so much seeming resignation and composure of mind. That is exactly the thing I have wished you all to do for me,—to be cheerful and perfectly resigned to the holy will of a wise and good God. I bless his most holy name that I am, I trust, in some good measure able to do the same. I am even "joyful in all my tribulations" ever since my confinement, and I humbly trust that "I know in whom I have trusted." A calm peace, perhaps like that which your own dear mother felt in view of her last change, seems to fill my mind by day and by night. Of this neither the powers of "earth or hell" can deprive me. Do not, my dear children, any of you grieve for a single moment on my account. As I trust my life has not been thrown away, so I also humbly trust that my death will not be in vain. God can make it to be a thousand times more valuable to his own cause than all the miserable service (at best) that I have rendered it during my life. When I was first taken, I was too feeble to write much; so I wrote what I could to North Elba, requesting Ruth and Anne to send you copies of all my letters to them. I hope they have done so, and that you, Ellen,[1] will do the same with what I may send to you, as it is still quite a labor for me to write all that I need to. I want your brothers to know what I write, if you know where to reach them. I wrote Jeremiah a few days since to supply a trifling assistance, fifteen dollars, to such of you as might be most destitute. I got his letter, but do not know as he got mine. I hope to get another letter from him soon. I also asked him to show you my letter. I know of nothing you can any of you now do for me unless it is to comfort your own hearts, and cheer and encourage each other to trust in God and Jesus Christ whom he hath sent. If you will keep his sayings, you shall certainly "know of his doctrine, whether it be of God or no." Nothing can be more grateful to me than your earnest sympathy, except it be to know that you are fully persuaded to be Christians. And now, dear children, fare well for this time. I hope to be able to write you again. The God of my fathers take you for his children.

Your affectionate father,

JOHN BROWN

In late November Mr. Lowry of Erie, Pennsylvania visited John Brown in prison. His comments were published by the *True American* on November 25th as follows:

I felt that it was due to the old man, and to my old friendship for him, to visit him in his prison, and bear to

---

[1]   Mrs. Jason Brown

him the salutations of his old neighbors in Northwestern Pennsylvania. I have just returned—having seen the misguided but honest old man, and brought a message from him. It is this—given to me as the door was closing between us: "*Say to those without, I am cheerful.*"

I obtained a letter from the adjutant-general of our state before leaving, and was well armed, in addition, with letters to Governor Wise, Senator Mason, Andrew Hunter, Colonel Washington and others, from friends in Philadelphia and Baltimore. I was informed for the first time when I reached Philadelphia that all Northerners who had been identified as friends of Brown had been warned from the State, and that the country about Charlestown was under martial law, and I was strongly warned not to venture any further on my journey.

Mr. Brown did not at first recognize me, but on my giving my name, he greeted me cordially and gratefully. He said there were many whom he had hoped to see, whom he had not seen, but he had not expected to see any of his old Crawford County friends. He alluded to Crawford as being very dear to him, as its soil was hallowed as the resting place of his former wife and two beloved children, and the sight of any one from that region was most cheering, I cannot pretend to give his language—it was the natural expression of a deep and impassioned nature, and as eloquent as words could be uttered.

I remarked to Mr. Brown that there had been a difficult version given to his Kansas exploits by the *Herald of Freedom* from that which his friends gave, and ventured the opinion that his reputation demanded an explanation. He replied that he understood my allusion but that I was mistaken in supposing that it needed any refutation from him. "Time and the honest verdict of posterity," he said, "will approve of every act of mine to prevent slavery from being established in Kansas. *I never shed the blood of a fellow man except in self-defense or in promotion of a righteous cause.*" He spoke in indignant terms of the editor of the *Herald of Freedom*, characterizing him as "selfish, unjust, revengeful, mercenary, untruthful and corrupt." I remarked that I regretted to hear him speak of G. W. Brown in such terms, as he was an old acquaintance of mine, and had been trusted and respected. His answer was—"Mr. Lowry, you are mistaken if you suppose that anything that George Washington Brown could say can tarnish the character of John Brown." During our conversation, the martial music (where Governor Wise was reviewing his army near the prison) made a great noise, and thinking it must annoy him I asked him if it did not? "No," said the man, "it is inspiring!"

And here, as I parted with him, telling him I would see him again, if possible, he repeated to me—"Tell those without that I am cheerful." My time was up and I was invited to leave.

I wished very much to see Brown again, and expressed a wish to stay in his cell all night, but they assured me that if my wish was even known, I might not be safe—and in accordance with the advice of these friends, I left on the morning train for Harper's Ferry. On the train I met Governor Wise. In a previous conversation with me the evening before, he had asked me whether John Brown was considered an insane man when he resided in Pennsylvania. I said that he was thought to be sane and honest. In the cars I asked the governor if he would commute the sentence of Brown, He said, "*If I dare to commute the sentence of Brown—the citizens of Virginia would acquiesce, but I will not do it.*" "Why," he said, "John Brown never asked to be pardoned. *And I doubt whether he would ask it, if he knew the asking of it would obtain it.*" He said that he would rather pardon Brown than Cook, but that he would pardon neither. I asked the governor if Brown's friends could have his body after his death. He answered, "The surgeons will claim his body." I said to the governor, that in my opinion Brown was a monomaniac, and as crazy on the subject of slavery as Gerrit Smith. He said, "Men of that kind of insanity ought to be hanged.

Recently an intelligent Virginia gentleman also by the name of Brown asked me, "what I wished to do with Brown's body?" I told him it would belong to his wife; *but if his friends would not claim it, I would, if they gave it to me, and bury it in my own burying grounds.* He remarked that it would be used for a different purpose if the North should get it; *that Massachusetts would take the head, and other Northern States other parts of the body, and each would erect a monument over its portion higher than Bunker Hill.*

Mr. Brown is a member of the Old-School Presbyterian Church and a decidedly religious man, though he strictly and sternly refuses to be aided in his prayers by the pro-slavery divines of Virginia. One of these gentlemen in conversation with me, said that he had called on Brown to pray with him. He said Brown asked if he was ready to fight if necessity required it, for the freedom of the slave. On his answering in the negative, Brown said that he would thank him to retire from his cell, that his prayers would be an abomination to his God. To another clergyman he said that he would not insult his God by bowing down with any one who had the blood of the slave upon his shirt.

I omitted above to say that Governor Wise told me there was one condition on which he would surrender

General Brown—which was that I should deliver up to him general sympathy for execution in his stead. The governor and the citizens are evidently more afraid of the latter than of the former.

The present panic among these brave Virginians demonstrates the correctness of Brown's estimate of them when he thought that a small body of slaves with those unearthly weapons in their hands, could rush down from the mountains, victors over a panic-stricken commonwealth.

The program for the execution of Brown was carefully orchestrated by Governor Wise. All good citizens would be requested to absent themselves from the scene and about the scaffold; the troops, two thousand strong, would form an immense square, with the object of keeping the people beyond the reach of Brown's voice, should he desire to deliver an incendiary speech. If Brown desired to address the public, he could do so in writing. The soldiers will have a jolly time, at the expense of Virginia. It will cost the treasury a quarter of a million dollars at least. Among sensible men no rescue is feared, or regarded as probable or practicable. But the masses, as has been noted, are frightened even by a cow.

Among the visitors to Charlestown on Saturday, November 26th, were Col. A. P. Shutt, of the Baltimore and Ohio Railroad, William Prescott Smith, Esq, Master of Transportation on the same road, and Captain Henry Clay Pate, of Kansas notoriety. All these gentlemen visited the prisoners and had conversations with them. The meeting between Brown and Pate was not of the most cordial character on the part of the former. Pate was captured by John Brown in one of his Kansas battles by a piece of strategy not recognized in honorable warfare. Brown declared that he met a great many men in his life possessed of more courage than Captain Pate, to which the Captain responded by charging Brown with all kinds of villainy, amongst them he intimated that Brown would at any time appropriate another man's property for his own personal use. Dr. Rawlins, a special correspondent and Mr. Burghams, artist of Frank Leslie's *Newspaper* also came into town and were taken before Captain Sinn and examined, but their traveling papers saved them from excessive trouble.

Brown was visited on Saturday by the Reverend James H. March of the M. E. Church. The Reverend Gentleman advanced an argument in favor of the institution of slavery as it now existed. Brown replied to him, saying, "My dear sir, you know nothing about Christianity. You will have to learn the A B C's in the lesson of Christianity, as I find you are entirely ignorant of the meaning of the word. I, of course, respect you as a gentleman, but only as a *heathen* gentleman." The Reverend Gentleman here thought it best to draw such a discussion to a close, and left immediately.

The other prisoners were awaiting the execution of the sentence passed upon them with seeming composure, with the exception of Cook, who was quite crestfallen since the visit of Governor Wise, as the only hope he had was blasted away by the positive assurance given him while Wise was here, that under no circumstances would he interpose to save him.

Every thing in the shape of business has been suspended, and the inhabitants seem to do nothing but make efforts to provide for the military people in Charlestown. Schools were suspended, and the school-houses occupied as barracks. Churches were in a manner closed, and a closed closet had to be resorted to by those whose thoughts were directed from things carnal.

The Boston *Traveller* of Saturday, November 26th said:

> George H. Hoyt, Esq., of this city, counsel for John Brown, arrived home this morning. He has procured the affidavits of eighteen different individuals at Akron and other places in Ohio, showing in the clearest manner that Brown's family, on his mother's side, had exhibited insanity in many instances. His grandmother was insane for six years before her death, and died in that condition. Three of her children were insane, and another of her children had insane children, cousins of John Brown.

The only sister of Brown was also liable to attacks of insanity. Several of the witnesses, relatives, or intimate acquaintances of John Brown himself, testified to certain facts which, in their opinion, went to show clearly that the heredity taint existed in him.

Mr. Hoyt had an interview with Governor Wise on Wednesday, and placed these affidavits in his hands. The governor assured Mr. Hoyt that he would give them the most careful consideration. By a law of the state he has the power, if satisfied that a sufficient reason existed therefor, on the ground of insanity, to postpone the execution and have the fact of insanity passed upon a jury.

A steamer arrived at Baltimore from Norfolk on Sunday, November 27th. It contained two companies of troops, numbering one hundred and seventy men, and they will go to Charlestown that night on a special train. Two companies left Charlestown on Sunday bound for Wheeling to guard the Ohio state line. The Virginia cadets and a company of over one hundred volunteers went to Charlestown in a special train in the afternoon. These reinforcements will make the force at Charlestown over one thousand strong. Every car that passed through was searched at all the stops in Virginia for armed men. There seemed to be a determination to keep up a panic. Companies from all parts of the state have tendered their services to Governor Wise. The citizens of Rockingham County have tendered a hundred men to proceed to any point the governor designated. The Richmond *Dispatch* urged the people of Virginia to stay away from the execution of Brown and his comrades. It also said that if visitors from other states were allowed to be present they would be assigned vantage points where they could do no mischief.

It was said that the new and extensive military movements grew out of a confident belief on the part of the Virginia officials that an attack and an attempt at a rescue would be made Sunday night. Governor Wise and Attorney-General Hunter professed to have received reliable information to that effect. The howitzer company of Richmond who went back with Governor Wise returned to Charlestown on Sunday also.

Sentinels have been firing at imaginary foes nightly, and a number of citizens have narrowly escaped their bullets. On Sunday night the military confidently expected an attack and the sentries were doubled. No disturbers appeared, however.

A large number of the companies have been boarding at the various hotels in Charlestown, so General Taliaferro made inquiries on Saturday as to the arrangements made for payment of board. In a short time it was reported to him by the quartermaster that the men were paying $1.00 per day board, and had trust that the commonwealth would reimburse them. The general immediately ordered that cooking utensils be furnished them, and that they be allowed rations for themselves, or 40 cents per day in its stead.

The Reverend Edwin M. Wheelock, of Dover, New Hampshire, delivered a discourse on Harper's Ferry, and its lessons in the music hall, at Boston, on Sunday morning. The Boston *Courier* gave the following sketch:

> Mr. Wheelock took the view that the insurrection in Virginia was necessary, seasonable and right. He did not consider it a failure nor a mistake. It was not, as some say, a beginning of civil war, but, rather a continuance of it in a new phase. In taking up arms, John Brown had only done aggressively what the North would have been compelled to do in a few years in self-defense. And now that the example had been given, there would not be wanting brave men to follow it, and to succeed in doing all that Brown intended. His aim was, the preacher said, to put servile insurrection on as enduring a basis as the underground railroad has. This he might easily have done, had he avoided the federal arm. What the three hundred or so Indians and fugitive slaves in Florida cost the government to subdue them, might be regarded as

the prefiguring of what a determined man, raising the standard of revolt in the mountains of Virginia, or in the Great Dismal Swamp, only tracked by the feet of the flying fugitive, might easily accomplish. John Brown had but little faith in parties, lie saw that the Republicans would do nothing for the next year but try to find the most harmless man for a presidential candidate, and so he made a bold push for liberty, on his own account. *But he was defeated.* Yes; and all first-class victories, from that of calvary downward, are defeats. But it is said that he is a fanatic and a madman. Yes, but the fanatics of this age will be the crowned leaders of the next, and the madmen of today are the heroes of tomorrow.

One such man, says the preacher, makes total depravity impossible, and proves that American greatness died not with Washington. *The gallows from which John Brown ascends into Heaven will be, in our politics, what the cross is in our religion.* It is fitting that he should die. He has done enough and borne enough for the world's freedom. On the 2nd day of December he is to be strangled in a Southern prison for obeying the Sermon on the Mount. *To be hanged in Virginia is like being crucified in Jerusalem; it is the last tribute which sin pays to virtue.* John Brown, in dying, leaves to us two legacies—one his unfinished work, and the other, the families whose husbands and fathers and brothers fell in defending the cause of the oppressed. May God help us to be faithful to these trusts.

O. Jennings Wise, the son of the governor arrived on Monday, November 28th, with dispatches from his father. The governor had received a pamphlet written in code, which was supposed to be of high import, but adds largely to his already heavy stock of tribulations. On Tuesday Governor Wise issued a proclamation, announcing that the state has taken possession of the Winchester and Potomac Railroad, and that on the first three days of December it will be used entirely for military purposes. He also warned the people of the state to remain at home on patrol duty on the day of the execution, to protect their homes. Women and children will not be permitted to approach the scene of the execution, and strangers are cautioned that there will be danger to them in approaching Charlestown or near it on that day; that, if it is deemed necessary, martial law will be proclaimed and enforced.

General Taliaferro also issued his proclamation announcing that all strangers who cannot give a satisfactory account of themselves will be promptly arrested; and that all strangers approaching Charlestown by railroad or otherwise, under the pretext of witnessing the execution of John Brown, will be met by the military and turned back or arrested. He also emphatically warned the people of the county to stay home and protect their property, assuring them that information from reliable sources indicated that by so doing they will best consult their own interests.

On Tuesday, November 29th John Moore, Esq, a very wealthy and estimable gentleman visited John Brown in his jail cell. Shortly after entering, Brown introduced the subject of slavery, but Mr. Moore told him that he had no disposition to discuss it. Brown asked him how many slaves he owned, and Mr. Moore replied he did not know the number, but he was sure he had one, a woman eighty years of age, whose eyesight, he was sorry to say, had failed. He said he had given a prominent physician $100 a few days previous for operating on them, and if it were possible to restore her vision he would give $5,000. Brown asked him what he would take for the old servant. Mr. Moore replied that all the abolitionists in the North were too poor to buy her. The conversation here ended.

Four companies of United States artillery arrived at Baltimore from Fortress Monroe on Wednesday. They were under the command of Colonel Lee and they arrived via the Norfolk boat early in the morning. Two of these companies took their position at Fort Henry, and the other two proceeded to Harper's Ferry where they will be stationed on the armory grounds. They took guns and camp equipage, and will remain until the executions are over. The military movements are all by special trains, and do not interfere with the through travel of the Baltimore & Ohio Railroad.

The report that cars were invaded by troops and the passengers searched for arms was highly overrated. Passengers were not taken to Harper's Ferry unless they previously satisfied the president and officers of the company that they had a legitimate business there, and by an arrangement with the governor they were issued passports.

Three passengers on the western train of the Baltimore & Ohio Railroad were removed from a passenger car on their arrival at Harper's Ferry by the military and imprisoned on Wednesday. The parties arrested were merchants of Cincinnati, Ohio who were on their way to Baltimore. At Grafton they were heard to express themselves quite freely in relation to John Brown and his family, expressing great sympathy for him and them. The conversation was overheard by a man, alleged to be a spy of Governor Wise, who telegraphed to Harper's Ferry an account of the matter, and a description of the parties. When the train reached there the volunteers entered with loaded muskets and carried the men away, notwithstanding they earnestly protested their innocence.

The railroad company refused to sell tickets for Charlestown until after the execution of the insurrectionists. Among the passengers on Wednesday was one John Brown, who had a permit from the governor. It was learned that a large party of excursionists (numbering 2,000 in all) were scheduled to come to the execution. Mr. Perham, the famous entrepreneur, got this up as a hot speculation, but the Baltimore & Ohio Railroad will certainly not allow the visitors to pass over their roads on any terms.

Mr. Edgerton, a member of Congress from Ohio was one of the recent arrivals. He was on a mission from Brown's son to obtain the body of his father, but he was informed on Wednesday that no decision had been reached as to the disposal of the body. The governor was expected to arrive hourly, bringing two hundred additional troops with him.

The following letter from Miss Fouke appeared in the St. Louis *Republican* on Wedndsday, November 30th. It is an account of how she saved the life of the insurgent William Thompson. The St. Louis *Republican* called her "The New Pocahontas!"

Harper's Ferry, Sunday, Nov. 27, 1859.

MR. EDITOR: I anticipate your surprise, when your eye shall rest on the signature attached to this sheet; but that surprise will vanish when you learn the why and wherefore I have taken the liberty of writing you a few lines. I have learned from the daily Missouri *Republican,* that you were under the impression that I saved the life of Thompson, the insurgent, when he was taken captive. He was brought into the public parlor of the hotel, some time before I knew that he and Stevens had been captured. When I first saw Thompson, he was seated in an arm-chair, with his hands tied behind his back, guarded by some of the citizens. Several questions were put to him, in regard to his motives and expectations, when he enrolled under the "provisional government." His answers were invariably the same: That he had been taught to believe the Negroes were cruelly treated, and would gladly avail themselves of the first opportunity to obtain their freedom, and that all they had to do was to come to Harper's Ferry; take possession of the armory and arsenal, which would be an easy matter, and then the colored people would come in a mass, backed by the non-slave holders of the Valley of Virginia. Some one remarked, "I imagine you regret that you did not succeed in running off the darkies." He replied that he regretted having engaged in the attempt, and if it were to do over again he would decline.

Very soon after, Mr. Beckham, one of our most esteemed citizens, was shot down, unharmed as he was. I went into the parlor, and heard one of the guards ask Thompson if he were a married man; his answer was that he had been married six months only.

I walked up to where the prisoner sat and said to him, "Mr. Thompson, you had much better have stayed at home and taken care of your wife, and pursued some honest calling, instead of coming here to murder our citizens and steal our property; that their first act was to kill a free colored man, because he would not join them in their wicked scheme." He said I spoke truly; but they had been basely deceived.

While I was talking to Thompson, several of the friends of Mr. Beckham, who were justly enraged at his cold-blooded murder, came in, with the avowed determination to kill Thompson on the spot. As they appeared with leveled rifles, I stood before Thompson, and protected him, for three powerful reasons: First, my sister-in-law was lying in the adjoining room very ill, under the influence of a nervous chill, from sheer fright, and if they had carried out their design it would have proved fatal to her without doubt. In the second place I considered it a great outrage to kill the man in the house, however much he deserved to die. Thirdly, I am emphatically a law-and-order woman, and wanted the self-condemned man to live, that he might be disposed of by the law. I simply shielded the terribly-frightened man, *without touching him,* until Colonel Moore (I think it was Moore) came in and assured me, on his honor, that he would not be shot in the house. That was all I desired. The result everybody knows.

One other error I wish to correct. Philip B. Fouke, of Belleville, Illinois, is my cousin only. I am happy to assure you that I have a birthright in the "Old Dominion."

Respectfully yours,

C. C. FOUKE

As the day for his execution approached John Brown maintained a wonderful equanimity, and was busied with correspondence and reading. No further interviews were to be allowed with him. His time and patience were exhausted by curious visitors. On being importuned for his autograph, he kindly but firmly declined, on the ground that he could not grant the favor and keep his faith with others.

John Cook, however, was very much shaken. His lip quivered, his hands shook, and his eyes wandered. He evidently anticipated his death with great horror. The other prisoners were much the same. Stevens's face was badly swollen, but his life will last long enough. The Negroes said they are "as comfortable as could be expected."

The execution of Friday, December 2nd, will take place in the large field behind the prison, to the rear of which are the mountains. The scaffold will be finished on Thursday morning. The arrangements for the hanging are in charge of Major General Taliaferro, Sheriff Campbell, Mayor Greene and Colonel Hunter, but as yet none of them have been disclosed.

Chapter 10

EXECUTION AND BURIAL OF JOHN BROWN

T HE DAY DAWNED bright and cheerful in Baltimore on Thursday, December 1, 1859, but everybody was aware that it was the eve of the execution of John Brown in Charlestown. Several persons, the editors of abolition newspapers published in the North, were ejected from the train going to Harper's Ferry. They had purchased tickets and were very anxious to proceed, but were refused on account of an arrangement entered into between Governor Wise and the president of the railroad. They left on the Washington train, declaring that were bound for Charlestown to see the execution, and would reach there by the Orange and Alexandria Railroad. When the president of that road was informed of the fact he wasted no time in promptly ejecting the passengers.

The *American's* Charlestown correspondent said there was no falling off of the wild stories of invaders and perpetrators. Although martial law was not proclaimed, there was a vigorous military surveillance kept up that subjected everyone—even ordinary citizens—to great inconveniences. The ordinary day-to-day citizen could not pass through the suburbs without arrest and examination. On the arrival of one of the trains two people, unable to give a satisfactory account of themselves, were hastily sent by an armed escort across the Maryland line. Four suspicious characters were arrested since yesterday morning, one thought to be Coppoc's brother. These people were all detained at Charlestown for the present. A proclamation was issued forbidding any person to leave his house after dark in the evening under penalty of a ten dollar fine.

The Ohio merchants arrested at Harper's Ferry yesterday were discharged after a short detention. It was learned that John Brown had admitted his participation in the Kansas massacre, but offered various excuses in palliation of it.

The work of erecting the scaffold for the hanging commenced yesterday. It was understood that the members of the press would not be allowed inside the line; so, no report would be made of Brown's last proclamation, should he make one. The execution tomorrow will definitely take place in the large field behind the prison. In the afternoon a corporal and some of his guards went to the field with a wagon load of white flags fixed on short stakes, which were stuck in the ground at twenty paces apart all around the lot, in two rows, the rows being twenty paces apart. These were intended to mark the posts of the sentries. Other similar flags showed the positions for General Taliaferro, with his staff, the several companies and troops, and a narrow strip on the town side, where worthy and well qualified citizens who came properly vouched for, could be allotted positions.

The rope to strangle Brown was only about three feet long. It was of hemp, made in Kentucky, and sent in a box to Sheriff Campbell by a planter for this express purpose. Other ropes had been sent from other sections. One made of South Carolina cotton, in Alexandria, has already been displayed. This would have been preferred beyond all the others, because of the eminent fitness of the moral it conveyed for the consideration of all sympathizers with this deluded *abolitionist*! But providence willed it otherwise; for upon testing it was unable to sustain a weight much less than that of a man's body. Another, almost as great a choice with our Charlestown friends, was of hemp, made in Missouri by the slaves of Mahala Doyle, and sent by her with a particular request that, for the sake of retributive justice, it might be used to hang the man whom she asserts murdered her husband and two sons. This was also tested, but it was also found wanting. No, the precious gift from Kentucky would have to be used for the purpose.

Tomorrow all communication between Charlestown and Harper's Ferry will be suspended, and no dispatches will be permitted to leave the latter place without first having undergone a strict inspection. All persons were solicited to stay away from Charlestown on peril of their comfort, if not their life.

John Brown was reported to have said he did not intend to make a speech from the scaffold, and that the precaution of a circle of troops to prevent his words being heard was needless. He said he had nothing in the way of a confession to offer. Governor Wise has sent orders that no person shall be admitted to the jail compound until after Brown's execution. Some reports were in circulation that demonstrations would be made on the occasion of the reception of the remains of Captain Brown. Mayor Henry of Philadelphia had been mentioned in connection with the application made by Mrs. Brown for the body of her husband.

Brown, in a conversation with his jailor, said that if he did not see his wife before he was executed, he would like to express his desires relative to the disposition of his body. Governor Wise had assured him that it would be at the disposal of his friends, and accordingly the jailor was requested to say to Mrs. Brown, or whoever came for it, that he did not desire to have it removed North, but wanted it placed upon a pyre and burnt, and the ashes put in an urn. He also requested that the bodies of his sons who were killed at the Ferry might be disinterred and disposed of in the same manner. The last part of the request could not have been complied with, however, as the physicians at Winchester had already used their bodies in the dissecting-room.

Mrs. Brown, while in Philadelphia, wrote a letter to Governor Wise, making application for the body of her husband after the execution. As it was feared that this letter would remain unnoticed among the immense number of letters which Governor Wise was receiving daily, a number of gentlemen, among whom was Reverend Henry A. Wise, son of the governor, called personally on Mayor Henry and requested him to enclose the letter in one of the city envelopes, so as to insure the governor's early attention to the contents. This request the mayor complied with, and accompanied the document with an explanatory note in which he vouched for the authenticity of the letter of Mrs. Brown.

Governor Wise promptly responded to the letter, and in the kindest manner acceded to her request for the custody of the body of her husband. He also inclosed an order for the disinterment of Brown's two sons who fell at Harper's Ferry, and a passport for herself and for her agent directed to General Taliaferro. The body was consigned to the city of Philadelphia where Mrs. Brown will await its coming. There were many rumors being circulated about the body lying in state, and that there would be a demonstration in the path of the funeral parade in Charlestown, but there was no truth whatsoever to those stories.

Before noon tomorrow, John Brown, the hero, the victim, the martyr, the murderer, will, in all human probability, undergo the ultimate penalty of law. Had a rescue been at any time seriously contemplated, the extreme caution and ample military and police provision made by the executive of Virginia, would have defeated the attempt. So far has this spirit of precaution been carried, that all strangers have been arrested on the lines of railroads converging at Harper's Ferry, communications have been cut off, and Northern reporters and visitors have been stopped at Baltimore, and obliged to seek other approaches to the scene of execution, which they will likely find equally closed to them.

Governor Wise requested the opinion of Attorney-General Tucker of Virginia as to the state laws upon the distribution of incendiary publications through the post office. Tucker wrote a long report on the subject, taking the position that the federal power to deliver the mail does not carry with it the power to publish and circulate, and therefore that local laws, affecting such publications as incendiary documents in question, may be enforced. After this decision the circulation of objectionable mail-matter in Virginia was regarded as definitely prohibited.

Captain Philip T. Moore, of the Montgomery Guards, stationed at Harper's Ferry, was on his way home from Richmond where he had been on a brief furlough on Wednesday, November 30th. While traveling from Baltimore to Harper's Ferry he was informed by Colonel Shutt of Baltimore who traveled with him that Mrs. Brown was on the train.

Before reaching Harper's Ferry Captain Moore, who was rather dashing, found Mrs. Brown in the next car and introduced himself to her and to a lady and two gentlemen who accompanied her. He informed them that he would have to take them in his charge upon their arrival at Harper's Ferry. Soon after the arrival of the train, the captain telegraphed to General Taliaferro, informing him of the presence of Mrs. Brown and her companions at the station. The general telegraphed back, ordering all the parties to be detained until further orders were issued.

Early Thursday morning a detachment of nine mounted riflemen were dispatched to Harper's Ferry with instructions to Captain Moore to have Mrs. Brown given to them in charge, to be escorted to Charlestown. Moore was also instructed to order the lady and two gentlemen who accompanied her to return on the next train back to Baltimore. When Mrs. Brown was informed that her companions would not be permitted to accompany her any further, she exhibited some signs of being upset. Captain Moore, seeing this, immediately tendered her his service as an escort, which she cheerfully accepted. They then stepped into a carriage, which was in readiness at the station to convey Mrs. Brown to Charlestown, and immediately set out for their destination under the escort of the mounted riflemen. As they traveled Captain Moore referred frequently to the unfortunate situation of Mrs. Brown's husband. She exhibited no sorrow or regret, so far as he could observe, nor did she manifest any particular anxiety to see him, notwithstanding that five months had now elapsed since she had last seen him.

Seeing that she was not moved by this reference to her husband's condition, the captain turned the conversation upon another subject. He remarked what a misfortune it was to her and her family that her husband had involved himself in his present difficulties. Her reply was that she would bear the affliction as well as she could. She did not show as much feeling "as"—to use the captain's own words—"I would if the least wrong were inflicted on one of my children."

As they passed along, the captain brought Mrs. Brown's attention to a number of Negro children whom they met along the route, and remarked to her how happy and contented they seemed to be. "You can perceive," he said, "from their appearance how well they are cared for. They are well fed, well clothed and kindly treated in every respect—as much so, in fact, as the white children." She seemed pleased at hearing this. The captain assured her that such was the course of treatment pursued in reference to the Negroes throughout the South, and explained to her how it was in the interest of slave holders to treat their slaves kindly. She stated that she never before dreamed that their condition was so good, or that they felt so happy as they appeared to her from her present opportunity of observing them.

There was a grand full dress military parade on the city streets all that afternoon, in which only those troops that were fully uniformed, equipped and drilled took part. There were between four and five hundred men under arms. The rest of the troops were either doing patrol duty or going through their drill in another part of the city. The sun shone brightly and warmly, bringing out the bright colors of the uniforms, and making the bayonets glisten as the men went through their manual exercise. The sidewalks and balconies of the adjacent houses were crowded with spectators

Upon entering the town, the captain let down the curtain of the carriage to prevent Mrs. Brown from being gazed upon by the crowd while passing to the jail. She observed that she felt no inconvenience from the sun, and that it was entirely unnecessary to take any pains to exclude it. The captain informed her that such was not his object in letting the curtain down, but that it was to save her the pain of being made the object of general observation by the crowd on the street, who, no doubt, felt considerable anxiety to see her.

On arriving at the jail the captain conducted her from the carriage to the jailor's quarters, where she was given over to the charge of Mrs. Avis, the jailers wife, to be searched before being permitted her to see her husband. Meanwhile, the captain went into Brown's cell in company with General Taliaferro, Mr. Andrew Hunter, Mr. Campbell, the sheriff of the county;

and Mr. William H. Lyons, a member of the general's staff. Captain Moore told Brown that Mrs Brown had arrived, having been accompanied by him from Harper's Ferry to this place, and he apprized Brown further that he would have to accompany her back to that town tonight. He expressed his willingness to do anything for him that would be consistent with his duty. Mr. Brown returned his thanks. The captain then asked him to endorse a check for fifty dollars, drawn in his favor by a Mr. Cavender, of Philadelphia, and given to him by one of the gentlemen who accompanied Mrs. Brown to Harper's Ferry. Mr. Brown endorsed the check writing, "Pay to the order of Mary A. Brown. (signed) JOHN BROWN."

At this stage of the interview, General Taliaferro said, "Mr. Brown, your wife, Mrs. Brown, will be here in a few minutes, and I am sorry I cannot afford you an opportunity for a long interview with her. The reunion of John Brown and his wife lasted from 4:00 PM on the afternoon of December 1st until 8:00 PM, at which time General Taliaferro informed them that the period allowed had elapsed, and that she must prepare for departure back to Harper's Ferry. The interview took place in the parlor of Captain Avis, and Brown was free of manacles of any kind. There was an impression of prison officials that the prisoner might possibly be furnished with a weapon or with strychnine by his wife, and so before the interview her person was searched by the wife of the jailor, and a strict watch was kept over her during the time they were together. On first meeting they kissed and affectionately embraced, and Mrs. Brown shed a few tears, but immediately checked her feelings. They stood locked in an embrace, she sobbing for nearly five minutes, and he unable to speak. John only gave way for a moment, and was soon calm and collected and remained firm throughout the rest of the interview.

They sat side by side on a sofa, and, after discussing family matters, proceeded to business. John stated that he desired his property to pass entirely into her possession, and appeared to place full confidence in her ability to manage it properly for the benefit of his younger children. He requested her to remain at North Elba, on the farm where she now resided, and which belonged to her. He desired that his younger children should be well educated; and if she could not obtain facilities for their education at home, to have them sent to a boarding school. He then dictated a will to Sheriff Campbell, which directed that all his property should go to his wife, with the exception of a few presents and bequests which he made. To one of his sons he gave a double spyglass, and to another a watch; while a third was directed to take a tomb or monument that marks the grave of his father at North Elba, and have his name, age, and the manner of his death, together with the cause for which he had suffered, engraved upon it. He directed that it should remain at North Elba as long as his family resided there. To each of his children he bequeathed the sum of fifty dollars, and to each of his daughters a Bible, to cost five dollars—to be purchased out of money coming to him from his father's estate. Also, he directed that a Bible, to cost three dollars, shall be presented to each of his grand-children, and that $50 each be paid to three individuals whom he named, if they could be found, and, if not, to their legal representatives. During the course of the conversation Mary asked John if he had heard that Gerrit Smith had became insane, and had been sent to the asylum at Utica. He replied that he had read of it in the papers, and was sorry to hear it, but immediately changed the subject.

The subject of the death of his two sons was spoken of, and Mrs. Brown remarked that she had made some effort for the recovery of their bodies while at Harper's Ferry, to which object she said Colonel Barbour had kindly consented to give his assistance. John Brown remarked that he would also like the remains of the two Thompson's removed, if they could be found, but suggested that it would be best to take his body, with the bodies of his four sons, and get a pile of pine logs, and make one big bonfire. It would be much better, and less expensive, to thus gather up all their ashes together, and take them to their final resting place. Sheriff Campbell told him that this would not be permitted within the state, and Mrs. Brown objected to the macabre proposition altogether.

Brown said that he contemplated his death with composure and calmness. It would undoubtedly be pleasant to live longer, but as it was the will of God he should close his career, he was content. It was doubtless best that he should be thus legally murdered for the good of the cause, and he was prepared to submit to his fate without a murmur. Mrs. Brown becoming depressed at these remarks. He bid her cheer up, telling her that his spirit would soon be with her again, and that they would be reunited in heaven.

With regard to his execution, he said, that he desired no religious ceremonies either in the jail or on the scaffold from ministers who consented or approved of the enslavement of their fellow creatures; that he would prefer rather to be accompanied to the scaffold by a dozen slave children and a good old slave mother, with their appeal to God for blessings on his soul than all the eloquence of the whole clergy of the commonwealth combined.

During the past week several letters containing checks and drafts had been forwarded to him by his friends in different sections of the country. These he endorsed, and also made payable to his wife, MARY A. BROWN (one of them was for $100 and one for $50) and handed them all to her.

Mrs. Brown regarded her husband as a martyr in a righteous cause, and was proud to be the wife of such a man. The gallows, she said had no terrors for her or for him. She stated that she had not seen him since last June, about six months ago, and that they had been separated, with the exception of a few days, for nearly two years. They had, however, corresponded, and she had always felt a deep interest in the cause in which he was engaged.

At close to 8:00 PM in the evening John Brown felt the need of further union with his wife and requested of General Taliaferro that she be allowed to remain with him the rest of the night. To this the general refused to assent. At the close of their reunion they shook hands, but did not embrace, and as they parted Brown said in a low monotone, "God bless you and the children." Mary Brown replied, "God have mercy on you," and remained calm until she left the room, at which point she broke out in tears for a few moments. She then prepared to depart for Harper's Ferry where she would remain on execution day. From 6:00 PM until 7:30 PM the carriage and escort which were to convey Brown's wife back to Harper's Ferry was waiting for her to start. Her stay was longer than had been intended. Sentinels with fixed bayonets guarded the streets on all sides and prevented all persons, even military men, from passing in front of the jail. At length all was ready and the carriage was brought directly to the door. The military took possession of the square, and with an escort of twenty men the cortegé moved off, Captain Moore taking a seat in the carriage next to Mrs. Brown. During the trip from Charlestown she seemed to grieve much more than before her interview with her husband. She wept silently most of the way, and the only consideration which seemed to reconcile her to the fate of her husband was that he was going to die a martyr. Her sorrow would apparently diminish with every reference to that destiny; and no sooner would allusion be made to his impending fate than she invested it with the honors of martyrdom, as if to console herself. At Harper's Ferry she would await the body of her husband, which would be forwarded to her immediately after the execution.

Mrs. Brown arrived at Harper's Ferry at about 10:00 PM, and was put up at the Wager House. The lady and two gentlemen who accompanied her had been permitted, at her request, to remain and accompany her to Baltimore in the morning. Several persons, members of the press in particular, anxiously sought interviews with her. All through the evening the armory band of Richmond performed pieces of music in front of General Taliaferro's quarters, and in other parts of Charlestown. It did not seem to occur to any of the commanding officers that this serenading was, all things considered, of somewhat questionable taste.

The New York *Times* reported:

> On Friday, December 2nd, 1859 Virginia will exercise her sovereign power and "vindicate the majesty of her offended laws," after a fashion equally strange and sad. Yes, it is strange and sad, assuredly, that in one state of the American Union, it should be found necessary to surround the scaffold of a condemned man with a guard of five thousand soldiers. In this man's honor the bells of churches will be tolling in other states and the voices of

Christian congregations will be lifted in holy prayer at the same hour of his writhing death.

It is idle to blink the fact that John Brown, who dies tomorrow as a criminal in Virginia, will be honored and lamented as a martyr by thousands of men and women in the Northern states. This fact our Southern kinsmen have thought it best and wisest to force upon the world's attention. The situation has been in their control; they have made of it what their wishes or their passions, or their sense of duty commanded. All that is left to be done in the matter now by Northern men who love their country and would see the rights of all its sections justly maintained, is to protest against the extravagant and inflammatory use which fanatical and reckless men in the North will now be swift to make of this decision and this deed in Virginia. By every sound principle of public law the life which Virginia will this day take was forfeit to the state. Whatever we may think of the wisdom and the policy of the consummation to which Virginia has ripened John Brown's enthusiastic dream of duty, we cannot doubt, and we must not silently suffer others to deny, that our sister commonwealth has been in her right from the first; and that, if we mean this Union to endure as a great national system, founded upon the equality and fraternity of the states, we must earnestly repudiate and to the best of our abilities repress the sympathy which thousands of easy enthusiasts will now be hastening to offer to the memory of a man in whom Virginia can only see the invader of her established order, and the implacable enemy of the social institutions by which she will chooses to abide.

The execution day started fair, and the air was warm and balmy. All strangers were excluded from the town. Indeed, no railroad trains were allowed to enter during the entire day. The gallows were erected starting at 7:30 AM. All preparations for the execution were completed as soon as possible, and the workmen who had toiled on the scaffold disappeared rather mysteriously. The military assembled at 9:00 AM and were posted on the field leading to the place of execution and also at various other points as laid down in the general orders. Everything was conducted under the strictest military discipline as if Charlestown were in a state of siege.

Mounted scouts were stationed in the woods to the left of the scaffold and picket guards stationed out towards the Shenandoah mountains in the rear. The military on the field formed two hollow squares. Within the inner square was the scaffold, and between the inner lines and the outer lines the citizens were admitted, but no one was allowed outside of the lines, except the mounted guards.

It seems that on the previous morning Brown was more than ordinarily cheerful. The jailor remarked that he hoped his fine show of spirits would continue. Brown replied that he "knew the community expected that I would show fear, but they would find themselves disappointed. They did not understand the stiff fiber of which I am made." After this remark, he made a hearty laugh

At a little before 10:30 AM John Brown was summoned and he appeared perfectly calm and collected. Brown executed an instrument empowering Sheriff Campbell to administer all property of his in the state, with directions to pay over the proceeds of the sale of the weapons, if recovered, to his widow and children. The sheriff then personally bid Brown farewell in his cell, the latter returning thanks for the sheriff's kindness, and speaking of Captain Pate as a brave man.

Brown was then taken to the cell of Copeland and Green. He told them to stand up like men, and not betray their friends; and he then handed them each a quarter, saying he had no more use for money, and bid them adieu. He then visited Cook and Coppoc who were chained together, and remarked to Cook, "you made a seriously false statement!"

Cook asked "What do you mean?"

Brown answered, "Why, by saying that I sent you to Harper's Ferry."

Cook replied, "Didn't you tell me in Pittsburgh to come to Harper's Ferry and see if Forbes had made any disclosures?"

Brown retorted, "No, sir, you knew I protested against your coming."

Cook, dropping his head, said, "Captain Brown, we remember things quite differently."

Brown then turned to Coppoc, and said, "Coppoc, you also made false statements, but I am glad to hear that you have contradicted them. Damn it, stand up like a man!" He handed Coppoc a silver quarter. He shook both Cook and Coppoc by the hand and they parted.

Brown was then taken back to his cell, where he exchanged a few last minute words with Aaron Stevens. Stevens said, "Good-bye Captain, I know you are going to a better land."

Brown replied, "I know I am." Brown told him to bear up, and not betray his friends. He also gave him a quarter. Brown did not visit Hazlett, as Hazlett always persisted in denying any knowledge of him.

At 10:55 AM the prisoner told Sheriff Campbell that he was ready. He had a black slouch hat on, and the same clothes he wore during the trial, a gray woolen undershirt and a colored shirt, without a collar. His arms were pinioned. He proceeded to the door, apparently calm and upbeat. He was escorted to the street by Sheriff Campbell, Mr. Sterry of Charlestown, Captain Avis the jailor; Mr. Saddler the undertaker, and a gentleman from New York.

As he came out, six companies of infantry and one troop of horses, with General Taliaferro and his entire staff, were deployed in front of the jail, while an open wagon, with a plain white pine box, in which was enclosed a fine oak coffin, was waiting for him. Brown looked around and spoke to several persons he recognized, and, walking down the steps, took a seat on the coffin-box, along with his jailor, Avis. He looked with interest on the fine military display, but made no remark. The wagon moved off, flanked by two files of riflemen in close order.

On his way to the scaffold John Brown entered into conversation with Mr. Saddler the undertaker, who was driving the wagon and sitting next to him. Mr. Saddler, on the spur of the moment, remarked, "Captain Brown, you are a game man." He answered, "Yes, I was so trained up; it was one of the lessons of my mother." Mr. Saddler then admitted, "Captain Brown, you are much cooler this moment than I am." John Brown replied, "That may be so, sir. I have suffered more from diffidence than from any feeling of physical fear. I have never known, even as a child, what that feeling was. It is constitutional with men; they are constitutionally brave or cowardly. The hardest of this is parting with friends, even though newly made."

On reaching the field where the gallows were erected, they saw that the military had already taken full possession. Pickets were stationed, and the citizens kept back at the point of the bayonet from taking any position but that assigned them. Through the determined persistence of Dr. Rawlings, of *Frank Leslie's* magazine, the order excluding the press was partially rescinded, and they were assigned a position near the major-general's staff. Brown asked Mr. Saddler, "Why are none but military allowed in the inclosure?" Mr. Saddler replied, "I am sorry but the citizens have been kept out. Captain, the house you see to our right hand is the residence of Mr. Brown, the clerk of the court. You remember him, I expect." John Brown replied, "Oh, yes. It is the cream colored one isn't it? Saddler replied, Yes, sir."

Brown then said, "What a beautiful country you have around here. It is the first opportunity I have had of really seeing it." Mr. Saddler replied, "Yes, this is a beautiful part of the country." The escort and wagon had by this time reached the front of the gallows, where it was stopped. Captain Avis, Jailor, first descended from the wagon. Captain Brown immediately took off his hat—the black felt one of the Kossuth type. Brown was assisted to the ground by Captain Avis. On reaching the gallows he observed Mr. Hunter and Mayor Green standing nearby, to whom be said, "Gentlemen, good-bye," his voice not faltering. The prisoner walked up the steps firmly, and was the first man on the gallows. Captain Avis and Sheriff Campbell stood by his side, and after shaking hands and bidding an affectionate adieu, he thanked them for their kindness. He then said, "I die alone responsible for my own operations, and ask for no sympathy. I am satisfied in my own belief—but desire no other man to believe as I do, unless his conscience and philosophy approve. I am singly responsible for my own acts, good or bad. If right or wrong, the consequence rests only upon myself."

Captain Avis put the cap on Brown's face and adjusted the rope around his neck. Avis then said, "Please step forward." Brown replied: "You must lead me, I cannot see." After he was placed on the drop, and the rope, which had a loop, was attached to a hook in the crossbeam above, the order "not ready yet," was given by an officer. The soldiers marched, counter marched, and took positions as if an enemy were in sight, and were thus occupied for nine and a half minutes. Despite this painful and trying time Mr. Campbell frequently raised the opening in the left hand side of the cap, as if he was letting the prisoner have air. As the prisoner was standing all this time, Avis inquired if he was not tired. Brown said, "No, not tired, but don't keep me waiting any longer than necessary." Everything now being ready, Mr. Campbell pressed the shoulder of Brown and said, "Good bye, Captain," and Brown's last audible word on this earth was "Good bye;" and as the sheriff left him he braced himself firmly, pressed his hands to his sides, and at 11:17 AM the drop fell. A slight grasping of his hands and twitching of his muscles were seen, and then all was silent.

The field was not more than a half mile from the jail. From the windows of his cell, Cook had an unobstructed view of the whole proceedings. He watched his old captain until the trap fell and his body swung into mid-air, when he turned away and gave vent to his feelings.

The body was examined several times, and the pulse did not cease until thirty-five minutes had passed. Brown's neck was not broken. The cord cut a finger's depth into Brown's neck, and a considerable distortion of countenance was said to have been produced. Brown's hold on life was strong. He just did not die easily, judging from appearances. Dr. Mason, the jail doctor, was the first to examine the body and pronounce him dead. The body was then cut down, placed in the coffin and conveyed under military escort to the depot, where it was put in a car to be carried to Harper's Ferry by a special train at 4:00 PM. All the arrangements were carried out with precision and with military strictness. The general conviction entertained by the jailors about an execution rescue was an egregious hoax.

Shortly after the execution, while the body was being taken to the depot, great excitement was raised by the arrival of a horseman, announcing that Wheatland, the late residence of George W. Turner, who was shot at Harper's Ferry, was on fire, and that the fire was extending to the farm and buildings of Mr. William F. Turner. The latter, who was in town, said that he had left home at 10:00 AM in the morning. He said that several of his horses had died very suddenly, and also some of his sheep. He intended to have their stomachs analyzed, as he believed that they were poisoned. The stock of Mr. Castleman and Mr. Myers in the same neighborhood had also died very mysteriously. The excitement caused by this was very great. Colonel Davis had the Faquier Cavalry in readiness to go out and inquire into the truth of the report about the fire.

THE HANGING OF JOHN BROWN

The body of Brown arrived at Harper's Ferry via the special train, and will be taken on by Mrs. Brown and her friends by express directly to Albany. It was desired to avoid all public demonstration, and it was determined that the body should not be visible anywhere on the route to North Elba, where it will be deposited in the family burying ground. Mrs. Brown spoke in the highest terms of the great kindness shown her by the citizens and authorities of the state. She was, of course, in great mental distress. She has most favorably impressed all who have met her as a great woman, a woman of fine feeling, and one of great affection for her husband.

The express train that evening brought a package of H. Clay Pate's pamphlets on John Brown and matters connected with the battle of Black Jack, which was intended to vindicate his own character for personal bravery. This document, which for mean blackguardism and scurrilous language, deserved a special notice. Mr. Pate, with the view of getting Brown and Cook to testify before witnesses in regard to his (Pate's) courage, went to visit them in jail, accompanied by two friends and Captain Avis. He met the prisoners in a most friendly manner, shaking their hands heartily, and appearing to commiserate their imprisonment. Under this guise of amity, this flag of truce as it were, he got them to acknowledge that he had shown personal bravery in their several conflicts. His end once secured, he left for the North to publish a pamphlet, in which he loaded it with every opprobrious epithet that his malice could suggest, calling Brown a greater liar than hell ever held, and Cook a white-livered scoundrel, and other choice appellations. If Mr. H. Clay Pate thought to establish a renown by such a cowardly conduct, he was greatly mistaken, for ultra Southern men have protested against this mean kicking of the dead lion in emphatic terms.

John T. L. Preston, one of the founders of the Virginia Military Institute and one of its first faculty members wrote the following letter to his wife about the hanging of John Brown:

Charlestown, Dec. 2, 1859

MY DEAR WIFE: The execution is over; we have just returned from the field and I sit down to give you some account of it. The weather was very favorable: the sky was a little overcast, with a gentle haze in the atmosphere that softened without obscuring the magnificent prospect afforded here

Between eight and nine o'clock, the troops began to put themselves in motion to occupy the positions assigned to them on the field, as designated on the plan I send you. To Colonel Smith had been assigned the superintendence of the execution, and he and his staff were the only mounted officers on the ground, until the major-general and his staff appeared. By ten o'clock all was arranged. The general effect was most imposing, and, at the same time, picturesque.

The cadets were immediately in rear of the gallows with a howitzer on the right and left, a little behind, so as to sweep the field. They were uniformed in red flannel shirts, which gave them a gay, dashing, Zouave look, and was exceedingly becoming, especially at the battery. They were flanked obliquely by two corps, the Richmond Grays (Greys) and Company F, which if inferior in appearance to the cadets, were superior to any other company I ever saw outside of the regular army. Other companies were distributed over the field, amounting in all to about 800 men. The military force was about 1,500.

The whole enclosure was lined by cavalry troops posted as sentinels, with their officers—one on a peerless black horse, and another on a remarkable-looking white horse, continually dashing round the enclosure. Outside this enclosure were other companies acting as rangers and scouts. The jail was guarded by several companies of infantry, and pieces of artillery were put in position for its defense.

Shortly before eleven o'clock the prisoner was taken from the jail, and the funeral cortege was put in motion. First came three companies, then the criminal's wagon, drawn by two large white horses. John Brown was seated on his coffin, accompanied by the sheriff and two other persons. The wagon drove to the foot of the gallows, and Brown descended with alacrity and without assistance, and ascended the steep steps to the platform. His demeanor was intrepid, without being braggart. He made no speech; whether he desired to make one or not, I do not know. Had he desired it, it would not have been permitted. Any speech of his must, of necessity, have been unlawful, and as being directed against the peace and dignity of the commonwealth, and as such could not be allowed by those who were then engaged in the most solemn and extreme vindication of law.

His manner was without trepidation, but his countenance was not free from concern, and it seemed to me to have a little cast of wildness. He stood upon the scaffold but a short time, giving brief adieus to those about him, when he was properly pinioned, the white cap drawn over his face, the noose adjusted and attached to the hook above, and he was moved blindfold a few steps forward. It was curious to note how the instincts of nature operated to make him careful in putting his feet as if afraid he would walk off the scaffold. The man who stood unblanched on the brink of eternity was afraid of falling a few feet to the ground.

He was now all ready. The sheriff asked him if he should give him a private signal before the fatal moment.

He replied in a voice that seemed to me unnaturally natural, so composed was its tone, and so distinct its articulation, that "it did not matter to him, if only they would not keep him too long waiting." He was kept waiting, however. The troops that had formed his escort had to be put into their position, and while this was going on, he stood for some ten or fifteen minutes blindfold, the rope around his neck, and his feet on the treacherous platform, expecting instantly the fatal act. But he stood for this comparatively long time upright as a soldier in position, and motionless.

I was close to him, and watched him carefully, to see if I could perceive any signs of shrinking or trembling in his body, but there was none. Once I thought I saw his knees tremble, but it was only the wind blowing his loose trousers. His firmness was subjected to still further trial by hearing Colonel Smith announce to the sheriff, "We are all ready, Mr. Campbell." The sheriff did not hear, or did not comprehend; and in a louder tone the same announcement was made. But the culprit still stood ready until the sheriff, descending the flight of steps, with a well-directed blow of a sharp hatchet, severed the rope that held up the trap door, which instantly sank beneath him, and he fell about three feet; and the man of strong and bloody hand, of fierce passions, of iron will, of wonderful vicissitudes, the terrible partisan of Kansas, the capturer of the United States arsenal at Harper's Ferry, the would-be Catiline of the South, the demi-god of the abolitionists, the man execrated and lauded, damned and prayed for, the man who in his motives, his means, his plans, and his successes, must ever be a wonder, a puzzle, and a mystery—John Brown—was hanging between heaven and earth.

There was profound stillness during the time his struggles continued, growing feebler and feebler at each abortive attempt to breathe. He knees were scarcely bent, his arms were drawn up to a right angle at the elbow, with the hands clenched; but there was no writhing of the body, no violent heaving of the chest. At each feebler effort at respiration his arms sank lower, and his legs hung more relaxed, until at last, straight and lank he dangled, swayed to and fro by the wind.

It was a moment of deep solemnity, and suggestive of thoughts that make the bosom swell. The field of execution was a rising ground, and commanded the outstretching valley from mountain to mountain, and their still grandeur gave sublimity to the outline, while it so chanced that white clouds resting upon them, gave them the appearance that reminded more than one of us of the snow peaks of the Alps. Before us was the greatest array of disciplined forces ever seen in Virginia; infantry, cavalry and artillery combined, composed of the old commonwealth's noblest sons, and commanded by her best officers; and the great canopy of the sky overarching all, came to add its sublimity ever present, but only realized when other great things are occurring beneath each.

The moral of the scene was its grand point. A sovereign state had been assailed, and she had uttered but a hint, and her sons had hastened to show that they were ready to defend her. Law had been violated by actual murder and attempted treason, and that gibbet was erected by law, and to uphold law was this military force assembled. But, greater still—God's Holy Law and righteous Providence was vindicated, "Thou shalt not kill"—"Who so sheddeth man's blood, by man shall his blood be shed." And here the gray-haired man of violence meets his fate, after he has seen his two sons cut down before him, in the same career of violence into which he had introduced them. So perish all such enemies of Virginia! All such enemies of the Union! All such foes of the human race! So I felt, and so I said, with solemnity and without one shade of animosity, as I turned to break the silence, to those around me. Yet, the mystery was awful, to see the human form thus treated by men, to see life suddenly stopped in its current, and to ask one's self the question without answer—"And what then?"

In all that array there was not, I suppose, one throb of sympathy for the offender. All felt in the depths of their hearts that it was right. On the other hand, there was not one single word or gesture of exultation or of insult. From the beginning to the end, all was marked by the most absolute decorum and solemnity. There was no military music, no saluting by troops as they passed one another, nor anything done for show. The criminal hung upon the gallows for nearly forty minutes, and after being examined by a whole staff of surgeons, was deposited in a neat coffin to be delivered to his friends, and transported to Harper's Ferry, where his wife awaited it. She came in company with two persons to see her husband last night, and returned to Harper's Ferry this morning. She is described by those who saw her as a very large, masculine woman, of absolute composure of manner. The officers who witnessed their meeting in the jail said they met as if nothing unusual had taken place, and had a comfortable supper together . . .

There was a very small crowd to witness the execution. Governor Wise and General Taliafaro had both issued proclamations exhorting the citizens to remain at home and guard their property, and warned them of possible danger. The train on the Winchester Railroad had been stopped from carrying passengers; and even passengers on the Baltimore Railroad were subjected to examination and detention. An arrangement was made ro divide the expected crowd into recognized citizens, and those not recognized; to require the former to go to the right and the latter to the left. Of the latter there was not a single one. It was told last night there were not in Charlestown ten persons besides citizens and military.

There is but one opinion as to the completeness of the arrangements made on the occasion, and the absolute success with which they were carried out. I have said something about the striking effect of the pageant as a pageant, but the excellence of it was that everything was arranged solely with the view of efficiency, and not for effect upon the eye. Had it been intended as a mere spectacle it could not have been made more imposing, or had actual need occurred, it was the very best arrangement.

You may be inclined to ask was all this necessary? I have not time to enter upon the question now. Governor Wise thought it necessary, and he said he had reliable information. The responsibility of calling out the force rests with him. It only remained for those under his orders to dispose the force in the best manner. That this was done is unquestionable, and, whatever credit is due for it, may fairly be claimed by those who accomplished it . . .

Thomas J. Jackson also from the Virginia Military Institute also described the execution later that day in a long letter to his wife, Anna Morrison Jackson:

John Brown was hung today at about 11:30 AM. He behaved with unflinching firmness. The arrangements were made under the direction of Colonel Smith. Brown's wife visited him last evening. The body is to be delivered to her. The gibbet was southeast of the town in a large field. Brown rode on the head of his coffin, from his prison to the place of execution. The coffin was of black walnut, enclosed in a poplar box of the same shape as the coffin. He was dressed in carpet slippers of predominating red, white socks, black pants, black frock coat, black vest, and a black slouch hat. Nothing was around his neck beside his shirt collar. The open wagon in which he rode was strongly guarded on all sides. Captain Williams, formerly one of the assistants at the institute, marched immediately in front of the wagon. The jailer and high Sheriff and several others rode in the wagon with the prisoner. Brown had his arms tied behind him, and ascended the scaffold with apparent cheerfulness. After reaching the top of the platform, he shook hands with several who were standing around him.

The sheriff placed the rope around his neck, placed a white cap over his head, and asked him if he wished a signal when all should be ready—to which he replied that it made no difference, provided he was not kept waiting too long. In this condition he stood on the trap door, which was supported on one side by hinges, and on the other (south side) by a rope, for about ten minutes, when Colonel Smith told the sheriff "all is ready," which apparently was not comprehended by the sheriff, and Colonel Smith had to repeat the order, when the rope was cut by a single blow, and Brown fell through about twenty-five inches, so as to bring his knees on a level with the position occupied by his feet before the rope was cut. With the fall his arms below the elbow flew up, hands clenched, and his arms gradually fell by spasmodic motions—there was very little motion of his person for several minutes, after which the wind blew his lifeless body to and fro . . .

After detailing where the cadets had stood throughout the ceremony, Jackson continued,

> I was much impressed with the thought that before me stood a man, in the full vigor of health, who must in a few minutes be in eternity. I sent up a petition that he might be saved. Awful was the thought that he might in a few moments receive the sentence "Depart ye wicked into everlasting fire." I hope that he was prepared to die, but I am very doubtful—he wouldn't have a minister with him.

> His body was taken back to the jail, and at 6:00 PM sent to his wife at Harper's Ferry. When it reached Harper's Ferry the coffin was opened and his wife saw the body—the coffin was again opened at the depot, before leaving for Baltimore, lest there should be an imposition.

Saturday, December 3rd arrived and the news of John Brown's execution began to spread. The event created a good deal of feeling throughout the country. New York City papers contained notices of meetings and other indications of sympathy, held in various sections of the Northern States. Two churches were opened in the city for public service—one the Shiloh church of colored worshipers, and the other the church of Dr. Cheever. No other public demonstrations took place there, and even at those churches the attendance was not large. In other places, a very small minority of the people took part in public proclamations of sympathy. In both branches of the Massachusetts legislature a motion to adjourn received but a very meager support. Half a dozen individuals, in any village, it must be borne in mind, can hold a meeting; or ring bells, or fire minute guns, and so attract as much attention at a distance as if the whole population had been engaged in the affair.

The New York *Times* reported:

It is but just to add, however, that hundreds and thousands of persons, in New York and throughout the North, were deeply moved by personal sympathy for Brown, who were still too thoroughly convinced of the legal justice of his execution, to make any outward showing of their commiseration. There is not, as we have had occasion to say repeatedly, any general or even any considerable sympathy with Brown's invasion of Virginia or with the object which took him there, in the North. But there is a very wide and profound conviction in the public mind that he was personally honest and sincere,—that his motives were such as he deemed honorable and righteous, and that he believed himself to be doing a religious duty in the work which he undertook. And the public heart always weighs the motives, as well as the acts, of men,—and gives its compassion and its pity freely to the man who stakes everything upon the performance of what he believes to be his duty. We do not believe that one-tenth of the people of the Northern States would assent to the justice of Brown's views of duty, or deny that he had merited the penalty which has overtaken his offense. But we have just as little doubt that a majority of them pity his fate and respect his memory, as that of a brave, conscientious and misguided man.

Now that the curtain has fallen upon this sad tragedy, we trust the public feeling will resume a healthier tone, especially in the Southern states, where it has risen to an unreasonable and a perilous heat. We take it for granted, the authorities of Virginia will not deem it necessary to continue their formidable display of military force, or further to agitate the public mind by apprehensions of invasion. We are not disposed to censure unduly what they have done hitherto in this direction. We can make just allowance for the circumstances which have surrounded them, and for the distrust and dread they have evinced. But the mass of the people in the North cannot understand and do not appreciate either. Knowing how narrow and how feeble is the sympathy felt in the North for such movements as that of Brown, our people deem it weak and puerile in the South thus to clothe herself in military array against imaginary dangers. And at this moment, throughout the North, the conviction is well-nigh universal, that the Virginians have been needlessly panic-stricken, or else that they have been victimized by political demagogues, who have sought the promotion of their own selfish ends by playing upon the fears and the resentments of the mass of the people.

So far as this outbreak of violent sentiment has been the work of partisans, it is quite useless to protest against it. Some of these men aim at disunion, and they naturally avail themselves of every opportunity to stimulate the distrust, resentment and hatred of the two sections towards each other. Others among them aim only at the ascendancy of their own sectional party in the national councils; and they use these incidents merely to unite the South and coerce the North into conformity to their desires. And still another class aim merely to crush some local competitor, or overbear some local clique, by arousing a public sentiment powerful enough to sweep away all who hesitate about yielding to its current. As these men are thoroughly and recklessly selfish in their aims, no considerations of the public good would check their insane endeavors. It is their determination to goad the South into the conviction that the whole North is bent on waging active war upon slavery in the Southern states, and that John Brown's troop was only the advanced guard of the general army. They deliberately and willfully falsify the sentiment of the North upon this subject. They represent the Northern people as all abolitionists,—all fanatics,—all reckless of Southern rights and Southern interests,—all ready to plunge Southern society into the horrors of anarchy and servile insurrection. Whatever ministers to this belief is lavishly used for that purpose; whatever corrects it, is ignored or discredited. The harangues of Phillips, the sermons of Cheever, the diatribes of our abolition orators and journalists, are greedily copied in Southern prints and put forward as illustrations of Northern sentiment; while the conservative declarations which emanate from our pulpits, our rostrums and our presses, are utterly unnoticed. We cannot wonder that, under such tuition and discipline, the people of the South come to regard every Northern man as their enemy.

It is easy to see to what all this must lead if it is suffered to go unchecked. It will produce increased distrust and alienation between the North and South, until, in some excess of popular passion, when reason and judgment and patriotism have all given away to blind and panic-stricken resentment, the selfish leaders of the mad crusade will plunge their followers into some crowning crime, which will involve their own destruction and menace the Union with dissolution. The remedy, we believe, lies exclusively with the conservatives of the South. That the North has duties to perform in this regard, we do not deny or seek to conceal; but, in the face of such a sentiment as now prevails in the Southern states, it is utter folly for any man or party of men in the North to do anything whatever. Indeed, nothing we could do would be regarded as of the slightest value. In its present mood what the South asks at our hands is simply irrational and impossible. Even our conservatism is scouted as the extreme of radical folly. When the *Journal of Commerce* is treated as a foe, and the New York *Herald,* with its incessant and malignant attempts to stimulate fear is regarded as part of our institutions, it is clearly hopeless to expect any rapid healing. The conservatives of the South, if they still desire and seek the public welfare, must not yield to this torrent of heated ultraism. They must resist and stem it. Even where they are overborne by it, they must still give signs to the North that reason and patriotic feeling have not wholly fled from the Southern states, and that there is still something there which renders the Union worth preserving. If the whole South desires disunion she can probably have it. If she expects her own condition to be bettered by it, a very brief experiment will dispel that delusion. But it would be much more rational and profitable, to all sections and to all in every section, to weigh well the consequences in advance, instead of learning wisdom only by that most costly of all methods—**experience**.

The conservatives of the Southern states can keep in check this movement, if they have the courage to undertake the task. And now that the immediate occasion of the panic is over, we trust they will find a favorable opportunity in the improved temper of the public mind, for refuting the falsehoods and correcting the mistakes by which they have been misled.

The remains of John Brown arrived at Philadelphia on Saturday, in custody of Mrs. Brown and Messrs. Hector Tindale and Miller McKim, of Philadelphia, on their way from Charlestown, Virginia, to Essex County, New York, where Brown will be interred. A large police force was detailed to preserve order. A considerable crowd, chiefly composed of colored persons, had assembled to witness the arrival of the train. The depot was cleared of most persons except the mayor, police, reporters and the reception committee. The train came in from Baltimore at Broad and Prime Streets at 12:40 PM in the afternoon.

The reception committee, at the head of which was the Reverend Dr. William H. Furness, was in waiting at the depot. When the train came in, Mrs. Brown, with two ladies who were with her, left the cars and passed down Washington Street, leaning on the arm of Mr. Tindale. At Eleventh

Street they took a city railway car and passed up to Arch Street. Mrs. Brown was firm in demeanor and was dressed in mourning.

In order to avoid the crowd, the body remained in the baggage car until 1:15 PM, when it was then taken out. The depot was cleared of all persons except a few policemen, reporters, and persons connected with the railroad company. The body was in a box, which was covered with a blanket of coarse cloth. A fur robe was lashed upon the top. A double line was formed by the policemen, and the body was carried by other officers to an old furniture wagon, covered with canvas, and drawn by an old bay horse, which was in waiting in the yard of the depot, on the south side of the buildings. Without any ceremony several policemen got into the wagon, and it was driven out of the gate onto Broad Street at about 2:00 PM.

These arrangements were not made with as much secrecy as was intended, for the boys who clambered upon the fence or peeped in through its interstices reported progress to the persons who were upon the outside, and by the time the wagon was driven out, there was an immense crowd, which was composed principally of colored people. The appearance of the vehicle with the body of Brown was greeted by loud cries, and the crowd chased after the wagon. There were three or four carriages, filled with colored persons, in the rear, but they had difficulty in keeping up with the wagon, which was driven as rapidly as the horse could trot.

The crowd, or at least as many of them as could keep up, followed the wagon to the Walnut Street wharf, while the women and the short-breathed among the men were compelled to lag behind, leaving a straggling mass to line the streets from the depot, at Broad and Washington Streets, to the wharf. The places of those who fell off were supplied by new-comers, while at the wharf there was a very large gathering. As the crowd ran along past the factories on Washington Street, the girls and men employed in them gathered at the doors and windows and shouted and screamed as the colored troop flocked along.

The remains of John Brown arrived in New York City at 6:30 PM by way of the Camden and Amboy railroad route from Philadelphia. J. M. Hopper of Brooklyn was in charge of the car in which the coffin was located. The body was inclosed in an oak coffin which was surrounded by a plain pine box. The body was accompanied by one of the sons of the deceased, who took charge at Philadelphia. Mrs. Brown arrived later at New York City via the New Jersey railroad at 8:30 PM, and crossed the ferry into the city in a closed carriage. She was met at the depot by several friends, with whom it had been arranged that she should spend Sunday in the city, in order that she might obtain the necessary repose before resuming her journey.

The large crowd of curious spectators who thronged the depots on Sunday at Baltimore and Philadelphia to obtain a view of the remains, rendered it necessary to observe some secrecy in their movements after arriving. The body was accordingly kept at the steamboat landing until 2:00 AM Sunday morning, when it was quietly conveyed to McGraw & Taylor, Undertakers, at No. 163 Bowery Street. The clothing which he had on was removed and the body placed on ice. During the afternoon, the place where the body had been temporarily deposited became known, and a crowd of persons gathered about the premises and endeavored to gain admittance to view the body. At one time it was feared that violence would be used to force open the gate which led to the rear of the building. The police, however, dispersed them. Afterwards several persons were admitted to the room, the lid of the coffin was removed, exposing Brown's face and breast. The body was found to be in remarkably good state of preservation. The features would have been instantly recognized as those of John Brown by any one who had seen his photograph. They were not in the least distorted, and wore a calm expression, as of one asleep. The lids were closed naturally, and there was a slight bruise perceptible on the side of his right eye. His body was dressed in the clothes he wore when he was executed.

No demonstrations of any kind took place in New York City with reference to the arrival or departure of the body, although it had been rumored that the remains would be conveyed to Dr. Cheever's Church of the Puritans, where funeral ceremonies would be preformed. A strong desire for such a demonstration in this city was expressed by many, but the movement was decided to be impracticable under the circumstances, beside being in opposition to the plainly expressed wishes of the deceased, concerning the disposition of his body. Arrangements were made for funeral rites upon the arrival of the train at Troy, New York.

Six companies of the Richmond and Wheeling military were ordered home, and about one-forth of the members of the other companies obtained furloughs for ten days, to return before the 10th, to attend the other executions. A military force was thus kept up, and martial law enforced throughout the county. The excitement has greatly abated, though there is still a great feeling of insecurity in the rural districts. The weather was cold and wet, and the military suffered greatly on picket guard and in their uncomfortable quarters.

Demonstrations of sympathy with the aims and the end of Brown continue to be reported from all parts of the North, and from Canada. Meetings were held at Cleveland and Rochester, formidable in numbers, and unmitigated in tone; while through New England hardly a town of note failed to have its utterance. To correct the impression these abolition manifestations will naturally make upon the South, a movement began in New York to hold a meeting expressive of Northern sympathy with the holders of slaves. The call, it is presumed, will find numerous signatures.

The Reverend Antoinette Brown Blackwell preached this Sunday evening with "Old John Brown" as a subject. She considered Brown and his followers as heroes and martyrs in the cause of freedom, but advocated moral persuasion as necessary to the work of anti-slavery. Discourses were also delivered today by Reverend Dr. Chapin and Reverend Dr. Cheever, both touching upon the fate of Brown—the former expressing conservative and the latter, as usual, radical views. A large meeting was held at the Corinthian Hall in Rochester, New York this evening, to signalize the execution of John Brown. Abram Pryne and Parker Pillsbury delivered addresses, which were listened to with profound interest.

John Brown's body remained at the New York City funeral home until 5:00 AM Monday morning when it was moved to the railroad depot on Warren Street, and went North by the 7:00 AM express train, Mrs. Brown and her son accompanying it. The casket arrived at Troy, New York at about 1:30 PM Monday, and was laid out in one of the rooms at the Union Depot. Wendell Phillips, Richard P. Hallowell, of Boston and James Miller McKim of Philadelphia were with Mrs. Brown. These gentlemen will accompany Mrs. Brown to North Elba, where the funeral will take place on Thursday of this week, and be interred according to the last wishes of the deceased. Mr. Phillips said that Massachusetts will eventually claim his remains for interment within her own soil, but that at present it was necessary to follow the directions of Mrs. Brown and the wishes of the family, that he should be interred at North Elba, Essex County, New York. Many of the family have not seen the deceased for several months, and they desired an opportunity of looking upon the last remains of one who was so near to them, and who lost his life in defense of a principle they all held so dear. Mr. Phillips said that the country cannot therefore claim him yet.

At Troy, the directors of the railroad gave the party a free pass to Rutland, Vermont, and provided them with temporary accommodations at the American House, a temperance hotel, where the deceased was in the habit of stopping when passing through the city. The proprietor of the hotel showed Mrs. Brown an autograph of her deceased husband, for which he had been offered $5 by a gentleman who promised to place it in a $10 frame. It was here, also, that Oliver Brown last parted with his wife previous to his journey to Harper's Ferry in company with his father. Mrs. Brown was quite unwell, and was unable to see any one. The severe ordeal through which she has passed has almost prostrated her, but it was hoped she will be restored enough to go on with the remains on the Renssalaer and Saratoga train in the evening. After a large dinner the party went to the depot, and took the cars bound for Rutland. They passed through Saratoga Springs, Whitehall, Castleton, and arriving at their destination safely, took up lodging at the Bardswell House at about 10:00 PM.

On the first day of the session of Congress, Senator Mason moved a committee of inquiry into all the circumstances of the affair at Harper's Ferry. Senator Trumbull, of Illinois,—a leading member of the Republican Party,—promptly assented to the propriety of such an investigation, and declared his confident belief that it would result in reestablishing public confidence in the disapproval by the North of any violent interference with slavery in the Southern states.

The New York *Times* reported:

> Mr. Mason took the proper course in this affair, and has been met in a proper spirit by Mr. Trumbull. The *émeute* itself would not deserve the formality of a public inquiry at the hands of congress, but the circumstances attending it, and the general belief in the South that it was countenanced and indorsed by the whole North, rendered it eminently proper that it should receive such attention. No opposition from any quarter was made to the resolution. It ought to pass by a unanimous vote, and without any preliminary debate. Heated discussion, indeed, in advance of evidence, would only aggravate the evils which make the inquiry necessary. There will be a strong inclination without doubt, on the part of partisans, to rush at once into the field of crimination and recrimination which was thrown so broadly and invitingly open. The wise and discreet men of all parties in Congress will resolutely discourage all such attempts to heat the public mind and trifle with the gravest interests of the country.

> Let us have the committee ordered promptly and unanimously; let the president of the senate select its members fairly and justly, from the soundest men of both parties; let it proceed at once with its investigations, and place before Congress and the country every fact which

the closest scrutiny can elicit concerning this bold but happily futile attempt to raise the black banner of servile insurrection on the soil of Virginia. The whole country can then form a clear and reliable judgment as to the character of the movement, and the responsibility which rests upon parties and politicians in connection with it.

The conviction is that the result of such an inquiry will be to divest the affair of much of the factitious importance, and to allay the feverish excitement to which it has given rise. But if it should prove otherwise, we are equally desirous that the investigation should be made. If prominent public men were parties to that outrage upon public law and the public peace;—if donations of money and of arms were made for the purpose of helping it forward,—and if it had the countenance and support of any considerable number of people in the Northern States, let the fact be known and the responsibility placed where it belongs. We hazard little in saying that the North itself will very promptly put the seal of its reprobation upon every man who can so far forget his obligations to the constitution and his duty to the country, as to lend the slightest countenance to a crusade which can only end in the ruin of the one, and the lasting injury and disgrace of the other.

We have assumed that the motive of the proposed inquiry was for the public good,—and that it will be made in the spirit of harmony and of union, and not of sectional hatred and dissolution. There is danger that in this matter we may be over sanguine. The spirit of partisanship is so general and so potent;—sectional animosity and distrust have already, to so great an extent, poisoned the springs of public action,—that we can scarcely count upon disinterestedness and patriotism in even the gravest and most solemn proceedings of our public bodies. If this inquiry is to be pushed, for the purpose of influencing the presidential election, it will do more harm than good. Its aim will be to feed rather than allay public excitement,—to foster partisan animosities and hatreds, and to plunge the country still more hopelessly into the heat and fever of sectional contention. This, however, is a peril from which we are never free; and we can only appeal to the patriotism and public spirit of the Senate, to save us from it.

The following correspondence was delivered to the New York *Tribune*:

Boston, December 3, 1859.

SIRS: I am happy to inform the friends of Osborne Anderson that he was *not* killed at Harper's Ferry, but is now in Canada. I have received this news from Francis J. Merriam, who succeeded in escaping, and is now at the town of Chatham, Canada, with Barclay Coppoc, the brother of the condemned prisoner at Charlestown. If it be true that a man named Coppoc has been arrested at Charlestown and that he is a relative of the prisoner, it is equally true that he was not at Harper's Ferry. Merriam, who was supposed to be dead, and was known to have been separated from his companions, succeeded, he states, in disguising himself near Carlisle, Pennsylvania and traveling North-star-ward, without suspicion or interruption, immediately after the arrest of Cook—that unfortunate boy whose undoubted bravery in Kansas is now forgotten in his recent quailing in view of a Virginia gallows. Let me say a few words in defense of this poor boy. He was tested in Kansas, and his courage admitted by our most daring guerilla bands.

There is no manner of doubt that he was a fearless fighter against the Southern invaders of Kansas, and an efficient aid in ridding the territory of Buford and his banded assassins. He was also a kind, generous, noble-hearted youth; but as his heroism was founded on the warm impulses of his heart only, not on principles the result of earnest thought, he is now in danger of dying with the reputation of a coward. They are mistaken who call him a coward; he is the victim of Voorhies and his brother-in-law. He would not have flinched if it had not been for them. God pardon them for corrupting that too plastic but generous-hearted youth!

Let us not believe that he recognized any one whom the other prisoners refused to know. Remember that the cowardly Virginians can now lie with impunity about him. I cannot believe that he is a corrupt man; *for no one has been implicated by his confession*, and he has said nothing that John Brown cared to conceal. He may have written some falsehoods; and if John Brown said so, he did lie; but who were his prompters and the more culpable men?

When at Chambersburg, he refused to give the name of his fourth companion—Merriam—even to his own lawyer in confidence; because he stated, he had not yet been implicated. John E. Cook is not a moral hero, but it is going too far to brand him as a coward. Let no one do it, at least, who did *not* go to Kansas to defend the cause of freedom there.

When Fort Titus was carried by the free state men, one of them found a carpet-bag containing $10,000 in gold and notes. He ran off with it, and succeeded in escaping from the territory. *Titus said that this money came exclusively from Virginia.* Does Virginia imagine that she lost that money? or that the Kansas men did not intend to pay the interest? Having failed to pay it at Harper's Ferry, Kansas asks for a further extension.

Sincerely,

JAMES REDPATH

The Brown party rose at an early hour on Tuesday, December 6th, and departed on the morning train for Vergennes, Vermont. They intended to cross Lake Champlain at this point and then travel over the mountains in wagons to North Elba. At Vergennes an employee of the Stevens House, Christopher Yallow, met the train carrying the funeral cortege. The proprietors of the Stevens House very generously refused to take any compensation from either Mrs. Brown or the gentlemen who accompanied her. John Brown, it appears, was well known in Vergennes, and the register at the Stevens House bore several of his autographs. None of the signatures were of recent date, but they are objects of special interest to the residents of the town, and highly prized. When the hour arrived for the departure of the cortege, the inhabitants, to the number of sixty or seventy, formed in procession, and amidst the tolling of bells the corpse was escorted out of the village on its way to the ferry. They took the turnpike from Vergennes through the town of Panton and on to Arnold Bay where the Adams Ferry was located. With the completion of the Champlain Canal in 1833 the Adams Ferry served as a transportation link between the farms in the Adirondacks and the cattle and sheep markets located in Vermont.

At the time the cortege arrived at the ferry there was a strong wind and a sleet storm blowing over the lake. Daniel Adams transported the party across Lake Champlain to Westport, New York, and the party arrived at Westport just in time for dinner. The Reverend Joshua Young of Burlington, who was asked to speak at the burial ceremony, missed the ferry's departure and had to cross the next day. The Brown party went to Person's Hotel where the proprietor of the hotel, Harry J. Person, who was an old friend of Brown's, refused to take any compensation. The inhabitants insisted on bearing the expense of transporting the party to North Elba, and provided the best of everything for their comfort while on the journey.

The passage over the Adirondack mountains at that season of the year was considered a most arduous trip, the region lying between Lake Champlain and North Elba being one vast wilderness. In order to give you some idea of the wilderness of the country at that time it might be mentioned that eight deer, two panthers, thirteen sable and one wild cat were killed there during that season by a single hunter. The distance from the lake to North Elba is only about forty miles, yet the journey was seldom accomplished in less than a day and a half, so rugged and mountainous was the path.

When the sleet turned to rain, the men in Westport changed from sleighs to wagons for the remainder of the trip. Just west of the village the funeral party entered the old Northwest Bay Road, a turnpike road with miles of ruts and mud, covered at points with wooden planks. After a tedious journey the party reached Elizabethtown, which is the seat of justice for Essex County, on Tuesday evening at 6:00 PM. At the Mansion House they halted for much needed rest and refreshment. The sheriff of Essex County, Elisha A. Adams Esq.,[1] who was the proprietor of the hotel there, received the party kindly and offered them the best his house afforded, and at his invitation the inhabitants formed a procession and conveyed the corpse to the court house, where it remained all night, guarded by six youths who volunteered for the task. Among them were O. Abel Jr., J. Q. Dickinson, Richard L. Hand and Mr. Haskell. The courtroom was soon filled by the leading residents of the town, eager to learn from Messrs. Phillips and McKim all the particulars of the execution. Among the gentlemen who paid their respects were Judge Hall; the Honorable Orlando Kellogg, late member of congress and G. L. Nicholson Esq. They

---

[1] Elisha A. Adams was the son-in-law of the famed Ruben Sanford of Wilmington, whose stand at the battle of Plattsburg was one of the treasured memories of the War of 1812. Earlier Adams had been the county clerk, but in 1859 he became the sheriff.

found it hard to realize that their old friend and fellow citizen, the man whom they had known so well, and only known to respect and admire, had actually been put to death. They did not think that, in the last extremity, Virginia would do the bloody deed. They did not see how Governor Wise could have deliberately consented to the death of such a man. Mr. Henry J. Adams, a son of the sheriff, volunteered to start off in the night, with a swift horse, to notify the family of the party's approach.

The journey was resumed Wednesday morning, December 7th. The party stopped at the house of Phineas Norton, living in the town of Keene, Vermont. Mr. Norton welcomed them most hospitably. He had known Mr. Brown well, and loved him dearly, and he had not been able to realize that the sentence of death would really be executed. The proof furnished by the coffin containing the dead body quite overcome him.

They stopped for rest and dinner, at his enthusiastic request. They had been all that time coming five miles! They then pushed on to North Elba. Slowly they climbed the mountain pass, and as slowly descended on the other side. The sun had set by the time they reached North Elba, and it was dark when they approached the house to which they were destined. As they drew close they saw moving lights, which, on their nearer approach, proved to be lanterns in the hands of friends who had come out to meet them. The meeting between Mrs. Brown and the surviving members of the family was not characterized by any loud demonstrations of grief. Tears did not flow as profusely, perhaps, as might be expected under the circumstances, but a close observer could perceive that the anguish of the household was intense. One by one they silently embraced their mother. First came Ruth, the eldest daughter, who married Henry Thompson; then followed Salmon and his sisters Anna, Sarah and Ellen, the latter being only five years old. Martha Brown, the wife of Watson Brown, who was killed at Harper's Ferry, was also present.

The coffin was brought into the house and deposited in one of the upper rooms, where it was the object of much curiosity among the neighbors who had crowded in. After tea the family surrounded Mr. McKim, and learned from him the particulars of the late scenes at Charlestown and

Harper's Ferry. The Reverend Gentleman testified to the courtesy of several prominent citizens in Virginia and Maryland, and the sympathy that was felt for Mrs. Brown all along the route from Harper's Ferry to North Elba. He said they had been treated with all proper respect, and made favorable mention of Mr. Garnett, president of the Baltimore and Ohio Railroad; Colonel Shutt, Dr. Phelps, Captain Sinn, Colonel Lee, Captain Moore, Colonel Barbour and others, who aided them materially in their mission South. At the close of the evening the lid was raised from the coffin and the body of Old Brown was exhibited to all present. The countenance of the deceased was more natural than it appeared in New York, and bore a placid and serene expression. An hour or so was then spent in conversation, and the household then retired for the night.

The homestead at North Elba was built upon a tract of land purchased by Gerrit Smith for a colony of Negroes, some fifteen years previously. The farm, in point of elevation, was said to be the highest in the state; hence it is not what might be called productive land. The inhabitants in that part of the country just manage to live on the product of their farms, and that is all. When Old Brown first settled at North Elba, about a dozen colored families followed him there, and it was believed by Gerrit Smith that a flourishing colony would grow up. Instead of increasing in population or wealth, however, the colony has decreased in both, and now there are no more than half a dozen Negro families in the place. The enterprise proved a complete failure, but Brown became quite attached to the spot, and refused to leave it. His family also resolved to make the place their future home, although few can see the inducement for spending a lifetime in such a dreary wilderness. The house was a medium-sized frame building, such as is common in that part of the country. It had four rooms on the first floor, and corresponding space above. The company was comparatively large, but ample accommodations were found for all; and although the night was intensely cold, a bountiful supply of good, warm bed-clothing kept all comfortable.

NORTH ELBA

Thursday morning, December 8th, dawned bright and clear. The sun shone brilliantly, and reflected with dazzling effect upon the snow clad peaks of Mount Marcy and the Keene Mountains. The thermometer was down to zero, but no one seemed to feel the cold, so deep was the interest in the ceremony that was about to be performed. Isabel Brown, wife of Watson Brown, with her babe five months old, arrived in the course of the morning, as also did Roswell Thompson and his wife, parents of William Thompson, who fell at Harper's Ferry. Later on the Reverend Mr. Joshua Young of Burlington, Vermont arrived with a young friend, Lucius Bigelow, having ridden all night over the mountains for the purpose of being present at the interment. Both were cold and shivering. Wendell Phillips greeted them and said to the Reverend, "Reverend Young, you are a minister; admiration for this dead hero and sympathy with his bereaved family must have brought you here, journeying all night through the cold rain and over the dismal mountains to reach this place. It would give Mrs. Brown and the other widows great satisfaction if you would perform the usual service of a clergyman on this occasion." Young replied that he would.

At about 10:00 AM the neighbors, to the number of two hundred and fifty, perhaps, commenced to assemble, and it was decided that the procession should start from the house at twelve o'clock. About twenty yards east of the house stands a large rock about eight feet high and oval like in shape. At the base of this boulder the neighbors dug a grave six feet deep. The work occupied considerable time, in consequence of the frozen state of the earth; but at noon all was in readiness to receive the remains.

At twelve o'clock the house was filled to its utmost capacity with the friends and relatives of the deceased. An hour or so was spent by the assemblage in taking a last farewell of the body. The entire family embraced the deceased, and then, falling back allowed the friends to come forward and view the corpse previous to its being conveyed to its last resting place. The procession started at one o'clock, preceded by about a dozen colored persons, singing "Blow ye the trumpet blow!"

> Blow ye the trumpet, blow!
> The gladly solemn sound
> Let all the nations know,
> To earth's remotest bound.
>
> (Chorus)
> The year of jubilee is come!
> The year of jubilee is come!
> Return, ye ransomed sinners, home.
>
> Jesus, our great high priest,
> Hath full atonement made;
> Ye weary spirits, rest;
> Ye mournful souls, be glad.
> Chorus.
>
> Extol the Lamb of God,
> The all atoning Lamb;
> Redemption in his blood

Throughout the world proclaim.
Chorus.

The gospel trumpet hear,
The news of heavenly grace;
And, saved from earth, appear
Before your Savior's face.
Chorus.

This was a favorite hymn of the deceased, with which he used to sing all his children to sleep. It was sung to the good old tune of Lennox. The coffin was borne from the house by six young men, and followed to the grave by the mourners in the following order:

The Corpse.
Mrs. Brown, supported by Wendell Phillips.
Mrs. Oliver Brown and her daughter Ellen
supported by the Reverend Mr. Young.

Henry Thompson and his wife Ruth.
Salmon Brown, his wife and child.
Roswell Thompson and wife.
Friends of the deceased and neighbors.

Arriving at the grave, the Reverend Mr. Young offered up a very impressive prayer:

Almighty and most merciful God! we lift our souls unto thee, and bow our hearts to the unutterable emotions of his impressive hour. Oh God, Thou alone art our sufficient help. Open Thou our lips and our mouth shall show forth thy praise. Thou art speaking unto us; in those grand and majestic scenes of nature, so in the great and solemn circumstances which have brought us together. Our souls are filled with awe and are subdued to silence, as we think of the great, reverential, heroic soul, whose mortal remains we are now to commit to the earth, 'dust to dust,' while his spirit dwells with God who gave it, and his memory is enshrined in every pure and holy heart. At his open grave, as standing by the altar of Christ, the most divine friend and Savior of Man, may we consecrate ourselves anew to the work of Truth, Righteousness and Love, forevermore to sympathize with the outcast and the oppressed, with the humble and the least of our suffering fellow-men.

We pray for these afflicted ones—this sadly bereaved and afflicted family. O! God, cause the oppressed to go free; break any yoke and prostrate the pride and prejudice that dare to lift themselves up; and O! hasten on the day when no more wrong or injustice shall be done in the earth; when all men shall love one another with pure hearts, fervently, and love with all their strength; which we ask in the name and as the disciples of Jesus Christ. **Amen.**

Mr. McKim, in pronouncing the funeral oration, said that words were utterly inadequate to the occasion. "These mountain peaks, this weeping group, the body of the martyr for liberty—what could he add to their eloquence?" And yet it was due to these stricken hoards that he should say something in honor of the hero whose remains were about to be laid in the distance—something to comfort those whose hearthstone had been left desolate. He had not known Captain Brown in life—had never looked upon his face till it was cold in death; but how he honored, admired and loved him, in view of the developments of the last few weeks, words could not tell. He felt it the highest honor of his life to take part in the burial of one so noble. He alluded to the tribute paid to the bravery and magnanimity of Captain Brown, even by those who had treated him as a criminal, and also to the respect manifested for Mrs. Brown during her sad and solemn journey to Virginia, to receive his remains. More than one Virginian sought to comfort her by paying a tribute to his bravery and consistency. A blunt militia officer said in her hearing, "I'll tell you what my opinion is of Brown; he's one of that kind of men that God does not put many of above ground." Another officer, thoroughly pro-slavery in his sentiments and feelings, had begged for some moments—his autograph, or some other relic, however trifling.

Mr. McKim then spoke of the last incidents before the execution, and described the manly and noble bearing of the old hero as he was led forth to die, and as he stood upon the scaffold. He would attempt nothing as a tribute to John Brown. The facts of his life and of his bearing in the face of death were his best eulogy. He sympathized most profoundly with the bereaved widow and children, and felt it a privilege to mingle his tears with theirs. John Brown and the sons and son-in-law who, with him, had sacrificed their lives in an effort to break the chains of the enslaved, were all benefactors, all martyrs in the sacred cause. Their lives had not been spent in vain, and the world would yet acknowledge itself their debtor. Their memory would be embalmed in history. Mr. McKim also spoke tenderly of those who were yet in prison, and read the following touching letter from Coppoc, brought to Mrs. Brown at Harper's Ferry, by the officers who accompanied her husband's body to that place:

Charlestown Jail. Va., Dec. 1, 1859

Mrs. John Brown.

DEAR MADAM: I was very sorry that your request to see the rest of the prisoners was not complied with. Mrs. Avis brought me a book, whose pages are full of truth and beauty, entitled, "Voices of the True Hearted," which she told me was a present from you. For this dear token of remembrance please accept my many thanks. My comrade, J. M. Cook, and myself, deeply sympathize with you in your sad bereavement. We were both acquainted with Anna and Martha. They were to us as sisters, and as brothers we sympathize with them in the dark hour of trial and affliction.

I was with your sons when they fell. Oliver lived but a very few moments after he was shot. He spoke no word, but yielded calmly to his fate. Watson was shot at 10:00 AM on Monday morning, and died about 3:00 AM on Wednesday morning. He suffered much. Though mortally wounded at ten o'clock on Monday morning he fought bravely against the men who charged on us at three o'clock in the afternoon. When the enemy was repulsed, and the excitement of the charge was over, he began to sink rapidly. After we were taken prisoners he was placed in the guard house with me. He complained of the hardness of the bench on which he was lying. I begged hard for a bed for him, or even a blanket, but could obtain none for him. I took off my coat and placed it under him, and held his head in my lap, in which position he died without a groan or a struggle.

I have stated these facts, thinking that they might afford to you and to the bereaved widows they have left, a mournful consolation. Give my love to Anna and Martha, with our last farewell.

Yours truly,

EDWIN COPPOC

Some of Captain Brown's friends, said Mr. McKim, seem to regard the result of the affair at Harper's Ferry as a disaster. Disastrous it was in some respects, but not a failure. It had developed the weakness, the imbecility, of a slave holding state, in such a way as must inevitably lead to emancipation. He has "built better than he knew." He had wielded "the sword of the spirit" against slavery with wonderful effect. His words had gone out to the world and were doing their work. They were inspired words, needing neither alteration nor addition. Thus with the sword of the flesh and the sword of the spirit, John Brown had performed a double mission, and the handwriting that doomed the system flamed out on the wall. Mr. McKim said that the grave of the martyr had been made in the very spot selected by himself. He also read the inscription for the family monument, which Old Brown wrote after the last interview with his wife, and which was sent to her with his dead body. The inscription was accompanied by some directions about his property, and also by the following appended note—the last, probably, that he ever wrote:

> MY DEAR WIFE: I have time to enclose the within and the above, which I forgot yesterday, and to bid you another farewell. "Be of good cheer," and God Almighty bless, save, comfort, guide and keep you to "the end."
>
> Your affectionate husband,
>
> JOHN BROWN

Mr. McKim closed with a few words of exhortation to the family and friends assuring them that by their sacrifices they had made large contributions to the cause of freedom and humanity, and that they had the earnest sympathy of thousands of the noblest and best men in the world.

Mr. Wendell Phillips then followed and spoke as follows:

> How feeble all words are here! You think you have known him. None of us seem to have known him. Walking serene to the scaffold, We say, "What courage!" Stooping to kiss that Negro child, he seems all tenderness. But he is only the center of a group. These quiet homes sent six to that score of heroes. How bravely they died—each standing in his post till his voice said "enough." And these weeping children and widows, how blessed, since in the last throbs of the brave young hearts at Harper's Ferry, thoughts of them mingled with love for God and hope for the slave. He has abolished slavery in Virginia. Some may say that is too much. Bunker Hill severed New England from the

mother country. Yet men that night pitied Warren. We see him cutting the link. George the Third ceased that day to rule here. History will date Virginia's emancipation from Harper's Ferry. When the tempest uproots one of these pines, it may live months, but it is timber, not a tree. John Brown has loosened the roots of slavery—it may gasp, but it is dead. He said he could take the town with twenty men, and did it. Who stopped him? Not Virginia; her he conquered. The Union seemed to check him. In reality God said "that work is done; you have proved that a slave state is only Fear in the mesh of Despotism; now come up highest by martyrdom—change a million hearts." Such a life was no failure. Virginia stands at the world's bar, on trial; round her victim stand the apostles and martyrs all, who have said, "God is God," and trampled wicked laws under their feet. He said, "My fathers have given their swords to the master; I give mine to the slave."

If God is ever the Lord of Hosts, "making one man chase a thousand," surely that band at Harper's Ferry may claim him as their captain. Men say, "how coolly brave!" But in him matchless courage seems the least of his merits. How gentleness graced it. When the frightened town wished to bear off the body of the mayor, a man said, "I will go under their rifles if you, Miss Fouke, will stand between them and me." He knew he could trust their gentle respect for women. He was right. He went in the thick of the fight, and bore off the body in safety. That same girl flung herself between Virginia rifles and your young, brave Thompson. They had no pity. The merciless bullet reached him in spite of a woman's prayers, though the fight had long been over.

Harper's Ferry was the flowering out of a long devoted life. These his sons and daughters show how wholly he lived for his idea, as each accepts so serenely his or her part in the movement—the share of toil and grief. As time passes, history will paint that gallows girt by thousands of armed men, guarding Virginia from her slaves, and ever against it that serene old man stooping to kiss the Negro child. Thank God for our emblem. May he move Virginia soon to blot out hers by repugnance and hide it with broken fetters.

We envy you your nearer place to these noble martyrs. Slavery will not go down by force. Hearts are stringer than swords. How sublime that last fortnight. His words are stronger than even his rifles. These crushed a state; those will yet crush slavery. God gave him better than a soldiers place—that of teacher. The echoes of his rifles have died away among the hills—his words millions treasure. God bless this roof—make it bless us. We dare not say, "Bless you children of this home," for you stand nearer to one whose lips God touched, and we bend for your blessing. God makes us worthier of him whom we lay among these hills. Here he girded himself with more of success than he ever dreamed God gave him. He sleeps in the blessings of the slave. Men believe more in virtue since he has lived. Standing here, let us thank God for a firmer faith and fuller hope.

The coffin was then lowered into the grave amidst deep silence. Just as it reached the bottom of the pit, and as the first shovel of earth grated harshly on the ear, the Reverend Mr. Young lifted up his voice, and in loud, impressive tones exclaimed, "I have fought the good fight; I have finished my course; henceforth there is laid up for me a crown of righteousness, which the Lord, the righteous Judge, will give me at the last day."

The work of filling the grave having been performed, Mrs. Brown and her relatives slowly wended their way back to the house, but the great bulk of the crowd remained idly gazing on the mound for an hour or so after it was all over. A large supper was provided for everyone and people ate and talked till late that night.

The first article of John Brown's will referred to a monument at North Elba, which he bequeathed to his son, John Brown Jr., with instructions to have his epitaph inscribed upon it. This stone was erected to the memory of the deceased's grandfather, who fell in the Revolution; but it was also intended as a monument for Brown himself, as demonstrated by the following extract from his will:

> I give to my son, John Brown Jr., my surveying compass and other surveyors articles, if found; also my old favorite monument now at North Elba, New York, to receive upon its two sides a further inscription, such as I will hereafter write; said stone monument, however, to remain at North Elba so long as any of my children or my wife remain there as residents.

The inscription that he speaks of was prepared the day before the execution, and given to Mrs. Brown. Of his own epitaph the following is a copy:

JOHN BROWN
Born May 9, 1800;
Was executed at Charlestown,
Virginia, Dec. 2, 1859.

For Oliver and Watson Brown he forwarded the following epitaphs:

OLIVER BROWN
Born 1839;
Was killed at Harper's Ferry,
Nov. 17, 1859.

WATSON BROWN
Born 1839;

Was wounded at Harper's Ferry Nov. 17, 1859.
Died Nov. 19, 1859.

Few persons were aware that Brown had a poetic turn of mind, and had written several pieces of rhyme. The following lines were dedicated to several of his children who died in their infancy:

Through all the dreamy night of death
In peaceful slumbers may you rest,
And when eternal day shall dawn,
And shades and death have past and gone,
Oh, may you then, with glad surprise,
In God's own image wake and rise.

It was now nearly 3:00 PM in the afternoon and Messrs. Phillips and McKim were anxious to be on their way home. A long and difficult journey was ahead of them and as the worst part was to be encountered at the outset, it was important that they start out as early as possible. The carriages were made ready, and a hasty but tearful leave taking ensued between the family and their friends from a distance. They were soon well over the mountains. Most of the party stopped at Keene for the night, but one or two pushed on to Elizabethtown. On the following evening Mr. Phillips had an engagement to deliver a lecture in the town hall at Vergennes.

Mr. Phillips carried a large amount of valuable matter from North Elba to Boston, intended for Mr. Child's promised memoir of John Brown. This matter consisted of original letters and other papers, and photographs of several members of the Brown and Thompson families. The memoir will not be published for some time, and the prospects of its appearance did not interfere with the sale of Mr. James Redpath's book about John Brown.[2]

---

[2] Which was published in 1860 by Thayer and Eldridge of Boston.

Chapter 11

GOVERNOR WISE'S
OFFICIAL MESSAGE

*T*HE FOLLOWING IS *the official message from Governor Wise to the Legislature of Virginia, at Richmond, Virginia, on Wednesday, December 7, 1859.*

To the Senate and House of Delegates of the General Assembly of the Commonwealth of Virginia:

GENTLEMEN: Up to a late period I had fondly hoped to close my official term and part from my executive duties with naught but cause of congratulations on the condition of the commonwealth. But the uppermost theme in this my last regular message must be, that our peace has been disturbed; our citizens have been imprisoned, robbed and murdered; the sanctity of their dwellings has been violated; their persons have been outraged; their property has been seized by force of arms; a stronghold in their midst, with its arms and munitions of war, has been captured, and the inhabitants cut off from the means of defense; a national highway through out limits, and its locomotive trains and telegraphic wires have been stopped; and state and national sovereignty have been insulted and assailed; and state and federal troops have been called out and compelled to fight, at the loss of several killed and wounded, to subdue rebellion and treason at Harper's Ferry, in the County of Jefferson, within our jurisdiction.

GOVERNOR WISE OF VIRGINIA

CHARACTER AND OBJECTS OF THE INVASION

This was no result of ordinary crimes, however highhanded and felonious. It was no conspiracy of bandits against society in general, with the motives which usually actuate criminals, confined to the individual perpetrators, and to be crushed by their arrest and punishment. But it was an extraordinary and actual invasion, by a sectional organization, specially upon slave holders and upon their property in Negro slaves. The home to be invaded was the home of domestic slavery; the persons to be seized were the persons of slave holders; the property to be confiscated was the property in slaves and the other property of slave holders alone, such as money, plate, jewels and other of like kind, which was to be taken to compensate the robbers for the trouble and risk of robbing the masters of their slaves; the slaves were not to be taken to be carried away, but they were to be made to stand by the side of the robbers, and to be forced to fight to liberate themselves by massacring their masters; the arsenal was taken to supply arms to servile insurgents; and a provisional government was attempted in a British province, by our own countrymen, united to us in the faith of confederacy, combining with Canadians, to invade the slaveholding states of the United States; and thus the night of the 16th of October last was surprised and the day of the 17th of October last was startled by the signal guns of rapine, murder, robbery and treason, began at Harper's Ferry for the purpose of stirring up universal insurrection of slaves throughout the whole South.

Sudden, surprising, shocking as this invasion has been, it is not more so than the rapidity and rancor of the causes which have prompted and put it in motion. It is not confined to the parties who were the present participators in its outrages. Causes and influences lie behind it more potent far more than the little band of desperadoes who were sent ahead to kindle the sparks of a general conflagration; and the event, sad as it is, would deserve but little comment, if the condign punishment of the immediate perpetrators of the felonies committed would for the future secure the peace which has been disturbed, and guarantee the safety which it threatened. Indeed, if the miserable convicts were the only conspirators against our peace and safety, we might have forgiven their offenses and constrained them only by the grace of pardon. But an entire social and sectional sympathy has incited their crimes, and now rises in rebellion and insurrection to the height of sustaining and justifying their enormity.

NORTHERN SENTIMENT RESPONSIBLE FOR THE INVASION

It would be pusillanimous to shut our eyes and to affect not to see certain facts of fearful import which stare us in the face, and of which I must speak plainly to you, with the firm and manly purpose of meeting danger, and with no weak and wicked design of exciting agitation. That danger exists, of no serious magnitude, there can be no doubt in the minds of the most calm and reflecting, and the way to avert it in all cases, is to march up to it and meet it front to front. If it has not grown too great already, it will retire from collision; and if it has grown strong enough already for the encounter, it had better be met at once, for it will not diminish by delay. I believe, in truth, that the very policy of the prime promoters of this apparently mad movement is purely tentative; to try whether we will face the danger which is now sealed in blood. If we "take the dare," the aggression will become more and more insolent; and if we do not, that it will either truckle or meet us in open conflict to be subdued;

and, in either event, our safety and the national peace will be best secured by a direct settlement at once—the sooner the better.

For a series of years social and sectional differences have been growing up, unhappily, between the states of our Union and their people. An evil spirit of fanaticism has seized upon Negro slavery as the one object of social reform and the one idea of its abolition has seemed to madden whole masses of one entire section of the country. It enters into their religion, into their education, into their politics and prayers, into their courts of justice, into their business, into their legislatures, into all classes of their people, the most respectable and most lawless, into their pulpits and into their presses and school-houses, into their men, women and children of all ages, everywhere. It has trained three generations, from childhood up, in moral and social habits of hatred to masters of African slaves in the United States. It turns not upon slavery elsewhere, or against slave holders in any other country, but is especially malignant and vindictive towards its own countrymen, for the very reason that it is bound to them by the faith and sanction of a confederate law. To set up that law to it is to enrage it by the sight of the law, because it is bound by it. It has been taught by the atheism of a "higher law" than that of a regular government bound by constitutions and statutes. It has been made to believe in the doctrine of absolute individual rights, independent of all relations of man to man in a conventional and social form; and that each man for himself has the prerogative to set up his conscience, his will and his judgment over and above all legal enactments and social institutions. It has been inflamed by prostituted teachers and preachers and presses to do and dare any crime and its consequences which may set up its individual supremacy over law and order. It has been taught from the senate chamber to trust in the fatality of an *"irrepressible conflict"* into which it is bound to plunge. Its anti-Christ pulpit has breathed naught but insurrectionary wrath into servants against their masters, and has denounced our national Union as a covenant with death for recognizing property in slaves and guaranteeing to it the protection of law. It has raised contributions in churches to furnish arms and money to such criminals as these to make a war for empire of settlement in our new territories. It has trained them on the frontier and there taught them the skill of the Indian in savage warfare, and then turned them back upon the oldest and largest slaveholding state to surprise one of its strongest holds. It has organized in Canada and traversed and corresponded thence to New Orleans and from Boston to Iowa. It has established spies everywhere and has secret agents in the heart of every slave state and has secret associations and "underground railroads" in every free state. It enlists influence and money at home and abroad. It has sent comforters and councillors and sympathy, and would have sent rescue to these assassins, robbers, murderers and traitors, whom it sent to felons' graves. It has openly and secretly threatened vengeance on the execution of the laws. And since their violation it has defiantly proclaimed aloud that *"insurrection is the lesson of the hour"*—not of slaves only, but all are to be free to rise up against fixed governments, and no government is to be allowed except "the average common sense of the masses," and no protection is to be permitted against that power.

RESULTS OF SUCH TEACHINGS

This is but an epitome, plain and unvarnished, without exaggeration. What is this but anarchy? What does it mean but "confusion worse confounded," and the overthrow of all rights, of all government, of all religion, of all rule among men? Nothing but mad riot can rule and misrule with such sentiments as these. There can be no compromise with them, no toleration of them in safety or with self-respect. They must be met and crushed, or they will crush us, or our Union with non-slaveholding states cannot continue.

The strongest arguments against this unnatural war upon Negro slavery in one section by another of the same common country is, that it inevitably drives to disunion of the states, embittered with all the vengeful hate of civil war. As that Union is among the most precious of our blessings, so the argument ought to weigh which weighs its value. But this consideration is despised by fanaticism. It contemns the Union, and now contemns us for clinging to it as we so. It scoffs the warning that the Union is endangered. The Union itself is denounced as a covenant with sin, and we are scorned as too timid to make the warning of danger to it worthy to be heeded. It arrogantly assumes to break all the bonds of faith within it and denies the attempt to escape oppression without it. *This rudely assails our honor* as well as our interest, and demands of us what we will do. We have but one thing to do; unless the numerical majority will cease to violate confederate faith, on a question of such vital importance to us and will cease immediately and absolutely cease to disturb our peace, to destroy our lives and property, and to deprive us of all protection and redress under the perverted forms and distorted workings of the Union, we must take up arms. The issue is too essential to be compromised any more. We cannot stand such insults and outrages as those of Harper's Ferry without suffering worse than the death of citizens—without suffering dishonor, the death of a state.

WHERE IS THE PROOF OF NORTHERN CONSERVATISM

For a quartet of a century we have been persuaded to forbear, and patiently to wait for the waking and working of the conservative elements in our sister states. We have borne and forborne, and waited in vain. We know that we have many sound and sincere friends in the non-slaveholding states. It may be that they are most numerous' for who abhor and detest such wrongs as these; but it is not to be disguised that the conservative elements are *passive,* whilst the fanatical are *active,* and the former are fast diminishing, whilst the latter are increasing in numbers and in force. But where is the evidence that the conservative elements are most powerful? Do we look to the schools and colleges? to the pulpits and clergy, and churches and congregations? to the press? to the journals? to the books? to the professions? the artisans? to associations, which are marked characteristics of the age? to politics? to public assemblies and speakers? to Legislatures? to Congress? to laws, either state or federal? to elections? to the administration of laws? to judicial decisions? Alas! Turn where we will, and to what we will, we find that the judgments of the courts are only with us, but that they have lost all reverence and respect, and we are left without protection, and the Supreme Court of the United States is itself assailed for not assailing our constitutional defenses. And these last are assailed in denying the rights of protection itself. A new sovereignty and a new law is set over the old, and we are denied protection itself. A new sovereignty and a new law is set over the old, and we are denied protection under both. Where the federal government has no power to oppress, it is assumed; and where it has the power and it is its duty to protect, it is not allowed to intervene. And the non-slaveholding states are in nearly solid array opposed to us. We, united, may contend for awhile by the aid of pluralities, but for a short time only, and uncertainly at any time, and at best have no majorities on which we can rely in at least sixteen states, having the power of the Union. The active has overcome the passive elements; fanaticism has subdued conservatism in all these states, and these can now, in our present condition, practically wield our destinies for weal or woe. Will they come back to the constitution, and abide its covenants or not? What those covenants are I have fully discussed in a reply to the resolutions of Vermont, which are herewith submitted, with my response appended, as a part of this message. I put it upon the archives of state as the most elaborate study of the subject of which I am capable.

SMALL NUMBERS NO EXCUSE

But no words can elaborate the issues to which we are now practically brought by the events at Harper's Ferry.

It is vain to point to the paucity of the numbers of the marauders. The daring of their attempt would prove not more their foolhardiness than their full assurance that they were to be joined by a force sufficient to be formidable. If they had not mistaken the number and disposition of the slaves who they expected to seize the spears, which they brought to capture an arsenal of arms, it is not known, and never will be known, how many other white fanatics would have swelled their numbers, nor how much blood and treasure it would have cost to quell their rebellion. Few they were, but they were fatal to the lives of several of our most worthy citizens; and insultingly dared the chances of doing immeasurable mischief to our entire Northern border.

THE INVADERS NOT INSANE

And it is mockery to call them monomaniacs. Maniacs they were, only as all great criminals; and monomaniacs they were, only as the subject of slavery makes men more insensate than any other one subject can. If these men were monomaniacs, then are a large portion of the people of many of the states monomaniacs.

Before these crimes, they were deemed sane soldiers in a notable crusade against slavery and slave holders. Many of those who now plead their insanity for them, put Sharpe's rifles in their hands, and enlisted, and trained, and trusted their wits for war in Kansas. Contributions were raised for them in churches. They had been puffed with the praise of the professedly pious, for being the very men of destiny for the mission against slave settlements. They had been furnished with money to make sharp spears of butchery for the throats and breasts of masters, and to supply munitions and stores of regular campaigns. They assembled together from parts as far between as they themselves were few. They were provided, supplied, and furnished with much beyond their own wants or means. And it is passing strange that they, madmen, should, few as they were, have been so many madmen, meeting from so far apart, so well supplied by others than themselves, at a point so well selected, and that they should have *conspired* with so much method as to be so successful, against such apparent odds. Were those parties, known and unknown, so situated, all mad? It is enough to say that the leader himself spurned the falsehood, hypocrisy and cowardice of this mawkish plea of monomania, and neither he, nor anyone of his men, nor their counsel, put it in upon their trials. He expected from his prompters and backers and sympathizers better pretense and more potent defense than that. Before his failure and defeat in what, in their correspondence with him they called a "glorious cause," their sympathy was all with his desperate daring and success; and now it is with his insanity for a plea against the legal penalties of his crimes, which had their origin in this very sympathy,—a sympathy which saw his insanity too late to snatch from his hands the weapons it had placed there; too late to save the lives taken by its own incitement; and too late to save him from a felon's fate.

By our laws, the plea of insanity could avail at any time, in any stage of trial, and after conviction, before sentence of the court; and after the judicial tribunals were done with the prisoners, and they were turned over to the executioner, the executive authority could forfend the law's sentence upon the insane. If either could show or prove insanity, either now or on trial, he could not be executed as long as I am the governor of the commonwealth, until cured in an asylum; and, if insane at the time of committing the offense, he could not be executed, cured or not cured, at all. But these men needed no menial cure; theirs was a moral malady of devils, which no power but divine could cast out. They were deliberate, cunning, malignant malefactors, desperately bent on mischief, with malice aforethought, gangrened by sectional and social habitual hatred to us and ours. Their vengeance was whetted by previous collisions hundreds of miles from us, and it whetted jagged-edged spears which it brought the hundreds of miles for our destruction. They came a few, like thieves in the night, did their deeds of death and were easily crushed; but they were prompted by an evil spirit of incendiarism which demoralized a numerous host of enemies behind them, who now blatantly sympathize with their deeds in open day before the world. These hired them to be assassins, robbers, murderers and traitors, without themselves incurring the risk of their crimes; and it is no wonder that they now sympathize with them even to madness, and that JOHN BROWN despised the hypocritical cant of their pretense that he was insane.

HISTORY OF THE CONSPIRACY

The details of this conspiracy, and of its *denouement* at Harper's Ferry, are given in the various accompanying reports. Much of the correspondence and many of the papers of the culprits were found. I have had them collected and copied by competent amanuenses, and they are hereto appended. Suffice it to say, in reference to my own official action, that the first intelligence of the outbreak reached me on the morning of the 17th October, and was very vague. Orders were dispatched immediately to Colonel Gibson, of Jefferson, to call out the necessary force of his own and adjacent regiments. But late in the evening of the same day, about 7:00 o'clock, the telegraph announced more serious and more precise causes of danger. The news was that 750 marauders had seized the arsenal at Harper's Ferry, with all its arms and munitions, and were arming the slaves, and that actual murder was done, and several citizens were killed and wounded. I immediately called out the First Regiment of Volunteers, and as many men of the 179th Regiment of militia as could get ready to move by the first train the following morning. And in one hour, at 8:00 PM. on the 17th, I departed in person, with Company F, Capt. Cary, for the scene. At Washington I was joined by Captain Mayre, of the Alexandria Rifles, and proceeded with ninety-one men and officers. At the Relay House, in Maryland, I received intelligence, on the 18th, that no more force was necessary, and I ordered back the force under Colonel August. And from that place I telegraphed Colonel Lee to make no terms with the insurgents. By 1:00 o'clock on the 18th I arrived with the force under my command. Colonel Lee made no terms, and had subdued the insurgents before my arrival. I immediately examined the leader, BROWN, his lieutenant, STEVENS, a white man named Coppoc, and a Negro from Canada. They made full confessions. Brown repelled the idea that his design was to run Negro slaves off from their masters. He defiantly avowed that his purpose was to arm them and make them fight by his side in defense of their freedom, if assailed by their owners or any one else; and he said his purpose especially was war upon the slave holders, and to levy upon their own property to pay the expense of emancipating their slaves. He avowed that he expected to be joined by the slaves and by numerous white persons from many of the slave as well as free states.

There was nothing for me to do but to arrest those who had escaped, to search for their hidden arms and plunder, to try to recapture the slaves they had taken, to get all their papers which could be found and to have them properly proceeded against according to law. Had I reached the place before they surrendered, I would have proclaimed martial law, have stormed them in the quickest time possible, shown them no quarter, have tried the survivors, if any, by court-martial, and have shot the condemned on the spot. But owing to the delay of the cars at Washington and the Relay House, and to the slow travel from the latter place to the Ferry I was too late. When I arrived they were subdued; they were prisoners and some of them wounded, and I was bound to protect them. I took them under the jurisdiction of Virginia; they were guarded from all violence; food and refreshment and surgical aid and every comfort at my command were given them; they were proceeded against regularly by the civil authority, under civil process from both state and federal governments, and I went in person with them under a military guard to Charlestown, and saw them safely lodged in jail in custody of the sheriff under civil and military guard. I remained a night to see that no violence was attempted from any quarter, and the next morning, after giving necessary orders to Colonel Gibson and furnishing him with arms, returned to Harper's Ferry. The services of counsel to assist the commonwealth's attorney were engaged by me for the state. Seeing, on the morning of the 18th, that the United States Marines were ordered away from Harper's Ferry, I ordered a police military guard for the confines around the arsenal. I did not remove the prisoners further into the interior, because I was determined to show no apprehension of a rescue; and if the jail of Jefferson had been on the line of the state, they should have been kept there, to show that they could be kept anywhere chosen in our limits. Soon after I returned to Richmond I notified the President of the United States that the reason so few men had captured the arsenal of the United States was that there was no military guard there, and that I had organized a guard to protect our frontier and, incidentally to protect the property of the United States. A neglected arsenal had been made a positive danger to us; we had been invaded by lawless bands from other states against which the United States were bound to defend us; we had been obliged to call out troops to defend the federal property, and at last had to guard it.

CONDUCT OF THE MILITIA

Thus the affair passed for the time being from the military to the civil authority. And here I cannot express too strongly what is due to the militia for the promptitude with which they volunteered for duty and obeyed my orders. The Jefferson, Berkeley and Shepherdstown militia were first at the scene, and manifested good courage and did some service; but they were restrained by a natural tenderness for their neighbors and friends who were held prisoners and hostages, and supposed to be in imminent danger from any attempt to storm their captors. The First Regiment of Volunteers, and Company F especially of that regiment, which was ready in an hour from the call, and a part of the 179th and the Alexandria Rifles, and the companies of Fredericksburg, Orange and Albermarle, all gallantly took arms and moved promptly. More than I called came, and were ready and anxious to do duty, and to be the first to encounter danger. A finer spirit and better temper of soldiers could not have been displayed.

TRIAL OF THE OFFENDERS

The state judiciary took the culprits in charge. Legal warrants were issued and served upon them; a court of examination was regularly held over those who did not waive it, and they were formally indicted in a court of competent jurisdiction. They had the full benefit of compulsory witnesses in their defense; had counsel assigned them, and counsel of their own selection; were confronted by witnesses and accusers, and were given, according to our Bill of Rights, as in all other cases, a speedy and fair trial by an impartial jury of the vicinage; upon their own confession, and upon other evidence, leaving no doubt of guilt, were legally convicted of several capital offences; were heard in person and by counsel why sentence should not be pronounced on them; were given every opportunity of applying for writs of *supersedeas;* did apply, and the court of highest resort, the court of appeals, sustained the judgment and sentence of the court which tried them. Never were prisoners treated. with more lenity of trial. And never in any case, in the history of trials, was justice administered with more forbearance, more calmness, more dignity and more majesty of law—never were such prisoners treated with as much benignant kindness as they have been by the people whom they outraged sufficiently to have incited summary punishment.

To prevent any such punishment on the one hand, and a rescue on the other, to guard justice, in a word, I called into service military guards to aid the civil authorities and keep the peace. Receiving information that organization of guards was necessary, I sent an aid to the scene, there to see what was wanting, to assist the adjutant-general and to pass my orders. Colonel J. Lucius Davis, a competent soldier, volunteered his services, and I accepted them, to organize the corps, to distribute arms, to post guards and to provide subsistence and quarters, and to call for whatever was wanting. These services he continued most faithfully and efficiently to perform, with my full approbation, until very recent events made it necessary to call for more troops, and Major General William B. Taliaferro, of the Fourth Division, repaired to the place and volunteered in person to take command. Many of the troops were from his division, and I could not decline the tender of his services. During the trial of the prisoners, and since, appeals and threats of every sort, the most extraordinary, from every quarter, have been made to the Executive. I lay before you the mass of these, it being impossible to enter into their details. Though the laws do not permit me to pardon, in cases of treason, yet pardons and reprieves have been demanded on the grounds of, first, insanity; second, magnanimity; third, the policy of not making martyrs.

APPLICATIONS FOR PARDON—REASONS FOR REFUSAL

As to the first, the parties themselves or counsel put in no plea of insanity. No insanity was feigned even; the prisoner Brown spurned it. *Since his sentence,* and since the decision on the appeal, one of his counsel, Samuel Chilton, Esq., has filed with me a number of affidavits professing to *show grounds for delaying execution, in order to give time to make an issue of fact as to the sanity of the prisoner.* How such an issue can now, after sentence, confirmed by the court of appeals, be made, I am ignorant; but it is sufficient to say that I had repeatedly seen and conversed with the prisoner, and had just returned from a visit to him when this appeal to me was put into my hands. As well as I can know the state of mind of any one, I know that he was sane, and remarkably sane, if quick and clear perception; if assumed rational premises, and consecutive reasoning from them; if cautious tact in avoiding disclosures, and in covering conclusions and inferences; if memory and conception and practical common sense, and if composure and self-possession are evidences of a sound state of mind. He was more sane than his prompters and promoters, and concealed well the secret which made him seem to do an act of mad impulse, by leaving him without his backers at Harper's Ferry; but he did not conceal his contempt for the cowardice which did not back him better than with a plea of insanity, which he spurned to put in on his trial at Charlestown.

As to the second ground of appeal: I know of no magnanimity which is inhumane, and no inhumanity could well exceed that to our society, *our slaves,* as well as their masters, which would turn felons like these, proud and defiant in their guilt, loose again on a border already torn by a fanatical and sectional strife which threatens the liberties of the white even more than it does the bondage of the black race.

As to the third ground: Is it true that the due execution of our laws, fairly and justly administered upon these confessed robbers, murderers and traitors, will make them martyrs in the public sentiment of other states? If so, then it is time indeed that execution shall be done upon them, and that we should prepare in earnest for the "*irrepressible conflict,*" with that sympathy which, in demanding for these criminals pardons and reprieves, and in wreaking vengeance or their refusal, would make criminals of us. Indeed, a blasphemous moral treason, an expressed fellow-feeling with felons, a professed conservatism of crime, a defiant and boastful guilty demoniac spirit combined, arraign us, the outraged community, as the wrong-doers who must do penance and prevent our penalty by pardon and reprieve of these martyrs. This sympathy sent these men, its mere tools, to do the deeds which sentenced them. It may have sent them to be martyrs for mischief's sake; but the execution of our laws is necessary to warn future victims not again to be its tools. To heed this outside clamor at all, was to grant at once unconditional grace. To hang would be no more martyrdom than to incarcerate the fanatic. The sympathy would have asked on and on for liberation, and to nurse and soothe him, while life lasted in prison. His state of health would have been heralded weekly as from a palace; visitors would have come affectedly reverent, to see the *shorn* felon at his "hard labor;" the work of his hands would have been sought as holy relics; and his party-colored dress would have become, perhaps, a uniform for the next band of impious marauders. There was no middle ground of mitigation. To pardon or reprieve at all was to proclaim a licensed impunity to the fanatics who are mad only in the guilt and folly of setting up their individual supremacy over law, life, property and civil liberty itself. This sympathy with the leader was worse than the invasion itself. The appeal was: it is policy to make *no martyrs,* but disarm murderers, traitors, robbers, insurrectionists, by *free pardon* for wanton, malicious, unprovoked felons! I could but ask, will execution of the legal sentence of a humane law make martyrs of such criminals. Do sectional and social masses hallow these crimes? Do whole communities sympathize with the outlaws, instead of sympathizing with the outraged society of a sister sovereignty? If so, then the sympathy is as felonious as the criminals and is far more dangerous than was the invasion. The threat of martyrdom is a threat against our peace, and demands execution to defy such sympathy and such saints of martyrdom. The issue was forced upon us: Shall JOHN BROWN be pardoned, lest he might be canonized by execution of felony for confessed murder, robbery and treason in inciting servile insurrection in Virginia? *Why* a martyr? Because thousands applaud his acts and opinions, and glorify his crimes? Was I to hesitate after this? Sympathy was insurrection, and had to be subdued more sternly than was John Brown. John Brown had surely to die according to law, and Virginia has to meet the issue. It is made. We have friends or we have not in the States whence these invaders come. They must now be not only *conservative* but *active* to prevent invaders coming. We are in arms.

RUMORS OF RESCUE

Information from all quarters, with responsible names, and anonymous, dated the same time, from places far distant from each other, came, of organized conspiracies, and combinations to obstruct our laws to rescue and seize hostages, to commit rapine and burning along our borders on Maryland, Pennsylvania, Ohio and Indiana, proceeding from these states and from New York, Massachusetts and other states and Canada. These multiplied in every form for weeks; and at last, on the 19th of November, a call was very properly and timely made by Colonel Davis for an additional force of 500 men.

These reports and rumors, from so many sources, of every character and form, so simultaneous, from places so far apart at the same time, from persons so unlike in evidences of education, could be from no conspiracy to hoax; *but I relied not so much upon them as upon the earnest continued general appeal of sympathizers with the crimes. It was impossible for so much of such sympathy to exist without exciting bad men to action of rescue or revenge.* On this I acted.

I immediately put in motion the troops of Richmond, Alexandria, Petersburg and Fauquier, who obeyed promptly—and in the time from 11:00 o'clock Saturday night to Tuesday morning, 503 men were added to the guards at Charleston. I again went in person with the troops, assembled the commanding officers, organized the command, issued general orders, and returned to Harper's Ferry, where I met Genweal Taliaferro, and accepted his services. Since then I have ordered an additional force of 560 men from Norfolk, and Portsmouth, and Petersburg, and Orange, and Albemarle, and Augusta, and Rockingham and Wheeling, and have called out a corps of howitzers, under Colonel Smith, of the Virginia Military Institute. And I have ordered Generals Rogers and Hunton to do whatever is necessary to guard the borders from the Point of Rocks to Alexandria, and the whole border is guarded west to Piedmont. I have exhausted this and the next year's quotas in issuing efficient arms, and have purchased arms of the best improved models, and issued them and coats and blankets to the troops. In a word, I have been compelled by apprehension of the most unparalleled border war, to place the state in as full a panoply of military defense as if a foreign enemy had invaded us. Indeed, one of the most irritating features of this predatory war, is that it has its seat in British provinces, which furnish asylums for our fugitives from justice and from labor; and sends them and their hired outlaws back upon us from depots and rendezvous in bordering states. There is no danger from our slaves or colored people. The slaves taken refused to take arms, and the first man killed was a respectable free Negro, who was trusted with the baggage of the railroad, and who faithful to his duty was shot running from the philanthropists who came to liberate the black race!

CONDITION OF SLAVES ON THE BORDER

But why do our slaves on the border not take up arms against their masters? We must look firmly at this fact before we take it as a solace. In the answer to that question lies the root of our danger. *Masters in the border counties now hold their slaves by sufferance.* The slave could fly to John Brown much easier than he could come and take him. The slaves at will can liberate themselves by running away. The underground railroad is at their very doors, and they may take passage when they please. They prefer to remain. *John Brown's invasion startled us; but we have been tamely submitting to a greater danger, without confessing it.* The plan which silently corrupts and steals our slaves, which sends secret emissaries among us to "stampede" our slaves, which refuses to execute fugitive slave laws, which forms secret societies for mischief, with the motto, "alarm to their sleep, fire to their dwellings, and poison to their food and water," and which establishes underground railroads, and depots and rendezvous for invasion, is more dangerous than the invasion of John Brown. Yet the latter excites us, and in the former we have been sleepily acquiescing. It is no solace to me, then, that our border slaves are so liberated already by this exterior asylum, and by this still, silent, stealing system, that *they have no need to take up arms for their own liberation.* Confederate states, as well as individuals, have denounced our laws and set them at defiance; they have by their laws encouraged and facilitated the escape of our slaves, and have made abolition a cancer eating into our very vitals.

We must, then, acknowledge and act on the fact that present relation between the states cannot be permitted longer to exist without abolishing slavery throughout the United States, or compelling us to defend it by force of arms.

CORRESPONDENCE WITH GOVERNORS OF STATES

On the 25th ult., I addressed letters to the governors of Maryland, Pennsylvania and Ohio, of which the accompanying are copies. From the governor of Maryland I have received a very satisfactory reply, herewith submitted. I have received a reply, by telegraph, from the Governor of Pennsylvania, who, I am proud to say, has promptly performed his duty in delivering up the fugitives from justice, and who protests that his state will do her confederate duty in all respects. He intimates that Virginia ought not to anticipate that Pennsylvania will neglect to prevent obstructions to or violations of the laws in her limits; but a watchful guardianship of Virginia's safety could not neglect to apprize Pennsylvania's authorities of crime meditated against either state (of which I was informed, and they were, probably, not informed) by way of intelligence, and warning. John Brown, with his associates, arms and stores, had just before already passed through Pennsylvania, and had remained at places in her limits, and he had enlisted one man, at least, a Negro, in one of her towns. I had not, therefore, anticipated the facts, but appealed to them for steps of prevention and precaution, after what had already occurred. And the governor of Pennsylvania, I presume, speaks more in the spirit of a just state pride than from such evidences of danger and cause of apprehension as the executive here is in possession of respecting combinations, depots and rendezvous in adjoining states for invading the borders of Virginia. From the governor of Ohio I have as yet received no answer.

LETTER TO PRESIDENT BUCHANAN— UNSATISFACTORY CHARACTER OF HIS REPLY

On the same day, the 25th ult., I addressed a letter to the President of the United States, of which the inclosed is a copy. On the 29th I received from him the accompanying answer, to which I have not replied, but upon which I must here comment.

He seems to think that the constitution and laws of the United States do not provide authority for the president to *"repel invasion,"* or to keep the peace between the states, in cases where the citizens of one state invade another state, unless the executive or legislature of the state invaded applies for protection. I differ from this opinion. Neither the framers of the constitution nor the Congress of 1795 were guilty of so gross an omission in their provisions for the national safety.

By the third clause of section ninth of article one of the constitution, the *states* are deprived of the power, "without the consent of Congress, to keep troops or ships of war in time of peace, or to engage in war, unless actually invaded, or in such imminent danger as will not admit of delay."

To compensate them for this privation of the power of preparation for defense, it is provided in section 4 of article 4, that *"the United States shall guarantee to every state in the Union a Republican form of government, and shall protect each of them against invasion; and on application of the* legislature, or of the executive, (when the legislature cannot be convened) against domestic violence."

Now, it is readily conceded, "United States" here is to be taken as synonymous with the words "the Congress." The clause is in juxtaposition with clauses defining the powers of "the Congress." And if they were not, by the 18th clause of section 8 of article 1, to "the Congress" is given the power "to make all laws which shall be necessary and proper *for carrying into execution*" its own powers, "and all other powers vested in the government of the United States, or in any department or officer thereof."

This duty and power then of guaranteeing protection to every state against invasion belongs unquestionably to Congress. Has it exercised the power? It has. Thus:

To the Congress also is given the power "to raise and *support armies,*" and "to provide and maintain a Navy," and these are called, specially, "the land and naval forces of the United States."

I presume that no one will gainsay the proposition that the chief object of these land and naval forces is "to suppress insurrections and to repel invasions."

But in addition to these powers another is specially added. "To provide for *calling forth* the militia to execute the laws of the Union, suppress insurrections and repel invasions." And I presume that no one will insist that the regular Army and Navy of the United States may not be ordered to execute the laws of the Union, and to suppress insurrections and repel invasions, without calling forth the militia, or though the militia may be called forth to execute the same purposes.

This granted, the Congress did pass the laws: 1st, to raise armies, and to provide and maintain a navy, as well as laws for calling forth the militia.

And then, by article 2, the President is vested with *the executive power.* He is sworn faithfully to execute the office of President, and to the best of his ability, to "preserve, protect and defend the constitution of the United States;" and he is made commander-in-chief of the Army and Navy of the United States and of the militia of the several states, when called into the actual service of the United States; *and he shall take care that the laws be faithfully executed.*

Now to revert to the 4th section of the 4th article:

In this section, there are two things against which the United States guarantees protection to *every* state:

1st, against *"invasion."* Not one kind of invasion or another, but simply *"invasion"* of all kinds from every quarter; *and no application* for *protection* is required against "invasion." Whenever it comes, however it comes, it is to be protected against. The word itself imports *force from without—any* force without the state indeed, whether from a foreign country, or alien enemies or Indian tribes; it is confined to no particular invasion. And against this the President has the means provided by Congress in the laws raising and providing a standing Army and Navy—the land and naval forces of the United States, which need not be "called forth," but are armies already raised and standing, and a Navy already *"provided and maintained."* The President is commander-in-chief of these, and may order them to repel actual invasion, as they are already in actual service without being "called forth." And he is surely as much bound to execute the constitution as the statutes of Congress. "The laws," to be executed, embrace both, and he has the means to execute both provided in the statutes for raising armies and providing a navy, as well as in the laws calling forth the militia.

But to proceed:

Second—The second thing that every state is to be protected against is, *"domestic violence."* These words import force from within—a *domestic* force, acting, in rebellion, or insurrection, or obstruction of the laws, against the state. To interpose against this, there must be an application of the legislature, or of the executive of the state, when the legislature cannot be convened.

And under this clause of this section, special acts of February 28, 1795, and of March 3, 1807, have been passed. They are wholly distinct from the laws of Congress raising armies and providing a Navy. The first clause of the first section of the act of 1795, relates to invasions of the *United States* "from any *foreign nation or Indian tribe.*" The 2nd clause of that section relates to *"insurrection* in any state against the government thereof," etc., to "domestic violence," in other words, and not expressly or impliedly to "invasion of any state." And the 2nd section of the act relates to obstructions of the laws of the United States, and not of any state. And the whole act, so far as it relates to the states, is an act to provide for *"calling forth the militia"* to suppress domestic violence and not for commanding the land and naval forces already in actual service against "invasion." *Invasion of any state is in fact invasion of the United States.* And the act of 1807 applies expressly to cases only of "insurrection or obstruction to the laws either of the United States or of any individual state or territory." And if the President's construction of his power be correct, this act which was intended undoubtedly to extend the act of 1795, and enlarge its provisions, would operate to restrict and contract its provisions. He could not use such part of the land and naval force of the United States as shall be judged by him, without having first observed all the prerequisites of the law for calling forth the militia. These acts, in a word, do not in word or meaning apply to cases of "invasion of a state," but so far as a state is concerned, to cases only of domestic violence; and where the militia are called forth on application of the legislature or of the executive of the state rebelled against.

There was no "insurrection;" no case of force from without. Invasion was threatened from without, by citizens of one state against another state. It is monstrous to say that there is nothing in the constitution or laws guaranteeing protection to a state in such cases. The constitution is express. It needs in fact the laws only which have been passed—the laws of the army and navy of the United States, and the laws for calling forth the militia, to execute both of the clauses of protection guaranteed by the constitution to "every state in this Union." The men of 1795 made no such gross omission. They understood their work too well for that. And what a spectacle *the United States* would have presented, if on the second instant an army of fanatics had invaded Virginia to rescue felons legally convicted, and a bloody battle had been joined, and the United States land forces at Harper's Ferry stood neutral spectators, guarding only the United States arsenal, and playing *posse comitatus* to a United States Marshal, but not allowed to aid in the execution of the laws of a state or to repel invasion, because the *United States* were not invaded "from a foreign country or by Indian tribes." The bare statement is revolting to the fourth section of the fourth article of the constitution, guaranteeing protection to every state *against invasion*" to every statute of Congress raising land and naval forces of the United States; to all the ends and purposes of those laws, and to peace; to the oath and executive office of the president of the United States to preserve, protect and defend the constitution, and to see the laws faithfully executed.

DIFFERENCE OF OPINION BETWEEN GOVERNOR WISE AND PRESIDENT BUCHANAN

Such are my views of the constitution and laws. The views of the President, it seems, are different. I notified him of a just apprehension that this state was threatened with "*invasion*" by a predatory border war to rescue prisoners convicted of high crimes and felonies, and to seize our citizens as hostages and victims in case of execution of the criminals, proceeding from several surrounding states.

He answers, that "It would seem almost incredible that any portion of the people of the states mentioned should be guilty of the atrocious wickedness, as well as the folly of attempting to rescue convicted traitors and murderers from the penalty due their crimes under the outraged laws of Virginia."

I reply to him, through you, gentlemen, that it is strange this should seem so incredible, when the very "convicted traitors and murderers" were portions of the people of the states mentioned, who had just been convicted of invading our border, and seizing a United States arsenal, and of perpetrating treason and murder against both the state and the United States authority. And I surely may be allowed latitude for acting on the mass of information I have received, of renewed invasion, when, perhaps, pardonable inattention at Washington to warning of the murder and treason at Harper's Ferry left an arsenal and a people defenseless against that invasion!

I did not call on the President to protect Virginia and would not do so. I apprized him of apprehensions "*in order that he might take steps to preserve peace between the states.*" I had called out our own militia, and they are a thousand fold ample to defend their state. They have had not only to guard their own border but to guard in part the arsenal of the United States. The president has, however, manifested a "cheerful and cordial" disposition to defend the *place ceded to the United States at Harper's Ferry*; he sent a small guard, as soon as informed it was unguarded, and has reinforced that guard, "not only to protect the public property clearly *within federal jurisdiction, but to prevent the insurgents from seizing the arms in the arsenal at that place,* and using them against the troops of Virginia." "Besides," he says, "it is possible the additional troops may be required to act as *a posse* comitatus *on the requisition of the Marshal of the United States for the Western District of Virginia, to prevent the rescue of Stevens,* now in his custody, charged with the crime of high treason."

THE PRESIDENT REFUSING TO PROTECT
THE STATES AGAINST INVASION

Then for these objects—1st, to keep arms of the United States out of the hands of the invaders of Virginia; and 2nd, to act as *"posse comitatus"* to a United States Marshal, the land forces of the United States may be used; but 3rd, *not to prevent "invasion" of one state by the people of another state.* And he says he can discover *nothing in any provision in the constitution or laws of the United States, which would authorize him to "take steps" for the purpose of preserving peace between the states, by guarding places in surrounding states which may be occupied as depots and rendezvous, by desperadoes, to invade Virginia."* As I understand his interpretation of the constitution and the laws, he cannot call forth the militia, nor employ the land and naval forces of the United States *"for this purpose."* He says it is the duty of the respective *state governments* to break up such depots, and to prevent their citizens from making incursions, etc.; but *that if the federal executive were to enter these states* and *to perform this duty for them, it would be a manifest usurpation of their rights. Were he thus to act it would be a palpable invasion of state sovereignty, and as a precedent, might prove highly dangerous.* Now, this is a new doctrine, and teaches even Virginia a lesson of state rights which destroys her constitutional guarantee of protection by the United States against "invasion" by abolition fanatics from other states. They are not from any foreign country, nor are they Indian tribes. The fanatics from free states, such as John Brown and Stevens, he says, in effect, are *not invading the United State when invading Virginia*; they are not "from any foreign nation or Indian tribe," rendering it lawful for the president to employ the federal forces to repel such invasion.

VIRGINIA MUST PROTECT HERSELF

These are alarming doctrines to invaded states. And however the argument or the error may be between the president and your executive, this at least is clear, *that if I am right in my views of our guarantee of protection in the case before us, imminent as it is, he, the executive of the United States, does not concur with me, and will not enforce the protection we need; and on the other hand, if he is right, and we cannot legally claim that the United States shall keep the peace between states, and guarantee one state against invasion from another, the federal executive cannot interpose to repel or prevent the invasion.* In either case, we are clearly thrown on our self-dependence. *We must rely on ourselves, and fight for peace! I say, then—to your tents! Organize and arm!*

The constitutional guarantee of protection is withheld, whilst we are invaded from all around, and this withholding will inspirit the sympathizers in felony against our property and lives. To defend ourselves, and to suppress sympathy in insurrection, which must multiply felons against our peace and safety; and if they did not intend invasion before, will make them enact it now; under this construction of state rights to disturb and state rights to defend the public peace, we will need all our forces for the conflict. I therefore recommend to you more energetic measures than the president compliments me for adopting on the side of *peace* against invasion.

I repeat:

1. Organize and arm.

2. Demand of each state in the Union what position she means to maintain for the future in respect to slavery and the provisions of the constitution and laws of the United States, and the provisions of state laws for its protection in our federal relations, and be governed according to the manner in which the demand shall be answered. Let us defend our own position, or yield it at once. Let us have action and not resolves—definite settlement, and no mere temporizing the constitution. and no more compromise.

EXECUTION OF BROWN

John Brown, the leader of the invasion of Harper's Ferry, was executed, according to the sentence of the Court, on the 2nd inst. His body was delivered, by my request, to the sheriff of Jefferson County, to the orders of Major-General Taliaferro to be guarded safely to Harper's Ferry, and there delivered to his widow, Mary Brown. The laws of the commonwealth have reigned in his arrest, trial and execution, and when dead under the sentence, they released his remains to his relatives, to whom they have, with dignity and decency, been handed over.

THE OTHER PRISONERS

The other convicts await execution, and will be executed on the 16th, unless the general assembly orders otherwise. I shall be guided in my course in respect to the reprieve, pardon or commutation of punishment of these, or in respect to their execution, by your resolves. This will meet the open invasion, but it acts only on the individual convicts, and it doesn't settle the question of our peace and protection against future aggression. To do that, we must cease to resolve, and take decided action. What action, is for you to decide. I have done my part, according to the best of my ability—and it remains only for me to offer myself, all that I am and all that I have, to the commonwealth, wherever she may order me or mine, in any service, when the term of my present office closes.

I submit detailed recommendations in another message. I am, most respectfully and devotedly, your obedient servant,

HENRY A. WISE

Chapter 12

VICTOR HUGO ON JOHN BROWN

*T*HE FOLLOWING LETTER *was written by Victor Hugo from the Hauteville House, on December 2, 1859.*[1]

To the Editor of the London Star:

> SIR: When our thoughts dwell upon the United States of America, a majestic form rises before the eyes of imagination. It is a WASHINGTON!

Look, then, at what is taking place in that country of Washington at this present moment.

In the Southern states of the Union there are slaves, and this circumstance is regarded with indignation, as the most monstrous of inconsistencies—by the pure and logical conscience of the Northern States. A white man, a free man, John Brown, sought to deliver those Negro slaves from bondage. Assuredly, if insurrection is ever a sacred duty, it must be so when it is directed against slavery. John Brown endeavored to commence the work of emancipation by the liberation of the slaves in Virginia. Pious, austere, animated with the old Puritan spirit, inspired by the spirit of the Gospel, he sounded to these men, these oppressed brothers, the rallying cry of freedom. The slaves, enervated by servitude,

---

[1] Hauteville House is on the Island of Guernsey. Victor Hugo purchased the house on May 16, 1856 and lived there in exile. It is a large white building with a garden overlooking the sea.

made no response to the appeal. Slavery afflicts the soul with deafness. Brown though deserted, still fought at the head of a handful of heroic men; he struggled; he was riddled with balls; his two young sons, sacred martyrs, fell dead at his side and he himself was taken. That is what they call the affair of Harper's Ferry.

John Brown has been tried, with four of his comrades, Cook, Coppic, Green and Copeland.

What has been the character of his trial? Let us sum it up in a few words:

John Brown, upon a wretched pallet, with six half-gaping wounds, a gun shot wound in his arm, another in his loins, and two in his head, scarcely conscious of surrounding sounds, bathing his mattress in blood, and with the ghostly presences of his two dead sons ever beside him; his four fellow-sufferers wounded, dragging themselves along by his side; Stephens bleeding from four saber wounds; justice in a hurry and overleaping all obstacles; an attorney, Hunter, who wishes to proceed hastily, and a judge, Parker, who suffers him to have his way; the hearing cut short, almost every application for delay refused, forged and mutilated documents produced, the witnesses for the defense kidnaped, every obstacle thrown in the way of the prisoner's counsel, two cannon loaded with cannister stationed in the court, orders given to the jailers to shoot the prisoners if they sought to escape, forty minutes of deliberation, and three men sentenced to die. I declare, on my honor, that all this took place, not in Turkey, but in America.

Such things cannot be done with impunity in the face of the civilized world. The universal conscience of humanity is an ever-watchful eye. Let the judges of Charlestown, and Hunter, and Parker, and the slaveholding jurors, and the whole population of Virginia, ponder on it well; they are watched! They are not alone in the world.

At this moment America attracts the eyes of the whole of Europe.

John Brown, condemned to die, was to have been hanged on the 2nd of December—this very day.

But news has just reached us. A respite has been granted to him. It is not until the 16th that he is to die.

The interval is a brief one. Before it has ended will a cry for mercy have had time to make itself effectually heard?

No matter! It is our duty to speak out.

Perhaps a second respite may be granted. America is a noble nation. The impulse of humanity springs quickly into life among a free people. We may yet hope that he will be saved.

If it were otherwise, if Brown should die on the scaffold on the 16th of December, what a terrible calamity!

The executioner of Brown let us avow it openly (for the day of the Kings is past, and the day of the Peoples dawns, and to the people we are bound frankly to speak the truth)—the executioner of Brown would be neither the Attorney Hunter, nor the Judge Parker, nor the Governor Wise, nor the State of Virginia; it would be, though we can scarce think or speak of it without a shudder, the whole American Republic.

The more one loves, the more one admires, the more one venerates that Republic, the more heartsick one feels at the contemplation of such a catastrophe. A single state ought not to have the power to dishonor all the rest, and in this case there is an obvious justification for a federal intervention. Otherwise, by hesitating to interfere when it might prevent a crime, the becomes a participator in its guilt. No matter how intense may be the indignation of the generous Northern states, the Southern states force them to share the opprobrium of this murder. All of us, no matter who we may be, who are bound together as compatriots by the common tie of Democratic creed, feel ourselves in some measure compromised. If the scaffold should be erected on the 16th of December, the incorruptible voice of history would thence forward testify that the august confederation of the New World had added to all its ties of holy brotherhood a brotherhood of blood, and the *fasces* of that splendid Republic would be bound together with the running noose that hung from the gibbet of Brown.

It is a bond that can only kill.

When we reflect on what Brown, the liberator, the champion of Christ, has striven to effect, and when we remember that he is about to die, slaughtered by the American Republic, the crime assumes an importance coextensive with that of the nation which would commit it; and when we say to ourselves that this nation is one of the glories of the human race; that like France, like England, like Germany, she is one of the great agents of civilization; that she sometimes even leaves Europe in the rear by the sublime audacity of some of her progressive movements; that she is the queen of an entire world, and that her brow is irradiated with a glorious halo of freedom, we declare our conviction that John Brown will not die, for we recoil horror-struck from the idea of so great a crime committed by so great a people.

Viewed in a political light, the murder of Brown would be an irreparable fault. It would penetrate the Union with a gaping fissure which would lead in the end to its entire disruption. It is possible that the execution of Brown might establish slavery on a firm basis in Virginia, but it is certain that it would shake to its very center the entire fabric of American Democracy. You preserve your infamy, but you sacrifice your glory.

Viewed in a moral light, it seems to me that a portion of the enlightenment of humanity would be eclipsed—that even the ideas of justice and injustice would be obscured on the day which should witness the assassination of emancipation by liberty.

As for myself, though I am but a mere atom, yet being, as I am, in common with all other men, inspired with the conscience of humanity, I fall on my knees weeping before the great spangled banner of the new world, and with clasped hands, and with profound and filial respect, I implore the Illustrious American Republic, sister of the French Republic, to see to the safety of the universal moral law, to save John Brown, to demolish the threatening scaffold of the 16th of December, and not to suffer that, beneath its eyes, and I add, with a shudder, almost by its fault, a crime should be perpetrated surpassing the first fratricide in iniquity.

For—yes, let America know it and ponder on it well—there is something more terrible than Cain slaying Abel; it is Washington slaying Spartacus.

An editorial appeared as follows in the New York Times of December 24, 1859 as to Victor Hugo's thoughts on John Brown:

> Victor Hugo, of all the exiles of French Democracy the most democratic, has spoken his mind in the matter of John Brown to the whole Republic of the United States. To say this is to say that he has spoken it well, with emphasis with fervor, in that clear and vigorous prose which is the prerogative of great poets. As a piece of literary composition, this voice which comes to us from the Isle of Jersey is highly note-worthy, glittering with antithesis, arising perpetually into a quite dithyrambic grandeur of statement, and full of that effective pathos of the footlights in which the taste of our time so greatly delights, and of which the author of the *Orientales* and *La Legende des Siecles* is an unrivaled master. Of course, our Southern friends will deny even this merit of form to a series of apostrophes twenty times more insulting to their patriarchal institution than the most reckless rhapsodies of a Cheever, or the most biting sarcasms of a Wendell Phillips. They will probably take measures at once to retaliate on the poet as they do on the North, by a decree of non-intercourse. To possess a copy of *Notre Dame de Paris* will doubtless become a capital crime in South Carolina, and the luckless wight who shall be caught hanging upon

the pages of *Les Derniers Jours d'un Condamné* in Virginia, will be instantly made to realize the situation which that work so thrillingly describes, and be set to meditating his own speedy demise in a Charlestown cell.

We at the North can afford to deal with the matter more calmly. We shall not affect any cheap and frivolous contempt for the prospective flagellation which Victor Hugo administers to us. The sincere convictions of a man of great genius, who has made his mark deeply in his day and generation, and who professes a sympathy, which his acts have proved, with the fundamental principles of our national institutions, are not to be lightly esteemed, nor met with vulgar scoffs. The picture which Victor Hugo presents to us of himself, "kneeling with tears before the great spangled banner of the New-World, and with clasped hands and profound and filial respect imploring the illustrious American Republic, sister of the French Republic, to see to the safety of the universal moral law, to save John Brown, and demolish the scaffold of the 16th of December," is not to be dismissed with a shallow sneer at its theatrical effulgence. Let us do all justice to Victor Hugo, that we may satisfy ourselves fairly whether Victor Hugo has or has not done justice to us. *Fas est et ab hoste doceri*, and Victor Hugo is by no means our enemy. He is a fanatic of liberty, and of liberty as our wildest demagogues understand it. He loves America because he hates Kings. He has just put forth, in the latest, and, in some respects, the most remarkable of his works, his conception of universal history in terms which would have made the heart of Jefferson tingle with delight had that enemy of all antiquities been living to enjoy them. For Victor Hugo all the evil of the world is summed up in the story of sovereigns. He has done his best, in vain, to brand the greatest of living Monarchs as the incarnate evil genius of the nineteenth century; and after failing to fix upon the Emperor of the French, the *sobriquet* of Napoleon the Little, he has devoted himself to proving that the son of Hortense is assuredly a more frail and fearful Beast of Darkness than was dreamt of in the Apocalypse.

When he tells us then that we are committing "a crime surpassing the first fratricide in iniquity," and horrifying the world with the spectacle of "Spartacus slain by Washington," we have every reason to believe that the tale of John Brown's raid may truly strike in this sense the minds of foreign enthusiasts, who build their best hopes of the future of mankind upon us and our success, and who would lament our failure as their own.

What, then, are the facts on which this awful indictment against America is founded?

In part it rests upon that wild and feverish haste with which the trial of Brown was conducted in Virginia. When we urged patience and the forms of a more grave and humane justice upon our Virginian friends, they angrily assailed us as foes of them and their honor. Here is a far-away foreigner, no foe of them and theirs, quite beyond the suspicion of a wish to be sent to Congress from a Republican district in New York, and beyond the temptation of making money by his opinions of Virginia, who takes these proceedings at Charlestown in an infinitely more intense disgust. Ought not this to show afresh to our friends beyond Mason & Dixon's line, the extreme stupidity of so managing their justice as to provoke such emotions in the observant mind of the civilized world? Ought it not, at least, to teach them that a desire to see John Brown mercifully dealt with did by no means argue the partisan sectionalism of those who felt it at the North?

So far, then, as this cause of his distress is concerned, we admit that Victor Hugo, loving America, had good reason to lament that an American state should even appear to have been driven by its fears for slavery into a hot and hasty administration of justice. So far, we cry *peccavimus*; the John Brown history does us here no credit; on the contrary, sore discredit. It was indeed a bad business badly managed. We accept the tears of the exile of Jersey. But does this make us criminals worse than Cain? Victor Hugo thinks the Union has murdered a man better than Abel, and that henceforth "the fasces of the splendid Republic will be bound together with the running noose that hung from the gibbet of John Brown;" that we "have preserved our infamy, but sacrificed our glory."

To this the answer is very simple. The Union has not murdered John Brown. Victor Hugo's zeal for American liberty, has outrun his knowledge of American institutions. The American Republic, which he invokes, is by no means a sister of the French republic, which he himself did so much to make impossible. In the American Republic, vested rights are as sacred as Victor Hugo would have personal theories to be. Ours is a liberty which grows by toleration, by the endurance of incongruities which cannot be suddenly removed, without tearing up the nerves and ruining the health of the whole body politic. Victor Hugo, hating slavery, nothing seems more simple than that slavery should be assailed, turned out, beaten to death. Our crime then clearly is, that we do not think with him on this matter. Our crime is the crime of the people of France, who decline to assassinate their emperor and invoke civil war, because a number of the best of Frenchmen dislike the *regime* of the Tuileries, and despise its courtiers. Victor Hugo cannot forgive them, and he, therefore, cannot forgive us. By a singular chance, the same day, the 2nd. of December, represents the obstinacy of both nations. It will now be doubly blackened in the poet's calendar. But Napoleon III. reigns, and has made France mightier and happier than she had been for forty years before he reached the throne; and the cause of freedom in America is assuredly not less advanced this day than it would have been had the Northern states invaded Virginia under the command of President Buchanan, hung Governor Wise and Mr. Hunter, and raised John Brown to the Presidency. Victor Hugo is a great poet, but he adds a fresh illustration to the old truth, that no prophets are so persistent as those whose prophecies are never fulfilled, and no teachers so strenuous as those whose lessons invariably turn to naught.

Chapter 13

ANOTHER ROUND OF EXECUTIONS

MILITARY MOVEMENTS WERE continuing in Charlestown due to the upcoming and final round of executions, and troops were arriving and departing daily. Captain James N. Nichols commanding the Petersburg Artillery left Thursday morning, December 9, 1859. These men made hosts of friends by their gentlemanly bearing and soldierly conduct. A large crowd assembled at the depot to bid them farewell. The Tenth Legion Artillery arrived on the same train on which the Petersburg Artillery left. The Tenth Legion company was from New Market, Shenandoah County, and was under the command of Captain Milton M. Siebert. It numbered over fifty men. With the company came Master Albert, the seven year old infant drummer, who was quite a prodigy. The company fifer, Jacob Hockman, was 75 years of age, but still managed to produce good music. The contrast between the two musicians attracted the attention of all.

Fifty of the Richardson Guards under Captain Welsh, arrived on the evening train from Madison County. This company had been most anxious to come on, and held themselves in readiness from the beginning of the affair. Later in the evening the Clarke Guards, Captain Bowen, from Berryville, Virginia, marched into town. The Guards have been organized but a few weeks, but their ranks were very full, 65 men being in the line.

The military force here on Friday, December 9th, consisted of the Portsmouth Guards, Woodis Riflemen, Mountain Guards, West Augusta Riflemen, Montpellier Guards, Petersburg Grays, Clarke Guards, Richardson Guards, Washington Guards and Jefferson Guards—in all over five hundred men—besides which, twenty-five of the Executive Guards under Captain Hunter were constantly on duty.

A local Charlestown newspaper reported "the inconvenience to which our citizens have been subjected for weeks has not yet been entirely overcome, and complaints of the interference of ignorant sentinels with the rights of our citizens have been made daily. The complaint, however, is not entirely urged against the sentinels, but citizens are beginning to talk loudly against those who were in power. The instructions to the sentinels were certainly in conflict with the commonest rights of citizenship, and the evil called loudly for remedy. An aged and infirm old gentleman, one of Charlestown's wealthiest citizens, was stopped at an early hour a few evenings ago. When within twenty steps of his residence, he was not allowed to pass into his own house. A half-dozen children, who had been to a pump for water, were marched to the guard-house by a vigilant sentinel. These cases were cited to show how ridiculous things had become."

The attention of the public was now turned from the hanging of John Brown to the approaching end of John Cook and his associates in crime. Cook's wife and sister have not yet arrived, but Cook looks for them daily. He is now in good spirits, though he often talks about Executive clemency, and endeavors to show the justice of it. Barclay Coppoc remains as stoical as ever, and awaits the time of his execution with an indifference almost revolting. The Negroes attract very little attention and no sympathy. It has been rumored here for some days that Governor Willard, of Indiana, will be here in a few days, and expresses his intention of going up on the scaffold with Cook. Mind you, its just a rumor!

It was the intention of the governor to have the military force here materially strengthened before the day of execution, and the same program will be followed as was enacted at the execution of John Brown.

The Cleveland *Morning Leader* published the following letter from the prisoner Cook:

Charlestown Jail, Va., Dec. 9, 1859.

To the Editor of the Morning Leader:

DEAR SIR: I had the pleasure of receiving a copy of your interesting paper yesterday evening. In its perusal I was somewhat surprised to see a copy of a letter which I had written to Mr. and Mrs. Seller, of your city. When I wrote that letter, I had no thought of its ever being published. But, as I see some false statements in regard to my fellow-prisoners and myself, which you have quoted from other papers, I am glad Mr. Seller took the liberty to give it publicity. I am also thankful to you *for the comment* you made upon those statements.

I will only say, such statements as have been made by the *Times*, in regard to my companions and myself, *are totally false. There has not been one single instance, in which I have felt, or shown any sign of fear or nervousness since I have been here. Neither has my comrade Coppoc, since he has occupied the cell with me, shown any such weakness, or dread of death.* We both dislike the mode of death to which we have been doomed. But notwithstanding, *we are cheerfully and calmly awaiting our fate, and trust we shall meet it like men.*

I will frankly admit that on one or two occasions I have been agitated by the reception of touching letters from *my wife and other relatives whose happiness is dearer to me than my life.* The doom that awaits me has not in the least affected my appetite, nor has it occasioned any loss of rest. I sleep as calmly here as in my boyhood home.

I have made these statements because I deem it *my duty* to my fellow prisoner and myself to do so. By giving this an insertion in your paper you will greatly oblige.

Yours truly,

JOHN E. COOK

P. S. I have just read in one of the papers published at this place an account of the farewell scene between Captain Brown, Edwin Coppoc and myself. To show the falsehood of these reports, *I will state just what passed at this farewell interview.* Captain Brown came in smiling, and shook both Coppoc and myself warmly by the hand. He asked kindly after our health. He then said to me that he was sorry that I had made a statement that was not true; as I would only gain contempt by it. I asked him what I had said that was untrue. He told me that it was the statement which I had made, "That he had sent me to the Ferry." *I told him he most certainly did tell me to go there.* He said he had no recollection of anything of the kind; but that he remembered distinctly of telling me not to go there. *I replied that I had a good memory, and had not the slightest recollection of anything of the kind.* He remarked that he thought that my memory must be treacherous, but it would do no good to talk about that; but that if we had to die, to meet our fate *like men*; that we had gone into a *good cause*, and not to deny it now. He then turned to Coppoc, and said that he had heard that *he* had made some false statements, but was glad to learn that those reports were untrue. He then asked if he could do anything for us. We answered in the negative. He gave Coppoc fifty cents, remarking that, as he owed Coppoc's brother $40 which he did not know if it would ever be paid, that a little change might do him some good. He then pressed our hands warmly, and bade us a last farewell. There was no one present except Captain Avis, John Brown, Coppoc and myself. Captain Avis will, I think, vouch for the truth of this statement, as will Edwin Coppoc. Please give this a place in your paper, and oblige yours truly,

J. E. COOK

There has been so much speculation relative to the companions of Captain Cook, who had accompanied him in his flight until he was arrested, and who subsequently made their escape to the North, that a brief factual narrative of their movements might be interesting to you. The following was published on December 10th by Mr. Arthur Franklin of Chambersburg, Pennsylvania:

Captain John E. Cook, Barclay Coppic, Owen Brown, Charles P. Tldd, and Francis J. Merriam, made their escape from Harper's Ferry together—Hazlett and Anderson (a Negro) also escaped from the Ferry, each traveling alone. All of them came into Franklin County, and first sought concealment in the South Mountain. Anderson made his escape, doubtless through the aid of Negro friends, and is now in Canada. I believe that no white man in our county saw him who knew him. Albert Hazlett was the first one of the fugitives arrested. He came into Chambersburg alone, at noonday, with his Sharp's rifle under his arm, wrapped up in his blanket. He was believed to be Captain Cook—the only fugitive who, at that time, had been described in the public press, and for whom a reward had been offered. Several persons followed him until he entered the house of Mrs. Ritner, with whom Brown and all his party had boarded when in that place. Hazlett met the wife of Captain Cook there, and she at once besought him to fly for his life, as she knew that persons were watching for the fugitives. He escaped out through the back yard, and all traces of him were lost until he was seen the next day walking along the Cumberland Valley railroad tracks, near Newville.

He was at once followed, and was arrested as he entered Carlisle, Pennsylvania. As soon as he was arrested, Governor Wise was telegraphed to, and he forwarded a requisition for Captain Cook; but when Virginians came on to Carlisle to identify Cook, they did not know the prisoner at all. Another requisition was obtained for Albert Hazlett, and other witnesses sent on, but they could not positively identify him either. One of the witnesses, however, did swear that he saw the prisoner participate in the insurrection and fire his Sharp's rifle upon the citizens. A third requisition was then obtained for Harrison, the name he gave as his, and on that he was remanded. The difficulty in identifying him delayed his delivery to the Virginia authorities for some two weeks after his arrest; hence Captain Cook, who was arrested a week later than Hazlett, was in Charlestown and on trial by the time that Hazlett reached there. Cook's delivery was also facilitated by the fact that a requisition was in Carlisle for him at the time he was arrested—the requisition having been sent on when Hazlett was first arrested, under the impression that he was Cook.

With the details of the arrest of Captain Cook you are all familiar. He was in search of food, and, not knowing the country, found himself most unexpectedly at Major Hughes' iron works, within hailing distance of some fifty men. The mountain opens very abruptly upon the works, and had he been acquainted with the locality he would certainly have chosen any other point than that one to purchase food. Strange to say, also, the first man he met was Daniel Logan, the most expert man to arrest a fugitive we have in the country. Mr. Fitzhugh was with Logan, or Cook would have passed without suspicion as Logan had not seen Cook's description; but Fitzhugh had noticed him particularly, and had no doubt of Cook's identity. At the moment he saw him he communicated his belief to Logan in a whisper, without exciting Cook's suspicion, or they would doubtless have both paid the penalty of their lives in attempting to secure him, as he was armed and uses a revolver with fatal precision. They asked him to go along with them to get meat, and in an unguarded moment they seized his arms. Cook made a desperate struggle to reach his pistol, but he was overpowered and the pistol taken from him. He was then bound and brought to Chambersburg.

On his way to Chambersburg, he confessed his identity to Logan, and endeavored to make a private arrangement to purchase his release. Whether he could have secured his release by paying his captors is doubtful; but as he had no money, and no one in Chambersburg who could vouch for him, the effort necessarily failed. He was taken before a justice, where Messrs. Brewer, McClure, and Carlisle appeared on his behalf; but his identity was conclusively established by papers upon his person, and he was committed to prison. In three days he was in Charlestown, and in three weeks he was under a sentence of death.

Earnestly as all rational men must condemn the conduct of Cook, and justly as the law demands his life, there are few who know him who will not lament his terrible fate. He is under thirty years of age, and of most effeminate appearance and stature. He weighs scarcely 125 pounds, and his long, light hair, large soft blue eyes and exceedingly fair complexion, added to his amiability and frankness of manner are well calculated to win up in any heart. He is a man of high culture, a graduate of one of the Eastern colleges, and has evidently been an earnest devotee of the fine arts. In prison his mind would involuntarily wander from himself, and he would discuss the great paintings of the old masters with all the enthusiasm of his nature. He is a stranger to the ordinary vices of the day, and, excepting his criminal infatuation on the slavery question, few men could boast of a higher standard of morals. Profanity never escaped his lips, and he never was intoxicated in his life.

But on the slavery question he was decidedly unbalanced—he was mad. He had passed through the Kansas difficulties; had seen his friends killed by his side; had, on various occasions, saved his own life only by his indomitable courage and skill; had gone for weeks, when pro-slavery men had taken possession of the territory, with a price set upon his head, to be paid whether he should be taken dead or alive; and these grievances, or persecutions, as he regarded them, dethroned his reason. From thence he was the mere creature of what he regarded a great moral principle, and which, with him, had become a passion more powerful then self. He was honestly and wholly devoted to it, and his humane and impulsive nature but served to cloud rather than aid his judgment. Thus was Cook impelled to stain his hands with murder.

None can complain of Virginia for the execution of her laws. Cook invaded her territory and, according to her laws, was justly convicted; and whether the extreme penalty shall be inflicted is for Virginia alone to determine. She has determined it, and Cook must expiate his offense upon the scaffold. I would that Virginia had decided otherwise, and mingled magnanimity with justice; but justly as he dies in obedience to the penalty of outraged law, John E. Cook will die widely lamented.

The facts in relation to the escape of Merriam, Owen Brown, Barclay Coppoc and Tidd are well known to the public here. Merriam is a young Bostonian, of scarcely 23 years of age. He passed through part of the Kansas war, and was fearless and untiring in his efforts against the Missourians who were at war with the free-state men. Subsequently he went to Hayti and spent a Winter there. He does not seem to have been immediately connected with John Brown in his Harper's Ferry insurrection until about the 1st of October. He came to this place about that time on his way to Harper's Ferry, and called with one of our attorneys and had his will drawn, properly executed, and mailed to the executor in Boston. He represented himself as a tourist on his way South and fearing accidents, wished his will prepared.

Merriam is a young man of fine address and evidently more than ordinary culture. He was not in the fight at Harper's Ferry, but was stationed at an outpost for some purpose—perhaps to receive and lead expected reinforcements. In company with Tidd, Coppoc and Owen Brown, he came to Chambersburg the night Cook was put in jail; and the whole four remained in this immediate vicinity for several days. They were seen frequently by different persons, and suspected to be the fugitives; but nothing was known of them, with any degree of positiveness, excepting by a few who were professionally or otherwise confidentially advised of their names and purpose. They slept in a barn near town for two nights, and were seen there; and they called at several houses in town after dark to get food. It is generally understood that they desired and contemplated a rescue of Cook from prison; but they were prevailed upon not to attempt it. They each had four revolvers, in addition to their Bowie-knives and rifles. It is believed that but one white person communicated with them directly during their stay here, and that person was a woman; though it is more than probable that they were advised indirectly by several of our citizens. Although it was well known that they were here, no one attempted to hunt or arrest them. No reward had been offered for them.

In fact, the Virginians believed that Tidd, Anderson and Brown were dead, and they did not know that there had been two Coppocs in the insurrection. Governor Wise was informed that four fugitives were in this neighborhood, and he at once offered a reward of $500 a head for them. But it did not tempt anyone to try the arrest; indeed, it was well known that they could not be taken alive. They might have been overwhelmed by numbers, and taken dead, or crippled; but, with each one prepared to fire twenty-four balls, with fearful precision, in as many seconds, the attempt would have been a most costly one.

After Cook had been remanded to Virginia, Merriam disguised himself, and went to Boston directly by railroad, passing through Philadelphia and New York City. In Philadelphia he stopped at the Merchants' Hotel, and, I believe, registered his name correctly. He was known to but very few persons out of Boston, and when he passed through Philadelphia the general belief was that he had died of wounds received at Harper's Ferry, and had been buried by his companions in the mountains. Obituary notices of him were published in several of the New York and Boston papers. He reached Boston, and from there he went to Canada, where he still remains.

Tidd, Barclay Coppoc and Brown, being better known, started for the North on foot through the mountains. Brown was wounded, and often had to be assisted by his companions, and at times they carried him to facilitate their progress. They reached the north mountain, near Strasbourg, in this County, and from thence passed on to Shirleysburg, in Huntingdon County. They were ten days reaching Shirleysburg, some forty miles distant. From that place they went on to the Juniata, at Bell's Mills, where they separated. Coppoc reached Canada first, and Tidd was some days behind him. Owen Brown never went to Canada; and is still in the Northern states, and will probably remain there.

Both Cook and Hazlett were arrested by citizens of Franklin County, and after having the law exhausted for their release, they were quietly remanded to the Virginia authorities by a due process of our courts, and not an arm or a voice was raised against it. No Virginian ever attempted to follow the fugitives. Even when it was known in Virginia that four of them were in this county, no one came to aid in their arrest; and the only two they have secured were given them by Pennsylvania police and Pennsylvania courts. In addition to this, had John Brown succeeded in exciting a servile insurrection; Franklin County, which is now and will remain decidedly Republican in politics, would have sent thousands of men, if necessary, to protect the families and the homes of the Virginians, *and not one would have joined the forces of* Brown! And yet a citizen of Franklin County cannot now enter Virginia. One of our mechanics started for Virginia a short time ago to work at his trade, and he had scarcely crossed the line until he was lodged in jail. What would have been his fate had not an acquaintance chanced to pass the jail, is hard to conjecture. In addition to this, Virginia is sounding the tocsin of civil war, and breathing disunion through her press and her officials. And for what? Because seventeen madmen, unaided by and unknown to the North—excepting, perhaps, a few scores of fanatics out of twenty millions—attempted to revolutionize their state.

Why this constant alarm? Why were these men, confessedly guilty, it is true, tried with indecent haste, in the midst of the wildest excitement, when a deliberate trial, in reasonable time, and with unbiased jurors, would have reached the same results? By no rule of law could the prisoners have escaped conviction, with a fair and dispassionate trial, and Virginia could well have afforded it to them. Such would have been a quiet but majestic declaration of self-reliance that the world would have respected, and the future would have no regrets for Virginia weakness and rashness in the administration of justice. When the present excitement shall have exhausted itself, and Virginia shall see that the North is, as ever, loyal to the Union and the laws, will her people look back with pride upon the trial, conviction and execution of the Harper's Ferry insurgents?

An extract from the official report of the Special Committee in Congress was received on Sunday, December 11th, in Charlestown from Washington, D. C. on the troubles that occurred in Kansas demonstrating that John Brown committed the massacre at Osawatomie Creek, though now denied by the author Mr. Redpath and others. The text reads as follows:

First in order of time were the murders committed on the night of the 24th of May, 1856, on the Pottawatomie creek. In that massacre it was known that five persons were killed on one night, viz: Allen Wilkinson, William Sherman, William P. Doyle, father, and William and Drury Doyle, sons. Various affidavits have been produced which have been appended and added to this report.

Allen Wilkinson was a member of the Kansas Legislature—a quiet, inoffensive man. His widow, Louisa Jane Wilkinson, testified that on the night of the 24th of May between the hours of midnight and daybreak, she thinks, a party of men came to the house where they were residing, and forcibly carried her husband away; that they took him in the name of the "Northern Army," and that next morning be was found about 150 yards from the house, dead. Mrs. Wilkinson was very ill with the measles. Here follows an extract from her affidavit:

I begged them to let Mr. Wilkinson stay with me, saying that I was sick and helpless, and could not stay by myself; my husband also asked them to let me stay with me until he could get some one to wait on me; told them that he would not run off, but would be there the next day, or whenever called for. The old man who seemed to be in command looked at me, and then around at the children, and replied, "You have neighbors." I said, "So I have, but they are not here, and I cannot go for them." The old man replied, "It matters not," and told him to get ready. My husband wanted to put on his boots, and get ready so as to be protected from the damp and night air, but they would not let him. They then took my husband away . . . after they were gone I thought I heard my husband's voice in complaint . . . next morning Mr. Wilkinson's body was found about 150 yards from the house, in some dead brush. A lady who saw my husband's body, said that there was a gash in his head and his side; others said that he was cut in the throat twice.

Mr. Wilkinson was a poor man, and his widow was left destitute but regardless of this fact they took away some property, including the only horse they had. Mrs. Wilkinson was presented at Westport, Missouri, with the necessary means to go to her father's, in Tennessee. She has two small children. Mrs. Wilkinson's description of the leader of the men who murdered her husband fits Captain John Brown, a well known character in the abolition party. She says that her husband was a quiet man, and was not engaged in arresting or disturbing anybody. He took no active part in the pro-slavery cause, so as to aggravate the abolitionists; but he was a pro-slavery man.

The circumstances attending William Sherman's assassination was testified to by Mr. Joseph Harris, of Franklin County in Kansas. Mr. Sherman was staying over night at the house of Harris, when, on the night of the 24th of May, about two o'clock Captain John Brown and his party arrived. After taking some property and questioning Harris and others Sherman was asked to walk out. Mr. Harris, in his affidavit, says, "Old man Brown asked Mr. Sherman to go out with him, and then Sherman went out with Brown. I heard nothing more for about fifteen minutes. Two of the 'Northern Army,' as they styled themselves, stayed with us until we heard a cap burst, and then these two men left. Next morning, about ten o'clock, I found William Sherman dead in the creek near my house. I was looking for him; as he had not come back, I thought he had been murdered. I took Mr. William Sherman's body out of the creek and examined it. Mrs. Whiteman was with me. Sherman's skull was split open in two places, and some of his brains were washed out by the water. A large hole was cut in his breast, and his left hand was cut off, except a little piece of skin on one side."

In relation to the assassination of James P. Doyle and sons, the affidavit of Mrs. Mahala Doyle, the widowed mother, was procured. William Doyle, one of the murdered, was twenty-two years of age. Drury Doyle, the other, was twenty years of age. Mrs. Doyle was left very poor, with four children—one of them only eight years old—to support. Mrs. Doyle testified that a party of armed men came to her house about 11:00 o'clock, she thinks, on the night of the 24th of May. They first inquired where Mr. Wilkinson lived, and then made Mr. Doyle open his door, and went into the house, saying they were from the "Army of the North," and asking them to surrender. Says Mrs. Doyle, "They first took my husband out of the house; then they took two of my sons—the two eldest, William and Drury—out, and then took my husband and the two boys away. My son John, sixteen years old, was spared because I asked in tears, to spare him. In a short time afterwards I heard the report of pistols—two reports; after which I heard moaning, as if a person was dying Then I heard a wild whoop . . . I went out the next morning in search of them and found my husband and William, my son, lying dead in the road, close together, about two hundred yards from the house. They were buried the next day. On the day of the burying I saw the dead body of my son Drury. Fear for myself and the remaining children induced me to leave the home which we had been living at, and I went to the state of Missouri."

The testimony of John Doyle goes to corroborate that of his mother. Here follows an extract, "I found my father and one brother (William) lying dead in the road, about two hundred yards from the house. I saw my other brother lying dead on the ground about one hundred and fifty yards from the house in the grass, near a ravine. His fingers were cut off, his head was cut open, and there was a hole in his breast. William's head was cut open, and a hole was in his jaw, as though it was made by a knife, and a hole was also in his side. My father was shot in the forehead and stabbed in the breast. I have talked often with Northern men and Eastern men in the territory, and these men talked exactly like Eastern men and Northern men talk—that is, their language and pronunciation were similar to those of Eastern and Northern men with whom I had talked. An old man commanded the party. He was of dark complexion, and his face was slim. My father and brothers were pro-slavery, and belonged to the Law and Order party."

There seems to be little or no doubt that a certain notorious leader of the free state party (as they call themselves) in Kansas, whose name it is not here deemed proper to give, was at the head of the party engaged in this fiendish massacre. Mr. Harris testified that one John Brown, one of the leaders of the free state party, was engaged in the killing of Sherman, and it will hardly be doubted that these men who murdered Sherman also killed the rest—all being murdered on the same night and in the same neighborhood. Those who were killed, it was testified, were pro-slavery people; and the undersigned has no hesitation in saying that these Ill fated men were deprived of their lives, and their wives and children made widows and orphans, in consequence of the insurrectionary movements instigated and set on foot by the reckless leaders of the Topeka convention.

Next in order are the outrages committed on the property of Morton Bourn and that of J. M. Bernard. The affidavit of Mr. Bourn shows that, on the night of Wednesday, the 28th day of May, 1856, a party of abolitionists entered his house forcibly, threatened to take his life if he did not leave the territory immediately; took all the money he had, which they said they wanted to use to carry on the war. They also took guns, saddles and horses, and then robbed his store of various articles. Mr. Bourn, on oath, says, "I own slaves, and have a crop of corn and wheat growing. I have never taken any active part with the pro-slavery party, only voted the pro-slavery ticket, and was for sustaining the laws . . . These men said I must leave in a day or two or they would kill me, or hinted as much—said I would not fare well, or words to that effect. I left for fear of my life and the lives of my family. They said that the war was commenced, that they were going to fight it out and drive the pro-slavery people out of the territory, or words to that amount. The men that robbed my house and drove me away from my property were abolitionists or free soilers . . . I believe they hated me so because I am a pro-slavery man, and in favor of the territorial laws, and because I served on the last grand jury at Lecompton."

But the most flagrant case of robbery that occurred while your committee were in Kansas was the plundering of Mr. Joab Bernard's store and premises. Mr. Bernard was quite a young man, and of a highly respectable family. While prosecuting his business he was warned that his life was in danger, and was compelled to leave his home for safety; and during his absence his store was robbed of nearly four thousand dollars worth of goods and money, and his premises of cattle and horses of the value of at least one thousand more. The facts of this case were testified to by Messrs. John Miller and Thomas S. Hamilton. Mr. Bernard testified himself as to his life being threatened, and the amount of goods in his store and other property on the premises. Messrs. Miller and Hamilton corroborated his testimony and the undersigned made their dispositions a part of his report. St. Bernard, J. M. Bernard's place is situated in Douglas County, on the California and Fort Scott road, about thirty miles from Lecompton. The robbery took place on the 27th day of May, 1856.

In his affidavit Mr Miller said, "I was in the store with Mr. Davis. While there a party of thirteen men came to the store on horseback, armed with Sharp's rifles revolvers and Bowie knives. They inquired for Mr. Bernard. I told them he had gone to Westport. One of them said to me, 'You are telling a God damned lie,' and drew his gun and pointed it at me. Some of them came into the store and the rest remained outside. They called for such goods as they wanted, and made Mr. Davis and myself hand them out, and said if we 'didn't hurry' they would shoot us. They had their guns ready. After they had got the goods—they wanted principally blankets and clothing—they packed them upon their horses and went away. Mr. Joab Bernard was a pro-slavery man."

Mr. Miller recognized one of the party as an active free state man. On the next day they came back with a wagon and took the remainder of the goods in the store, except about one hundred and fifty dollars worth—including flour, sugar, coffee, bacon and all kinds of provisions, as well as two fine horses, three saddles, two bridles, and all the money that was loose in the store. In the conclusion of his affidavit Mr. Miller said, "When they first came they looked up at the sign over the door and said they would like to shoot at the name." The affidavits accompanying this report are full and explanatory, and the undersigned begs to make them a part of his report. They are sworn to before a Justice of the Peace for Jackson County, Missouri, and the seal of the Jackson County Court is attached to the clerk's certificate, as to the official character of the Justice of the Peace. The undersigned thinks that, in reviewing these outrages, he did not inappropriately characterize the Pottawatomie Creek murders as instances of "savage barbarity and demoniac cruelty." The robberies of Bourn and Bernard are almost without parallel in the history of crime in this country. In this connection, the undersigned deems it proper to state that the report so currently circulated throughout the country, to the effect that the lamented Wilkinson, Sherman and the Doyles were caught in the act of hanging a free state man, and were shot by a party of free-soilers, is without the least foundation in truth—that it is entirely false.

In the Virginia Senate on Monday, December 12th, the Honorable A. H. H. Stuart arose and said: "Mr. President, I was called upon by a gentleman from a distant state, who entrusted to me a memorial, at the request of the governor, to be presented to this body in behalf of Edwin Coppoc, now under sentence of death at Charlestown. I called to see the governor, and he authorizes me to say that, from his personal knowledge, and from information gathered by him during his stay at Charlestown, the case of this man stands upon a very different footing from that of the other individuals who have been mentioned. He informs me that he is a youth of about twenty-three years of age, and that he had borne an unexceptional character up to the time of this difficulty.

There are present here in our lobby several members of the Society of Friends, who have an intimate knowledge of this man since he was seven years of age. He was an orphan at the age of six, and was placed in charge of one of these gentlemen, where he had remained until he attained the age of sixteen. The gentleman then removed from the state of Ohio to the state of Iowa, and he was placed in charge of another member of the Society of Friends, with whom he remained until August last. These gentlemen inform me that he was their trusted agent in the transaction of business, and frequently in the collection of money, and that in all circumstances he acquitted himself with fidelity and truthfulness. They express the deepest sympathy for him, and the governor informs me, moreover, that this young man, while he was in the engine house at Harper's Ferry, was the means of saving the lives of the prisoners who were captured by the marauders; that he frequently remonstrated with them about the exposure of their persons, and pointed out places of safety, which he insisted they should occupy, while he remonstrated against the murder of others on the street by some of his associates. I know nothing of the facts myself, and I give them to you as they have been communicated to me. In view of the near approach of the day of execution, I trust that speedy action will be had upon it. I move its reference to the Committee of Courts of Justice.

Mr. Coghill: I move that the committee meet at four o'clock to consider the question.

Mr. Wickham: I had supposed that all subjects referring to the Harper's Ferry affair were to be sent to the joint committee already appointed to consider the several matters concerned with this invasion. Would it not be well to give that destination to the memorial just presented?

Mr. Stuart: This is a matter peculiarly belonging to the Committee of Courts of Justice.

Mr. Thomas of Fairfax: I desire to hear that memorial read. For my part, I should prefer that the Senate should act upon it in the committee of the whole, for it seems to me there is something in it which requires that it be taken out of the regular course of legislative proceeding. It is essentially necessary that we should have full information on this subject, and that the governor himself should appear before us to give whatever facts he may have in regard to a matter of so much importance as this is.

Mr. Stuart: I had presumed that the proper course would be to commit the memorial to the Committee of Courts of Justice, because that committee could investigate the facts of the case and have the evidence before them. The committee might, if they choose, have a conference with the governor and summon before them those gentlemen from distant states who are now present. A committee of the whole House, I presume, would be too large to examine into all the details of this question, while the Committee of Courts of Justice, from the nature of its constitution, would have more facilities to obtain all necessary information and examine the subject more fully. The report of that committee would carry with it that weight which would induce the Senate to act upon it as they would upon any other grave question. I trust the memorial will be permitted to take the destination which I have indicated and that the committee will act upon it as speedily as the necessity of the case demands.

Mr. Thomas called for the reading of the memorial.

The Clerk then proceeded with the reading of it, as follows:

MEMORIAL FOR THE COMMUTATION OF THE SENTENCE OF EDWIN COPPOC

RICHMOND, Virginia, December 10, 1859.

To the Senate and House of Delegates of the Commonwealth of Virginia, convened in General Assembly: The memorial of the undersigned, a citizen of the State of Iowa, respectfully represents that Edwin Coppoc, a citizen of that state, is now in the jail at Charlestown, Jefferson County, Virginia, under sentence of death for his participation in the late deplorable affair at Harper's Ferry. Your memorialist would most respectfully ask your honorable body to commute the said sentence to imprisonment in the penitentiary, and in support of said request begs leave to submit the following facts:

Edwin Coppoc was left an orphan at the early age of six years. He is quite a young man, not having yet attained his twenty-fourth year, and has heretofore sustained an excellent reputation. Your memorialist has been well acquainted with him during the last nine years and can truly bear testimony that up to the period of his most unfortunate acquaintance with John Brown, be was an honest, industrious, truthful and law abiding person.

Your memorialist would further represent that the acquaintance of Edwin Coppoc with John Brown is of recent date, and that he had no knowledge of or acquaintance with him whatever in Kansas. Your memorialist would respectfully refer to the evidence adduced on the trial of these parties, which goes to show that Edwin Coppoc was not fully apprized of John Brown's designs, that he had no intention whatever to commit either treason or murder, and that, in fact, no one fell by his hands.

Your memorialist would also respectfully refer to the evidence, which abundantly proves that Edwin Coppoc's conduct towards the prisoners whom Brown held at Harper's Ferry was marked throughout by a kindly feeling, and a desire frequently expressed that they should place themselves in positions where they would be shielded from injury, as he did not wish to see any of them hurt.

Your memorialist would further urge, on behalf of this young man, that during his imprisonment in the jail at Charlestown, his conduct has been commendable, and his correspondence entirely unexceptionable, accompanied by a heartfelt repentance for the wrong he has committed; and that there is at Harper's Ferry and Charlestown, where the facts are known, a general desire that his sentence should be commuted, in consideration of his meritorious treatment of Brown's prisoners. On these considerations, and others which might be offered, your memorialist bases his appeal to your honorable body on behalf of Edwin Coppoc, and trusts that in the exercise of a dignified moderation, you will in his case "temper justice with mercy."

THOMAS WINN

Mr. Thomas: I do not know that I shall object to the course indicated by the Senator from Augusta, (Mr. Stuart) inasmuch as the memorialist presents some circumstances, certainly, of alleviation in the case of Coppoc. It would be better, perhaps, that the examination should be made by the Committee for Courts of Justice. It would be necessary, however, in order that that committee may perform efficiently the important duty imposed upon them, that they should have power to send for persons and papers if necessary, and I make a motion to that effect, in addition to the motion to refer the memorial to the Committee for Courts of Justice.

Both motions were agreed to.

A copy of the same memorial was presented in the House of Delegates by Mr. Barbour, of Culpepper, and referred to the Committee of Courts of Justice.

Mr. Wyndham Robertson, of Richmond, offered the following resolution in the House of Delegates today:

Resolved, That it be referred to the committee on the affairs of Harper's Ferry to inquire into the expediency of so modifying the existing law as to make Negroes competent witnesses in all cases of conspiracy with or inciting slaves to rebel, or make insurrection, or circulating written or printed matter designed to that end, of stealing or carrying off slaves, or of advising slaves to abscond, that may arise under existing laws, or under any laws that shall hereafter be passed to punish these or like offenses; and that the same committee further inquire what measures can and may be taken by this state to countervail the hostile and unconstitutional legislation of those states which have passed laws designed to defeat the execution or impair the efficiency of the laws of the United States for the surrender of fugitive slaves, or have otherwise violated the rights of owners of slaves, or of the slave holding states.

The resolution was adopted.

The question of taxing oysters, in conformity with the suggestion of Governor Wise, was today referred to a select committee.

Rood, the agent for the *Eclectic Magazine*, passed through here a day or two ago on his way North, after being released from the clutches of the law in Charlottesville. He swears, we understand, that he will never attempt to sell a book again south of the Mason and Dixon's line. Northern agents, peddlers and drummers have entirely disappeared from this latitude. A druggist in this city said, one or two days ago, that against an average of twenty-five calls a week heretofore made by persons of this class, not one a month is now made. Business men look upon this as a decided advantage, for these fellows were intolerable pests. They seem to have realized a proper appreciation of the state of feeling in the South when they so wisely determine to remain away. Their passage through Virginia now, or any part of the South, would be a very thorny one, and they would do well to keep that conviction before their minds for the future.

The press was informed yesterday that a brother of the notorious Hinton Helper is passing in disguise through Virginia, or at least has been very recently, distributing his "*Impending Crisis.*" He passes, we understand, under the guise of a pension agent looking up claims. If he succeeds in propagating these documents, it must be in some strictly private manner, for their character is now so well and so generally known as to prevent their being gotten off as counterfeits. If this fellow is apprehended, that will be the end of him, we imagine.

Both committees to whom the memorial in favor of Edwin Coppoc was referred met again the evening of December 11th, for the purpose of considering it. Governor Wise was summoned before them to state what he knew regarding Coppoc's course in the Harper's Ferry affair. He gave a full detail of all he had ascertained from the prisoners taken by Brown—Colonel Washington and others—and stated that had not Coppoc been convicted of treason, and therefore placed beyond his jurisdiction, he would have commuted his sentence, if every man in the state was opposed to it. He said that Coppoc should not be placed in the same category with Brown, Stevens and the others now under sentence. The committee agreed to report in favor of a commutation of his sentence to imprisonment in the penitentiary for life.

Mrs. Kennedy, the mother-in-law of John Cook, visited him in his cell on Monday, December 12th. Upon her approach they embraced affectionately, recognizing each other as mother and son. She remarked that he looked thin. He replied he was well, at least as well as he could be under the circumstances. After a general conversation, she said, "Had I only known your business at Harper's Ferry, you would not have been here, John." In the conversations, Mrs. Kennedy said she had gone down into the Ferry to find him twice on the morning of the 17th, and referred to the narrow escape of a young friend, who came near being killed by Cook's fire from the opposite side of the river. He expressed his pleasure at this, but said nothing in reference to other parties who were in range of his rifle. In speaking of his arrest, he said, "Had I got possession of my pistol I would not have been here." Mrs. Kennedy replied, "Perhaps, John, it is better than if you had used it." After his arrest Mr. Logan, under a promise of absolute secrecy, obtained from him his name, and also his commission as Captain in John Brown's forces, and Cook bitterly complained that he was guilty of betraying him. He spoke in terms of eulogy of his lawyers, and said they had done their whole duty, the whole evidence being so positive and direct against him. He read a portion of a letter from his brother-in-law, notifying him of the appearance of his wife and sister, which said, "he (the brother-in-law) already looked upon the little boy as his own son." His mother-in-law, before leaving, exhorted him to keep nothing back, and said, "Tell me all you know." Cook replied, "I have nothing further to tell—I have told you all I know of it."

Governor Willard, of Indiana, brother-in-law of John Cook, and two sisters of Cook, were expected here Tuesday. Also expected is Mr. Voorhies, Cook's eminent counsel. The action taken by the Legislature last week in regard to Cook and the other prisoners has, we presume, very clearly shown Governor Willard that there is now no hope whatever of a pardon, or rather commutation of the sentence. Cook's wife is also expected here in a few days. From what one can see of Cook, and from what we hear of him, it is generally thought that he will show the "white feather" next Friday.

Extensive preparations were being made at Charlestown on Tuesday, December 13th for the approaching executions. Nineteen companies of military were now on duty, and guards were stationed at every street corner and cross-road. Picket guards patrolled the surrounding country, and six more companies were announced as on their way here. The citizens found difficulty in passing from one part of the town to another. They were brought to a halt and marched to the guard-house if they were unable to give the countersign.

Green and Copeland will be hung at 11:00 AM Friday morning, and Cook and Coppoc at 3:00 PM in the afternoon. All these men are composed, and look calmly on their approaching doom. Their bodies will be given to their friends, if claimed.

The town is quiet and unexcited by rumors. Military discipline was kept up, however, as if it were encompassed by a besieging army. The people look forward with great pleasure to exemption from military surveillance, and when the Civil government is restored there will be quite a jubilee. The people would willingly consent that Stevens and Hazlett should spend the rest of their days in the penitentiary, rather than have another military siege at their execution.

Strong efforts will be made to save John Cook from his ignominious fate by Governor Willard, of Indiana, his brother-in-law, and other friends; but it is sure it will be without avail. A strong attempt in Coppoc's favor was also made to the Virginia Legislature, but that body refused to commute his sentence; so that both prisoners will have to meet their terrible doom on Friday.

The arrival of Governor Willard, accompanied by Mr. Voorhies, Mrs Crowley and Mrs. Stanton, sisters of Cook, and Miss Hughes, a cousin of Cook's wife, created great interest, and was the theme of various comments. Mrs. Crowley and Mrs. Stanton, escorted by Governor Willard, visited the jail and were admitted to see Cook. Sheriff Campbell accompanied them to the room. When Captain Avis, the jailor, opened the door of his cell, Mrs. Crowley rushed into the cell, screaming, "Brother! oh my poor

Brother! I never thought or expected to see you thus," throwing herself in his arms and sobbing hysterically for many minutes. Captain Avis said he couldn't stand it, and had to leave the cell. It was the duty of Sheriff Campbell to remain and be a witness to the disturbing interview, and it required all the fortitude of which he was possessed to keep from shedding tears. When the time for parting came—they remained with Cook for about three hours—Captain Avis came to the door to let them out. He said that the scene was really and truly heartrending; such a picture of woe and extreme sorrow he has never seen. After Governor Willard had taken final leave of Cook he rushed from the cell, threw himself upon Captain Avis, clung to him for support, and wept and sobbed for many minutes.

Tuesday evening, about 8:30 PM Governor Wise and those accompanying him took their departure for Harper's Ferry on their way to New York City, where they will remain until the body of Cook is sent on. The ladies were treated with the most marked kindness and respect, and every attention shown them. Our worthy Mayor, Thomas C. Green, invited Mrs. Crowley, Mrs Stanton and Miss Hughes to make his house their home while they remained. His kind invitation would have been adopted but for the short time they remained.

On that same Tuesday Edwin Coppoc wrote his uncle Joshua Coppoc as follows:

CHARLESTOWN, December 13, 1859.

MY DEAR UNCLE: I seat myself by the stand, to write for the *first*, and last time to thee and thy family. Though far from home and overtaken by misfortune, I have not forgotten you. Your generous hospitality towards me, during my short stay with you last spring, is stamped indelibly upon my heart, and also the generosity bestowed upon my poor brother, who now wanders an outcast from his native land. But thank God he is free. I am thankful that it is I who has to suffer, instead of him. *The time may come when he will remember me, and the time may come* when he will still further remember the *cause in which I die.* Thank God, the principles of the cause in which we were engaged *will not die with me and my brave comrades.* They will spread wider and wider, and gather strength with each hour that passes. The voice of truth will echo through our land, bringing conviction to the erring, and adding *numbers to that glorious army who will follow its banner.* The cause of everlasting truth and justice *will go on conquering,* to conquer, until our broad and beautiful land shall rest beneath the banner of freedom.

I had hoped to live to see the dawn of that glorious day. I had hoped to live to see the principles of the Declaration of our Independence fully realized. I had hoped to see the dark stain of slavery blotted from our land, and the libel of our boasted freedom erased, when we can say in truth, that our beloved country is the land of the free, and the home of the brave.

But this cannot be. I have heard my sentence passed. My doom is sealed. But two more short days remain for me to fulfill my earthly destiny. But two brief days between me and eternity. At the expiration of those two days, I shall stand upon the scaffold to take my last look of earthly scenes, but that scaffold has but little dread for me; for I honestly believe that I am innocent of any crime justifying such punishment. But by the taking of my life, and the lives of my comrades, Virginia is but hastening on that glorious day, when the slave shall rejoice in his freedom. When he can say, *"I too am a man,* and am groaning no more under the yoke of oppression.

But I must now close. Accept this short scrawl as a remembrance of me. Give my love to all the family. Kiss little Josey for me. Remember me to all my relatives and friends. And now farewell for the last time.

From thy Nephew,

EDWIN COPPOC

P. S. Thee wished to know who was here with me from Iowa. Thomas Winn is here and expects to stay until after the execution; and then will convey my body, to Springdale. It is my wish to be buried there.

I would of been glad to see thee or any of my other relatives, but it is now too late. I did not like to send for any of you, as I did not know whether any of you would be willing to come.

I will say, for I know that it will be a satisfaction to all of you, that we are all kindly treated and I hope that the North will not fail to give Sheriff Campbell and Captain Avis due acknowledgment for their kind and noble actions.

E.

There was a meeting in Washington on December 14, 1859 of the Select Committee appointed to inquire into the late invasion and seizure of the public property at Harper's Ferry. The committee consisted of three pro-slavery Senators and two from the North, headed by Senator James M. Mason, of Virginia. The resolutions annexed were:

Resolved, That a committee be appointed to inquire into the facts attending the late invasion and seizure of the armory and arsenal of the United States at Harper's Ferry, in Virginia, by a band of armed men, and report—

Whether the same was attended by armed resistance to the authorities and public force of the United States, and by the murder of any of the citizens of Virginia, or of any troops sent there to protect the public property;

Whether such invasion and seizure was made under color of any organization intended to subvert the government of any of the states of the Union; what was the character and extent of such organization; and whether any citizens of the United States not present were implicated therein, or accessory thereto, by contributions of money, arms, munitions, or otherwise;

What was the character and extent of the military equipment in the hands or under the control of said armed band; and where and how and when the same was obtained and transported to the place so invaded.

That said committee report whether any and what legislation may, in their opinion, be necessary on the part of the United States for the future preservation of the peace of the country, or for the safety of the public property; and that said committee have power to send for persons and papers.

On Thursday December 15th the hotels and private houses here in Charlestown were all crowded. Strict surveillance was kept on strangers, though these who come from curiosity and were well vouched for on the question of our "peculiar institutions" were allowed to remain.

After receiving the letter sent by Edwin, Joshua Coppoc went at once to Charlestown. Today he talked over matters of mutual interest with Edwin and Thomas Winn. Edwin changed his original burial request, expressed in his letter, to a preference for burial near his birthplace in Columbiana County. The last letter written by Edwin Coppoc was a short note to his resourceful friend Mr. Thomas Winn as follows:

MY DEAR FRIEND THOMAS WINN: For they love and sympathy, and for they unwearied efforts on my behalf, accept my warmest thanks. I have no words to tell the gratitude and love I have for thee. And may God bless thee and thy family, for the love and kindness thee has always shown towards my family and me. And when life with thee is over, may we meet on that shore where there is no parting, is the farewell prayer of thy true Friend,

EDWIN COPPOC

Governor Willard's interview with Cook on Wednesday evening, when delivering a message to the prisoner from his sister, Mrs. Willard, was very affecting. The governor was strongly attached to the prisoner, and wept over him as if he were his own son. His lamentations could be heard throughout the building.

The prisoners were all calm and resigned today, and engaged, with seeming devotion, in spiritual exercises, under the direction of the Reverend N. C. North, a Presbyterian clergyman. The gallows will be re-erected this evening, The Negroes will be hung between eleven and twelve o'clock and the whites between twelve and one.

The prisoners were visited this afternoon by Reverend Mr. Nassau, Reverend Mr. Dutton, Reverend Mr. North, of the Presbyterian Church, and Reverend Beverly Waugh, of the Methodist Episcopal Church. The services in the cells were of an interesting and solemn character, and were participated in by all the condemned men, though it is now evident, from subsequent events, that Cook and Coppoc, at least, were playing 'possum, as their minds must have been fixed on hopes of life and liberty, rather than on death and eternity, at the time they were making outward protestations of resignation. They all gave unqualified assent to the convictions of religious truth, and each expressed a hope of salvation in the world to come.

Cook and Coppoc were loudest in their professions of a change of heart, and in the hope of divine forgiveness. They freely admitted their guilt, and acknowledged their doom a just one, and that in the main they had been treated with the utmost kindness by all, though they thought some of the witnesses were rather harsh in their testimony. The ministers imagined they discovered a decidedly favorable change in the condition of Cook's mind since his interview with his sisters. Up to that time his calmness and bravery were regarded as proceeding from a lack of feeling, and on leaving him yesterday in the afternoon they reported that he had been led to seek forgiveness for his sins as the only hope of salvation, and that Coppoc was also equally in earnest in his protestations of religious convictions and hopes of forgiveness—all of which was undoubtedly intended to hoodwink people as to their project of escape.

Cook had been visited throughout his imprisonment by the Reverend N. Green North, at the request of the prisoner, as also of Governor's Wise and Willard.

The Reverend Mr. North was present at an interview between Coppoc and Mr. Butler, a Yankee gentleman from Ohio, who raised the prisoner. He described the interview as an affecting one, and spoke highly of Mr. Butler's Christian deportment and advice to the prisoner. Mr. Butler said that Coppoc was a trusty, but very willful boy. An uncle of Coppoc, of the same name, from Ohio, his father's brother, visited him also yesterday, the interview lasting over an hour. He seemed much distressed at the sad fate which awaited his relative.

This was the condition of the town, prisoners and military up till 7:00 PM Thursday evening. All apprehensions of an intended rescue had long since been banished, and nothing was thought of but the approaching execution, whilst the overflowing throng of strangers were hunting quarters for the night. The bar-rooms were all crowded with people discussing the resignation of the prisoners to their fate; and so firmly had this conviction settled in the public mind, that military duty was regarded as a bore, and the *finale* of the tragedy regarded as almost reached.

The supper table of the Carter house was crowded for the fifth or sixth time, and all was moving on calmly and quietly till a little past 8:00 PM, when an alarm was given and the whole town thrown into commotion by an attempt of Cook and Edwin Coppoc to escape from the jail.

At 8:10 PM in the evening there was a loud report of a rifle being fired near the wall of the jail, followed by several other shots from the vicinity of the guard-house, near the jail. The military were called to arms, and the excitement was intense beyond anything that has yet occurred during our ever-memorable era of military occupation. In a few minutes the streets and avenues of the town were in the possession of the armed men, and it was with some difficulty that the cause of all the turmoil could be ascertained. Rumors of every description were afloat, and it was at one time thought that the prisoners had overpowered their guards and made their escape, and then that an attack had been made on the jail by parties attempting to rescue the prisoners. It was dangerous for a citizen to go out to ascertain the true cause of the excitement, and rumors of a most extensive character floated in, to be contradicted by momentary new arrivals of citizens driven in from the streets.

The sentinel stationed near the jail reported that at 8:10 PM he observed a man on the jail wall. He challenged him, and, receiving no answer, fired at him. Another head was also seen above the wall but it disappeared as soon as the first one had been fired at. The man on the top of the wall seemed at first determined to jump down, but the sentinel declared his intention of impaling him on his bayonet, and he then retreated into the jail yard with Coppoc, and both gave themselves up without further resistance. Cook afterwards remarked that if he could have got over and throttled the guard, he would have made his escape. The Shenandoah Mountains were within a ten minutes' run of the jail wall, and had he reached them, with his thorough knowledge of the mountains, his arrest would have been difficult—especially as but few of the military could have followed him during the night. They had succeeded, after two weeks' labor, whenever alone, and at night when the bed-clothes muffled the sound of the saw they had made out of an old Barlow knife, in cutting their own shackles, so that they could pry them off at any moment when they should have their other work completed.

They had also made a sort of chisel out of an old bed-screw, with which they succeeded, as opportunity would offer, in removing the plaster from the wall, and then brick after brick, until a space sufficient for them to pass through was opened all to the outer brick. The part of the wall on which they operated was in the rear of the bed on which they slept, and the bed being pushed against the wall completely hid their work from view. The bricks they took out were concealed in the drum of a stove, and the dirt and plaster removed in the course of their work was placed between the bed-clothing. They acknowledged that they had been at work a whole week in making the aperture in the wall. Their cell being on the first floor, the aperture was not more than five feet above the pavement of the yard, and when freed of their shackles their access to the yard was quite easy. Here, however, there was a smooth brick wall, about fifteen feet high, to scale. This difficulty was, however, soon overcome with the aid of the timbers of the scaffold on which Captain Brown was hung, and which was intended also for their own execution. They placed these against the wall and soon succeeded in reaching the top, from which they could have easily dropped to the other side, had not the vigilance of the sentinel on duty so quickly checked their movements. They were arrested in the jail-yard by General Taliaferro and the officer of the day, who rushed to the jail the moment the alarm was given.

General Taliaferro immediately telegraphed to Governor Wise, informing him of the frustrated attempt of the prisoners. His answer directed that the military should immediately take possession of the interior of the jail, and guard the prisoners until they were executed. Sheriff Campbell and Captain Avis were, of course, much chagrined at this near escape of their prisoners, especially as they had resisted all interference of the military with the interior discipline of the jail. The prisoners were shrewd and cunning fellows, and were undoubtedly without any accomplices in their undertaking. Their friends, who were still here, were also fearful that they might be suspected of knowledge of their attempt. The general impression is that it they had waited till midnight or later, they might have reached the mountains. But it is presumed they were fearful of being watched during the night, or desired to have as much as possible of the darkness, to gain a good distance before daylight would allow a general pursuit.

At daybreak Friday morning *reveille* was sounded from the various barracks, announcing the dawn of the day of execution, and soon the whole community was astir. The anxiety to learn a true version of the events of last night, caused the streets to be thronged with people at an early hour. The military, most of whom had been on duty all night, or sleeping on their *arms,* looked less fit for the active duties of the day than was anticipated at the time of parade yesterday. The weather was bright and beautiful, and much milder than for several preceding days. At 9:00 AM, the entire military force in attendance was formed on Main Street, and the officers reported ready for duty at headquarters. Those companies detailed for field duty around the gallows, immediately took up the line of march, and at 9:30 AM were in the positions assigned them on the field. Those companies detailed for escort duty took up their positions in front of the jail, awaiting orders.

The following is Cook's last letter to his wife written from the prison:

Charlestown Jail, Dec. 16, 1859.

MY DEAR WIFE AND CHILD: For the last time I take my pen to address you. For the last time to speak to you through the tongue of the absent. I am about to leave you and this world forever. But do not give way to your grief. Look with the eyes of hope beyond the vale of life, and see the dawning of that brighter morrow that shall know no clouds or shadows in its sunny sky—that shall know no sunset. To that eternal day I trust, beloved, I am going now. For me there waits no far-off or uncertain future. I am only going from my camp on earth to a home in heaven; from the dark clouds of sin and grief, to the clear blue skies, the flowing fountains and the eternal joys of that better and brighter land, whose only entrance is through the vale of death—whose only gateway is the tomb.

Oh, yes! Think that I am only going home; going to meet my Savior and my God; going to meet my comrades, and wait and watch for you. Each hour that passes, every tolling bell, proclaims this world is not our home. We are but pilgrims here, journeying to our Father's house. Some have a long and weary road to wander; shadowed o'er with doubts and fears, they often tire and faint upon life's roadside yet, still all-wearied they must move along. Some make a more rapid journey, and complete their pilgrimage in the bright morn of life; they know no weariness upon their journey, no ills or cares of toil-worn age. I and my comrades here are among that number. Our pilgrimage is nearly ended; we can almost see our homes. A few more hours and we will be there

True, it is hard for me to leave my loving partner and my little one, lingering on the rugged road on which life's storms are bursting. But cheer up my beloved ones; those storms will soon be over; through their last lingering shadows you will see the promised rainbow. It will whisper of a happy land where all storms. are over. Will you not strive to meet me in that clime of unending sunshine? Oh! yes, I know you will; that you will also try to lead our child along that path of glory; that you will claim for him an entrance to that celestial city whose maker and builder is God. Teach him the way of truth and virtue. Tell him for what and how his father left him, ere his infant lips could lisp my name. Pray for yourself and for him. Remember that there is no golden gateway to the realms of pleasure here, but there is one for the redeemed in the land that lies toward the stars. There I hope we may meet when you have completed your pilgrimage on the road of life. Years will pass on and your journey will soon be ended. Live so that when from the verge of life you look back you may feel no vain regrets, no bitter anguish for misspent years. Look to God in all your troubles; cast yourself on Him when your heart is dark with the night of sorrow and heavy with the weight of woe. He will shed over you the bright sunshine of his love, and take away the burden from your heart . . .

And now farewell. May that all-wise and eternal God, who governs all things, be with you to guide and protect you through life, and bring us together in eternal joy beyond the grave. Farewell, fond partner of my heart and soul. Farewell, dear babe of our love. A last, long farewell, till we meet in Heaven.

I remain, in life and death, your devoted husband,

JOHN E. COOK

At 10:30 AM General Taliaferro, with his staff, numbering about twenty-five officers, having given orders to prepare the two Negro prisoners, Shields Green and John Copeland, for execution, took their departure to join the main body of the troops on the field. The military then formed in a hollow square around the jail, and an open wagon, containing the coffins of the prisoners, drew up in front, with a carriage to convey Sheriff Campbell and his Deputies.

The crowd of citizens and strangers was very great—at least five times as numerous as on the occasion of Brown's execution—most of whom were already on the field, whilst others waited to see the prisoners come out. The religious ceremonies in the cell of the prisoners were very impressive, and were conducted by Reverend Mr. North, of the Presbyterian, and Reverend Henry Waugh, of the M. E. Church.

At 10:45 AM the prisoners, accompanied by the Sheriff and the Reverend Mr. North, appeared at the jail door, and with their arms pinioned moved slowly forward towards the vehicle in waiting for them. They seemed downcast, and wore none of that calm and cheerful spirit evinced by Brown under similar circumstances. They were helped into the wagon and took their seats on their coffins, scarcely looking to the right or left. The escort now commenced to move and the wagon was close flanked on either side by a company of riflemen marching in double lock step.

At 10:53 AM, the procession entered the field occupied by the military, and the prisoners cast a shuddering glance towards the gallows erected on the rising ground in its center. In two minutes more the wagon stopped at the foot of the gallows, and while the prisoners were alighting, the companies forming the escort moved off to the position assigned them on the field.

The prisoners mounted the scaffold with a firm step, and were immediately joined by Sheriff Campbell. After a brief prayer by the clergyman, the caps were drawn over their heads, and the ropes affixed around their necks. During the few moments they thus stood, John Copeland remained quiet, but Shields Green was engaged in earnest prayer up to the time the trap was drawn, when they were both launched into eternity. They fell at 11:11 AM.

Green died very easy, his neck being broken by the fall. The motion of his body was very slight. Copeland seemed to suffer very much, and his body writhed in violent contortions for several minutes. They were accompanied on the gallows by Reverends Waugh, North and Leah, to whom they bade an affectionate farewell, and expressed the hope of meeting them in Heaven. The bodies were placed in poplar coffins and carried back to the jail. They will be interred tomorrow on the spot where the gallows stands, but there is a party of medical students here from Winchester who will doubtless not allow them to remain there long.

The bodies of the two Negro prisoners were brought back to the jail, at about 11:45 AM and notice was given to Cook and Coppoc that their time was approaching—only one hour more being allowed them. The military movements, similar to those at the first execution, were repeated, and the wagon with two more coffins was standing at the door waiting at 12:30 PM. The same military escort was in readiness while the closing religious ceremonies were progressing in the cell. The prisoners had been visited by Reverend North, Reverend Waugh and Reverend Leach. Previous to their departure for the scaffold, the prisoners were engaged in washing their feet and putting on their under-clothing. Captain Avis said that if they had anything to say they could say it then, in the presence of fifteen or twenty persons. Cook replied that he was grateful indeed for the kindness shown him by Sheriff Campbell, the jailor and the guards. To the ministers, who had manifested such interest in his welfare, and Messrs. Joseph F. Blessing and John J. Locke, as well as the citizens generally, for their kindness to him, he was very grateful.

At this point Edwin Coppoc looked up and said, "Them's my sentiments, too, gentlemen." John Cook then gave directions in regard to one or two articles—one, a breastpin, he did not want taken off then, nor at the scaffold. He wished it eventually given to his wife or to his boy. Within his shirt-bosom, on the left side, was a daguerreotype and a lock of his sons hair, which he wished given to his wife. Since the failure of their attempt to escape last night, their assumed composure and apparent resignation had given way, and they now looked at their fate with the full conviction of its awful certainty. They were reserved, and rather quiet, but fervently joined in the religious ceremonies. On their way down stairs they were allowed to advance to the cell of Stevens and Hazlett, and bid them farewell. They shook hands cordially, and Cook said to Stevens, "My friend, good-bye." Stevens replied, "*Good*-bye, cheer up; give my love to my friends in the other world." Coppoc also made a remark to Stevens which was unheard by the crowd, but Stevens replied, "Never mind." Both then shook hands with Hazlett, and bade him "good-bye," but did not call him by name. On emerging from the jail Cook recognized several gentlemen, and *bowed* politely. Both Cook and Coppoc requested that their arms should not be pinioned tight enough to stop the circulation of their blood, which was complied with. A blue cloth tallith was thrown over Coppoc and a dark one over Cook. During these proceedings, Coppoc was struggling to keep down his emotion, and Cook was striving to be calm. The Quaker gentleman then remarked that "it is hard to die," to which Coppoc responded, "It is the parting from friends, not the dread of death, that moves us."

They were helped into the wagon and took seats on their coffins. Their appearance was rather indicative of hopeless despair than of resignation, and they seemed to take but little notice of anything as the procession moved slowly on to the field of death. The wagon reached the gallows at 12:45 PM, and the prisoners ascended the scaffold with a determined firmness, that was scarcely surpassed by Captain Brown. On approaching the trap a brief prayer was offered up by one of the clergymen, the rope was adjusted, and the caps were drawn. Edwin Coppoc turned towards John Cook and stretched forth his hand as far as possible. At the same time Cook said "Stop a minute; *where* is Edward's hand?" They then made contact and shook hands cordially. Cook, with great emotion said, "God bless you." After the rope was adjusted, Cook exclaimed, "Be quick—as quick as possible;" which was also repeated by Coppoc. They both exhibited the most unflinching firmness, and said nothing further. In seven minutes after they ascended the gallows they were launched into eternity. They died almost instantly, the rope having been adjusted by a surgeon so as to assure a speedy and less painful death. After hanging for about half an hour, both bodies were taken down and placed in black walnut coffins, prepared for them. That of Cook was placed in a poplar box, labeled and directed as follows: "Ashbell P. Willard and Robert Crowley, No. 104 William Street, New York City; care of Adams' Express." Joshua Coppoc and Thomas Winn brought the body of Edwin in a coffin provided by the State of Virginia to the train depot, awaiting the next train that would take them to Iowa. The bodies of Green and Copeland were handed over to the surgeons from Winchester for such disposal as they deemed necessary.

Mr. Chilton published the following letter in the *National Intelligencer*, on Saturday, December 17th, in explanation of his agency in procuring the affidavits of the insanity of John Brown:

Washington, Tuesday, Dec. 13, 1859.

GENTLEMEN: A card in your paper, signed Germaine, dated December 7, 1859, which came to my notice only last Saturday, renders it proper, in my judgment, that I should address you a brief communication under my own name. Urgent business engagements have prevented it at an earlier date. I do this very reluctantly, as I am sure I shall be credited by all who know me when I say I have no desire to see my name in the newspapers.

In my absence from home some time ago my partner, A. B. Magruder, Esq., caused to be inserted in your paper a card in answer to a communication from a letter-writer at Charlestown, Virginia, to the Baltimore *American*. saying that I was engaged in collecting affidavits by which it would appear that John Brown had been insane br several years. This was denied in the card. The denial was strictly true. I never did collect or procure an affidavit directly or indirectly, touching the subject, nor have I ever seen one. If I had been at home I do not think I should myself have noticed the communication. If evidence had been furnished to me of Brown's insanity, in the opinion of those who had known him, I should not, as his counsel, have hesitated to take their affidavits and use them as best I could for his defense, either before or after conviction. When I accepted the employment by the relatives and friends of Brown to appear as his counsel, I held myself bound to render him my best services, as fully and zealously as I would have served the most distinguished man in the nation.

I trust that in my professional career I shall never know or observe any difference between clients, whether they be high or low, rich or poor, popular or unpopular. When I engage as counsel, while it is always gratifying to me to have the approval of my friends and the public in the discharge of what I deem my duty, yet my own sense of propriety must be the tribunal of ultimate resort with me, and whithersoever duty points the way I will not fear to tread.

Your correspondent Germaine says he desires "to vindicate the truth of history." What particular object be aimed at accomplishing by such vindication I do not distinctly understand. If he intended to attack me, (he acquits my partner) I think before he wrote his communication he might have inquired of me, a resident of the same city with himself—perhaps an acquaintance and friend—what was the exact truth of the matter about which he was writing, so that truth might be *fully* vindicated. If he had done so before he published his communication, it would probably not have appeared, because he would have feared that it would utterly fail in the vindication he proposed to effect. It may be justly said that the truth of history has ever suffered most at the hands of those who write and publish without proper inquiry.

I have already said I have never seen one of the affidavits presented to Governor Wise touching Brown's insanity. Nor did I ever write or present, or cause to be written or presented to him any petition in Brown's behalf. Nor was I aware that any such petition had been presented to him until I saw the fact stated in his message. Yet I take occasion to say I would have presented a petition on behalf of Brown to Governor Wise, not such a one as was presented, because that is obnoxious to the criticism the governor makes upon it, viz: that it betrays a want of knowledge of Virginia law, which I am not willing to admit on my part, and but for this fact I do not think I should have troubled you now.

The whole explanation is this: While I was in Richmond attending the Court of Appeals in Brown's case, I received a letter from Mr. Hoyt, a young lawyer in Boston, who was one of my colleagues in conducting Brown's defense before the circuit court of Jefferson County, at Charlestown, Virginia, saying he had sent by express the records in two other cases of the Charlestown convicts, requesting that William Green, Esq., my colleague in Richmond, and myself, would, in the event we were successful in our application for a writ of error in Brown's case, apply as counsel for similar writs in the other cases; saying also that be was on his way to Ohio to procure affidavits of Brown's insanity, upon which to found an application for an issue under the statute of Virginia. It seems that he and others, friends of Brown, had been misled, as they allege, by an editorial of the Richmond *Enquirer* published after Brown was sentenced, stating in reference to his alleged insanity, that it was still not too late to have the question of insanity tried upon an issue and relief afforded, if it was found to exist. I have never seen the editorial in question.

I returned from Richmond on Sunday, and on Monday morning, on my way to attend the Alexandria circuit court, I casually met Mr. Hoyt. He said he had just returned from Ohio with a large number of affidavits touching Brown's sanity, and wished to consult with me. I replied that he must come down to Alexandria if he wished to see me, as I should most probably remain there during the week which I did. I have neither seen nor heard from Mr. Hoyt since.

I learned for the first time on yesterday that Governor Wise came through this city on his return from Charlestown. Unexpectedly I was absent, and as Brown's execution was fixed for a day not distant, Mr.

Hoyt prepared the affidavit and signed my name to it as counsel and submitted it, accompanied with the affidavits, himself in person to Governor Wise. If I had been at home I should certainly, as counsel for Brown, have presented to the governor a petition accompanied with the affidavits, but should not have prayed for an issue, as I knew that after sentence there could be no issue ordered by any authority, unless the Legislature did it by a special law. After conviction and before sentence an issue might, upon good cause shown to believe him insane, been ordered by the court which tried him. Nor should I have petitioned for pardon, as I knew that by the law of Virginia the governor had no power to pardon in cases of conviction for treason, which was Brown's case. I should simply have submitted the affidavits to him to be dealt with as he thought fit and proper.

If there be any private or public interest felt in having the truth of the history of this transaction accurately ascertained and recorded as a part of the history of the times, I trust I have furnished your correspondent Germaine, and all others who may desire it, full information upon the subject, and the material for making up an accurate and complete record.

SAMUEL CHILTON

Cook and Coppoc, after the failure of their attempt to escape from the Charlestown jail, drew up the following statement, which was handed to the correspondent of the Baltimore *American* for publication:

Charlestown Prison, Friday, Dec. 16, 1859.

Having been called upon to make a fair statement in regard to the ways and means of our breaking jail, we have agreed to do so from a sense of our duty to the

Sheriff of the County, and jailor and jail-guard. We do not wish that any one should be unjustly censured on our account.

The principal implements with which we opened a passage through the wall of the jail was a Barlow knife and a screw which we took out of the bedstead. The knife was borrowed from one of the jail guards to cut a lemon with. We did not return it to him. He had no idea of any intention on our part to break out. Neither did the sheriff's jailer nor any of the guard have any knowledge of our plans.

We received no aid from any person or persons whatever. We had, as we supposed, removed all the brick except the last tier, several days ago, but on the evening previous to our breaking out we found our mistake in regard to that matter. We had intended to go out on the evening that my sister and brother-in-law were here, but I knew that it would reflection them and we postponed it—but I urged Coppoc to go, and I would remain, but he refused. We then concluded to wait.

I got a knife-blade from Shields Green, and with that made some teeth in the Barlow knife, with which we sawed off our shackles. We had them all off the night previous to our getting out. Coppoc went out first and I followed. We then got up on the wall, when I was discovered, and shot at. The guard outside the wall immediately came up to the wall.

We saw there was no chance to escape, and as it was discovered that we had broken jail, we walked in deliberately and gave ourselves up to the Sheriff, Captain

Avis, and the jail guard. There was no person or persons who aided us in our escape. This is true, so help us God.

(Signed)   JOHN E. COOK

EDWIN COPPOC

Back in Salem arrangements had been made for a quiet funeral for Coppoc in accord with Quaker custom. Neighbors came in large numbers to attend Coppoc's funeral at Winona, Ohio in Columbiana County on Sunday, December 18th. Until late in the afternoon they continued to come, some through curiosity, but most generally through sympathy. All were respectful. The number that came was estimated between two and three thousand, and the simple rite turned into a large public funeral.

In the little room at the home of Joshua Coppoc where the body lay, a neighbor woman, Rachael Whinery, from an adjoining farm, rose and delivered a eulogy which she had only prepared the evening before. As evening approached the body was borne out into the yard and permitted to rest a short time while the silence was broken briefly by a solemn voice closing with the appeal, "Let us here over this lifeless body and as if standing at the altar of Christ, consecrate our lives anew to go and battle manfully for truth and righteousness, and for the overthrow of the bloody system that sacrifices millions of our fellow men."

As the setting sun passed below the horizon, the remains of Edwin Coppoc were lowered into the grave in the Friends' Churchyard, among the hills and valleys of his childhood days. When the shadows of night had fallen and the funeral crowd had vanished, a few men entered the Friends' Church with rifles to guard the dead, for a rumor had been passed around that an effort would be made to rob the newly dug grave.

Edwin Coppoc's funeral took place in Ohio on December 18th. On Monday a correspondent of the Cleveland *Leader* said:

Yesterday I attended the funeral of Edwin Coppic at the Friends' Meeting, near Whinery's Mill. Joshua Coppoc, an uncle of his living near there, left here last Wednesday for Charlestown to procure his body, having received a telegraph dispatch the day before to do so, from the Virginia authorities. He, with one or two other friends, returned last Saturday to this place with the body on the evening express, when notice was given that the burial would take place the next day at 3:00 o'clock. Before their return it was expected that the body would be taken to Iowa, but for reasons satisfactory to his friends it was decided to bury him here.

The time was very short, but the word was rapidly circulated through the neighborhood, and a larger funeral I was never at. It is said that not less than 2,000 persons came to look at the victim of Virginia's revenge and malice, during the few hours from morning till the burial took place. Of course there would have been a much larger attendance had a longer time been allowed. I heard several say today that they would have attended if they had known it. Coppoc's friends are members of the Society of Friends, and of course the funeral was conducted according to their rules.

A very deep feeling appeared to pervade among the people, and a great deal of interest to hear of the doings during the last hours of Coppoc's life; and I have not the least doubt but every anti-slavery man and woman left the ground with a deeper hatred of the vile system of American slavery. All could not gain admittance into the house to see the corpse. It was taken into the yard and placed on a table, and as each one came to the side of the coffin they appeared to linger over it with more than usual interest and sympathy, notwithstanding the disfiguration of the face, caused by the mode of death.

The body of John E. Cook, one of the four associates of John Brown, executed at Charlestown on Friday, arrived at Jersey City about midnight on Saturday, coming by Adams Express. It was at first designed to remove the remains to Willamsburg in a hearse, but, fearing that public attention might be attracted, that vehicle was dispensed with, and an express wagon employed instead. Governor Willard, of Indiana, and Mr. Robert Crowley brothers-in-law of the deceased, followed in a carriage. By some oversight, a permit to take the body through the city had not been obtained, and the express man was stopped at the Jersey City ferry, with the warning that without complying with this formality he could not pass. Governor Willard and Mr. Crowley however, gave the most positive assurances that the permit should be forthcoming in the morning, and they were then allowed to proceed into New York City. The same delay occurred at the Willlamsburg Ferry but with the same result. Immediately upon its arrival, the body, which was left precisely as it had been taken from the gallows, was conveyed to the undertaker's to be prepared for interment. Upon opening the coffin, the features of the deceased were found to be somewhat distorted from strangulation, and there was some extravasation of blood.

The fact of the arrival of the corpse in the city was very generally known, and hundreds of people, many of whom had been personally acquainted with the deceased while he was a resident of Willamsburg, called at the undertaker's with the hope of seeing his remains; but the face was so much discolored that it was not thought advisable to expose it until the process of embalming had been completed, when it is hoped that all unnatural appearances will be removed. The body was dressed in a black suit, and had suspended around its neck a miniature picture of an only child of the deceased. Mrs. Cook, with her child was stopping yesterday in Williamsburg. It is but seventeen months since she was married, and her first acquaintance with the Northern relatives of her husband is at his grave. For obvious reasons she was not permitted to view the body yesterday.

So confident were the friends of John Cook that Dr. Porter's Church would be opened for the funeral services, that a circular was printed inviting different ministers and congregations to be present. Dr. Porter himself was called upon, and expressed himself perfectly willing to preach the funeral sermon in his church, and desired to have the body brought there. As Mr. Robert Crowley, brother-in-law of Cook, had been associated with the church for fifteen years, and had been a member of the consistory for the last seven years, the family had no suspicion that any objection could be made to the contemplated services. The consistory held a meeting and passed a resolution to the effect that an undue excitement might be created, endangering the temporal and spiritual interests of the church, and it was afraid that it would be impossible to protect the church if it were opened for the purpose proposed, and it therefore could not consent to the measure. A counter proposition was submitted to the family to the effect that the consistory would consent to the obsequies in the church, if the body was not brought there. But to this the family would not consent. They wanted the body to be in the church, and there receive a Christian burial according to the customary forms. A third proposition was then made that the funeral services should take place in the church, and the body be taken there, but that the face of the deceased should not be exposed to public view.

To this the family objected, on the ground that they waited to bury their relative as they would one of their own number, and as a man who had professed to die in the Christian faith. They only wished that the deceased should have paid him the last sad rites of the Christian Church and felt exceedingly grieved that this privilege should be granted only on the conditions named, and that this refusal should come from a Church with which he was so nearly allied. They believed that there was very few in the congregation who would indorse the action of the consistory of the Church, and it would seem that Doctor Porter himself had anticipated no trouble, as he not only had his sermon written, but had suggested the names of several gentlemen whom he desired to participate in the services.

This unexpected decision of the consistory caused much embarrassment to the family of the deceased—so little time was left to make the necessary arrangements; in the words of a near friend, "the blow was felt even more keenly than that of the unfortunate death of their relative." After this refusal an effort was made to procure Doctor Tompkins' New England Church, but it was understood that the consistory were opposed to granting the edifice for the purpose proposed. The South Baptist Church tendered the use of its hall, but the room was found to be too small. A number of gentlemen immediately came forward in this emergency, offering the bereaved family the use of their private houses, and it was finally determined to hold the funeral services at the residence of Mr. Samuel L. Harris, No. 114 South Ninth Street, Williamsburg, at 10:00 AM on Tuesday. The remains would then be conveyed to the Cypress Hills Cemetery for interment. The coffin, which has been prepared was made of rosewood. It was handsomely mounted with silver-headed screws, handles, etc. A silver-plate on the lid bore the following inscription

John E. Cook
Died Dec. 16, 1859,
Aged 28 years.

The facts given above regarding the action of the Consistory of Doctor Porter's Church were obtained from the deceased. A statement was published in the *Evangelist* of last week in which the consistory explained and defended the course which it had taken.

The friends of the family placed in contrast with the action taken by Dr. Porter's Church the kind conduct of the Virginia authorities toward them. To Colonel Washington, especially, they were very much indebted, for his assiduous attention while they were discharging their sad mission at Charlestown. They stated that they would have found no difficulty in procuring the use of a church in Charlestown, where Cook was executed, for the performance of such services as they saw fit.

The last number of *Frederick Douglass' Paper* contained a letter from the fugitive editor, who had arrived safely in England. Douglass confessed that his sudden journey was undertaken in fear of arrest. He said:

It is probably quite well known that I sailed, not from the United States, but from Canada—not from Boston, where I had intended to take passage, but from Quebec. Nor is it necessary to state that the Harper's Ferry troubles, and the evident purpose of Messrs. Bennett and Buchanan to involve me in them, caused me to take my present route, though not my present journey, for that was already determined upon more than a year ago, and the arrangements partly made for it.

Of John Brown, he says:

To fail is madness. To succeed is the highest wisdom. Had John Brown pursued his original plan—avoiding a fight altogether, keeping himself and his men scattered abroad in the ravines, caves, and the ten thousand Sevastopols to be found among the Alleghany range of mountains—adding to his number all such as desired to be free, and were willing to suffer hardships and perils to gain it—the insurrection would not have seemed the mad and fruitless thing it now seems. But John Brown has not failed. He has dropped *an idea*, equal to a thousand bombshells into the very Bastille of slavery. That idea will live and grow, and one day will, unless slavery is otherwise abolished, cover Virginia with sorrow and blood.

After the funeral of Edwin Coppoc, it was, of course, the big topic of conversation about the country firesides for many miles around, and there was much sympathy and resentment in the town of Salem. Dissatisfaction was felt at the quiet funeral. Fear was expressed that the body would be removed by pro-slavery sympathizers. Someone said in the midst of a crowd of listeners that it was little short of a disgrace to permit the body of this young martyr to remain in a coffin furnished by the slave state of Virginia. This view soon found frequent expression. There was a demand for a more public funeral in order that the sentiment of Salem and the surrounding country might have adequate expression. An announcement was made in the newspapers and in a handbill signed by prominent citizens setting December 30, 1859 as the date for the <u>second</u> and final burial of Edwin Coppoc at Hope Cemetery in Salem.

The following letter from Mr. Crowley gave some explanation of the problems attendant with Cook's funeral:

Williamsburg, Tuesday, Dec. 20, 1859.

To the Editor of the New York *Times*:

I need not say how painful it is, under the circumstances, to be compelled to notice in this public manner anything which may appear in the Press concerning my unfortunate deceased relative, John E. Cook, but justice to myself, and to all his other relatives, requires me to notice a statement which has been made in regard to the arrangements for his funeral and burial services. It is untrue that either I or any of his relatives or kindred desired that any effort should be made in the funeral services to make an ovation to the memory of John E. Cook.

After I became satisfied that all efforts which had been made by his counsel and his friends would fail to spare him from death, I parted from my brother-in-law, Governor Willard, at Washington,—I to come to New York City to prepare for the funeral services, he to go to Charlestown and make arrangements for the transportation of the body to New York. Where the body was to be buried, neither I nor Governor Willard knew. That was a question to be decided by the deceased himself. No man can believe for one moment, when he reviews the circumstances which attended his trial, the defense made by his counsel, in the presence of myself and Governor Willard, that either he or I desired any display at the funeral I and my wife were members of the Reformed Dutch Church, Fourth-street, Willamsburg. I was also a member of the Consistory. I had the highest assurance which I could receive from man, that my brother-in-law believed in God and hoped for salvation through the sacrifice that Christ had made. Thus believing, I thought it but right and proper that he should receive a Christian burial, in accordance with the forms and usages of the church of which I and his sister were members.

I made the application first to the pastor, Reverend Elbert S. Porter. He assured me that the funeral services should take place in the church, and signified to me what gentlemen he desired to assist him. Relying upon his word, I published notices fixing the time and place for the funeral. Afterwards, I was waited upon by two gentlemen—members of the consistory—and requested to attend a meeting of that body. I went, in obedience to the invitation, and was informed by them that the services could not be performed in the ordinary way—that the body of my brother-in-law could not be taken into the church, there to be seen by his kindred and friends. Various reasons were assigned for this action. One was that there would be danger in the damage which might be done to the property of the church. I assured them that I would be responsible for every pecuniary loss. Another was the great excitement which would be created, and there was fear of violence. I told them that I would provide ample police force to secure peace and order. After all this, they denied to me the right to have the service in the Church. Feeling deeply attached to the church, I made no arrangements for the funeral until a member of the consistory, who was absent at the first meeting, called at my house, and said that he thought all things could be arranged, and that he regretted the hasty action of the consistory. I, therefore, believing that it would be to the dishonor of a Christian church to deny any man a Christian burial who died declaring his faith in the Christian religion, made no final arrangements for the funeral until after the meeting of the consistory on Sunday afternoon.

The house which I am building for my future residence not being completed, many sympathizing friends kindly tendered me the use of their dwellings. I accepted the one offered by Mr. Samuel L. Harris. The funeral services were there performed, and those who supposed that the remains of my unfortunate relation would not be treated with respect by the citizens, I suppose are satisfied, from the events which there transpired. To those friends and acquaintances who have sympathized with me in this calamity, and the public generally, for the decent regard which was today shown for the *proper observance of Christian duties,* I return my fervent thanks.

R. CROWLEY, No. 63 South Tenth Street.

In spite of the incessant rain on Tuesday morning, December 20th, several hundred persons attended the funeral of Captain John E. Cook, at the residence of Samuel L. Harris, Esq., in Willamsburg. A large police force prevented the overcrowding of the house, but so anxious were the hundreds in the street (including many ladies) to view the remains, that they stood in the storm until the services indoors were concluded.

About one hundred and fifty persons were admitted to the dwelling, including the relatives of the deceased, Governor Willard and Attorney-General Voorhies, of Indiana, Judge Culver, of Brooklyn, who adjourned his court for the occasion; the Honorable C. W. Fisher, T. W. and S. A. Fields, the officiating clergymen, Reverend Doctor Caldicott of the South Baptist Church, Reverend W. H. Josephson, City Missionary, Reverend C. T. Mallory, Methodist, Revwerend William Goodell,

Reverend S. S. Jocelyn, Congregationalist, and a number of well-known and respected citizens.

At 10:00 AM the relatives of the deceased left the residence of Mr. Robert Crowley, on South Tenth Street, and proceeded to the home of Mr. Harris for the funeral. Reverend Dr. Caldicott, commenced the services at 10:30 AM. He said:

> We will now enter upon this solemn service, for we are assembled today to bury the dead. We are here to pay the last rites of burial for the dead, and to administer sympathy and religious consolation to the living. We are here today neither to justify nor condemn the act for which the deceased died, neither to justify nor condemn the sentence by which he died. We are here today for a higher and holier purpose than that; we are here not to add a single drop to the seething cauldron of political agitation, but we are here to pour the oil of consolation into bleeding and suffering hearts. Let us then today lay aside every thought—let us look at this death in the light of our holy religion. Let us listen to the oracles of God, that we may know the voice of Revelation.

The Reverend Gentleman here read a number of passages of scripture of consolation to the afflicted, and recommending a trust in Divine Providence in the hour of trial. He continued as follows:

> As I stated in introducing the Oracles of God, we are here today to minister consolation and instruction to sympathizing friends. In services like this we shall gather consolation from two sources—from the past life of the deceased, and from the professions and promises of Jehovah in the Gospel. We gather consolation, if possible, from both; if not from the living experience of the deceased, yet we do from the compassion and mercy of our God. But, when we look back upon the life of the

departed, is there no light? Is there no evidence, no proof, that he was the child of God? We think the evidence is abundant. There are lights in the human character that, under the influence of peace, go out one by one, till the last is extinguished, and that last light is the love of father, and mother and friends. These lights were never extinguished in the life of the deceased. Although of a peculiar mind and of strong impulses, and led sometimes by those impulses to leave home and friends, his heart was always there. If he had, as he supposed, a higher and holier object in view than staying at home, his sense of duty impelled him to pursue that object unto its attainment. It has been incorrectly reported that he was a willful and disobedient child. That mourning father who sits there testifies "It was not so; John was a loving, affectionate son." We will trust his testimony today rather than idle reports. It is true, he left his home, but he never forgot his home. It is true, he left his friends, but he never ceased to love them, or yearn for their society. He never lost his respect and love for the Christian religion. He never forgot his prayers; he never forgot the sound of the Sabbath bell; he never ceased to love the Sabbath school or the blessings of religious instruction for the young. He never denied his Savior or ceased to believe in the efficacy of His atoning blood.

If John Cook made any mistake in his life—for it was the controlling passion of his life that brought him to his death—it was that he thought he was pitying those over whom Christ wept; he thought he was laboring for the good of Christ's oppressed ones. We are not here to settle the question of right or wrong; that can be done elsewhere. We are simply here to state facts, and from those facts to draw that consolation that may sustain these mourning, bleeding hearts today. And then, even though we have to take a sterner view of the act by which he died—as a guilty act, is there no hope? Must his memory be consigned to infamy because he was wrong? Oh you who would cast reproach upon that memory, think of the Savior's saying to the Pharisees "He that is without sin among you, let him cast the first stone." Think of the Savior's love of the dying malefactor, "This day shalt thou be with me in Paradise." And then listen while I read the last words of the deceased to his friends. They are not penned under nervous excitement, every line and stroke is as plain as though he was sitting in bowers of peace with the prospect of a long life before him.

After the final hymn all those who stood in the drenching rain formed a mournful procession that wended its way to the Cypress Hills Cemetery where the remains were interred in a plot belonging to Mr. Robert Crowley.[1] There were eleven pallbearers including Samuel L, Harris, Ed. Howard and John Evans.

It occurred to one of the anti-slavery leaders of Salem that a copy of the handbill announcing the burial of Edwin Coppoc should be sent to Governor Wise of Virginia. The following letter was sent:

Salem, 12th Month 28th, 1859.

HENRY A. WISE: It been on my mind for some time to address a few lines to thee but have waited until the great tragedy in which thee has been engaged is over.

I am satisfied that an awful doom rests over Virginia, not only for her hugging the accursed system of slavery so close to her vitals, but for the wilful murder of some of the best men that have graced the pages of history

---

[1] On August 10th, 1868 John Cook was re-interred at the Greenwood Cemetery in Brooklyn, Kings County, New York. He is located in section 36, lot 5243.

for many generations. I mean John Brown and his most noble followers.

Inclosed thee will find an advertisement. We expect to have eight or ten thousand people present on its occasion.

Thine Respectfully,

DANIEL BONSALL

N. B. We shall not bury Edwin Coppoc in the Virginia coffin, but would be rejoiced if her governor would come, or send for it.

D. BONSALL

The appointed day for Edwin Coppoc's funeral brought a very large crowd of people to Salem to attend the final obsequies. The Salem *Republican* of December 30th said:

In the morning the people began to arrive, some of them from a considerable distance. Long before the appointed hour, 1:00 PM in the afternoon, the town was thronged with thousands of strangers, who came to pay the final tribute of respect and sympathy. The body of the dead youth was still well preserved but his face, so lifelike at the former funeral, had begun to dis-color. It was shrouded in a costly metallic coffin to which it had been transferred. Alfred Wright at the head of a committee of arrangements had charge of the funeral. The body lay in the Town Hall, which had so often, in the years gone by, rung with appeals for the cause that took Edwin Coppoc to Harper's Ferry.

The Reverend James A. Thome, of Ohio City, now a part of Cleveland, offered a prayer, which he followed with brief remarks. He declared that Coppoc's purpose was righteous and that he died "a martyr to the sacred cause of liberty."

"I visited this place more than twenty years ago," he said, "before this young man was born, to defend the doctrine of human rights. Here before me lies the victim of that irrepressible warfare upon human rights, waged by the bloody system of the slave states."

Through the Town Hall passed the throng, estimated at six thousand, unusually silent and solemn, even for such an occasion. Later the body was taken out of the hall to the hearse and the procession moved to the grave on the hill in the following order:

The near relatives.
The pall bearers.
The colored people (for whose race the deceased had given his life).
Citizens on foot.
Citizens in carriages.

The coffin was lowered into a strong plank box, in a grave of unusual depth. In the evening all that could enter the town hall listened to the impressive funeral discourse by the Reverend Thome. The meeting was organized by calling to the chair Jacob Heaton, who for years had been a recognized leader in the anti-slavery cause. After prayer by Reverend Burke of Wayne County, the congregation sang the stirring hymn, "Blow, ye trumpet, blow." Reverend Thome took as his theme, Daniel and the writing on the wall, declaring that "like the message to Belshazzar was John Brown's to enthroned iniquity." "Here," he said, "is grandeur; here is God's own work and grace, here where it is treason to proclaim God's truth; here in an age of sounding brass—are these great souls, like living organs through whose trumpet notes God has blown an anthem that shakes the land like an earthquake."

The sermon was described as remarkably eloquent—such as one hears but only once in a lifetime. And thus the remains of this unpretentious youth, this warrior in the anti-slavery cause, found a final resting place in a spot that he had known since his childhood days.

Chapter 14

THE END OF THE ROAD

IT WAS GENERALLY supposed that Aaron D. Stevens, one of the accomplices of John Brown in the Harper's Ferry affair, had been handed over to the Federal authorities, and was to be tried in the United States courts. It seems, however, that this was not so. George Sennott, Esq., of Boston, wrote to the president for information on the subject, and was informed by a letter from Andrew Hunter, Esq., on Wednesday, January 4, 1860 that "the authorities of Virginia have definitely decided that he is to be tried in Charlestown," and that the trial will probably come off in the present month, although that was not certain.

It was suggested that this change had been resolved upon in consequence of the appointment of an investigating committee by the United States Senate. The original object of Virginia in allowing the trial to take place in a federal court was so that witnesses might be compelled to attend from other states. It was understood however, that Dr. Howe, Wendell Phillips, and others, would be summoned to attend the committee, and that their testimony would thus be secured. A special session of the state court for Stevens' trial was ordered by the Virginia Legislature.

Mr. Raymond of the New York *Times* made the following remarks at the Union meeting in Albany on Thursday January 12, 1860, about the invasion of John Brown, its effect upon the South, and the actions of Governor Wise:

Under these accumulated influences, the Southern mind had become profoundly sensitive. They felt that they were menaced by dangers the precise nature of which they could not trace, and which were all the more terrible on that account. Just at this moment, while they were in this condition, came John Brown's invasion of Virginia and his attempt to excite an armed insurrection of her slaves. It startled the South, very much as a flash of lightning would startle men who had built their dwellings under the eaves of a powder magazine. Its very audacity clothed it with terror. We who live here in security, free from any pervading element of social peril, incline to look upon the alarm of the South as out of all proportion to the magnitude of the actual danger. But no one who will take the pains to inform himself as to the actual condition of social life in the Southern states, can be surprised that such an attempt should have carried terror and dismay into every plantation of every Southern state.

If the danger had been met with the calmness of cool courage, with the self-possession which disarms danger by never overrating it, the alarm would have been comparatively local and temporary. But Virginia had a governor who was not given to such common-place achievements. No one doubts his courage, his ability, his excessive eagerness to face danger and challenge the world in arms. But unfortunately he is not content to be brave, unless he can also impress the world with the conviction of the fact. He is nothing if not theatrical. In his hands the whole transaction became essentially and thoroughly melodramatic. He was quite willing to have the South understand that the affair was one of the most formidable invasions ever set on foot by a powerful nation,—because the greater the peril the more profound would be their gratitude to the hero who had rescued them from it.

He treated the raid of Brown, with his handful of whites and Negroes, as if it had been the full outpouring from the loins of the multitudinous North. Everything he said and did was calculated to convey the impression that it was only the premature explosion of an enormous conspiracy; that thousands and tens of thousands of men in the Northern states were organized for the onset, that money in vast abundance was at the command of the crusaders, and that the movement had the profound sympathy and active cooperation of the great body of the people in the North. Other influences combined to aid the impression Governor Wise was thus making upon the Southern mind. The abolitionists in the North improved the opportunity. They seized upon the excitement which the perpetration of any great crime, upon a conspicuous theater and under peculiar circumstances, never fails to arouse, to promulgate their sympathy with Brown, their approval of his attempts, and their profound conviction that it was only the beginning of the war under which slavery must speedily be extinguished in blood.

Partisan presses, eager to make political capital out of so promising an event, sought to fasten the responsibility for John Brown's acts upon obnoxious and formidable opponents—a portion of the Republican press teemed with expressions of sympathy for Brown and with apologies for his acts; and that great bulwark of Southern rights and general champion of public peace and tranquillity, the New York *Herald*, (laughter) devoted itself with unwearied assiduity to the task of hunting up every utterance of abolitionist fanaticism, dragging it from its native obscurity and parading it before its credulous and admiring readers in the Southern states as proof of the sentiments universally entertained throughout the North, concerning slavery and the slave holding section of this Confederacy. (applause and cries of "good!") It is not strange that under such influences the South should have been—as I believe they were, and still are—profoundly alarmed by what they believed to be the sentiments and intentions of the people of the Northern states. They would be something more, or something less, than human if they failed to be impressed by the demonstrations which have passed before their eyes. They undoubtedly believe today—the great mass of the people in the Southern states believe today—that the great body of the people of the North sympathize with the act of John Brown, and approve entirely of the attempt in which he failed. And it is to that belief that the hostile movements so rife in that section of the country are mainly due.

The following letter was written by Aaron Stevens to Anne Brown:

Charlestown Jail, Friday, Jan. 13, 1860.

Dear Annie: I am quite cheerful and happy, never felt better in my life. It made me feel sad, to part with my companions, but I think they are in a better land, and a great comfort to me.

I was in the same room with your father. He was very cheerful all the way through, and appeared as happy on the morning of his execution as I ever saw him. Watson was shot about a half minute before me, that was on Monday about 8 o'clock, and he lived until Wednesday morning. I had a very hard time of it, for about four or five weeks, but I am as well now as ever, except my face is paralyzed on one side, which prevents me from laughing on that side, and a bone was thrown out of place and my teeth do not meet as they did before, which prevents me from chewing anything very fine.

The boys met their fate very cheerfully. I cannot tell you when I shall be tried, but I think in two or three weeks.

Sincerely,

AARON D. STEVENS

The following letter was written by John Brown's wife Mary Brown:

North Elba, January 17, 1860.

To the Editor of the New York *Tribune*:

SIR: Through the columns of the *Tribune*, I wish to correct some misrepresentations afloat in the country through the medium of a small book, namely, that Mr. Brown was guilty of several murders, among which were the wives of two men, whose bodies (the wives) he burned to ashes to escape detection. Now, permit me to say to whom it may concern, that it is not at all strange to me that pro-slavery men should rack their inventive genius, fired by frenzy, even to the last extreme and desperation, to fabricate and set afloat false statements to prevent a sale of the memoirs of the life of one whose influence, with that of others, in the scale of liberty, operates so powerfully against them, both morally and politically. False witnesses appeared against the great Savior of men, both before and after his death; and is it not enough for the servant if he can fare as well as his Master did? The public may rest assured that Mr. Brown never committed the murders and the burning of the bodies of murdered wives to ashes, which are so maliciously alleged against him; nor ever confessed any such thing. Neither do the reading, thinking, liberty-loving part of the community believe that such reports have even the shadow of a foundation.

The spirit and tenor of his letters, his speeches, and his deportment, read by the civilized world during the last few weeks of his earthly career, testify conclusively and unmistakably to the character of the man.

MARY ANNE BROWN

The following letter from Judge Conway, of Kansas, in vindication of the memory of John Brown appeared in the Boston *Journal*:

LAWRENCE, K. T., January 23, 1860

SIR: I am very much surprised to find, in a late number of your paper, a letter from your excellent correspondent, Albert Deane Richardson, Esq., in which my name is used to corroborate a most atrocious slander upon the memory of Old John Brown, of Osawatomie. Mr. Richardson does not himself indorse this wicked calumny, but refers to a conversation he had with me, in which he says that I informed him that Brown admitted to me that he was engaged in the killing of Doyle and others, on the bank of the Pottawatomie, in 1856. He also cites a conversation with Captain Walker, to the same effect. This, sir, is a mistake so far as it relates to me, which I cannot see how a gentleman of Mr. Richardson's intelligence could contrive to fall into. Mr. Richardson must, therefore, pardon the directness of my answer, when I assure him emphatically that *I never told him, any such thing*. Captain Walker will also pardon me, when I say to him, most courteously, that I do not believe that Brown ever told him any such thing. It is, indeed, a wonderful circumstance, taken from any point of view, how many persons have recently sprung up to whom John Brown long since confided a dreadful secret—a secret which, if exposed would have cost him his life, and which, not being exposed, made any one in it liable to the penalties of a capital offense. And still more wonderful, that those persons are of a class with which Brown never had any sympathy, and toward which he always maintained a profound aversion!

These witnesses are certainly too swift. They pretend to have been the bosom friends of the old man; to have shared with him the most awful secrets of his soul, and yet they are among the loudest in execration of his memory. They pretend to be in possession of a secret which could only have been conveyed under bonds of the most sacred private friendship; and yet they are ready to expose this secret to blacken the name of their friend. This is unnatural and impossible; I distrust all such testimony. From what I know, *I am convinced that Brown never had any personal participation in the killing of the men on the Pottawatomie*, and that, of course, he never told anybody he had. My recollection of what I said to Mr. Richardson, on this topic, is very distinct, and to this effect—namely, that John Brown, said to me in Boston, two years prior, that he was *not* at the killing on the Pottawatomie, but that he approved it. Mr. Richardson could not have been doing me the honor of giving me his attention at the time, or he would not so far misapprehended me. This statement made to me by Brown was precisely the same made by him to all his best and most confidential friends touching the subject, and may be very safely taken for the truth, the whole truth, and nothing but the truth, in the matter.

The fearful story of his seizing five or six men in their beds at night, tearing them away from the arms of their weeping wives and children, killing them by slow degrees, within hearing of their families, and then wantonly mutilating their dead bodies, was invented and propagated by one of the most notoriously lying rascals in the United States; an individual who has been doing all manner of base work for the past three years, in this vicinity, for the Democratic party, and getting paid for his wretched services in hard cash. It was of course seized on by all the enemies of Old Osawatomie as soon as it appeared, and hawked about the country as embodying the indubitable record of the "Pottawatomie Massacre." But it is utterly unworthy of credit, and should be discarded by every honorable mind as a malignant attempt to injure the fame of one who, whatever, in the estimation of some, may have been his errors or his crimes, was the purest embodiment which the county affords of exalted self-sacrifice; and, as such, dear to any friend of humanity.

It may, perhaps, add something to the estimation in which this tragical romance of the Pottawatomie should be held, to inform the public that, since it was first published, the author has fled the country in disgrace. The weekly journal edited here by him has become extinct, and his wife has filed a petition in the county court, praying for a divorce charging him with being an "inhuman monster," which, from my own knowledge of the animal, I will very promptly testify to, if summoned as a witness in the case. Retributive justice is sometimes speedy, as well as always sure.

Very respectfully, yours,

M. F. CONWAY

On Monday, January 23rd, both branches of the Virginia Legislature passed a bill appropriating $150,000 to help defray the expenses of crushing the Harper's Ferry rebellion. This bill appointed the Secretary of the Commonwealth, the auditor and Attorney General's Board to audit the claims and issue warrants to be paid by the auditor, provided not more than $150,000 be so paid; and that all claims would be presented within six months; and provided, if doubts should arise as to the claims, that they would be reported to the House. The bill also excepted, and required to be reported to the Legislature, the claims of all general, staff and field officers, and all railroad companies.

The New York *Times* of January 24, 1860 reported Senate procedures relative to Harper's Ferry as follows:

> The new Senate chamber in Washington witnessed, for the first time, a scene which recalled the great debates of the nation in that old hall made illustrious by the elegance and patriotism of Webster and Clay, and of Calhoun and Benton. It was crowded in every part, from floor to gallery on Monday, January 23, 1860. The Representatives left their own hall; the citizens of Washington, the foreign diplomats, the whole floating population of the capital, thronged the huge gilded saloon in which the Senators held their high council, to hear the gravest questions affecting the relations of a state with states in the Union discussed by the champion of Popular Sovereignty. Thus much at least it is due to Mr. Stephen A. Douglas to say, that he dealt with the themes suggested by the crisis in which the nation was now struggling, in a temper and in a tone worthy of their importance. The proposition which he laid before the Senate is one which has already been demanded with less of form and detail by conservative men out of Congress, in speeches made before popular assemblies in various parts of the country, and through the columns of the press.

> The Senator from Illinois very briefly, clearly and forcibly stated the case arising out of John Brown's arrest, between the governor of a single commonwealth and the president of the Union. Virginia found herself threatened with invasion, not by a foreign foe, but by an organized band of American citizens from a sister state. On application for protection to the federal executive,

she was informed that no provision had ever been made for meeting such a contingency. It could hardly be thought discreditable to the sagacity of our fathers that this should be so, since even after the angry sectional collisions of the last few years, the tidings of John Brown's raid took the whole nation by surprise. But it will be very discreditable to ourselves, as Mr. Douglas boldly and distinctly put it, should we now refuse to meet an issue which has actually arisen, and the recurrence of which cannot be safely regarded as improbable unless measures shall be taken to render it impossible. For while nothing can be more certain than that the attempt to render the Republican party or its leaders, now dominant in the North, directly responsible for the deliberate conspiracy of John Brown, was a most senseless and indecent abuse even of the large license of partisan warfare, nothing at the same time can be more clear than that John Brown's conspiracy would never have been dreamed of, had not a widespread practical hostility to slavery wherever it exists been developed throughout the Northern states during the fierce sectional conflict which followed the repeal of the Missouri Compromise.

That this wide-spread practical hostility to slavery—a sentiment much more intense, much more demonstrative, much more irreconcilable with the permanent peace of the Union than the general anti-slavery feeling by which the North has always been pervaded—still exists, and is still formidable, no man in his senses can deny. The numerous meetings held in different parts of the Northern states to do honor to the memory of John Brown, and the absolute refusal of such extreme and fanatical journals as the New York *Tribune* to stigmatize the invasion of Virginia as a crime, sufficiently illustrate this truth. It is against this sentiment that the South has a right to ask protection from the Union; and all conservative men at the North, of all parties, will agree with Mr. Douglas in offering this protection even before it has been asked. We cannot but regret, therefore, that Mr. Fessenden, of Maine, in the debate of yesterday, should have even apparently committed any portion of the great party to which he belongs to what must he regarded as an attempt to evade an act to which no tenable objection can be offered. That the affair at Harper's Ferry is still under consideration by a committee of the Senate, certainly does not affect the palpable fact that John Brown went into Virginia with a company of Northern men for the purpose of disturbing the whole social order of that commonwealth; or the equally palpable fact that the men who defended the rights of the free settlers of Kansas in 1856 have been most unjustly saddled in 1859 with the responsibility of this great wrong attempted upon Virginia.

If Mr. Fessenden, instead of patronizing and commiserating with Mr. Seward for what he deems the rhetorical mistake of the Senator from New York in condensing his doctrine of the *"irrepressible conflict"* into a single phrase which everybody could remember, or fencing upon the Fugitive Slave law, had taken up the proposition of the Senator from Illinois in the spirit in which it was offered, and proved to the Senate and the country that the Republicans of the Northern states are ready, as a unit, to extend the guarantees of the constitution in the spirit of the constitution, wherever the progress of events shall make their application necessary, the debate of yesterday in the Senate might be contemplated with unmixed satisfaction by every patriot.

The Boston *Traveller* of Tuesday, January 24th reported that a summons for S. G. Howe to appear before the Harper's Ferry Investigating Committee at Washington was left at the door of his residence that evening. Dr. Howe had just left for Canada, to fulfill an engagement for an exhibition by the blind pupils of the Perkins asylum. James Jackson, an uncle of Francis J. Merriam, to whom, as it appeared by certain documents, he had sent money, was summoned before the same committee. Franklin Benjamin Sanborn, of Concord, Massachusetts, was also summoned to Washington to testify before the committee.

Mr. Sanborn was waited upon at Concord by an United States official and tendered his witness fee to the official, which he refused to accept. Before other measures could be taken he had disappeared, and was thought to have gone to Europe.

United States Marshal Johnson was at Cleveland, Ohio on Tuesday January 24th, to serve a summons on Joshua R. Giddings and John Brown, Jr. of West Andover, Ohio to appear before the Senate committee. Mr. Giddings was in the State of New York, but was telegraphed to, and was expected to proceed to Washington forthwith. Mr. John Brown Jr. could not be found, but a copy of the summons was left at his house, and the probability was that he would obey. Both were summoned to appear on the 30th of January, 1860.

The joint committee on the Harper's Ferry affair in the Virginia Legislature have made a voluminous report, which closed with resolutions urging the arming and equipping of the militia, and the passage of laws encouraging domestic manufactures, and for the more prompt punishment of persons attempting to incite slaves to insurrection, and vindicating the course of Governor Wise throughout the Harper's Ferry affair. Five thousand copies were ordered to be printed.

Charlestown was thronged on Wednesday, February 1, 1860 to witness the proceedings of the start of the trial of Aaron Stevens, one of the Harper's Ferry conspirators. At 11:00 AM the Court went into session with Judge John Kenny, of Rockingham, presiding, Judge Parker being engaged in holding the regular town court in Hampshire County. The grand jury, of which R. V. Shirley was the foreman, was sworn in. The judge delivered his charge, and in referring to the Harper's Ferry invasion, said:

It is known to you, and is now a part of the history of the country, that on the night of the 18th of October last past a band of traitors, murderers and incendiaries stealthily made a descent on the soil of Virginia, in the County of Jefferson, and wantonly murdered several of our citizens and people, with the design to incite our slaves to revolt and to subvert our government. Some of these desperadoes, and others the dupes of designing cowards, were captured, tried, and punished according to their deserts. But there are some engaged, or supposed to have been engaged, in this foray who have not as yet been apprehended, and others who are believed to have been actively engaged in this tragedy, but who are not yet known to the public. It will be your duty, and I believe your pleasure also, to inquire who were guilty of polluting our soil and attempting to dishonor the sovereignty of Virginia. I deem it unnecessary for me to recommend to you to conduct your inquiries with that coolness, justice and good sense which has distinguished your predecessors in their inquisitions, and which have met with the approbation of the good and patriotic and honorable citizens of our common country. So conduct your inquiries that the bright escutcheon of our beloved state shall not be dimmed by passion, prejudice or groundless suspicion, and also let them be conducted without fear, favor or affection, that you may elicit the truth, the whole truth, and nothing but the truth.

The jury then returned to their room, and the witnesses in the case of the commonwealth vs. Aaron D. Stevens were sent up. Before the jury retired Mr. Harding, District Attorney, made an address to them, and after an absence of an hour they returned with a bill against Stevens, charging him with murder and treason, and conspiring with slaves to create a rebellion.

The witnesses in the case of the commonwealth *vs.* Hazlett were then sent up, and an indictment of the same character was shortly afterwards returned against him. The work of impaneling the jury, in the case of Stevens, was postponed a day, in order to allow counsel time to examine the indictment against him. Stevens and Hazlett were to be defended by Mr. Sennott. The commonwealth was represented by Andrew Hunter. It was deemed unnecessary to increase the military force now in the area to any extent. The only addition that was made was a company of twenty cavalry from Shepherdstown.

The court opened at 10:30 AM on Thursday February 2nd, Judge John Kenny presiding. Mr. Stevens was brought in by the jailor and his guard and he seemed in perfect health. Mr. Sennott suggested to the commonwealth the propriety of announcing whether it would elect to try one or all of the counts, or whether they relied upon one or all for conviction. He also read a letter from President Buchanan in reply to inquiries in regard to the trial. He thought the commonwealth had acted in bad faith towards the prisoners, in removing the case to the Federal court, and then receding from that determination, and thought the indictment should be quashed. He appealed to the mercy of the court, for it certainly would be an act of mercy to send the prisoner to Staunton for trial.

Mr. Harding, for the commonwealth, had not made a proposition for removal, and had strongly protested against it throughout the trial. He was at first willing to turn them all over to the Federal authorities, but after the state decided to try them he was opposed to any change of trial. He did not consider that Governor Wise had authority to make the change.

Mr. Hunter denounced as utterly untrue the assertion of Mr. Sennott that Stevens was forced to plead at the late term of the Court. Mr. Sennott disclaimed any intention to reflect on anyone, and spoke eloquently of the State of Virginia, hoping his tongue might wither before he would speak in any but terms of praise of that state. When the offer was made to send Stevens to Staunton, he thought he should better accept the offer, for it was a matter of life and death, and he might share the fate of Brown.

Judge Kenny, after stating his understanding of the motion of Mr. Sennott, said there was nothing to show that Virginia ever made a legal surrender of the prisoner. He would pay no attention to political influences, and the prisoner should have as fair a trial as any Southern man could have. He could only look upon it as an appeal of the counsel for the defense to the state to transfer the case, and would have to reject the appeal.

Mr. Harding moved a *nolle prosequi* on the old indictments, as the prisoner would have to be tried on the indictments brought in yesterday. Mr. Sennott requested the commonwealth to select one count in the indictment, in order to render the case less complicated and in justice to the prisoner. Mr. Hunter replied, quoting a number of authorities to show the legality of the course taken, and declining to recede from any count in the indictment, deeming them all necessary.

Mr. Harding objected to the motion of Mr. Sennott to select one indictment and argued that all the counts were of the same degree as all were punishable by death. Each was an indictment in itself, and all were necessary to render the case free from embarrassment. He quoted a number of authorities to show the correctness of his position.

Judge Kenny said that it was conceded there was no rejoinder in the case. It was insisted that this was calculated to embarrass the prisoner in his defense, but he could not see how it could embarrass him by a joinder of all the counts. The object was to give the prisoner all the chances in his favor, but still the commonwealth had the right to maintain that the prisoner is regarded as innocent until he is proved guilty. He therefore rejected the motion of the counsel for selecting one count.

Mr. Sennott stated that he would present his exceptions to the ruling of the judge at the proper time. The arraignment of the counsel occupied more than two hours, and Stevens was not called upon to plead to the indictment till after 12:00 noon. The reading of the indictment occupied ten minutes, and during that time the prisoner stood up in an erect manner, not moving a muscle. He answered the charge in an unfaltering voice.

The empaneling of the jury then commenced, and the usual number of twenty-four was exhausted without assembling the jury.

Before the court adjourned Mr. Hunter said that he had just been handed papers from Governor Letcher informing him of the arrest of a brother of Coppoc in Iowa. Judge Kenny gave orders for another jury which will meet at 10:00 AM tomorrow.

Mr. Stevens made his appearance in court in a new suit, and seemed in good spirits. The room was crowded. The case would certainly occupy several days. Hazlett was discharged until Monday. The jurymen for this case were summoned from Frederick County. It was impossible to get them here right away.

The trial of Albert Hazlett, the last of the Harper's Ferry captives, was begun on Monday, February 6, at Charlestown. The jurymen selected from Frederick County were exhausted before the jury was completed, and an adjournment until the next day became necessary. Messrs. Botts and Green appeared for the prisoner. Nine witnesses were examined on Tuesday, and their testimony was conclusively to the point that Hazlett was one of Brown's party. The only difference in the testimony was as to the color of the prisoner's hair, some stating that it was red and others that it was a light color. His hair, at the present time, was reported to be dark, though it had the appearance of being colored using hair-dye. Among the visitors in attendance at the court Monday was the Reverend Mr. Newton of Vermont, who had previously been before the Senate Investigating committee. The number of witnesses summoned for the commonwealth amounted to about forty, but all would not be examined. The testimony for the defense in the case of Hazlett was closed on Thursday, February 9th. The court then adjourned until 10:00 AM Friday morning, to give the counsel time to prepare his arguments. No doubts were entertained as to the conviction of the prisoner, as the testimony given during the morning session was unfavorable to the defense.

The court room was crowded on the morning of February 13th, to hear the sentence of the judge passed upon Hazlett and Stevens. Some time was occupied by counsel in presenting bills of exception in the case of Hazlett, and it was 12:00 noon before Stevens was brought into the court house. Stevens was brought into the court by the sheriff, jailor and men of the Jefferson Guards. Both prisoners wore an unconcerned air, and seemed utterly serene at the awful position in which they have placed themselves. The clerk asked the prisoners if they had anything to say why sentence should not be passed upon them. Both responded that they had.

Stevens then said:

> May it please the court, I have a few words to say. Some of the testimony given against me was untrue. One of the witnesses stated that I said. "Let us kill the sons of bitches and burn the town down." To those who know me it is useless to make a denial of this charge, but I deny here, before God and man, ever having made such a proposition. I wish to say I am entirely satisfied with the conduct of my counsel, Mr. Sennott. I think he did all in his power on my behalf. I desire also to return my thanks to the officers who have had charge of me, for their universal kind treatment, and to my physician for the services rendered me while suffering from my wounds. When I think of my brothers slaughtered and sisters outraged,[1] my conscience does not reprove me for my actions. I shall meet my fate manfully.

Hazlett then spoke as follows:

> I have a few words to say also. I am innocent of the charge on which I have been convicted. I deny ever having committed murder, or ever having contemplated murder, or ever having associated with any one with such intentions. Some of the witnesses here have sworn to

---

[1] This is understood to be the treatment of his Northern brethren and sisters during his Kansas broils.

things which I deny, and which were positively false. For instance, in reference to my beard; I have never in my life, until my imprisonment in jail, allowed my beard to go more than three weeks without shaving, and all testimony, therefore as to the length of my beard is false. Again, Mr. Copeland testified that I was sitting on a stool when he entered the cell at Carlisle; this I deny. I was sitting on a blanket, back against the wall, and another man was on the stool. Copeland also said there were only two men in the cell; this is false, as there were four other white men in the cell with me, and we comprised all the white prisoners in the jail. Others of the witnesses made false statements, but I forgive them all. I have been treated kindly since my confinement much better than I had expected—and I must say I now think much better of Virginia. I wish also to return my thanks to the counsel who have so ably defended me; they have done more in my behalf than Northern counsel could possibly have done. I repeat, I am innocent of murder, but I am prepared to meet my fate.

The prisoners having concluded, Judge Kenny then proceeded to read the following sentence, during which he seemed most affected, and at times could only with difficulty give utterance to the sentence:

Aaron D. Stevens, you have been indicted and tried by a jury of the county, and after being defended with zeal and ability by counsel of your own choice, from your own section of our common country, you have been found guilty of advising and conspiring with slaves to rebel and make insurrection, and for conspiring with John Brown and others to rebel and make insurrection.

And you, Albert Hazlett, have also been indicted by a jury of this county, and found guilty of murder in the first degree, in wilfully, deliberately, feloniously and of malice of forethought, killing and murdering George W. Turner, Fontaine Beckham and others, and you have also been defended by counsel of this county, assigned to you at your request by the court, with an ability seldom equaled, and with a zeal and attention to every point in your case, whether of law or fact, that could not have been surpassed had they been defending a citizen of their own county.

You have been prosecuted with great ability by the counsel representing the commonwealth, and with an interest the magnitude of the charges required, yet, in a manner the most fastidious could not except to. The painful duty is devolved upon me to announce thus publicly the penalty the law affixes to the crime whereof you are now found guilty.

When I look upon your comparative youth, your genteel appearance, and consider the mental agonies you must have endured during these protracted trials, I cannot help pitying you; and could wish, if the honor and dignity of Virginia, the security of her citizens and their property would authorize it, the law imposed a less penalty than death.

The crimes in which you participated, and which were so tragical in their incipient steps, if carried to the extent contemplated by you and your accomplices and associates in arms, for horror and fraternal perfidy would have had no parallel in modern civilization since the massacre of St. Bartholomew's eve.

But I will not attempt to harrow your feelings by a rehearsal of the scenes at Harper's Ferry in October last—this is now a part of the history of our common country; and will, I hope, for years to come, constitute its darkest page.

I prefer diverting your attention to your awful situation, for I declare to you that I believe you ought not to indulge in any hopes of pardon or commutation of your punishments or of the suspension of it's execution, (unless there is some error in the proceedings of the court, or in its opinions, and there is none, I most surely think) and to urge you to devote the few days remaining to you in preparing to meet that judge before whom you and I, your jurors and counsel, and all, must appear to render an account of the deeds done in the body.

You who have been raised in the Christian world must have learned that there is a gracious Redeemer, who invites all, even the greatest criminals, to believe in Him, to repent of their crimes, and partake of the blessings of his atoning blood. If you can realize your awful position, and call on the ministers of out holy religion, they will cheerfully, gladly wait on you—they will instruct you in the way that leads to life everlasting. They will pray with you and for you; they will accompany you to the edge of the grave, and commend you to the great Captain of our salvation, in whom if you confide and on Him rely, by His "rod and staff" He will conduct you safely through the "dark valley of the shadow of death."

He then proceeded to sentence each of them to be hung publicly on Friday, the sixteenth day of March 1860, between the hours of 10:00 AM and 2:00 PM. Immediately after passing sentence the court remanded the prisoners back to jail, and the crowd that had drawn to witness the proceedings quietly dispersed.

Captain Avis told of finding Hazlett and Stevens engaged the day after their sentence in "chucking" pennies in the prison yard. As the jailor stood there Stevens tossed the coin and called out, "Heads or tails?" "Tails!" shouted Hazlett.

"Its heads—I've won!" said Stevens, and he went over and picked up the coin. Captain Avis said, "What have you won?"

"The privilege of selecting you to put the hangman's noose around my neck!" was the facetious reply.

The official Senate Harper's Ferry Investigating Committee had another meeting on Monday, February 27th, and for the first time elicited something of interest, and this not directly connected with John Brown's invasion of Virginia. Horace White, Esq., Editor of the Chicago *Press and Tribune*, and formerly Secretary of the National Kansas Committee, was called before the committee and sworn, testified as follows:

> The National Kansas Committee was organized by a mass convention at Buffalo in 1856. It consisted of one member from each Northern state, except Maine, New Hampshire and New Jersey, together with three members from Illinois, to wit, J. D. Webster, H. B. Hurd, and George W. Dolh, of Chicago, who constituted the executive board, meeting every day for the transaction of business. The committee received and disbursed in all, about $120,000 of which less than $10,000 was expended in the purchase of arms. Considerable quantities of arms were received as contributions from first hands. The witness first saw John Brown in August, 1850. Subsequently, he saw him three times; the last time at the general meeting of the National Kansas Committee, at the Astor House, in New York City, in January, 1857. Brown petitioned the committee for two hundred Sharp's rifles, then stored at Tabor, Iowa; originally purchased and forwarded by the Massachusetts state committee. He also asked for money and clothing, as he was organizing a military force to repel the Border Ruffian invasions of Kansas.

> The petition was debated by the committee at considerable length, and was warmly opposed. Finally, the

rifles were voted back to the Massachusetts committee, at the urgent request of the representative of that organization. The committee, however, voted Brown twelve boxes of clothing, which the witness shipped to his order at Nebraska City in March, 1857. Brown then left New York for Boston, and the witness never saw him afterwards. The committee had previously given Brown $150 at Chicago, and sent him twenty-five navy revolvers, but the latter never reached him. The witness also presented his two sons, Watson and Owen, one rifle each, and bought them a small amount of much-needed clothing. This comprises the sum total of the committee's transaction with Brown. The committee went out of existence in March, 1857. Brown never told the witness of any plans outside of Kansas. He never told any member of the committee in the presence of the witness. The witness was acquainted with John E. Cook, Richard Realf and James Redpath. He had seen none of them since 1857. They never told the witness anything about Harper's Ferry, or any of Brown's plans. They never alluded to any designs against slavery, except, in Kansas, to the committee. In short, the witness knew nothing whatever about the subject of the Senate investigation. The witness was proceeding to explain why the two hundred Sharp's rifles were detained at Tabor, Iowa, instead of being forwarded to Kansas.

The committee decided that the testimony was irrelevant.

The witness then said he wished to correct a misapprehension which perplexed the former witness, Mr. Stearns, who had been surprised that the arms were not sent straight through to Kansas. Senator Mason asked the witness how he knew anything about Stearns' testimony. The witness replied that he read it in the newspapers. Senator Iverson asked the witness if he had not been long enough in newspaper life to know that a great deal of irresponsible, untruthful stuff got into print.

The witness proceeded to state that the rifles were detained in Iowa because the Border Ruffian invasion in Kansas had ceased for that season, and it was deemed unwise to scatter arms in irresponsible hands throughout the territory, where they could not be reached in a time of real danger. The committee decided that the testimony was not proper to go on record. The witness had learned, from time to time, of Brown's being in Chicago since January, 1857, but never saw him since that date.

Governor Letcher of Virginia made a requisition to Governor Dennison, of Ohio, in early March for the arrest of Owen Brown and Francis Merriam, two of the Harper's Ferry insurgents, who were reported to have been in Ashtabula County. Indictments were found against them in Jefferson County, Virginia. On the 5th of March United States Marshal Johnson delivered the paper to Governor Dennison, who, in a letter dated the 8th of March declined issuing warrants, and stated that his reasons for this conclusion were communicated to Governor Letcher.

In Richmond, Virginia, the Committee of the Virginia Legislature on Courts and Justices reported it inexpedient to take any action in regard to the commutation of sentence or reprieve of either Stevens or Hazlett.

The following is the substance of the argument made before the Virginia Legislature on Tuesday, March 13, by George Sennott, Esq., in favor of reprieving Stevens and Hazlett, sentenced to be hung on Friday next for having participated in the Harper's Ferry affair:

> I begin by thanking you, and through you the Legislature of Virginia, for a courtesy without example. I know no one in Richmond. I came on business not agreeable to you. I walked up to the capitol, addressed the first gentleman I found, told my name and errand, and immediately this hearing was granted, by the unanimous consent of both Houses!

> I may mistake, but I do not believe that such an act of courtesy would be performed for a person, coming on

such an errand, by any other legislature in the world. May it be an omen of better things yet to come! I say this much, gentlemen, because it is true and I will say also, because you cannot be expected to know me, that no legislature, or committee, or person, however exalted, ever did or could extort from me a word of undeserved acknowledgment. Your courtesy leaves me embarrassed. I had prepared a speech which I shall not deliver. I would have spoken it in a court of justice, or wherever I had rights to assert, unflinchingly. But I am admitted here by courtesy alone; and while, as a Northern man, I ought to be sincere, and not hide my hatred of slavery, as a gentleman I cannot take a contemptible advantage of your patience to make you listen to disagreeable things.

As to the case: There are two prisoners. There were *seven* capital indictments all in vitality against them at one time—four against Stevens, and the others against Hazlett. On the first indictment Captain John Brown was tried, and to it Stevens was forced to plead. Of that indictment, if the most strenuous study of the criminal law in its principles—if the greatest pains to understand how every species of indictment, complaint or information should be framed—and if the most careful and laborious reading of a great number of indictments, with a view to trial—if all these things give me an opportunity to judge, or a right to speak on the subject, I say that indictment was *very bad.* But your Court of Appeals thought there was enough of it good to hang Captain Brown and his companions. Stevens, however, was supposed to be dying. He had five bullets in his body; he fell from fainting fit into fainting fit, and the Judge determined not to try him, when a message from the then governor, Henry A. Wise, proposed to transfer him to the courts of the United States. Stevens had been brought in on a bed, and the people, who showed very little sympathy for the others, appeared deeply moved when this young man was laid on the court house floor. The case was not transferred, but only continued, and you know, gentlemen, better than I what efforts were made here to have a special session in February, when the regular session of the circuit court was to be as early as May. The law passed, and I was notified by—the newspapers!

Gentlemen, I left my distant home at a very great disadvantage and loss; and when I arrived in Charlestown I found the bad indictment *nol pros'd*, as we call it, and three others, newly made, with all the errors cancelled which eleven lawyers had pointed out. I defended Stevens on the indictment for conspiracy. Two Virginia lawyers, Thomas C. Green and Lawson Botts, defended Hazlett, and it gives me great pleasure to say, of my own knowledge, that a more eager, thorough and careful defense I never witnessed. It gives me the greater satisfaction to say so, because they were unkindly and, I am sure, unjustly accused of collusion with the government in the case of Brown! I was disgusted to hear that. I did not believe it then. I feel sure now it was without foundation, since I saw what they did for Hazlett. Hazlett, however, was convicted, and so was Stevens—the first for murder, and the second for conspiracy to make slaves rebel. In that case, I thought, and think now, and I am sure that the evidence proved a conspiracy to run off Negroes, and for that offense he should have been convicted. The court, however, thought differently, and the jury followed the court. There are then, two indictments remaining. One against Stevens for murder, and another for treason; and one against Hazlett for treason, and another for conspiracy. Let me now explain how I come before you, since the law gives you no power to pardon any crime but treason, and leaves all other pardoning exclusively to the governor. The difficulty was raised the moment I arrived here; but a little reflection enables us to see that it is more apparent than real. I suggested that, even under the code, the Legislature might *recommend* the pardon of criminals whom they could not pardon themselves. This was agreed to, and the result is that you are listening to me, for which I thank you.

But we do not propose to ask your good offices for too much. The state of public feeling here I am informed is not favorable for a full pardon. We are in the *ground-swell* after the hurricane. I could not help believing that such a request might be thought unseasonable as yet. So having no power or influence of any kind, we thought it better to ask for a little, and get it, perhaps, through your kindness, than for much, and fail to get anything.

Surely we cannot mistake. Surely, the people of Virginia, who might refuse a pardon, will not be inhuman enough to refuse a *reprieve*. This is all we ask you to recommend. I know the governor will attend respectfully to any such recommendation. And Aaron D. Stevens, for whom I ask a bare reprieve—only a few days longer of such light and air as a dungeon affords him, is not an alien foe, or a domestic foe, or an enemy of any kind, but a young man of our own stock, handsome, powerful, youthful, in the first bloom of manhood—indeed hardly 28 years old! And he will be publicly strangled to death in eight days from now, if you do not recommend him to mercy!

Gentlemen, do it for humanity's sake! Do it for the credit of our common America! Do it for the honor this grand old commonwealth, and thank Heaven for the opportunity of covering with everlasting confusion those *malignant philanthropists*, who long for another death, that in every corner of the civilized world they may exhaust the resources of human language, and tire the tongue of the speaker, and blunt the pen of the writer, and wear out the pencil of the artist, in blackening and cursing the noble Virginian name! Do it, and the blessing of those who are ready to perish will fall upon each of you and upon his house! You can do it with a word—just one little word—**Mercy;** the word which is to die upon your own quivering lips when you enter with awful misgivings into the presence of Him who is to forgive *as we forgive those who trespass against us!—as we* FORGIVE them! Just one little word, which costs you but a breath to utter; and yet it is of that divine force that it will not only save two lives, but it will surely tranquilize a nation, and be the beginning of peace on earth and good will to men down to the remotest generations of American mankind!

The laws of Virginia must be executed, I am told. True, but permit me humbly to suggest to you a way to gratify your obedience to law and your humanity at the same time. A reprieve is a strictly legal transaction. Recommend it, and when granted it will be as legal as a hanging, and ten thousand times more to your honor and advantage. And that you can *retract.* The governor reprieves at his pleasure. Now, if you give us of the North a *chance,* there may be a restoration of ancient good feeling. If not, you can hang your prisoner when you please. But the villainous peculiarity of capital punishment is, that once inflicted you may regret it, but there is no remedy. On that ground alone all men hesitate to inflict it, and the wiser and better men become the longer they hesitate—and the wisest and best decline to countenance it at all. Only the absolute necessities of self-preservation excuse, without justifying it to the leading minds of our time, whether they lead in action or in speculation. Remember the case of Coppoc—how he was hung for a letter, which turned out to be written by Cook, and how sorry everybody was when sorrow was unavailing!

If necessity alone can excuse it, how are we necessitated? What overpowering force is upon us, that we can do nothing but kill and kill? What obliges you to look with sickening heart upon hands smoking with the blood of a misguided boy? Ah! there is our case, gentlemen. He was misguided—he was deluded. Do not delude yourselves into the fatal belief that he was a common murderer, or a low criminal. No, nor any of his associates. It was no common murderer or low criminal that convulsed the state of Virginia. It is only belittling the commonwealth to say it, if true, and trifling with our own dignity if we do not believe it, when we say it. No! empty your penitentiary into the street, and nobody but the prison guards will so much as chase the criminals. These men are *fanatics*. At the word the veils of dead centuries are lifted, and I see a tremendous host sweeping down from their deserts upon terrified Christendom, like the fire upon grass! I see the awful eyes of Mohammed—the waving arm of Ali; I see the dreadful face of Khaled, black as night, casting the frown of death over kneeling Damascus. I see his bloody scimitar uplifted—I hear his inexorable voice, "O, Christian dogs! say *God* is God, and Mohamed is the Prophet of God, or instantly sink into the flames of hell." And this man, who could swim his war horse in the blood of his own saber had poured out, was he a murderer? Or was it a murderer who was all but worshiped for ages, from the Pillars of Hercules to the Sea of Japan! Yet the very least of the slaves of his successors often slew more human beings in one assault than Stevens ever saw assembled together.

I look again, and behold the innumerable, invincible, steel-clad swarms of the Crusade! I behold Godfrey and Tancred and Bohemond and Hugh the Great. I see them toil under the flaming sky of Syria. I hear their thundering shouts, "Deus vult! Deus vult!" I see them pour into the Holy City a river of steel. I see their sad procession, and strangest sight of all I see their immense assembly, uncovered, unarmed, bare footed, kneeling, groaning with real anguish before the sepulcher that once held the human body of the Son of God! I see them rise. I see them put on the weighty armor. I see them draw the broad-bladed dagger and sway the two-handed sword, and trample with bloody, remorseless cruelty, under their iron shoes, the hearts of distracted multitudes in the great mosque of Omar!

Yet what school boy does not know that the knight who had cleft the skulls of a hundred Saracens would have had his golden spurs chopped from his heels with a cleaver, and would have been hung on the nearest tree by the hands of his own neighbors, for fatally felling the poorest Christian camp-follower, in a moment of passion, with the stock of his lance?

The darkest as well as the most enlightened ages have always made this distinction, and history runs over with examples of it, which, it seems, I am obliged to call attention to this day. Allow me one more rather striking illustration of this distinction between a common criminal and a fanatic.

A young Frenchman once read a small book, Las Casas' account of the cruelties of the Spaniards to the Indians of America. It is a very remarkable book, gentlemen, in subject, style and illustration, for it was full of pictures by the greatest masters of the then new art of engraving, and it had a circulation greater than the Waverley novels, or the works of Mr. Dickens, or of Thackery, or of

Dumas—enormously greater if we consider the difference between now and then in facilities of publication. Not all the soldiers of France, nor all the ships of England struck such a blow at the power of Spain as that one little book; for wherever it went—and it went everywhere—no tongue was too tender to frame a curse, and no heart too feeble to throb with hatred for the Spaniards. That book filled the young Frenchman's heart with madness. A race, he thought, capable of cruelties so monstrous, must be accursed of God. They ought to be exterminated—and he! he must be the agent of God's justice! How he acted on that conviction may be seen in the bloody annals of the Buccaneers. Other men robbed the Spaniards, but blood alone could satisfy the deadly hatred of L'Olonnois. Now according to the plainest common sense, according to the dictates of the most ordinary honest dealing, according to the dictionary and the Bible, and the shop and the stable, and the street—what *was* this man? A murderer! And yet Stevens, who as it happens, never killed a human being—for it is notorious that he actually hurt nobody—and who yet walked into the commonwealth almost alone, did nothing unusual, nothing to distinguish him either in act or intent from a common murderer or criminal. A man takes Harper's Ferry with twenty-one men, and actually remains there when he can leave, and captures and locks up men, just as if he was a constable with a warrant, or a sheriff with a writ, whom you obey, of course, unless you are crazy. A man does this, and much more, and I am asked, "Don't you think him a common criminal?" I do not. I think of him as an extraordinary fanatic, and I think it is wrong to hang him, as if he were raving mad.

I am told, with much simplicity, when I say so, that he cannot be a fanatic—he is so *cool* and shows so little passion! Why, gentlemen, I hardly know what remark to make; but I must answer, I suppose, so I will try. Passion, Mr. Chairman, is a matter of temperament. Many men who have much passion exhibit very little, because they have control or lack expression. Many who have not much, express all they have, and appear to have more than actually belongs to them. But fanaticism goes deeper than mere passion of any sort. It is a disorder of the entire man, which makes him see things as they are not. It affects every kind of man, without regard to his passion any more than to his stature. The late Mr. Calhoun, for example, was a perfect fanatic. And yet whoever heard him say—who ever saw him do—one unpleasant, one unbecoming, one passionate thing? No one. I have not the slightest doubt that for the later years of his life his powerful but disordered mind imagined itself to be *thinking!* Read his books and you will find a most extraordinary state of things—a use, for instance, of the forms of demonstration not to be found outside of a book of geometry, and an application of them not to be imagined outside of bedlam! General Jackson, on the contrary, was not fanatical at all. If any man ever lived who saw things as they are, it was General Jackson. But he was a passionate man. Mr. Calhoun, who wanted South Carolina to take the United States, never swore, probably in the whole course of his dignified existence. General Andrew Jackson, on the contrary, swore a great deal during the early part of his not very dignified, but exceedingly useful life.

Am I told that Brown slaughtered his own countrymen? If he did Stevens did not. You say Stevens prepared to help him. Perhaps;—but the reply is as obvious as it is common-place. If the man fanatically attacks his own family, it is not that fact which makes the crime more horrid. It is the fanaticism which takes away the moral responsibility!

As to slaughtering his own countrymen, George Washington did that by the hundred, and expected to be hung as Brown was if taken. No *moral* blame whatever can attach to a fanatical outage, and it is an outrageous abuse of language to argue that it does. Well, then, say the advocates of death, must you turn a lion or tiger, an irresponsible wild beast, loose into the streets, and not kill it? Stevens, I answer, is not a beast, but a man. Kill your beast, and then, perhaps you lose; but it is certain that the most unprofitable use to be made of a man is to hang him.

But one charge which I have very, very often heard since I arrived here must be answered, for I am told it affects many. It is that the North sympathizes with these men, and that *therefore*, they ought to be hung! Leaving the exceedingly odd *sequitur* for a while, look the first charge in the face. If we do, can we help it? And is it wrong? We are very apt to sympathize with almost anybody who is going to be hung. It is human to feel that way, and you feel so yourselves just as often as we do. But if the sympathy goes any further, yourselves are partly to blame for it. I have an excellent chance to know the feeling on boh sides; for though my own party always is so "conveniently small" that you can have them all for acquaintances, yet, owing to some singular accident, the greater number of my personal friends are abolitionists, or Republicans. The surprise, then, was complete. The Democrats were furious; and as for the other side, I happen to know that Dr. Howe—upon whom you are very severe, without in the least knowing him—was as surprised as anybody. At his instance we tried to gain time for the trial, and at last, in consequence of an urgent letter from Brown to His Honor Judge Russell, we started for Charlestown. Up to that time we—that is, the public—thought Brown was a madman, or, at the very utmost, that he was a cool and courageous fanatic; and for that we had the high authority of Governor Wise.

At Charlestown we found an excitement, and a suspicion that looked like insanity. People from the North were followed about the street—stared at—questioned and bored, not only by the authorities, but by super-serviceable men, very likely unknown to them. And I have often remarked that people who are not interested in slavery, to the amount of the thousandth part of a drop of the sweat of a Negro, are its most absurd and offensive advocates. Ladies coming to see the prisoners, as ladies always will, were stared at through windows, publicly threatened, and advised to leave in the country papers. A sculptor, who came in the interest of the fine arts, had to accomplish his object by stealth. But all this might never have been heard of but for the inconceivable simplicity which extended the same treatment to the reporters, particularly after the first reports came in. Now, if a newspaper in my own city chooses to say I was a murderer, or even a thief, I doubt if I should venture beyond the mildest form of denial. For how can you contend with a gentleman who can talk about you one hundred thousand times every morning? It is on no use, as I should think had been ascertained by one Virginia gentleman—who undertook to contend with Mr. Bennett. It is very well known that artists, authors, and reporters, *et id genus omne*, are the most irritable of men, and accordingly, being exasperated at this, to them, novel treatment, they revenged themselves in their own fashion. In a few days in every town in the North, from Portland in Maine to Portland in Oregon, was full of unfavorable notices of the people of Charlestown. I desire it to be expressly understood that I am not now finding fault with the precautions of the authorities, though they irritated me greatly at the time. I am merely telling you the impression made upon me and others by what happened, and showing you how to account for much newspaper "sympathy" for John Brown.

Mr. Sennott then attested to the fact that anyone charged with enormous crimes commonly enlisted much sympathy, whether guilty or not. He referred to numerous cases, such as the Jumpertz case, the Lemoine case, and spoke of the sympathy shown by the ladies of Richmond for Professor Webster—"a stolid old wretch, who cut up his friend's body like a sheep, and went to tea with his family almost without cleaning his hands—a cool-blooded animal, whose only regret at leaving life appeared to be that he could have no more dinners from Parker's;—and were your lovely and sympathetic ladies murderous because they unknowingly pitied him?"

Mr. Sennott continued:

You sympathized with O'Connell—did you desire a bloody revolution in the British Empire on that account? But the case of Lopez, gentlemen, I particularly recommend to your reflections. He went to Cuba exactly as Brown came here. He influenced young men to enlist with him. They went and were shot, and did you not sympathize with them? I am sure I did, and very glad was I when the Spanish government liberated the remnant of his force, as we hope you will the poor remains of Captain Brown's. And it is clear that if pitying Brown makes us abolitionists, pitying Lopez makes us filibusters, Negro thieves and land pirates. I can count all the active abolitionists, even in Boston, on my fingers. I know they make much noise, but so does a parrot at my hotel. He is an excessively noisy bird, and shrieks and scolds the entire neighborhood from morning to night. But he is hardly a fair representative of the population of that house, though he makes a greater disturbance than all of them put together. Neither do our abolition or our Republican politicians represent to you the feeling of our people—and let you arm yourself against us! And you refuse to pardon Stevens because we wish you would! Gentlemen, this may be a *reason*, but it requires great practice in arguing about the resolutions of 1798 and 1799 to enable one to comprehend it . . .

Does public safety require these executions? Safety from what? A slave insurrection? I have not thought you feared any. People at the North say you do, and go so far as to state that you dare not pardon anyone connected with Brown on that account. Now, I know—first, from actually living in a slave state, what the reciprocal sentiments of the slaves and their masters are. Secondly, I know from general principles that if I had been brought up among slave children—if I had joined their childish sports as a child always will—if I had played hide-and-seek with a little black boy around a wheat-stack, or had him beat me for running off with his marbles, or fought and made-up with him over a hundred childish disputes—I might think that a meddling scamp would make him leave me some day, but I should as soon think of cutting his throat as of cutting mine. No! the days of barbarism are over, unless you choose to reinstate them. Treat your Negro as you do, and the kindness, submissiveness and improvidence of his nature will keep him where he is—your faithful, humble, lazy, useless and most burdensome slave. And if he were the fiercest savage of Africa, we are white men, and twenty to one. I say we—I mean we, the citizens of the United States. For whatever you may think, or whatever politicians may say, we are all of one mind on that and kindred points; and though I detest war, I think a small defensive war with some foreign power might be useful just now, if it did not last too long. A union of the Massachusetts Regiment and the Palmettoes, under the orders of Colonel Memminger, to defend this capitol against a British incursion—or a union of the Green

Mountain Boys and the Seventh Regiment on board a fleet of Massachusetts transports loaded with weapons of the newest Yankee pattern, to arm the people of Savannah and Charleston against the enemy, would be a Union meeting we could believe in! Even the muscle which must exist somewhere in the anatomy of our most distinguished Union-saver to originate his circulation might be fairly supposed capable of expanding with something more than muscular irritability in a Union meeting like that.

When we consider attentively how we have been brought to the very brink of destruction from a condition of nearly perfect happiness, it really does appear as if the Omnipotence and Omniscience of God had to be exerted in order to keep in advance of the exquisite absurdity of men. Up to 1834, it is certain that no people out of Heaven were happier. Separated from every enemy on every side—overflowing with riches and with strength—with productions so diversified and so co-relative that what one had the other needed, and thus we could not rival each other or compete with each other any more than one man can rival woman, or woman compete with man—crowned with a common historic glory—proud of a common and most illustrious ancestry—governed by a common law, and bound together in the loving, melting, heart-moving music of a common mother tongue—what madness has overwhelmed us all that we and ourselves are suddenly glaring at each other with blood on both our hands; and, merciful God, what blood! What has caused it? Who did it? What spirit of satanic malignity—what heart and brain set on fire of hell first entered our Western Eden, and set us on each other? Ah, fellow-citizens of the dis-United States, it was no infernal spirit from the other world that wrought us so dire a mischief. It was a small source from which these horrors sprang. The thing that did it all was neither heart nor brain. It has only a tongue and a belly—a tongue to twaddle and a belly to fill. It is that feeblest production of the decay of American statesmanship, to wit—the professional politician. A statesman, the gift of Heaven to distracted nations, is as rare as a prophet. But the race of politicians is cheaply propagated, and is as numerous and as useful as the thistle and the burr. It was after the establishment of the Missouri compromise that this miserable breed began to annoy us. The great old statesmen who had laid the foundation of our greatness, broad and deep, were going calmly to their great reward. It was emphatically an era of good feeling. We were all one people, and many men still living remember with regret the happy and cordial interchange of benefits and good wishes between the fine old Southern gentlemen and the princes of the Northern commerce who met round the hospitable tables of the capitol to felicitate each other on the magnificent progress of a common country.

All at once a small society appeared in the city of Boston. It was a very insignificant company then—very much resembling a missionary or a peace society, and composed apparently of time same sort of people—enthusiastic men, and respectable, benevolent and sympathetic women, old and young. Its purposes were entirely peaceful. Its numbers were utterly insignificant, and its *personnel* of no manner of influence, except that some of the ladies belonged, I believe, to high Bostonian society. Such as they were, the member of Congress at that time did no think them of sufficient consequence to notice their questions on the subject of slavery. Happy would it have been for us all if his successors and their opponents and friends had ever since followed his example. But it was not so to be. Instigated by some contemptible political rogue, an unruly mob of well-dressed blackguards surrounded their place of meeting—offered insult to the assembled ladies—drove them out of their hired hall, and in open day, and in the heart of the most peaceful and orderly city in the whole civilized world, actually put a rope round the neck of one of the men to hang him. That rope may one day strangle the life out of the American constitution. The man was William Lloyd Garrison. About the same time other and similar outrages were perpetrated in various cities of the North, and one of the earliest and most vivid recollections of my childhood is the horror I felt when I was told that the man I saw pelted down the street by a shouting crowd was a "vile abolitionist." I did not know what that meant then, but thought it must be a monster of course. I grew up almost to manhood with similar feelings, and can truly say that for a long time I saw an abolitionist about as often as I saw a Negro—a race of men not much encouraged in the North.

At school and at college it was nearly the same. An abolitionist was seldom heard of or seen, and when he was, he was pretty severely snubbed. If, during these years, a Southerner or anybody else had told us that the North was to be abolitionized, or that we thought about the South in any way except as a country full of generous, hospitable people, we would undoubtedly have thought him unsound in mind. We were full of our own affairs, and never, I venture to say, so much as thought of your existence, except to your advantage. The South to us had a traditional reputation for courtesy, magnanimity, and even for statesmanlike and scholarly men. In those happy, and it may be, irrevocable days, a Northern man would come here without being thought to be an abolition sneak, and a Southern man could visit us without being considered a blustering humbug. Southern men respected us, and we loved them. Yet today, owing to the machinations of foolish, unprincipled politicians alone, and from no other earthly cause, it is safer to be a murderer dripping with blood in many parts of the

South than to hail from the illustrious Commonwealth of Massachusetts or the imperial Republic of New York. Permit me to tell you, though you know it well, what sort of a thing a politician is. In the North he is likely to be a bankrupt shoemaker, who prefers to swindle and go half starved rather than work and pay his honest debts; in the South he is more than likely to be a lawyer without a brief, and often without a book, whose practice is confined to the bar of the village hotel. The whole stock in the trade of one is anti-slavery gabble; the whole stock in trade of the other is pro-slavery bluster. The respectable people of their several localities are too busy, and in the North they are certainly too much occupied in money-making, to vote them down, but they shun these brawlers like an unmentionable disorder; they abandon the polls to them; they stay at home in Massachusetts to the number of 120,000 votes. The fellow-loafers of the two specimens of rogues elect them; and now two men are appointed to look after the interests of the country who are not acquainted even with its geography. And they are intrusted in the business of the nation who have been chiefly remarkable for the reckless and fraudulent neglect of their own. These men meet each other perhaps in the halls of Congress—not to consult, for they can only vituperate—not to counsel, but to harangue—not to enact useful laws, but to invent ways and means to get themselves reelected. And thus they have done again and again by abusing men and institutions of which they respectively know nothing, and playing upon and trading with the passions of the most frivolous of the people.

Such is the material that makes up the bulk of what we are pleased to call eminent politicians on both sides of Mason and Dixon's line. Such are the men whose want of sense and want of principle have led, step by step, to the unpremeditated horrors of Harper's Ferry.

You may say, if you please, that abolition teaching did this. But what produced abolition teaching and gave it its widespread effect? I will tell you. It was a political rascality undertaking to put down freedom of speech by force, that made men help on the abolition movement who were not then and who never will be abolitionists. Let me prove it, gentlemen, by well-known historical facts. The mobbing of abolitionists by their own fellow-citizens had hardly ceased, when a few people petitioned Congress to abolish slavery in the district, and also the internal slave-trade. The petitioners were then just as inconsiderable as they had been when first dispersed and half hanged; for they were the same people who had experienced that treatment without being contented or improved by it. And now, were they left unnoticed? Were they quietly and sensibly sent about their business? No. If any quiet and sensible council had prevailed, the politician's occupation was gone. The mischief-makers then in Congress seized it as a godsend. They wanted something to twaddle about and they reached into the ark of our covenant for their support. They laid their dirty hands upon the sacred right of petition. belonging as a birthright to the sovereign people of the United States. Now, gentlemen, allow me to give some information that I hope will not displease you. If it does, excuse it, for it is true, and presented from good motives. I know the sentiments of the people where I live. I mean the people, not the politicians, who have no sentiments that they are not ready to sell. We are all sound on the slavery question; for we all detest slavery—all of us. We cannot help detesting it. But we ardently desire to let it alone. It is your institution—not ours, thank God! "Hands off—let it alone—mind your own business," these are the expressions that suit us to use, when Northern men attempt to meddle practically with you. But then we have an institution which is ours if not yours—It is freedom of speech, and we do not want you to meddle with that.

Allow us to say what we please at home about slavery. Do not especially try to suppress any discussion, or to punish directly or indirectly those who discuss, as long as they do not meddle with your property. If they do that, punish them, and no one can object. We hate slavery of course. But we need not talk, nor do we propose to talk, abolition to your Negroes. There are places and times for all things. The science of physiology, for example, in all its branches, is eminently useful and proper to talk of—but not in general society. The abolition of slavery in like manner is a very important subject of discussion even here—but not so to a crowd of ignorant slaves. So long as we observe on our side that safe and proper rule of action, do you on your side take no liberties with our discussions. Let us alone—hands off, if you please. Mind your own business. It is our turn now to cry out; and, however much we detest slavery, don't undertake to keep us from saying so or thinking so, as long as we never meddle practically with you and yours. That meddling, foolish men, on both sides have undertaken to interfere in practice with what did not concern them at all, is the cause of all our difficulties. Letting each other's peculiar business alone will probably bring about the cure of them—and now help us by a good beginning on your side. Your broken laws have been dreadfully avenged. The active invaders are nearly all destroyed. The rocks, the river and the hungry gallows have devoured the blood of most of them, and the poor remnant is waiting in a dungeon the result of your deliberations. Let it result in mercy, we conjure you. Money is a word which should drop easily from your Virginia lips. Your commonwealth owes its existence to an act of mercy. Your founder, like my client, was the invader of a people who had never harmed him; like him he was taken in the act of invasion; like him he was tried with all the solemnities of savage law as Stevens was under the forms of a civilized code; like him he was sentenced to death according to the profoundest axioms of those poor barbarians. Who knew no better or safer way than always to kill all their enemies. But he was saved by Mercy, incarnate to that sweet Indian maid, whose image glows through the twilight of history with all the loveliest hues of young romance! May the parallel not fail us here in its noblest part! May those whose hearts proudly beat around me with the more than regal—the richer than imperial blood of Pocahontas—remember their illustrious ancestors this day! May they emulate her merciful spirit! May they prove their pure descent by their magnanimous actions! May they not refuse to extend, without risk, to a young countryman wholly in their power, the mercy which she risked her life to show to a stranger, an alien and an enemy!

Mrs. Pierce who was Aaron Steven's sister, and Miss Jennie Dunbar of Ohio visited the prisoner on Thursday, March 15th, the day before the execution. Miss Dunbar had just returned from a visit to Richmond where she had pleaded with Governor Letcher for the lives of Stevens and "Harrison." Miss Dunbar arrived at Richmond on February 14th and was received with civility. Governor Letcher said in substance that Stevens was the worst of the Harper's Ferry insurrectionists and remarked that he was "reckless, hardened and dangerous to society." Mr. Letcher said he felt it to be a duty to rid the world of him. Both ladies stayed at Charlestown Wednesday night.

Charlestown was thronged with visitors on Thursday, and several companies of militia were in attendance. On the last morning Mrs. Pierce and Jennie Dunbar had breakfast with Stevens and Hazlett. Stevens was dressed in fresh clothing, his chains had been removed and Miss Dunbar remarked, "I had never seen him looking better, he seemed fitter to live than ever on the morning of his execution." Mrs. Pierce was quite overcome and had to leave the table to recover herself. Tears welled down from Miss Dunbar's eyes. Stevens packed a little trunk with items designating various gifts for different persons and chatted as if he were going to see them soon again. He polished his shoes and brushed his clothing, saying "I wish to look well when I go up on the scaffold." Miss Dunbar, in taking her last farewell said, "You have done a great deal for me, inasmuch as you have shown me that the moralist's faith will do to die by."

"Oh! yes," he replied, "I am perfectly confirmed in the belief that God rules over all and that he is too loving a God to make his creature unhappier than they make themselves."

On Execution day, March 16th, the New York *Times* discussed the "Vengeance of Virginia" as follows:

> When Mr. Henry Wise resigned the gubernatorial seat of Virginia to his successor, Mr. John Letcher, we hoped that the political Jack Ketch of the Old Dominion might be about to retire from office with her pyrotechnic Palinurus. The country, while it lamented the passionate obstinacy with which the hero of Harper's Ferry had pursued his purpose of putting to death a fanatic whom death was sure to invest with the martyr's aureole, could yet make allowances for the author of this stupendous blunder, and did, In fact, make them. It is not only a Virginian, but, we fear, an American trait to exaggerate every emotion, and to sacrifice the gravest considerations of sense and dignity to the ecstasy of an intense sensation; and when we saw that Virginia had gone simply mad with mingled rage and fear, we could not fairly demand that Virginian statesmen should risk their influence and their future in an attempt to stem the furious torrent of the popular folly. We deplored the infatuation before which those who should have ruled the people felt themselves constrained to bow; but we knew that even a Virginian governor is, after all, a man of like passions with ourselves,

and we felt that it would be neither charitable nor just to expect of a provincial executive, at such a moment, the courageous discretion which we might have had a right to look for from a statesman of loftier position dealing with a more reasonable because a more powerful community.

It is a mere truism to say that all human passions become exasperated exactly in proportion as the circle in which they move is narrowed. A village mob is, of all imaginable mobs, the least amenable to any argument but force; and such is the constitution of society in Virginia that, for all practical purposes, the whole state was converted by the Harper's Ferry excitement into a mere hive of village mobs. Governor Wise must have been a very great man, indeed, if he was to find in himself the strength to resist and disregard the angry clamors of this hive. And as we had no reason to insist that Governor Wise should be a very great man, we could afford to see him throw the reins for a time on the popular neck, without berating him immoderately. But the deed which Virginia proposes to do today, is far worse than the blunder which brought John Brown to the gallows, and the Governor of Virginia who has sanctioned it has dealt in cold blood a heavier blow at the character of his own commonwealth, and at the peace of the country, than was struck by Wise in the fever of the popular rage.

Virginia will hang two men today. They are young, intelligent, and vigorous men—Americans by birth and blood, for treason to an American state. And this, not in any moment of panic. She has waited until the feelings of inter-sectional hostility had begun to subside in the hearts and the language of inter-sectional recrimination to die away on the lips of the people in the North and in the South. In the tempest of the first days which followed those scenes at Harper's Ferry, we all grew terribly familiar with the notion of an *"irrepressible conflict,"* a truly irrepressible conflict of passions, apt to bloodshed and to rapine, between the different sections of our common Union. Virginia would have it so: she would make us accept John Brown as the incarnation of a deliberate Northern policy and a determined Northern purpose. Upon the sheer insanity of this course it is too late for us now to waste words. It did its wild and wicked work: work which we may yet have no little trouble, we or our children, to undo. But after the storm came a calm. We were beginning to think whether it could be possibly true, after all, that John Brown was seriously believed at the South to represent us of the North, our feelings, and our will. Southern men, we are sure, were beginning to ask themselves whether this fearful mistake of the Virginians could not in some way be set right. We were reflecting, all of us, on the peril and the scandal of such an interpretation as we had invited mankind to put upon the history of Harper's Ferry. It was coming back to us in so many unpleasant shapes!—returning to plague the original interpreters, with foreign prognostications of the impending downfall of the Republic, and with foreign sarcasms upon the imbecility of slave holding communities. Even the petty states of South America have been enjoying their fling at us; and it is worth noting that, on the very day on which the American Secretary of Legation at Lima left that city for Washington with the insolent refusal of the Peruvian government to acquit certain acknowledged claims of American citizens, a journal *El Commercio* of that city, contained a long and portentous article setting forth the terrible nature of the convulsions which had already begun to shake the proud Northern Empire to its foundations. Much wiser in their day and generation than the counselors of Virginia were these rulers of Britain who refused to the Irish revolutionists of 1848 the glory of the gallows and the axe, and dealt with treason contemptuously as an anachronism and an absurdity which madmen might mediate in Utopia itself, but which had become practically impossible in a prosperous, free and Christian state.

Then, too, the thought of capital punishment, inflicted for a political crime upon men who—as Mr. Sennott, the counsel of Stevens and Hazlett, very justly put it the other day, in his eloquent plea for the prisoners before the Virginia Legislature—were really as little like common murderers as the Crusaders or Caliphs; the thought of capital punishment inflicted upon such men has been allowed thus enough to dilate before the public mind, till we can all of us begin to see how hideous a thing it is, here in the democratic American Republic, and in the year of our Lord 1860. We must shrink instinctively, the least thoughtful must shrink from the incongruous reappearance in the midst of our free modern civilization of the "royal justice" which pursued the followers of Nathaniel Bacon for years after their leader's death with the gibbet and the cord, over all the regions of the James River Colony. Nathaniel Bacon did far more damage to life and property in his successful war than John Brown had so much as dreamed of. Jamestown laid in ashes, and a whole community given up for more than a year to perpetual skirmishing and forays, make up a much sterner account than the raid upon the Arsenal. Nor were Bacon's objects one whit more legal than those of Brown. Brown set society at defiance that he might "liberate his own soul" and the slaves of other people. Bacon convulsed a colony that he might coerce a sluggish government into doing its duty. Both were traitors, no doubt; but no impartial man will ever read their stories without the deep conviction that the justice which hunts down the misguided followers of traitors such as these through weeks and months and years, it is not justice at all, but vengeance—vengeance which has been scornfully defined as the "pleasure of fools," and which assuredly is very fat from being the wisdom or the strengths of states.

At 8:30 AM on Friday March 16th, Miss Dunbar and Mrs. Pierce left to wait at Harper's Ferry for the remains of the two brave men. They were hung at 12:05 PM in the afternoon. They appeared resigned to their fate. Stevens died very hard, while Hazlett perished without a struggle. Both exhibited great firmness and resignation. There were no religious exercises at the gallows, as the prisoners persisted in refusing all the kindly offices of the ministry in their last moments. They were both spiritualists, and had a peculiar religion of their own. Both their bodies were forwarded to Mr. Marcus Springs in South Amboy, New Jersey. The caskets reached Baltimore on the early Saturday morning train, and were soon on their way to New Jersey. Plans were made to bury them on the Eagleswood estate.

It was now divulged that the friends of John Brown were always concerned with the prisoner's lives and eager to do anything to aid them. The failures of their efforts to rescue John Brown from death on the scaffold only increased the determination of his three militant friends, Thomas Wentworth Higginson, John W. LeBarnes[2] and Richard J. Hinton, to cheat the Virginia hangman of some of his victims. Before they could do much four more raiders, John Cook, Edwin Coppoc, Shields Green and John Copeland were executed on December 16, 1859. Actually Cook and Coppoc almost escaped on their own the night before their execution.

With these deaths only Aaron D. Stevens and Albert Hazlett remained alive at the Charlestown prison. Under pressure for some action, Richard J. Hinton telegraphed Captain James Montgomery of Kansas for help. The two met when they assembled at Harrisburg, Pennsylvania on February 16, 1860. Higginson was going under the name of Charles P. Carter

---

[2] He became a lieutenant of a German company in the Second Massachusetts Infantry during the Civil War.

while Captain Montgomery was referred to as the "master machinist." Higginson had obtained permission from John Brown's widow to use part of the funds placed in his hands for the benefit of the Brown family in his endeavor to save Hazlett and Stevens. The publisher's of Redpath's book on John Brown, William W. Thayer and Charles Eldridge, were enlisted in the cause and contributed $800 partly as an outright gift and partly as a loan. Wendell Phillips promised $100 and Sculptor E. A. Brackett $200. All in all, $1271 was raised in the undertaking.

Mr. Higginson immediately tried to get in touch with any of the raiders who escaped through the mountains. He succeeded in locating Charles Plummer Tidd, who was then in hiding in Ohio. Tidd came to Boston in February to counsel with Higginson, Thayer and Eldridge. He stated his belief that a plan of rescue conceived by Higginson of an overland dash to Charlestown through the mountains was impossible due to bad winter conditions. In the meantime John W. LeBarnes had returned to New York City to enlist a group of German revolutionists. Their willingness to start out was never actually tested, but LeBarnes and Richard Hinton saw to it that they were armed.

There was no difficulty in getting men together in Kansas under Montgomery's leadership. From Linn County came John Brown's friend Augustus Wattles. Captain Montgomery, signing himself "Henry Martin," telegraphed Higginson from Leavenworth on February 10, 1860. The coded message said he had eight men ready to depart. Captain Montgomery and his men arrived at Harrisburg, Pa., in the guise of cattlemen. Montgomery speedily found Higginson who was renting rooms from Dr. William W. Rutherford, an abolitionist, and probably the only man in Harrisburg entrusted with the secret.

The problems of a rescue involved cross-country travel, crossing the Potomac River, and charging a building defended by two sentinels outside and twenty-five men inside a wall fourteen feet high. Montgomery insisted that he had to scout the country by himself. He went with a friend by the name of Soulé straight to Charlestown and discovered the well-armed Virginia patrols, with which the roads teemed. Soulé stopped at every inn along the way and entered Charlestown in such a state of intoxication that he was speedily locked up in the very jail with the men he had come to rescue. Soulé obtained an interview with Stevens and Hazlett who both declared a rescue impossible due to a constant guard of 80 men. Their kind jailor, Captain Avis, they knew would fight to the last. They did not wish liberty at the cost of his life.

In the Drover's Tavern in Harrisburg a council of war was held. Soulé made his report of Steven's and Hazlett's wishes. A severe snowstorm which had just occurred was the final deciding factor, and Montgomery reluctantly submitted. Higginson, who presided at the conference asserted that he consented reluctantly to the abandonment of the enterprise upon which he had built high hope. To the great disappointment of Hinton and LeBarnes who were in New York awaiting word, Stevens and Hazlett were left to their final fate and did not cheat the hangman.

The Senate Investigation Committee wound up its business on June 14, 1860. The next day Senator James Mason of Virginia presented a majority report signed by himself, Senator Jefferson Davis of Mississippi and Senator G. N. Fitch of Indiana. The minority of the Committee, Senators Jacob Collamer of Vermont and James R. Doolittle of Wisconsin also presented a short report. The minority expressed no sympathy with John Brown or his purpose. Their chief effort was to offset any political effect the majority report might have in connecting the North with John Brown and his men.

The majority report of the committee was entirely ineffective from the slavery point of view. It was disappointing considering that such able men as Jefferson Davis and James Mason constructed it. Their report presented the facts of the invasion without any attempt at coloring. They dwelt upon John Brown's desire to incite insurrection among the slaves and declared that "it was owing alone to the loyalty and well-affected disposition of the slaves that he did succeed in creating a servile war . . ." The majority report admitted that John Brown's reticence was such that "it does not appear that he intrusted even his immediate followers with his plans, fully, even after they were ripe for execution." Finally Messrs Mason, Davis and

Fitch could suggest no legislation that would be adequate to prevent like occurrences in the future. The invasion to them was simply the act of lawless ruffians. The two reports attracted little attention when printed and distributed.

Chapter 15

OWEN BROWN'S STORY

In March of 1874 John Brown Jr. had a two-story frame house on the eastern shore of Put-in-Bay Island on Lake Erie. It was far from the hustle-bustle of the mainland and out of the way of summer visitors to the resort hotels which dotted the region. The main road on the island threaded its way through many grape orchards. The house sat up high and there was a lawn all the way down to the lake front. As one looked out from this point one could see Kelly's Island and the Ohio mainland in the distance. Put-in-Bay Island was only one in a number of grape laden islands in this region. They glittered in green and purple in the hot summer afternoons. How idyllic a place to live and grow old.

John Brown Jr. came into this quaint place after fighting his enemies in Kansas, and after being hunted from place to place for the attempt at Harper's Ferry, although he was not there. He moved here in 1863 when the pleasant vineyards were wild land, after having to leave the Civil War battlegrounds on account of a disease contracted in his first battles against slavery. He was so modest and unassuming such that you would never know he had ever fired a gun in anger in his life.

When Mr. Ralph Keeler called at his house and inquired for Mr. Brown, a plain motherly-looking woman came to the door and asked which Mrs. Brown he wanted, John or Owen. This mild voiced matron turned out to be John Brown Jr's wife, who had shared the dangers and hardships of the Kansas border-life with her husband, and it was from her, then and there, that Keeler learned that Owen Brown was also on the island. She told Keeler that the two brothers were mowing grass in a neighboring field. Keeler walked over the rise and found John; a large well built man and Owen, slender but still tall; and of the two he was more like the old Captain of Osawatomie. They both wore a full beard, sandy, as their father's was once, and beginning to whiten as his did at their ages. Owen showed his forty-nine years while John looked younger at fifty-two. They both wore hickory shirt sleeves and farm trousers of blue drilling, but they were both striking in looks.

John Brown Jr. came over to the fence where Keeler stood. He was the quiet, genial, warm-hearted farmer who was an amateur geologist and land surveyor. Owen Brown was leaning on his scythe. He was the sole survivor of the little party he led through the mountains to escape Harper's Ferry—and, if we believe that Osborne Anderson the mulatto, was dead—the only one living in all that company which accompanied Captain Brown to Harper's Ferry.

At that first interview Keeler could not get them to speak much about the affair but the Brown brothers were interested in Keeler's adventures as well. They were particularly curious about certain rarely visited places beyond the sea that Keeler had visited. They parted late that night. It was not until Keeler had met with them often did Owen Brown consent to tell the story of his escape. John Brown Jr. was at his home in Ashtabula County, Ohio at the time of the attack. He had just returned from Canada where he had been organizing the most trustworthy of the slaves who had escaped to some of the border towns. He would have been at Harper's Ferry if his father had not been driven to begin operations before the appointed time. His object, as we now know, was to make slave holding so unsafe and unstable as to render it unprofitable, and so lead to abolition. He and his company had already in effect driven slavery out of Kansas, and lessened the value of slaves in Missouri and the border states to the amount of a million dollars. It was John Brown's desire to show the slave holders from the first the humanity of his intentions, that caused him to delay his escape from the engine house at Harper's Ferry until it was too late.

Owen Brown was spoken of as a cripple. He injured his right arm in throwing a stone when a boy, and has since had only the partial use of it. He was a bachelor. Keeler was invited to his one-room shanty, a little way from his brother's farm house. Upon the wall just above his head hung an overcoat which was once worn by Captain Brown, and on a bench beneath the window lay the gun used by the old warrior at the fight of Osawatomie. This place, indeed, was full of mementoes. Owen Brown told Keeler that he had not told the story of his escape for the last twelve years. He then plunged into the daring account of his escape. It was a thrilling tale:

The last time I saw my father was on the Sunday night of the attack on October 16, 1859. At about 11:00 PM our small company started from the Kennedy farm five miles north of Harper's Ferry. My father left Barclay Coppoc, Frank J. Merriam, and myself to guard the arms and ammunition stored on the premises, until it should time to move them, either to the school-house, a mile from Harper's Ferry, or to the town itself. Barclay Coppoc was, as mentioned previously a brother to Edwin, who was hung soon after my father at Charlestown, Virginia. The mother of the Coppocs was a Quakeress and their father was dead. Before the Coppocs joined up with my father they lived in Springdale, Iowa, but they originally came from Columbiana County, Ohio. Barclay Coppoc, who was with me throughout the escape, was a medium sized young man not over twenty-two or twenty-three years old. He did not look very healthy, but he was hardy. He was not as learned or as well educated as his brother who was hanged.

Frank J. Merriam was from a wealthy family in Massachusetts. He was twenty-nine or thirty years old at the time. He had an easy-going manner but he intensely hated slavery. Neither of these two men were with me and my father in Kansas, so I thought it best that I should stand guard at night letting the other two sleep. We knew nothing of the events which were occurring at the Ferry until 5:45 AM Monday morning when we heard firing in the direction of the town. Rain, starting out Monday morning was at times heavy, and continued intermittently all day long and into the night.

At about 11:00 AM a slave of Colonel Lewis Washington came up with a four-horse wagon and requested a load of arms. One of Captain Brown's men came with him. The two men knew less about the details of the fight than we did. While they put their team in the barn and fed them, I got dinner for them. I had been the cook just about every day at the Kennedy farm. After a nourishing meal we loaded the wagon as quickly as we could with boxes of revolvers and Sharp's rifles, which my father managed to have shipped to him under the name of Isaac Smith & Sons. The wagon then drove away headed for the school house where the arms were to be stored.

Between two and three o'clock that afternoon we heard a great deal of firing in the direction of the Ferry. At about 4:00 PM a black man came up on horseback and asked us to go over to the Ferry and help in the fight. He said his name was Joe. I really didn't know on what basis he had made this request. He must have come from the school-house where some of Washington's and Allstadt's slaves were congregated.

At any rate I put things in order, feeling with fatality that I would never return. I told some of the neighbors where they could help themselves to provisions and other things if they wanted them. I also tied up the puppy dog called "Cuff" to a post so that he would not follow along. (We heard much later that he grew to be a big ferocious dog from the people who afterwards took possession of the vacant boarding house.) Then armed with rifles and revolvers we started for the Ferry through the rain on foot; Joe riding his horse. We traveled a mile or so when we saw three men approaching us on mules. The sun was setting and the light was poor. I ordered them to halt, which they did with frightened readiness. They weren't looking for us and knew nothing about what was going on at the Ferry. All they knew about affairs was that folks were shooting one another down there, and they wanted to get to their homes as fast as their mules would carry them. We let them pass and went on our way.

A short time later we saw an armed man and I ordered him to halt. He hesitated, but we suddenly recognized each other. It was Charles Plummer Tidd, one of my father's men. He was once a lumberman in his native state of Maine. He had been with us in Kansas and was a buddy of Stevens, one of my father's Captains. Tidd was one of the men on duty at the school-house. He told us that our men were all hemmed in at the Ferry and that many of them were killed, and that there was no chance of escape.

"The fact is, boys," said Tidd, "we are all used up and the best thing we can do is to get away from here as fast as our legs will carry us."

"But Charlie we shouldn't desert our friends," I said, and I proposed to go to the school-house, collect the slaves left there, and then cross the ravine up through the forest to the point of rocks upon the mountain opposite Harper's Ferry. At this point we might be able to divert or frighten away the enemy with our long range Sharp's rifles, and let our people escape. Coppoc and Merriam were with me all the way.

Tidd thought that the case was hopeless but consented to go along with us up to the school-house. We had not traveled over a mile farther when we saw another man approaching in the dark. I yelled out, "halt!"

"Halt yourself!" was the reply. We recognized the voice of John E. Cook, the same Cook that was with us in Kansas. "Our men are all killed but seven," said Cook. "Your father was killed at 4:00 PM this afternoon." He didn't know whether my brothers Oliver and Watson were among the dead or not. He told us how the remaining band of men had surprised and taken the town and the army and held it, fighting all day long. But at last military companies came in from the surrounding towns in Virginia, and eight hundred troops turned the tide.

Cook said, "In my opinion the best and only thing for us to do is to make good our escape." I was opposed to leaving my friends behind who might want to escape with us and we argued the case right there in the rain and darkness. Cook said he had been exchanging shots with the enemy not far from the school-house and now he expected to find it occupied by hostile Virginians. I reluctantly prevailed on Cook to go to the school house for provisions and to see what had become of the liberated slaves.

When we finally came in sight of the school-house Tidd and I left the others concealed in a thicket. Approaching nearer, we whistled and called out, "Are you there? Where are you?" We received no answer. This seemed to confirm the idea of enemies there. Tidd hesitated, (but perhaps I ought not to tell you this about a comrade) and I had difficulty in getting him to go with me into the school house. He followed me, though, revolver in hand, and I lit a candle and we looked in. The school house seemed deserted so we entered. There was a barrel full of sweet biscuits which I had made myself earlier, and I hurriedly thrust as many of them as I could into a bag. I took about twenty pounds of sugar in another bag. That's about all the provisions we took. We knew that we dared not build fires in our flight so it would be cold fare for the foreseeable future.

Coming out of the school house we joined Cook, Merriam, Coppoc and Joe the Negro. We stayed in the area for perhaps an hour calling out every so often for stragglers. The only thing we heard in the darkness was the rain and the sporadic firing at Harper's Ferry. We saw no more of the liberated slaves. They probably went back to their plantations and owners.

It was plain that we could not go to the top of the mountain opposite the Ferry before Tuesday morning. I hated to give up the idea of helping our friends to escape, but I had to. We might have been lucky and killed one or two of the enemy, but it would have surely cost us our lives. We finally decided to go back to the Kennedy farm and get our India rubber blankets and other necessary things. I put my bags of biscuits and sugar across Joe's horse, and as we moved out I made my plans for our escape. I had some valuable experience as an engineer on the underground railroad, and I had been a woodsman all my life. I told the boys if they stuck by me I felt sure I could get them safely through to the North, and to Canada, if necessary.

By this time the firing became louder, showing that the people were thoroughly aroused, and on the alert. We had a hasty supper at the Kennedy farm and hurriedly seized what things we could carry away, resolving to sort them out in the woods at daylight. We could bury those things we did not absolutely need. I picked up an empty shot bag to put salt in, but in my rush I forgot to put any salt into it. The bag, however, would prove valuable later on.

We resolved to camp on the mountain as close to the farm as we dared, so as to aid in the escape of any other stragglers who might find their way there. Afterwards I learned that two of our men actually reached the farm-house the next day after we had gone. They were Hazlett and Anderson. Hazlett was caught and hung with the rest. Osborne Anderson made his way into Canada. I heard later that he went to Liberia in Africa, and if he is still living, he would be the only other survivor of all my father's company at Harper's Ferry.

When we began our ascent of the mountain I asked Joe to turn his horse loose. "Why," he exclaimed, "dat horse is worth more'n a hundred an' fifty dollars!" I had hard work to convince him that his life was worth more than the horse. Near the base of the mountain, about a mile from the farm, we halted in the laurel and made our beds. It was still raining and very cold. We had not learned, as we did afterwards, to keep warm by sharing the same bed. We spread our India rubber blanket upon the earth, then a woolen blanket for a cover, and another India rubber blanket on top of all.

Here I told the boys my plan, here in this God awful spot in the woods. I explained that the mountains there extended in a northeasterly direction. We must therefore follow the mountain ranges, making to the northwest when we could; traveling only at night upon the edges of the clearings; sleeping and hiding by day in the thickets on the uninhabited mountain-tops; shunning all traveled roads at all times, except as we were obliged to cross them in the night; building no fires; buying or stealing no provisions; in fact only speaking in whispers until we could get beyond Chambersburg, Pennsylvania.

About this time Joe, who had been despondent all along, began to complain of rheumatism. He was afraid he couldn't go on with us. I told him that he was certain to lose his life if he went back, and I felt reasonably sure I could get him his freedom if he kept with us. We then went to bed. I had not slept in two days and two nights, but I sat up against a tree and watched. I was suspicious that Joe would bolt and I thought I better keep an eye on him. He, of course, knew what I was thinking. He knew his only hope of saving his life would be in turning us in. Our beds were about twenty feet apart. After a while Joe began to groan and complain of his rheumatism again; said he couldn't lie comfortably and wanted to sit up. I got up and walked past him and then sat down on the nearest bed. I must have fallen asleep for five or ten minutes or more; I don't know. But when I woke up and looked for Joe he was gone. I hunted and yelled for him but in vain. Then I roused up all the boys in a great hurry. They agreed with me that we must move at once, and change our plans as much as possible. All we could do to mislead our pursuers was to make for a different range of mountains which would take us in the same general direction. There was a new road just three miles from us across the mountains from the valley where the Kennedy farm house was to a place called Pleasant Valley. Our lives seemed to depend on our getting north of that road before daylight.

We got rid of a number of items including Joe's guns which he had not taken with him. We buried these items in the ground. We each took two Sharp's rifles with one or two revolvers apiece, besides a full cartridge-box to a man. I carried about fifty pounds of provisions. The others were opposed to taking so much to eat. We started up the mountain diagonally. It was hard work getting through the laurel and up the steep slopes with our loads. We had to stop often to rest. I was actually able to fall asleep for a few minutes at each stop. My father used to sleep while riding horseback. He got a good deal of his rest in Kansas in that way.

We reached the top of the mountain at daylight on Tuesday. The rain had stopped but it was foggy. We could see the Kennedy farm-house some two or three miles below. There seemed no one around, but we heard occasional shots in the direction of Harper's Ferry. We traveled the greater part of a mile perhaps, along the mountain top before we came to the road which we were so anxious to cross. The fog was rising a little now with the sun. We were not quite out of sight of the thicket on the northern side of the road when we heard the sound of horses' hoofs upon the wet ground. Eight (yes, I counted them!) armed men rode briskly past us over the mountain. We kept hidden until they had disappeared, and we stole further into the thicket, where the five of us hid away for the day. The horsemen didn't see us. Did Joe betray us? I couldn't tell for certain.

For all our narrow escapes I slept soundly that day in the thicket. We awoke in the late afternoon and ate some of our biscuits and sugar and discussed the situation in a whisper. Cook, in his fiery, quick thinking way proposed some bold hazardous measures. To some extent he influenced Tidd and Coppoc. They were in favor of stealing some horses and riding into the face of death. Was there a reward on out heads? Yes, I believe so. How much? I couldn't even guess. Cook's wife,—he was the only married man in the party,—was then in Chambersburg, and he was bent on going there. So were Tidd and Coppoc. Merriam always abided by my decision. Poor fellow, he began to show symptoms of giving out. I waited for him and helped him along, especially in steep or rocky places.

It was not my plan to go to Chambersburg, but I was out-voted. They were all younger than I was. While we were lying there arguing in a hoarse whisper a gray squirrel attracted by our colorful blankets went up the tree right over us and chattered noisily. Soon after he was joined by a black squirrel and they both chattered at us. I had all I could do to keep Cook and Tidd from shooting them. I could not keep the boys from going down to the edge of the clearing before dark. It was cold and we had to keep moving to stay warm. I insisted on going ahead. I told the boys that if I saw anyone I would make a signal and they should all drop down. Just as we approached the clearing where we could see Pleasant Valley I saw a man coming along the path through the woods. He was carrying a sack of flour on his shoulders. I made the signal, and we all dropped down not far from the path. I think the man saw us but he saw that there were five of us, with two guns apiece. He walked right past without speaking or turning his head.

I had no difficulty in prevailing upon the boys to wait until later in the night before attempting to cross the valley. And when we finally did start, we were no more than half way through the first field, when we saw and heard a horseman at full run upon the nearest road, and making the most terrible noise I ever heard come from mortal lips. He was alarming the whole valley. I learned later that the man was shouting to the people that Cook's men were coming down from the mountains to massacre them all. They all knew Cook because he had been teaching in the neighborhood of Harper's Ferry for the past year. I heard that the inhabitants of Pleasant Valley fled for their lives precipitantly across the Potomac into Jefferson County and some of them as far away as Winchester.

There was nothing for us to do but press right on across the field toward the next mountain range east of the valley. Reaching the mountains we pursued our journey along its side just above the clearings. Towards daylight we went up to the top and concealed ourselves, eating our sugar and biscuits and sleeping. Of course we were traveling very slowly. When we got up in the afternoon Cook wanted to travel by the roads, and since the provisions were getting low he insisted that we should go to buy more. To appease him I offered, and he took, all my share of the biscuits and sugar. I was only able to live upon the dry, hard Indian corn which we found still standing in the fields. I occasionally found some wild potatoes which we ate raw.

I had forty or fifty dollars in specie; the others, excepting Merriam, had merely two or three dollars apiece. On Wednesday evening a cold rain set in. Towards morning it changed into snow. All day long the trees sagged with it and our bed was covered with it,—the one bed into which the whole five of us crawled, as I have told you, to keep warm. We slept well. Shortly after dark we came to where the mountain gave an unexpected turn to the east, and we were compelled to cross a valley to the next range. We crossed a large stream and at least five miles through the snow and wet, before we reached the mountains again. We found some pine shavings and some wood, and in spite of all I said the boys made a fire. We were all wet and cold and exhausted for want of food, and I suppose the temptation was too strong.

It was not yet daylight and our fire was dying out. Just then we were startled by an owl. He took his perch on a neighboring tree and hooted at us. About a half hour later while we were munching on our wild corn we heard what were unmistakable human voices, calling to one another in the valley below. Soon we heard the baying of hounds, evidently in pursuit of something. The idea that we were being followed immediately flashed upon us. We were not a minute in putting out the fire and scattering and covering every stick and ember in the snow and earth. Then we started up the mountain and into the thistle. We could hear the hounds in the distance. We pressed on till well after daylight. All of a sudden we came upon a clearing with a house on it and a road running along the summit of the mountain. A man came driving along with a load of wood but twenty-five or thirty feet away. Though the noise of the hounds was coming nearer and nearer we had to wait until the man and his team were out of sight. Fortunately he did not see us. We traveled on perhaps a mile until the day was so bright and the hounds so near that we made up our mind that we would either have to hide or fight. I counseled the boys, however, not to shoot the dogs unless there were men with them. I never saw a dog that would bite me. Dogs are like men,—if you pretend to know them they are not sure what to do. There is a convincing peace-making mystery about it.

So we stopped and waited for the hounds. In a little while a red fox with his tongue out, showing that he was bushed, broke past us down towards the valley. Had they been put on our track? I don't think so. If they were, they pursued the fox, instead, being no doubt more used to that sort of hunting. We went on a mile or two further and there we camped, seeing no more of anybody else that day.

We heard enough firing that day and night to show us how thoroughly the country was aroused and after us. Already the want of salt, the scarcity of food and the fatigue of carrying Merriam's luggage besides my own, and the bag of dry corn for all of us began to make me dizzy. We would almost always fall asleep when we sat down to rest, and we would sleep soundly, no matter how frosty it was.

We were looking for a pike below Boonesboro which would lead from Hagerstown to Baltimore. I knew we would never be safe until all of us should get across that pike. The clue to finding the pike was that it would appear in a gap in the mountains. The next day we became aware that we were approaching the perilous gap in the mountains. When we came in sight of the pike in question I heard the baying of hounds again,—big hounds and little hounds and all sorts of dogs. I never heard so much barking in my life. At a sudden bend in the mountain the gap spread out in front of us. What a sight it was! There must have been a hundred fires in view,—alarm fires, we took them to be, of those who were watching for us. They had heard that Cook had a large party of men and they had gone in to head them off. I saw that our chances of getting away were very slight indeed. I did not say it to the boys, however. I told them that this was no place for us. They were quite ready to follow me. We retraced our steps half a mile or so, came upon a road, and followed it down the mountain until we came to a spring, where we hastily gulped down some cold water and washed our faces.

We supposed that we were in the Cumberland Valley. Our object was to get across away from the gap and the people watching for us there. It was now nearly midnight. We could not tell exactly, as nobody had a time piece. We had to get across the pike and valley to the mountain beyond before daylight. Nothing but the excitement of the moment enabled us to accomplish what we did that night.

Imagine our disappointment when we found that we had reached not Cumberland Valley, but a ravine with a steep mountain right in our way on the other side. There was nothing to do but climb it. It was nearly morning before we got down into the Cumberland Valley. Pursuing our way toward the pike we were startled again because we found ourselves marching straight up to a toll-gate. Getting to the side of the path we crossed the pike about three hundred feet further on, just as the first light of morning appeared. A few minutes later we were obliged to wade across another large creek. I happened to look back and found that Merriam was no where to be seen. Hurrying back to the steep bank of the creek I discovered Merriam, poor fellow, unable to climb over it. I tried to help him, but he was too tired and weak.

I called Tidd and took hold of Merriam rather impatiently, and in pulling him up, he was bruised against a projecting rock. We rushed on through a lately plowed field. I was worried because our tracks would be very plain to the hundreds of pursuers. And there we were in the middle of the field, when clatter, clatter along the pike came forty or fifty armed horsemen galloping in plain view down toward the gorge in the mountains. Away we went up the mountain struggling to find a hiding-place. We rushed about finding no place to be safe or hide. On the summit we came upon a sort of observatory, in the shape of an unfinished tower. A white rug was flying from a pole at the top of it. Satisfying myself that no one was about I went up the winding stairs in the building to take a view of the surrounding country. The others were too fatigued to go with me. I could see what I believed to be the outskirts of Boonesboro and enough of the valley we had crossed to give me a vivid picture of the danger we had escaped. It seemed the whole country was under arms. Descending hastily I had little difficulty in impressing upon the boys how necessary it was that we should remain in concealment. Yet we followed along the ridge at that mountain-top for as much as three miles in broad daylight without finding a safe place to halt.

Finally as we were about to sink under fatigue we came to a large fallen tree, and made our bed in the branches. Tired as I was I spent an hour or so cutting laurel branches to hide us. We were soon all fast asleep and had got through the day safely. In our night travel it was so rough that one of Cook's boots gave out. Luckily I had a needle and thread with me and I stitched up Cook's boot as well as I could, using my knife-blade for an awl. Later on Cook fell down a steep rocky place along the trail. I heard something snap when he fell, and thought it was his leg, but it was the limb of a tree which had broken with him. He was now pretty bruised; but we helped him on and he limped along with us.

We walked not only all night but into the afternoon of the next day. The woods were then so thick and extensive on the mountain-top that we thought it might be safe to travel in the day. Leaving Cook, Merriam and Coppoc in the timber I took Tidd and went to see if we could prudently cross the valley by daylight. We went about a mile and a half when we came in sight of a road with teams coming and going. Farther on we could see a farm house. While we were discussing the merits of day travel we could smell something like doughnuts cooking. What a delightful smell! It was too much for Tidd's endurance. He vowed he wouldn't go a step further without food. "You'll be all winter," he said, "and never get through after all; you'll starve and freeze to death. It is just as well to expose ourselves one way or another." He took a long breath of the distant frying. I promised Tidd that as soon as we got three nights north of Chambersburg I would steal all the chickens, milk and apples we needed.

Tidd, however, clung to the delightful, maddening odor and his determination to go and buy food. Everyone but myself agreed with Tidd, and Cook was especially anxious to be the person to go. I told them I needed food as much as any of them; and if they <u>should</u> go and get it it would be foolish of me not to help eat it. I had a large red silk handkerchief with white polka-dots on it given to me by Gerrit Smith. This with the empty shot bag that I intended to fill with salt I gave to Cook and told him if he insisted on having food bought, he would wield the glibbest tongue and tell the best story—he should indeed be the man to go.

Since I had more money than the rest I made Cook take some of my gold pieces to pay for it. But I begged him to the last <u>not to go</u>. In Cook's confession he said <u>we</u> sent him for food. That is the way it was. Cook was gone about three hours and came back with a couple of loaves of bread, some salt in the bag I gave him, some good boiled beef and a pie. He had a splendid visit, he said. He had stayed for dinner which happened to be a little late that day with some people of the town. He told them that he was part of a hunting party too far from home to get back to our dinners. The feast that day was extraordinary. The shadow of danger hanging over us did not seem to affect the others and they were exceedingly merry. After our meal we all went to sleep for an hour or so.

Before sundown out lives were again imperiled. Cook had brought with him an old fashioned single barrel pistol that belonged to General Washington and which he took from Colonel Lewis Washington at Harper's Ferry. Well Cook took this old pistol and strolled off shooting it in the air around the area. This got Tidd mad and he ordered Cook to stop. Cook said he knew what he was doing and would not take any orders from him. "I am carrying out the story of our being hunters," Cook said. The quarrel went on loudly and angrily. They were fast coming to blows and to pistol shots, when I rushed over between them, Coppoc assisting me. Merriam lay quietly on the ground. It was not easy work to separate Cook and Tidd, but we finally got them still.

In the course of that night we came to a wide creek which we had to ford. Cook's boots wouldn't come off so I offered to carry him across, if he would hold my boots and luggage. His weight, the two bundles, four guns, revolvers and ammunition, upon my bare feet on the sharp stones became unbearable. I told Cook I must drop him, and drop him I did about two-thirds of the way across. He got soaked, but kept the guns and ammunition dry.

We crossed two valleys and a mountain and got into the woods of another mountain before day-break. I was especially anxious to get as far as possible from the place where Cook had purchased the provisions. The forest was so heavy and extensive here we thought it might be safe to go on by daylight. We traveled on in what we thought was the direction of Chambersburg till the middle of the afternoon, seeing no trace of inhabitants. All day long Cook grumbled to me about his quarrel with Tidd, making threats against him. His anger seemed to increase rather than decrease. He also talked a great deal about the prospective meeting with his wife and son in Chambersburg.

We stopped at a clear spring that afternoon, and ate the last of the provisions bought the day before. Then the boys said it would be a good time to go and get a new supply. More earnestly than ever I tried to dissuade them, but to no avail. Coppoc wanted to go this time. I said since they were determined that somebody must go, Cook was the man most fitted for the mission and I gave him most of my money, and the same red silk handkerchief. He moved out with one revolver between three and four o'clock in the afternoon. I am only guessing because no one had a time-piece in the party. We also lost reckoning of the days of the week. That is my excuse if some of them are incorrect in this narrative.

Cook hadn't been gone long when two large black crows flew over our heads cawing dismally. You may think it queer, but it struck every one as a bad omen. We waited till dusk, but Cook did not return. We waited till dark and the stars came out—still no Cook. At midnight we were really worried. We scurried about, calling and watching for him until at least 2:00 AM. Cook never came.

We knew nothing of his fate till more than a week afterwards when we got hold of a newspaper at a Pennsylvania farm house and read of his capture. The story that I heard was that he came to a clearing and came upon two men chopping wood, and told his hunting party story to them, and asking where to buy food. They appeared very friendly and walked along talking to him—one on each side of him. The report said—but I did not believe it—that Cook told them who he was. At a given signal they rushed upon him and seized his arms. Poor Cook was then taken that night to the Chambersburg jail, fourteen miles away. I forgot the name of one of Cook's captors, but the other one was called Daniel Logan. They got the huge reward offered for him and drank it up in bad whiskey. They were both killed later in the rebel army.

Daring to wait no longer for Cook we made a bold push for the road. It was interesting to note that Tidd, his mortal enemy, took most of the things left behind by Cook. The rest of shared the remainder. I still have Cook's rifle belt. By the way, there hangs the coat I escaped in. Do I keep it here in this shanty as a relic? Oh, no! I wear it sometimes though. The fact is, I have always been a pack rat since that hungry trip. From that day to this, I have never seen the least morsel of any kind of food wasted without pain. I shall never get over that, I suppose.

We risked traveling for a while on the public road to see if we might in some way find Cook. It was quite a while before we reached the village of Old Forge. We walked right down the main street, seeing only a few people. A half mile or so beyond the village we struck through a corn field, helping ourselves to that dry, hard corn, to which we were again reduced. I guess I wanted to get to the outskirts of Chambersburg. I didn't approve of going there at all, you understand, but the others insisted upon it. They wanted to go to the house of Mrs. Ritner, a widow lady whose husband had been a conductor on the underground railroad as well as upon a real railroad. All of us had been at Mrs. Ritner's before Father and Kagi boarded there. Just across the corn field we came upon a wide public road evidently leading to Chambersburg. Here Coppoc and Tidd astonished Merriam and myself by announcing that they were going to leave us. They said Merriam, in his weak state, could not get into Chambersburg before daylight the next day since it was at least fifteen miles away. They knew that I had pledged myself not to abandon Merriam. So, leaving a gun or two extra for us to carry, and promising to meet us the next night at a point beyond Chambersburg, they started off as fast as they could walk.

It was a dumb thing for them to do. Weak and worn out as Merriam was, he saw as well as I did that they were endangering us as well as exposing themselves. Picking up the guns they had left we started after them in the belief that it was a walk for life, and I have no doubt it was. On and on we went unchallenged through toll-gates and past farm houses. For the whole fifteen miles Tidd and Coppoc never got over five hundred feet ahead of us. Some time before daylight Coppoc went up to a house asking the way to Chambersburg! Tidd was sitting on a fence post waiting for him as Merriam and I came up. Coppoc had not yet come out of the house when a man came riding along the road. He had a fine horse, and looked like an officer of some kind. It is strange but we felt like killing the man. We had been chased and hunted, and had lived like wild beasts so long that we felt blood thirsty. He rode out of sight before we did anything rash.

Coppoc came out and we were on our way again—in the direction we had been taking all the time. As we approached Chambersburg I told the boys that it was not fair to expose Mrs. Ritner. We finally stopped by a house on the corner of the street which led to Mrs. Ritner's place. Merriam, who had over-exerted himself, dropped down in the middle of the street and lay with his baggage for a pillow. As Tidd and Coppoc left us I begged them to come back if nobody was at home. They knocked at Mrs. Ritner's door but received no reply. Tidd threw a pebble at a second story window. Mrs. Ritner put her arm out of the window and motioned him away. Tidd said, "Mrs. Ritner don't you know me? I am Tidd."

"Leave, leave!" came back in a frightened stage whisper.

"But we are hungry."

"I couldn't help you if you were starving," she whispered back again. "Leave; the house is guarded by armed men."

It always seemed to me next to a miracle that Tidd and Coppoc were ever allowed to get away from that house. They were pretty well frightened and utterly discouraged. "What shall we do? What shall we do?" they asked in despair. "I'll tell you what to do," I said, picking up my bundle, "but you will have to follow me this time!"

After we started out I turned to look for Merriam, but he was nowhere to be seen. I went back and found him still laying in the middle of the street. I jerked him up and told him his life depended on walking a half mile or at most a mile farther to a hiding place. Poor fellow! Before we reached a thicket which I intended to hide in, the daylight became too bright for safety. A mist which lay low nearby saved the situation. We finally came to a patch of briars in the middle of the thicket and crawling into it, made our bed. We didn't even sit up to talk before retiring.

A railroad ran by one side of the field and we could distinctly see the trains pass during the day. A little before noon we heard martial music approaching us, not at all a pleasant sound under the circumstances. It stopped and ten minutes later a train went by. The martial music started up again, at what we supposed to be a railroad station. I learned later that it was the escort that took poor Cook from the jail to the depot; and the train we saw was the one which bore him away to Charlestown, and as you know, to his death. We, of course, were not aware of this at the time.

A cold rain with snow and sleet set in about 1:00 PM. It was great protection. While we were lying there we had determined that in the exhausted condition of Merriam it would be best to run the risk of sending him out on the railroad. I mended his overcoat which had been torn in our mountain travel to a state of what I called suspicious shabbiness. Being a bachelor, I had a pair of scissors with my needles and threads, so I clipped his beard as close as I could shingle it. Did you know Merriam wore a glass eye, and the eye fitted him so well that he could turn it nearly as well as he did the other one. That, and his beard gone, Merriam was pretty thoroughly disguised. We discussed Merriam's leaving more or less for the rest of the day. Coppoc wanted to go with him. I whispered myself hoarse, trying to convince him that he ought not to go. I told Coppoc he would excite suspicion if he went with Merriam. "We need you with us," I said, "and you need yourself with us,—for defense, and especially to keep warm at night. When it is safe, you shall be the next to go."

The snow and sleet stopped for a while as we were still arguing and I looked over at Coppoc; and I could see that great tears had fallen and hung quivering on his waistcoat. None of us spoke for a long time. Towards night a boy came riding on horseback into our field. He was not over ten years old. Suddenly his face brightened as he saw some lost cattle in the field. He rounded them up and departed. I do not think the boy saw us. It was my plan to keep us on a northwesterly direction, which would take us through Meadville and to some old friends in Crawford County, Pennsylvania. We thought it best to leave all of Merriam's arms behind in the briar patch except a pistol and some ammunition which he could carry on the railroad. Tidd, Coppoc and I left everything behind in the way of arms except our navy revolvers and one heavy gun apiece. Merriam would not take five dollars from me when making his preparations to part with us.

A driving snow set in that night and it was pitch black. We started for the road bordering the railway. Tidd and Coppoc bade Merriam good bye and God-speed. Leaving them at a fence-corner I took Merriam by the hand—it was so dark and he was so feeble—and led him to the railroad track. Then I walked a little way down the track with him so that he would be sure to take the direction away from Chambersburg, and reach the first station outside of that town before taking a train. So I left him on the track and found my way back to Tidd and Coppoc through the darkness and blinding snowstorm. I heard later that Merriam got away safely.

Tidd, Coppoc and I, leaving the public road, now started across the country. After a while we came to a creek swollen by the recent rains until it was about forty feet across. There was nothing to do but wade across. The water was swift and up to our hips. When I got to the other side I could not feel my bare feet on the snow, they were so numb. We went past a farm house on a road with a barn on the other side. It was so dark we were not sure of our direction, so after going about a mile we decided to return to the barn and seek shelter in defiance of the dog living there. We made our bed in a shed at the end of the barn nearest to the road. The dog quit barking. Then it stopped snowing and the stars came out. So we resumed our way in a northwest direction. We could see the mountains in the distance but we could not reach them before daylight. The snow was two or three inches deep. Just before sunrise we passed another farm house and a mile beyond that we found a brier-patch in the midst of which we spread our blankets and went to sleep.

At about noon the sun was strong enough to melt some snow and wake us up. A boy came close to us during the day and at about dusk two pigs came wandering toward us. I tried to catch one for about an hour, but gave up. We stayed in the briar-patch until dark and then we made our way toward the mountains. Along the way we came to one of those Pennsylvania barns, which we were sure was red without being able to see it. I caught an old Jersey Blue hen and a rooster and wrung their necks without allowing them to make any noise. Putting them into the provision bag I hurried on with my companions. On the mountain we came upon a gorge where we built a fire and went to dressing our hen and rooster. We ate them just about raw. Tidd, burning the bones, ate them also. It was a thickly settled country and men and teams passed not far from us all day long.

The next night as we were crossing a pleasant valley we heard voices along the road. We hastily crouched in the shadow of a fence corner, and there walked by in the bright moonlight, two pairs of young people with locked arms and hugging each other affectionately. They were evidently returning from a late country fair. That same night we surprised an apple-orchard and helped ourselves plentifully, and filled our provision bag. Not till the second or third night after eating the hen did we dare build a fire to cook the rooster. It was a pleasant spot where we roasted him; beside a spring in a little hollow surrounded by beech and hemlock trees, the mountain-top towering just above us, and bristling against the sky with pitch-pine. We had salt! Tidd, besides eating perhaps too many apples, also ate the burned bones of the rooster.

The next night I had the luck to catch four or five chickens in a barn. These of course went better, when we got a chance to cook them. That was not until we came to a little shanty in a wild place on the mountain-top. It had been built, we could see, by tannery men. We came to this shanty just before daylight in the rain. It was a mere hut of logs, covered with bark. Some stones were laid up in a corner for a fire-place. The bare earth was the floor. We knew that the tannery men worked only in the spring, and so we felt comparatively safe and happy. That is all but Tidd, who had been complaining ever since he ate so many hen and rooster bones. We built a comfortable fire in the hut, and cooked a couple of spring chickens, and ate what apples we had left. It was the first house we had been in for many a day and many a night; it seemed several weeks,—I shall not attempt to tell you how many it really was, for I should make some mistake. Coppoc and I slept splendidly as the rain poured down on our bark-roof. Waking up in the afternoon we found Tidd still complaining. Coppoc and I, wandering about the mountain saw a flock of wild turkeys, but could not get a shot at them. When we reached the hut again we found Tidd groaning and unable to go on that night. I left Coppoc to nurse him, and after dark went down the mountain for more provisions. About three miles away, I discovered an orchard, and filled my bag with apples, climbed back again, and found Tidd pretty sick. Coppoc and I did not sleep much that night, taking care of Tidd. It was almost providential that we had a roof and a fire for the poor fellow, or he might never have recovered. It rained the next day, and we stayed at the hut with Tidd, who began to feel better. Late that night he felt ready to travel, and we started out. Our course was to the northwest, and we left the mountains altogether. It took us from one range to another, instead of along the tops and sides, making our work much slower and more tedious. Still, by way of compensation we helped ourselves pretty freely to the chickens and apples of the wealthy Pennsylvanians as we passed; occasionally milking their cows for them, too. One night I got hold of a guinea-fowl, and she made an infernal noise; but we cooked her, nevertheless, in the neighboring mountains. Once an old cow would not stand to be milked, and I went after some corn to persuade her. The granary was within a few feet of the house where the people were sleeping; I could not reach the grain from the outside of the granary, and so I had the temerity to open the door and climb in, and fill my pockets with corn. The cow yielded now, and I milked her dry. One night a red fox came around our bed and barked at us, in the way foxes do, circling off and coming back six or eight times. It might have been dangerous for him if he had been good to eat; as it was, he finally disappeared unharmed.

We ventured after a while to travel on the public roads by night. This become our regular practice. I developed a terrible sick headache. I crawled up in the woods and lay down, telling the boys I couldn't go any further. I slept one or two hours, got up perfectly well, and walked on with the others. I never cured a sick headache so easily before or since. The next day we washed ourselves in a clear spring and put on clean shirts and mended our clothes. I cut both of the other fellow's hair.

I had heard that there were Quakers at a place called Bellefonte and I hoped we might be somewhere near there. Quakers, you know, were always out friends being great anti-slavery people. A man told us that Bellefonte was a good way on, but he didn't know exactly how far. We were about ten miles from the Juniata River he told us. When we got to the river we were ferried across by a woman who sold us some doughnuts and some bread and butter. There was a canal on the other side of the river. We kept on till long after dark when a canal boat overtook us. We asked the captain where he was going. He said Hamilton Falls, I think,—about seven miles away and invited us on board. The captain refused to take any money for our ride and we left him at the town (whatever its name was) before daylight and continued on towards Bellefonte.

We finally went off the road and waited for darkness. We knocked at the door of a farmer and obtained permission to stay for the night. The farmer's wife gave us a tasty dinner. The farmer in a casual sort of way mentioned Harper's Ferry and then we asked him for the day's news. We had already learned from our host that it was Friday the 4th of November. Thus we had been about three weeks in our wanderings. The farmer let us read the newspaper and Tidd started reading aloud. The first thing that caught his eye was the account of Cook's capture.

Somehow my two brothers Watson and Oliver had not been mentioned. I did not have the heart to ask about them. The 4th of November was my birthday and that was the most remarkable one of my life. After breakfast the next morning, having paid our host, we asked for directions to Bellefonte, and for the name of Quaker families along the road. We had determined the previous evening what names we would assume; mine was Edward Clark, Tidd's was Charles Plummer and Coppoc's was George Barclay. We got to a small village and Tidd went into a store to buy a pocket map. We told everybody we were wood-choppers looking for work. This was, if I am not mistaken, Saturday and at sundown we came to the private road leading to Mr. Wakefield's house. The Wakefield's were Quakers. We thought best to have Tidd go ahead to the house. He found Mr. Wakefield and his son loading wheat. Tidd asked if we could be put up for the night. "Thee and thy friends may come," said Wakefield. But when we approached with our guns he held up his hands in awe and told us we could not bring any weapons into his house. We hit upon the lucky compromise that we would take all the ammunition out of the guns. When we went inside he told us in a calm fashion that he knew we were from Harper's Ferry. We asked him how he knew that. He said we were so gaunt looking. We found the house nice but plain. His two trim daughters were the housekeepers. (The mother I think was dead.) The daughters put on a splendid supper. While they were preparing the meal we went out and helped load the wheat. After supper we had a long talk about slavery and the struggles of our family in Kansas.

Mr. Wakefield made us stay over till the next day. He told us that we should travel for a while only at night. He knew that we were being pursued. He gave us provisions to last two or three days and would take no money. He showed us the way on our pocket-map. We were to go about forty miles to a cousin of his, a Quaker living a mile from a place called Half-Moon. We parted Sunday night and traveled on two more days. Having eaten all the provisions given to us by Mr. Wakefield we took to eating apples and corn again. Late that night we approached the village indicated by Wakefield as being near his cousin's. We had the good fortune to meet a man just outside the town who showed us the way to the Quaker's place. We walked boldly through the village out to the farmhouse, and knocked very loudly on the door. The man of the house opened the door. I have forgotten this Quaker's family name, I am sorry to say. We told him that Mr. Wakefield had sent us to him, and he seemed happy to let us in. Just at that moment a window on the second floor of his house opened and three night-capped heads were thrust out. "No, you can't come in," they cried in chorus. They knew who we were; we were traitors and our lives were forfeit. We said that we had merely risked our lives for the freedom of millions of helpless slaves. They replied that they were <u>not</u> in favor of slavery but they were also not in favor of putting it down by force. And there we had it with the night-caps. We offered to pay them twice any sum they would ask. What was money to them when we were traitors and carried wicked guns, besides?

There was some commotion inside. Then the two younger voices said, "Well father, if you want to take in murderers, you may, but don't ask us to wait on them!" and the two young night-caps disappeared and the window went down. It might seem amusing to you, but it was pretty serious to us; and we stood there wondering what was to be our fate. Just then the Quaker gentleman told us we might enter, and he showed us to our rooms immediately.

At breakfast the next morning the mother and her two daughters would not eat with us, and the man would not take any money for our room and board. So we all went out into the field with him and fell to husking corn. At dinner time the women folks seemed to be somewhat mollified and we prevailed upon them to take some silver coins we had. Tidd and Coppoc went to work in the field in the afternoon and I went to the village to see about selling our guns and of sending Coppoc home by stage coach and railroad. I bought a nice carpet-bag for each of us. (I still have mine—see it there on the wall?)

I went looking for a box which we could use for storing some of our things and also all the little things once Cook's which we wanted to preserve. Returning to the Quaker's house with the box on my shoulder, I proceeded to pack it. One of the things I put in the box was the pistol formerly carried by General Washington, the one that Cook had pilfered at Harper's Ferry. By the way, Colonel Washington wrote the next year to Thaddeus Hyatt, I think, pleading for his ancestral relic. We sent it to him, asking for some things of ours, but we never heard from him. The next morning we shipped the box along with Coppoc to Salem in Columbiana County, Ohio. Coppoc very joyfully took the stage and arrived safely at his old home among the friendly Quakers.

The Quaker women were more friendly at supper time that day and got up quite a sympathy with treason before we parted. The Quaker himself still persisted in not taking any money from us. Tidd and I started on foot with our new carpet-bags the same morning on which Coppoc took the stage. We still pretended to be wood-choppers looking for work. We each kept our good navy revolver and cartridges, and we were resolved not to be taken alive—ever. Our plan was to go directly to an old friend of mine at Townville. We went by daylight, averaging twenty-five miles a day, even though it rained or snowed most of the time. At Brookville Tidd wrote a letter and I mailed it to some of his people. It was about the time that Father, in the Charlestown jail, heard of my safety, and sent me some money and that opera-glass there.

Passing through Clarion and Shippensville, Ohio we eventually came to Franklin, the present center of the coal and oil region. We stopped at a tavern on the outskirts of the town. The oil business was just beginning at the time. From Franklin we went up Sugar Creek to Randolph where we stayed a day or two with old Mr. Gilbert who helped my father build the first tannery in Richmond, Pennsylvania.

A few afternoon's later we walked to Townville and into the store of another old friend Mr. George B. Delamater. He wasn't in but his partner Mr. Orange Noble, of Erie, Pennsylvania took me aside and said he recognized me from descriptions he had seen. He whispered to me that I might feel perfectly safe. When Delamater finally came in he recognized me immediately although we had not met in twenty-five or thirty years. He took us both to his house. Under assumed names we went to work for him. After about a week Tidd was sent down to Oil Creek, where he stayed a long time. I stayed at Townville several weeks until some suspicious persons came about looking for me. I went with my brothers John and Jason to Oil Creek, and Elk Creek, and finally to Ashtabula County, Ohio. Jason had lived at Akron, Ohio.

On the 4th of July 1860, after my father's death all of our family got together at North Elba, New York. Tidd was still in the oil regions and so didn't show up. Through the efforts of Miss Kate Field, and the liberality of herself and many friends in North Elba, the farm was purchased and given to our family. That 4th of July was the last time that our family has ever been all together. John and I have been here on this Island for some years. My step-mother, with my half-brother Salmon, and three half-sisters—one of them married—lives in Rohnerville, Humboldt County, California. My brother Jason lives at Akron, Ohio and my sister Ruth, married to Henry Thompson, lives in Wisconsin.

Thus, you see Mr. Keeler there are still eight of us children. Father's was the last death in the family. As a family we would have been all long lived if we had only been allowed to live,—that is, if we hadn't been murdered in Kansas, and shot and hung in Virginia.

Chapter 16

THOSE WHO LIVED

Osborne Perry Anderson

MARY ANN SHADD was born a free woman in Wilmington, Delaware on October 9, 1823. In 1839 she organized a school for children of color. In 1851 she moved to Toronto, Canada where as a champion of racial integration she found herself at odds with Henry Bibb, who was a supporter of segregation. Bibb published a newspaper called *The Voice of the Fugitive* in which he attacked Shadd's views, with the motto, "Self Reliance is the Final Road to Independence." Shadd then founded the paper *Provencial Freeman* in which she challenged Bibb's assertion from separation. She married Thomas F. Cary of Toronto in 1856. They lived in Chatham, Canada, where Mary continued work on her *Provencial Freeman.* In 1858 John Brown had a secret convention at the home of Mary Shadd's brother Isaac, a meeting which intensified Mary's concern for the anti-slavery cause. Thomas Cary died in 1860, and Mary moved to Washington, D. C.

Early in 1861 Mary Ann Shadd published Osborne Anderson's *A Voice From Harper's Ferry.* At the time of his book's publication, Anderson, a Pennsylvania-born African American, was known as a shy and unobtrusive printer. He was also the longest-surviving black member of John Brown's original army of liberation. Anderson had escaped with a white comrade, Albert Hazlett, who was also a native Pennsylvanian. They separated in Pennsylvania, and Hazlett was captured and returned to Virginia, where he was tried and hanged a few months after John Brown. Anderson was aided in his passage through Pennsylvania at the Underground Railroad station in Chambersburg, by Henry Watson; in York by William Goodridge, who owned a photography studio; and in Philadelphia by William Still. He made good his escape.

Anderson had been outraged at the coverup of the support of local slaves for John Brown. All the other members of Brown's original army were killed or captured. The Civil War had not yet begun, and the lives of those who helped were in great danger. He was in the position of trying to set the record straight without saying too much, so that local people, both free and enslaved Africans, would not be personally identified. He attended the first memorial to John Brown at the farm in North Elba on July 4th, 1860, and was recognized by Annie Brown, who had been with her father at the Kennedy Farm in Maryland in the summer of 1859.

Anderson continued his militant commitment to end slavery by recruiting slaves for the United States Colored Troops in Indiana and Arkansas, in association with the Shadd family. Mary Ann Shadd was commissioned by Martin R. Delany, and then by the governor of Indiana, to be an active war recruiter. Some references have stated that Osborne Anderson served as a non-commissioned officer, but the actual regimental records were never found to substantiate the claim. He may have served under a pseudonym, as did Charles Tidd, a member of Brown's army who escaped from Maryland with four other white raiders who were moving captured arms.

After the Civil War, Anderson moved to Michigan and participated in a black convention as a delegate from Battle Creek in 1866. He became associated with another recruiter of slave troops, A. M. Green, and lived with him in Philadelphia, and then in Washington D. C. Osborne Anderson visited Harper's Ferry in 1871 and pointed out the scenes of battle to Richard Hinton, another of Brown's active army who had been stationed by Brown just outside the area of the fighting during the raid, in the crossroads town of Hagerstown, Maryland.

Anderson died in Washington D. C. at a friend's house on the morning of December 11, 1872, at the age of forty-two. His funeral was at the 15th Street Presbyterian Church and his pallbearers were active leaders of both the Civil War and Reconstruction period. The most well known pallbearers were the Honorable Josiah Walls, a member of Congress, and Lewis H. Douglass, who served in the 54th Massachusetts Infantry and edited the *New National Era*. Other pallbearers included two members of the Purvis family of Pennsylvania, early staunch abolitionists; and George T. Downing, a friend. The eulogy address at the memorial service on December 19, 1872 was made by D. A. Straker, who asked that Anderson be "remembered to the latest generations." He was buried in the Columbian Harmony Memorial Park Cemetery on Rhode Island Avenue.

There is no memorial at Harper's Ferry to Osborne Perry Anderson. Instead, there is one to Hayward Shephard, the black railroad worker killed by John Brown's men, an "industrious and respected colored freeman" who "in pursuance of his duties as an employee of the Baltimore and Ohio Railroad became the first victim of this attempted insurrection," the plaque said. It was erected in 1931 by the United daughters of the Confederacy. When it was later deemed too controversial by National Park officials the Shephard memorial was covered up. The plywood sheathing was removed in 1995, but not without protest, and a new interpretive plaque was added.

Mary Shadd Cary went back to school and studied law, but she continued to write and support women's rights. She became the first black female lawyer in the United States when she graduated in 1870. She died in Washington D. C. of stomach cancer on June 5, 1893, and was also buried at the Harmony Memorial Park Cemetery. [1]

---

[1]   This cemetery was moved in 1959 from the Rhode Island Avenue location to Landover, Maryland.

MARY SHADD CARY

Owen Brown

Owen Brown was the last living white survivor of the John Brown raid. He was one of the seven who escaped from Harper's Ferry through the mountains, swamps and forests. He finally reached his brother John's home at Put-in-Bay, Ohio. Owen remained there until the early1880's harvesting grapes, teaching mathematics and science to the islanders and doing some surveying. Owen lived in a small cabin on his brother's land, and spent the winter months on nearby Gibralter Island serving as a caretaker to Jay Cook's summer home.

In 1884 Jason and Owen Brown took a homestead on a bench of mountain land five or six miles north of Pasadena, California, at a settlement now called Las Casitas. This they subsequently sold. They then took land higher up the mountainside, built a cabin, cleared and worked a few acres, and lived there—two feeble old men, and quite alone. (Jason had been with his father in the Kansas struggle, but not at Harpers Ferry.)

They were visited by tourists and citizens, some out of mere curiosity but others from a warm sympathy with the historic career of the family.

Jason and Owen made a good passable wagon trail up to their mountain hermitage, and were planning to continue it as a donkey path to the top of the mountain known as Brown's Peak, but it was never completed. On December 30, 1888 the aged brothers came down to Pasadena to attend Colonel Woodford's two day gospel temperance meeting in the tabernacle. Owen Brown was taken sick and had a chill after going to his sister Ruth's home after the meeting, and in a week he died of typhoid pneumonia. He had been failing for some months, and this had been noticed by his relatives and friends. He walked over two miles to his sister's house, after the meeting. These over-exertions were probably the immediate cause of his pneumonia.

At the women's meeting on Tuesday, January 1st, he and Jason were elected honorary members of the Women's Christian Temperance Union. He was much pleased with this, and said there was no cause he would more gladly contribute his $1.00 membership fee to aid. He was later buried with the W. C. T. U. white ribbon on his breast. The last words he uttered that could be distinguished were: "It is better-to be-in a place-and suffer wrong-than to do wrong."

Owen died in Pasadena on January 8, 1889, at the residence of his brother-in-law Henry Thompson. The last rites were paid to his mortal remains on Thursday, January 10th, 1889. It was a historic day in Pasadena. The tabernacle was well filled, with about 2000 people in attendance. The exercises were conducted by the Reverend R. H. Hartley, pastor of the Friends Church. The choir was filled with singers who sang appropriate hymns with fervor and pathos as if the very spirit of the Browns had woven itself into heavenly music.

Prayer was offered by the Reverend Dr. Bresee, which went to the heart of the historic occasion and was an uplift of soul in all noble aspirations. Remarks were made by Reverend Mr. Hartley; also by Reverend D. D. Hill, pastor of the Congregational church; Reverend E. L. Conger, pastor of the Universalist church; Colonel George Woodford, the gospel temperance evangelist; and by H. N. Rust, a life-long friend and neighbor of John Brown and his family in East Hampton, Massachusetts. The city trustees, who were all old-time Republicans, attended in a body and took seats on the platform, as a token of respect for the memory of John Brown and his sons.

The students of the Pasadena Academy attended in a body. Members of the Grand Army of the Republic and Sons of Veterans who could leave their business places also attended the funeral. At the conclusion of the services the casket was removed to the corridor and the face cover removed. Then the vast audience passed in columns by each aisle on each side of the bier and all had an opportunity to view the face of Owen Brown. It appeared perfectly natural—a little paler than in life and looked as though he was only taking a nap. The bier was covered with floral emblems and tokens of love: A cross, a wreath, and bouquets composed of calla lilies, roses, violets, marguentes, sweet elysium, geraniums, smilax and feather palms.

Relatives present at the funeral included Jason Brown, brother of the deceased, and Ruth Brown Thompson, sister of the deceased, with her husband, Henry Thompson, and their youngest daughter, Maimie. Mr. Thompson had been one of John Brown's soldiers in Kansas. Also present were Mrs. Grace Simmons, daughter of Mr. and Mrs. Thompson, with her husband and son, who resided at Las Casitas, and Mrs. Town, another daughter, with her husband and son, who also resided at Las Casitas. Mrs. Hand came from Wellington, Ohio. She was a sister of John Brown, and an aunt to the deceased, now visiting her daughter, the former Mrs. Hood of Pasadena. Mrs. Hopson, cousin of the deceased, came down from Sacramento, and Mrs. Quinn, a cousin from Saratoga Springs, N. Y. arrived at the last moment. Owen Brown had wanted to be buried at the top of Brown's Peak, but because the donkey trail was incomplete he was buried on the mountain homestead instead.[2]

---

[2]   Chester, T., "Where Is the Grave of Owen Brown?" Internet accessed on 2 April 2006, http://tchester.org/sgm/lists/faq.html#brown.

It is quite remarkable that there should have been found so many men who were associated with John Brown in Pasadena, California. In charge of the pall bearers was Mr. H. N. Rust, President of the Pasadena Library Association. Among the other pall-bearers, James Townsend of Spring Dale, Cedar County, Iowa, who was John Brown's intimate and confidential friend, was most prominent. John Brown had taken his last meal at Townsend's house before starting from West Liberty, Iowa, to Chicago with his men and twelve escaped slaves. At that time John Brown, who had a $2,000 reward offered for him dead or alive, took a group of slaves in a railroad train to the cities of Davenport, La Salle, Joliet, Chicago and finally on to freedom in Canada. From there he moved on to his final operations at Harper's Ferry, Virginia.

In 2002, 113 years after Owen Brown was buried on that Altadena hilltop, the headstone marking his grave and the concrete block that held it in place disappeared. The Altadena residents who often visited his grave, which was along a popular hiking trail were baffled. Local conservationists were enraged. The landowner, long battling residents about trespassing on his property, said he was extremely upset over the whole situation.

Barclay Coppoc

F. C. Galbreath reported the details of Barclay Coppoc's escape. He stated that Barclay Coppoc proceeded with dispatch to Salem, Ohio on November 24, 1859 by railroad where the box of arms had been shipped. Here he remained for a short time with relatives and friends to rest and regain strength. From Ohio Barclay went to Canada and then down to Niagara Falls. He then went east as far as Rochester, New York. Feeling blue he went to his home in Springdale, Iowa via Buffalo arriving on the 17th of December, the day after his brother died on a Virginia scaffold. He met a most warm and tearful welcome from several hundred persons who were anxiously awaiting his arrival.

William McCormick of Muscatine, Iowa wrote to Governor Wise of Virginia on December 23rd apprizing him that Barclay Coppoc "is with his mother in Springdale and was in Muscatine yesterday. I do not see why he could not be arrested without much trouble. He is in the country away from any town of any note, but am told that he has many friends among his neighbors."

Coppoc's mother, in a letter to James Whinnery of Salem, Ohio dated "Springdale, Iowa, 1st Mo., 22nd day, 1860," wrote, "Barclay is at home and seems determined to stay, although there are reports almost continually of somebody being in search of him. He says he has hurt nobody, and will not *run* nor will he be taken . . . I think Barclay's friends will take care of him, as they are both numerous and resolute."

How his friends had prepared to "take care of him" is indicated in the following letter, written by a neighbor who, like Mrs. Coppoc and her family, had earlier left Columbiana County, Ohio, and gone to Iowa. It is interesting because it shows that the village of Springdale and the surrounding countryside were thoroughly aroused, and that the non-resistance creed of the Quakers who lived there was gradually giving way under the stress of the times. It is a singular combination of the "plain language," guts and the assurance that Springdale "was right on the goose:"

Springdale, Cedar County, Iowa, Feb. 12, 1860.

SIRS: The object of thy anxious inquiry (Barclay Coppoc) has not been taken from Springdale, nor is it intended that he shall be taken. Springdale is in arms and is prepared, at a half-hour's notice, to give *them* a reception of 200 shots; and it will be necessary for the marshal to find him before he can be taken. There is a well-organized body here. They meet two or three evenings each week to lay their plans and take the necessary steps to have them carried out in case of necessity. There are three of their number who always know of his whereabouts, and nobody else knows anything of him. He is never seen at night, where he was during the day, and there are men on the watch at Davenport, Muscatine, Iowa City, Liberty, Tipton, and all around, and the first sign of an arrest in any quarter a messenger will be dispatched to Springdale, and larger companies than the Virginians can raise will follow immediately after them. Muscatine has offered to send 400 men at the very shortest notice. But it is intended to baffle *them* in every possible way without bloodshed if possible. The marshal was at Des Moines City two weeks ago for a requisition, and the governor refused to grant it on account of informality; then swore they would take him by mob. The citizens dispatched a messenger immediately to this place. He rode four horses down on the way, and came through in two nights and a day, it being 165 miles. We understand that the marshal has gone the second time to Des Moines for his requisition, and his return is looked for daily. But I have no doubt he will be baffled in some way, and be assured Springdale is right on the goose.

F. C. GALBREATH

Just as Governor Willard of Indiana was personally involved in the Harper's Ferry raid through his brother-in-law John E. Cook, Governor Samuel J. Kirkwood of Iowa [3] was officially drawn into the aftermath of that event by the return of Barclay Coppoc to his home in Springdale.

In his inaugural address of January 11, 1860, Governor Kirkwood devoted considerable attention to John Brown's invasion of Virginia. Like many other men in office at the time, he expressed strong disapproval of the Brown movement, and like others of his political faith he made it pretty clearly known that he considered this a result of the unfair treatment that the free state men had been accorded for years in the territory of Kansas. This sentence in his inaugural address stirred up his political foes to active and open hostility:

---

[3]   Later United States Senator and Secretary of the Interior.

While the great mass of our northern people utterly condemn the act of John Brown, they feel and express admiration and sympathy for the disinterestedness of purpose by which they believe he was governed and for the unflinching courage and calm cheerfulness with which he met the consequences of his failure.

This expression precipitated a storm in the Iowa legislature. The governor was severely criticized by his political opponents in that body and they finally went on record in a scathing protest. Here matters rested for a time until January 23, 1860, when Mr. Camp, an agent sent by Governor Letcher of Virginia who had succeeded Governor Wise, appeared in Des Moines and presented to Governor Kirkwood a requisition for the arrest and surrender of Barclay Coppoc. Two members of the Iowa legislature, Edward Wright and B. F. Gue, both abolitionists, entered the governor's office while the interview between Camp and Governor Kirkwood was in progress. This is what happened, as subsequently reported by Mr. Gue:[4]

We found in conference with the governor a pompous-looking man, who seemed to be greatly excited. Governor Kirkwood was calmly listening to the violent language of this individual, who was swinging his arms wildly in his wrath. The governor quietly suggested to the stranger, that "he had supposed that he did not want his business made public."

The rude reply was: "I don't care a damn who knows it now, since you have refused to honor the requisition."

The pompous man then proceeded to argue the case with the governor, and we soon learned that he was an agent from Virginia bearing a requisition from Governor Letcher for the surrender of Barclay Coppoc.

---

[4]   "History of Iowa," B. F. Gue, Vol. II, p 20.

In reply to a remark by the agent that Coppoc might escape before he could get the defect in the requisition cured, the governor, looking significantly at us, replied, "There is a law under which you can arrest Coppoc and hold him until the requisition is granted," and the governor reached for the code. We waited to hear no more, but, saying to the governor that we would call again when he was not engaged and giving him a look that was in response to his own, we walked out.

Promptly afterward a conference was held with other anti-slavery members of the legislature and a messenger was sent posthaste on horseback to distant Springdale to warn Coppoc and his friends. The messenger bore a note advising that the governor would probably be compelled to issue the requisition. The messenger arrived in due time and the friends of Coppoc prepared to give the Virginia agent a warm reception if he should appear.

In the meantime Governor Kirkwood's keen and sympathetic eye had detected certain material flaws in the requisition papers and he refused to order Barclay Coppoc's arrest for the following reasons:

First—No indictment had been found against him.

Second—The affidavit was made before an alleged notary public, but was not authenticated by a notary's seal.

Third—The affidavit did not show that Coppoc was in Virginia aiding and abetting John Brown.

Fourth—It did not legally charge him with commission of any crime.
When this action of the governor became publicly known, the legislature was again thrown into commotion and the following resolutions were offered by a partisan opponent:

> *Whereas,* A requisition was made on the governor of Iowa by the governor of Virginia for Barclay Coppoc, an

alleged participant in the difficulties at Harper's Ferry, Virginia, as a fugitive from justice, and

Whereas, The governor of Iowa has refused to deliver up said Coppoc under said requisition, alleging technical defects therein, therefore be it

Resolved, That the governor of Iowa be requested to lay before the House a copy of the requisition directed to him by the governor of Virginia, and all matters connected therewith; also to inform this House whether he possessed any knowledge in regard to a rumor that a special messenger was dispatched to inform Coppoc of his danger; and if so, by what authority said messenger was dispatched to inform Coppoc of his danger.

The governor very promptly laid before the House of Representatives a ringing defense of his action. After criticizing the conduct of the agent from Virginia and denying that he had sent any word whatever to Barclay Coppoc or his friends, he said:

Permit me to say in conclusion that one of the most important duties of the official position I hold is to see that no citizen of Iowa is carried beyond her border and subjected to the ignominy of imprisonment and the perils of trial for crimes in another state otherwise than by due process of law. That duty I shall perform.

If Governor Packer of Pennsylvania had been as deliberate in his action before surrendering Hazlett and Cook to Virginia, it is probable that neither of them would have ended their career on the gallows.

In this connection it is interesting to recall the attitude of Governor Dennison of Ohio. He promptly referred the requisition for Owen Brown and Merriam to the attorney general of Ohio who very soon found a number of defects that were ample excuse for the governor not to authorize the arrest of either of these men.

Finally, a second requisition from Virginia, which avoided the defects that Governor Kirkwood had pointed out in the first one was presented at Des Moines and a warrant was issued for the arrest of Barclay Coppoc. Coppoc, however, could not be found. His friends had been promptly notified and, along with Thaddeus Maxson, he was conveyed with an armed guard to Mechanicsville. Later the two men proceeded by rail to Chicago and on to Detroit. It was stated that they crossed over to Canada. If they did so they remained a very short time, for they soon went to Ohio where Barclay was in hiding with friends near Salem and later joined Owen Brown and F. J. Merriam at the home of John Brown, Jr., in Dorset, Ashtabula County, Ohio.

Throughout all this time a reward was offered for the capture of Coppoc, and he was in continual danger of arrest. It is not likely that Governor Dennison would have been instrumental in this if he could have consistently avoided it, but he feared that the United States authorities might at any time seize any of the members of the John Brown party that had escaped from the Ferry. It was therefore important that these men and their friends should be constantly on guard. It was at this time that Barclay Coppoc and Thaddeus Maxson visited the home of Daniel Bonsall, a prominent anti-slavery activist living near Salem. Charles Bonsall, who was living at the age of eighty-two, gave his reminiscences of the visit of these two men as follows:

> In the spring of 1860, sometime in April, as I remember, Barclay Coppoc and Thaddeus Maxson came to the neighborhood of Winona and remained for some time. They spent the time with well-known abolitionists. I distinctly recall their visit to the home of my father, Daniel Bonsall. When they first called, my father was away from home and I met the two men. As soon as they knew who I was and that they were safe they made known

their identity. I suspected this before they spoke. Barclay Coppoc, after his escape from Harpers Ferry, had returned to Springdale, Iowa. From that place he had come back with Maxson to his native neighborhood south of Salem to organize secret leagues to oppose the Fugitive Slave law. The principles of this league had been formulated by Parker Pillsbury and printed along with the constitution in pamphlet form.

The name of this organization was the Order of the League of Freedom. It was founded in Ashtabula County and it was the purpose of its members to extend it to other states. Through the kindly interest of Mr. and Mrs. T. B. Alexander, a copy of this document, which was secretly printed, is now in the possession of the Ohio State Archaeological and Historical Society. The preliminary declaration is as follows:

Whereas, Our fathers founded this federal government upon the "self-evident" truth that all men are endowed by their Creator with equal and irrepressible rights to enjoy *life, liberty,* and the pursuit of happiness; and by the constitution provided, that no person shall be deprived of *life, liberty*, or property, without due process of law; and we, believing that the African and all other races of men are included in these provisions; and

Whereas, We believe slave-holding in the United States is the source of numberless evils, moral, social and political; that it hinders social progress; that it embitters public and private intercourse; that it degrades us as individuals, as states, and as a nation; that it holds back our country from a splendid career of greatness and glory, and is in direct violation of the principles laid down in the Declaration of our National Independence.

We are, therefore, resolutely, inflexibly, at all times, and under all circumstances, hostile to its longer continuance in our land.

It soon became known to many people of Salem that Barclay Coppoc was in the neighborhood. A citizen of Salem, who was something of a private detective, declared that he would get the reward offered for the arrest of Coppoc and that in a short time he would be returned to the Virginia authorities. When Barclay Coppoc heard what this would-be detective proposed to do, he sent to him substantially this message:

> I understand that you propose to arrest me and turn me over to the Virginia authorities. I will not go to Salem to afford you the opportunity to make this arrest but if you wish to get me you can find me where I am at almost any time. I suggest that you get at least five men to aid you and I assure you that they will have plenty to do before they succeed in capturing me.

Mr. Charles Bonsall, a Civil War veteran who served in the Third Kansas Regiment, said that it was well known that friends in the neighborhood would stand by Coppoc and no one had the courage to attempt to arrest him. He also recalled Coppoc's excellent marksmanship: "A gray squirrel ran up a tree at some distance away and was passing to another tree. Coppoc drew his revolver and fired, apparently while the squirrel was still moving. At the first shot it fell to the ground!"

It was while Barclay Coppoc was with friends near Salem that he went to see a panorama of the Harper's Ferry raid presented in that town. Mrs. Mary Lease, of Salem, Ohio, eldest daughter of Dr. J. C. Whinnery, thus recalled Barclay Coppoc's presence at this exhibition:

> When Barclay Coppoc returned to Salem, after his return from Harper's Ferry and Canada, he was kept secreted and constantly guarded. During this period a traveling company with a panorama of Harper's Ferry, the

arsenal, the scaffold, and the route that Barclay traveled to
Iowa, came to Salem. Barclay insisted on seeing it, despite
all pleadings and dissuasions, notwithstanding that there
was a reward of $1,000 offered for his head, and the fact
that some of the people were watching for him. So he
went, disguised and surrounded by his friends, the whole
party well armed. It was agreed that no one of the party
should speak a word, in the building; but that Barclay
should indicate his approval of what was correctly shown
by slightly inclining his head. But he became so absorbed
as to forget all precautions and when a scene came on that
displeased him he raised his hand in a violent gesture and
I caught and held it just in time to prevent his betraying
himself.

On July 4, 1860, a number of the followers of John Brown, including
Barclay Coppoc, were said to have been at the home of John Brown, Jr.,
in Ashtabula County. Later that year Coppoc returned to Kansas, and
with a few other men went into Missouri, where they liberated and ran
off a number of slaves. Later he very nearly lost his life in a trap set by a
man under the assumed name of Charley Hart, who pretended to favor
the Free State cause and the freedom of the Negroes. This man persuaded
Coppoc and some of his associates to make another raid into Missouri to
help some Jackson County slaves to freedom. They were ambushed and
Coppoc almost lost his life. Two of his party were killed, the others escaped.
The "Charley Hart" who planned the capture of the party was himself
an Ohio man, who afterwards was known as the infamous Confederate
guerrilla, "Quantrill," whose name became a terror on the western border
early in the Civil War.

The election of Abraham Lincoln in 1860 and the threat of Civil War
radically changed the status of Barclay Coppoc. There was now no longer
serious thought of hunting down the remnants of the John Brown band.
Barclay returned to his old home in Springdale and once more settled
down quietly to farm work.

The year 1861 marked the marshaling of arms and the beginning of the Civil War. It is scarcely necessary to say that with his past record, his adventurous spirit and his hostility to slavery Barclay Coppoc could not long remain inactive in the quiet village of Springdale. He was no longer a fugitive from justice. The part that he had taken at Harper's Ferry had ceased to make him an object of aversion to all except his closest friends. Occasionally he was pointed out to strangers as one of John Brown's men who had escaped from the foray into Virginia. His part in that event was gradually making him an object of distinction rather than reproach. Possibly, as he thought over the past, he recalled the words of his brother Edwin in a letter to his uncle Joshua:

> The time may come when he will remember me and the time may come when he will still further remember the cause in which I die. Thank God, the principles of the cause in which we were engaged will not die with me and my brave comrades. They will spread wider and wider, and gather strength with each hour that passes. The voice of truth will echo through our land, bringing conviction to the erring, and adding numbers to that glorious army who will follow its banner.

The army was now forming under the flag of the Republic and a call was sent out for volunteers. Barclay Coppoc responded and on the 24th day of July, 1861, he was commissioned First Lieutenant in Company C, Third Regiment, Kansas Volunteer Infantry, and was mustered into service six days later. And now in a uniform of blue he was given the job of recruitment. As the days passed, in spite of his modest demeanor and reticence, he was more and more an object of interest to his comrades because of the dangers that he faced at Harper's Ferry and in the long flight through Pennsylvania and Ohio. What distinction might not come to him in the great conflict between the North and the South?

Coppoc was sent to Iowa to recruit young men of Cedar County who desired to serve in a Kansas regiment. On his return to Kansas he took the Hannibal and St. Joseph Railroad east from St. Joseph, Missouri on September 3, 1861. The Confederates had been waging active guerrilla warfare in Missouri. They had blown up culverts and committed other bold assaults in the northwestern part of the state under the cover of night. The train on which Coppoc was a passenger had been delayed. All danger was thought behind them and he was confidently expecting to reach his destination. Suddenly the train plunged through a burning bridge into the Platte River of Missouri, and the darkness was rent with the shrieks of the wounded and dying. The Confederate guerrillas had set the bridge on fire and, without a word of warning, the train, crowded with passengers, plunged a distance of forty feet into the river. About twenty-five passengers were killed. Among those fatally injured was Lieutenant Barclay Coppoc. One of the survivors of the wreck, Mr. W. R. Ramsey, of the Government Printing Office in Washington, would write about the tragedy in 1899:

> Of the ninety or more passengers on board (men, women, children and soldiers) very few escaped uninjured and many (about twenty-five) were killed, among the latter being Lieutenant Coppoc. I saw him at the St. Joe Hotel the day after the accident, and how he survived twenty-four hours with the frightful wound in his head was a miracle, as very few men could have withstood the shock.

The Daily *Conservative* of Leavenworth, Kansas provided a full account of the disaster at the Platte River bridge in its issue of Thursday, September 5, 1861. The article described how the train plunged into the river at about eleven o'clock at night. The heavens were clouded and a heavy darkness overhung the scene of the tragedy. A few of the passengers escaped uninjured and these made heroic efforts to save the others. Some went to St. Joseph, nine miles distant, and others to Easton to bring aid. It was 4:00 AM the next morning before a relief train arrived.

The *Conservative* of Friday, September 6th contained an account of the funeral as follows:

The burial of Barclay Coppoc and Carl Fording, two of the victims of the unparalleled atrocity of last Tuesday night, took place yesterday at the Mansion House.

Coppoc, recently from Iowa, was a young man of noble soul and undaunted courage, and held the position of lieutenant in the company of Captain Allen, in Colonel James Montgomery's regiment. Barclay Coppoc was with John Brown in the raid on Virginia; his brother Edwin was captured and hung but Barclay escaped. He fled in company with Captain Cook and succeeded in eluding pursuit when his companion was taken. There was nothing of the bravado about him. Religiously anti-slavery, he endeavored solely to do what he considered his duty. Carl Fording was a young man who was coming with him from Ohio to join the same company.

The Home Guards, Fencibles, and the Old Guard led the procession while a large concourse of our most influential citizens followed the hearses containing the remains to the cemetery on Pilot Knob. The companies of Captain Swoyer and Jenkins were with the procession part of the distance. At the graves Reverend Mr. Paddock delivered an earnest, soul-stirring prayer, and a about 5:00 PM the remains were committed to the ground. A military salute was then fired over the graves.

Francis Jackson Merriam

Francis Jackson Merriam was not in the attacking party at Harper's Ferry, but had remained to guard the arms with Cook, Tidd, Barclay Coppoc, Anderson and Owen Brown at the school-house on the Maryland side.

After escaping from Harper's Ferry, Merriam worked his way through the South Mountain and reached Philadelphia. He then went to the Merchant's Hotel where he registered using his true name. From there he went to Chatham, Canada. He was there at the time of the executions of December 2nd and 16th. He returned to Boston and was there at the time of Stevens' and Hazlett's executions on March 16, 1860. He had visits from Wendell Phillips, Mr. Sanborn and his Uncle James Jackson. He went to North Elba for the reunion on the 4th of July.

Merriam then visited Hayti in the interest of a revolutionary movement which embodied an uprising of slaves. He was full of plans for a new "invasion" and would not at first return to Canada where he would be safe. But he was finally talked into it, and went to the Fitchburg Railroad station to take the night express train for Montreal. But in his distraught state of mind he took the wrong train and ended up early in the evening at Concord, Maine. He had to pass the night there. He had the presence of mind to remember that Franklin Sanborn lived in Concord, and he went to Sanvorn's house, where he was welcomed and sheltered for the night. Sanborn insisted on calling him "Lockwood" out of regard for his safety. The next morning he was driven in a friend's carriage by Henry Thoreau to the neighboring railroad station of South Acton where he took the first train for Montreal, and returned to Chatham. Mr. Thoreau only knew him as Lockwood, and though suspecting him to be one of the Harper's Ferry fugitives, was cautious not to mention that trip to anyone.

After the Civil War broke out Merriam wrote on January 31, 1861, dating it "Third month of the Crisis," that:

> I hail with exultation the emancipation of six million Southern whites—and I care not for the abnormal manner they use their newly acquired liberty.

> They seized power to rivet the chains of their black felons,—they have freed themselves and will soon accomplish the freedom of the remaining four million.

> While others see only anarchy and the ruin of our
> country, I see permanent peace, founded on justice,
> through a veil of then, though dark, war clouds.

Early in the Civil War Merriam met and married Minerva Caldwell of Galena, Illinois. She was the daughter of a prominent physician, and also became a doctor of note. Merriam fought with the Union army in a number of campaigns. David Thayer, another medical doctor, wrote to author Robert J. Hinton with the information that Merriam was killed in the Battle of Fredericksburg in 1862.

"I went down," Thayer said, "to Washington to claim his body." In his search through all the hospitals of the District of Columbia he saw thousands of wounded and dying soldiers. As Thayer was searching in one particular field hospital he heard someone call out, "Dr. Thayer, is that you?" Thayer replied, "Who is it?" and went in the direction of the voice. Someone said, "It's me—Francis!" Thayer looked and found it was Merriam. "God, it's great to see you, but Francis, this is all wrong." Merriam replied, "My friends in Chicago know where I am, but I could not keep out of it."

Merriam went to the South Carolina Sea Islands in 1863 to recruit colored soldiers for the Union cause as a captain in the Third South Carolina Colored Infantry. Early in the summer of 1864 Congress approved a law allowing each state to recruit Southern Negroes and to deduct the number enlisted from the state's draft quota. Merriam died in New York City on November 28, 1865, from wounds he had incurred in battle. No obituary appeared in the New York newspapers, and his exact burial location was not reported.

Charles Plummer Tidd

Charles Plummer Tidd, usually known as Charles Plummer, had been a captain in Brown's army. He emigrated to Kansas with the party of Dr. Calvin Cutter of Worcester in 1856. After the insurrection he made a trip to Canada and Ohio under the name of Charles Plummer. He lived for a while at Edinboro in Erie County, Pennsylvania, where he got interested in the oil business.

In the summer of 1860, Tidd settled in Massachusetts and renewed his friendship with the family of Doctor Calvin Cutter. Dr. Cutter was already quite famous. In 1847 he began his compilation of "Cutter's Physiology," a textbook for schools and colleges, which sold about a half million copies. He was an early abolitionist and in 1856 he was selected by the Massachusetts Emigrant Aid Company to supply Sharp's rifles to the Free State men of Kansas. Later that year Cutter led the "Jim Lane Army" to Kansas, commanding that group for about a year before becoming surgeon of the Twenty-First Massachusetts Infantry.

Tidd entered the army on July 19, 1861 as Charles Plummer in Company "K" of the 21st Regiment of the Massachusetts Volunteer Infantry, influenced by the fact that Dr. Cutter was the chief surgeon of the regiment. He was soon made an orderly sergeant, and it wasn't long before Dr. Cutter became Charles Tidd's father figure.

At the end of January 1862 Tidd shipped on the steamer *Northerner* as part of the Burnside expedition to North Carolina. Tidd was selected to command a band of sixty scouts organized by Colonel Maggi. They were to scout the hostile country. Dr. Cutter's daughter also sailed with her father on the Burnside expedition to North Carolina, as a nurse. She was probably the first female to enter her country's service in the Civil War. On February 7, 1862, shortly before they landed, Tidd was prostrated with enteritis. He decided he wouldn't stay behind because his old nemesis Henry A. Wise was the general in charge of the Confederates. He was forced to remain in bed when the regiment entered the boats, and died of his illness just before landing on February 8, 1862. Carrie E. Cutter was present to close his dying eyes. Ex-Governor Wise lost his son, Owen Jennings Wise, in the same battle. Charles Plummer Tidd was unceremoniously buried on Roanoke Island, North Carolina. Doctor Calvin Cutter died on March 25, 1872.

It is interesting to note that Carrie E. Cutter became the only woman to be buried in the National Cemetery at Newbern. Learning that her betrothed, Charles E. Colledge, a private in the Twenty-fifth Massachusetts, had been stricken with typhoid fever, Cutter went to Newbern Harbor to nurse him. He died, and she, heartbroken, fell an easy prey to the same disease. She was just nineteen years and eight months old. Her last wish was that her remains could rest forever beside the man she loved and admired so well. Special permission was granted by Congress, and their graves are located side by side in section 10 of the National Cemetery. His remains are buried in grave number 1697 and hers in grave 1698.

Chapter 17

HARPER'S FERRY REDUX

IN 1904 MR. Joseph Barry, a resident of Harper's Ferry, was invited
to speak about the future of Harper's Ferry after the insurrection
and to speak about the affairs of the residents who were involved in that
fateful event back in October, 1859. Mr. Barry recalled:

You will remember that John Brown picked out ten of the most
prominent of his prisoners as hostages and retreated into a brick building
near the armory gate, called the engine house. This little building was
afterwards famous under the name of "John Brown's Fort," and, from
the time of the invasion until the spring of 1892, it was an object of
great curiosity to strangers visiting the place. It was sold in 1892 to a
company of speculators headed by Adoniram J. Holmes of Boone, Iowa
for exhibition at the World's Fair in Chicago, and with it much of the
glory of Harper's Ferry departed forever.

The building was taken apart with the utmost care, the pieces numbered
and the various parts were boxed separately, and shipped to Chicago. It
was re-erected outside the exposition grounds, and was opened to public
view in September 1892. The exposition came to an end in 1893. The
venture was not a financial success and the historic building passed from
the sheriff's hands into those of wreckers, and it was again taken down to
make way for a department store.

Back in Washington Miss Kate Field, a noted journalist, worked out
a plan for returning the engine house to Harper's Ferry. Miss Field had
been interested in John Brown for many years and in fact in 1875 she

raised funds to purchase the John Brown's farm at North Elba. After a few visits to Harper's Ferry to look for a site for the engine house she secured permission of the owners to take possession of the pile of bricks and timbers without cost to her. Now the problem was to secure funds to carry out the rest of her plan.

Miss Field raised the remaining dollars she needed in 1895 from Mr. McAvoy, who owned one of Chicago's largest breweries. She also obtained seven acres of farm land from Alexander Murphy on Bolivar Heights, about two miles from its original site. She was given free transportation by the Baltimore and Ohio Railroad for all materials sent from Chicago to Harper's Ferry, and free passes for all persons connected with the work of restoring the John Brown Fort.

The next problem involved finding someone to supervise the job. A Mr. Edward Cummins was selected and departed to Harper's Ferry to begin work. Miss Field went to Hawaii in September 1895 and entrusted to her friend and Attorney Robert McCabe the completion of the work she had begun, and made him sole custodian of the remaining funds. While in Hawaii Miss Field received letters of disapproval of what was going on back at Harper's Ferry. She sent an urgent message to Mr. McCabe to go at once to the Ferry and see what it was all about. Upon his arrival there Mr. McCabe immediately consulted the station agent Mr. E. B. Chambers who told him that the problem rested with the contractor who had come from Chicago to do the job. Chambers said, "Cummins has outraged the community and called our people rebels. He is abusive, lazy and good for nothing. He has never paid his workers, and all he does is spend all his time fishing. This man must be removed."

Mr. McCabe went to see Mr. Cummins. He proved to be obstinate and insisted he would do the job his way. McCabe went back to Mr. Chambers and reported his inability to reason with the man. "Suppose," said Chambers, "I throw Cummins into the Potomac. I won't hurt him, but I think he will be ready to leave." The plan was agreed upon. Later, about midnight, Mr. McCabe was awakened at his hotel and was told that a woman insisted on seeing him immediately. It was Mrs. Cummins, and she had come to report that her husband had been thrown into the river, and he barely managed to save himself. McCabe told her that it looked like a dangerous situation. Needless to say Cummins was on the next train for Chicago.

Now a new contractor had to be found. Mr. Chambers was proficient along those lines and was held in high regard by all the local citizens. He accepted the responsibility of supervising the restoration of the John Brown Fort on the site chosen by Kate Field. The Harper's Ferry station agent saved the day. Miss Field died in Honolulu on May 19, 1896, soon after the work of restoration had been completed. The project languished, however, and the plan for a park seemed to collapse.[1]

The gallows on which Brown was hung was a vast source for souvenirs of the Brown invasion. Of the many thousands of soldiers who were stationed in Jefferson County from the day of Brown's execution until the last regiment disappeared, more than a year after the Civil War, almost every other man had a portion as a souvenir of his sojourn in Virginia. I saw a piece of wood and fragments of rope purporting to have formed parts of the structure—enough to build and rig a large man-of-war. If the soldiers believed they had genuine relics they were as well contented as they would be if they had the truth and it would be cruel to ruin their joy of owning a piece of history. The true history of that scaffold is rather interesting. It was built by a carpenter of Charlestown, named David Cockerell, expressly for the execution of Brown. When this purpose was accomplished the builder took it to his home, and put it away as a curiosity. When the Civil War broke out Cockerell joined the Confederate army and acted as engineer on the staff of Stonewall Jackson. Fearing

---

[1] The Fort stood all alone out in the countryside until 1909, the fiftieth anniversary of John Brown's raid. At this time the structure was taken over and removed to the campus of Storer College in Harper's Ferry, a co-educational institution for Negro students, and now the Mather Training Center for the National Parks. Again it was restored, to be used as a museum to house mementoes of Harper's Ferry and John Brown. In 1968 it was again moved by the National Park Service to the old armory yard near its original location!

that in his absence from home his family might be annoyed by soldiers coming to see the relic or, if possible, to steal it, he ordered it to be built into a porch attached to his house and the whole structure to be painted in the same color so that no stranger could guess at anything beyond the common in the ordinary looking porch. Cockerell died some years after the war, and it is said that his heirs disposed of the famous scaffold to some Washington D. C. speculators, who proposed to exhibit it at the World's Fair in Chicago in 1893.

For several months after the raid a brisk trade was carried on by the young men of Harper's Ferry selling "John Brown pikes" to railroad passengers who, everyday now stopped at the station from curiosity and, as the number of genuine pikes was not very large, the stock must have been exhausted in a very short time. It is said, however, that some ingenious and enterprising blacksmiths in the neighborhood devoted much of their time and capital to the manufacture of imitations, and it is certain that the number of pikes sold to strangers exceeded, by a great many, the number supposed to have been captured at Brown's headquarters.

Mr. Barry then said, "I am sure you are interested in the citizens who were killed at Harper's Ferry during the insurrection. I recall very well what happened to these people."

Shephard Hayward, the first man killed by Brown's party, was a very black Negro aged about forty-four years. He was uncommonly tall, measuring six feet and five inches, and he was a man of great physical strength. He was a free man, but, in order to comply with a law then existing in Virginia, he acknowledged Mayor Beckham as his master. The relations of master and slave, however, existed only in name between them and "Hayward" became fairly well-off and owned some property in Winchester. It is supposed by many that the killing of this man was the only thing that prevented a general insurrection of the Negroes, for some of the farmers of the neighborhood said that they noticed an unusual anxiety among the slaves on the Sunday before the raid. If it is true that the Negroes knew anything of the intended attack, it is probable that they were deterred from taking a part in it by seeing one of their own race the first person sacrificed.

Thomas Boerley, the second man killed, was Irish. He was also a man of great physical strength and he was noted for courage. He measured about six feet in height and weighed about two hundred pounds. He was a blunt, straight-forward man in his dealing and he was very popular on account of his easy-going and fun-loving nature. Many years before he had a fisticuff fight with an equally powerful man named Joseph Graff, who, at that time, resided at Harper's Ferry. The fight was conducted in the old border style of "rough and tumble," including biting and gouging. Darkness alone terminated the encounter and the combatants parted with their mutual respect greatly augmented and with a great accession of glory to both. The admirers of each party claimed a victory for their champion, but the principals themselves wisely divided the laurels and never again jeopardized their reputation by renewing the contest. Mr. Boerley's age at the time of his death was about forty-three years. He was married and had three children. His youngest child, Thomas, junior, still resides at Harper's Ferry and is quite a prominent citizen. The state of Virginia granted a small pension to his widow but when the war broke out shortly afterwards, the payments stopped. After the war her claim was brought to the notice of the state authorities, and from that time, until her death a few years ago, she was paid punctually. Mr. Boerley kept a grocery store. Thomas Boerley, junior, became the mayor of Harper's Ferry and arrested and brought to justice Erwin Ford, the brutal murderer of Elsie Kreglow, of the District of Columbia, in 1896.

George Turner, the third citizen killed was a very fine looking man, aged about forty years. He was educated at West Point and was distinguished for his great polish and refinement of manners. He was unmarried and left a good deal of property when he died. He was a native of Jefferson county, Virginia, now West Virginia.

Fontaine Beckham, the fourth and last of the citizen's party killed, was like the others, a tall, powerfully built man. His age was about sixty years. He was a native of Culpepper County, Virginia, and a brother of

Armistead Beckham, a master-armorer. He had been for many years a magistrate of the county of Jefferson and the agent of the Baltimore and Ohio railroad company at Harper's Ferry. At the time of his death he was the mayor of Harper's Ferry. He was a widower and two sons and a daughter survived him. Mr. Beckham was in many respects a remarkable man. It was said that he was the best magistrate that Jefferson county ever had, his decisions being always given with a view of justice to all. He was sometimes very whimsical, and some amusing scenes used to be enacted between him and "Hayward"—his factotum. Frequently, the squire would give unreasonable or contradictory orders to his servant who never hesitated on such occasions to refuse obedience, and it was no uncommon thing to see Hayward starting out from the railroad office with a bundle on his back en-route for Winchester, and swearing that he would not serve the squire another day for any consideration. He never proceeded very far, however, before he was overtaken by a message from his master conveying proposals for peace and Hayward never failed to return. Notwithstanding their frequent rows, a strong attachment existed between these two men through life; and in death they were not parted. Mr. Beckham's sister was the wife of Mr. Stubblefield, superintendent of the armory, and his niece, Miss Stubblefield was married to Andrew Hunter, of Charlestown, one of the most eminent lawyers of Virginia. Mr. Beckham's wife was the daughter of Colonel Stevenson, of Harper's Ferry, and, thus, it will be seen that he was connected with many of the most influential families of the Northern Neck. Mr. Beckham's death was mourned by everyone as a great public loss. He had all the qualities that go to make a lovable man and a good citizen.

Mr. Barry paused and then said:

I would now like to talk about the hostages taken by John Brown in the engine house. I shall first mention Colonel Lewis W. Washington who was at the time a very fine looking man of about fifty years of age, with that unmistakable air that always accompanies a man of true patrician birth and education. He was the soul of hospitality and Cook used to visit him at his home for pistol shooting contests, an art in which both were experts. On these occasions Colonel Washington used to exhibit the sword and some other relies of his great namesake and grand-uncle, and, thus it was that Cook and his companions in the conspiracy gained so intimate a knowledge of Colonel Washington's household arrangements and were enabled to find at once the place in which the relics were stored and to capture the owner without difficulty. Cook was entertained hospitably whenever he visited the generous Virginian, and the ingratitude manifested towards Colonel Washington was, perhaps, the worst feature of the whole transaction. The grand-nephew of the founder of our nation, it is said, exhibited a great deal of the dignity and calmness which characterized his illustrious kinsman and his fellow captives used to speak of his great coolness under the trying circumstances of his situation.

Colonel Washington, in his testimony before the Select Committee of the United States Senate, appointed to inquire into the outrage, gave a graphic description of his capture by the party. He described them as having consisted of Stevens, Tidd, Taylor and the Negro, Shields Greene. Another, named Merriam, was supposed to be about the premises, but he was not seen by Colonel Washington. In his recital no mention was made of Cook's presence at the capture, but it was ascertained afterwards that though he was not there in person, the captors had got from him all necessary information and that they acted under his instructions. It may be remarked that Merriam, although he was known to have been connected with the enterprise, was not seen by me in the skirmish at Harper's Ferry. Colonel Washington was one of those who disagreed with me as to the identity of Stewart Taylor. In my opinion Anderson and not Taylor accompanied the party to make the seizure. The colonel had several narrow escapes from death while in the hands of "the Philistines."

About the time when Mr. Beckham was killed, Brown was sitting on the fire engine near the engine house door, rifle in hand, apparently watching for an opportunity to make a good shot. Colonel Washington noticed him fingering his gun abstractedly, and like a person touching the strings of a violin and, being somewhat struck with the oddity of the idea, he approached Brown, for the purpose of inquiring if he had learned to play the fiddle. It is easy to imagine the answer the stem, old Puritan would have returned, had there been time enough to propound the question. As

Colonel Washington came near Brown, a bullet from the outside whistled immediately over the head of the latter, penetrated the handle of an axe that was suspended on the engine and passed through Colonel Washington's beard, striking the wall near him and sprinkling brick dust all over him. Brown cooly remarked, "that was close," and Colonel Washington postponed his inquiry, thereby consigning posterity to ignorance on the momentous question as to whether John Brown played the fiddle or not. The colonel deeming it prudent to leave that neighborhood, moved a little to one side, when he entered into conversation with Mr. Mills, another of the prisoners. Their faces were not four inches apart, yet through this narrow passage, another bullet sped and the friends finding one place as safe as another continued their conversation.

Colonel Washington at that time owned a dog of very odd appearance and habits and apparently of a nasty disposition. His name was "Bob" and he was of the common bull species. With other peculiarities, he was remarkable for having been born without a tail. Nature, however, with that tendency to compensation which our common Mother exhibits in awarding gifts to her children, gave him more than an equivalent for the caudal deficiency by providing him with an extra allowance of brains. He made it a point to visit the laborers on the plantation several times every day and, if there were more than one party of them, he would inspect each in turn, and eye the Negroes suspiciously, after which he would return to his bed which was in front of the main entrance to the house. He never made free with any person, not even with his master, who tried frequently, but in vain, to induce his surly dependent to follow him 'round the farm. His morose disposition and the jealous eye with which he always regarded the Negroes gave rise to superstitious dread of the animal among the servants and a belief that in him was the soul of some defunct plantation overseer who, with the ruling passion strong after death, continued to exercise his favorite avocation. Pythagoras himself would, no doubt, have agreed with the Negroes, had he known "Bob" and his peculiarities, and it may be supposed that the philosopher would have pointed triumphantly to this overwhelming proof of the Metempsychosis.

On the night of Colonel Washington's capture, however, Bob's whole nature appeared to undergo a change. He accompanied his master to Harper's Ferry, stuck by him all day on Monday and, when Colonel Washington was confined in the engine house as a hostage, his faithful though hitherto undemonstrative dog followed him into close captivity. Brown and his men tried to eject him and even his master endeavored to induce him to go out, but in vain. When Colonel Washington was released, he lost Bob in the dense crowd, but, on reaching home an Tuesday night, he found the metamorphosed overseer waiting for him at the gate and exhibiting signs of the most extravagant joy at his return. After this, the dog was regarded with more favor and many of the Negroes from that time rejected the former theory of transmigration as a slander on the faithful animal. Many years ago, at a ripe canine age, poor Bob was gathered to his fathers, and he sleeps in an honored grave in the plantation garden, but, as slavery has been abolished in the United States and bids fairly to disappear from the whole earth, it might puzzle even Pythagoras himself to find a suitable tenement for the now unhappy shade of the overseer. Colonel Washington died at his residence near Harper's Ferry on October 1st, 1871, much regretted by all who had the pleasure of his acquaintance.

Mr. Allstadt was a gentleman then about sixty years of age, of very unassuming manners and amiable disposition. He, too, was examined before the senate committee and gave a lively picture of his adventures while a prisoner. His son, Thomas, then a young man of eighteen, was taken prisoner with his father and voluntarily accompanied the party to Harper's Ferry to watch for the old gentleman's safety. Mr. Allstadt, senior, has been dead for some years, but Thomas yet survives, now a well-matured man, and he is probably the only one of the prisoners who were confined in the engine house who survives, with the possible exception of Messrs. Mills and Schoppe, of whom nothing has been heard about at Harper's Ferry for the last forty years.

John E. P. Daingerfield was then a man of about forty years of age and of a very delicate constitution. He bore up very well, however, and when he was released by the marines his physical strength had not given way, as his friends feared it would. At the breaking out of the war he moved to North Carolina and there he died suddenly a few years ago while on a hunt in the woods. It is supposed that his death was caused by too severe exertion while he was prosecuting a favorite sport.

Armistead M. Ball was at that time a man of about forty-six years of age. He was very corpulent but, notwithstanding his great bulk, his health was delicate. He died in June, 1861, of apoplexy. As before said, he was a man of great mechanical ingenuity. He invented a rifling machine which was used for several years in the armory, and was regarded as an excellent piece of mechanism. Many people, however, believed that Mr. Ball owed much of his reputation to ideas borrowed from a man named John Wernwag who, at that time and for many years before and afterwards, lived at Harper's Ferry and whose name will hereafter appear in this history in connection with a thrilling adventure in the great flood of 1870. Mr. Wernwag was, confessedly, a great genius in mechanics, but, as he was a man of very retiring habits and taciturn disposition, he never made any show of his ability and, consequently, only a few were aware of the wealth of mechanical genius that was possessed by this unassuming man, but was lost to the world through his unfortunate bashfulness. He and Mr. Ball used to take long and frequent hikes over the neighboring heights, and it was supposed that in their conversation on those excursions the latter got many hints which he improved and practically elucidated in his mechanical devices.

Benjamin Mills was a man of about fifty years of age at the time of the Brown raid, small in stature but muscular and active. Soon after the insurrection he returned to his home in Harrodsburg, Kentucky. It is not known when he died. John Donahue was at the time quite a good looking young man of about thirty-five years of age. He was a native of Ireland, but a resident of this country from his childhood. For many years his home was at Harper's Ferry, where he was highly respected for his integrity and business qualifications. His life was one of many vicissitudes and he died in the spring of 1892 at Hagerstown, Maryland.

Terrence Byrne was about forty-eight years of age at the time of the raid. He was, as far as is known here, the last survivor of the hostages, except for young Allstadt. As his name indicates, he was of Irish extraction. He was in comfortable circumstances and resided near the Kennedy farm where, unfortunately for him, he became well known to Brown and his men. Mr. Byrne was examined before the senate committee and testified that the party who captured him was composed of Cook, Tidd and Lehman. They visited his house early on Monday morning and conducted him as a prisoner to Harper's Ferry. Mr. Byrne died in about the year 1898.

Israel Russell, Justice of the Peace at Harper's Ferry, was then about fifty years of age. He was for many years a magistrate of Jefferson county, and was very much respected. He died in 1902 from a disease of the jaw, caused by the extraction of a defective tooth. It is strange that men will often escape unhurt from the most appalling dangers to succumb to apparently trivial ailments or casualties. Of Mr. Shope little is known at Harper's Ferry. He was a resident of Frederick, Maryland, and his connection with the raid was due entirely to his accidental presence at the scene of disturbance on the memorable 17th of October.

Of the grand jury that indicted Brown and the petit jury that tried and condemned him there is but one survivor, as far as I know, Mr. Martin, now of Virginia. Judge Parker, who presided at the trial, and the lawyers Hunter and Harding—who prosecuted, have all "crossed the bar." The sheriff Campbell who officiated at the execution, and all his deputies, have passed away. Lee and Stuart are dead, and it is believed that of all who figured prominently in this remarkable tragedy the juror above referred to is the only survivor, with the exceptions before named and Lieutenant Israel Green of the marines.

Lieutenant Green was dismissed from the marines on May 18, 1861 because he resigned to go South. Although from Vermont he joined the Confederate Marine Corps with the rank of major and adjutant on March 16, 1861 and served throughout the war in that position. After having come out of the war and experienced the abolishment of slavery he had to move his family away from the South to avoid pro-Union sentiment and he chose Mitchell, South Dakota, for his residence. His farm was two miles east of town. He was one of Mitchell's first civil engineers and surveyed the first east-west road to the Black Hills of South Dakota from Yankton.[2]

Mr. Barry concluded his talk on a note of melancholy. He said:

John Brown's fame is on the increase and time enhances it, call him what you will. It is remarkable that the gentlemen who were Brown's prisoners displayed little or no vindictiveness towards the man who had subjected them to so much danger. I frequently noticed in conversations with them that they invariably dwelt on his extraordinary courage and that the animosity, which it was natural they should feel on account of his treatment of them, was lost in their admiration for his daring, though misguided bravery. Mr. John Donahue visited him in prison and, very much to his credit, exhibited towards his fallen foe a generosity characteristic of the man himself and the gallant nation of his birth.

---

[2]   Green died in Mitchell, South Dakota on May 26, 1909 in his 86th year.

Chapter 18

REBURIAL

C APTAIN E. P. Hall and Dr. Thomas R. Featherstonhaugh, both
of Washington, D. C., returned to the capital on July 31, 1899,
from Harper's Ferry, where they had been exhuming the bodies of eight
of John Brown's raiders. They were assisted by Professor O. G. Libby
from the University of Wisconsin. The two great "stove boxes" containing
the corpses were found some three feet below the surface of the ground.
They were, of course much decayed, but from being constantly wet by
being near the Shenandoah river, were remarkably preserved. Most of the
smaller bones had crumbled away, but the long bones of eight men were
recovered. The bodies were sent to North Elba, New York by Dr. Libby
where they were buried near the grave of the leader under whom they
fought and died.

There was no question as to the identification of the remains. The
particular locality of the graves, the peculiar method of burial,—all being
packed in two great boxes,—the memory of a number of the older citizens
who witnessed the burial, and the affidavit of the man who buried the
bodies placed the matter beyond controversy.

The other two raiders who were killed at Harper's Ferry were buried
separately. The remains of Watson Brown were recovered and buried near
John Brown's body in 1882. His body was taken from Harper's Ferry to
be used at the medical college in Winchester for anatomical purposes.
During the Civil War a Union army officer stationed in Winchester
discovered Watson's body at the college. Realizing that it was the body
of John Brown's son, he took it north where he gave it to a lodge he

belonged to. For years the lodge used the body for its secret rituals. But upon hearing that Mary Brown, who then resided in California, would be traveling through his area in 1882, the officer moved the body to a doctor's office and arranged for Mrs. Brown's son, John Jr., to identify it. This done, Mary took Watson's body to North Elba for burial. Where Jeremiah G. Anderson's body was no one could tell. He was probably taken from Harper's Ferry to the same medical college as Watson.

Miss Katharine E. McClellan of Saranac Lake, was kind enough to assume the labor of making all the arrangements for the funeral at the John Brown farm, in North Elba. At her solicitation the town presented a handsome casket with silver handles and a silver plate bearing the names of all the men, with the date of interment. The remains were all placed together in this one casket, and a grave was dug by the side of those of Captain John Brown and his son, Watson, under the shadow of the huge bolder that Captain Brown wished to stand sentinel over his last resting-place.

Ceremonies were to be held at the new John Brown grave site, and it was said that the Reverend Joshua Young of Groton Massachusetts, who buried John Brown and who *suffered* social ostracism for it, would take part. A monument was eventually erected over the graves. The bodies recovered were those of Oliver Brown, Stewart Taylor, W. H. Leeman, William Thompson, Dauphin O. Thompson, John H. Kagi, Dangerfield Newby and Lewis Sheridan Leary. A few weeks before the Harper's Ferry raid some friends of John Brown sent a lot of great blanket shawls to the Kennedy farm as a gift. On the night of the raid each man had taken one of these shawls and used it instead of an overcoat. Many witnesses spoke of those blankets, and how the short Sharp's carbines were kept from the rain beneath these protectors. The men had evidently been buried in these shawls, for great masses of matted wool were found enveloping each body. A great deal of the clothing had been marvelously preserved. There were portions of coats and vests with the buttons still in position upon them, and even from one of the vest pockets dropped two lead pencils, all sharpened and ready for use.

The date for the reburial of the bodies of the comrades of John Brown at North Elba, Essex County, New York was changed from Saturday, August 26, 1899 to Wednesday, August 30. This news came via Plattsburg, New York on August 25th, 1899. This date was chosen for the re-interment ceremonies because it was the 43rd anniversary of John Brown's victory at the battle of Osawatomie in Kansas, the event which brought him to national prominence and which ultimately led Kansas to become a free state. On that Wednesday afternoon fifteen hundred visitors and neighbors witnessed the ceremonies at the re-interment of John Brown's followers in the little graveyard at the John Brown Farm at North Elba, about two miles from Lake Placid.

During the preparations for the funeral, Mr. E. P. Stevens of Brookline, Massachusetts, a nephew of Aaron D. Stevens, one of the raiders who was hanged at Charlestown, accomplished the task of having his uncle and a companion, Albert E. Hazlett, who was also hanged, disinterred from their graves at Perth Amboy, New Jersey. They were dug up on August 28, 1899 and shipped to North Elba, New York, where they were placed beside those of the others of the party. The bodies had been brought to New Jersey from Harper's Ferry just after the execution by Mrs Rebecca Marcus Spring, who sympathized with Brown and his men. Mrs. Spring buried them on property owned by her at Perth Amboy. The bones of the men, when disinterred on the 28th, were found to be in good condition, and even the clothing they wore was still in a fair state of preservation.

The hymn "Onward, Christian Soldiers" was sung at the opening of the ceremony at 2:00 PM in the afternoon and the entire audience joined in. Prayer was offered by the Reverend E. A. Braman, after which the Reverend Joshua Young, D. D., of Groton, Mass., who had also preached at John Brown's funeral sermon forty years previously, made a few appropriate comments. The Epps, a colored family who were brought to North Elba years ago by John Brown, then sang "There is a land that is fairer than day."

Captain James H. Holmes of New York City, who fought with John Brown and fired the first gun at the battle of Osawatomie in the Kansas raids in 1856 delivered the key address. The talk kept everyone in rapt attention. Author Richard J. Hinton of Brooklyn delivered a historical address, which included a biographical sketch of each of the men, many of whom he had personally known. The audience then joined in singing "John Brown's Body Lies a—Moldering," after which Bishop Potter of New York spoke briefly, and introduced Whitelaw Reid of New York. Mr. Reid, who was visiting Bishop Potter at his camp on Mohawk Island, Lake Placid, spoke of the Brown raid at Harper's Ferry, Va., and of the bravery of the men. The funeral procession was under a military escort from the Twenty-sixth United States Infantry, Plattsburg, with Lieutenant's Connell and Ball in command. A military salute was fired over the open grave; the benediction was then pronounced by the Reverend Joshua Young, and the large crowd slowly dispersed.

The designation of the North Elba farm as a National Historic Landmark occurred in 1998 and was the federal government's official recognition of the national importance of the property. On Monday, August 30, 1999, State Parks Commissioner Bernadette Castro marked the centennial of the re-interment of the ten raiders at Harpers Ferry at the John Brown Farm State Historic Site in North Elba, New York. Mr. Castro dedicated a plaque designating the farm as a National Historic Landmark.

The re-interment centennial commemorated the 1899 ceremony at which the remains of eight of John Brown's followers who were killed during the Harpers Ferry raid, and two who had been tried and hanged for their part in it were moved and interred at the farm site near the graves of John Brown and his two sons.

"The life of John Brown and his commitment to the anti slavery cause helped shape the history of our nation," said Commissioner Castro. "It is fitting to memorialize his lifelong commitment to the abolition of slavery, and that of his sons and comrades, in this humble setting he called home." Joining Commissioner Castro were State Senator Ronald Stafford; Elizabeth O'C. Little, member of the State Assembly; Shirley W. Seney, Supervisor of the Town of North Elba; and William Bolger of the National

Park Service, Director of the National Historic Landmark Program. Commissioner Castro said, "Also attending were great-grandnieces of two of John Brown comrades. Mrs. Douglas Sutcliffe is the great-grandniece of Aaron D. Stevens, who was hanged for his participation in the Harpers Ferry raid and is now buried at the farm. Mrs. Ann Chetsky is the great-grandniece of Oliver Brown, who was killed at Harpers Ferry and re-interred at the farm."

The North Elba property is now owned by the New York State Department of Environmental Conservation (DEC) and is currently managed by the New York State Office of Parks, Recreation and Historic Preservation (OPRHP).

Chapter 19

NORTH ELBA LIVES ON

The New York *Times* of January 10, 1896 reported that Henry Clews, as trustee for the owners of the John Brown farm, in the Adirondacks, at North Elba, where the great abolitionist was buried, transferred the property on January 9, 1896 to the state, to be used forever as a park or reservation. The property had been offered at auction, when Kate Field decided to save it. On January 11, 1870, she and her friends bought it for $2,000. The subscribers to the fund were Miss Field, Mrs. R. C. Watterson, Isaac H. Baily, John E. Williams, William H. Lee, George A. Robbins, George Cabot Ward, Henry Clews, D. Randolph Martin, Le Grand B. Cannon, Charles Stewart Smith, S. B. Chittenden, Isaac Sherman, Jackson S. Schultz, Elliott C. Cowdin, Thomas Murphy, Charles C. Judson, Salem H. Wales, Sinclair Tousey, and H. B. Claffiin.

Mr. Clews took the deed, as trustee for the subscribers. It was given to him by Alexis Hinckley of North Elba, Essex County, who had obtained the farm from Mary A. Brown, John Brown's widow. The deed described the property as consisting of 244 acres in lot 95, township number 12, of the old military tract, Thorn's survey, Essex County, New York. It reserved from conveyance "so much of the land as has been inclosed as a burying place, and in and upon which the remains of John Brown are interred, together with the right to pass to and from said reserved tract, said reserved tract containing about one-quarter acre."

Mr. Hinckley had accepted this restriction from Mrs. Brown, and it appeared in Mr. Clews's deed to the state. The grave was marked only by a boulder. It was the intention of the subscribers to build a more appropriate monument.

The farm had been rented since the subscribers owned it. The accumulated funds were to be used for the monument in the yard. The state was expected to keep the farmhouse in which John Brown lived in its present condition, which was fairly good. Miss Field reported that there were many visitors to the grave every year. Of the twenty original subscribers to the purchasing fund nine had died. The value of the farm had been multiplied many times since 1870 by improvements in that section.

Mr. Epps, one of the Negroes brought from the South by John Brown, continued to live on the farm at North Elba, given him by Gerrit Smith. He was a music teacher of rare natural ability, and according to the New York *Times* was respected by all who knew him. He was a close friend and confidant of John Brown.

One of the interesting and characteristic features of the burial service of John Brown at the grave at North Elba on Dec. 8, 1859, was the singing of Mr. Lyman Epps and his family. The hymn sung was "The Year of Jubilee," beginning "Blow Ye the Trumpet, Blow."

At the public exercises at the time of the transfer of the John Brown farm to the State of New York, to be held forever as a public park, which took place at the old homestead at North Elba on July 21, 1896, Mr. Epps and family sang again, by request, "Blow Ye the Trumpet, Blow." Mr. Epps later remarked "What a contrast between the sentiments of this great assembly today and the general sentiment of 1859!" Simple funeral services were held at his late residence on March 26, and the burial took place in the public cemetery at North Elba. The death of Lyman Epps occurred at his home at North Elba, on Wednesday, March 24th, 1897.

The New York *Times* also reported a six-ton bronze memorial to John Brown, depicting him with his arms about the shoulders of a Negro boy, was unveiled at ceremonies at Lake Placid on May 9, 1935. The huge statue, more than eight feet tall, shows the Negro lad, who appears to pull backward as if frightened, his face upraised to Brown's. The granite for the pedestal was taken from the mountains near Ausable Falls, about twenty-five miles away from the memorial amid the Adirondacks.

More than 1,500 people, many of them Negro pilgrims to the grave of John Brown, crowded about the site of the memorial. The statue was unveiled by Lyman Epps, Jr., 87 years old, who was present as a young boy at the funeral of the abolitionist in 1859. He was assisted by Mrs. Anna Franklin, President of the Lake Placid Chapter of the John Brown Memorial Association. Dr. J. Max Barber of Philadelphia, elected president of the association for the ninth year, said in his dedicatory address, "After John Brown's death, there could be no peace with slavery in the land."

Accepting the statue for the State, Conservation Commissioner Lithgow Osborne extended the greetings of Governor Lehman, and said,

The State of New York accepts the monument with pride that its soil nurtured such a stalwart body, such a rugged unflinching soul, accepts it with gratitude that the admirers of John Brown have seen fit to erect it here; accepts it with happiness in the state's pledged faith to care for and cherish it as it merits.

Another ceremony took place at North Elba on Saturday, May 9, 1959 at the grave of John Brown's grave. It was the 159th anniversary of his birth. The ceremony was conducted, as it had been annually since 1921, by the interracial John Brown Memorial Association, and it commemorated the centennial of his trial.

The program was not as full as it usually was. It consisted merely of an invocation, an address and laying of wreaths at John Brown's grave and at the foot of the Brown statue that stands on the property. The reason was because a larger ceremony was planned for July 12th, the date when the Department of Education of New York State, which has jurisdiction over the farm and the homestead which Brown built in the middle of it in the Eighteen Fifties, would officially open and "activate" it, following a most meticulous restoration of the homestead to its condition in Brown's day. Officials of the New York State's Board of Regents conducted the July 12th event, and Governor Rockefeller was invited to attend.

The work of restoring the shabby little frame house took several years, two of them spent in research under the direction of Anna K. Cunningham, supervisor of New York State Historic Sites, working with Dr. Albert B. Corey, the State Historian. The research involved study of thousands of documents of the period and records of many kinds. Of great value, according to Colonel Charles B. Briggs, caretaker of the property, were two drawings by the famous cartoonist Thomas Nast. Nast had been assigned to report the burial of John Brown, and the sketches which he made on the scene show exterior views of the house.

The original doors and woodwork of the house had been covered with layers of paint by successive owners. The newer paint was carefully removed, leaving the original homemade stain. The stain was made by boiling hemlock bark on the kitchen stove and adding salt as a fixative. Several of the windows, composed of two sashes—an upper sash of six panes and a lower one of four—still have their original glass, now so weathered as to be virtually iridescent: One window, facing the west, and the prevailing winds, had been boarded up by a later tenant, but was discovered only after the removal of the newer woodwork. A cupboard and a bookcase, built by a member of John Brown's family, remain as they were.

The restoration involved what Miss Cunningham described as "archaeological research"—examination and identification of features of the house to ascertain their approximate dates. In this way, floor boards, nails and the like were identified as from the Brown period.

The little kitchen garden set out by John Brown's wife Mary was tilled for the first time in many decades. Additions to the original house were removed, and landscaping around the place restored the contours of the land which John Brown trod.

John Brown had been attracted to the bleak region of North Elba because Gerrit Smith, a philanthropist of the day, had set aside 100,000 of his acres there to be colonized by runaway slaves. (The colonization was never very successful, mostly because of the rigorous climate.) Brown himself bought 244 acres from Smith, at a price of one dollar an acre. The land remains virtually intact.

The fiery zealot, who counted his life—not to mention a number of others—as nothing compared to his cause, took great care in directing the disposal of his remains. He had already brought the tombstone of his grandfather, Captain John Brown, killed in the Revolutionary War, to North Elba, where for years it leaned against the wall of the farmhouse. Now, Brown directed, his own name should be added, with the inscription, "born May 9, 1800, was executed at Charlestown, Va., December 2, 1859." He also directed that the names of two of his sons, killed at Harper's Ferry, should be added.

He chose as his burial place a space in front of a great glacial boulder, about one hundred yards east of his house. There he was buried, his two sons beside him in a second grave, and a dozen of his followers in a third. The gravestone was set in place there, and plaques fixed to the boulder record the names of Brown's followers who lie there.

The boulder is shaded by a great tree, and the graves are surrounded by a high iron fence. It is now a place of tragic memories, and, standing there, as 20,000 visitors did during 1998, it is quite understandable how Federal troops at Civil War, two years after the old zealots death, could sing that "his soul goes marching on."

On Saturday, May 1, 1999, the New York *Times* reported that more than 300 people gathered at the John Brown Family Farm in North Elba, New York to commemorate the 199th anniversary of the birth of the great abolitionist. They came from the area around Lake Placid, from New York City, Boston, and as far away as Iowa and North Carolina. Among them were students, community activists, and two busloads of church people from Brooklyn. They came in response to the Call put out by the

New Abolitionist Society and signed by novelists Russell Banks and Toni Morrison, and twelve other artists and scholars.

As guests arrived at the Trinity Chapel in North Elba they were greeted by music from Scott M. X. Turner and the Devil's Advocates, from Brooklyn, who also led everyone in singing "John Brown's Body." After welcoming remarks by Noel Ignatiev of the New Abolitionist Society, the crowd moved to the cemetery next to the chapel, where Lyman Epps and William Appo, Sr. were buried. Epps worked with Brown in the Underground Railroad and Appo, whose son fought in the Civil War, lived in Timbuctoo, the black farming community that drew Brown to the area. Following a recounting of their lives by historian Charles Thomas, the crowd walked to the John Brown Farm nearby, where the bulk of the ceremony took place. There were shuttle buses for those who could not walk.

Manager of the John Brown Farm Terry Noe welcomed the guests. The gospel group *Voices of Glory* sang several songs, including one of their own composition called "Old Souls," celebrating Brown, Harriet Tubman, Frederick Douglass, and Malcolm X. They also sang the Methodist hymn "Blow Ye the Trumpet, Blow." The singing was followed by an invocation given jointly by Reverend Johnny Ray Youngblood of the St. Paul Community Baptist Church and Reverend David Haberer of the Community Bible Church, both from Brooklyn.

William Banks, a ranger at the Harper's Ferry National Historic Site, gave a moving reading from a speech by Frederick Douglass on Brown. Carolyn Sutcliffe read powerfully from the diaries and letters of Aaron Stevens, who fought with Brown at Kansas and Harper's Ferry and was hung shortly after the Old Man. Ms. Sutcliffe, of Sanbornton, New Hampshire, is a direct descendent of Stevens. In preparation for John Brown Day, Ronald "Cornbread" Owens, a former prisoner, had written and circulated an appeal to prisoners to take part in the day's events. His appeal elicited a number of responses, from which he and a young friend read to the crowd.

Russell Banks, author of *Cloudsplitter*, a novel based on the life of Brown, read from Brown's last speech at his trial. Banks pointed out that Brown was not merely extremely courageous but probably "the most eloquent man of his time." Following the collection by Reverend Haberer there was an open mike at which people read from past writings on Brown and spoke of his contemporary relevance. People gathered afterwards at the Cascade Cross Country Ski Center for a lunch provided by local chef Vicki Cram. That evening the crowd danced to music of the Devil's Advocates. The next day about sixty people gathered in the barn to discuss continuing the legacy of John Brown. Following the meeting, Ed Cotter, former caretaker at the Farm, gave an excellent slide presentation on the life of Brown.

Local people worked hard to organize the event. Students from Lake Placid High set up, ushered, and staffed the tables. Advance donations, the collection at the farm, and sales of literature and T-shirts more than covered the costs. Before, after, and during breaks in the ceremony visitors toured the Farm and looked at the plaques commemorating Brown and his family members and comrades at arms who are buried there. The scene was beautiful, and the weather perfect. Last, but not least, the children caught pollywogs in the farm pond.

In October 2009 the United States celebrated the 150th anniversary of John Brown's raid. The largest celebration occurred at Harpers Ferry National Historical Park at Harpers Ferry, West Virginia. The symposium was held at the Stephen T. Mather Training Center with keynote sessions in the Curtis Freewill Baptist Church.

North Elba, in the vicinity of Lake Placid, New York also commemorated the life and legacy of John Brown on December 4th and 5th 2009. A series of talks which examined the life and actions of John Brown as well as the effects that still influence us to this day were presented.

A Sesquicentennial commemoration occurred at Charles Town on March 16th 2010. It was the 150th anniversary of the execution of Aaron Stevens and Albert Hazlett and took place at the Jefferson County

Courthouse where the trials were held. Following the narrative of the two trials a procession was held to the execution site, about four blocks from the courthouse.

John Brown's 150th Sesquicentennial was surely **"A great time of Ritual, Reflection, Remembrance and Renewal."**

John Brown
Alias List

H.F. stands for Harper's Ferry
The infamous 22 Brown Men ✖
One of the ten hostages in the engine house ❿
Citizen killed ✓
Citizen wounded ⍻
Those Hung Π
Those not hung, date of Death ☦

Last	First	Middle	Identification
Alburtis Alberts Albertis	(Captain)		Led the Martinsburg men on an attack of the engine house and released prisoners.
Allstadt Alstedt Alstadt Alstadtt Allsteadt	John	H.	❿ 51 year old farmer located 2.5 miles above H.F. Hostage.
Allstadt Alstedt Alstadt Alstadtt Allsteadt	John	Thomas	Eighteen year old son of John Allstadt. Accompanied his father to the engine house.
Anderson "Andress"	Jeremiah Jere "Jerry"	Goldsmith	✖ John Brown insurgent from Iowa. Rank of Lieutenant. Killed at H.F.
Anderson	Osborne Osborn	Perry	✖ Negro Brown follower. Canadian, who escaped from H.F. ☦ on December 10, 1872.

Last	First	Middle	Identification
Avis	John	B.	Jailor at Charlestown prison.
Ball	Armistead Armstead Armisted	M.	❿ Master Machinist at H.F. armory, and chief draughtsman.
Baylor Bayler	(Colonel) Robert	W.	Senior officer of the Virginia militia, Commandant 3rd regiment, cavalry.
Beckham Brekham Breckham Becham	Fontaine Fountain Fountaine		✔ 60 year old Mayor of H.F. and railroad agent.
Bell	Benjamin	T.	Stationed at the Galt House in Captain Botts's company.
Beller	James		Citizen at H.F., with George Chambers.
Boerley Burnley Boerly Burley Burleigh Btrley	Thomas Joseph		✔ Irish Grocer at H.F. Shot standing in his own doorway from Shenandoah Street.
Boteler	Alexander	R.	Congressman and resident of Shepherdstown. Viewed assault at the Rifle Works and interviewed Brown after he was taken into custody.
Botts	Lawson		Son of General Thomas H. Botts of Virginia. He was a lawyer who commanded the "Botts Greys" from Charlestown. Refused Brown's surrender terms, and wanted to storm the engine house immediately. He was assigned as a defense lawyer for John Brown, but understandably quit at an early point in the trial.
Bowman			✅ Conductor from Martinsburg.

Last	First	Middle	Identification
Brown	John "Osawatomie"		✖ Commander-in-Chief of the Insurrection. Wounded at engine house. ∏ on Dec. 2, 1859.
Brown	Owen		✖ 35 year old son of John Brown. Rank of Captain. Escaped from H.F. ✝ on January 8, 1889.
Brown	Oliver Ottawa Oteway Otteway		✖ Son of John Brown. Rank of Captain. Born in Ohio. Killed at engine house.
Brown	Watson		✖ Son of John Brown. Rank of captain. Born in Essex County, New York. Killed at engine house.
Brown	Mary	Anne Ann	John Brown's second wife.
Brown	Anne Ann Annie		Daughter of John Brown.
Brown	Martha		Daughter of John Brown.
Brua Brewer Burd	Joseph	A.	❿ Armorer at H.F. arsenal. Hostage. Went out a few times with a flag of truce.
Butler	V. (Captain)		Commanded the Hamtramck Guards.
Byrne O'Byrne Burns	Terrence Terence		❿ Farmer 3 miles northwest of H.F. and 1.5 miles south of Kennedy farm. Hostage.
Campbell	James	W.	Sheriff of Jefferson County.
Chambers	George	W.	Resident of H.F. He lived near the public square, and was the town clerk. He owned the Galt House, a tavern near the arsenal and in view of the armory yard.
Child	Lydia	Maria	Prominent abolitionist from Wayland, Mass.

Last	First	Middle	Identification
Chilton	Samuel		D.C. lawyer appointed as additional counsel for John Brown during the trial.
Cockerell	David		He was a carpenter and built the gallows for the execution of John Brown.
Cook Cooke	John	Edwin Edward Esten	✖ John Brown insurgent. Held a captain's commission. ∏ on Dec. 16, 1859.
Copeland, Jr.	John	Anthony	✖ Black insurgent from Ohio. ∏ on Dec. 16, 1859.
Coppoc Coppic Coppie Coppich Coppick Coppee Copdic	Edwin Edward		✖ 24 year old insurgent from Iowa. Rank of lieutenant. He was captured in the engine house. ∏ on Dec. 16, 1859.
Coppoc Coppic Coppie Coppich Coppick Coppee Copdic	Barclay		✖ Brown insurgent. Edwin's younger brother. Rank of private. Escaped from H.F. ✝ on September 4, 1861.
Crayon	Porte		Nom de Plume. See Strother, David H.
Cromwell	Jacob		Baggage master for B & O Railroad
Cross	Reason Rezin		Resident of H.F. Good friend of Mayor Beckham.
Currie Currie	Lind	F.	School teacher and farmer.
Daingerfield Dangerfield	John	E. P. E. R.	❿ Paymaster Clerk of the armory at H.F. Hostage.

Last	First	Middle	Identification
Davenport	(Colonel) Braxton		Presiding judge of magistrate court where Brown was indicted.
Diffey			Master of trains at Martinsburg.
Donahue Donohue Donohoo	John		❿ Clerk of Baltimore & Ohio Railroad. Hostage.
Dorsey	Evan		✔ Martinsburg conductor.
Douglass	Frederick		Famous colored acquaintance of John Brown.
Edgerton	Charles (Brigadier General)	C.	In charge of Baltimore Second Light Brigade. Only accompanied the marines part way to H.F.
"Emperor"			See Green, Shields.
Evans	Allen		Misnomer for Aaron Stevens.
Faulkner	(Colonel) Charles	J. K.	Accompanied the marines to H. F. Court assigned counselor for John Brown, but did not serve.
Forbes	Hugh		Wealthy early Brown supporter.
Fouke Foulke Foulkis	Christine Christina Christiana	C.	Woman who begged for the life of William Thompson.
Gibson	(Colonel) John	T.	Directed the Militia of Jefferson County and attacked the Rifle factory where Copeland was captured.
Green	(Lieutenant) Israel	J.	In charge of the marines. Stormed the engine house. ✟ on May 26, 1909.
Green Greene	Thomas	C.	Ex-Mayor of Charlestown, Virginia. Assigned as assistant to counsellor Lawson Botts for the defense of John Brown.
Green	Shields		✖ Douglass friend who went with Brown. Known as the "Emperor." ∏ on Dec. 16, 1859.
Grist Griest	Albert		Elderly H.F. citizen seized at bridge and taken to armory.

Last	First	Middle	Identification
Griswold	Henry Hiram		Cleveland lawyer who arrived during the trial to act in Brown's defense.
Hallett Hollett			✓ Conductor at Martinsburg. Wounded.
Hammond	Henry		✓ Son of Dr. Hammond of H.F.
Harding	Charles	B.	Prosecutor for the state against John Brown.
Harris	(Colonel)		Mistaken for Colonel R. E. Lee.
Harrison	William	H.	"Alias" for Albert Hazlett.
Hayward Heywood Haywood	Shephard Shepherd Sheppard		✓ Negro railroad porter.
Hazlett Hazlitt Haslett	Albert Elbert		✖ Brown insurgent. Rank of lieutenant. Wounded and captured on Oct. 22nd, 1859. ∏ on March 16, 1860.
Higgins	Patrick		Train Watchman at H.F.
Hobbs	Benjamin		Armory worker.
Hoffmeister Huffmaster Hoffmaster Heiffmaster	Jane		Nosy female resident near the Kennedy Farm.
Holt	James	H.	Resident of H.F. who captured John Copeland in the Shenandoah River.
Hood			Baggage master. Taken prisoner.
Hooper	N.		✓ Resident wounded by insurgents.
Hoyt	George	H.	Young counsellor for John Brown who arrived at the trial early on October 28, 1859.
Hunter	Andrew		Assistant of Charles Harding prosecuting John Brown.
Hunter	Henry		Went to H.F. with Charlestown Guard and saw Beckham killed.
Kagi Kagg	John	Henry	✖ Second in command and adjutant for John Brown. "Secretary of War." School teacher from Ohio and killed at Harper's Ferry.

Last	First	Middle	Identification
Kelly	Alexander		Resident of H.F. Saw Turner & Boerley killed.
Kelty	H.		Telegraph operator at Frederick.
Kennedy	(Dr.) Booth Andrew		Deceased owner of the Kennedy Farm near H.F.
Kitzmiller Kittmiller Kiltzmiller Kitzmeiller Kilzmeiller	Archibald	M.	Chief clerk at armory, and acting superintendent in place of Mr. Barbour. He was a Brown prisoner.
Krouse Knouse Koise			H.F. man who told Conductor Phelps he could proceed with his train.
Leary	Lewis	Sheridan Sherrard	✖ Colored insurrectionist from Ohio under Brown. Was killed at H.F.
Leeman Lehman Leman	William	Henry	✖ Youngest of the Brown raiders from Maine. 18 years old. Rank of lieutenant Was killed at H.F. by George D. Schoppert.
Linn	(Captain)		See Sinn (Captain)
Logan			Passenger from Baltimore who was arrested on bridge and searched for arms.
Mason			Head watchman for Potomac River Bridge.
Mason	James	M.	U.S. Senator from Virginia.
Merriam Meriam Marion	Francis Frances	Jackson	✖ Brown raider who escaped from H.F. Rank of private. ✝ on November 28, 1865.
Mills	Benjamin "Mayor"		❿ Master Armorer of H.F. arsenal. Hostage.
Moore	(Captain) Philip	T.	Member of the Montgomery Guards at H.F. who accompanied Mrs. Brown to Charlestown.
Murphy	George	H.	✓ Paymaster who was wounded in the leg at H.F.
McByrne			Passenger on train.

Last	First	Middle	Identification
McCabe	Edward		✅ Citizen wounded at H.F.
Newby Newly	Dangerfield		✖ 44 year old colored follower of Brown. Raised in Virginia. Spiked to death at H.F., and had his ears cut off.
Nicholls			Ran a boarding house near H.F. Brown and the Brown women boarded there for a few days.
Nichols	(Captain) James	N.	Commander of the Petersburg Artillery from Virginia.
Ould	Robert		United States District Attorney for the District of Columbia who took the steps for the trial of the prisoners in the Federal Courts of Virginia.
Parker	(Judge) Richard		Circuit Court judge who tried John Brown for treason and murder.
Phelps	Andrew	J.	B. & O. Train conductor.
Phil	"Big"		Black servant of Mr. Allstadt who poked openings in the engine house for shooting holes.
Phillips			Name mistaken for Patrick Higgins, watchman at H.F.
Plummer	Charles		See Tidd, Charles Plummer.
Quinn Quin	(Private) Luke		✔ Marine Corps private shot in the attack on the engine house.
Reynolds	(Major)		In charge of 400 troops dispatced to H.F.
Rhinehart Rienahart	(Captain) Jacob		Shepherdstown troop commander.
Richardson	George	W.	✔ Martinsburg resident and train conductor.
Riley			Martinsburg telegraph line repairer.
Rosengarten	John	G.	Director of Pennsylvania railroad and friend of Governor Wise. Witnessed death of George W. Turner.
Rowen	J. (Captain)	W.	Commanded the Jefferson Guards from Charlestown.

Last	First	Middle	Identification
Ruppert Rupert Ruffert	(Private) Mathew		✓ Marine private. Slightly wounded in the face at engine house.
Russell	Israel		❿ Justice of the Peace at H.F. Carried a flag of truce from Brown in the engine house. Hostage.
Russell	(Judge) Thomas		Mr. and Mrs. Russell visited Brown in jail. The judge had intended to defend Brown.
Russell	(Major)		Accompanied the marines to H.F.
Schoppert Schoppart Schoeper	George	A.	Virginia militiaman who shot William Leeman. He deliberately placed his pistol at the boy's head before firing.
Seaman	William		Misquoted for William Leeman.
Sennott (Esq.)	George		Boston lawyer who defended most of the insurrectionists except John Brown.
Sheats	John	L.	Aide to Captain Avis at the Charlestown prison.
Shephard Shepherd	Hayward		(Error) See Hayward, Shephard.
Shope Shoppe	George	D.	❿ Citizen of Frederick City, Md. Hostage.
Shriver	(Colonel) Edward		Head of 16th Regiment Maryland Volunteers stationed at Frederick. Interviewed Brown at armory.
Shutt	(Colonel) A.	P.	Employee of the Baltimore and Ohio railroad.
Siebert	Milton	M.	Captain of a military company from New Market, Virginia.
Simpson	Luther		Baggage Master from Monocacy Station.

Last	First	Middle	Identification
Sinn Senick Simms Simmes Linn	(Captain) J.	T.	Captain of a company from Frederick, Maryland.
Spring	Rebecca		Mrs. Marcus Spring was an abolitionist from Perth Amboy, N. J. Visited Brown and later Hazlett and Stevens in prison.
Starry	(Doctor) John Lewis	D.	Practicing physician at H.F.
Stevens Stephens	Aaron	Dwight C.	✖ 28 years old. Rank of captain. He was wounded at H.F. Ⅱ on Mar. 16, 1860.
Strider Snider Stricler	Samuel		Senior Citizen of H.F. who carried a surrender summons to Brown. Identified by his malaproprisms
Strother Strouther	David	H.	Known as "Porte Crayon." He sketched many scenes connected with the Harper's Ferry insurrection, and also made pronouncements about the raid.
Stuart Stewart	J. E. B. James	(Ewell Brown)	Marine lieutenant, First Cavalry, and aide to Colonel Lee.
Taylor	Stewart Steward Stuart		✖ Brown follower from Canada. Rank of private. Killed at H.F.
Thompson	Dauphin Dolph Adolph	O. Adolphus	✖ Brown follower from New York. Rank of lieutenant. Brother of William and stabbed to death at engine house in H.F.
Thompson	Henry		Son-in-Law of John Brown. Married to Brown's daughter Ruth. Brother of Dauphin and William. Did not go to H.F.

Last	First	Middle	Identification
Thompson	William		✖ Brown follower from New York. Rank of lieutenant. Brother of Dauphin. He was shot to death at H.F.
Throgmorton Throckmorton	W.	W.	Clerk at the Wager House in H.F.
Tidd Todd Tydd	Charles	Plummer	✖ From Maine. Rank of captain. Escaped from raid on H.F., and went into hiding in Ohio. ✝ on February 8, 1862.
Turner	George	W.	✓ West Point graduate and revered citizen of Wheatland five miles from Charlestown. Killed on the street in H.F.
Tyler	(Doctor) William		Attended Luke Quinn, a marine who was mortally wounded.
Unseld	John	C.	Resident living in outskirts, one mile from H.F.
Washington	(Colonel) Lewis	W.	❿ Distinguished 46 year old farmer living in outskirts of H.F. Hostage. ✝ on October 1, 1871.
Watson			Seventy-five year old man who had his rifle shattered when he raised it to his shoulder to shoot at the insurgents.
Ways	C.		Telegraph operator at Martinsburg.
Westbrook	C.		Superintendent of the Baltimore & Ohio Telegraph company.
Whelan Whelen	Daniel		Watchman at armory gate on night of Sunday, October 16, 1859.
White	Charles		Citizen of H.F. Minister of Presbyterian Church.
Williams Williamson	William	M.	Watchman on the on Potomac River bridge.

Last	First	Middle	Identification
Wise	Henry	A.	Governor of Virginia. ✝ on September 12, 1876.
Wollet Wollett Woollet Woollett	George		✅ Headed up a force of 20 Martinsburg men. Broke in door to armory and liberated 18 of the prisoners.
Wooley	William		Train engineer.
Young	Samuel Thomas	C. P.	✅ Resident of H.F. He was shot and crippled for life. He was mis-identified for George W. Turner in dispatches. (i.e. West Point graduate and having noble qualities.)

Framework of the Proposed Revolutionary Government

Baltimore, Maryland, October 19, 1859.

T HE FOLLOWING DOCUMENT, found among Brown's papers was indorsed, "Provisional Constitution and Ordinances for the people of the United States:"

PREAMBLE.—*Whereas,* Slavery throughout its entire existence in the United States is none other than the most barbarous, unprovoked and unjustifiable war of one portion of its citizens against another portion, the only conditions of which are perpetual imprisonment and hopeless servitude, or absolute extermination, in utter disregard and violation of eternal and self-evident truths set forth in our Declaration of Independence:

Therefore, we, the citizens of the United States, and the oppressed people, who, by a recent decision of the Supreme Court, are declared to have no rights which the white man is bound to respect, to respect, together with all the other people degraded by the laws thereof, do, for the time being, ordain and establish for ourselves the following provisional Constitution and ordinances, the better to protect our people, property, lives and liberties, and to govern our actions.

ARTICLE 1.—QUALIFICATIONS FOR MEMBERSHIP.—ALL persons of mature age, whether proscribed oppressed and enslaved citizens, or of proscribed and oppressed races of the United States, who shall agree to sustain and enforce the provisional constitution and ordinances of organization, together with all minor children of such persons, shall be held to be fully entitled to protection under the same.

ARTICLE 2.—BRANCHES OF GOVERNMENT.—The provisional government of this organization shall consist of three branches, viz.: the Legislative, the Executive and Judicial.

ARTICLE 3.—THE LEGISLATIVE.—The Legislative Branch shall be a Congress or House of Representatives, composed of not less than five nor more than ten members, who shall be elected by all the citizens of mature age and sound mind connected with this organization, and who shall remain in office for three years, unless sooner removed for misconduct, or inability or by death. A majority of such members shall constitute a quorum.

ARTICLE 4.—EXECUTIVE.—The Executive branch of this organization shall consist of a President and Vice-President, who shall be chosen by the citizens or members of this organization, and each of whom shall hold his office for three years unless sooner removed by death or for inability or misconduct.

ARTICLE 5.—JUDICIAL.—The Judicial Branch shall consist of one Chief Justice of the Supreme Court and four Associate Judges of the said Court, each of them constituting a Circuit Court. They shall each be chosen in the same manner as the President, and shall continue in office until their places have been filed in the same manner by an election of citizens.

Articles 13 to 25 provide for the trial of the President and other officers and members of Congress, the impeachment of Judges, the duties of President and Vice-President, the punishment of crimes, army appointments, salaries, etc., etc. These articles are not of special interest, and are therefore omitted.

ARTICLE 26.—TREATIES OF PEACE.—Before any treaty of peace shall take full effect it shall be signed by the President, Vice-President,

Commander-in-Chief, a majority of the House of Representatives, a majority of the Supreme Court, and a majority of all the general officers of the army.

ARTICLE 27.—DUTY OF THE MILITARY.—It shall be the duty of the Commander-in-Chief, and all the officers and soldiers of the army, to afford special protection, when needed, to Congress, or any member thereof, to the Supreme Court or any member thereof, to the President, Vice-President, Treasurer, and Secretary of War, and to afford general protect to all civil officers, or other persons having a right to the same.

ARTICLE 28.—PROPERTY.—All captured or confiscated property and all property the product of the labor of those belonging to this organization and of their families, shall be held aa the property of the whole equally, without distinction, and may be used for the common benefit or disposed of for the same object. And any person, officer or otherwise, who shall improperly retain, secrete, use, or needlessly destroy such property, or property found, captured, or confiscated, belonging to the enemy, or shall wilfully neglect to render a full and fair statement of such property by him so taken or held, shall be deemed guilty of a misdemeanor, and on conviction shall be punished accordingly.

ARTICLE 29.—SAFETY OR INTELLIGENCE FUND.—All money, plate, watches or jewelry captured by honorable warfare, found, taken, or confiscated, belonging to the enemy, shall be held sacred to constitute a liberal safety or intelligence fund, and any person who shall improperly retain, dispose of, hide, use or destroy such money or other article above-named, contrary to the provisions and spirit of this article, shall be deemed guilty of theft, and on conviction thereof shall be punished accordingly. The Treasurer shall furnish the Commander-in-Chief at all times with a full statement of the condition of such fund and its nature.

ARTICLE 30.—THE COMMANDER-IN-CHIEF AND THE TREASURY.—The Commander-in-Chief shall have power to draw from the treasury the money and other property of the fund provided for in article 29, but his orders shall be signed also by the Secretary of War, who shall keep a strict account of the same, subject to examination by any member of Congress or general officer.

ARTICLE 31.—SURPLUS OF THE SAFETY OR INTELLIGENCE FUND.—It shall be the duty of the Commander-in-Chief to advise the President of any surplus of the Safety and Intelligence Fund, and he shall have power to draw the same, his order being also signed by the Secretary of State, to enable him to carry on the provisions of article 17.

ARTICLE 32.—PRISONERS.—No person after having surrendered himself a prisoner, and who shall properly demean himself or herself as such to any officer or private connected with this organization, shall afterwards be put to death or be subjected to any corporeal punishment without first having the benefit of a fair and impartial trial, nor shall any prisoner be treated with any kind of cruelty, disrespect, insult, or needless severity, but it shall be the duty of all persons, male and female, connected herewith at all times and under all circumstances to treat all such prisoners with every degree of respect and kindness that the nature of the circumstances will admit of, and insist on a like course of conduct from all others as in fear of the Almighty God to whose care and keeping we commit our cause.

ARTICLE 33.—VOLUNTEERS.—All persons who may come forward, and shall voluntarily deliver up slaves, and have their names registered on the books of this organization, shall, so long as they continue at peace be entitled to the fullest protection in person and property, though not connected with the organization, and shall be treated as friends, and not merely as persons neutral.

ARTICLE 34.—NEUTRALS.—The persons and property of all non-slave holders who shall remain absolutely neutral shall be respected, so far as circumstances will allow of it, but they shall not be entitled to any active protection.

ARTICLE 35.—NO NEEDLESS WASTE.—The needless waste or destruction of any useful property or article by fire, throwing open of fences, fields, buildings. or needless killing of animals, or injury of either, shall not be tolerated at any time or place, but shall be promptly and peremptorily punished.

ARTICLE 36.—PROPERTY CONFISCATED.—The entire personal and real property of all persons known to be acting either directly or indirectly with or for the enemy, or found in arms with them, or found wilfully holding slaves, shall be confiscated and taken whenever and wherever it may be found, in either Free or Slave States.

ARTICLE 37.—DESERTION.—Persons convicted, on impartial trial, of desertion to the enemy, after becoming members, acting as spies, or treacherously surrender property, arms, ammunition, provisions or supplies of any kind, roads, bridges, persons, or fortifications, shall be put to death and their entire property confiscated.

ARTICLE 38.—VIOLATION OF PAROLE OF HONOR.—Persons proven to be guilty of taking up arms, after having been set at liberty on parole of honor, or after the same to have taken any active part with or for the enemy, direct or indirect, shall be put to death, and their entire property confiscated.

Articles 39, 40 and 41 require all to labor for the general good and prohibit immoral actions.

ARTICLE 42.—THE MARRIAGE RELATION—SCHOOLS— THE SABBATH.—Marriage relations shall be at all times respected and families be kept together as far as possible, and broken families encouraged to reunite, and intelligence offices shall be established for that purpose. Schools and churches shall he established as soon as may be, for the purpose of religious and other instructions, and the first day of the week shall be regarded as a day of rest, and appropriated to moral and religious instruction and improvement, to the relief of the suffering, the instruction of the young and ignorant, and the encouragement of personal cleanliness; nor shall any person be required on that day to perform ordinary manual labor, unless in extreme urgent cases.

ARTICLE 43.—TO CARRY ARMS OPENLY.—All persons known to be good character and of sound mind and suitable age, who are connected with this organization, whether male or female, shall be encouraged to carry arms openly.

ARTICLE 44.—NO PERSON TO CARRY CONCEALED WEAPONS.—No person within the limits of conquered territory, except regularly appointed policemen, express officers of army, mail carriers, or other fully accredited messengers of the Congress, the President, Vice-President, members of the Supreme Court or commissioned officer of the army, and those under peculiar circumstances, shall be allowed at any time to carry concealed weapons; and any person not specially authorized so to do who shall be found so doing shall be deemed a suspicious person, and may at once be arrested by any officer, soldier or citizen, without the formality of a complaint or warrant, and may at once be subjected to thorough search, and shall have his or her case thoroughly investigated, and be dealt with as circumstances on proof shall require.

ARTICLE 45.—PERSONS TO BE SEIZED.—Persons living within the limits of territory holden by this organization and not connected with this organization, having arms at all concealed or otherwise, shall be seized at once, or be taken in charge of by some vigilant officer and their case thoroughly investigated, and it shall be the duty of all citizens and soldiers as well as officers, to arrest such parties as are named in this and the preceding section or article, without formality of complaint, or warrant, and they shall be placed in charge of some proper officer for examination or safe keeping.

ARTICLE 46.—THESE ARTICLES NOT FOR THE OVERTHROW OF GOVERNMENT.—The foregoing articles shall not be constructed so as in any way to encourage the overthrow of any State Government or of the General Government of the United States, and look to no dissolution of the Union, but simply to amendment and repeal; and our flag shall be the same that our fathers fought under in the Revolution.

ARTICLE 47.—THE PLURALITY OF OFFICES.—No two offices specially provided for by this instrument shall be filled by the same person at the same time.

ARTICLE 48.—OATH.—Every officer, civil or military, connected with this organization, shall, before entering upon the duties of office, make a solemn oath or affirmation to abide by and support the Provisional Constitution and these ordinances. Also, every citizen and soldier, before being recognized as such, shall do the same.

SCHEDULE

The President of this Convention shall convene, immediately on the adoption of this instrument, a Convention of all such persons as shall have given their adherence, by signature, to the Constitution, who shall proceed to fill, by election, all offices specially named in said Constitution, the President of this Convention presiding and issuing commissions to such officers elect, all such officers being hereafter elected in the manner provided in the body of this instrument.

Origin of the "Irrepressible Conflict."

Being an extract of a Speech
by the Honorable William H. Seward, of New York.
Delivered at Rochester, New York on Monday, October 25, 1858

F ELLOW CITIZENS: THE unmistakable outbreaks of zeal which occur all around me show that you are earnest men—and such a man am I. Let us, therefore, at least for a time, pass by all secondary and collateral questions, whether of a personal or of a general nature, and consider the main subject of the present canvass. The Democratic Party—or to speak more accurately—the party which wears that attractive name, is in possession of the federal government. The Republicans propose to dislodge that party and dismiss it from its high trust.

The main subject then, is whether the Democratic Party deserves to retain the confidence of the American people. In attempting to prove it unworthy, I think that I am not actuated by prejudices against that party, or by prepossessions in favor of its adversary; for I have learned, by some experience, that virtue and patriotism, vice and selfishness, are found in all parties, and that they differ less in their motives than in the policies they pursue. Our country is a theater which exhibits, in full operation, two radically different political systems—the one resting on the basis of servile or slave labor; the other on the basis of voluntary labor of freemen. The laborers who are enslaved are all Negroes, or persons more or less purely of African derivation. *But this is only accidental.* The principle of the system is, that labor, in every society, by whomsoever performed, is necessarily unintellectual, groveling and base, and that the laborer, equally for his own good and for the welfare of the state, ought to be enslaved. The white laboring man, whether native or foreigner, is not enslaved only because he cannot, as yet, be reduced to bondage.

You need not be told now that the slave system is the older of the two, and that once it was universal. The emancipation of our own ancestors, Caucasians and Europeans, as they were, hardly dates beyond a period of five hundred years. The great melioration of human society which modern times exhibit, is mainly due to the substitution of the old system of voluntary labor for the old one of servile labor, which has already taken place. This African slave system is one which, in its origin and its growth, has been altogether foreign from the habits of the races which colonized these States and established civilization here. It was introduced on this new continent as an engine of conquest, and for the establishment of Monarchial Power by the Portuguese and the Spaniards, and was rapidly extended by them over all South America, Central America, Louisiana and Mexico. Its legitimate fruits are seen in the poverty, imbecility and anarchy which now pervade all Portuguese and Spanish America. The Free Labor system is of German extraction, and it was established in our country by emigrants from Sweden, Holland, Germany, Great Britain and Ireland.

We justly ascribe to its influence the strength, wealth, greatness, intelligence and freedom which the whole American people now enjoy. One of the chief elements of the value of human life is freedom in the pursuit of happiness. The slave system is not only intolerant, unjust and inhuman towards the laborer, whom, only because he is a laborer, it loads down with chains and converts into merchandise, but scarcely less so to the freeman, to whom, only because he is a laborer from necessity, it denies facilities for employment, and whom it expels from the community because it cannot enslave and convert him into merchandise also. It is necessarily improvident and ruinous, because, as a general truth, communities prosper and flourish, or droop and decline, in just the degree that they practice or neglect to practice the primary duties of justice and humanity. The free-labor system conforms to the divine law of equality, which is written in the hearts and consciences of man, and therefore is always and everywhere beneficent.

The slave system is one of constant danger, distrust, suspicion and watchfulness. It debases those whose toil alone can produce wealth and resources for defense, to the lowest degree of which human nature is capable, to guard against mutiny and insurrection, and thus wastes energies which otherwise might be employed in national development and aggrandizement. The free labor system educates all alike, and by opening all the fields of industrial employment and all the departments of authority to the unchecked and equal rivalry of all classes of men, at once secures universal contentment and brings into the highest possible activity all the physical, moral and social energies of the whole state. In states where the slave system prevails, the masters, directly or indirectly, secure all political power, and constitute a ruling aristocracy. In the states where the free-labor system prevails, universal suffrage necessarily obtains, and the state inevitably becomes, sooner or later, a Republic of Democracy.

Russia yet maintains slavery, and is a despotism. Most of the other European states have abolished slavery and adopted the system of free labor. It was the antagonistic political tendencies of the two systems which the first Napoleon was contemplating when he predicted that Europe would ultimately be either all Cossack or all Republicans. Never did human sagacity utter a more pregnant truth. The two systems are at once perceived to be incongruous. But they are more than incongruous, they are incompatible. They never have permanently existed together in one country, *and they never can.* It would be easy to demonstrate this impossibility, from the irreconcilable contrast between their great principles and characteristics. But the experience of mankind has conclusively established it. Slavery, as I have already intimated, existed in every State in Europe. Free labor has supplanted it everywhere except in Russia and Turkey. State necessities, developed in modern times, are now obliging even those two nations to encourage and employ free labor, and already, despotic as they are, we find them engaged in abolishing slavery. In the United States slavery came into collision with free labor at the close of the last century, and fell before it in New England, New York, New Jersey and Pennsylvania, but triumphed over it effectually, and excluded it for a period yet undetermined, from Virginia, the Carolinas and Georgia. Indeed, so incompatible are the two systems that every new state which is organized within our ever extending domain, makes its first political act a choice of the one and an exclusion of the other, even at the cost of civil war, if necessary. The slave states, without law, at the last National election, forbade, within their own limits, even the casting of votes for a candidate for President of the United States supposed to be favorable to the establishment of the free labor system in new states.

Hitherto the two systems have existed in different states, but side by side, within the American Union. This has happened because the Union is a confederation of states. But in another aspect, the United States constitute only one nation. Increase of population which is filling the states out to their very borders, together with a new and extended network of railroads and other avenues, and an internal commerce which daily becomes more intimate, is rapidly bringing the states into higher and more perfect social unity or consolidation. Thus these antagonistic systems are continually coming into closer contact, and collision results.

Shall I tell you what this collision means? They who think that it is accidental, unnecessary, the work of interested or fanatical agitators, and therefore ephemeral, mistake the case altogether. It is an *irrepressible conflict* between opposing and enduring forces, and it means that *the United States must and will, sooner or later, become entirely a slave holding nation, or entirely a free-labor nation.* Either the cotton and rice fields of South Carolina and the sugar plantations of Louisiana will ultimately be tilled by free labor, and Charleston and New Orleans become marts for legitimate merchandise alone, or else the rye fields and wheat fields of Massachusetts and New York must again be surrounded by their farmers to slave culture and to the production of slaves, and Boston and New York become once more market for trade in the bodies and souls of men. It is the failure to apprehend this great truth that induces so many unsuccessful attempts at final compromise between the slave and free states, and it is the existence of this great fact that renders all such pretended compromise, when made, vain and ephemeral. Startling as this saying may appear to you, fellow-citizens, it is by no means an original or even a modern one. Our forefathers knew it to be true, and unanimously acted upon it, when they framed the Constitution of the United States. They regarded the existence of the servile system in so many of the states with sorrow and shame, which they openly confessed, and they looked upon the collision between them, which was then just revealing itself, and which we are now accustomed to deplore, with favor and hope. They knew that either the one or the other system must exclusively prevail.

President Lincoln Discusses John Brown

Being a portion of a speech
by the Honorable Abraham Lincoln, of Illinois.
Delivered at the Cooper Institute,
New York City, on February 27, 1860.

T HE HONORABLE ABRAHAM Lincoln of Illinois, the great protagonist of Senator Douglas and Republican Party Candidate gave a lecture on National Politics on Monday evening, February 27, 1860 at the Cooper Institute in New York City, and touched on the Harper's Ferry Disaster. Although there was an admission fee for the benefit of the Plymouth Church[1] course of lectures, the seats of the great Hall were nearly all filled, and a large number of people preferred standing to sitting in the rear seats.

Mr. Lincoln, after prolonged applause, commenced,

MR. PRESIDENT AND FELLOW CITIZENS OF NEW YORK: The facts with which I shall deal this evening are mainly old and familiar; nor is there anything

---

[1] Reverend Henry Ward Beecher's Church in Brooklyn, New York

new in the general use I shall make of them. If there shall be any novelty, it will be in the mode of presenting the facts, and the inferences and observations following that presentation . . .

You charge that we stir up insurrections among your slaves. We deny it; and what is your proof? Harper's Ferry! John Brown!! John Brown was no Republican; and you have failed to implicate a single Republican in his Harper's Ferry enterprise. If any member of our party is guilty in that matter, you know it or you do not know it. If you do know it, you are inexcusable to not designate the man and prove the fact. If you do not know it, you are inexcusable to assert it, and especially to persist in the assertion after you have tried and failed to make the proof. You need not be told that persisting in a charge, which, one does not know to be true, is simply malicious slander.

Some of you admit that no Republican designedly aided or encouraged the Harper's Ferry affair; but still insist that our doctrines and declarations necessarily lead to such results. We do not believe it. We know we hold to no doctrines, and make no declarations which were not held to and made by "our fathers who framed the government under which we live." You never dealt fairly by us in relation to this affair. When it occurred, some important state elections were near at hand, and you were in evident glee with the belief that, by charging the blame upon us, you could get an advantage of us in those elections. The elections came, and your expectations were not quite fulfilled. Every Republican man knew that, as to himself at least, your charge was a slander, and he was not much inclined by it to cast his vote in your favor. Republican doctrines and declarations are accompanied with a continual protest against any interference whatever with your slaves, or with you about your slaves. Surely, this does not encourage them to revolt. True, we do, in common with our fathers who framed the government under which we live, declare our belief that slavery is wrong; but the slaves do not hear us declare even this. For anything we say or do, the slaves would scarcely know there is a Republican party. I believe they would not, in fact, generally know it but for your misrepresentations of us, in their hearing. In your political contests among yourselves, each faction charges the other with sympathy with Black Republicanism; and then, to give point to the charge, defines Black Republicanism to simply be insurrection, blood and thunder among the slaves.

Slave insurrections are no more common now than they were before the Republican party was organized. What induced the Southampton insurrection, twenty-eight years ago, in which at least three times as many lives were lost as at Harper's Ferry? You can scarcely stretch your very elastic fancy to the conclusion that Southampton was got up by Black Republicanism. In the present state of things in the United States, I do not think a general, or even a very extensive slave insurrection, is possible. The indispensable concert of action cannot be attained. The slaves have no means of rapid communication; nor can incendiary free men, black or white, supply it. The explosive materials are everywhere in parcels; but there neither are, nor can be supplied, the indispensable connecting trains.

Much is said by Southern people about the affection of slaves for their masters and mistresses; and a part of it, at least, is true. A plot for an uprising could scarcely be devised and communicated to twenty individuals before some one of them, to save the life of a favorite master or mistress, would divulge it. This is the rule; and the slave-revolution in Hayti was not an exception to it, but a case occurring under peculiar circumstances. The gunpowder plot of British history, though not connected with slaves, was more in point. In that case, only about twenty were admitted to the secret; and yet one of them, in his anxiety to save a friend, betrayed the plot to that friend, and by consequence, averted the calamity. Occasional poisonings from the kitchen, and open or stealthy assassinations in the field, and local revolts extending to a score or so, will continue to occur as the natural results of slavery; but no general insurrection of slaves, as I think, can happen in this country for a long time. Whoever much fears, or much hopes, for such an event, will be alike disappointed.

In the language of Mr. Jefferson, uttered many years ago, "It is still in our power to direct the process of emancipation and deportation, peaceably, and in such slow degrees, as that the evil will wear off insensibly; and their places be, *pari passu*, filled up by free white laborers. If, on the contrary, it is left to force itself on, human nature must shudder at the prospect held up."

Mr. Jefferson did not mean to say, nor do I, that the power of emancipation is in the federal government. He spoke of Virginia; and, as to the power of emancipation, I speak of the slave holding states only.

The federal government, however, as we insist, has the power of restraining the extension of the institution—the power to insure that a slave insurrection shall never occur on any American soil which is now free from slavery.

John Brown's effort was peculiar. It was not a slave insurrection. It was an attempt by white men to get up a revolt among slaves, in which the slaves refused to participate. In fact, it was so absurd that the slaves, with all their ignorance, saw plainly enough it could not succeed. That affair, in its philosophy, corresponds with the many attempts, related in history, at the assassination of kings and emperors. An enthusiast broods over the oppression of a people, till he fancies himself commissioned by Heaven to liberate them. He ventures the attempt, which ends in little else than in his own execution. Orsini's attempt on Louis Napoleon, and John Brown's attempt at Harper's Ferry were, in their philosophy, precisely the same. The eagerness to cast blame on old England in the one case, and on New England in the other, does not disprove the sameness of the two things.

And how much would it avail you, if you could, by the use of John Brown, Helper's book, and the like, break up the Republican organization? Human action can be modified to some extent, but human nature cannot be changed. There is a judgement and a feeling against slavery in this nation, which cast at least a million and a half votes. You cannot destroy that judgment and feeling—that sentiment—by breaking up the political organization which rallies around it. You can scarcely scatter and disperse an army which has been formed into order in the face of your heaviest fire, but if you could, how much would you gain by forcing the sentiment which created it out of the peaceful channel of the ballot box, into some other channel? What would that other channel probably be? Would the number of John Browns be lessened or enlarged by the operation?

But you will break up the Union, rather than submit to a denial of your Constitutional rights.

That has a somewhat reckless sound; but it would be palliated, if not fully justified, were we proposing, by the mere force of numbers, to deprive you of some right, plainly written down in the Constitution. But we are proposing no such thing . . .

References

1. Barry, Joseph
   "The Strange Story of Harper's Ferry" With Legends of the Surrounding Country
   Thompson Brothers
   Martinsburg, W.V., 1903

2. Boteler, Alexander R.
   Recollections of the John Brown Raid, with Comment by F. B. Sanborn
   The Century Magazine
   July, 1883

3. Boyer, Richard O.
   The Legend of John Brown—A Biography and a History
   Alfred A. Knopf
   New York, 1973

4. Craven, Avery
   Edmund Ruffin Southerner—A Study in Secession
   Archon Books
   Hamden, Ct., 1964

5. DeWitt, Robert M., Publisher
   The Life, Trial and Conviction of Captain John Brown
   George Russell and Company
   New York, 1859

6. Featherstonhaugh, Thomas
   The Final Burial of the Followers of John Brown

New England Magazine and Bay State Monthly
April, 1901

7. Galbreath, C. B.
Barclay Coppoc
Journal of the Ohio Historical Society, Vol. 30.
October, 1921

8. Gee, Clarence S.
John Brown's Fort
West Virginia History, Vol 19, No. 2.
January, 1958

9. Higginson, Thomas Wentworth
Cheerful Yesterdays
Houghton Mifflin & Company
Boston, 1898

10. Hinton, Richard J.
John Brown and his Men
Funk & Wagnalls
New York, 1894

11. Internet Acquisitions.

12. Keeler, Ralph
Owen Brown's Escape From Harper's Ferry
Atlantic Monthly
March 1874

13. Nolan, Jeannette Covert
John Brown
Julian Messner
New York, 1850

14. Nelson, Truman
    The Old Man; John Brown at Harper's Ferry
    Holt, Rinehart & Winston
    New York, 1973

15. Newspapers, Contemporary

16. Redpath, James
    The Life of Captain John Brown
    Thayer and Eldridge
    Boston, 1860

17. Robertson Jr., James I.
    Stonewall Jackson: The Man, The Soldier, The Legend
    Macmillan Publishing USA
    New York, 1997

18. Quarles, Benjamin
    Allies for Freedom, Blacks and John Brown
    Oxford University Press.
    New York, 1974

19. Rosengarten, J. G.
    John Brown's Raid
    Atlantic Monthly
    June 1865

20. Sanborn, F. B.
    Life and Letters of John Brown
    Roberts Brothers
    New York, 1885

21. Select Committee, U. S. Senate
    Invasion at Harper's Ferry
    Gryphon Editions
    New York, 1993

22. Stavis, Barrie
John Brown—The Sword and the Word
A. S. Barnes & Company
New York, 1970

23. Villard, Oswald Garrison
John Brown, 1800-1859: A Biography Fifty Years After
Alfred A. Knopf
New York, 1943

24. Walcott, Charles F.
History of the Twenty-First Regiment, Massachusetts Volunteers . . .
Houghton, Mifflin and Company
New York, 1882

25. Wise, Barton H.
The Life of Henry A. Wise of Virginia
The Macmillan Company
New York, 1899